HUNTING

NORTH AMERICA
1885-1911

HUNTING
NORTH AMERICA
1885-1911

Edited by
Frank Oppel
and
Tony Meisel

CASTLE

HUNTING
NORTH AMERICA
1885-1911

Copyright © 1987 Castle,
a division of Book Sales, Inc.
110 Enterprise Avenue
Secaucus, NJ 07094

Printed in the United States of America.

ISBN:1-55521-155-0

CONTENTS

1.
THE WAIL
OF THE GUIDE
(1892)

The Wail of the Guide.

BY

FREDERIC
COLBURN
CLARKE.

Yo' city chaps comes ter th' woods
  With yo' new-fangled guns,
'N 'low yo' prime ter shoot th' hide
  Off anything 'et runs:—

Yo' grumble at the grub I cook,
  Yo' shirk at rain 'r fog,
'N when yo've nathin' else ter do
  Yo' tease 'n kick my dog.

* * *

Who cleans yo' guns 'n tends th' camp?
  Who built that 'ere canoe?
You think yo'd larn them tricks in books,
  'N maybe larn me, too.

There ain't no guide in seven States
  Kin track a moose like me,
'N I kin smell a caribou
  As fer as yo' kin see;
I'd like ter see yo' tote th' load
  O' stuff yo' make me pack,
From lake ter lake along th' run—
  Yo'd break yo' dog-goned back.

Who keeps yo' out o' traps 'n snares?
  Who calls yo' moose 'n deer?
Who showed yo' whar ter find a b'ar
  That day yo' run so queer?—
Don't guy yo' country guide, my friend,
  Tho' he don't know yo' creed—
Thar's heaps o' things a man kin larn
  As well as larn ter read.

2.
MOERAN'S MOOSE
(1899)

MOERAN'S MOOSE.

A HUNTING STORY.

ONE of the best fellows among the hardy lot who have run the trails and paddled the lonely tributaries of the upper Ottawa was Moeran. No bolder sportsman ever went into the woods, and few, or none of the guides or professional hunters could rival his skill with rifle or paddle. The tough old "Leatherstockings" fairly idolized him, for he got his game as they did, by straight shooting, perfect woodcraft, and honest hard work; and most of them, while they usually charged a heavy price for their services, would have gladly thrown in their lots with him for an outing of a month or more, and asked nothing save what he considered a fair division of the spoils. He was also a keen observer and a close student of the ways of bird and beast. The real pleasure of sport seemed to him to lie in the fact that it brought him very near to nature, and permitted him to pore at will over that marvelous open page which all might read if they chose, yet which few pause to study. His genial disposition and long experience made him ever a welcome and valuable companion afield or afloat, and the comrades he shot with season after season would have as soon gone into the woods without their rifles as without Moeran. Physically, he was an excellent type of the genuine sportsman. Straight and tall, and strongly made, his powerful arms could make a paddle spring, if need be, or his broad shoulders bear a canoe or pack over a portage that taxed even the rugged guides ; and his long limbs could cover ground in a fashion that made the miles seem many and long to whoever tramped a day with him.

And this was the kind of man that planned a trip for a party of four after the lordly moose. Moeran had, until that year, never seen a wild moose free in his own forest domain, and needless to say he was keenly anxious to pay his respects to the great king of the Canadian wilderness. He had been in the moose country many times while fishing or shooting in the provinces of New Brunswick, Quebec, Ontario and Manitoba ; he had seen the slots of the huge deer about pool and stream, on beaver meadow and brule; he had spent more than one September night "calling," with a crafty Indian to simulate the plaintive appeals of a love-lorn cow; he had heard the great bulls answer from the distant hills — had heard even the low, grunting inquiry a bull moose generally makes ere emerging from the last few yards of shadowy cover, and revealing himself in all his mighty strength and pride in the moonlit open. More than once he had lain quivering with excitement and hardly daring to breathe, close-hidden in a little clump of scrub, about which stretched full forty yards of level grass on every side—lain so for an hour with every nerve strained to the ready, with ears striving to catch the faintest sound on the stillness of the night, and with eyes sweeping warily over the expanse of moonlit grass and striving vainly to pierce the black borders of forest, somewhere behind which his royal quarry was hidden. Upon such occasions he had lain and listened and watched until he fancied he could see the moose standing silently alert among the saplings, with ears shifting to and fro and with keen nose searching the air ceaselessly for trace of his mortal enemy. The occasional distant rattle of broad antlers against the trees as the big brute shook himself or plunged about in lusty strength had sounded on his ears, followed by the faint sounds of cautiously advancing footsteps seemingly bent straight toward the ambush. Then would follow a long agonizing pause, and then a snap of a twig or a faint rustling told that the crafty bull was stealing in a circle through the cover around the open space before venturing upon such dangerous ground. At last a deathlike silence for many minutes, and then a faint, far snap of twigs and "wish" of straightening branches as the great bull stole away to his forested hills, having read in breeze or on ground a warning of the foe concealed in the harmless scrub. All these were disappointments, but not necessarily bitter ones. The long night-vigils were after all rarely spent entirely in vain, for each brought to him some new ideas, or let him a little further into the dark mysteries of the great wild world's nightly moods and methods. The skilled craft of his Indian "caller;" the strange voices of the night that came to his ears, telling of the movements of creatures but seldom seen or heard by day, were full of interest to a genuine woodsman. And then the fierce though subdued excitement of the weird watch for the huge beast that never came, and yet might come at any moment full into the silvery moonlight from out the black belt of silent wood — these were each fascinating to such a nature as his. But still he had never once seen his long-looked-for game, though several seasons had slipped away and the month of July, 18—, had come and half passed by. Then Moeran got ready his fishing tackle and camping gear and vowed to find a good district for the party to shoot over the coming season, even if he had to remain in the woods an entire month. Right well he knew some of the likeliest points in New Brunswick, Quebec and Manitoba, the eastern portion of the latter province being the best moose country now available, but none of them met the requirements of the party, and so he decided to go into northern Ontario and prospect until he found what he sought.

In the region of the upper Ottawa River, and in the wild lands about the Mattawa River and about the lakes forming its headwaters, is a country beloved of moose. Thither went Moeran, satisfied that his quest would not be in vain. Early in the third week of July he and his Peterboro canoe and outfit reached the railway station of North Bay, on the shore of noble Lake Nipissing. While awaiting the arrival of the guide and team for the next stage of his journey, he put rod together and strolled out on the long pier which extends for a considerable distance into the lake. Reaching the farther end and looking down into the clear, green depths below, he saw watchful black bass skulking in the shadows, and lazy pickerel drifting hither and thither, in and out, among the great piles which supported the pier. To tempt a few of these to their doom was an easy task, and soon the lithe rod was arching over a game black gladiator and a master hand was meeting every desperate struggle of a fighting fish, or slowly raising a varlet pickerel to his inglorious death. In time a hail announced the arrival of the team, and after presenting his captives to the few loungers on the pier, he busied himself stowing canoe and outfit upon the wagon.

"IT SLOWLY ROSE HIGHER AND HIGHER."

THE OLD BULL.

Their objective point was on the shore of Trout Lake, a lovely sheet of water distant from Nipissing about four miles. The road was in many places extremely bad and the team made slow progress, but there was plenty of time to spare and about noon they reached the lake. The guide, as guides are given to do, lied cheerfully and insistently every yard of the way, about the beauty of the lake, the countless deer and grouse upon its shores, the gigantic fish within its ice-cold depths, the game he, and parties he had guided, had killed, and the fish they had caught. He did well with these minor subjects, but when he touched upon moose and bear he rose to the sublime, and lied with a wild abandon which made Moeran seriously consider the advantage of upsetting the canoe later on and quietly drowning him. But he was not so far astray in his description of the lake. It formed a superb picture, stretching its narrow length for a dozen miles between huge, rolling, magnificently wooded hills, while here and there lovely islands spangled its silver breast. After a hurried lunch

they launched the good canoe, the guide insisting upon taking his rifle, as, according to his story, they were almost certain to see one or more bear. The guide proved that he could paddle almost as well as he could lie, and the two of them drove the light craft along like a scared thing, the paddles rising and falling, flashing and disappearing, with that beautiful, smooth, regular sweep that only experts can give. For mile after mile they sped along, until at last they neared the farther end of the lake, where the huge hills dwindled to mere scattered mounds, between which spread broad beaver meadows, the nearest of them having a pond covering many acres near its center. All about this pond was a dense growth of tall water-grasses, and in many places these grasses extended far into the water which was almost covered, save a few open leads, with the round, crowding leaves of the water-lily. A channel, broad and deep enough to float the canoe, connected this pond with the lake, and, as the locality was an ideal summer haunt for moose, Moeran decided to investigate it thoroughly and read such "sign" as might be found. Landing noiselessly, he and the guide changed places, Moeran kneeling forward, with the rifle on the bottom of the canoe in front of him, where he alone could reach it. "Now," he whispered, "you know the route and how to paddle ; work her up as if a sound would cost your life. I'll do the watching."

Slowly, silently, foot by foot, and sometimes inch by inch, the canoe stole up the currentless channel, the guide never raising his paddle, but pushing with it cautiously against the soft bottom and lily-roots. It was a good piece of canoe work, worthy even of Moeran's noted skill, and he thoroughly appreciated it. By motions of his hand he indicated when to halt and advance, while his eyes scanned sharply every yard of marsh revealed by the windings of the channel. Not the slightest sound marked their progress until they had almost entered the open water in the center of the pond, and were creeping past the last fringe of tall grass. Suddenly Moeran's hand signaled a halt, and the canoe lost its slow, forward motion. He looked and looked, staring fixedly at a point some twenty yards distant, where the growth of grass was thin and short and the lily-pads denser than usual, and as he gazed with a strange concentration, a wild light flashed in his eyes until they fairly blazed with exultant triumph. Straight before him among the faded greens and bewildering browns of the lily-pads was a motionless, elongated brown object very like the curved back of a beaver, and a foot or more from it, in the shadow of a clump of grass, something shone with a peculiar liquid gleam. It was an eye—a great, round, wild eye—staring full into his own—the eye of a moose—and the curving object like the back of a beaver was naught else than the enormous nose, or muffle, of a full-grown bull. Something like a sigh came from it, and then it slowly rose higher and higher until the head and neck were exposed. The big ears pointed stiffly forward, and the nose twitched and trembled for an instant as it caught the dreaded taint; then with a mighty floundering and splashing the great brute struggled to his feet. It was a

THE CAMP BY THE LAKE.

"LOOK, LOOK AT HIM!"

grewsome spectacle to see this uncouth creature uprise from a place where it seemed a muskrat could hardly have hidden. For a few seconds he stood still.

"Shoot! Shoot!"

Moeran simply picked up the rifle and brought it level.

"Load! 'Tain't loaded—the lever—quick!"

He made no response, merely covered, first the point of the shoulder and then the ear, and then, as the bull plunged for the shore, he covered the shoulder twice more, then lowered the rifle, while a horribly excited guide cursed and raved and implored by turns in vain. And just how great was the temptation was never known, but it certainly would have proved irresistible to most men who call themselves sportsmen. In speaking about it afterward Moeran said: "It would have been a crime to have murdered the beast under such conditions, and out of season. I covered him fair four times, and could have dropped him dead where he stood—but we'll attend to them later on." For there were, in all, four moose in the pond, and, shortly after the big bull commenced his noisy retreat, a tremendous splashing and plunging from the other side of the pond attracted their attention. They turned just in time to see a grand old cow and two younger moose struggle through the last few yards of mud and water, and then crash their way into the cover at the rapid, pounding trot peculiar to the species.

Moeran's mission had been accomplished much easier than was expected, and he certainly had discovered a most promising locality for the trip with his friends. After a day spent fishing, he departed homeward, leaving his canoe and camp outfit in charge of the guide, whom he also bound by most solemn pledge neither to betray the secret of the beaver meadow, nor to molest the moose himself, before Moeran and his friends returned in time for the first lawful day.

The last day of the close season saw the party and the guide snugly encamped at a point half-way down the lake. His three friends had unanimously agreed that Moeran should have the honor of visiting the beaver meadow first, and alone if he desired. He was the surest shot and by far the best hand at this sort of business, and he had discovered the moose, while all hands knew how keen he was to secure a head to his own rifle. So at earliest dawn Moeran put lunch and rifle into his shapely Peterboro and sped noiselessly away through the ghostly vapors curtaining the sleeping lake, and they saw him no more for many hours. The guide had questioned the others about their comrade's shooting (of his ability at the paddle he had somewhat sorrowful remembrance), and then, strange to say, had advised Moeran to go alone.

"So much more glory for you," he said, "and I'll look after these other gentlemen and give them a day's fishing." But his manner was shifty, and Moeran mistrusted him.

In due time he reached the little channel leading to the beaver meadow, and, as the sun lifted clear of the distant hills, he began working his way to the pond. He hardly expected to find the moose there then, but he had made up his mind to steal into the high grass and hide and watch all day, if necessary, and, at all events, study the thing out thoroughly. As the sun rose higher a brisk breeze sprang up, but as it came from the woods toward his station he did not mind, although it would have been fatal to his chance, probably, had it come from any other point of the compass. Presently his nose detected a strong, sickening odor of carrion, which, in time, as the breeze gained force, became almost overpowering, and he started to investigate. Paddling straight up-wind he came at last to a small pool, and the trouble was explained. The half-decomposed body of a full-grown cow moose lay in the pool and Moeran muttered savagely his opinion of all such butchery when he saw that not even the feet had been taken for trophies. Then he poled his canoe to the edge of the meadow and scouted carefully entirely round the open, seeking for any possible sign of the remainder of the quartet. To his utter disgust he found the remains of another moose, one of the younger animals, lying just within the borders of the cover, and, as in the other case, the butcher had not troubled himself to take away any portion of his victim. Moeran understood, of course, that the guide had played him false, and if that worthy had been present he might have seriously regretted his wrong-doing, for he it was who had guided a learned and honorable (?) American judge to the sanctuary of the moose a month previously, and, for a consideration of twenty-five dollars, enabled his patron to gratify his taste for the shambles.

Moeran's careful search discovered no fresh sign, and he made up his mind that the two survivors, the old bull and the yearling, had fled the scene and had probably sought another expanse of beaver meadow and ponds the guide had mentioned as being about ten miles from Trout Lake. Moeran knew that some sort of a trail led thither, and he resolved to find it and follow it to the end and endeavor to locate the moose.

Of the ensuing long, hard day's work it will be unnecessary to speak in detail.

At nine o'clock that night his three friends·sat near their roaring camp-fire on the lake shore, wondering at his protracted absence. The guide had turned in an hour previous, but the three were anxious, so they sat and smoked, and discussed the question, piling great drift-logs on their fire till it roared and cracked in fierce exultation and leaped high in air to guide the wanderer home. Its long, crimson reflection stretched like a pathway of flame far over the black waters of the lake, and the three sat and waited, now glancing along this glowing path, anon conversing in subdued tones. The lake was as still and dark as a lake of pitch, and some way the three felt ill at ease, as though some evil impended. At last the veteran of the trio broke a longer silence than usual :

"Boys, I don't like this. It's ten o'clock and he should have been back long ago. I hope to Heaven——"

A touch on his arm from the man at his right caused him to glance quickly lakeward.

Forty feet from them, drifting noiselessly into the firelight, was the Peterboro, with Moeran kneeling as usual and sending the light craft forward in some mysterious manner which required no perceptible movement of the arms nor lifting of the paddle. It was a fine exhibition of his skill to thus approach unheard three anxious, listening men on such a night, for he had heard their voices good two miles away. His appearance was so sudden, so ghostlike, that for a few seconds the party stared in mute surprise at the forms of man and craft standing out in sharp relief against the blackness of the night ; then a whoop of delight welcomed him.

He came ashore, swiftly picked up the canoe and turned it bottom upward on the sand for the night, carried his rifle into camp, then approached the fire and looked sharply round.

"The guide's asleep."

"Oh, he is;——him!" Then he flung himself down on the sand. Something in his tone and manner warned his friends not to talk, and they eyed him curiously. His face was white as death and drawn with an expression of utter exhaustion, and marked with grimy lines, showing where rivulets of sweat had trickled downward. As they looked, his eyes closed ; he was going to sleep as he lay.

Quietly the veteran busied himself getting food ready, and presently roused the slumberer.

"Here, old chap, have a nip and eat a. bite. Why, you're dead beat. Where on earth have you been ?"

A strangely hollow voice answered :

"To the back lakes."

His listeners whistled a combined long-drawn "whew" of amazement, for right well they knew the leagues of toilsome travel this statement implied.

"See anything ?"

"Wounded the old bull badly, and trailed him from the lakes to within five miles of here. That cur sleeping yonder sold us ; but you hear me !" he exclaimed with sudden fierce energy, "*I'll get that moose if I have to stay in the woods forever!*"

The three looked at him in admiring silence, for they guessed that, in spite of his terrible day's work, he intended starting again at daylight. In a few moments he finished his meal and staggered to the tent, and fell asleep as soon as he touched his blanket.

When the party turned out next morning the canoe was gone, though the sun was not yet clear of the hills. After breakfast they started in quest of grouse, working through the woods in the direction of the beaver meadows, and finding plenty of birds. About ten o'clock they heard the distant report of a rifle, followed in a few minutes by a second, and the veteran exclaimed, "That's him, for an even hundred, and he's got his moose, or something strange has happened."

At noon they returned to camp laden with grouse. No sign of the canoe as yet, so they had dinner, and lounged about and fished during the afternoon, casting many expectant glances down the lake for the laggard canoe. Night fell, with still no sound or sign of the wanderer, and again the camp-fire roared and flamed and sent its glowing reflection streaming far over the black waste of water. And again the three sat waiting. At ten o'clock the veteran rose and said, "Keep a sharp lookout, boys, and don't let him fool you again, and I'll get up a royal feed. He'll have moose-meat in the canoe this time, for he said *he'd get that moose if he had to stay in the woods forever.* He'll be dead beat, sure, for he's probably dragged the head out with him." So they waited, piling the fire high, and staring out over the lake for the first glimpse of the canoe. Eleven o'clock and midnight came and went, and still no sign. Then they piled the fire high for the last time and sought the tent. At the door the veteran halted, and laying a hand on the shoulder of his chum, drew him aside.

"Why, whatever's the matter with you?"

The old man's face wore a piteous expression, and his voice trembled as he whispered:

"Hush! Don't let *him* hear you—but there's something wrong. Something horrible has happened—I feel it in my heart."

"Nonsense, man! You're sleepy and nervous. He's all right. Why, he's just cut himself a moose steak, and had a feed and laid down——"

The sentence was never completed. A sound that caused both men to start convulsively tore through the black stillness of the night. A horrible, gurgling, demoniacal laugh came over the lake, and died away in fading echoes among the hills. "Woll-oll-all-ollow-wall-all-ollow!" as though some hideous fiend was laughing with his lips touching the water. They knew what it was, for the loon's weird cry was perfectly familiar to them, and they laughed too, but there was no mirth in their voices. Then one sought the tent, but the veteran paced up and down upon the cold beach, halting sometimes to replenish the fire or to stare out over the water,

until a pale light spread through the eastern sky. Then he too turned in for a couple of hours of troubled, unrefreshing slumber.

The bright sunshine of an Indian summer's day brought a reaction and their spirits rose wonderfully; but still the canoe tarried, and as the hours wore away, the veteran grew moody again and the midday meal was a melancholy affair. Early in the afternoon he exclaimed:

"Boys, I tell you what it is: I can stand this no longer — something's wrong, and we're going to paddle those two skiffs down to the beaver meadow and find out what we can do, and we're going to start right now. God forgive us if we have been idling here while we should have been yonder!"

Two in a boat they went, and the paddles never halted until the channel to the beaver meadow was gained. Dividing forces, they circled in opposite directions round the open, but only the taint of the long-dead moose marked the spot. Then they fired three rifles in rapid succession and listened anxiously, but only the rolling, bursting echoes of the woods answered them.

"Guide, where would he probably have gone?"

"Wa'al, he told you he'd run the old bull this way from the back lakes— thar's another leetle mash a mile north of us; it's an awful mud-hole, and the bull might possibly hev lit out fur thar. Enyhow, we'd best hunt the closest spots first."

The picture of that marsh will haunt the memories of those three men until their deaths. A few acres of muskeg, with broad reaches of sullen, black, slimy water, its borders bottomless mud, covered with a loathsome green scum, and a few pale-green, sickly-looking larches dotting the open—the whole forming a repulsive blemish, like an ulcer, on the face of the earth. All round rose a silent wall of noble evergreens, rising in massive tiers upon the hills, with here and there a flame of gorgeous color where the frost had touched perishable foliage. Overhead a hazy dome of dreamy blue, with the sun smiling down through the gauzy curtains of the Indian summer. Swinging in easy circles, high in air, were two ravens, challenging each other in hollow tones, their orbits crossing and recrossing as they narrowed in slow-descending spirals. "Look, look at him!"

One bird had stooped like a falling plummet, and now hung about fifty yards above the farther bounds of the muskeg, beating the air with heavy, sable pinions and croaking loudly to his mate above. Closing her wings, she stooped with a whizzing rush to his level, and there the two hung flapping side by side, their broad wings sometimes striking sharply against each other, their hoarse, guttural notes sounding at intervals. A nameless horror seized the men as they looked. Their hunter's instinct told them that death lay below those flapping birds, and with one impulse they hurried round on the firmer ground to the ill-omened spot.

The veteran, white-faced but active as a lad, tore his way through the bordering cover first, halted and stared for an instant, then dropped his rifle in the mud, threw up his hands and exclaimed in an agonized voice:

"Oh, my God, my God!"

One by one they crashed through the brush and joined him, and stood staring. No need for questions. Ten square yards of deep-trodden, reeking mud and crushed grass, a trampled cap, and here and there a rag of brown duck; a silver-mounted flask shining in a little pool of bloody water; a stockless rifle-barrel, bent and soiled, sticking upright; beyond all a huge, hairy body, and below it a suggestion of another body and a blood-stained face, that even through its terrible disfigurement seemed to scowl with grim determination. Throwing off their coats, they dragged the dead moose aside and strove to raise Moeran's body, but in vain. Something held it; the right leg was broken and they found the foot fast fixed in a forked root the treacherous slime had concealed. In the right hand was firmly clutched the haft of his hunting knife,

and in the moose's throat was the broken blade. The veteran almost smiled through his tears as they worked to loosen the prisoned foot, and muttered, "Caught like a bear in a trap; he'd have held his own with a fair chance." Carrying the poor, stamped, crushed body to the shade, they laid it upon the moss and returned to read the story of the fearful battle. To their hunter's eyes it read as plainly as printed page. The great bull, sore from his previous wound, had sought the swamp. Moeran had trailed him to the edge and knocked him down the first shot, and after reloading had run forward to bleed his prize. Just as he got within reach the bull had struggled up and charged, and Moeran had shot him through the second time. Then he had apparently dodged about in the sticky mud and struck the bull terrific blows with the clubbed rifle, breaking the stock and bending the barrel, and getting struck himself repeatedly by the terrible forefeet of the enraged brute. To and fro, with ragged clothes and torn flesh, he had dodged, the deadly muskeg behind and on either side, the furious bull holding the only path to the saving woods. At last he had entrapped his foot in the forked root, and the bull had rushed in and beaten him down, and as he fell he struck with his knife ere the tremendous weight crushed out his life. The veteran picked up the rifle-barrel, swept it through a pool and examined the action, and found a shell jammed fast.

In despairing voice he said, "Oh, boys, boys, if that shell had but come into place our friend had won the day, but he died like the noble fellow he was!"

With rifles and coats they made a stretcher and carried him sadly out to the lake.

"*He would get that moose, or stay in the woods forever!*"

3.
MODERN NOTES ON UPLAND SHOOTING
(1888)

THE WOODCOCK AT HOME.

OUTING.

SEPTEMBER, 1888.

MODERN NOTES ON UPLAND SHOOTING.

BY FRANK CAMPBELL MOLLER.

ANY fine early autumn morning when the farmers are cutting and sheaving the husks and cornstalks, one may hear the gregarious, cheery little quail, who loves the cultivated lands about the old homestead. The first rattle of the ox-cart may start them from the stubble-field to the shelter of bog tussocks or of the cat-brier coppice by the spring drain in the meadow.

The grouse, with plumed head and regal ruff about his shapely neck, whirls up with a noisy flight from its hiding-place beside the lumber path on the wooded hillside, where at evening the far-off tinkle of the cow-bell causes the farmer's boy to grumblingly trudge along the track of the past winter's logging, in search of the kine, wandering where the dusk is gathering under the mountain laurel and feathery pine. But the woodcock—that long-billed, night-loving bird, whose high set, big dreamy eyes mirror the moonlight in which he loves best to travel—is the least known of all our upland game birds in the mysterious gloom of his swamp-shaded life.

The rapid and extensive growth of our large cities, in the vicinity of which most of us do our shooting, and the changes incident to such growth in the climate and topography of the surrounding country, have produced radical changes in the habits of several of our most valued species of game birds. "Frank Forester" wrote in his "Field Sports," thirty years ago, relative to the fall flight of woodcock, that "after a black frost not a bird is to be found in the country." To-day, the main body of birds is not known to frequent the spring-fed ferny turf on the southern slope of the birch-clad hills, or to lie under the black-stalked alders that o'ershadow the stream in the meadow flat, until a good black frost has skimmed with thin ice the horse-trough in the stable-yard, or laid low the sturdy red and yellow dahlias in the kitchen-garden.

In shooting woodcock during the autumn, the birds are rarely found in the same grounds whereon they bred in April and May, but in swampy woodlands, under whose shade, thick with undergrowth alders, sluggish streams creep through banks of soft loamy soil tufted with clumps of skunk-cabbage and rank ferns, I have known

THE WOODCOCK'S VESPER FLIGHT.

them to remain late in July, until they left for the moulting-grounds.

It was, and to many is still, a matter of speculation why woodcock disappear from their midsummer haunts.

The absence of the few woodcock hatched and matured, which have escaped legal or illegal shooting, as certain States may hold the law, may readily be accounted for. They merely betake themselves, scatteringly and singly, to the drains on the mountain side, or to the thick covert dells where the fern-beds, watered by some rock-born spring, grow luxuriantly in the damp shade of black birch and giant rhododendron. There I have shot them in the pin-feather of the August moult ; there I have found them while beating for ruffed grouse in September ; there many remain until some one tramping the hills, with gun and dog, in "cheery nut-brown October," finds them on what is designated "early fall ground."

Later, as the nights become colder, under the full moon and frosty breath of the queen of the autumn months, they descend to like lyings lower in the valley, especially to the neighborhood of bright streams of running water bordered by high turfy banks and shaded by saplings and second growths. At this season they no longer particularly affect the mud-lined streams of the swamp woodlands. Here the worms have burrowed from the frost, which may lie all day under the cold, darksome thicket, too far for even the woodcock's long, searching bill. The "flight birds" will now be found on the springy, mossy turf that covers the alder and birch-roots, and where the little angle-worms lie close under an earthy carpet, warmed here and there by stray rays of mellow sunlight stealing through the half-denuded branches of the spinney stretching beside the murmuring water.

The birds which in the spring migrated

farther to the north and there bred, return in the autumn by short nightly journeys and reappear day by day in the local coverts.

This passing flight lasts about three weeks. It commences, generally, with the full of the moon which ushers out October or lights up, in fitful gleams, the cloud-swept early November night, when the hoar-frost lies long into the day under the shadow of barn, tree, and stone-wall. The moonlight itself, however, is not, as commonly supposed, essential to the southern migration of the woodcock, although they are in some way influenced by the phases of the orb itself. In the autumn of '77, which, by the way, was a very poor one for this species of sport, I found the only flight of consequence on my old shooting-grounds during a week of incessant rain and nights of inky darkness, but at a time when the moon, had it been visible, would have shone in its third quarter. The main body of woodcock shape their migratory course by the line of some long, broad body of water, independent of the little brooks and rivulets, beside which they may pitch as they turn off to rest in the wilds of the back country. Along the Hudson, for instance, opposite Yonkers, and the Connecticut side of Long Island Sound, many cock are shot every fall where a bird is never seen in the summer months. By the end of November, the flight has passed south of the Jersey swamps, albeit an occasional bird may be started for a week or

two later by some warm, sheltered spring-hole. I have killed stray, big, strong-flying birds—those of white forehead, jet-black bills and pink-colored, thickly-feathered thighs—as they whirled up into the first snowstorm of the season under the leaden sky of a Thanksgiving afternoon by a Putnam county pond, the shores of which were ice-coated.

Is there any truth in the theories expounded thirty years ago and advocated to-day by those who fail to find woodcock in August and September, that there is a second general migration still farther northward; or else a general gathering on the nearest mountain-tops in the vicinity? If so, why have we not heard, during all these past years of sporting, travel and exploration, of August flights over the Canadian border or in the Hudson Bay Country; or, in the other case, of large collective "moults" on our local mountains?

In August a few of these birds undoubtedly remain in their early summer lyings. During this month a low-lying corn-field within easy flight of the neighboring swamp, is a favorite resort for them, particularly after a rain-storm has softened up the rich, deeply furrowed mould between the rows of green stalks. Here, if the corn reaches above one's head, it is often impossible to catch a glimpse of the cocks when they rise from the row parallel to the one followed by the gun. But good sport may sometimes be had in such places by one of the party, with a dog, beating the field,

FEMALE GROUSE.

while the other stands on top of the encompassing stone-wall. An easy shot is obtained at the bird swiftly winging across the broad-leaved stalks, which sway, with their heavily fruited, tasseled ears, a mass of emerald light and green shadow in the summer wind.

Again, where the patches of standing blackberries grow in semi-open reaches of the swamp side, or a dwarf apple-tree drops its small juicy fruit on some little elevation of rich soil by the old snake-fence running through the brake, a moulting August woodcock may often be found. Here he loves to probe his bill into the succulent recesses of the cool, worm-eaten fruit, and riot in the supply of ants their decay furnishes. A couple of hundred yards away the muddy shores of the stream may contain numberless borings made overnight; but not a bird will be started in beating along the banks where they were always flushed a few weeks earlier in the season. The presence of fresh tracks and patches of swamp earth honeycombed with billings, and the absence of the birds, have puzzled many sportsmen in that most unsatisfactory of all sports—August woodcocking. Such are some of the vagaries of the woodcock.

On being flushed in the covert, he springs, with his *tremolo*, rising whistle, about ten feet in the air—just high enough to clear the willows and alders, and glides over the undergrowth and between the oak and maple tops for fifty or sixty yards. Then as his high set, and, by day, short-sighted eyes discern some glade or opening in the coppice, he turns quickly, and darting suddenly down, runs two or three feet into the covert shades. Woodcock, unlike quail and grouse, never force their way through the thicket when alighting, but always seek to drop in some cleared spot on the edge of the brake. A knowledge of this fact is most essential to mark them properly. The oftener this bird is flushed, the wilder is each successive rise, and longer the following flight. If not killed on the third or fourth finding he will vacate altogether the shelter of the swamp, and drop perhaps in some perfectly open field far up the hillside. When a bird once quits the swamp, thoroughly frightened away, it is useless to hunt for it more until it has had a chance to return in the still quiet of the night to the old feeding haunts, which before late Autumn it is nearly certain to do; but a flight bird lost in this way never returns again to the same covert.

A woodcock, when only wing-tipped, rarely, if ever, runs like other game birds after falling to earth, but squats as concealed as may be within a few feet of where he fell, and watches with big round eyes the pointer sent to retrieve. He seems wisely aware of the generally fruitless actions which cause a slightly wounded quail or grouse to lead the setters a long, puzzling foot-scent before it is seized between the red, saliva-coated lips of the trailing dog. A quick turn of the sportsman's wrist, and death comes quickly and mercifully with the dislocation of the neck; the lids half close over the bright eyes, and a convulsive shudder shakes a few feathers flying earthward, or to lodge on one's shooting jacket.

Those who go for summer woodcock shooting must be on the ground the first few days, as the birds, when once shot off, are not replaced by others as in the autumn flight. The scattered and diverse lyings affected in August and September will hardly repay one for a trip into the country for the express purpose of woodcocking, though during the latter month it may be combined with ruffed grouse or "partridge" shooting, under a hot sun and in the thickest covert from which, for a month yet, no leaves will fall. But if one is resident, at the time, at a country house about which there are fair coverts, an early morning or late afternoon tramp after woodcock and grouse may yield an agreeable change from the monotony of the tennis-court or the glare of the black bass pond. It may also result in most acceptable adjuncts to the next day's dinner table. It surely will, at least, render one as anxious for the cold shower tub and fresh raiment as an hour on the river with the sculls or a bout with the gloves at the end of the billiard-room.

It will take you past the nooks where cattle stand knee-deep in willow-shaded streams; where the wild-roses exhale a perfumed heat at the edge of the tangled brake. Ascending the dark ravine where the breath of fragrant pines is borne along on the gentle rush of water, you reach the stream head on a flat in the mountain side. Here, between the fluffy white tresses of the trailing clematis, which hang in transparent veils from mountain laurel to silvery birch, the country side rolls away in the sizzling heat along the valley, the summer wind caresses your heated brow, the ferns wave at your feet, you are in the September home of the grouse and woodcock. For the late summer drought always forces the former bird from the dry slopes to the spring-watered gullies. The flesh of the moulting woodcock is as good, and his flight as strong as in the month of July, but his winging is lazy and his instinct dull compared with the full-feathered, sagacious October bird.

The acme of woodcock shooting comes with the autumn flight, which, alas ! is becoming smaller and smaller every year. I always time my annual fall outing to include, in its four weeks' scope, the swift-flying, full-plumaged woodcock. In the alder coppice, which lies a patch of dismal brown between the red and gold of the wooded hill-slope and the running blue of the meadow stream, one may flush our three varieties of upland game, woodcock, quail and grouse, within gunshot of one another, and perchance see the red-brown hare scurry away over the dead leaves covering the most bottomland.

I have often noticed, in current sporting publications, descriptions of ruffed grouse or "partridge" shooting in counties neighboring to New York or Boston, wherein, amid glowing delineations of October coloring, atmospheric effects and rural settings, the dogs always managed to secure points before the first rise of these birds. For myself, shooting within a hundred miles or so of our Eastern cities, and with the best adapted dogs, I am rarely able to obtain points on matured grouse after they have left the maternal guidance and straggle about their wild and rugged solitudes either singly or in twos or threes. Naturally, in this paper devoted to country sport, all references are excluded to those tamer birds of tree-alighting proclivities, which furnish but few opportunities for wing-shooting in the Adirondack woods and the Maine and New Hampshire wildernesses. The grouse of our adjacent rural counties rarely tree.

In early September, when the coverts hang thick and unthinned by the frosts, and the packs are yet unbroken, and up to the time unmolested, they admit of a close approach of the dog and gun. On being flushed, they scatter and lie as closely as quail in a hedgerow, but the full-grown and educated October bird, with his largely developed aural cavities, will spring up forty and, aye, sometimes seventy yards ahead of the dog, which he hears pattering over the crackling dead leaves. It is this first wild rise that loses this magnificent bird to many unobservant sportsmen. Take his line, which may be indicated but by the shadow of a wing, gliding through the woodland. Follow it. The ruffed grouse invariably fly in a direct line, making only a short curve to the right or left as they lower their flight in alighting. Now keep the dog at "heel" until the bird flushes again of his own accord, and this time perhaps within gunshot.

With the grouse, unlike the woodcock, each successive flight is shorter, and he lies correspondingly closer. If not found to flush up with his noisy, defiant hurtling after the second or third moving, the sportsman should order on the dog to beat the ground whereabout you have marked him down or think he has probably alighted. Here, thoroughly frightened at last, he may be kicked up almost underneath the dog's nose, which is now held low and close over the steaming scent. Your sportsmanship has triumphed. You have a ruffed grouse lying to a point. Now step up, flush and kill him if you can, as he whirs with the accompanying thunder of his rise through the wall of mountain laurel and sails with outstretched pinions and fan-like tail up and between the hemlock tops. Comparatively few grouse are shot over a full point. I kill the majority of those birds that I bag as they rise wild, and my dog is either following at heel or beating at close range. In this sort of shooting, the setter's or pointer's utility is in most cases limited to retrieving or to trailing the wounded.

Ruffed grouse are uncertain birds to find in any stated haunt. Although the lives of most of them are spent within a square mile or two of the hillside whereon they were hatched, they do a vast amount of traveling about the home coverts, wandering down the mountain to the swampy woodland ; sometimes sunning themselves in an old rag field ; wallowing in the warm dust of the lumber track as it crosses the sunlit clearing, or where a secluded buckwheat stubble fringes the wooded hilltop. The early autumn droughts may force them from the hills to the bog-tufted swamp where thick covert is afforded by dense undergrowths of rhododendron and alder, and the juicy poke-berries hang close by the ground. The cold nights of late autumn will have the same effect. Yet on the same morning that one has been started in such places you, perhaps, continue your beat up the warm southeastern slope of an adjacent hill. Here, in softly measured cadence, the odorous breath of whispering pines caresses the velvety bloom on the little frost-grapes' cheek. Beneath those tangled, sweetly smelling vines the grouse loves to lie with his crop full of the luscious purple globules. Here the increasing power of the rays of the heightening sun steals through the twisted stems, warming luxuriously the dead moss and leaves whereon the big-breasted bird is squatting with the black, velvet-like gloss of his outstanding ruffs tipped with the early golden light. On such ground I have some mornings started twelve or fifteen of these birds, and where the following day not one was to be found.

Old grouse, when ousted often from fre-

bird lie sufficiently close. But he will depend mainly on the other guns to render an account of the birds thus driven past the openings.

There is no other branch of sport which calls for more acquaintance with the country-side, knowledge of the secrets of rural field-craft, patience and unlimited powers of rough walking than beating for October and November grouse. Absolute silence is indispensable. Nothing startles this bird so much as the sound of human voice. This I have discovered often to my cost; for when I have been following the course of some wild grouse, a loud call or an-

ON THE WING.

quented haunts, form certain courses of flight as well as the wild deer that have their forest "runs." The only killing way to hunt these birds is, when two or three are of the shooting party, to post the guns along the covert side, by wooded paths and glades, past which you know, from previous observation, that they will fly when started. Then, when time has elapsed for the men to gain their vantage points, the handler of the dogs, crashing through the brush, takes his chance for a snap shot should a

swer to my companion would again start it up out of gunshot. Had I remained quiet I might have approached to within twenty or thirty yards. The experience of past years has taught me never to set out for the exclusive purpose of ruffed grouse or "partridge" shooting, as it is more commonly called. It is too uncertain. However, I am glad enough to shoot at them when flushed from the mixed covert of quail or woodcock ground, or to follow them into their indigenous thickets when such lie in the line of my beat for the other game of the uplands.

I have in recollection a perfect day in November. One of those hazy Indian summer noons—a blending of swiftly-moving cloud-cast shadow and golden sunlight, stippling with changing yellow lights the browns and madders of the landscape. We were coming down the faded green slope of a pasture hill on the other side of which we had been having good sport with the quail as they rose over the cat-briers and withered flags of a moist bottom valley. A dense swamp woodland lay before us. Across the northern end ran a wide cow-path with a rotting corduroy bridge spanning the tree-hidden stream. In this little triangular-shaped end I had, the previous day, flushed a grouse amid the matted vines and closely-growing osiers. I could not see where he went, but surmised that he cleared the outside bogs and surrounding open fields and sought refuge on the hill beyond.

We stood on the bridge and in low voices made our plans. One, with the dog, was to work through the thicket on either side of the shallow stream. Another was to follow the open on the cleared slope beyond and keep, as near as he could judge, about thirty yards ahead of where the dogs should be work' g. Grouse, when flushed, rarely quarter back. I, after exchanging the No. 10 quail shot in my left choked-bore barrel for a shell loaded with No. 6, backed with coarse, strong powder, followed the field along the right edge of the swamp.

Beyond the apex of this three-cornered woodland the stream emerged, to flow in winding course through flats of dun-colored stubble or the dead green of the frost-killed meadows. Afar off, beyond a snake-fenced lane crossing the meadows, gabled roofs and brick chimney-pots showed above brown orchard tops. The only sounds that broke the golden silence of that autumn noon were the harsh, metallic tinkle of the blue-jay, or the sonorous caw of the crows flocking toward a distant mountain. The washed-out green of the pines against the dark rust of the hills, and the warm red flanks of the yoked oxen standing in a brown fallow field were the only pronounced bits of coloring in that neutral-tinted landscape. All this I saw as I walked by the covert side. Did I not see such sights, and were it not for the picturesque adjuncts of field sporting, shooting to me would prove a mere butchery. Its attendant excitement would be found as well behind the pigeon traps as in a fifteen-mile gloriously exhilarating tramp in quest of the charming distraction amid romantic and harmonizing surroundings.

But now comes a low whistle from within the covert. It is a signal to ask our positions as a necessary precaution for mutual safety, as the high covert conceals each one of us from the other. I reply with the soft call of the quail; to answer by voice would stop the grouse, should one be ahead of us, from breaking cover on this side. "Careful, Dash," says a low voice from the break. Then one can just make out the orange and white body of the pointer as he nears a thinning in the brown-stemmed undergrowth, only to round back and creep out of sight with slow and stealthy pace. He is evidently drawing on a running bird. Now a whirring is heard in the thicket, followed by the loud call of "Mark!" Will he come out over this edge? one anxiously asks himself as the gun is held well out, while the right hand grasps the pistol-grip and the nervous forefinger hovers between guard and trigger.

Then a speeding feathered object darts out about thirty yards ahead, having gained, in the rising angle of his flight, the heights of the maple-tops. It gives one that high, open and perfectly unobstructed shot, as a rule only offered by the wild duck as he flies past your "blind" over some watery waste. The gun is pitched well ahead of him as he is speeding high across the field toward the woodland on the ridge. As the trigger is pressed and the piece instinctively lowered, one perceives an immediate cringing as a few feathers drift away from the mass moving forward by its previous momentum. Then it suddenly seems to collapse and topples over, and with down-hanging neck and a broken pinion fluttering uppermost in its light resistance to the air, it falls earthward to flutter for a few seconds with a convulsive kicking of its heavily feathered thighs. Such is the killing of a wary old cock-grouse.

These birds are supposed to be the hardest to kill of any that fly over the uplands, but, for myself, I know that I miss, proportionately, more quail in thick covert than "partridges." The latter bird will rise, almost always, to an angle of thirty degrees, as he darts upward, giving one a chance to shoot as he ascends to the height of the undergrowth, or else his big body and powerful winging leave a surging wake to fire into through the covert wall, so as to kill him, perhaps, when he has entirely passed from sight. The woodcock will have to top the alders before gliding away, and flying across a bit of open is the easiest bird of the three to kill. But a quail, in a dense thicket-bottom, will start from beneath one's feet, skim close to the ground, between the stalks of the undergrowth, and is lost to sight in a second. In the open bogs and stubbles, quail afford comparatively easy shooting. I have noticed men who are capital covert shots at woodcock and partridge—high-flying birds—often shoot indifferently at quail, as they mostly hold under this bird, whose flight is rarely higher than four feet from the ground.

Quail in our Eastern States are the most uncertain to find, as to time and place, of all our upland game. You flush a bevy in a stubble or boggy bottom one morning, yet the next day or for the next week, perhaps, fail to find the same lot again, although you may be certain that they have not wandered a mile away from the farmstead. You may be always sure to find woodcock in the same seasonable lying in summer or late autumn if there are any birds at all in the country, but the quail can live and feed almost anywhere.

This peculiarity is well noticed while looking for partridges and woodcock in September and early October. You know that several birds have mated in the vicinity, and have heard their cheery calls in the soft spring eventide, but in October one finds them not where in the latter part of the season of past years they were always flushed.

Where are they? Everywhere! In the orchards, on the hill-sides, where the grasshoppers whiz and the crickets chirp. Shooting has not yet driven them to the shelter of the thicket-bottom, or cold nights killed all insect life and forced them to live between the stubble-fields for their feed of grain and seed, and the bog-meadow for warm shelter at night, or to the swamp or cat-brier thicket for a harbor against the sportsmen of the earth and the hawks of the air. Until the frost has smothered the nocturnal note of the katydid, the flesh of the quail is soft and squashy.

At this time of the year you may have hunted all over the farm for a bevy known to frequent its shelter, even worked again, perhaps, that little woodcock swale where you found them yesterday at noontime, where they had doubtless run in to drink, and to lie snugly hidden until the long shadows falling across the old fields should warn them that supper-time was at hand. You kennel your dogs—quail shooting is the only sport in the East in which a man can work two dogs with advantage, one being all that is needed on the wild grouse or solitary, thicket-loving woodcock—and as your pen lies idly in your hand, as you look an hour or two later, from your study window, over the autumn landscape, you hear their plaintive call from among the cornstalks yet standing in your garden. Such are the vagaries of the quail of the Eastern uplands.

I have not intended in the foregoing to express any ornithological detail descriptive of haunt and habit which may be found in any of the works on field sports—mainly compiled, at veracious length, from Audubon or Wilson. Nor have I intended to give any rules for general guidance of sportsmen, but simply to state some peculiar characteristics which may aid some one, who has had less opportunities for observation than has the writer, to add, in the coming shooting season, a bird or two more to his bag in the course of the day, than if he were not cognizant of some "Modern Notes on Upland Shooting."

4.
SOME MILES
OF MARSH MEADOW
(1903)

SOME MILES OF MARSH-MEADOW

By EDWYN SANDYS

DRAWINGS BY HENRY S. WATSON

THE jarring thump on the door was suggestive of the hand of Justice reaching for the unregenerate. The safest reply to such a knock is, "Come in," and presently he came. There is that about some men which at once suggests a picture, and as I stared at the intruder, before my mind's eye spread a vision of broad English fens and wild-fowling as it was in the olden days.

Imagine a long, lean figure, loose-jointed, yet powerful, and garbed in the grimiest of moleskins; topping it off, a face nut-brown and seamed by long years of exposure to the keen marsh wind, and fringed by whiskers which suggested a lot of very rusty wire. Add to these a nose with a color worthy of an ancient meerschaum and a pair of shrewd, yellow-brown, extremely foxy eyes, and you have a fair idea of old Matt—the hardiest of all the hardy crew who yearly took their heavy toll of fur and fin and feather from our marshes.

The history of this man is identical with that of a thousand of his kind. Born oversea and inheriting that deathless love of sport which in a country like Britain makes the tireless and incurable poacher, this type of man has to choose between the certain though oft-evaded prison and the emigrant ship. Matt chose the latter, partly because his natural sound sense told him it was the safer selection, and partly owing to what he heard of the game and sporting possibilities of the broader land this side the Atlantic. At the time of his call upon me he had become thoroughly Americanized in everything except appearance; and what he had not learned of the game and wild life of the district was scarce worth bothering about. To be candid, so far as game-laws were concerned he was about as thorough-going a rascal as ever I met; yet sportsman and rigid protector as I profess to be, I freely forgave his small lapses for the sake of his many sterling qualities. Game and loyal as a bull-terrier to his friends; grim and defiant to whoever he fancied was a foe, he also possessed many qualities which would have made great a man in the higher walks of life. That he was an invaluable companion in the field may readily be imagined. In his own peculiar way he had got very close to nature, but while his knowledge of high and low lands was broad and comprehensive, his true preference was for the marsh. He *liked* deer, turkey, grouse and quail and all things pertaining thereto; but he *loved* the wastes of rush, rice and lily-pads and all web-footed and long-billed things that haunt them.

In a few minutes he explained his visit by unfolding a plan which his appearance prepared me for. As he put it—"We ain't had a shoot together for a couple of years, and I just dropped in to find out if New York has spoilt what *used to be* a pretty good feller." Now there was a deal of sarcasm in his words "used to be," and I instantly resolved to give him a practical demonstration that the alleged used-to-be had not altogether lost the old-time knack of keeping his end up fairly well. I sniffed a joke, too, because all unknown to Matt I had just put in a solid month on fast water in the North, and a stretch like that, half the time at the paddle, really leaves a fellow pretty fit.

"Oh! you'll go, eh?" he finally remarked; "I guessed you would, so I made ready before seein' you. The boat's in the river right below, so if you'll chuck them store clothes and get fixed like you should be, we'll be off in mighty few minutes."

To get into shooting-gear, buy a box of shells and get fairly squared away occupied little more than half an hour, and presently we were headed down river under an ash breeze of my raising, which was strongly aided by Matt's paddle astern. Within a mile we had struck the old all-day stroke, and as there was no possibility of game before some eight miles had been covered, we swung steadily along, smoking and chatting as two old hands will. On and on we slid till the banks began to get low and the breeze came whispering of the

"First came broods of gray ducks."

great plains close below, where the ponds spread like glassy pages o'er-written by wind-driven pens of living green. And the big heart of Matt was planning, for as the easy-running craft slid past a bend which marked the last of the farmlands proper and the first of the bronzy-grassed fen which spread for miles, he suddenly exclaimed, "Run ashore and we'll shift things a bit; there's apt to be a chance most any time below here." What he meant was that I should take the bow, with both guns before me, and do things to any fowl that might rise from either side. When two men are in a boat, this is the one allowable method, for none but a fool would let the rear man have a gun in skiff or other small craft. Some people are careless in this respect, but it is a criminal form of carelessness which too often has resulted in fatal or very serious accidents.

The dozen decoys were already snugly stowed in the bow, so all I had to do was to shift the grub and blankets and prepare a soft pad for my knees. Then with my own gun in hand and the other within easy reach, I knelt in comfort, ready for whatever chose to demand attention. After a stiffish pull, this sort of thing comes like a sweet session in an earthly Eden. A stream like the one in question is the laziest thing imaginable. Its currentless waters lie like so much oil, with only a veering cat's-paw of air to wrinkle its smiling surface. The damp banks rise barely a foot above the water, and that slight rise is hidden by a wall of sturdy bullrush and trembling rice, before which spreads a rod-broad mat of flattened water-grasses and the warped discs of the water lily. Many coots and not a few of the river-ducks are given to loitering in just such places, and often all one sees of them are dark forms and jerking heads as their owners plow small furrows through the outlying mat, and creep into the friendly shelter of the standing stuff nearer shore. Here and there, too, are short stretches of muddy, beach-like form, and these are worth a keen scrutiny, because several very interesting things look at a distance extremely like rounded lumps of mud.

As we neared one of these muddy spots, Matt muttered, "Look out—teal," and instantly my eyes were busy examining a series of brownish protuberances which looked like tufts of half-burned grass. It is hard to distinguish the rounded form of the teal amid such surroundings, but presently a slight movement betrayed the dainty quarry. When the teal rises from such a place, he gets under way almost as smartly as a grouse, so the chance is not easy. In a moment, and precisely when I thought they wouldn't, three small, swift bantams of duck kind sprung into the air, and it was so easy to miss with the second that I did it with a foot to spare. One teal, however, tarried, and Matt chuckled out, "The first was all right, but old York sighted that second barrel." Yet fate was kind; for as I picked up the dainty, wee gray thing, watchful Matt sung out, "Mark left!" and lo! there were the others coming back to seek the lost one. They found him, too, for as they drove straight past, flying as only teal do, the spreading lead covered both, and the quick spat-spat on the water ended their story.

From this point on, the action gained speed. Even the trifling reports of "smokeless" warned the marsh folk far ahead that there was "a chiel amang 'em" takin' shots, and those which did not sneak to cover were alert and nerved for speed. Big, lumbering coots splashed and kicked the water as they half-ran, half-flew for the farther side, but they had nothing to fear. Silent, rubbery grebes twisted their snaky necks and went under as though greased; but now and then a teal, and occasionally a big gray duck, rose and either paid the penalty, or went winnowing off to alarm every relative for a mile below. In an hour seven victims had been booted, while nearly as many intended victims had proved the truth of that old line about "Vainly the fowler's eye"—yet we were very well satisfied.

I am very partial to this form of shooting, not necessarily because the other fellow is doing most of the work, but rather because of the constant expectancy of what may rise. Then, too, the great majority of shots are at longish range, which, coupled with the fact that the fowl are apt to rise unexpectedly, adds to the interest of what is by no means an easy kind of shooting. The sport also is full of surprises. Once, as we were sliding past a great wall of rushes which prohibited any extensive view of the marsh beyond, there sounded a sudden hollow booming and a wedge of gray fairly ripped its way across the open. In that living wedge probably were a dozen fowl, and though the gun seemed to be swung the proper distance ahead, not a feather answered the double hail. The noise and speed of the fowl betrayed that comparatively rare and interesting species—the shoveler.

Keen as he is, Matt never postpones a meal unless compelled, so I was not at all astonished when, after a slight let-up in the

elers? 'Twer'n't a very long shot,'' growled Matt through a muffle of bread and meat.

"Hanged if I just know. I thought I allowed them plenty; but just watch me next time. I'd give a dollar for another crack at them; haven't killed a shoveler in five years," I replied. A moment later Matt gave a start, dropped his sandwich and hissed out, "Here they come now!" I just caught a glimpse of a dark mass

" Here they come now."

sport, he ran the skiff ashore where a bit of almost bare, firm ground and a stranded log formed a convenient spot for a stretch and a bite. Under the circumstances it seemed wise to take one gun ashore, for a flock of fowl might pass at any moment, so the weapon was rested against the log while we tackled some sandwiches. Because the available space was rather limited, we squatted close together, the gun within easy reach of either.

"How'd you happen to miss them shov-

rushing toward us at electric speed ; then, thoughtless of the sandwich, but keen to remedy the previous error, I grabbed for the gun. I failed to see the other arm stretched toward it, but the unexpected resistance caused me to shift my eyes from the roaring flock, and lo! Matt's snapping peepers were blazing straight into mine. "What the ——?" was all he could stammer, for both hands appeared to be double-riveted to the weapon. "Boo-oom!" went the flock not forty yards away, but the mischief was done.   At the instant, each remembered and each did the same thing—let go of the gun—and there we sat like twin fools while the roaring wedge cleft its sounding way unharmed.   Matt slowly rose, stared a moment at the vanishing flock, then bent well over and muttered, "Give it to me good and hard"; and because a rubber boot doesn't hurt much, but more because I felt that way, I slammed it to him as hard as was safe for my toes in such gear.   And therein I most grievously erred.   The old brute just hunched a trifle, then remarked, "There's some of that comin' to you too, I reckon—turn around there!"   Then our very souls seemed to rush together, and I almost bit the end off my tongue trying to remain on the earth. Then and forever I remembered that marsh-men run barefoot and get hardened.

For an hour after lunch we slipped along, Matt's tireless hands manipulating the paddle with that smooth, soundless action which only the expert displays.   About every half-mile reasonable chances offered, and I had done very well.   The stream was broader now, and distant flocks of fowl proved we were approaching the line of regular flight.   Yet some miles below was the lake, with its thousands of acres of closely-preserved marsh, from which the dull "rump-rump" of big guns proved that some of the old-timers with their ten-gauges were enjoying those privileges which accrue to the men who can afford to control extensive shootings.   We knew that the late afternoon and evening flight would furnish the best sport, and Matt had just explained how we would go to a certain point of rushes a mile or so below, when a peculiar thing happened.

We were now so far into the lowlands proper that we could see for miles either side, and away in the misty distance a dark spot was dimly visible.   Matt eyed it for some seconds, then drove the skiff close in under the reeds.   "It may be an eagle or a loon—there's no tellin'—get down an' be ready, 'cause it might be a goose," he warned, and instantly I was keenly interested.   The one thing at which I had any license to teach Matt was goose-shooting, and this he knew.   Long as he had been in the marsh, he never had mastered the goose-call, which, by the way, comparatively few men ever do, while I had carefully studied the ways of geese and their

language till, as the marshmen put it, I could "talk goose" at long or short range.

By chance the low-flying, dark form was headed almost directly for us, and as soon as seemed proper I voiced the sounding "Aw-wunk—wa-hunk" of friendly greeting.   The now plainly visible goose at first made no response; indeed it seemed to veer a point or so from its original course; but a second cautious challenge had better effect, and the fowl swerved and bore dead on.   It was flying very low, merely a few yards above the growth, and a something about its flight seemed strange.   But in goose-shooting the wise man never looks too long, so we flattened down and waited in half-breathless expectancy.   At last a low croak of inquiry caused me to rise, and there was the goose, scarce twenty yards distant.

As the barrels followed the slim, black, out-thrust neck, I half-saw a something dangling, and the instant after pressing the trigger the thought flashed through my mind that this might be somebody's half-tamed decoy with a bit of its tether trailing. It was not an exhilarating idea, but the goose went down like a rag, and we started to investigate.   My half-formed regret speedily vanished, for the fowl proved to be a young wild goose which bore the painful jewelry of a musk-rat trap firmly gripped upon a leg.   The killing really was a merciful thing.   This was the second goose wearing that sort of ornament I had seen killed, and one other flew past me with the chain of a trap hanging in plain view.   Presumably some musk-rat trappers had placed their traps upon the roosting-places of the geese, and probably with no intention of taking the winged quarry.

Where a long point of mingled rice and rush jutted forth from leagues of marsh-meadow, Matt put out his decoys.   It was a treat to watch his method, for years of observation had taught him why the wooden lures should be so far apart and arranged just so.   In a few moments the lot were riding to their anchors as wary old black and gray ducks ride when 'tis time for the idling before the homeward flight through the dusk.   The dun-colored skiff was forced into the rushes, and with eyes toward the lowering sun we watched and waited.   We knew that when the red rim passed below the water 'twas time for sportsmen to lift decoys, but an hour or more of the best of the day yet remained.

And the expected happened. First came close-bunched broods of gray ducks, an occasional quack and guttural response telling the fiction that all was well. They did not decoy with the offhand friendliness of red-head and blue-bill, but the sight of the painted lures caused them to swing in from side to side, because, in their limited reasoning, where a flock of any sort of duck could ride in quiet was a good place to be. They came, they saw, they concurred, when the sharp summons called a halt; and after them the warier black fellows—the ones of hoarser quackings and singing wings. A dark mass hissing athwart the reddening sky; the quick, insistent re-ports; the hissing falls and dull crash of reeds, or sounding falls in open water—these every duck-shooter knows. And now and then the teal, swift, small and noisy-winged, like cannon-balls in feathers, come in. It may be a small brood, or a single bird singing with speed, flashing across that magical west, where the last fires of the sun flicker amid graying ashes.

Then indeed we held far ahead, and as the dark forms bent from the line of flight and went plunging down, we told each other that this was the very cream of wild-fowling and worth all the slow toil of win-ning one's way through the long intricacies of miles of marsh-meadow.

5.
A Sporting Vacation in Montana
❀ ❀ ❀
Moose Hunting in New Brunswick (1895)

Painted for OUTING by Marc Lucas.   (See "A Sporting Vacation in Montana.")

"THE BIRDS ROSE RATHER WILD."

A SPORTING VACATION IN MONTANA.

By G. M. Dillard.

IF ever two over-worked men suddenly felt the burdens that lay upon them fall from harassed shoulders, they were my good friend C—— and the writer. At last, after many disappointments, we were actually started upon our holiday journey to far Montana.

A mutual friend, K——, a ranchman and a thorough sportsman, had written as follows from Lewistown, Montana:— "Am spending the summer on our ranch. Come, if you like. Good bird shooting and trout fishing; can also fit you out for the mountains and big game. Bring a good dog and as many friends as you please."

The "good dog," Frank, was safely chained in the baggage car; we had complete, yet compact outfits checked to our final railway station, and all we asked for, in addition to existing comforts, was safe and rapid transit, for we were keen as only the men of few holidays can be.

We left St. Paul in the evening, and all the following day we were whirled over Dakota prairies. About nightfall we entered the famous Bad Lands of western Dakota.

Bad Lands! What a picture these words present to one who has seen that district! What wonderful freak of nature formed those thousands of mounds and pillars and bee-hives and ant-hills and cones, of naked earth and rock; those Indian tents and pyramids, with innumerable roadways and lanes and streets, without life, or tree, or shrub of any kind. A city of nature, deserted and destitute, covering hundreds of square miles of territory.

Next morning we sped up Yellowstone River, to Billings, Montana, where we breakfasted. Thence, by a stage ride of one hundred and forty-two miles, to Lewistown, where nice distinctions were abolished and Frank was admitted as a first-class passenger on the stage.

We started northward, across the valley, and ascended the rocky cliff that leads to the great world above, of prairie and alkali and sedge and dust. About sunset we approached the Musselshell river, which was marked by a long line of green and yellow cotton-wood trees, extending east and west far ahead of and below us. We descended into the valley, fifty miles from Billings, with feelings of great relief produced by the presence of water.

Here we saw the first sage hens; four or five feeding quietly near the trail, so much to Frank's astonishment that instead of pointing, as he has a habit of doing, he dashed after a young bird, the size of a full-grown pheasant, which flew for a great distance down the valley, constantly just out of his reach. An express bullet left enough of the largest cock for closer examination. It resembled in size and markings a Plymouth Rock fowl, though lighter in color and having a spot of rich black in the breast. In appearance it is a perfect type of game bird, but feeding on the sage leaves almost unfits it for food. We saw no more game until after we had reached the ranch, and the varying discomforts of the last stage of the journey need not be dwelt upon.

The ranch is situated at the foot of the southern peak of the Judith Mountains and close to the northern extension of the Snowy range. The space between the two ranges makes a narrow pass about six hundred yards below the house, where the ranch road leads out; and a walk of ten minutes from the house takes one out of the basin, in full view of the limitless open country to eastward. On the mountain side, half a mile above the house, beautiful fir trees grow, and an ice-cold spring flows perpetually, where deer constantly go to drink and lie in the cool shade during the warmest part of the day. Above this, on the mountain summit, is a level, grassy park, containing a thousand acres, enclosed on all sides by tall fir trees.

K——, our host, had been detained while visiting his home in Helena, and a letter from him directed us to take possession of the ranch, during his absence, and that the foreman, McG——, and Song would administer to our wants. The log-house is very comfortable, for this is a civilized ranch. The first room is the sitting-room, and of the other four rooms one is the dining-room and the three remaining are bedrooms—all furnished very much as such rooms would be in the East.

Next morning, after breakfast, we saddled our horses, provided a large sack-bag, called out Frank, Toby, a finely-trained pointer, and Sailor, an Irish setter and a grand retriever, and started for chicken.

As we rode out of the pass below the house all the dogs turned to the right and disappeared in a ravine. Quickly the heavy sound of chickens' wings notified us that game had been found. Two big birds had flushed and gone to the hill-side beyond, but the dogs held their point. C—— dismounted for a shot. As he approached the brink of the ravine, seven or eight birds rose in quick succession, and three shots from him laid out two birds to be retrieved by Toby and Sailor. I marked the other birds down on the hill-side, and we thought it would take only a few minutes to bag them all. So leaving the horses, we separated apace and ascended the hill. The ground was too open this time for a point, and the birds rose rather wild. Up they went above us, in quick succession; one, two, three, four, five, six. Bang! bang! bang! bang! bang! and five fine birds testified that the guns were held right. Their rising had not been too rapid to prevent one of us reloading and getting an extra shot. With the seven birds we started to recross the ravine to the horses, when a point from Frank arrested our progress. This time C—— scored.

Concealing our bunch of birds in the ravine, we remounted and continued our course. A few hundred yards, and another interruption. A point from Frank, backed by Toby and Sailor. This time eight chickens rose, and we divided the covey evenly. The four that escaped, after a flight of one hundred yards, settled in the low, thick, berry bushes. Before our guns had cooled the dogs pointed at the bushes, and we walked in and flushed. This time only three birds were added to the bag. Remounting, we started, but soon had to halt to another point. The birds were in high weeds along the little stream, and they got up in an irregular way that enabled us to bring down six or seven in quick order. The others were not worth following. To avoid further delay we took to the hill-sides, riding through a beautiful group of firs. The dogs quickly took a trail and worked it up finely. A rustle, a whir and a roaring flight, and a bang! with more flying and other shots, and three beautiful grouse lay dead. Without further search we rode over the high, open prairie eastward, constantly descending into deep depressions and ascending again to the common level beyond, till our attention was attracted to a favorable looking cluster of willow bushes, half a mile to the left.

The dogs coursed ahead, reached the nearest bushes, and at once established a point. Four chickens rose at our approach, and made off down the narrow brake of bushes and weeds. Moving on, a fine covey of twelve or fifteen birds flushed and settled again in the bushes. C——and I dismounted and took opposite sides of the brake. Rapid work followed. One dog retrieving, one pointing, and the other roading at the same moment. Next, all retrieving at once. Birds kept rising, two or three every minute. I had five down at once on my side, and C—— as many on his. Two flew, quartering from C——. His first shot missed, but the second killed both birds. Before these were exhausted, one or two other coveys rose and mingled with the survivors of the first. On we went to the end of the brake, firing every minute, with the dogs pointing and retrieving too rapidly to take note of their actions. The birds were too heavy to carry, and had to be left in bunches on the ground. We changed sides, and beat back with even better shooting than while going down. We had disposed of all the wild birds, and those left lay closely, and afforded excellent practice for the dogs. Three or four times we hunted up and down this brake, all within the space of a few hundred yards ; and each time had fine points and good shooting.

Finally we collected the birds—sixty-four ! Should we go on, or cry enough and return ? We decided upon the latter, and as the ranch was reached, a bunch of blue-wing teal rose from the ice-pond, and one for each of us concluded the day's shooting.

The Montana "pheasant" (the ruffed grouse) is the same as the bird found in the mountains of Virginia and the East generally ; having, however, not so rich a color. The prairie chicken (sharp-tailed grouse) is the well-known bird of British America, seven or eight hundred miles north of central Montana, and is a little lighter in color than the chicken.

Another grouse found in great numbers in the foot-hills, early in fall, but which later seeks the fir forests, high in the mountain ranges, is larger than the chicken or pheasant, with longer tail, wings and neck, of a dark gray or lead color, and is exceedingly delicate and graceful.

And now for big game, and how we got our first white-tail.

One snowy day C—— and I rode over the prairie vainly seeking a shot at antelope. We were eating lunch, overlooking a deep *coulèe*, when it was determined to finish the day after deer. We had seen a number of them about the ranch, but always out of rifle-range. Mounting, we rode along the edge of the precipice in quest of a practicable crossing, and had gone perhaps a quarter of a mile, C—— in advance, when we directed the horses down the steep, rocky side. As C—— reached the bottom of the *coulèe*, up jumped a grand buck, not ten yards from his horse. "Here he is, now," exclaimed C——, as the buck darted under the brush and aimed for the hill beyond. Taking in the situation at a glance, I leaped from my horse and, as I touched the ground, C—— fired the first shot. I saw the splendid animal going, as on wings, up the rocky cliff above us, and sent a 44-calibre bullet after him that shattered his right hind quarter, and turned him somewhat to that side. A second shot from C—— sent a bullet into the left flank, but, running on three legs, the buck disappeared over the cliff, while

we pursued with horses on the full run. I expected more shooting on reaching the top, but was mistaken. The buck lay dead, twenty yards beyond. A more perfect and beautiful animal cannot be imagined. His head, which has been finely mounted, gives but an impression of the perfection of the whole animal.

We found it no easy matter to place this two-hundred-and-forty-pound game on horseback, but finally succeeded in doing so, after backing the gentler horse into a narrow gully. The eight miles homeward, across cañon and *coulèe*, in the face of a furious storm of rain, hail and snow, were disagreeable enough; but still we felt repaid.

The white-tail deer is especially prized as food, and this one was astonishingly fat and tender. Song was an expert at cooking steaks and roasts, and we freely admitted that till one has eaten of white-tail deer, he has not tasted the finest meat on earth. It is rather a mark of good hunting to kill this kind of deer, as they are very smart, and never or rarely seen, except running. They inhabit the foot-hills and *coulèes*, while the black-tail deer live in the main mountain ranges and fir forests.

The arrival of our host, after we had been in possession of the ranch so long, was naturally a great pleasure. After a few days' bird shooting, we prepared for a trip into the mountains after larger game.

Our outfit consisted of a team and covered wagon, a large double buggy and team, and two extra saddle horses. The wagon was loaded with an abundance of blankets, a large tent cloth, several extra guns and rifles, cooking utensils, canned fruits, bacon, flour, butter, sugar, coffee; fishing rods and tackle, and in fact a supply of what was actually needful. Song and Pete, the teamster, were placed in charge of the wagon, while K——, C—— and I rode in the buggy, or on horseback. Frank and Mack, a genuine Chesapeake retriever, were allowed to play with prairie dogs and gophers till they were tired, and then to ride in the wagon.

On the afternoon of the second day we entered the foot-hills of the Belt range, and trailed up the Judith river. Our destination was the home of Jake Hoover, a veteran bear hunter and pioneer, who lives alone in the mountains, on the south fork of the Judith. Reaching the South Fork we ascended a hill, several miles in extent, that led up to the barren, rocky walls of the mountain ahead. The slight track which we had been following turned aside and entered a ravine, which closed in till it became a mere crack in the solid mountain, so narrow that the hubs of the wheels would be sometimes scraping the rock. A quarter of a mile of this brought us suddenly again into the dry bed of South Fork, and the cañon where it issues directly through the main range. Precipitous walls of rock rose hundreds of feet above us on both sides, and above that grew the dark green fir, while the stream bed was marked by bright yellow cotton-wood trees.

Here we saw the first evidence of habitation—five panels of fence laid across the stream bed, between the cañon walls; and those five panels barred the entrance to perhaps twenty thousand acres of fine grazing land, within the embrace of mountain heights too great for cattle to cross. Ascending, we soon reached flowing water, and then a bold stream. Eight or ten miles above the cañon, the mountains separated sufficiently for rich meadows to intervene between them, and we soon reached Jake's comfortable cabin. He was at home and invited us to camp there, but we preferred a wilder site, and kept on as far as the wagon could be taken, a mile above his house. Here, we pitched camp in the upper end of a little park, a few acres in extent. The location was well taken, with a few conical shaped pines and cedars immediately around camp, the clean, level park or lawn stretching out in front, bordered on the left by a fringe of yellow cotton-wood along the stream, and on the right by overtowering fir forest. The stream afforded fine trout, subject to our order for every meal, and deer, pheasants and grouse could be killed in sight of camp.

According to an appointment, Jake called at our camp, bringing with him, besides the horse he rode, three others, for carrying packs and game. We also took one extra horse. Our pack consisted of bedding and provisions for three or four days, with a tent large enough for four of us. Song, Pete and the dogs were left in camp. So off we went, eight horses and four riders. We left the meadow in a moment, struck into an open park that extended high up the mountain, and at once began a sharp ascent. Across the park, five hundred yards away, two white-tail deer were playing in the shade of the forest line, but before we could dismount for a shot they disappeared in the darkness of fir. Presently, we too entered the forest.

Jake had blazed the trees for three or four miles through this wonderful mass of timber, and by his marks we wended our way in single file, in and out between the trees, underneath an almost solid canopy of fir branches which excluded the sun-rays. We could see only a few yards in any direction, but presently we emerged into a small park, with an ice-cold spring and good grass. Here we picketed horses and pitched tent in a level corner of the park, beneath tall trees, and prepared for an afternoon hunt. Signs on all sides proved that deer were plentiful, but we wanted a lion or bear.

Jake assured us that we were on the main range of the black-tail, as they go south to Wyoming and Colorado in fall; that they travel in a narrow range, varying from a quarter of a mile to a mile or two in width, and a few days later they would begin to run, when one man might kill twenty deer a day.

The hunt commenced by our advancing, with only the horses we rode, through another short space of timber into the main park, which occupies a site of wonderful beauty, perhaps a thousand feet below the mountain summit, enclosed between three great peaks—one timber-covered to its top, as we viewed its northern side, and the other two, viewed from the south, barren and rocky—a difference due to snow lying on the north side in spring, affording moisture and vegetation.

Crossing the park, we descended into the timber between the mountains beyond, when Jake and C—— took one direction, and K—— and I another. We found many signs of bears and some of elk, but could not start the game. Returning to the park, K—— and I separated and started through to camp.

K—— was ahead and got the first shot. A big buck and doe met him, turned, ran, then stopped and faced him, in an open space on the mountain side. Dismounting, he fired several shots, but the deer escaped. Without knowing of K——'s bad luck, I returned to camp, left my horse and went on foot over the hill, to the other end of the little park.

It was growing dark, and one could not see distinctly more than a hundred yards. Glancing about, I saw the well-defined image of a large deer, standing in the open park, facing me, and about ninety paces away. Thinking it a perfectly easy shot, I aimed at its chest and fired. With a bound or two it was behind a bush and off in the timber. I followed some distance, expecting to find it dead, but did not. It was a miss. I returned to the park, and was astonished to find another deer that had entered from the other side, during my brief absence, facing me at about the same distance as the first. With extra caution and determination, I again fired, and the farce of the first disappearance was repeated. I returned to camp to ponder over the inquiry, why it is more difficult to hit a deer's body than a squirrel's eye. The afternoon was a failure, but next morning we were industrious, and by breakfast time had two large black-tail bucks and a doe lying before our little tent.

After a good breakfast we remounted and started for a steep climb to the mountain top, in search of bear. Jake had killed two large silver-tips there a year before. We re-entered the big park, then the timber on the mountain side above, then dismounted and led the horses straight up toward the rocky ledge above the timber. It was a test for the wind and sure-footedness of both man and beast.

The tall tree-tops along the park were now far beneath us. We were ascending the end of a mountain range, with a deep cañon behind us, and then the commencement of another range. We gained the summit of this first mountain terrace and found a beautiful table-land, covered with high, yellow grass, over which we rode to the foot of the second terrace, higher and steeper and rockier than the first. It seemed absurd for man or beast to think of ascending such a precipice ; but in the West nothing seems impossible, and in a short time we were riding across the second table-land, through a fir grove and up the last terrace, to the very mountain top, and the grandest table-land of all, where alternate forests and parks stretched away for miles.

We separated, and I saw my friends no more until camp was reached that night. After a time, I found a fresh track of a bull elk, which led me in and out of long stretches of forests and high grass, along the eastern side of the mountain top, but I failed to obtain a sight of the antlered king. Later, I followed the track of an immense bear, but the snow remained only in patches, and it was impossible to track him surely, and impossible to find him without tracking, except by chance. Crossing westward the distance of a mile, to the limit of the mountain plain on that side, I turned campward, realizing that my companions had preceded me, and that I was alone in this world in the skies. Rousing up my horse, I hastened toward the terraces, in order to make the descent by that only way before dark. The sun, descending, gave a thousand varying shades and shadows and forms throughout the cañons and mountains beneath. It was a scene to remain with one through life.

From this camp we descended to the main camp, hoping that the snow, which had been so abundant while we were on the ranch, would return and enable us to kill a bear or two. But after several days' rest, during which we caught trout and shot grouse and "pheasant" and a deer or two, realizing· that our time was limited, we again camped on the range, in an opposite direction from that first taken.

Again the scenery was splendid and our camp site wild and beautiful, but we killed only deer and smaller game, though signs of bear and elk were numerous—we still lacked snow. Once I distinctly heard a lion's call, and the animal came so close that I heard the twigs stirring as it moved, but the thick growth of timber deprived me of a shot.

This camp was remarkable for the number of grouse about it, and had K—— taken up his shot-gun and dog, I have no doubt but that he might have bagged a hundred of these fine birds each day.

Our guide, Jake, told us many interesting yarns of adventures in these wilds. He is one of the most noted hunters in the West, and is well acquainted with the history of Montana, since its early days. He acted as hunter to General Crook's army, and has had some lively affairs with Indians on his own account. He has killed one hundred and seventy bears with the rifle, besides numbers that he caught in traps. He shoots his 44-calibre Winchester with wonderful rapidity and accuracy, and has several times had his life depend on a single shot, at close quarters with bears.

One of his experiences with mountain lions, as he relates it, and he is too true a sportsman to intentionally misrepresent it, is more romantic and wild than fiction could have drawn it.

He had ridden out in the snow to shoot deer, and had killed three out of a band of ten, when he noticed the track of a lion that had also joined in pursuit of the remaining deer. This did not disturb Jake in the least; in fact, it added so much to his eagerness to overtake the deer, that he quite forgot that these lions walk in the tracks of one another, so that you cannot judge of their number from their tracks. Proceeding cautiously, he again came in sight of the deer, some distance ahead, up the mountain. They had climbed a ledge of rock that extended all along the mountain side, and were passing through a forest of burnt timber. Almost at the same time he saw, above the ledge and a little beyond, the ears and head of a lion, as it sat watching the deer. Jake rose in his saddle to place a bullet, as he said, midway between those ears, when a powerful lion leaped from behind a tree on the ledge of rock above, and striking him in the chest, carried him off his horse, head-

long down the mountain, and his horse ran wildly away. A moment later Jake was lying on his back in the snow, his head up-hill, and the beast standing over him with one paw planted firmly on his chest, the other slightly lifted, and wagging its tail in delight, while its hot breath was exhaled into Jake's face. His first impulse was to hold down his chin tightly, to prevent his throat being torn open, while he cautiously felt for his knife. He found the knife and as he drew it a slight grating sound caused the lion to rebound at his feet, and as it did so, it uttered a scream which Jake knew gave him only the chance of a moment. It was a call for the other lion. Fearing to make a motion of escape or resistance, he moved his hand back in the snow, in search of his rifle, which had been lost in the fall. His finger touched the stock. He cautiously pulled it down by his side, and still looking his captor straight in the eyes, slowly turned the rifle till its muzzle faced the lion. The bullet passed through its heart and it sank on Jake's feet. Before he could move from his helpless position, the other lion bounded over the precipice, and somewhat overleaping his mark, lit in the snow, and instantly received a bullet in its brain. The two lions lay dead, not ten feet apart, and Jake arose master of the field.

This, and many another thrilling experience, Jake described in plain hunter's language as we lounged about the camp-fire; and, though we bagged neither bear nor lion, we finally broke camp satisfied. We had plenty of sport with deer, grouse, duck and trout; we had enjoyed every hour of our long holiday, and, best of all, we had found rugged health lurking in the changeful scenes which marked our never-to-be-forgotten vacation in Montana's picturesque wilds.

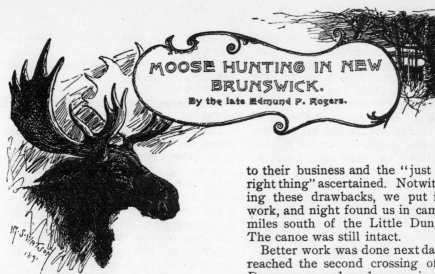

MOOSE HUNTING IN NEW BRUNSWICK.

By the late Edmund P. Rogers.

THE season was at its best when I reached Boisetown, on my way to a favorite range of the moose. At Campbelltown I had picked up my Indian, Peter, and at Boisetown I found the men, the teams, and my favorite bark canoe awaiting my arrival. I had conceived the idea that this canoe would be very useful upon certain long stretches of dead water, and so had resolved to risk the experiment of transporting it one-hundred and fifty miles into the woods. Some of the natives assured me that the canoe would be kindling-wood before it had traversed half the distance, but I was determined to risk it.

After carefully packing impedimenta and securing some necessary stores, we started upon the first stage of our trip into the wilderness. We made good progress until noon, when we halted for rest and food at a farm-house, the last upon our route. About dusk we made camp at the portal of the forest primeval, and all hands soon turned in, for all knew that the real labor of the trip was yet to come.

A lovely crisp morning found us early astir. The precious birch was secured to its sled, and anxiously watched by all hands as it bumped its way over bowlders, stumps and ruts. As on all first days, whether packing in the Rockies or sledding on the wood roads of Canada, numerous vexatious stops occurred, till ropes were stretched, horses settled to their business and the "just exactly right thing" ascertained. Notwithstanding these drawbacks, we put in good work, and night found us in camp, four miles south of the Little Dungarvon. The canoe was still intact.

Better work was done next day. We reached the second crossing of Little Dungarvon, and made camp in a lovely spot; a gentle slope to the river, knee-deep in grass. The white canvas lean-to of the guides, surrounded with the packs, sleds, harness, etc., my tent about twenty yards off, and the four horses enjoying their succulent supper, all made a picture that would stir any sportsman's heart.

We started the next morning through a succession of heavy showers and gleaming sunshine, and mid-afternoon found us at the rough log fish-house on the Big Dungarvon.

All anxiety about our beloved canoe had vanished, for we had accomplished a piece of portaging that was probably the first of its kind. The only accident was at once unexpected and amusing. We had halted at the head of a sharp descent, where all hands took a rest and a smoke. We little dreamed that one of our nags would use the bow of our birch as a scratching post; but this, to our horror, he did. His vigorous swaying started the bark sheathing, but fortunately high up, and a little rosin and cloth soon repaired the damage.

After lunching, we bade adieu to our teamsters, launched and loaded the canoe and started up-stream, finally making camp at Beach-nut Cove. Here we were joined by the men who had been sent on a week before to clear our trails, select camping grounds, etc. These hardy woodsmen, backing packs of from eighty to one hundred pounds each, tramped over the mountains.

Sunday found us in permanent quarters, on the dead waters of the Renouse. As this was to be our main camp of supplies, two days were taken to fit it up, while B—— and I scouted' about in quest of sign.

On one of these expeditions we saw a striking example of the beavers' ingenuity. Finding our route barred by one of their dams, we broke away about six feet of it. Two days after we found the breach repaired and it was almost impossible to detect where the repair work began and ended. In deference to this workman-like job, we pulled the canoe over, and left our ingenious and industrious friends in peace.

After completing our main camp and securing stores against that arrant thief and epicure, the bear, we started for Lewis lake. This is a magnificent sheet of water, about three miles long and two wide, and abounding in trout. Our useful craft, the catamaran, which had been hauled out the previous fall, was quickly launched, and after poling to the head of the lake we soon had our old quarters in comfortable order. Then we killed a dozen big trout, had supper and turned in.

While fishing, we had an amusing experience with that skillful thief, the mink. B—— had taken several fish, which he had tossed on the beach behind him. Presently he heard a purring noise and on looking around, he found a mink helping himself to choice tidbits. The thief paid, later on, somewhat bitterly for his rascality. B—— happened to leave his tackle lying near the water. On the hook was a piece of pork, which the mink endeavored to filch, and in so doing hooked himself fast. He was haled at end of the line up to camp. He fought like a terrier at every effort to get hold of him, and it was only by slipping him into an empty bag that he could be secured, and even then the hook had to be filed off. The time made by that mink from camp to lake was a two-minute gait, and we were not again troubled by his visits.

Round Lewis lake, at a distance of from one to two miles, are large barrens dotted with lagoons. Sign was plentiful, the barked saplings and their twisted limbs showing that the moose were rubbing off the velvet and sprucing up to make a gallant show before their lady-loves.

One morning Peter said to me, "You get moose to-day."

"Why?"

"Me dream of blood, sure sign;" and so indeed it turned out.

Picture to yourself a perfect Autumn afternoon, the air just cool enough, a light breeze ruffling the lake, and the surrounding hills gorgeous in their varied and brilliant tints. We started about three o'clock for a large barren, about a mile away. Just as we struck the opening of the trail to the little lake, we saw on the opposite shore a bull moose. His antlers flashed in the sun with every motion, and his coat appeared almost as black as ink. Crouching at once in the friendly screen of the alders, we quickly made preparations to call.

The bull was taking things in the most leisurely style, cropping a bit of moss or sipping a mouthful of water, but at the first note of the challenge he became an active, fierce opponent. Raising his lordly head, he uttered an answering roar that carried "biz" in every note. He was eager and ready for fight, and he started at once to come round the edge of the lagoon, giving with each step, a short, sharp grunt, as much as to say, "I'll cook your mutton, presently."

The distance he had to come was about a quarter of a mile, and he stopped every now and then to give forth a bellow in answer to our renewed invitation to "come and have it out."

The sight of that great, raging brute was one never to be forgotten. In all my previous experiences in hunting I had seen nothing to equal it, for it must be remembered that the bull was in full view for nearly two hours. It is impossible to describe our feelings. The fear that some whiff of wind might carry the taint of our presence to his keen scent; the dread that some slight defect in the call would alarm his sensitive hearing; the necessity to remain as quiet as the grave in our hiding; his partial disappearances when the trail led around some large bowlder or a few yards into the forest, kept our excitement at fever heat.

When he was within a hundred yards

Painted for OUTING by Marc Lucas.

"THE KING OF CANADIAN WOODS."

or so of us, he halted. He was evidently stripping for work. Tossing his head, striking his horns against the saplings, pawing up the mud and moss, and throwing it over his back, he presented a sight rarely granted to the hunter. His stop troubled us, as he might fool about till dark. A whispered consultation was held. The feasibility of trying to creep nearer to him was discussed. We dreaded to risk another call, as the slightest failure in its tone would be fatal. Finally, in desperation, we uttered one more call, and so perfect was it that the bull at once started forward. We could hear the rattling of his antlers against the trees, and the welcome bark given with each step. Nearer and nearer came the sounds, till at last they ceased, and a bellowing challenge followed, so close to us, that it made the few hairs on my head fairly stand on end.

"Reckon you had better give it to him," whispered B——.

Simple advice enough, but fraught with indescribable import to the chap behind the gun. The moment so desired was at hand, and the next would see well-earned success, or ignominious defeat.

Rising, I beheld a sight which few city men have seen. Within ten yards, his magnificent antlers towering over his massive head, his eyes red and savage, and his mane erect and bristling, stood the King of Canadian Woods.

A rash movement, a tremor of the arm, might have spoiled it all, and the probability that a wound would send him charging down upon us (woe betide us in such event), did not tend to steady me. Aiming until I could see the very curl in the centre of his forehead, I pulled trigger.

Though blinded for a moment by the smoke, I knew from the thrashing going on, and B——'s triumphant shout, "You've got him," that the game was mine. Aroused by the shot, Peter and Pringle came tearing along the trail, and presently pronounced the head to be far beyond the average.

The hands of three skilled woodsmen soon finished their task. In half an hour the head so longed for was on Peter's back, and succulent steaks and liver in the hands of the others. With flaming torches of birch bark we marched back to camp, a triumphal procession indeed.

We went to the same barren next morning, and, somewhat to our surprise, saw a moose feeding. Its head was concealed by foliage, so that we could not decide its sex. We made a careful stalk down the bed of a small stream, and to our regret, found a cow moose browsing on the lily pads near the shore. We quietly watched her for five minutes or so, and then rose with a shout and waved our caps. She quickly disappeared in the forest.

The old adage, "It never rains but it pours," proved itself to be a true one. That evening a noble bull, evidently having found one of our trails to the barrens a convenient route, deliberately walked into camp. He came within twenty yards of the main fire, where all hands were talking and smoking, and cooly took in the situation. Unfortunately, before I could reach my rifle, he concluded to leave, which he did at a cracking gait.

Another rencontre occurred, but it was a very ludicrous one. Peter and I had tramped over to the main camp for some supplies. On our return, when we were within a few yards of the catamaran, with Peter leading with a substantial pack on his back, he suddenly stopped and shouted, "Bear, bear, shoot!"

"Where shall I shoot, Peter?" I asked, not seeing the animal.

"No matter, shoot, shoot anywhere."

I don't know whether the poor little bear or Peter was most frightened. They had met face to face, and both were too startled to know exactly what to do.

Black bear are numerous in this portion of New Brunswick, but I never found much excitement in hunting them. We killed two nice ones with beautiful fur, and one morning we saw a she bear and her two cubs swimming near the opposite shore. After a man has once hunted grizzly he is apt to neglect black bear, except he is after skins. These I cared little about, and not once did we hunt in earnest for the fat black fellows. Had we done so, several skins might have been added to the handsome trophies that we brought out of the woods when our pleasant holiday was done.

6.
DUCK SHOOTING ON SOUTHERN BAYOUS
(1903)

In some places no blind is needed ; you may push your boat in behind the rushes, put out your decoys and be sure of soon getting a shot.

DUCK SHOOTING ON SOUTHERN BAYOUS

By H. S. CANFIELD

FIFTY years ago, in the gray of the late autumn evening, a man stood at the point of a little headland which jutted into Bayou Têche. He was six feet high, and eighteen inches wide, and his gun was nearly as long as himself. Blue cottonade trousers covered his thin legs; a hickory shirt was on the upper part of him; a wide straw hat came down to his ears; his bare feet were thrust into rawhide shoes. His small dark eyes were alert and keen.

The gun was a muzzle-loader of 14-gauge. Its barrels measured thirty-eight inches; they were beautifully damascened, and so soft that the ends of them might be trimmed with a dull knife; if overloaded they swelled at the breech, and had to be beaten into shape with a wooden mallet. The stock was of finest rosewood, scrolled and carven. The hammers, even when drawn back, projected much above the line of sight. This gun had been a flint-lock weapon, but in the progress of things had been changed to use percussion caps. Before leaving his cabin that afternoon, the man had loaded it carefully, then stuck a needle into the tubes to make sure that the passage was clear, then primed the tubes with grains of hard black powder, then fitted on nicely a couple of "G. D." caps. The loads were each of three drams of powder, brown paper wadding rammed down until the rod leaped from the barrels, an ounce of soft No. 4 shot, and more brown paper sent lightly home. He wanted these loads to go off, because he had no meat in the hut. With him literally it was duck or no dinner. He intended to be sure, because he had no more ammunition. In fact, he was afraid that the charge in the right barrel was a little light, for the powder in the horn had run low. The Têche steamboat, which connected with the Mississippi steamboat, which came from New Orleans, which was to bring him five pounds of powder and two sacks of shot, would not arrive for two days yet.

He stood on the point, facing south, his eye glancing to the east, for he knew that any passing ducks would come from that way, bound westward to the swamp for roosting. The sunset was red, and the beards of Spanish moss wagging in a little breeze were dyed to blood. He was at ease, leaning upon one foot. The gun rested upon its stock in front of him, and the muzzle came nearly to his chin.

Around a bend half a mile to the east, shot two small dark objects. They were mallards, drake and hen, the drake twenty feet in the lead, and both going for all that was in them. They were late and on business, for they had twenty miles to fly to the deepest fastness of the unknown swamp, and there is no twilight down there. Sixty feet above the bayou, thirty yards out from its shore, they cut the air with necks stretched far forward, and shimmering wings bowed and quivering. There was a whinnying whistle as they passed. A mocking-bird on the topmost bough of an oak ceased his song for a moment as they dashed by him; a blue heron, a lonely and desultory fisherman on the bank, cocked his head sideways, and watched their going.

The man saw them when they rounded the bend, and dropped to one knee; then he was rigid. The half-mile was covered in forty seconds. The long brown barrels came up quickly. Right at the end of the gun the man saw the leading drake. He switched his weapon forward until five feet of space showed, and, still swinging it steadily, pulled the forward trigger. The drake's head dropped instantly, he whirled on his back, and then in a series of somersaults struck the water far below, sending it up in spray. Before he was half way down, the second barrel had spoken. The hen had swerved widely and furiously as the powder cracked, going up and out, but she was not fast enough. The heavy shot caught her under the lifted wing and she went dead, sinking on a long slant. It was clean work, pretty work, and the shabby hunter smiled broadly as he scrambled down the westward bank of the point and into a pirogue. There floated his dinner and his breakfast, and his luncheon and his supper, and he could wait a day for the coming of the ammunition. He told himself in patois that he was as good a shot as Jean Baptiste de Coco farther up the bayou, as good a shot as any man in the parish, and very probably he was. The heron had flown down the stream in the fast-falling dusk, scared and wondering, and the mocking-bird's song was still.

Long ago the 'Cadian marksman swallowed and digested the drake and hen—may they have made his nerve steadier and the modern who too often stands on the headland is armed with a cheap and chipper "repeater." If he misses the drake with the first shell, he pumps five more after him, and counts his score by the number of birds he butchers, not by the number of times he shoots. Things have altered in many ways for the worse, and few ways for the better. It is to be doubted that any choke-bored, hammerless, breech-blocked, automatically ejecting double-barrel of the present shoots any more strongly than the old muzzle-

Rising for a Shot in the Open Waterway Blind.

and his eye keener—and then went to his fathers. Still the mallards swing along the bayou at sunset, and other marksmen with sallow skins and small brown eyes mow them down. Only, alack! the old muzzle-loader which was made in France, and cost many napoleons, has gone to the junk-pile, loader—two out of two is hard to beat—but the guns they make now are hard on the game because of the rapidity with which they may be fired. In the old days, when a man stood on a pass he got two barrels into a fleeting flock, and while he was reloading some dozens or hundreds had a chance to go by in safety. Now he empties four shells into one flock, two more into a flock immediately following, and then is reloaded with six charges in a tenth of the time consumed by the former method. One of the strangest things about wild fowl is the manner in which they have borne up against the continued assaults by continually improved weapons.

Southern Louisiana is the winter home of tens of thousands of all sorts of ducks and geese which make their way down along the Atlantic coast, or by way of the Great Lakes and the Mississippi River. When far down, a big detachment of the birds swings westward over Texas, and goes to the southwestern coast of that State between Corpus Christi and Brownsville; many of the flyers which escape the guns of hunters in the Dakotas go to the same place. Yet Louisiana continues to receive its share. Certainly no finer shooting of the kind is to be had anywhere in the world than in the rich country which lies below New Orleans and extends westward to the Sabine River. Not only are big bags to be made, but they are made in comparative comfort, there being no freezing temperatures to encounter, and they consist of pretty nearly every variety of duck known to American ornithology. There, in a winter's shooting, a man may learn the looks and habits and disposition, and flights of them all. Whether he becomes a good shot or not, will depend upon the way nature fashioned him. An old dog-Latin sentence has it that "Reading and writing may be bought of the schoolmaster, but a crack shot is the work of God." He will, at any rate, become an informed ducker, able to talk of ducks interestingly, and to tell most men things about them. Canvas-backs, red-heads and mallards, pintails, widgeons and gadwells, blue-bills, butter-balls and teals, wood-ducks, squealers and sawbills, duskies, and a dozen others are there; and even the beautifully marked "southsoutherly," from Chesapeake Bay, goes down sometimes to mingle its soft notes with the more raucous voices of its cousins. A man may not kill individuals of all of these varieties in a day, because they inhabit differing water and use differing feeding grounds, but it will not be uncommon for him to get back to camp after

an evening shoot with six or eight kinds in his pockets.

The bayou shooting of Louisiana is in a measure pass shooting, because the ducks fly up and down it, either in search of food or in going to or coming from roost. They use it as a highway because, commonly, it runs through a massive forest. They are compelled either to get clear above the tops of the interlocking trees and fight the wind, or else use this natural canyon through the vegetation. Bayou Têche, mentioned in the opening of this story, is a big navigable stream, south of the center of the State and not noted for ducks, though a half-century back it was thickly peopled by them. It is on the lagoons which seam the coast part of the country that most of the shooting is had, and they are populous aërial and aqueous roadways.

A man using a gun there does not have to bother about blinds, for nature has provided them. He does not have to worry about heavy underclothing and waterproof trousers, and a coat that will "break the wind," for nature has obviated all of that too. In the severest weather he will need clothing of no greater weight than is worn North in the fall. He will not have to worry about decoys, for he can always kill a duck or two, and, setting them out on the water, with sharp sticks under their chins to keep their heads up, he can kill more. He travels flying light, and if his feet gets wet it will not hurt him. Residents, if told of the Wisconsin formula for good duck weather, that the water must freeze upon the backs of the decoys until they turn belly upward, stare incredulously. They have no ice to mention down there. Now and then, in cold which they term fearful, a thin sheet of it may form along the edge of bayou or pond, extending out for a foot, but it is gone by nine o'clock in the morning.

A man needs little furniture except a suit of corduroy, stout shoes, a slouch hat, his gun, shells and a boat. Decoys are little used except in the widest, stillest portions of the bayous, where they become miniature lakes, because the ducks shot are commonly bound to and from some place and are not stopping to feed. Consequently a man gets a great number and variety of crossing shots, and it is fine practice. Two weeks there ought to teach him how far to hold ahead of any sort of duck within killing distance, and in all the lore of duck shooting, that is the hardest thing to learn. The ducks cross two feet above the water, and forty yards out, and they cross a hundred feet above the water. They cross going with the wind, and against the wind. They will sometimes see the man crouching in the thick growth of the bank and dart straight upward. It takes a giant strength of wing to check and alter swift progress, but the duck has it. Many shells will be wasted by the man who tries bayou shooting for the first time, but unless hopelessly inaccurate by natural limitation he will improve with experience.

From a bayou seventy-five yards wide, winding its slow course into and through a swamp to flow finally into a big swamp lake, stretch at intervals smaller bayous, running at right angles and little more than creeks. The ducks fly down these in the late afternoon until they strike the big bayou, and then they hurry down the big bayou to the lake where they roost. The air above the big bayou where it empties into the lake is dark and clamorous with the fall fowl as the sun sets, because all the streams of ducks which have swept down the smaller bayous converge there, and they rush outward over the lake in a hurrying, pulsating mass that fills all nature with the beatings of its myriad wings. The shooting is not often good at the point of debouchment, because the birds seem instinctively to fear danger, and as they sweep toward the open water rise until they are two hundred yards above it. They are beaten down sometimes by high winds, and forced to fly lower than the tree tops, and then a couple of men standing at the bayou's mouth may kill a quantity of them, limited only by the fading light.

Shooting on the smaller bayous is of a different kind, for there the birds, being compressed between the lines of trees, pass much closer to the shooter. Some of these black sluggish streams are not more than twenty yards wide, and the timber comes down to their edges. The ducks are thus close at hand, the shooter being invisibly hidden; but the bayous are so tortuous, the bends are so sharp and numerous, that a bird is rarely in sight for more than fifty yards. They come and are gone, hurtling by between the drawing and expulsion of a breath, and quickness and accuracy are needed to stop them—quickness because they are for only a little time in view, and accuracy because at the close range the shot, even when sent from a cylinder-bore, have little space in which to scatter. It, indeed, sometimes happens that a mallard or sprig, centered by a pattern at ten yards, is shot in two, or shot to pieces, and is worthless. The choke-bore at that distance throws the pellets practically in a lump, and little is left of any bird hit squarely.

Most difficult of all bayou shooting, however—probably most difficult of all forms of duck shooting—is pass-shooting in the woods. It sometimes occurs that in making for the big bayou which empties into the lake, or in making for the lake itself, the fowl establish a pass through the forest where the trees grow thinly. Sometimes this pass will be half a mile long, and will cross two or three of the smaller bayous. No fair shooting is to be had along it, because the overhanging limbs of trees and the pendulous masses of moss interfere. The ducks must be taken as they cross one of the small bayous or sloughs. This is duck snap-shooting of the most rigid kind. The birds flash out of the woods on one side of the narrow stream, and flash into the woods on the other side. The space covered from forest wall to forest wall is not more than thirty yards; often it is not more than twenty yards. They are flying from forty to fifty feet above the ground, and as they are bound to roost, or bound for early morning feeding grounds, they are going at their speed limits.

No time is afforded for deliberation. The man must shoot or not shoot, and do it mechanically or instinctively. If there is any hesitation, there is no shot. The eye catches a glimpse of the passing bird; the gun leaps to the shoulder; the man does not see the gun, for he has no time to observe it; he sees only the glinting target, and if the weapon does not fall into line with it, the target is missed. It does not take a duck of any variety a great space of time to go across an opening thirty yards wide. Probably not a second is occupied in the appearance, the shot, the death, or the miss. Men act faster under such circumstances. They must act faster than the wonderfully fast duck, or they would never shoot at anything save empty air. A mallard or sprigtail or gadwell, flying across an opening of this character, is distinctly visible for a little while. The hunter can see at least that it is a duck, and even detect the variety from its form and wing motion. But a single teal, either blue or green-winged, going across is an indistinct vision of something going, and that is all. The shooter is unable to say whether it looks like a round black ball as big as a baseball, and seen for a fleeting section of a second, or whether it is a long black streak that stretches clear across the opening. There is a whizz, and silence. If the teal has crossed twenty yards from the stand, and the gun has been pitched at a proper elevation, in line of its flight, and some twenty feet ahead of it, and the trigger snatched back promptly, and the muzzle kept swinging at a velocity to equal the velocity of the teal, a kill has been made; and if any single condition among the foregoing conditions was lacking, the shot went wide and the teal went on.

It will be seen that at this kind of cross-bayou shooting a high average is not made. It is chancy work. Yet the deadliness of a man so placed will depend much upon his practice, for it is trick-shooting after all. A beginner will score probably twenty misses to a kill; one who has had three or four trials should get a bird in six; an old hand will get one in three.

Occasionally a man is found who develops a remarkable expertness at this form of wing-marksmanship. Some years ago there lived a market-hunter in St. Louis whom all knew as "Eugene." He did a great deal of cross-bayou shooting in duck passes reaching the Illinois River, and could kill more ducks in that way than in any other. "Eugene," week in and week out, would average two out of three, sometimes running strings of eight and ten straights on all kinds of ducks, and most of his birds were hit well forward, many of them through the head. He seemed to know sub-consciously the kind of duck that was crossing, and also sub-consciously to regulate his speed accordingly. The ordinary man never knows

until he picks it up whether his prey be blue-wing or canvas-back.

The ducks of the Louisiana woods and bayous, when killed between the first of of December and middle of February, are' in prime condition, their flesh taking on a rich, fat, and nutty flavor impossible to describe, but delightful to any educated palate. This is due to the amount of mast which they consume. They get many kinds of acorns, nuts of various sorts, duck-grass, corn, rice and celery. Their food supply is measureless and inexhaustible, the extent of water great, and it is these two things conjoined which bring them to that region in millions, year after year. Ducks will be there in the cool months so long as there are ducks in America. The shooting will fail there only when it has become a memory everywhere else, for the delta of the Mississippi provides for all aquatic fowls as much of a refuge as they can find anywhere, and an exhaustless storehouse. It is a sight worth remembrance to see the ducks pouring in or out evening or morning. The observer, placed upon some point which rises above the surrounding lowland, will come to think that all the sky is made of fowl. From zenith to horizon there is a shifting panorama of wings and bodies, with every hue that painter has dreamed of, flashing in the rays of the sun. The air is tremulous with wings, and resonant with calls. Overhead rushes a flock of mallards, passing, as if they were standing still, a laboring line of sandhill cranes or flamingoes. Below them a bunch of avocats flies in wide swoops. To the right an immense gang of the bronzed ibis circles over the land, uncertain where to pitch; to the left are hurrying clumps of redheads, wood-ducks, blue-bills, or squealers; outspeeding them all, miracles of flight, go the teal in a band numbering possibly a thousand individuals. The guttural creaking note of the heron falls; the bittern booms; flashing kingfishers spring their rattles; the multitudinous ducks clamor as they go; and far up, driving strenuously through thin cool air, the wild goose, barytone trumpeter of the skies, winds his solemn horn.

7.
THREE DAYS' DUCKING ON LAKE CHAMPLAIN
(1899)

Painted for OUTING by Jas. L. Weston.

"HEY! COME BACK AND GIVE US THE PROVISIONS."

THREE DAYS' DUCKING ON LAKE CHAMPLAIN.

BY ELLIOT C. BROWN.

THE woods were turning red and yellow, the nights getting cold, and the whole world seemed to be greeting a splendid autumn. All the fellows were preparing for their fall shooting, but, on account of some business, I was unable to join them. As one after another passed by my office window, bearing a gun or some other implement of the craft, I felt something drawing me to Sandbar Bridge—my favorite grounds—and a longing to get away for two or three days grew and grew, until, at last, upon an invitation from my friend Douglas to keep him company on the *Francis* for a short trip, I promised to go with him.

I knew he did not expect to do any shooting, for he was one of those strange mortals that said he "didn't see the fun in it, any way," but upon being asked if he had ever tried it, had to acknowledge that he hadn't. I determined to give him a try, and then let him decide ; and Mansfield, my brother, made a plan by which we might lure him into shooting with us, for my brother was also going. Accordingly, I sent my little twenty-five-foot launch on up the lake, with orders to wait until I was heard from.

The next morning, everything being ready, we started up the lake in the *Francis*, as fine a little boat as I ever saw. She was thirty-six feet long, with a cabin capable of holding eight persons in a pinch, so with only three on board it was quite roomy. A strong southeast wind was blowing, and we made splendid time for about an hour, when Douglas proposed crossing the lake. We both protested, saying that the northern part was much better, so he again headed north. Mansfield and I winked knowingly to one another, for the first part of the plot had been successful.

About noon we passed Rock Point, and behind us was seen a launch rapidly overhauling us, for the wind had fallen.

She passed about a mile to starboard, and Douglas remarked that she looked very much like mine. I replied that it was indeed strange, and proposed that we should spend that night in Mallett Bay. All giving their assent, again there were winks and self-satisfied expressions !

That afternoon we ran past Mallett Head and into the Bay. I had taken particular pains to be at the wheel at this time, and so, upon sighting a launch lying at the entrance to a creek, I headed directly for her. She was the same one we had passed earlier in the day ; and, upon a nearer approach, Douglas recognized her as the *Eilen*, and looked from one to the other of us, demanding an explanation in his very amazed look alone. We refused to gratify his curiosity until he was seated with us at supper that night on the *Eilen*, and then made a full confession of our plan. After some hesitation he promised to accompany us on our shoot the next morning and see whether he liked it or not.

The sun set in a bank of gold behind the Adirondacks, and the curtains were let down to keep out the cold night wind. We all lay in our blankets on the *Eilen*, pipes going full blast. All were just getting warm and comfortable, when a change in the wind forced us to go up the creek for about three hundred yards, leaving the *Francis* behind, for she was well off-shore and there was no danger of her anchor dragging.

There was no wind on the creek, so the curtains were again raised, and we lay in the light of a quarter moon. Everything was absolutely quiet, except for the song of some campers farther up the creek. After a while, upon looking over the side, I was just in time to see a muskrat go under with a "chung." Those little fellows would come paddling up, and then lie there, motionless, blinking at the boat, but upon the least sound would go under with a splash. Whenever I woke up during the night, I could hear these rats about the boat.

That unrelenting demon, the alarm-clock, woke us at three o'clock the next morning. While still half asleep, we started the engine and moved slowly down the creek. Having lit the lanterns, we took a look at the *Francis*, which swung about her anchor, the very picture of beauty in the half light, and started for Sandbar Bridge.

Day was just breaking when, the launch having been hidden, we were installed in the blind with guns out and shells placed on the little wooden shelf. With the sun's first rays the air was cleared from all mist. The decoys were bobbing merrily up and down, twenty-five yards in front of the blind. Pipes had been laid aside, and we were patiently waiting when there came a whirr-r over our heads and a small flock of blacks went past. Mansfield and I got in a shot apiece, but poor Douglas was taken so much by surprise that one of the ducks lay in the water before he realized what had happened. Then, bursting out into a hearty laugh, he exclaimed :

"Well, boys, I've seen some quick shooting myself with a rifle, but this shot-gun business beats me !"

"Wait a moment, Douglas, and you will have a chance to see them before they're on top of you, next time. It was mere luck we got that one, anyway. By George ! here come some now."

Even as said. A long line of whistlers were coming from the north, heading down the lake. They headed straight for us. "Hold slightly ahead of them, and fire just as they begin to back water," was my whispered advice to the novice.

Nearer and nearer they came. Twice they swung away, and twice came on again. We could now hear their wings whistling, and soon they circled, coming directly for the decoys. "Now," whispered Mansfield, and we answered with a vim. Four reports rang out almost simultaneously, followed by a roar like an explosion. We were enveloped in smoke, and were at a loss to know what had happened. The smoke cleared, and there on the ground sat Douglas with the gun beside him. The sight was so ludicrous that we all commenced laughing, until Douglas, who had by this time risen, called our attention to the decoys.

We were brought back to the stern realization of facts in a most forcible manner. The heads of four decoys, together with five ducks that had dropped, were floating away. One of the latter was making desperate efforts to rise, so Douglas was told to see if he could hit it, and he surpassed our wildest expectations by killing it instantly. He explained how the giant report, smoke, and disastrous effects had been caused, saying :

"Somebody left two shells in the *Francis*, and I brought them along. This morning I thought it just as well to slip them in first. They must have been loaded with black powder—even I can tell that ; and they must have shot out the wrong end, judging from the way my shoulder feels and the way they sat me down ! Boys, do you know, I think I pulled both triggers together, for both shells are empty."

The ducks recovered and the mutilated decoys brought in, we were again ready.

"Lucky they weren't live ones," mused I, as I looked down on my carefully made decoys.

"Lucky it wasn't your head," replied Douglas.

"Look out now; here comes something."

"Butterballs."

"Let Douglas have them all to himself," pleaded brother Mansfield.

"No, don't kill any ; we can't use them."

"Do you think I would shoot and *kill* a harmless little bird ?" asked Douglas absent-mindedly, putting an empty shell in one barrel.

"I think you can shoot at them all right, but as to the last part, well, I have my doubts. Go ahead and shoot at them, though, for I want one to stuff."

They had by this time swung up to the decoys, and Douglas fired, somewhere near them. One fell, a clean kill. Mansfield and I supported each other until we could fully comprehend the state of affairs, while Douglas calmly put the muzzle of his gun to his mouth in order to blow the smoke out. Upon examination the bird was found to have been hit by just one pellet, in the eye.

"You said you wanted him to keep," said the hero of the shot, "so I just laid one pellet in his eye, where it won't disfigure him, you know ; they will put a glass one in any way."

Line after line of south-flying ducks went down the lake, but did not seem disposed to come in any more. Nevertheless the sport was good up to twelve o'clock, when we moved down to Keeler's Bay, where we found the same trouble—none would come into the decoys or by calling, so we went back to Mallett Bay.

It was now nearing sundown, and Douglas wanted to go out for an hour or so to get some bass. We said that we would also go along, and found that the *Francis* was as well stocked with lines and rods as the *Eilen* with guns. We were soon seated in the tender off a point near the river, and the fun began. In three-quarters of an hour we had caught eight, Douglas getting the best, a small-mouth weighing three and three-quarter pounds. We returned to the boat well tired out, but, to our amazement, our companion wanted to go up the river to try for a heron he had seen there the previous day. We let him go, giving him a rifle and shot-gun, and accompanying him up the creek as far as our camping place. Here we left him, and went off to get some wood. Soon a nice fire was crackling on the beach, and all we waited for were Douglas and the boat, which contained the food. Soon we heard the crack of a rifle, and then two quick reports.

"I wonder if he's living," mused Mansfield.

"No, but his bird is ; look there."

A big blue heron was flying over the meadow on the opposite side of the river. Even while we looked, without any forewarning, he tumbled over and over to the ground ; but in a moment was off again. About one hundred yards farther on he took another fall, but got up and went off again. Douglas came in sight, pulling as though his life depended on it.

"Have you fellows seen a monstrous bird go past ?" asked he.

"Yes, and he's on his way over the lake now, but you had better hurry up if you want to get him. Hey ! come back here and give us the provisions." No use ; he was off again and quickly lost to sight. Twenty-four hours before, he had said "There isn't any fun in it any way ;" and here he was now, crazy with excitement.

"I guess he is a sure convert," laughed Mansfield.

Of course, supper had to wait until the food and Douglas arrived, tired but victorious. He had finally shot the heron

a quarter of a mile from shore, after it had fallen in the water and was unable to rise. It was one of the finest specimens I had ever seen. Douglas wanted to have the bird mounted, so we carefully placed it in the tender.

The sight that met my eyes the next morning upon issuing from the *Francis* cabin was long to be remembered : fog, fog, fog everywhere ; and the thickest, heaviest, wettest one I ever saw ! A consultation was held, and we decided to go to a blind about two miles off, near the entrance of the bay, and take the chances of a wind rising and blowing off the fog. Soon the launch was ready, and we moved slowly down the bay. Arrived at the island, we anchored the launch well inshore on the landward side, and then rowed around to the opposite shore. By this time we were drenched to the skin.

The decoys could hardly be seen, water and fog blending twenty yards distant. If fifty ducks had passed at thirty yards not one would have been seen. Soon it was evident the birds were flying, for the swift swish-swish of wings could be heard over the water. Not a breath of wind was stirring, so the conditions were about as unfavorable as they could well be. How we prayed for a wind that would scatter the fog and bring in the ducks !

Nearly two hours had passed, when I saw something moving about among the decoys. The bird was so indistinct, it was like shooting at a shadow. Twice I found myself holding for a decoy, and it was fully ten minues before I could get in a shot without endangering the heads of two or three more decoys. The bird lay flapping in the water, so I silenced it with my second barrel. As luck turned, it proved to be a butterball, but we kept it to put beside its fellow, which Douglas had shot the day before.

After another long wait some birds appeared beyond the decoys. I instantly knew them to be pied-billed grebes. These birds are as quick as loons in diving, and we found it was a more difficult task to get one than we at first supposed. They kept coming nearer and nearer, and soon two were picking at the decoys. They came on, and when just inside the decoys Douglas and Mansfield both shot. As I watched the proceeding it seemed to me that the grebes disappeared as soon as, even sooner than, the reports of the two guns ; but they were too quick for the boys and got away without the loss of a feather.

A flock of whistlers passed over our heads, mere flitting, shadowy forms in the fog, so it was impossible to get any. Can anyone imagine a more tantalizing condition of affairs than this? Whole flocks of ducks flying past, and yet not be able to get one ! It was simply exasperating, and we were just going to leave when several grebes swam into view. The curiosity of these birds is great, and these came on to inspect the decoys.

All of us were determined to get one at least, so we waited until they were in very close range before firing. This time success favored us, for two beautiful birds floated on the water. We all wanted something to mount after we returned home, and so, since Douglas and I each had something, the grebes were given to Mansfield.

The *Eilen* was soon under way, and we were slowly feeling our way up the bay when four specks disentangled themselves from the fog, and there, scarcely three boat's-lengths away, lay four ducks. Fortunately the engine had been stopped, and we were now "coasting." I got out on the bow, but on account of a swell found great difficulty in maintaining my balance. As we passed I got one. The rest rose and flew straight away, except one, which wheeled and flew directly over the boat. Mansfield snatched up his gun, and got him with one of the most difficult, yet one of the prettiest, shots I ever saw. Leaning out over the side, in order to get from beneath the canopy, he held onto the boat with one hand, making a one-handed shot with the other. The bird collapsed in mid-air, a clean, straight kill. The ducks—two blacks—were recovered, and we went on toward the *Francis*.

That afternoon, a good wind having risen and broken the fog, sail was raised on the *Francis*, and we turned her bow homeward. Upon reckoning being taken, we found that the sum total of our two days' fun amounted to eight blacks, seven whistlers, two butterballs, two grebes, one blue heron, and, let me not forget, several bass

8.
AFTER BIG GAME WITH PACKS
(1899)

AFTER BIG GAME WITH PACKS.

BY CAPTAIN JAMES COOPER AYRES, U. S. A.

WITH PICTURES BY JAY HAMBIDGE.

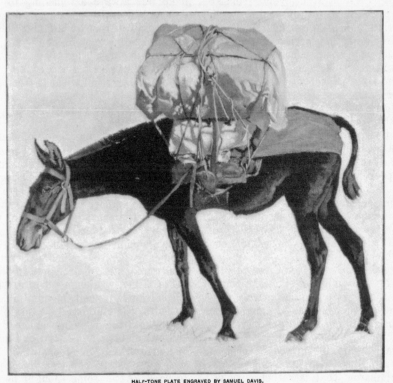

HALF-TONE PLATE ENGRAVED BY SAMUEL DAVIS.

THE METHOD OF PACKING A MULE.

FEW probably know that the United States possesses, near Cheyenne in Wyoming, a practical school for the instruction of that much-abused but indispensable animal, the government mule. This higher education is not for the ordinary draft-animal, but is confined to such individuals as have been selected for the loftier service of packing.

Pack-mules have been used in all our Indian wars. Generals Crook and Miles used them constantly in their campaigns in Arizona, and General Brooke employed them at Pine Ridge in 1890.

The feature about a mule that makes him available for packing is the fact that he becomes what the packers call "struck on" a horse. That is, mules, when once infected with this strange infatuation, will follow a horse wherever he goes, never stray far away from him, crowd about him, try to rub him

with their noses, and display other symptoms of affection. This fact makes it possible to conduct a pack-train. The horse has a bell strapped to his neck, and is called the bell-horse. The cook of the outfit leads him on the march, and the packs require no driving. They vie with one another in keeping close to their beloved bell.

It is not all plain sailing for the packers, however, as they have to keep incessant watch over the mules, for loads are constantly getting loose and must be readjusted. Occasionally, after going over a steep hill or through a bog, the whole train will have to be "worked," that is, virtually repacked.

Packing is an exact science. Weights must be adjusted so as to ride well up on the back, in order not to compress the lungs of the animal when he is cinched. They must be balanced by raising one side or lowering the other. The load must be fastened so that no amount of jerking or rubbing will detach it, and at the same time it must be so tied that it can be released in an instant when camp is made.

The organization at Cheyenne consisted of two pack-trains, or rather the nucleus for the formation of two trains, should they be required for actual service. A pack-train should consist of a pack-master, or cargador, a cook, and nine packers, who handle one bell-horse and sixty mules. Deducting the animals for riding and the reserve which is always liable to be necessary, as the packers ride farther and harder than the pack-mules travel, the available train for cargoes amounts to about forty-five mules.

For the two trains at Cheyenne there were a chief packer and the full quota of officers for each train; but only ninety-three mules were kept there, and eight ordinary packers. In an emergency more mules could be added, and, with the assistance of the skilled packers, the additional men necessary could quickly be broken in.

This pack-train was given a daily drill and was always in the highest state of efficiency. Besides the drills a regular march of two or three weeks during the summer, subject to all the conditions of actual service, was required.

No tactics are prescribed in print for packing a mule, but the packers have fallen into a rigmarole that is rather curious to listen to. The cargador, who is responsible for the proper packing of the loads, and a packer stand on opposite sides of the mule, whose eyes are covered with a leather blinder, as he will ordinarily neither start nor kick when prevented from seeing. The orders and replies are something like this, depending upon the conversational talent and the exuberant fancy of the participants.

CARGADOR. Rope; throw it pretty, now. (*Receives and returns rope.*)

PACKER. Got her.

CARGADOR. Good shot. Tied.

PACKER. All right?

CARGADOR. Bet your life. Go it when you 're mad [ready]. (*Both take in slack of ropes.*)

PACKER. Lots of rope.

CARGADOR. Come down. (*Pulling on rope.*)

PACKER. Good.

CARGADOR. Come down.

PACKER. Right.

CARGADOR. No rope.

PACKER. Tie her loose.

While this rather bewildering conversa-

tion is going on, the diamond hitch is being adjusted, ropes are flying about, and the poor mule is being cinched within an inch of his life. The rapidity with which two good packers would adjust the loads on a pack-mule was always astonishing to me. The diamond hitch is a mystery in itself to tenderfeet. The ropes whirl about apparently in the most inextricable confusion, the packers "come down" on them with all their weight, a loose knot is tied, and the mule can roll down a hill without freeing himself from his pack. Two expert packers will pack a mule, when everything is ready, in about one minute.

Mr. Thomas Moore, the chief packer, was a gentleman of great experience and wonderful resources, who had, notwithstanding his rough life, found time to read a great deal and keep up with the times. He invented various appliances connected with packing, planned the best army-wagon that has yet been devised, and was the patentee of a double boxing for wagon-wheels that has a promising future. When General Flagler, afterward chief of ordnance in the United States army, was engaged in getting up at Rock Island Arsenal the admirable packing outfit for the Hotchkiss mountain gun used throughout the army, he sent for Mr. Moore and was materially assisted by him.[1]

I once asked Mr. Moore what he considered the most difficult thing he had ever had to pack. After some thought he said that he believed that "about the most unhandy thing he had ever tackled" was a millstone weighing eleven hundred and fifty pounds. Now, the ordinary load for a mule is about three hundred pounds, so here was evidently an opportunity for mind to triumph over matter.

Mr. Moore overcame the difficulty in this wise: He got out two stout hickory poles about thirty feet long, and supported the ends on either side of two of his strongest mules. The stone was placed on these poles and lashed securely, but in such a way that it could be made to slide along the poles. On level ground, of course, the stone would be kept at the middle point of the poles. In going up a hill the rear mule would evidently have more than his share of the load, so the stone was moved up toward the foremost mule, while in going downhill the reverse

[1] The above was written in 1894. I regret to state that Mr. Moore died about two years ago, but his work survives, and some of his pupils performed splendid service on the road from Daiquiri to Santiago, last summer.
J. C. A.

would obtain, and the stone was moved nearer the rear mule. It was, of course, a very heavy load, but they carried it through without a sore back. Great ingenuity has been displayed in packing mill machinery, though the pieces are seldom so heavy as this millstone. A wire rope would sometimes take ten or twenty mules, coils of two hundred pounds being packed on each animal, with a slack of fifteen or twenty feet between.

The mules of the Cheyenne train are taught to form line in front of their aparejos, or pack-saddles, with almost as much

made, but others are grotesque in the extreme. The embroidery is generally what the ladies would call appliqué, and in colors. The packers assert that some of the mules know their own coronas and always take their proper places in the line, but this I am inclined to doubt.

The value of a thoroughly organized pack-train has always been fully appreciated by the general officers who have commanded the Department of the Platte. So much of the country in Wyoming, Utah, Idaho, and South Dakota is inaccessible to a wagon-

ELK "MILLING."

regularity and promptness as a company of soldiers. The bell-horses of the two trains are stationed at the ends, and the mules fall in between. The aparejos are set up generally in a straight line, with the blankets and coronas on them. The corona is a pad of felt or blanket that is placed next to the animal's back. Then come the blankets, and on them the aparejo. Each mule has his own corona, and to distinguish them they are embroidered with particular designs.

As far as possible the name of the mule furnishes the design. For instance, Polly has a parrot, Sullivan a pair of prize-fighters, Minnie some minnows, Nibsy a fish, Buck, Cub, Fly, etc., their appropriate pictures. Some of these designs are very well

train that the packs have frequently been called upon. The late General Crook gave the pack-train great attention, and often made practical work for it in time of peace by using it in hunting big game. His wonderful success in Indian warfare was probably due more to the knowledge of the country and of the various tribes obtained on these extended hunting expeditions than to anything else. The Indians have the greatest respect for a good hunter, and the Gray Fox, as General Crook was called, had their implicit confidence until his death.

When General Brooke was in command of the department, he gave great attention to his pack-train. He has seen its necessity in every part of the West, for his knowledge of the plains and mountains goes back beyond the Civil War, in which he won the two stars of a major-general at the age of twenty-five. In the campaign of 1890 and 1891 the importance of the packs was further impressed upon him in the Bad Lands, near Pine Ridge, and he always gave the pack-train a thorough overhauling when he

The hunt of 1893 was in the Sierra Madre and Park Range mountains of southern Wyoming. We left our comfortable car at old Fort Steele, once a well-built military post on the Union Pacific Railroad at the crossing of the North Platte, but since abandoned and looking more cheerless than the catacombs. Our course was south,

HALF-TONE PLATE ENGRAVED BY S. G. PUTNAM.
HOW BAT SHOOTS.

visited the post, Fort D. A. Russell, of which Cheyenne Depot is a part.

The general is also a Nimrod of no small fame, and it was his custom annually to test the efficiency of his train by taking it on a hunt in the mountains. It is astonishing what a difference a few days of actual field-work under the immediate supervision of the general make. Camp is pitched as if by magic, the loads of the mules seem to fall off at their proper places without the slightest friction, the fires are going and water boiling, mules are cared for, supper is eaten, and the packers are singing "After the Ball" before green hands could have put up a tent.

and our first march to Saratoga, twenty-eight miles, was rather a long one for a starter. We got into camp, however, in good shape, just in time to escape a little flurry of snow.

On the third day, as we journeyed southward, we crossed a vast plain which possesses great historical interest. Here was once the Nijni Novgorod of America, and years ago this place was even more wonderful than the remarkable city on the Volga, that perennially blooms into a huge metropolis and again fades into a hamlet.

The creek that runs through it, and the mountain that looks down upon it, were called the Grand Encampment, but the great meeting from which they are named is a thing of the past.

Thirty years ago, as soon as the grass of this broad savanna became green, a universal peace was tacitly declared among the Indian tribes, and caravans started for the Grand Encampment from every point. Soon the banks of the creek were dotted with tepees, thousands of ponies grazed on the fertile meadows, and the wilderness became an immense market. For weeks war was forgotten and the arts of peace were cultivated.

Scattered in picturesque groups, these children of the plains and mountains made their bargains, raced their ponies, showed their marksmanship, displayed feats of agility on foot or on horseback, while the squaws labored in the camp and applauded the exploits of their lords. How often has a whole tribe been ruined because one pony could run faster than another! How often has a buck lost his all, not excluding his better half, by his ill luck with the stones or bones, his rude substitutes for dice!

With that wonderful sign-language, the Volapük of the plains, the various tribes easily conversed. The encampment was a vast market. The sheep-keeping Navajoes brought their famous blankets, so closely woven as to be impervious to water; the Pawnees, always great hunters, brought buffalo-robes, elk teeth, and bear claws; the Shoshones, eagle feathers for war-bonnets and clay for peace-pipes; the Osages, osage-orange wood, the *bois d'arc*, for bows; the warlike Utes, flints for arrow-heads, sinews for strings, and skins for clothing and tepees: every tribe brought something and carried away something else.

The Grand Encampment is a thing of the past. The Indians have little to trade, and the killing of the buffalo and other game on the plains has made it impossible for them to make long journeys. The valley is now dotted with ranches, and its post-office bears the inappropriate name of Swan.

We had intended to establish our camp on the summit of Grand Encampment Mountain, but we found that the snow was already two feet deep there. This would drive the game to better grazing-grounds, and besides make very uncomfortable hunting, so we continued our course south to the Colorado line.

We crossed and recrossed the State line several times, and finally, after a long, hard march, camped after dark by the light of pine fires beyond the continental divide, on a branch of the Snake River.

Our hunter and guide *par excellence* was

Baptiste Garnier, or "Little Bat," as he was generally called. He was five feet six inches tall; his frame was well knit; every muscle was developed; his lungs were as sound as an antelope's; his eye had the power of a microscope; and a rifle had been his plaything since boyhood. His father was French and his mother Indian, and he inherited the energy, bravery, and endurance of the old Canadian voyageurs, with the remarkable observation and instinctive knowledge of topography and of the habits of animals of the aborigines of the plains. His mission in life seemed to be to kill, and probably his aggregate bag would surpass that of any other hunter in this country. He kept a record only of the bears he killed, and that record had then reached eighty-five. Mr. Webb Hayes, son of the late ex-President, who was one of our party, called him "the greatest hunter in the world." His wonderful powers of trailing game were our admiration. He would ride along on his pony and occasionally make such remarks as, "Two mountain-sheep crossed there yesterday," or, "A blacktail deer and fawn passed along here this morning," and we would look in vain for a sign. He would trail a deer or an elk at a trot, and presently remark, "He's over in those bushes," and, sure enough, there he would be.

He had the true Indian taciturnity about his success as a hunter. Mr. Collins of Omaha likes to tell a story of one of Bat's elk hunts. He was on a hunt with General Crook some years ago, and one afternoon strolled off alone and on foot. When he returned at dark, Mr. Collins said, "Well, Bat, did you see anything?" "Saw thirteen elk," was the reply, with an intonation that seemed to end the conversation. Mr. Collins persevered: "Did you get any of them?" "Yes; I got them." He had actually slaughtered the whole band of thirteen elk.

This was a possibility in one way: If the leading bull was killed and the hunter remained unseen, the cows and young bulls would lose their heads and get to "milling," as it is called; that is, they would revolve about their dead leader, too frightened to escape. This was what had happened in the case of Bat's band, and he had relentlessly shot them all down.

Mr. Hayes, to whom I referred a moment ago, once participated in a little bear episode that very narrowly missed putting the White House in mourning. Hayes, then a youngster, was hunting deer with General Crook, but had strayed from the main party, unattended except by a colored cavalryman named Hawkins. In the course of their wanderings they accidentally found a bear-hole. The ambition to kill a bear captured Hayes. He did not know much about killing bear, but the first thing evidently was to find out whether Bruin was receiving that day. So Hayes stood guard while Hawkins took a peep into the cave, which was some ten feet up the bank. Hawkins presently dropped down, with eyes like search-lights. "He 's dar sure 'nough, Marsa Webb."

This was encouraging; but the bear was comfortable and declined to give up his nap. Then these two enthusiasts proceeded to throw stones into the hole from a distance of only a dozen feet. Hawkins finally landed one that hurt, and the bear came "a-running," with a roar that took half a dozen shades out of Hawkins's face. There was nothing to do but shoot, and Hayes shot, and fortunately lodged his bullet in the neck of the beast, breaking his backbone.

As hunters generally calculate upon putting something like a pound of lead into a grizzly before he succumbs, and as this one could easily have eaten up both Hayes and Hawkins if he had had another minute to live, it is evident that the shot was a remarkably good one.

The day after we made permanent camp we started early and went out in couples, so as to cover as much territory as possible. The first day is always more of a reconnaissance than a hunt, as it is necessary to discover where the game is likely to be found.

The only two who had any luck were the general and Bat. They had found a band of elk and had killed four out of it, and Bat had shot a blacktail deer that he said would persist in getting in his way. They had seen a number of blacktails besides, but did not shoot them, because the firing would have frightened the band of elk. The general had killed a magnificent bull with immense antlers and felt correspondingly happy.

The following day five of us went out with Bat to make another attack on that band of elk. We took some pack-mules along to bring in the elk killed the day before and those that we hoped to kill. Under Bat's leadership we wound through a pine forest, up a valley, over a range of hills, and finally debouched upon an opening on the mountain-side. Here Bat ordered a halt. He dismounted and examined every point of the country with his field-glass. In a moment he announced that there was a band of elk on the slope of the second range of hills in front of us. Presently we could see them

with the naked eye, looking like moving specks on the distant hillside.

Bat immediately signaled us to move forward down the hill, keeping well covered by the pine-trees. He then proceeded leisurely to roll a cigarette. We made out that the elk would probably cross over the ridge of the hill they were on, and that we would then be able to approach them. Where we had seen them there was no cover. We waited fully half an hour, and then mounted and followed Bat's lead down a steep gulch, through fallen timber and over a mountain stream. The road he took us was no boulevard.

At length we came out on the top of a hill from which we could see the elk, not five hundred yards distant. There were about forty of them. Bat left us here and again reconnoitered. We ate our lunch and waited. Every few minutes the indescribable whistle of a bull-elk would sound upon the crisp, wintry air. Their whistle is a beautifully clear note, sometimes covering nearly an octave. I know of no musical instrument that could exactly reproduce it. Perhaps a silver flute would come nearest to it.

After a while Bat came back and took us by a circuitous route to a still nearer point. It would be a fair shot at an animal as large as an elk at five hundred yards, but an Indian likes to have a sure thing, and if he can find cover, will crawl up till he can almost touch the game with the muzzle of his rifle. Then he will carefully adjust the two sticks that he always carries so as to form a rest, and only when he thinks he is perfectly sure does he pull the trigger. Bat is a splendid snap-shot, but he always uses the sticks if he has time, and never shoots beyond a hundred yards if he can help it.

This time he brought us up to within fifty yards of the elk, but they saw us as soon as we did them, and were off. We kept up a fusillade as long as they were in sight, and then proceeded to take account of stock.

We found we had killed six out of the band, four bulls and two cows—not a bad day's work. It is not always easy to pack fresh meat, and an elk head with antlers is especially obnoxious to a mule. Blinders are always put over a mule's eyes when he is being packed, but even when his eyes are covered he will often object to the smell of blood. His nose must then be well rubbed with blood, and sometimes it is necessary to tie his legs together before he will allow the disagreeable burden to be placed upon his back. In this instance there was no special difficulty, and we were soon on our way to camp, each of us claiming all six of the elk, as we could not tell who had killed them.

On the march in, Bat, with his conscience-less mania for killing, shot a snow-shoe rabbit. This is a species I had never seen before. The feet are webbed like those of a duck, a provision of nature to enable the animal to make his way over the snows that are almost perpetual where he makes his home.

When the sun went down the mercury made such a decided drop that the poetical camp-fire of huge pine logs was not comfortable, and we found the prosaic Sibley stove in our big circular tents much more conducive to story-telling. The Indian hits it pretty well when he says, "White man makes big fire and can't get near enough to it to get warm. Indian makes little fire and keeps warm."

Those tent-walls listened to some startling fishing and hunting stories, as the smoke from cigar and pipe coiled around the tent-pole.

One of our party had led a very adventurous life on the plains. After the Civil War, which he left as a captain, though only a boy, he joined his brother, who was United States marshal at Salt Lake City, and became his deputy. During the Mormon troubles he personally arrested Brigham Young. Thousands of Mormons had gathered, and a sign from their prophet would have precipitated a conflict that would have exterminated the Gentiles in Utah for the time being. The sign was not given, and the prisoner was marched to the court-rooms.

The mob, however, could not be dispersed, and finally an appeal was made to Brigham Young. He stepped to the window, looked out upon the dense mass of fanatic saints, and simply said, "Go to your homes now; when I want you I will send for you." The crowd melted away like a fog, and the officials had no further trouble.

The two brothers afterward established stage lines all over the Western country from Omaha to Salt Lake. At one time the younger brother, who was paymaster and inspector, traveled over twelve hundred miles of stage lines every month. Let our railroad managers who cruise about their lines in well-stocked private cars think of this record. Only a man of the splendid physique of our friend could have stood the strain.

Some of his stories rivaled Mark Twain's matchless tales of Slade and the road-agents in "Roughing It." By the way, he had a little anecdote of Slade that displayed a curious phase of his character. Slade was eating dinner at the hotel at Laramie City when an army officer entered with a friend who knew Slade. The officer was a slim and rather undersized young fellow, only recently from West Point. His friend wanted to do the polite thing, and introduced him to Slade. Slade stretched out his hand for the inevitable shake, but the officer drew back, and said in a perfectly audible voice, "I do not want to know the murdering scoundrel." Everybody began to get ready to dodge, expecting Slade's ready pistol to answer this deadly insult, but he merely laughed and went on with his dinner.

When gold was found in the Black Hills, the brothers had a stage line from Sidney, on the Union Pacific, to Deadwood, and thousands of adventurers rushed to that point. All the coaches and wagons and horses that could be obtained were put into service, but it was simply impossible to carry the crowd. Through tickets were sold by the railroads at Eastern points, and the stage line was expected to take care of all comers.

A railroad magnate who knew the situation pretty well asked our friend one day how he managed. "First-rate," he replied: "those who have first-class tickets have their baggage carried, and ride *if there is room;* the second-class passengers have their baggage carried and walk; the third-class walk and carry their own baggage." This was almost literally true. Wagons were sent out piled up with bags and satchels, forty men following on foot.

Stages were "held up" daily. The company carried valuables in a treasure-coach, but no treasure on the passenger-coaches, and the robbery of the passengers was of no consequence. In fact, this systematic plundering benefited the company, for it compelled the fortune-hunters to send their valuables by express, for which service they were charged *seven per cent. of their value.* The treasure-coach was built of boiler-iron and accompanied by six men armed to the teeth. In their bullet-proof citadel they could successfully stand off half a hundred road-agents.

Scott Davis was the Slade of this line, without Slade's shady record previous to becoming superintendent. Davis was a man of powerful physique, dauntless nerve, and wonderful endurance, with an eye like an instantaneous camera, and a trigger finger that could follow the lightning flash of his eye.

Hundreds of stories are told of his prowess. One or two will suffice as samples. One day he was lying at a stage-station, wretched and feverish from a bullet-wound he had received in the leg, when it was reported that seven stage-horses had been stolen by three men. He got up at once, mounted his horse, although every movement of his leg was agony, rode twenty miles, and overtook the thieves at a haystack where they had put up for the night. Davis first reconnoitered and then fearlessly attacked them single-handed. He killed one man, and the other two fled, leaving the horses behind. Exhausted, he slept soundly that night on the hay beside the dead robber. At daybreak he was again in the saddle. He rode all day to Green River, managed to get the drop on the two thieves in a saloon, and marched them both to jail. They afterward served sentence in the Wyoming State penitentiary.

At one time six men combined to kill Scott Davis. They went to the stage-station, "held up" the hostler, whose name was Mike (his other name is lost to history), and tied him securely in the barn. As a special favor, Mike begged to be taken into a shed at the rear of the barn, for he said that barn would be no place for a Christian when Davis got there. When the stage arrived, of course Mike did not appear. This aroused Davis's suspicions, and he leaped from the box to the side of the coach opposite the barn, and got behind a tree. The six conspirators opened fire, but could only hit the tree. Finally one of them brought out Mike, and using him as a shield, advanced toward the tree. Davis let them come half-way, and then quietly said: "Mike, don't you think you had better stop? If you come any farther, I shall have to shoot that thieving scoundrel *through your body*." Mike was not in an enviable position, to say the least. With a six-shooter at his ear and a Winchester at his heart, he was far from happy. He knew Scott Davis, however, and not another step would he budge. His convoy finally retreated, and Davis successfully held the whole six men at bay until assistance arrived.

Delaney, the pack-master, came in one night much excited, and reported that he had found a bear-hole with many fresh "signs" near it, but no bear. He thought Bruin had gone off on a berrying expedition and might be back the next day. So the following day he guided Bat and myself to the hole, which was in a deep ravine, about thirty feet from the bottom. Sure enough, fresh signs were abundant. We could see the grizzly's tracks and the fresh dirt thrown out by his powerful claws.

We reconnoitered carefully. Bat was general-in-chief. We all waived rank, even to the general himself, when Bat took command. He posted me on the other side of the ravine, immediately opposite the big hole, which was so deep and so much inclined that we could not see into it. Delaney took station above the hole on the same side, so as to rake him fore and aft if my broadside failed to make him strike his colors. Then Bat examined his gun carefully, cocked it, and rolled stones down toward the hole. No results. Then Bat redistributed his forces. I moved up a little nearer, and Delaney was posted in a tree within forty paces of the hole. Bat threw some more stones, and succeeded in dropping some into the hole. Still no bear. Then Bat took a stand behind a tree on the opposite side from Delaney, came to a "ready" with his rifle, and directed me to fire into the hole. Without flinching, I sent three shots from my Winchester into that hole, but still the enemy failed to appear.

Bat then motioned to Delaney, and they approached the hole cautiously and peered in. Would that I could state that Bruin lay at the bottom of the hole with one of my bullets through his heart; but truth compels me to say that the hole was empty, but one wall was frescoed with three bullet-holes. Bat decided that the bear had abandoned the hole two or three days before, for some unknown reason, and gave it as his opinion that he would not return.

One day we had a snow-storm that lasted until late in the afternoon. After the snow ceased falling I mounted my trusty mule and made a circuit of a couple of miles, hoping to find the fresh trail of an elk in the snow. I returned to camp without seeing anything. Shortly afterward Bat came in from an expedition on foot, and reported that he had crippled two elk only a hundred yards beyond where my trail turned back. This was a little discouraging. He said it was too dark to go after the elk that night, but that he would get them in the morning. Bright and early we started out next day, and easily found one elk. The other had mysteriously disappeared.

Suddenly Bat bristled with excitement and announced that a bear was after the wounded elk. We followed the trail rapidly on horseback until it became pretty fresh and plunged down a ravine. Bat dismounted, and two of us elected to accompany him on foot. We know better now. It was not so bad while we were going downhill, but presently the bear decided to run up a hill, and after that he made it a practice to go up a hill as soon as we were beginning to get any semblance of breath.

We were ten thousand feet above the level of the sea, and my wind is not the best at any time. I never was half so completely blown in my life. Bat trotted along as fast as we would let him, not minding it in the least. Presently our bear was joined, as shown by the trail, by another large bear and two smaller ones. We now evidently had the whole family before us, and were reminded of Goldilocks and her surprising adventures with the great big bear, the middle-sized bear, and the little wee bear. The big bear in this instance must have been a monster, for he had a trail like his Post-tertiary cave prototype.

Once the bear family halted, and Bat, who was in the lead, got in a shot. After that the big tracks had a red stain alongside them, but the pace only seemed to grow hotter, and it was soon evident to Bat that he could never overtake the enemy with his full-blown assistants.

He reluctantly gave up the chase and mounted to the summit of a neighboring hill that commanded a turn in the course of the gulch. From this point we rolled boulders down into the ravine for half an hour, hoping to dislodge the grizzlies and drive them up the opposite side, where we could get a shot at them.

Bat brought out the whole force of hunters the next day, and gave his entire attention to that bear family for a whole day, but we never found them again. A grizzly bear is no fool, and has no desire to stay in the vicinity of a man who has killed eighty-five of his species.

The general was a thorough sportsman, and would countenance no wanton destruction of game; so as soon as we had all the elk meat we could properly use, we broke camp and started for the railroad. We had few farewells to make. Only a camp-robber (a pretty and lively little gray-bird) and a squirrel had called upon us, though the long leaping trail of a mountain-lion ran within fifty yards of our camp, and we had several times heard his unearthly scream.

We were a hundred miles from our car; it took us four days to make the march; but we had had a great hunt: every cell of our lungs had expanded to drink in the glorious mountain air, and we felt equal to a ride of a thousand leagues over those glistening peaks and through those fragrant forests.

9.
THE MOUNTAIN SHEEP OF AMERICA
(1902)

THE MOUNTAIN SHEEP OF AMERICA

By ANDREW J. STONE

IT IS very near to the century mark since our introduction, but only within a few years that we really began to know these creatures. We heard of them as living in the rugged mountains, growing massive horns and capable of doing many wonderful things, prominent among which was that they would, without hesitation, leap from lofty peaks, landing on their heads among the rocks many feet below without injury.

Audubon wrote of them in 1852; but his description is no longer of value, other than as a bit of history, and many ideas that the naturalist then entertained have given place to the more perfect knowledge obtained through extended observation.

They are a part of a group that constitute the genus *Ovis* of zoölogists. They are ruminants, and belong to the hollow horned section, *i. e.*, those having persistent horns composed of conical epidermic sheaths, encasing and supported by processes of the frontal bone. In all the wild sheep of America the horns are present in both sexes, though much smaller in the

"They were so fat I concluded they must have feared the sun would melt their fat."

In the Sheep Country of the Nahama Mountains.

female. They are trigonal in section, having always three more or less distinctly marked surfaces, the upper one being divided by edges running longitudinally to the axis of the horn, in some species sharply prominent, in others rounded off. They are also marked by numerous transverse ridges, more or less prominent, varying, with different species, and they present a strong more or less spiral curve, which varies in direction in different species. The teeth resemble, generally, those of the other *bovidæ*. The upper incisors and canines are entirely wanting, their place being taken by a callous pad against which the lower front teeth bite. These are eight in number, all much alike and in close contact; the outer pair represent the canines, the rest the incisors.

The mountain sheep of America are the proudest and handsomest of our wild animals. They are the most perfect combination of strength, hardihood, endurance, agility, beauty, and grace. They are the most delicate in their tastes, and the most artistic in temperament. Their home is the most picturesque, and their food the daintiest. They are extremely timid in the

presence of their enemies, but courageous in battling with the many forbidding elements to which their lives in the high mountains are exposed.

They range through the greatest depth of latitude of any family of the ruminants on the continent, and are instinctively wild. No wild animals are further removed from domestication; they find the most congenial home in the pure air of the wildest mountain countries, and so far, all efforts to transplant and domesticate them have been failures.

According to Indian tradition they once lived in the low lands when the earth was yet in darkness, but when the earth was lighted and the rays of the sun burst suddenly upon them, they were seriously frightened and fled to the mountains, where they have ever since remained.

Indians are not our most reliable source of knowledge in tracing the early history of our animal life, but their story is not entirely improbable, for we have records of much greater changes having taken place in the habits of many of our wild animals.

Many names have been given to the first species of mountain sheep discovered in

Ovis Canadensis is the Largest of the Mountain Sheep.
The Horns Grow to a Circumference of Twelve Inches.

America, and it has required careful investigation to trace the priority between *canadensis* and *cervina*. They were described by Desmarest as *Ovis cervina* in 1804, but it is now generally admitted that Shaw described them as *Ovis canadensis*, in 1803, and there is but little doubt that *canadensis* will be recognized in scientific circles as the name they are fully entitled to bear, and it is now pronounced by many of our best informed zoölogists as of unquestionable priority.

The type locality of the *Ovis canadensis*

to their relatives farther north, nor do their pastures become dry and parched like those ranged by their relatives in California and Mexico. They graze the little mountain meadows just in the upper edge of tree growth, are often found grazing among the timber patches well down the mountain sides, and not uncommonly come down into the valleys to the banks of the large streams. They are the largest and have the heaviest bones of any of the American wild sheep. The horns of the males are massive, curve close to the head,

"The horns of the *Ovis stonei* are delicate in pattern, curving gracefully out from the head."

Shaw, is the Rocky Mountains of Alberta, Canada. The high mountain ranges from the Colorado River and Arizona north to the head waters of the Frazer and the Peace rivers are the limits of their range from north to south. The Bad Lands of North Dakota and the Cascade Mountains in Washington are their most easterly and westerly ranges.

The territory occupied by the *Ovis canadensis* is most likely the best suited to the development of these animals of any range occupied by wild sheep in America. They do not experience the long winters known

are deeply corrugated on the upper edge, are very much flattened, and acquire a greater size than those of any of the other varieties. Many of them in very old animals grow to a circumference at the base of more than 20 inches, and I have measured them $19\frac{1}{2}$ inches in circumference at the base and $52\frac{1}{2}$ inches long around the curve. The tips are directed forward and up, and are usually very much broken in the older animals.

The color of almost all animals varies with the different seasons of the year and the condition of the pelage, and the various species of the sheep do not give us any exception to this rule. The general color of *canadensis* is a bluish gray, shading to light brown or tawny color when the coat is short, but as the coat grows longer, it grows darker, until in many of the adult males it reaches a deep wood brown tinged slightly with a bluish gray or lead color. There is a dorsal stripe somewhat darker than the rest of the hairs usually prominent, the face is ashy brown, the body brown, the under and inner sides of the legs tawny.

Eighty-one years elapsed before a second variety of mountain sheep in America was discovered. Then was the white sheep of northern North America discovered by Mr. E. W. Nelson, in 1884, and named *dalli* in honor of Professor Dall, of Washington, D. C.

Dr. D. G. Elliott, of the Field Columbian Museum, Chicago, in a synopsis of the mammals of North America, gives the type locality of the *Ovis dalli* as Fort Reliance on the Upper Yukon. Dawson City is the type locality of the newly discovered *Ovis fananni*, or saddle back sheep, described by Wm. T. Hornaday, director of the New York Zoölogical Society. Old Fort Reliance and Dawson City are in the same locality, and I cannot believe it possible that both varieties live in the vicinity of Dawson and Reliance. Whether Mr. Nelson secured specimens at this point in the flesh, or simply secured some dry skins of Indians that had brought them to Fort Reliance from some distant hunting ground I have no means of knowing, but I am persuaded the latter must be correct, as I do not believe the white sheep range near Dawson or anywhere on the Upper Yukon. The white sheep *(Ovis dalli)* range all of the Rocky Mountains from the Liard River north to the Arctic Coast and west to the Noatak and Kowak rivers in northwestern Alaska. Their range extends south from the head waters of the Colville River, across the Koyukuk River and across the Yukon, following the general trend of the Yukon hills into the mountainous country around the head waters of the Kuskokwim River; from there it spreads to the east and west. Extending east through the great range of mountains at the head of the Kuskokwim, through the Sushitna country, and in the mountains west of the Tanana River, then south to the Copper River, west to the Kinik, down into the Kenai Peninsula country, and further west around the north of Cook Inlet on the Upper Nushugak and throughout the region of Lakes Clark and Illiamna.

The *Ovis dalli* occupy the most northerly range of any sheep in the world, and the most extensive of any in North America. They are white the year round, but in summer the ends of the hairs are tipped with rust, giving the coat an appearance as if soiled by sleeping or rolling in clay. In winter the coat gets very heavy and is almost perfectly white. They are not so large as *Ovis canadensis* and their bones are not so heavy. Their horns grow to nearly as great a length as those of *canadensis*, but are never nearly so heavy, rarely exceeding fifteen inches in circumference at the base. They are more round, much lighter in color, not so deeply corrugated, and extend farther from the head. The *Ovis dalli* range entirely above the timber line, very rarely coming down into the timber at any season of the year. This might be attributed to the fact that their country is much troubled with wolves, and they can more readily detect the approach of such enemies in the high open countries. They range very nearly the same character of country the whole year through, the only exception being that the old males climb into slightly more rugged and secluded regions in the summer months.

The next to be described were the black sheep of sub-Arctic America, discovered by the writer in the Che-on-nee Mountains at the head waters of the Stickine River, Northwest British Columbia, in 1896, described by Dr. J. A. Allen, curator of vertebrate zoölogy at the American Museum of Natural History, New York, in 1897, and named *stonei*, in honor of the discoverer. The *Ovis stonei* range throughout the mountains north from the head waters of the Peace and Frazer rivers as far as the source of Pelly River. They are the handsomest of the American wild sheep and the darkest, shading from a grayish brown to almost black. The adult males are extremely dark in the fall, being almost black over the shoulders, chest, brisket, and legs, shading somewhat lighter on the neck, body, and across the loins; light to medium gray in the face and white on the rump, under the belly, and on the inside of the thighs. They are marked by a dark dorsal stripe.

Like the *Ovis dalli* they range entirely above the timber line. They and the *dalli* are almost identical in size, and their horns are alike very light in color, but the style of horn grown by the *Ovis stonei* is entirely different from that of any of its relatives, being delicate in pattern and curving gracefully out from the head in a sweeping coil that readily distinguishes it; in this it more nearly resembles the *Ovis poli* of Central Asia than any American sheep. The white rump patch is very white and is in such great contrast with the dark color of the sides of the animal as to render it very striking. The type locality of the *Ovis stonei* is in the Che-on-nee Mountains, the very heart of the range.

Closely following the description of the *Ovis stonei* in 1897 came that of the *Ovis nelsoni*, discovered by Mr. E. W. Nelson, of the Death Valley expedition in the northern continuation of the Funeral Mountains, locally known as the Grape Vine Mountains, along the boundary line of Nevada and California, and described by Dr. C. Hart Merriam, of the Biological Society of Washington. Ten specimens were secured, from which their peculiar characteristics were traced.

The geographic range of the *Ovis nelsoni* is not yet known, but it is probably the semi-barren desert country of New Mexico and the Southern United States from Texas to California.

Says Dr. Merriam: "Compared with *Ovis stonei* recently described by Dr. Allen, the contrast in color is even more marked; but the patterns seem to be the same, and the darkening of the under parts and legs is also a character of *stonei*." Type locality, the Grape Vine Mountains, or the barren deserts of Southern California.

Dr. Merriam describes the *Ovis nelsoni* as similar to *Ovis stonei* in pattern of coloration, but much paler; rump patch small and completely divided on median line; tail short and slender; molar teeth very small; upper parts, except rump patch, pale dingy brown; under parts and legs much darker, contrasting sharply with white areas; inner aspect of thighs and posterior aspect of fore and hind legs, white.

Almost four years elapsed after the description of *Ovis nelsoni* without additions to the number of species, when Wm. T.

Hornaday's description of the *Ovis fananni* was closely followed by Dr. C. Hart Merriam's description of the *Ovis mexicanus*.

The specimen examined by Mr. Hornaday was that of an adult male, secured by Mr. Henry Brown, near Dawson City, N. W. T., and named in honor of Mr. John Fanin, curator of the Provincial Museum of British Columbia. The specimen was taken in midwinter and described as follows: Entire head and neck, breast, abdomen, inside of forelegs, and rump patch for four inches above insertion of tail, snow white. Entire body except as above, brownish gray, giving the appearance of a white animal covered by a gray blanket. This color is produced by a nearly even mixture of pure white and blackish brown hairs. The gray color covers the shoulders from the insertion of the neck downward to the knee, where it fades out. On the outside of the thigh the gray color grows paler as it descends, until at the hock joint, it fades out entirely. The posterior edge of the thigh is white. The lower portion of the inner surface of the thigh partakes of the gray body color, but is somewhat paler.

On the front edge of the thigh, and extending down to the hoof, is a conspicuous band of dark brown, 1½ inches wide, which, below the hock joint joins rather abruptly the pure white hair which covers the sides and rear edge of the leg. A similar brown band extends down the front of the foreleg, from knee to hoof, similarly backed up posteriorly with white. The tail is similar in color to the body, but much darker, and a thin line of dark brown hair connects it with a gray mass of the body. The horns are clear, transparent, even amber-like, similar to the horns of *Ovis dalli*, when clean; annulations, numerous and well defined; a slight groove under the superior angle is not so deep as that of *Ovis stonei*. In the type specimen the horns do not spread as in *Ovis dalli* and *stonei*.

During extensive travel in the north I went completely around the habitat of this new species and frequently obtained information concerning it, but never directly penetrated its country or collected any specimens. Its range comprises a very large portion of the watershed of the Upper Yukon, covering the extensive mountain country of the lower Stewart

River, the Macmillan, the Pelly, the Lewis, and White rivers, ranging west from the western slope of the main range of the Rockies to the mountains east of the Tanana River. They go more into the timber than either the *dalli* or *stonei*.

The last of the series to be described was *Ovis mexicanus*, collected by Mr. E. W. Nelson and Mr. E. A. Goldman in the barren mountains about Lake Santa Maria, Chihuahua, Mexico, in 1899, and described by Dr. Merriam in April, 1901. It is described as being large in size, much darker in color than *nelsoni*, but lighter than *canadensis;* horns massive, dark, not strongly outcurved; hoofs and molars larger than in *Ovis canadensis;* ears long and large, nearly double the size of those of *canadensis;* tail long and slender; color pattern similar to that of *canadensis*. There is no trace of dorsal stripe on the *mexicanus*, and the muzzle is much paler than the rest of the face. The geographical range of the *mexicanus* is not yet known.

Dr. Merriam having found differences in the skulls of the sheep of the western Dakotas and those of Montana, and Alberta, has described the sheep of the western Dakotas as a sub-species of *Ovis canadensis* and named them *Ovis canadensis auduboni* in honor of Audubon, who obtained some specimens from there in 1843.

The females of all the different species wear horns the character of which are very much alike. They are quite flat, slightly annulated, grow upward and backward and outward to a height rarely exceeding eight inches.

The distribution of the northern varieties and the range occupied by each is pretty clearly defined. There is more to learn, however, concerning the ranges of the southern varieties, very especially of those in Mexico, and it will be extremely interesting to know just how far south their ranges extend.

The maximum age of wild sheep, I believe to be about sixteen years.

The general range of the sheep is now pretty well known, and it is hardly probable that many more species will be added to the list. The following table gives the measurements (in millimeters) and the dates of description of the species at present known:

	O. canadensis.	O. dalli.	O. stonei.	O. nelsoni.	O. fananni.	O. mexicanus.
	1803.	1884.	1897.	1897.	1901.	1901
Total length...		1476	1676	1280	1525	1530
Height...	1000 to 1070 } 991		...	830	865	900
Tail vertebra...	102	89	100	102	130	
Hind foot...	419	...	360	...	425	
Length of horn over curve...	928 to 1143 }	375 to 990	762	...	1030	...
Circumference of horn at base...	356 to 458 }	219 to 368	324	...	405	...

The following is a list of measurements from a splendid series of *Ovis dalli* taken by me in the Rocky Mountains 66.30 N. in the summer of 1898 (measurements in inches):

	Adult male.	Adult male.	Adult female.	Adult female.	Lamb.	Lamb.
Length	58½	53½	51	54	38	39
Tail	4	4	3	3½	2½	2¾
Tarsus	16½	15½	15¼	15	12½	12½
Femur to humerus	36	34½	27½	33	22½	23
Across chest	10½	10	7¾	9¼	6	6
Height at shoulders	39	38½	34¾	33½	24	24
Depth of body	18	17½	14¾	15½	10½	10

The habits of the sheep are very regular and very interesting. I have spent days up in the mountains watching them feed and rest and travel. In winter all ages mingle in large bands of various numbers, according as they are plentiful in any given locality. They will paw the snow from the grass where it is only a few inches deep, but they usually keep to high tablelands where the winds keep the snow blown off. The character of their coat is such as to give them great protection against cold and storm, and it is rare that the northern herds seek any more protection from the elements than what they find among the cliffs of rock. The *canadensis* are more accustomed to being in timber and often seek the higher belts of timber during storm, and sometimes come down to the very bottom of the canyons.

The *dalli*, the *stonei*, and the *fananni* simply defy the elements throughout the long Arctic and sub-Arctic winters. Like most animals they do not feed much during severe storms, and will huddle closely, the little fellows crouching alongside the older ones for warmth and protection, while many of the adult males and stronger animals get restless, and prowl about, walk the highest ridges, and nibble indifferently at the single spears of grass found peeping through the snow here and there. When the storm breaks they will at once set out to some feeding ground of which they have a most perfect knowledge. They know their own home, and always know where to look for food, even when it would seem that every foot of their country was buried deep in snow. It not infrequently happens, however, that during storms they remain in some small rocky cave and the winds drift the snow across their only avenue of escape so deeply that they find their way out with difficulty. The old males are always the first to break their way out and their superior strength is often put to a severe test, but the road made by them is of great advantage to the weaker and younger animals. During the winter season the older males always lead the way from one feeding ground to another.

All through the northern mountains there are high tablelands of varying extent, where the winter winds keep the snow swept away sufficiently for the sheep to reach the tiny blades of grass, and it is on these they range mostly and may be found in bands varying from a very few head to as many as three hundred.

The *dalli* is the only species found in Arctic America, and the long Arctic nights hold no very great terror for them.

I will never forget with what wonder I viewed a small bunch of these animals in midwinter. It was the middle of December and I was traveling east from Herschel Island along the Arctic Coast. We were cutting across a point of land that extended into the sea and had reached quite a high elevation at the foot of some very rugged mountain ridges. The weather was very cold (the thermometer registering about 40° below, Fahr.), but clear and quite calm at the foot of the mountains where we were. It was about noontime, and, although we could not make lunch or boil tea for want of fuel, I decided to give the dogs a short rest after their long, hard climb. There had been no sun in this latitude for weeks, and storms of the worst sort had been frequent. The country was barren of trees and shrubbery of every kind, and the white mountains looked buried deep in snow. I usually kept moving moderately while our dogs were rest-

ing, and on this occasion I was pacing a little knoll viewing with admiration the wonders of my surroundings. To the north lay the great white limitless frozen ocean; to the south rose the towering white mountains. The scene was a perfect, spotless white. One of my Esquimaux called me to look. Glancing in the direction that he was pointing I could make out the outlines of moving objects on the very crest of one of the highest and most rugged mountain ridges. Through my field glasses I discovered a bunch of sheep, almost as white as the snow, and only the fact that they were moving, outlined against the sky, enabled us to first sight them. There were two magnificent rams with heavy horns, three females, and two young ones, and they followed one behind the other in this order, frequently stopping for a moment to glance about, but were making no effort to feed and were evidently following this ridge from one feeding ground to another. The sky was just sufficiently lighted to give their outlines perfectly, and I never gazed at animals with more admiration than I gave those two magnificent rams, as they walked proudly, with heads thrown back, silhouetted so perfectly against the cold blue and purple sky.

They live for months in those high, barren, snow-covered, and storm-swept mountains, with no protection of any kind, not even the cheering rays of a winter sun!

When the sun grows warm in the spring the old rams leave the general herd and steal into the highest mountains, gradually working their way, as the snow leaves the higher elevations, into the very highest meadows. These are generally small, but numerous, and almost always shut in by rugged peaks, making them very secluded and rendering them almost entirely free from every kind of enemy, even a very large per cent. of the most ambitious big game hunters. In these high pastures, surrounded with patches of eternal snow and ice that are piled so deep in many places that the short summers cannot destroy them, they live a quiet, peaceful life, and exchange their old coats for new ones. They have their entire new coat by the middle of July, and it is then they begin to take on flesh rapidly. By the last of September they are very fat; in fact I have seen them in August so fat that they seemed burdened under the great weight of flesh.

I was once with two companions, one a white man and the other an Indian, high up in the Che-on-nee Mountains, N. W. B. C., hunting *Ovis stonei*. We reached a very high point about 11 A. M. from where several high ridges extended in different directions. I decided we would take up positions overlooking these ridges and watch for game, and accordingly my party located themselves for the purpose, no two being over one hundred yards apart. We had kept our places about an hour, and besides being chilled by the high mountain winds, though the sun was really shining warm, I was growing tired of the inactivity. I never had very much patience in waiting for animals to come to me (the great feature of an Indian's hunting), and I was just thinking of abandoning my position when I heard a low whistle, and, looking around, saw the Indian beckoning. When I reached him he pointed to a patch of snow almost a mile away, and taking my glasses I could see two sheep, one standing and the other lying down on the snow. It was then in the month of August and the Indian remarked, " Sun warm; big ram heap fat; 'fraid his glease will melt."

The two animals soon left the snow and worked their way up the ridge to within a quarter of a mile of us, and again lay down on a patch of snow, where they remained, lying down most of the time for more than three hours. I secured the pair just before sundown and they were so fat that I concluded the Indian was right; they must have feared the sun would melt their fat.

These animals feed in the early morning and evening—always descending the mountain sides to a convenient pasture, working their way to a high ridge for their noonday siesta, and again at evening, when they paw out a shallow basin in a bed of decomposed shale, a resting place for the night. If they are left undisturbed they will keep to the same locality all summer and may at night always be found on one of two or three ridges best suited to them. Rarely more than three to five adult rams are found together in the summer.

The ewes seek the larger plateaus of slightly lower elevation and, with the disappearing snow the last of April and first of May, bring forth their young. Sometimes twins, but not often. It is really a

wonder that they rear any, but they do bring up a goodly per cent. in spite of wolves, wolverines, eagles, and other animals. The ewes generally keep together in considerable numbers and a single band of them will range back and forth over a few miles of these mountain plateaus, throughout the entire summer.

I never found a more interesting study than in following a bunch of these mothers with their young during the latter part of July in the Che-on-nee Mountains. The ranges suited to them are more restricted in numbers, and are often more difficult to locate than those of the rams. I had hunted the Che-on-nee extensively in '96 without finding a single trace. In '97 I determined to find them, because I wanted to secure specimens and I wanted to know in what kind of country they ranged. With one companion I made the usual hunt for several days without success. I then resolved to travel straight away through the mountains until I found some trace of them. The days were very long then and, selecting from my camp outfit one canvas sheet, one pair of blankets, two small pots, one for tea and one for oatmeal, a little oatmeal, bacon, and tea, we started early one morning for a high level plateau that I had often seen from the summit of the mountains.

At four o'clock in the afternoon, we climbed a high wall and found ourselves on the edge of this plateau. For a mile or so I saw no sign of sheep, and the pasture was not suited to them, all of which was very discouraging. Then skirting a little clump of low rounded knolls we suddenly came in full view of a bunch of ewes and lambs. Retiring behind the knolls undiscovered I led the way behind a series of small elevations with the favor of the wind until I was within five hundred yards of the band. They were feeding in a little swale where the grass, though very short, was kept green by the constant trickling of water from the numerous patches of snow which lay against the sides of the low rounded hills that rose here and there from the surface of the plateau. I watched these animals until nearly dark and then retired to a deep canyon for the night. For three days in succession I sought this bunch of sheep about sunrise every morning, and followed them all day, keeping advantage of the wind and dodging them by making long detours around hills. With a pair of powerful glasses I could often bring them so close as to carefully study the color of their coats. There were seven lambs, no two with one mother. There were nine ewes of different ages, two three-year-old rams, and three younger animals. During the three days they did not leave the one plateau, whose width was about four miles; and they often fed for half a day within a radius of a quarter of a mile, moving back and forth as gently as if swayed by the wind. No one animal fed constantly, but as the bunch moved forward, those in the lead frequently lay down and waited for the others to feed past them, when they would jump up and join the rear ranks and go to feeding again. They seemed to lie down and to get up instantaneously, as though not a second of thought was given to the act. Sometimes the animals lying down would allow the bunch to feed past them some distance, when they would spring up as suddenly as if frightened and run rapidly until they overtook their mates, then stop and go to grazing as quickly as if their lives depended on immediate food. The lambs would play and frolic about very much as domestic lambs do, but would never bleat. Most wild ruminants live the greater part of their lives in extreme quiet, and our sheep live in greater silence than any other hoofed animals with the exception of the mountain goat. Never, during the three days' watch, did I hear a single bleat. Every night this band would sleep at the top of the little rocky ridges which crossed the plateau, and every morning about eleven o'clock they would leave the grass and climb to the top of one of those ridges, remaining among the rocks and lying about on the decomposed rock or shale until three or four o'clock in the afternoon. None of them would lie down long at a time and there were always five or six of the bunch playing around in a careless, lazy sort of manner. But there were no sentinels on watch, as we so often see pictured.

At the end of the third day I secured one female as a specimen and aimed to get her lamb, but it was behind some rocks and off with the herd too quick for me. The band was terribly frightened and left the plateau entirely.

The next morning I set out to follow them in hopes of securing a lamb. I had traveled about three miles and was climbing a very rocky hill, when just as I was nearing the summit I saw a lone animal some distance ahead coming toward me. I had been following on the trail of the bunch and my first impression was that I might be near them again, but I soon discovered that the animal coming toward me was a young one, perhaps a lamb, and I hid among the rocks to await results. It did not see me and kept coming in my direction, walking slowly for a hundred yards or so at a time and then stopping to look around for a moment. When it came quite near I could hear it bleat occasionally, but very low. It was hunting its mother on the back track of the band. It was the only bleat I ever heard come from a wild sheep, with the exception of once or twice in the case of a wounded animal. My heart sank within me at the thought of shooting it, but it seemed the most merciful thing to do, and besides I *must* have a specimen.

It is rare that a wounded sheep utters any cry. They always face death bravely and silently. The young females always remain with the ewes all the summer through, and the yearling males remain with them most of the time, but the two and three-year-old rams are the trail makers. I have often followed the trail of the wild sheep through the mountains with the greatest interest, wondering at the many hoofs it must have taken to wear the furrows I found in the solid rock. The young rams are the travelers, and they are largely responsible for the well-worn trails. They never know what to do with themselves. They feel that it is not just dignified to remain with the ewes and youngsters, and the old rams high up in the mountains disdain their company. So in this restless, unsettled position they travel back and forth between the two, often following the same route scores of times each summer. They never acquire the flesh that the old rams do, for which this restless travel is responsible. In the fourth year the males begin to assume the dignified manners of the adults and, although not fully grown until in the sixth year, they commence to try their strength for supremacy. It is not, however, until they are fully grown that they really do battle royal. No animals fight more viciously than a pair of full-grown rams by butting;

they back up, and run at each other with all their power, coming together with awful force. It is in the head that they can stand the heaviest blow, and when one of the combatants allows his antagonist to strike him in the body, he generally suffers seriously. The only sound ever made in battle is that of the pounding together of heads and horns; the vanquished always accepts his defeat in silence. The victor rarely displays any mercy and will often follow his victim for hours in an effort to inflict further wounds. The southern animals are the greatest fighters and the ends of the horns of the *Ovis canadensis* are nearly always battered off because, being so close to the side of the head, the ends of the horns often receive the full force of the blow from the base or heavy part of the antagonist's horn. The male adult *canadensis* almost always has the appearance of having a Roman nose. This is largely due to bruises on the front of the nose received in battle, which cause the skin to grow very thick. I have killed specimens where this skin was fully five-eighths of an inch thick and almost grown fast to the nasal bones. And in many instances the hair was completely worn off. The males of the northern varieties fight, but not so viciously, and in a large number secured by me in different localities I rarely found either the horns or the noses of the animals seriously battered. The old story that the rams jump from cliffs alighting on their heads among the rocks many feet below without injury, is a myth. They practise no such thing. They leap down rugged places, but they always aim to land on their feet. Wherever the rams go the ewes and young will go, and the latter have no heavy horns.

In scaling dizzy heights the *Ovis dalli* has no superior. I once located three young rams while hunting the *Ovis dalli* in the Northern Rockies, that were resting on a ledge seemingly not more than a foot in width on the face of an almost perpendicular cliff fully five hundred feet below the top. I watched them some time by lying down and peering over the top of the wall. I directed my Indians to throw stones at them, knowing that when they were disturbed they would find some route to the top of the cliff. Pretty soon I could hear them traveling the face of the cliff and I could tell by the sounds which way

they were going. I ran as fast as I could in the same direction and saw two of the animals show up on the brink of the high wall about four hundred yards ahead. I fired a hurried shot, just as they saw me and were turning to run, but failed to hit either of them, and they were soon safely out of reach.

I kept going and was within one hundred and fifty yards of where they had stood when the third animal showed up. I fired, missing him the first shot, but bringing him down with the second. In his death struggles he went over the face of the cliff and rolled down to a little bench about three hundred feet below. With me were three splendid young Indians and one of them had with him a long rope, but with the aid of this and by trying every possible means of descent we could not get down that cliff any place, even where the animals came up, and were compelled to leave our specimen untouched, although we were badly in need of food and that ram represented the only food in sight.

In the possession of Mr. Madison Grant, secretary of the New York Zoölogical Society, is the head of a four-year-old ram which I secured in the Rockies, about 66° North latitude, whose performances are worthy of record as showing the footing and endurance of these animals. The Indians I had with me on this trip were as wretched hunters as Indians can possibly be. One of them reported in camp one evening that he had crippled a ram but failed to secure him. This fellow had previously used up nearly two hundred rounds of ammunition without securing a single animal, and I did not believe that he had really crippled one. I am very much averse to leaving cripples in the mountains, however, and I decided to take all my help the following morning and look for this one. We rounded the crest of a high plateau in the country the Indian claimed to have hunted, and on reaching a certain point, he told me to wait, saying that he was going into the canyon below to look for the fellow. My other two Indians wandered off in another direction hunting, and I remained alone to await results. Two or three hours had elapsed when I heard a hallooing, and looking down the canyon in the direction from which the sounds came, saw the Indian working his way up the bottom and could make out the ram hobbling along among the rocks some distance ahead of him. I could not at first understand what the Indian was trying to do, but soon concluded that he had determined on driving the specimen to the top of the plateau where I was, rather than to help carry it up, believing I would be on the lookout and finish it when it reached the top. I felt pity for the poor cripple and could I have reached it in time I should have tried to save it the climb, but as it was I could only wait. I had no thought of failing to put an end to its life when it came up at the head of the canyon, and had taken a seat on a rock about one hundred yards from where I expected it. As it stood on top, I saw that its left thigh was crushed, the leg hanging entirely helpless, and the whole thigh and rump were red with blood, presenting a ghastly sight. It stood still for a moment on three legs, and, turning its head in my direction, looked straight at me without moving. I raised my rifle and fired at its shoulder. It dropped to the ground and rolled completely over. I was so satisfied that I had killed it that I dropped my rifle and started forward. I had scarcely risen to my feet when the ram was up and off, going at a remarkable speed, his left hind leg swinging in the air like a pendulum. I was so astonished that I never thought of my rifle until he was out of my reach, and then I went after him, rifle in hand as fast as I could go, but he disappeared over a canyon wall before I could get a shot. The Indians soon joined me in the chase, but the first we saw of him he was perched on top of a high spiral rock that rose abruptly from the face of the canyon wall about two hundred yards below us. I could not shoot him there, for if I did he would have tumbled off and gone to pieces on the rocks below. I sent the Indians down to drive him from the top of the rock, expecting they would kill him when he landed on the slide below. I stood watching the fellow, wondering what he would do next and feeling half sick at the thought of his suffering. When he saw the Indians coming he went down the side of that rock almost as if he had wings, and was soon far ahead of them down the canyon.

The Indians then separated and commenced a long chase up and down that canyon after the ram, keeping it up until

two of them gave out and came back to where I was. I could see every move, and I began to think that the ram must possess several lives. The third Indian kept on, but was a long way behind the ram, which had turned back toward our position. It came up the canyon until just about even with us, when it turned directly toward us up a little side canyon. Climbing to a position of not more than two hundred yards below it found its way up a very abrupt cliff wall and disappeared. Adjusting my glasses I discovered that it had entered a large cavern in the face of the cliff, and I could very clearly make out the outlines of its white body in the shadows of the cavern, and could see that it was lying down. At length the Indian climbed to where he could see the ram, but he could not get it, and I knew that if he shot it where it was, he could not get it. He commenced pelting the wounded ram with stones and it jumped up, came to the mouth of the cavern and after a moment's hesitation, turned directly around the face of the cliff, that to all appearances was almost perfectly straight up and down without any visible foothold. It proceeded for about thirty feet around the face of the cliff, and then, as if to show us just what a ram could do, it turned completely around and walked back to its starting point and leaped to the rocks fully fifteen feet below, falling as it landed. Another chase took place, the Indian bringing it down with a shot a half hour later. It was so fearfully mangled and its white coat so saturated with blood that I could save only the head, which was a very pretty one. The only ball I had fired at it had struck it in the left side, just behind the shoulder and ranged upward and backward not far from the heart, passing out at the right flank. It had sustained most painful injuries the day before, had bled profusely from the wound I gave it, both externally and internally, and yet it not only clung to life, but performed in a way almost beyond the belief of those who witnessed it.

Wild sheep depend for greatest protection on their climbing capabilities. They travel where no man can follow and often in climbing use their knees instead of their forehoofs. Their first instinct at the approach of an enemy is to start for the mountain top, aiming if possible to get

Lying in Wait.

In Winter the Coat of *Ovis Dalli* is Almost Perfectly White.

above and keep above the enemy. The greatest exception I ever found to this rule was among the white sheep of the Northern Rockies, which have run straight away from me down the mountain, crossing deep canyons below in preference to skirting the mountain I was on. The stories told of rams always standing on watch while the rest of the herd is at rest are purely visionary. Many artists have accepted this idea and many hunters believe in it, and honestly enough, too. But I have frequently seen bunches of every class of these animals perfectly unconcerned, without a single member of the herd making any pretense at standing guard. The movements of sheep are rather remarkable; they will trot, gallop, and lope, but the trot is very little indulged in, and the gallop is a gait they always take very leisurely. When they are alarmed or travel rapidly they lope and often jump stiff legged for long distances at a time over every sort of country.

Although surefooted they often get falls, sometimes quite serious ones. On several occasions I have killed a female whose lower jaw had been broken, evidently from a fall on the rocks. They are fond of salt, especially in the spring, and often visit licks or places where salty or brackish water oozes from the earth, where they will lick and gnaw at the ground.

Wolves, wolverines, and eagles are their most common enemies, and the lambs suffer extensively from these. Wolves are capable of taking down grown animals, but in summer hunger seldom induces them to make the struggle, and in winter they prefer lower altitudes. There are many stories told of the lordly ram doing battle with wolves, which are on a par with the story of their leaping from dizzy heights. The old rams are cunning and in this lies their greatest safety. They are perfectly at home on rocky ledges, where the wolf is not, and if they can gain such a position they will, with one charge, hurl the wolf to the rocks below. But by this method of battle only can sheep defend themselves against wolf or wolverine. It is not uncommon for a band to start a snowslide and the whole lot to go down with it to their death, but the loss from such causes is inconsiderable.

The prospector and the white hunter who live in the mountains, and the Indians, who now all carry firearms, are responsible for the destruction of these beautiful animals. The Indians used to snare them and kill them with bows and arrows by hiding behind rocks near their trails.

On what is known as Black Mountain, just inside the Arctic Coast and to the west of the Mackenzie delta there yet stands a stone fence constructed by the Tooyogmioots, a tribe of Eskimo now extinct, for the purpose of snaring the sheep. They left openings in the fence at regular distances and at these openings set their snares.

Almost all the northern Indians and the Eskimo to the west of the Mackenzie, in Northwest Territory and Alaska, use the skins of the sheep extensively for clothing, and the horns of the animals are split and steamed and bent into shape for spoons, some of them very artistically.

If American ruminants lived in flats, the buffalo would be on the first floor; the moose, elk, and deer on the first and second floors; the caribou on the second and third floors; the sheep on the third and fourth floors; and the goat on the top. In this way one may locate their relative positions as to altitude.

Sheep hunting is an adventurous sport, full of excitement and hard climbing. While it does not demand the skill and woodcraft of still-hunting, it is one of the grandest sports indulged in by American big game hunters, and is experienced by fewer of them than any other sort of big game hunting.

I have been caught in cold rains, hail storms and in sleet and wet snows, high up in the mountains when it seemed my life would be chilled out of me in spite of my best efforts to keep my blood warm. I have been caught on the face of rugged

Field Work in Taxidermy.

mountains where I could scarcely hold on, when wind storms would come sweeping down and take such hold of me as to almost break my hold on the rocks. During weeks in the Rockies between 66° and 67° North I have lived almost without shelter, experiencing every sort of storm. I have traveled all day in the cold rain and with only a single pair of blankets slept in the rain all night. One might live a rather luxurious camp life while hunting the *Ovis canadensis*, but if one would get to *know* such animals, he must actually live

weather was perfect, so we never put up shelter during the entire trip, but slept in the open. Near where we slept was a little mountain lake, clear as crystal, through which flowed a stream of water, just from the snow and almost as cold as ice. Around us rose the rugged canyon walls and at the foot of one of these was a great stretch of snow many feet deep. We kept our fresh meat buried in the snow, which proved a most convenient ice box. Every day we would climb these high ridges and travel them for miles hunting sheep and viewing

The Sheep Is Very Tenacious of Life, This One, Several Times Shot, Led the Hunters Many Miles Over All but Impossible Cliffs.

in their country, prepared to follow them at all times of the year and under all kinds of conditions. I have spent months high in the mountains, and studying and hunting these animals without tasting food from civilized lands, sharing the life of my savage help and facing the elements without sickness or a cold.

Once, on the other hand, I camped in the Che-on-nee mountains just in the mouth of a canyon and at the foot of high ridges where the sheep were accustomed to range. Our only fuel was a few small scrub balsam and alders, but it was August and the

one of the grandest panoramas of mountain scenery in the world. I left our camp one day with two men, a small piece of canvas, one pair of blankets, and a frying pan. We had but little care as to where night should overtake us, and just before sunset I killed two magnificent rams. We cooked our fresh steaks on a fire of dead willows and the three of us slept warm and comfortable on top of the piece of canvas with the one pair of blankets over us.

This is the cheerful side of sheep hunting.

10.
DEER HUNTING
ON SANHEDRIN
(1897)

DEER-HUNTING ON SANHEDRIN.

By Ninetta Eames.

SANHEDRIN or Sanhedrim, as the mountain is locally called, is a noble eye-rest for the California traveler, from whichever way he approaches its wilderness of peaks and pines. History does not tell us who gave to this interesting landmark its musical Jewish name, but it was my good fortune to run across an old hunter who told how, in the early fifties, one Pierre de Léon, an educated Frenchman, came to live with the Indians hereabout, and how when troubles arose between the several tribes, a council of chiefs took place on this central mountain, and De Léon, who was present, was said to have begun an eloquent speech with the declaration, "We are the Great Sanhedrin of the Nomalackie tribes."

The name thus dramatically introduced into Indian nomenclature, has since clung to the traditions of this vast "council-chamber"—Nature's "Hall of Gazzith"—whose superb appointments of tree colonnade, rock sculpture, cloud-picturing fountains, a rich mosaic of flora for pavement, and the whole burnished heavens for roof, fit it more for the meeting place of gods than for white hunters or Diggers in war-paint.

Viewed from the Russian River valley, Sanhedrin runs its ten miles of noduled ridge against the northern blue, its height hardly less than the snow-scarred cones of Mount Hull, St. John, and Snow Mountain. This group of Coast Range summits forms the upper apex of a rugged spur whose trend is from northeast to southwest, the whole including what is known to the few as the best deer-preserve in California.

When, therefore, Sam Paxton and Doctor George wrote to us to join them in their regular summer's hunt on Sanhedrin, the invitation was gladly accepted.

There were five of us in the party, with hunting equipments, saddles, blankets, and "grub-box," all snugly packed in a stout spring wagon and cart. Pedro, the Doctor's deer-dog, shared the back-seat with the Commodore. Not one of us, unless it be Pedro, is likely to forget that morning's drive out the orchard lane and on up the long, shining valley with its dimplement of river blue, the wind sweet and cool in our faces, a broad sunrise brilliance on the mountains, and all the shaggy wild-wood of the foot-hills gathering to us. Sixteen miles on up stream, and we trace the Russian River to its head in Potter Valley, where modest farm-homes peep at the passers-by through loops of hop-vines and windows framed in apple-boughs.

Beyond the peaceful valley the road turns leftward to let us squeeze between the steepled bowlders that overlook Coal Creek. Thence on we zigzag across broken uplands, down whose gardened cañons the snow treasures of Sanhedrin come cascading to the south fork of the Eel River.

At this season the Eel River has a summer flow measuring no greater depth than reached our wagon-bed. But winter shows a different phase—a foaming torrent impossible to ford; and the occasional pilgrim to Sanhedrin solitudes must submit to be swung across, from bank to bank, in a basket hanging from a cable.

In climbing out of Day's Vale, our interest in the landscape grew apace; we were beginning the ascent of Sanhedrin. The forest became denser—not massed in solid shades, but grouped in beautiful open groves, the dark plumes of conifers in lovely contrast to the foliage of oak and madroño and the pale green of hazel.

High and still higher we mount, every foot of the ascent bringing fresh wonderment at the vastness and grandeur of the mountain world about us. The colossal gap between us and Mount Hull and Iron Mountain is the roadway of Eel River, its lofty walls smoothed out of jagged feature by sweeps of forest and chemisal, the whole as wild as if newly created. At times we catch the glint of water from depths of gorge. We lunch by a bowlder-choked stream, and eat the thimble-berries on its banks for dessert. After an hour's rest we are again on the road.

This glorious wilderness is a choice feeding-ground for deer. The broad forests on the east and south of Sanhedrin are, as yet, practically inaccessible to lumber traffic, and no pick of miner has defaced the comfortably-cushioned rocks. Even stock-raising is at a disadvantage, as the snow lies so late on these alpine highlands that only migratory flocks and herds come up from the valleys to graze in the short warm season.

The deer's favorite browse is chemisal—"chemise brush" it is commonly called; the name is supposed to be of Indian origin. Whole mountain fronts grow this thorny, dull-colored shrub, and, shortly after the uninviting pasture has been swept by fire, deer greedily feed upon the sprouting twigs. These high woodlands also furnish unlimited supplies of other browse—leaves, buds, shoots, moss-fiber, acorns—any of which deer prefer to the sweetest of young grass. When winter sets in, small bands, led by masterful old bucks, work their way gradually down to warmer altitudes, keeping as much as possible to sheltered passes.

Each steep we gained—hunters assert there are twelve distinct summit-ridges to Sanhedrin—was housed and dreaming under living towers of cedar and pine. I have never seen mightier specimens of these trees in the Sierra or northern Coast Range than are marshaled here in stalwart clans four thousand feet above sea-level.

We wound up the south slope of the mountain, through mile above mile of primeval forest. The sun darted javelins through the dim vault of the trees, the young oaks clapped their leaves joyously, there was a spiced coolness in the air, and the vigorous splash of Cedar Creek made tumult in the ravine that walled in the road. A sign-board was nailed to an obtrusive fir, and the Commodore hailed us to "heave to till he made out the colors."

Our "sailor man" spelt out the straggling letters of "Bachelor's Camp," and the horses were turned off the road, when they crashed uphill through a tangle of berried shrubbery. A few rods of this, and the great pines stood aside to make room on a sunny glade

for sapling oaks. Sam and Burk were already here and unloading the cart. There were two hours yet of sun, and we all turned to at the jolly work of regulating camp.

Nature seemed to have done the planning for us, and with a felicitous regard for the relations of beauty and utility. You saw at once which niche she intended for the dining-room, the sun-proof boughs of a fir for ceiling, and walls of interlocked alder and pepperwood. A kitchen square alongside had an indoor water supply to delight the heart of the most exacting housekeeper. While Sam energetically proportioned off the stream into "spring-house," sink and cellar, the Doctor was intent upon building the kitchen-range, his hands fitting the rocks and clay-mortar with the nicety of a stone-mason. In the meantime the Commodore constructed table, benches and stools, the boards having been brought from a little mill a mile up the divide. Burk and I busied ourselves at various odd jobs, and finally settled to cutting fir-boughs for beds.

When it came to getting supper, Sam naturally fell into place as head cook, his experience in the army and in many a summer's hunt since, making him exceptionally expert in outdoor cooking. Add to this a painstaking knowledge of woodcraft and deer-lore, with unfailing good humor and helpfulness, and Sam's virtues as a comrade may be readily understood.

While we lingered over supper, a young man with two hunting-dogs rode up and handed us a can of fresh milk. There were general "how d'y' dos" and hand-shakings, followed by the eager question:

"Seen any deer lately, Jimmie?"

The answer was not so encouraging as we expected:

"There was plenty awhile back, but last week a couple o' 'Frisco hunters was all up an' down here an' Panther Cañon, a-shootin' every digger-squirrel an' chipmunk they see, so of course scared off a lot o' deer."

Jimmie could not wait just then to further advise us; he said he "guessed he'd better git a move on, as them girls was alone at the cabin"—meaning his wife and sister—but he promised to guide us to the best hunting on the mountain.

After the exertion of the day, we

were tired and sleepy, and made little ceremony of hurrying to bed. Our tent was spread in the upper chamber of the grove, and in all the magnificent castle of out-of-doors there was never a more inviting or convenient apartment. Two giants, a pine and a fir, upheld the stately arch of doorway through which we looked down upon the "lower story," our eyes fascinated by the weird night-effect of the scene. The smoldering fire lit fitfully the cavernous dark of the kitchen, where Sam's gaunt form moved to and fro, setting things to rights. Outside the dim circle made by the light, the black trunks of the trees stood like a stockade, and beyond them the immeasurable gloom of the forest.

One novelty in our tent was a miniature well, a foot or two wide and of equal depth—a break in the crust of earth above an underground stream. We had our bed directly over this stream, and from my pillow I could dip my cup into the fern-fringed bowl. I lay back in an ecstasy of privacy and rest, my limbs acquainting themselves by slow degrees with the yielding, fragrant mattress, and my senses deliciously lulled to sleep by the tinkle of the running brook.

The next day we spent in overhauling traps and straightening up camp, lazying off a bit now and then in the irresponsible way that is half the charm of out-door living. Near sunset Sam shouldered his rifle, and with Pedro at his heels, sallied forth to satisfy himself of the whereabouts of deer, for we planned an early hunt in the morning.

In Northern California, and more particularly Mendocino, the chase is usually carried on with trained hounds, some of which cost their masters no inconsiderable sum. A sheepman willingly gives one hundred dollars for a good "varmint dog," and often numbers six to a dozen in his pack.

A shepherd-dog is generally considered the best for deer, though a cross with a foxhound and a bloodhound will often produce a mongrel superior to either parent for deer-hunting. "A dog can have too good a nose," as Sam expressed it; that is, a pure bloodhound will cause delay and trouble by sticking too long to a trail.

There are two varieties of black-tail deer — *Cariacus columbianus* — found to-day on Sanhedrin: the forked-horn Pacific or Coast deer, and the "sprangled"-horn, the latter by far the more numerous.

When Sam sauntered into camp an hour or two later, our neighbor was making his nightly call with the milk. Sam asked him "Which way had we better go in the morning?"

There was a momentary scratching of the dark, curly pate.

"Well, I reckon we jump more deer down on the river, an' that's your best chance. Last time me an' my wife was there, she says, 'There lays a deer!' An' sure 'nough there was a big 'sprangled'-horn buck, an' 'long side o' him a yearling. I had only Dad's old Winchester, but I let fly an' jest shaved the old feller's rump, an' he lit downhill fifty feet at a jump, an' I lost him. Cap and Spot [his two dogs] headed off the little spike till I got in a shot an' killed him. It had something cur'ous 'bout it; its horns was hard with the velvet on. I never see one that-a-way before."

It was agreed that the four of us should call for Jimmie as soon after daybreak as possible, Burk promising to stay and keep camp. Accordingly, at four in the morning, I was jarred awake by something like a bomb exploding close to my ear. It was Sam, whooping outside the tent. The Commodore snorted, sleepily, "Ay, ay, sir!" and then floundered back to bed, and drew the blankets over his bald head. This would never do. I lit a candle, and stuck it with melted tallow to a box, then felt for his neck-band, and shook him till his eyes stood out, and he bawled lustily, "Belay that!" After this effectual "eye-opener" we both hurried into our clothes and joined the others in the firelight.

A hasty breakfast was eaten, while Pedro stood about, his eyes and tail eloquently mindful of what was in prospect. When we took the guns from their cases and made a start for the horses, the intelligent brute trotted from one to the other of us in an exuberance of understanding; he was as sure of the hunt as if he already scented the game.

The morning broke with perfect weather, the wide blue of the sky propped by ponderous peaks, the risen sun a glory on the world, a breeze waking to music the vibrant pines, and every falling stream a tuneful undertone to infinite harmonies. It was not so early but a digger-squirrel scurried over the dry leaves and cones in ostentatious search for his breakfast of pine-nuts. The bark of this plebeian of the *Sciuridæ* is so evidently an impertinence, that one is provoked to silence it even at the risk of putting to flight nobler game.

We rode single file down the mountain. When we reached Jimmie's cabin, the family was eating out-of-doors, the dogs nosing about the legs of the table.

The delay at the cabin was a short one, as Jimmie's horse was saddled, and soon he was in advance, piloting us over a south exposure of wild mountainside to the Eel River cañon. We spoke under our breath, as deer are keen to detect the human voice, but are often indifferent to sounds made by cattle and horses. In this rough-country hunting a horse is used as much as possible to lessen the labor of the chase. Sam's Billy seemed to enter quite as intelligently into the sport as his master, who related instances where he loaded one or two deer on him and then sent him alone back to his partner in camp, while he—Sam—continued the running down of a wounded buck.

When well over an intervening ridge bristling with chemisal, Jimmie called the dogs after him and struck out alone down the river to make the drive with the wind. A deer's sense of smell is so acute that the greatest caution is necessary to keep to leeward, until he is brought by the hounds within range.

For some silent minutes the rest of us walked our horses on an obscure trail midway up the slope, where we overlook a sweep of upper and lower hillsides and ravines. On crossing a verdant dip where springs gush, we see sharp-toed hoof-prints, and judge that five deer at least have been here to drink within an hour. Thence on, our excitement and eagerness augment with every step, and our eyes rest searchingly upon each object that bears a likeness to the game.

Suddenly the hounds give tongue—a portentous outburst which the mountains catch and give back in a thousand stirring echoes. With bounding pulses we urge our horses toward a group of oaks. Sam hears Pedro's prolonged, mournful bay in the lead, and cries exultingly:

"He's jumped a deer! Just hear the music. Now for luck, boys."

They are grand—those urgent, death-thirsting yells, which make cataracts of our blood! Flinging ourselves out of stirrups into the shade, we tie up quickly; then with rifles held so as to clear the chemise brush, we stumble heedfully over the lip of the scarp. Sam is on ahead, and as Pedro's trumpet challenge grows nearer and more furious, keeps calling to us in an extravagance of relish, "Listen to that music! *Isn't* it beautiful?"

We are all equally enthusiastic, but the Commodore seems at a loss to understand. He glows with sympathy, but is evidently confused. His eyes wander from point to point in a puzzled way, and when Sam again exclaims, "Just hear that chorus, boys! Great guns, but that's the music for me!" he bursts forth:

"Music? I don't hear any music! If those dogs would keep still, I might."

It was said in all simplicity, but Sam looked such daggers of disgust that I hastened to interpose by asking where each of us was to be stationed.

Sam's ardor had received a heavy shock, and his answer is cold and straight to business:

"You and the Commodore stay where you are. Doc, you had better get up on that big rock below, and I'll go still farther down to those trees."

Sam is a general at a deer-drive, and we obeyed without question. From our several vantage grounds within halloing distance of each other, we commanded the mouths of three small ravines which opened into the main defile of the river. A deer is not apt to run across a cañon, but up or down it; and, judging from the direction the dogs were heading, it was certain the Commodore and I would get the first shot.

A few minutes' breathless waiting, and then a mad plunge through brush, and the bump-bump of bounding hoofs, a startling glimpse of flying horns and dun hide, and the clamorous hounds break cover within a hundred yards of us. Bang! my bullet overflies the mark by a good foot—a common mistake in downhill shooting; and the Commodore, who had never before seen a wild deer, stares open-mouthed and forgets he has a gun. Crack again! A curl of blue smoke below us, and the Doctor gets off his pedestal with more haste than dignity, and running across a strip of open ground, disappears behind a parapet of rocks.

We made the precipitous descent at breakneck speed, coming upon the scene just as the Doctor was imperturbably shifting the position of a big buck so as to turn the head downhill, that the blood might better run from the gaping wound in the throat. The dogs, panting but elated, crowded around us, and Sam coming leisurely up, the bullet - hole was pointed out to him.

"Phew! Spine cut in two as clean as a whistle. Doc ain't much of a hunter, but fetch along your deer and he's the best running-shot in the country."

The Doctor's jolly laugh set the woods agog, and a blue jay, perched on the polished red of a madroño bough, squalled vociferously in company. We all voted the buck a noble prize; fat, glossy of rump, and with an imposing frontlet of soft horn wrapped in beautiful mouse-gray velvet.

The next thing in order was the

AN EXHAUSTING SCALE.

pouching of the deer for packing. The skin was split down the back of the front legs from knee to dew-claw, the knees then unjointed, and the limp ends crossed diagonally and used as toggles through the slit gambrels of the hind legs. By this ingenious manipulation the hunter adjusts the carcass to his shoulders as he would a knapsack, and is thus enabled to carry the weight with the least possible friction and fatigue.

After an exhausting scale of the hot cañon wall, each of us taking turns at packing the deer, we emerged from the jungle of chemisal to the sheltering oaks, where Jimmie was waiting with the horses. The sun being now high, we were of one mind to return to camp to refresh and cool off. All were as hungry as cannibals, so it was a great relief to find that Burk had the dinner well under way when we got there, and Sam had only to put the finishing touches by doing to a turn some venison steaks. His practiced fingers delicately disposed the floured pieces in the smoking grease, and the appetizing odors that arose made my mouth water. Burk puttered about the wood-pile, and the Doctor in brown "Mother Hubbard" overalls, a flowered calico neckerchief knotted loosely around his neck, a towel slung over one arm, and a long steel fork held ready for use—cut a comical figure as second cook.

"Deer liver" declared Sam, "ain't really meat, but hunter's bread. I've cut it just like a loaf and spread butter on. If cooked right, you can't eat enough of it to hurt you."

That night, for a late supper, we had deer meat in another form—a "digger roast," as the boys called it. A saddle of venison, sprinkled with salt, was rolled in greased brown paper, and dipped in water. The logs of the fire were then pushed back, a hole dug in the hot ashes, the roast fitted in and covered with live coals. During the hour it was to remain we sprawled before the blazing pitch-pine, a forest of firewood to our hand, and the whole night—the all-contenting, star-hung night—before us.

When the dusk was deepening, Jimmie's wife came along with our nightly supply of milk. She laughed at our fears to let her return alone through the woods, and after a grateful "good night," both horse and rider were swallowed up in the black of the forest. The Doctor looked after her, with uneasiness:

"It doesn't seem just right to let her go alone!"

As if in answer to the kindly thought a ringing note of song reached our ears, the words indistinguishable, but the air wild and musical. It was repeated again and again, each time sounding fainter and sweeter through the hushed pines.

"She is nearly home," said the Doctor, as he gave a relieved poke to the fire.

Shortly after we had a picturesque intruder—an old hunter, called "Dad." He was well known to the boys, who made him heartily welcome. Dad had on the conventional overalls, a gray flannel shirt, minus a button at the neck, and a faded vest, with a whole row of buttons off. His old felt hat might have been the original, so battered and full of holes was it. He seated himself upon one end of the long bench, and the Commodore sat cross-legged on the other, both doing their best to balance their seat on the hummocky floor. Then we drew our visitor on to a graphic recital of how he killed the biggest panther ever seen on Sanhedrin—a ferocious beast that measured over nine feet from tip to tip and weighed two hundred pounds. In his excitement Dad rose to better slap his thighs, the bench gave a vicious tilt, and behold, the Commodore's legs beating a wild tattoo in the air as he keeled completely over !

For four consecutive mornings we rode to various hunting-grounds, all within five miles of camp, and only once came back without bigger game than quail and grouse—the latter a splendid game-bird, slaty-blue in color and as large as a domestic hen. We kept to "station-hunting," there being less work about it, and more certainty of success. The biggest kill we had was the morning the Doctor shot three deer, all before they could run a hundred feet. That day the camp was overstocked with venison—four deer strung up to the same stout limb. We made a handsome divide of spoils with Jimmie and the men at the mill, and as a team happened to be going through to Ukiah, sent a choice hind quarter to a friend there.

I had my first luck over beyond Windy Flat, with the Doctor and Pedro to make the drive. On making the ascent of a pine-tipped steep, we came upon a couple of deer-beds—two oval depressions, each about three feet long. The soil and leaves inside were worked up fine and pressed down by plump bodies, and the signs of recent occupancy so fresh that we half believed the beds were yet warm. Pedro scented the trail, and his tail went up.

We agreed to work down the south fork of a cañon, which spread its arms at our feet. The long hollows and hillsides were skirted with copses that deer love to haunt, and bowlders, moss-spotted and whiskered, were tumbled on the sunny patches between. Sam stationed himself on a furzy shelf across the stream, and stood erect, gun in hand, as fine a figure of a mountain hunter as one cares to see. The Commodore stood his ground directly opposite, where he fidgeted and perspired like a man hard beset. As a sportsman he was from first to last a self-confident failure, but not once did he lose pluck and energy.

From my position midway I faced a romantic glen whose summer foliage was all alight and murmurous. Anon was the rap-tap-tap of that little carpenter, the woodpecker, or the cheerful clatter of quail in the hazel brush, but altogether it was tedious waiting. At last Pedro opened—a faint bellow, but fast growing louder and fiercer. I knew the honest fellow was talking deer, for he never gave a false alarm, and so my fingers played nervously with the trigger.

Then came the sharp report of Sam's rifle. I thought, "There goes my chance," when crash ! thump ! an antlered head broke from behind a rock not a hundred yards off, and with no consciousness of taking aim I blazed away. I saw that I had winded him, for he stumbled and turned from sight downhill, by which I judged him hard hit ; for a deer severely wounded is sure to drag himself gulchward.

I ran to see, and Pedro, leaping the runnel below, I signed him to the spot. He bounded ahead, and, when I came up, was having a spirited bout with a six-pointer, the buck half lying, but making desperate resistance with his sharp horns and hoofs. The knife ended it, Pedro muttering savagely meanwhile.

Sam, too, was not to be outdone that morning. He had brought down a two-pointer ; so we considered ourselves well repaid for a long forenoon out.

To Sam is due the credit of shooting the one Pacific forked-horn seen by us on the trip. The fifth morning he went off on a still-hunt to Summit Lake—a pond or deer-lick seven miles from our camp, on Cedar Creek. He returned by the middle of the afternoon, and the buck he had slung across Billie was altogether the largest we had yet come upon, and its horns the handsomest. We drew closer to demand particulars.

"I guess it was just a 'happenstance,'" Sam said, with an adroit wink and thrust of his tongue. "Generally a man don't wait to see a deer, but just shoots at what might be a part of one—a patch of brown or gray, the bush above a pair of slim sticks that look like legs, or somewhere below two tips of ears or a bit of horn that the sun strikes. One time a bowlder I'd been watching, up and jumped twenty feet in the air, an' plunged downhill like an avalanche ; so there's something in knowing a deer when you see it. But this time I had a whole broadside to aim at, an I tell you it was a picture—smooth an' fat, head up and horns branching, ears flaring an' the shiniest eyes staring straight ahead. I wished I could see him in the short blue—then a buck's the prettiest animal in the world. I knew he couldn't scent me, so I lay low a spell to watch him. Well, it wa'n't long before he concluded he hadn't heard anything, so he up with his hind hoof an' scratched his ear, an' then fell to browsing. Have you ever noticed how a deer can't keep still a second ? He kept shaking, stamping an' wiggling his tail, always fighting the fleas and buck-flies. I didn't dare wait too long, so I drew a bead an' took him back of the shoulder."

We helped string up the buck, and then all hands napped in the shade for a couple of hours. When I roused up, there was Sam methodically at work on his deer—cutting off the head, separating the horns from the skull, and skinning the carcass — lamenting, meanwhile, that he had not done the last while the animal was yet warm.

"Comes a sight easier," he said, and then showed me what I persistently try to forget is there—the nest of maggots always secreted in the cavity just below the eyes in a deer.

"Ugh ! that's worse than a ship's biscuit," the Commodore exclaimed.

Despite eternal vigilance on the part of a deer, a fly gets up its nostrils and lays eggs, with the result related.

When Sam had made a neat job of the dressing, he proceeded to sack the deer—"put on its nightgown," as the Doctor had it. He first whittled out a peg, and punched a hole in the bottom of a burlap sack. Then drawing the string that held the deer up through the hole, he passed the end around the limb of a oak, pulled on the cord, and swung the venison out of reach of the "varmints."

"You see," he explained with complacency, "by punching the hole instead of cutting it, the mesh closes tight around the string and keeps out the flies."

Sam was a master at handy tricks. But the sack did not reach more than half-way down, so he drew another sack over the exposed parts that it overlapped the first, and then secured it by baling rope about the middle.

The day came all too soon for the Commodore and me to leave Bachelor's Camp, the rest of the party having decided to stay yet a week longer. By getting an early start, we would reach the nearest stage-line in time to catch the down coach for Ukiah, and thence finish our journey by rail—one hundred and fifty miles from Sanhedrin to San Francisco in one day.

On our last night a crescent moon rocked in the gap between two fir-pinnacled domes. A subdued radiance stole abroad, and the profound stillness of the mountains was better than music to soothe one. We wandered happily under the sugar - pines, above whose swinging tops the stars flashed through thin, voyaging clouds. Such armfuls of scented cones as we carried to camp for that last night's burning ! They were the largest I ever saw, measuring all the way from fifteen to eighteen inches in length, and when piled artistically, made the prettiest, crackliest camp-fire imaginable.

We were up at three in the morning, and by four o'clock had breakfasted and harnessed the horses. The Doctor was elected to drive us down Sanhedrin—a risky undertaking, for as yet no streak of dawn pierced the thick forest on Cedar Creek. Sam and Burk did their best to give us a cheerful send-off. They built a pyramid of gummy cones at the head of the road, and put a match to it when we were ready to start. The Doctor mounted to the front seat, took up the reins and whip, and set one foot on the brake; and while Pedro howled and tugged at his chain, I climbed up beside his master.

At the final moment Sam seized the handles of two blazing cones, the Commodore snatched a couple more, and in the general illumination the procession began a reckless dash, down grade, Sam's spectral figure running on foot in the lead, his torch held high, the Commodore prancing after and brandishing his flaming cones till the fiery smoke and sparks trailed back like the tail of a comet. It was wildly fantastic and exhilarating—the illusory figures of the two men, the weird lighting of the road, which looked like a tunnel through the pits of blackness upon either hand, the dumb challenge of highwaymen boles as they stepped forth and retreated with startling abruptness—our wheels grazing the unflinching granite on one side and the brow of a frightful abyss on the other, and overhead the pale stars slipping from sight one by one.

At times a dead pine, preternaturally tall and white, menaced us with fixed, ghostly arms; or a prostrate, disjointed fir reared its hydra-headed roots, like a dragon threatening us as we tipped crazily toward its ambush. When Sam's torch gave a dying flicker, he tossed it over the cliff and threw up his arm with a shout of farewell. The horses plunged ahead, and I looked dizzily back; nothing could be seen of our friend, only a second's glimmer of the yet burning torch—a star flung into infinitude.

We stopped for the Commodore to get in. He had carried our beacon bravely until both hands were blackened and scorched with burnt pitch. The Doctor cracked his whip at the off horse. It did not seem possible for mortal eyes to be sharp enough to keep the restive brutes in that ribbon of road. I made myself as small as I could, for our driver appeared to need all the seat. His heavy body, with the elbows held well out, balanced from right to left, the shoulders bent a trifle forward, his hat pushed back and eyes bulging with their intent lookout. With gasp and unfinished sentence, I clung to the farther end of the seat, the Doctor gently but firmly insisting that he must have "elbow-room."

It was like trying to keep to one place in a cyclone. We lurched from right to left, spinning around sharp angles, plumping into gutters, lunging ahead up rocky steeps, always a desperate dodging of shadowy trees which set themselves determinedly in our way, and then a final lightning race down a precipice, with a dismembering "fetch-up" at the bottom. We timed ourselves from "Oat Gap" to the foot of the mountain—a long four miles—and found we had made it in fifteen minutes. It was the most superb feat in mountain-driving I ever witnessed.

11.
TURKEY HUNTING ON THE WEKIVA, FLORIDA (1897)

TURKEY-HUNTING ON THE WEKIVA, FLORIDA.

By Leon L. Canova.

A TURKEY hunt in the Gulf Hammock had been arranged by my brother, his son and myself. I had written to Captain Wingate, a jovial old English gentleman, who settled in the Hammock at the close of the "late unpleasantness," requesting him to secure the services of Clayton, a negro guide who knew every cattle-path and tree in that part of the Hammock, and was equally conversant with the habits of the game.

Monday afternoon, preceding Thanksgiving, found us at Otter Creek near Cedar Keys. Here a team was awaiting to convey us to our destination, nine miles away. Into the wagon our guns, ammunition, luggage and persons were quickly bundled, and away we went through the pine woods, a most uninviting stretch of country. Our hearts were light, however, for we knew that four miles of this brought us to the Hammock, famed for its richness and abundance of game. The tract of heavily-wooded land is from six to twelve miles wide, extending from the Suwanee River to the headwaters of the Withlacoochee, a distance of about one hundred miles. It is known as the Gulf Hammock from the fact that it triangulates the shore-line of the Mexican Gulf.

As we entered the Hammock night came upon us as it so hurriedly does in this Southland, and the moon in its fullest splendor, which was so bright in the opening, was now almost totally obscured by the tops of the tall hickories, magnolias and oaks, which met overhead. The five-mile drive through the Hammock scarcely gave us time to enjoy all the anticipation to be derived from the morrow's hunt; and at half after seven we were awakened from our reverie by the barking of dogs, and as we rolled up to the "Lodge," as it is called, the cheery voice of Captain Wingate was heard calling to us to come right in to supper, which was waiting for us.

Jumping from the wagon the first person to meet me was Clayton. My joy at meeting him was surpassed only by the news he imparted. That afternoon he had "roosted" a flock of turkeys, and if we wanted to go out that night we could get some of them before bedtime. We were discussing an immediate raid when Captain Wingate hustled us into the old-fashioned dining-room, telling us that there was plenty of time to talk about such an ordinary thing as killing turkeys.

Was it our journey or was it the spread before us that gave us such appetites? Fried brook-trout, caught from the Wekiva, not fifty yards away; baked wild turkey and broiled venison invited us to eat like gourmands, and we accepted the solicitation. After the repast we went out in front of the house and threw ourselves on the lawn, where we lay in the moonlight planning a depredatory expedition against all turkeydom. Clayton assured us that the roosting turkeys would remain where they were, and our chances would be better early in the morning of securing some of them. It was therefore decided that we sally forth at half after three in the morning, and shoot the drowsy birds at the first streak of dawn.

We all turned in at an early hour, having first seen to our guns, shells, and the alarm clock which was to awaken us at three o'clock. I was a little disappointed when I was advised to leave my rifle, and told to take instead my number ten shot-gun.

We retired, but not to sleep; visions of roasting turkeys kept us awake. Several times during the night I arose and struck a match to see what time it was; the hours dragged so slowly I feared the clock was slow or had failed to work. Finally I dropped off to sleep, to dream of guns and gobblers, and had not been asleep more than ten minutes, at least it did not appear longer, when the burr-r-r-r-r of the alarm clock brought me to a standing position in an instant. A rap on the partition was sufficient to awaken my brother and nephew, and the three of us pulled on our clothes regardless of consequences.

When we left the house, a few minutes later, we found our faithful guide awaiting us; and, following him, we went down the wagon-road about half a mile, when we turned into a cattle-path, which although quite plain when we returned, was most vexing and confusing when we entered. Thorned vines were hung across the path, just high enough to catch one under the throat; huge spiders had built their nets, and one would unwittingly have a veil spread over his physiognomy, and a subdued expression of disgust would betray the fact to his companions. Those who were in the lead would brush aside a chincapin bush, and the branches, in swinging back, would cause profanity when their sharp-pointed leaves struck the face or more likely the ears. The leaves on the ground never seemed more brittle, and to us who were trying to proceed cautiously, our progress was loud and dangerous to our chances for success.

The moon was down, and we had a practical illustration that "the darkest hour is just before the dawn," but after groping around the windings of the path, we reached a point when we had to leave it and cut across to the trees in which our quarry slept. This was the critical part of our journey. Clayton whispered words of caution, and we proceeded as noiselessly as possible, but a crash seemed to follow every step we took. At last we reached the three clustered magnolia trees, and sat upon the ground to wait for daylight.

Day was certainly behind time. There we sat craning our necks to locate the glorious birds, but it was too dark to see them in the foliage of the magnolias. When the sky began to clear up we took standing positions, and made our necks ache by looking upward. I was the first to see the game, and this one was directly over my head; and it was only a few moments more when each, except the boy, was sighting along his gun-barrel waiting for the word "Ready." All of us pointed out a splendid shot to him, but his eyes were stubborn and he could not see the turkey we had selected for him. One moment he would see him, and, when we were all ready, he would say "Wait," in a stage whisper. The turkeys had discovered that something was wrong, and were sounding their signals of alarm in shrill "pits" and "puts."

We were especially anxious for the boy to bag a turkey, as he had never killed one. When we did get ready to shoot, my neck was almost broken. As the four reports rang out in concert, two fine turkeys, a gobbler and a hen, fell to the ground, the victims of my brother and nephew. The rest of the flock flew away in the wildest alarm.

Everybody has seen a gobbler strut, but the pride of the male turkey was surpassed by my nephew that morning, as he shouldered his first turkey.

We made haste to return to the "Lodge," where breakfast awaited us. After satisfying the inner man, we made preparations for an all-day's hunt on that point of land lying between the Wacasasa and the Wekiva, where game usually abounds. All of us carried our shot-guns with shells loaded for turkey and some for deer, as the "sign" was very plentiful and we were likely to jump one almost at any moment.

The territory over which we hunted was a series of islands separated only by small rivulets which could be easily crossed on logs. When we had crossed to one of these islands the guide and my nephew would work one shore, while my brother and myself would hunt the other, both parties meeting on the opposite side; then we would cross to another.

I would take my course along the borders of the little brooks, on the low ground, and my brother take his back upon the higher ground about a hundred yards distant, and thus we would hunt side by side until we met the other party. Sometimes we were in each other's view, and at times patches of scrub or palmetto would prevent us from seeing each other.

We had been over several of these islands without any success, but from the manner in which the ground had been scratched up we knew that plenty of turkeys were about and the many deer-tracks gave us hopes for larger game; in fact I had almost forgotten about turkeys when I heard a rapid rustling of the dry leaves some yards before me. I took it for nothing more than the flight of a wood-rat or a lizard, but with a hunter's caution I stopped in time to see a flash of bronze pass from a patch of scrub behind a large cypress log. My gun went to my face, and I threw it on the opening at the opposite end of the log, intending to drop the bird as he came in the range of my vision. The distance was so great that I had cocked the left-hand barrel, which contained buckshot.

Instead of the frightened bird continuing his race he came to a full stop, and in a moment I saw his red head peering from above his effective bulwark. No sooner had my eyes detected him than my gun spoke; but with a turkey's head as a target, ninety yards away, and only nine buckshot in your gun, one has a slim chance of success. So it proved in my case. For, although I never saw that gobbler again, my brother caught a glimpse of him going like a race-horse across the island, but too far for shooting.

I ran up to the log, expecting to find him, as I had not seen him fly; and as I was standing on the log, surveying the ground, I heard another rustling. As I looked up I saw a hen dash out of the scrub not more than fifty yards away, and I cut down on her. She fell in a heap, but as I started to run toward her she rose to her feet, and taking two or three short jumps soared skyward and sailed directly over my head toward a bit of cypress swamp. When I saw that she was likely to escape I hurriedly broke my gun and inserted loaded shells; and as she was sailing in a straight line away from me I sent a charge of number four shot after her, which stopped her and gave me a mark of honor.

We then went on another island, and stopped at the end of the foot-log on which we had crossed, to eat our lunch. We were hungry and had little to say while we were eating. As we sat there munching our food I heard a rustling of the leaves, which was drawing nearer all the time. The word "turkeys" was passed around, and in a moment every man had his gun in his hand, awaiting with eagerness their first appearance.

While we were in this position I saw a dark object pass a little opening in the underbrush some forty yards away, and as it did so I sent a charge of number eight shot to a point where I thought it would reach the game. My aim had been accurate, for an ear-splitting "squee-e-e" resounded through the woods, followed by the "goush-goush" of a fleeing wild hog, which told us that he was suffering with stinging sensations, for that is all the effect number eights have on the tough exterior of one of these animals. The merriment this created made us unfit for further hunting that day, so we returned to the "Lodge," well satisfied with the result of our hunt in the Gulf Hammock.

Painted for OUTING by J. L. Weston.

"IT GAVE ME A MARK OF HONOR."

12.
GOOSE SHOOTING
ON THE PLATTE
(1892)

GOOSE SHOOTING ON THE PLATTE.

BY OSCAR K. DAVIS.

WE were four old college chums on an outing— the first we had had together. In fact, it was the first meeting since that bright summer day we said our good-byes down in the old ivy-covered fraternity hall. Oddly enough, we had gone four different ways in pursuit of fortune and fame, and had embraced four professions. Law, medicine, business and journalism had each an advocate in the brown tent pitched among the willows on the river bank. "Doc," as we all called him, had a brother who had lived in Nebraska and knew something of the game to be found there. Doc himself was overworked and needed a rest, so when his brother wrote to him that there would be good shooting on the Platte in the spring, Doc wrote to me to know if I would go along for a few weeks. I never need persuasion on the subject of lugging a gun or wearing waders. So I penned a gleeful acceptance, and proposed asking Morton and Crane. That had already occurred to Doc.

Well, the boys agreed, of course, and the trip was promptly planned. We met in Chicago and determined to go to North Platte, Nebraska. The baggageman stared a little when we piled our "truck" into his bailiwick. There were six guns, a comfortable wall-tent, a camp-stove, and the general camp equipage—and ammunition. We had appliances enough for a regiment. We had two dogs, a beautiful Irish spaniel with big, soft eyes that matched his hair, and a knowing wag of his head that said as plainly as words, that he knew what was going on. Doc had a little black, stump-tailed cocker, which he vowed was the "knowingest" quadruped in the Northwest. Some big boxes of shells, wading-boots, geese and duck decoys, and a marvelous cupboard with intricate recesses which were supposed to contain the rarest delicacies of camp life, completed the outfit. We finally reached the valley of the Platte and from there on to North Platte we ran beside the big treacherous river over country as level as a floor. To the south, across the river, lay the big bluffs where we expected to get our game. To the north beyond a few miles of the level valley land lay the counterparts of the southern bluffs, except that they are not so steep nor so ragged.

At North Platte we arranged with an old farmer who lived near the river, to transport our impedimenta to the clump of willows which we selected for our camp site. We worked half a day setting up our canvas and making all things snug. The farmer had two boats, which we attached "for a consideration." He also furnished us with milk and sometimes eggs and butter and knickknacks which Morton gathered after he had collected wood for the camp-stove on which Crane displayed astonishing skill and originality. Doc kept the tent and camp in order while I washed the dishes and lariatted the boats. That old clump of willows saw the jolliest camp ever pitched. After one of Crane's marvelous suppers the pipes would come out and for an hour or so stories of old college life or our after experiences added to the pleasure of the day's sport.

The first night of our life under canvas, after making everything snug, we turned in early to be ready for a good start next day. Before the sun was up Morton had a roaring fire going and was off for the milk. He had been gone but a few minutes when he came crashing back exclaiming,

"Where's my gun? where's my gun? there's more'n a million geese right here under the bank!"

We were all out in an instant and at once saw that there was some foundation for his excitement in the fact that a small flock was sitting on the edge of a bar close to shore but a few hundred yards below our camp. We decided that as Morton had discovered them he should make the trial alone. He made a wide detour coming up toward the bank when Crane signaled that he had gone far enough. Morton had never shot a goose in his life, and the way he "sneaked" on that bunch showed how ardently he desired to bag his game. Flat on his face, shoving his gun before him over the sand, and forcing himself along with elbows and toes, he worked up to within forty yards of the unsuspecting birds before Crane signaled to him to shoot. Then he jumped up and ran toward the bank. With a great honking and splashing the frightened geese flapped the water in their efforts to rise. There was a flash, and a sharp report, another flash and another report, and when the little cloud of smoke cleared away we beheld our dignified business man charging over the river bank after a fine brace of Canadas—the first of the season. It mattered nothing to him that the water was four feet deep, or that the dogs were almost at his heels. They were his first geese and he scorned assistance in securing them. But it was with a decidedly wet and rather crest-fallen appearance that he acknowl-

edged in response to our shouts of laughter that "he guessed he got rattled, but any way he got the geese." The rest of that day he spent in camp bewailing his impetuosity, while he carefully dried his "leathers" as he called his hunting boots.

Our usual time to turn out of the blankets was half-past three in the morning. By four, bread and coffee had been discussed and we were in our "togs" starting for the hill shooting. Two of us tried bluff-cover and the other two went on into the corn fields. To select good bluff cover a sportsman must know his game. If he does, his blind will probably be in the same place on no two mornings, for it is not at all likely that the conditions of wind and weather will be exactly alike any two days, and these things are the greatest factors in determining the path of the principal flight, under which the best blind is, of course, to be had if proper cover can be found. If the morning is cold with strong wind find a low spot between two bluffs; if the wind is very high get into the deep-

"HOLD ON," HE SHOUTED, "THEY'LL BUNCH."

est draw you can find, for the geese will have all they can do to " raise " the bluff, and they will choose the very lowest point to go over. Get a bunch of good, long grass. That is better than a clump of plum trees or sumac bushes, for the geese are suspicious of such places, while the grass always looks just the same. All you have to do is to cover yourself up so they can't see you, and wait. And, when a flock comes out over you, don't get rattled and blaze away before they reach you, or until they are low enough so that you can see their eyes. If you do you will waste your powder and spoil your own temper. Let them get squarely over you ; you can't shoot through their feathers when they are coming unless you have a rifle, and you can't hit them with that. When they are nicely over you and low enough so that you can see the crook in their necks, blaze away. Hold just on the line, pick your bird and let his bill come over the muzzle. Then give it to him, and the odds are very long that you have killed a goose.

If there is no wind there is little shooting. A high place opposite the bar, where the most geese are, will probably give the best results, but you can generally make sure that the shooting will be at long range and hard, and you may have to " push on the gun" to get game.

Cornfield shooting is different again. You can use decoys there and make any kind of a blind. An experienced cornfield shooter gets his location and has his decoys out before the flight begins. He chooses a low spot or a side hill almost invariably. For a blind he selects a row of standing stalks not more than forty yards from his decoys, in the path of probable flight, if he can. Bending them together he backs them up with a big bunch of loose stalks, gathered near by. Behind the blind he has a pile of stalks into which he can crawl clear out of sight, though seeing very well himself. We didn't know these things at first, but we found them out before we had been many days on the bluffs.

But with all our knowledge and the good advice of the old farmer, we did not succeed in making the tremendous bags we had supposed it would be easy to bring down. The geese were very wary. The old farmer laughed heartily at our disgust. " The trouble with you fellers," he said, " is't ye hain't got no ' receet ' ; ye don't know how to do it." And we were obliged to confess that if a " receet " was a means of getting game we did not have one.

The afternoon flight is but a repetition of the morning, and each day just like its predecessor. The last week of our vacation began with our prospects no brighter. We were having a jolly time of it, and enjoying ourselves immensely. As Crane said, we were " gathering great gobs of health," but the failure to gather great bags of the game that was on every side of us was desperately provoking. We lay around the fire in the evening and tried to devise some scheme by which we could trap the wily honkers. But every new scheme followed in the paths of the old. One day Doc and I laid behind a big log on the end of a bar which the night before had been the resting-place of thousands of the sharp birds. We discussed the results of the trip rather ruefully. Doc finally announced that he had a scheme which he believed would work. He would not divulge it, but asked me to help him carry it out. Of course I cheerfully agreed. I was ready to do anything which would assure success.

" Well, come on, then," he said ; " we will have to go to town for the stuff."

We pulled up our decoys at once and went back to camp. We got the old farmer to take us to town, and on the way Doc told me that his plan was to sink barrels in the bars flush with the sand and use them just as sink-boxes are used on the Chesapeake. I did not believe that the scheme would work, and I was sure that barrels would not be large enough. But he was very sanguine, and it was at least worth trying. As I expected, we found that barrels were too small, but we were able to procure two crockery tierces, which were sufficiently roomy for a man to sit down in very comfortably and with space enough left for a dog. These we had hooped up at a little cooper shop so that they would not leak, and, loading them on the wagon, went back to camp.

How the boys laughed when they saw what we had. But the laugh was soon on our side of the tent. It was an awful job getting those clumsy affairs out on the bar without upsetting the boat, but we succeeded and set to work at once to sink them. The bar was not more than ten inches out of water at the point we selected, and before we had a hole half a foot deep it filled with water and put an end to our digging ; for as fast as we dug the sand from the center, that at the sides slid down, and instead of getting deeper, the hole simply grew in circumference. Doc earned his title of "the schemer" then. Setting his barrel up in the hole we had started, he jumped into it and began to wiggle it back and forth. It sank slowly into the sand, just as a man's foot sinks further into the quicksand if he moves it. We kept at this work until the barrel had sunk to within a foot and a half of its top. Then by rapidly digging the sand from around the barrel we succeeded in getting it down to within four inches of the top. There it stopped, but we finished the good job by heaping sand up around it until completely hidden. Then throwing water on the sand where it had been trampled up, to give it a natural appearance, the blind was complete. The same process answered for the second barrel, and it was far into the night before we left the bar. The geese and ducks had been whistling around us all the time. We could not see them, but were sure their flying augured well for our scheme, for it showed they wanted to light on that bar.

In the morning we did not go out to the bluffs with the boys, but made up some of the sleep we had lost sinking the barrels. About seven o'clock we started out. The first flocks were beginning to come in from the fields as we reached our novel blinds. With a newspaper man's instinct, I had managed to find time while in town the day before to hunt up a lot of papers. I did not have much faith in the new blinds, so I took these papers with me. We set out our decoys and got into the barrels to wait. I had made a little stool to sit on, and was altogether very comfortable as I sat and smoked and read my papers. Doc had the dog with him, and I was so thoroughly comfortable that I went to sleep in short order. I was waked up by the report of Doc's gun, and jumped up to find him bringing in a fine big Canada goose. He was greatly elated with his success, and we got back into the barrels in high glee, confident that we would surprise the boys on their return to camp.

But something seemed to be wrong with our decoys. Before we had the barrels we thought the difficulty lay in the blinds. Now that we had them we transferred our objections to the decoys. So we pulled them up and lugged them back to the boat. The boat was about half way up the bar, and as a matter of further precaution we dragged it a couple of hundred yards further away.

While we were doing this the wind had been having fun with my papers, and when I got back to my barrel they were scattered all over that end of the bar. I was skirmishing after some of them when a shout from Doc sent me flying to cover. A big flock of white brants was bearing straight down upon us. We watched them as they came on, and inwardly cursed those fluttering papers. Doc skillfully worked his call, and the flock came straight on and set their wings to light right among the papers. They were within twenty-five yards of us before we raised up out of the barrels and fired, and when they sailed away four of their number lay on the bar. The reason of their action came to me like a flash. "Doc," I shouted, "the papers decoyed them. They thought the papers were white geese."

That surely was what had done it. We succeeded in securing a number of the papers, and tearing them into three or four pieces, threw sand on the pieces to keep them from blowing away. The loose edges fluttered in the breeze and gave them the appearance of life. The new-fangled decoys worked to a charm. I never saw any device that would approach in effectiveness or in the ease of its use, the simple scheme of plain white paper. I have used them since that hunt, as we used them then with wonderful success. We soon discovered that the best method was to roll a piece of plain white paper into a cornucopia and to stand it up on the big end. Then a handful of sand on the long corner of the base would fasten it down, while the loose corners would flap in the wind and give the novel decoy a realistic appearance of life. The judicious use of a good goose-call adds materially to the effect. I have seen geese drift a mile against a strong wind to light into a flock of these paper decoys, and no combination of iron and paint that I have ever seen—and I have used every kind I ever heard of—proved a hundredth part as successful as these simple white papers. The black geese go where the white ones do, and the white ones are seldom decoyed by iron.

Our morning's work in the barrels showed the success of the new scheme. The first flock that came in after we had fixed up the papers was a large bunch of "gabblers." They came off the bluff, about a mile above us, and flew straight to the river, as if uncertain whether to go up or down. Doc was a master with a goose-call, and he kept it going all the time they were between the bluff and the river. As they reached the river, they turned down toward us and began to "cut" down to the water. I never heard any other word used to describe the peculiar way in which geese descend rapidly from a great height. They set their wings as if to light, and then turn sidewise and "cut" down fifteen or twenty feet at a time until they are just above the water. When we saw this flock begin to cut we were pretty sure that some of them would not go further than our bar.

As they came nearer, Doc called less and less frequently, and we soon saw them making straight for the decoys. Crouched low in the barrels, with the guns leaning against the edge in front of us, we waited for them. We had agreed not to shoot until they set their wings to light. I took two extra shells in my left hand for a second shot. Nearer and nearer came the unsuspecting gabblers. How big they looked as they loomed up over the water scarce a hundred yards away! Once they circled to light, then on they came again, till I could see their bright eyes. They set their wings and settled down over the decoys, so close that the joints of their legs were plain to be seen. I jumped up and saw Doc standing in his barrel.

"Hold on," he shouted; "they'll bunch."

And they did. Startled by our sudden appearance they bunched together and began a tremendous flapping of wings trying to rise straight up out of harm's way. Then we shot, Doc to the right, I to the left. I dropped a brace with my first two barrels, and instantly reloaded. They had turned and were going down the wind. One big fellow was clumsy in turning and lagged behind. The gun swung up again, and I glanced along the barrels at him and pulled the trigger. He wavered, and I could see that he was

hard hit. The second barrel cracked and he fell, but into the water. I whistled to the dog and with an eager yelp he was away. Doc had good luck too. A fine brace had answered his call.

With the little frames we had prepared for this use, but had not had occasion before to try, we propped up the dead birds among the decoys. Nine geese from two flocks! What would Morton and Crane say now? How they would laugh at our barrels! They had been firing away out on the bluffs all the morning, but we had rarely seen a goose fall in their direction, and we were eager for their return. But we had not much time to talk about our luck. The flight was nearly over, but stragglers kept coming our way all the time and another small flock tried to light with our papers, so that we added eight more geese to our string that morning, besides a good many duck. We were waiting for the boys when they came into camp. They had three geese and a pair of duck and thought themselves lucky. "How do your barrels work, Old Sport?" Crane asked Doc.

Doc took him by the arm and silently led him to the boat. "Jumping Jehosophat, Mort, look here!" Crane shouted; "they've killed 'em all."

That afternoon he and Morton started to town for barrels and paper, and while Doc and I added a string of a dozen to our experience and score, they were toiling away on a lower bar, sinking a couple of despised barrels. The next day the old farmer came down to visit us. As we showed him the string of game hanging in the trees, he remarked with subdued admiration, "By Jove, you fellers hez got more luck 'n sense! Ye must ha' found thet receet."

The day before we broke camp was dark and cloudy and game flew all day long. Up and down the river there went a steady procession of geese and duck. The score we made that day forever wiped out the memory of all former failures.

During that outing we learned three things of great value to goose shooters: —the use of barrel blinds in sand-bar shooting, the use of white papers for decoys, and the use of number six shot. For a first-class vacation give me a barrel in a sand-bar in the Platte in goose time, plenty of fine shot and white paper, and a few genial companions.

13.
WINTER HUNTING OF GOAT AND SHEEP IN THE ROCKIES (1901)

"ON THE EDGE OF A CLIFF, WELL TOWARDS THE SUMMIT OF THE MOUNTAIN."

WINTER HUNTING
OF GOAT AND SHEEP IN THE ROCKIES

By J. W. Schultz

WHEN viewed from the plains of the eastern slope in winter, the northern Montana Rockies present a most forbidding aspect. Except where patches of timber darken their sides, they loom up cold and white, covered with a mantle of snow many feet in depth, and for days at a time their summits and needle-like peaks are lost in a swirl of gray storm-clouds.

One would naturally think that at this inclement season the sportsman, no matter how enthusiastic, would be content to look at them from the windows of his cosy ranch instead of planning how to invade their snow-bound fastnesses. But autumn after autumn I had traveled among them with a pack-train, and I had come to believe that if certain obstacles could be overcome, a winter hunt might prove a better way in which to secure a head or two of mountain game.

I have tried it, and talk no more to me of pack-trains and the back of a wall-eyed cayuse, ye summers-day hunters! I have experienced all the woes inseparable from their use. Have I not cut trails for them through miles of down timber, brush, and lodge-pole pines standing as thick as hair on a dog's back? Have I not helped yank every animal out of each succeeding mud-hole and bog? Have I not run until my breath was spent, and fallen a thousand times, and skinned my shins, and had my eyes nearly gouged out by the brush, in vain attempts to drive the beasts back into the trail which they never would follow? And haven't I been moved to deep anger at their obstinacy? I am done with them forever! I have found more tractable servants; the snowshoe has taken their place. In my stable hangs a long row of pack-saddles, panniers, swing and lash ropes, and cinchas; I shall give them to my bitterest enemy, and advise him to go on a long mountain hunt with a pack-train.

On each of our winter hunts we divided our hunt into two parts. First, a few days on the summit of the range for goats, and then a short trip to the mountains of the eastern slope for bighorn. We were accompanied both trips by Jack Monroe and Joe Carney, two of the best guides and mountain men in the West, and to whose untiring efforts our success was in a large measure due.

Leaving the cars at Bear Creek section-house, seven miles west of the summit, inside of an hour we had our packs all arranged, and strapping on our snowshoes walked northeast for three miles, through a low pass, to Oley Creek. The snow was very deep, some seven or eight feet on the level, and from twenty to thirty where it had drifted, but it was so well settled and firm that the bows of our shoes did not sink below the surface. At the end of the pass we descended a long, steep hill into the valley, and turned up it towards the summit of the great range.

We had made barely a quarter of a mile when we came to a yard of elk, but did not molest them, as they were not the kind of game we were after; and, then, no sportsman would take such a mean advantage of them. Their trails from patch to patch of willows were so deep that their backs were nearly on a level with the surface of the snow, and as they could make but little progress should they leave these trails, there was no help for them had we chosen to turn butchers.

Oley Creek valley is very narrow, seldom exceeding two hundred yards in width. On each side of it the mountains rise to a great height, those on the north being generally a succession of bare, rocky ledges rising one on top of another to the very summits, while those on the south side have more gradual slopes and are heavily timbered. Proceeding up the valley for four miles, we came to our old camping ground, a sheltered place under the spreading branches of a mighty fir.

THE FIRST GOAT.

It was barely three hours since we had left the section-house. It had taken us a long summer's day a year or two previous to make the same journey with pack-train. And how contentedly, how easily we had skimmed over the level surface of the snow, which deeply covered the brush and down timber, the bogs, and boulder-strewn stream

TIRED! PASS BETWEEN BEAR CREEK SECTION AND OLNEY CREEK.

we had formerly labored so hard to get our horses through! There can be but one better way than on snowshoes to enjoy a mountain hunt, and that will be when we are provided with aerial ships.

With our one shovel, and snowshoes answering the same purpose, we soon cleared a space upon which to erect our tent, cutting small, dry firs for the ridge and supporting poles. Then we made a bed of balsam boughs two feet thick in the back half of the tent, placed a wagon-sheet on it, laid our sleeping bags on that, all in a row, and folded the sheet back over them. Next we put up our stove, and the camp was complete. I must say a word about the stove; it was a bottomless, flat-folding affair, with three joints of telescoping pipe, presented to us by Mr. W. H. Mullens, of metal boat fame. For its foundation and bottom we built a platform of large, flat rocks, which absorbed great quantities of heat when a fire was going, and gave it out so slowly at night that the tent was always warm and comfortable. Often, before morning, our thermometer out in the brush registered 30° below zero and more, yet water in the bucket inside never froze.

When we arose in the morning, while all was still and pleasant in the valley, a severe wind-storm was raging higher up, concealing the mountains in one vast whirl of flying and drifting snow. Our Eastern friends were much disappointed at the prospect, as there was no use of trying to hunt while the wind blew so fiercely, and they had each hoped to kill a goat that day. We managed, however, to put in the day and evening quite comfortably, cooking and eating half a dozen meals, napping, and planning the morrow's campaign.

The next day was cold and clear, the mountains looming up on all sides with dazzling brightness. After an early breakfast Jack and G. started to climb the mountain directly north of camp, while M. and Carney went up the valley to hunt the next one beyond. It was my day to cook, but about noon, having everything in shape, I started out with my telescope, a powerful glass of thirty-five diameters, to have a look at the country.

There was a bare crag jutting out from the hillside just above camp, affording a good view of the mountains on the opposite side of the valley, the southern faces of them, where the goats remain in winter. Having arrived at the top, I made a seat of the snowshoes, adjusted the glass, and began to look for goats and some signs of my companions. There was the trail of Jack and G., where they had climbed a long, open gash in the mountain side, the result of a snowslide in years gone by. Their shoeprints were visible clear to the upper end of it, and then were hidden by ǝ projecting ledge.

On the east end of this mountain there were three goats, a nanny, a yearling, and a kid, leisurely crossing a narrow ridge which the wind had swept bare of snow. Turning the glass on the next mountain east, a large billy-goat came into the field at once. He was sitting on the edge of a cliff well towards the summit of the mountain. Yes, sitting down on his haunches just as a dog or cat does! The goat is the only ruminant which assumes such a posture, and he certainly presents a most ludicrous figure when he does it. Having no neck to speak of, his head seems to have been shrunk to the body, his buffalo-like hump and long, coarse mane rising even above the slender and scimetar-like horns. The expression of his countenance—if the term may be used—is one of silly vacuity; the narrow forehead is dished, the muzzle long and coarse, and on his chin he wears a patriarchal beard simply absurd. Another peculiarity is that his fore legs are covered to the knees with a growth of very long and fluffy hair.

As I continued to study the outlines of this particular ungainly beast he arose and walked to the back of the ledge, and then returned and seemed to stare at something below him and to his left. Dropping the glass in that direction, M. and Carney appeared, crossing a long and very steep incline, where the snow was so hard that they had removed their webs and were punching holes with their gunstocks to secure footholds.

Not far ahead of them the incline ended against a series of cut walls and ledges, and on a narrow shelf, below which there was a sheer fall of several hundred feet, I discovered another billy, a very large old fellow, comfortably sprawled out beneath a stunted and spreading pine. Occasionally he would reach up and nip a mouthful of needles from the overhanging boughs, chewing it with as much relish apparently as if 'twas the choicest of green and tender grasses. Throughout the winter the leaves of the evergreens—the pine, fir, spruce, and juniper—seem to be the goats' only food.

Owing to the convexity of the incline the hunters were crossing, this billy was all unconscious of the danger approaching him; but the other one, several hun-

FISHING THROUGH THE ICE
AT TWO MEDICINE LAKE.

dred yards higher up the mountain, was getting rather uneasy, walking back and forth on the ledge, and stamping his fore feet, as if uncertain what to do. Finally, with one last foolish stare at the men below, he left the cliff and climbed up over the summit of the mountain. He didn't run; a goat has to be very badly scared to do that, and when he does strike such an unusual gait, he lumbers off about as swiftly and gracefully as a fat old cow.

M. had now approached within fifty yards of the goat, and was preparing to shoot; the animal had raised up on its fore legs and was looking at him, when he brought the gun to his shoulder, and a second later I saw the beast collapse, give one convulsive kick, and slide down to the very edge of the cliff, where it lay quite still. The little 30-30 Winchester had done good work, as usual. I saw no smoke, heard no report.

The goat lay in such a position that it was an extremely perilous task to get to him, as the ledge had a steep slope from where he had lain to the verge of it where he had fortunately stopped. But Carney was equal to the occasion. I held my breath, though, as I watched him slowly descend, cutting footholds as he went, for a single misstep would have taken him down over the high, beetling

MIDDLE TWO MEDICINE LAKE.

cliff. At last he reached the animal, fastened his rope to its head, and then as carefully ascending to where M. stood, they dragged the animal up and out on the incline. Even that was not a very safe place, for had they slipped, they would have gone sliding down over the hard snow for five hundred yards or more to the foot of the mountain.

In an hour or so M. and Carney returned to camp with the head and skin of the big billy-goat, well pleased with their success. A little later the others came in, very tired, and cursing guns and gunmakers generally. After a long and difficult climb they had managed to get within fifty feet of a fine billy, and G. had pulled the trigger on every one of his ten cartridges, but not one of them would explode. Finally, after the goat had

calmly climbed up to the next ledge, and sat down to stupidly gaze at them again, they examined the rifle, and found that the point of the firing pin was broken off. It was a new weapon, had been tested and resighted in New York only a week previously, and had then been in perfect order.

The next morning M. declared that he was more than satisfied with the trophy he had secured, and would hunt goats no more that season; so G. took his rifle, and with Jack went up to where they had left the goat the day before. They were back in camp at three o'clock with its head and hide. We packed up then and there, and shortly after nightfall arrived at Bear Creek section-house, well pleased with our goat hunt.

At one o'clock the next morning the east-bound Overland Flyer stopped on a stretch of bare, bleak prairie at the edge of the foothills, and let us off. It was bitterly cold, and a keen west wind was blowing, as it ever does on these plains in winter. But we didn't mind that; having got our duffle out of the baggage-car, we crawled into our sleeping bags and rested well until daylight. One of the party said that four or five freight trains passed by during the night, but the rest of us heard them not.

Crawling out of sleeping bags at daylight, we ran over a little hill and down to the cabin of a settler, whom we aroused and induced to cook breakfast, and then haul our outfit to the head of Two Medicine Lake, some five miles northwest of his ranch. We arrived there at three o'clock, and had everything in shape before dark.

This north fork of the Two Medicine has its source in some basins far back in the mountains, and is fed by the everlasting ice and snow which lies on the flanks of the main range. There are three beautiful lakes on its course through the mountains, and our camp was situated on the lower one. On both sides of us the mountains were rather low, sloping, and easily climbed, and their sides and summits were covered with patches of short grass, which the wind kept bare of snow. It is this grass which attracts the bighorn from their summer range farther back in the mountains, and here they remain from November until late in May, until after the young are born, when they once more return to the higher and more inaccessible peaks.

For three days after we pitched camp here there was such a severe storm in the mountains that we did not attempt to climb them. But there were other things to do to keep us busy; the lake teems with trout, and we kept the table well supplied with them by fishing through holes cut in the ice. A most unsportsmanlike proceeding, 'tis true, but excusable, as our commissary was running low, and 'twas fish or starve. Then there were grouse, ruffed, blue, and Franklins, and we managed to secure a number of them by diligently tramping through the thick pines and willows.

At last, one morning the sun arose in a cloudless sky; G. had luckily borrowed a rifle from the old settler, and after a hasty breakfast we started out, Jack and G. up the valley, the rest of us towards the first mountain northwest of camp. After going a mile or two, we saw fresh tracks along its side and summit, and with our glasses counted twenty-three sheep, but none were the kind we were looking for—old rams. So, instead of climbing it, we kept well down in the timber until we had passed its upper end, where a wide, sloping basin separates it from the next mountain beyond.

We were just rounding a point of reef rock, and fortunately still in the timber, when we sighted a band of eleven sheep on the farther side of the basin, and pretty high up. Bringing the glasses to bear on them, we found that they were rams, all but two of them carrying immense horns. We saw, too, that there was no possible way of getting within five hundred yards of them. Well, we sat there in the pines all day, hoping that they would come down the hill or move to some place where they could be approached; but they didn't do any such thing, remaining on a bare grass patch not two hundred yards square. They were, as ever, extremely restless, alternately feeding and lying down every few minutes, but never forgetting to keep a sharp lookout on the heights above them and in the valley below. We stayed watching them as long as we possibly

OUR SNOWSHOES.

could, and then sneaked away unobserved. We found G. and Jack at camp, and the evening meal awaiting us. They had been up the valley as far as the middle lake and had seen a number of sheep, but no rams.

The next morning M. asked G. to go with him after the eleven rams, but the latter refused. "It's your bunch," he said, "and one man can approach them more easily than two. Never mind me;

IN CAMP AT TWO MEDICINE LAKE.

Jack and I will try to find some up above the next lake."

That was quite sportsmanlike and proper; but, alas! how many men I have known who called themselves sportsmen who would have rushed out to that ram patch without an invitation, and spoiled every one's sport.

VERILY, PATIENCE HATH ITS REWARD!"

For six consecutive days M. and Carney started out at daylight and tried to get within range of those eleven rams, but something always interfered with their plans; either the wind was wrong, or the band was in an inaccessible place, or a blizzard came up, or a band of ewes were between them and the coveted prizes. In the meantime G. succeeded in killing a fine ram, and it was lucky that he did, for we had nothing but a little flour left in the commissary.

On the morning of the seventh day we breakfasted on meat straight, washed down with cold water, which Carney declared was a sign of good luck; and so it proved to be. Arrived at their lookout place, the hunters found that the rams had moved around to the right side of the basin, and that by keeping behind a low rock-reef it might be possible to get within three hundred yards of them. M. essayed it, leaving Carney in the pines. There was an open space of five hundred yards to be crossed before the reef would shut off a view of him, and it took three long hours of crawling and sliding through the snow to do it. When the sheep had their heads down, feeding, he moved on, and when they looked up he laid still, often remaining in the latter position so long that he got thoroughly chilled.

At last the reef arose between them, and he walked quickly up to its base, rested a moment, and peered around the end; then up went the rifle to his shoulder and he fired at the uppermost ram. The bullet hit him, for he was seen to flinch, and then, bunching up, the whole band came pell-mell down the mountain straight by where M. stood behind the rock. Now was his opportunity come, indeed; as they rushed by him, he fired four shots, and, one after another, four fine rams keeled over in the snow within a space of thirty yards. "Verily, patience hath its reward!"

So ended our second winter's hunt, and we all agreed that the only easy way to get at sheep and goats is on snowshoes. We have also proved, to our own satisfaction at least, that there is no hardship in camping out in the coldest weather. The Klondike has no terrors for us now.

14.
HUNTING THE
VIRGINIA DEER
(1902)

HUNTING THE VIRGINIA DEER

By T. S. VAN DYKE

DRAWINGS BY CARL RUNGIUS

"**B**UT what will I do with all my deer? I won't sell them; the country is so wild I cannot even give them away, and I won't kill any to throw away."

Such thoughts formed the only spot on the bright rainbow that spanned my path as, in the fall of 1867, I made my way into the heart of the great forest that robed northern Wisconsin. Don't laugh. I had almost been born in the woods. They were the first place for which I had always started when school was out and where all my Saturdays and vacations were spent. I was twenty-five, had been hunting constantly since the age of twelve, was distinguished for keenness of sight and skill with pistol, rifle, and gun among far older companions even at the age of seventeen. I had seen deer run before hounds and helped cripple some with buckshot for the dogs to run down. What then more natural than to suppose I was a natural still-hunter that needed only opportunity?

Never since have I seen so many signs of deer, though I have been in many an almost untrodden wild. There was no looking for tracks. They were looking at me from every direction. The first glimpse of a leaf cut through by sharp hoofs, or pressed into damp ground, or the fresh earth pawed up around some bush, made me cock the rifle and look eagerly around while chills gamboled up and down my spine and hot flashes played around my ribs. But the grand buck I expected to see in imposing attitude in one of the most imposing corridors of the forest failed to appear. And the more plentiful tracks grew, the stronger the evidence of a great number of deer feeding on the oak-clad ridges where the acorns were falling, and the fresher every sign appeared, the more that handsome buck failed to keep the appointment I felt sure fate must have made.

Day after day passed with the golden haze of Indian summer sleeping more deeply upon the most lovely of virgin forests and the most hopeful of hearts threading them in vain though the tracks of deer were more and more plentiful. I was walking with the utmost care and keeping the sharpest watch in every direction. Yet the nearest I could come to seeing a deer was an occasional set of plunging jumps some fifteen to eighteen feet apart that had scattered the fresh earth in all directions, showing too plainly that the deer had in some way learned I was in the woods. But with my keen eyes that had always been so quick to find squirrels hidden in the tree tops or hares in their forms, why could I not even see one run? And in the still air why could I not hear the hoofs that must have descended seven or eight feet in clearing some fallen log?

Discouraged? No, delighted, rather. From the first days I read about hunting moose I envied the Indian who found the game and felt contempt for the white machine that merely did the mechanical part of pulling the trigger. Hunting was always more of a charm than shooting, and game that knew how to get away was always my first choice. To be surrounded by scores of invisible spirits aware of my presence while I was not keen enough to be aware of theirs, to feel that I only was at fault, and that the time would yet come when I could play in the game without being laughed at, was to me the loftiest form of pleasure in the pathless woods. The remark of the settler with whom I was stopping, "There's no use huntin' now; the woods are too noisy," was only a spur to my ambition. That I could not touch the dry leaves lightly enough to prevent a deer from hearing me and running so far away that I could not even see him or hear the thump of his feet, instead of being a reason for stopping, was only the strongest possible reason for keeping on. And after seeing much of the best shooting of America I must say that the most charming of all days were those—eleven successive days—I hunted from morning till night, never

out of sight of tracks made that very morning yet without catching the faintest glimpse of a deer, until the evening of the eleventh day, and then it was so far away that I was at first in doubt about it. There are fools among the wildest animals, and the more one hunts deer the more apt one is to feel a painful suspicion that the greater part of success comes from stumbling over a fool. Nothing much worse can befall the tenderfoot at first, for he is apt to feel himself a born hunter and learn little more. But such was not my fortune, and I became so interested that that hunt lasted several months and was repeated every fall until I moved to California.

Most beginners have much the same experience in still-hunting, and it arises mainly from the difficulty of comprehending — in practical form — the extreme acuteness of the senses of a deer and the constant watch the animal keeps on man, even in the wildest woods. When you consider that a deer can hardly distinguish a man at perfect rest from a stump only a few yards away the quickness with which those same eyes can detect your slightest motion across tree trunks, logs, or stumps, even three hundred yards away, and even when a thousand limbs are swaying with the wind, surpasses all comprehension. It will take you long to understand it, long to realize that when in sight of a deer you

cannot afford to raise any more of your head over a ridge than is absolutely necessary to see, and that you cannot afford to do even this except slowly. Nor is it safe to keep the rifle on your shoulder when looking over a ridge, for the slightest whirl of it as you take it down may catch the watchful eye. Many a shot has been lost by the attempt to get a rest for the rifle and many another by moving just a trifle to get a clearer view of game so hidden in brush that it seems impossible it can see you. But you never can realize this power of the deer until you follow the track of one you have started, as we shall see farther on. It is the quickness of detecting a motion almost as much as the acuteness of its ears that enables this slippery game to live within sound of the backwoodsman's axe long years after the elk and the moose have made their last run. When we consider how vast an area of wilderness is necessary to protect the larger game and how deer can defy man for months, and even years, without leaving a circle of three miles in diameter, bother him in a circle of two miles, and make him very weary even in a circle of one, we feel unbounded respect for the senses that enable them to do it. And these are mainly sight and hearing, for it is quite possible to avoid the nose, keen as it is. To avoid the other two successfully requires the happiest combination of snow or wet ground for still walking with the utmost skill and care on the part of the hunter, aided by eyes almost as keen as those of the game.

When you begin to comprehend the sharpness of the eyes against which you have to play you are still about as far as ever from understanding the nose of a deer. The idea that the game can smell you even hundreds of yards away when you do not discover any wind blowing, or when it is moving more slowly than you are moving, and when the current that carries your scent is twisted and whirled about by a thousand cross currents, is quite astounding to the novice. And still more so is the

"Almost always the head is well erect and all senses keen for danger."

Sometimes in Rutting Time a Grand Old Buck May Stop and Stand
Like a Stone Statue Within a Few Yards of You.

idea that when the slightest particle that rides the tainted air reaches that keen nose it acts like the electric spark that fires the mine. When a deer is alarmed by noise or an unusual sight he will often stop to assure himself that it means danger. He often relies on his judgment in such matters as if hating to admit that he could be scared at nothing. But when the scent of man reaches his nose there is no room for the play of reason. He knows too well what it is; the feet spurn the ground in a twinkling and rarely stop until far out of danger. And then the back track is watched so long that you might better seek another deer.

It is generally quite useless to explain this to the beginner. He cannot be made to realize it except in the severe school of experience. And here he cannot make a special test of it as he can of the deer's eyes by following his track. Nor can he have such plain evidence almost any day as he can easily have of the acuteness of the ears of his game. It will generally cost him years, with many days of bitter disappointment, to learn that under no circumstances can he trifle with the nose of the deer. But as the years roll on and you do much hunting on snow or ground bare enough to enable you to see tracks easily you will find many a fresh bed with the long jumps leading away from it tearing up the ground in a way that shows high speed. And the tracks the deer left in the bed show it rose as if lifted by dynamite. So you will find the same where the deer has been feeding at some bush or on the ridge where the acorns are falling. And many a time when the tracks begin to show that the deer has quit feeding and is straggling slowly about and making ready to lie down for the day, you will find them suddenly turned into fifteen foot leaps that clear the loftiest logs in full career. You will find so many of these at distances where it is impossible for the game to hear you on soft snow, where intervening ridges make it still more impossible for the game to see you, that you know it must have smelt you, though the air seemed to you quite still. And if you ever hunt much in open rolling hills, such as the bluffy region of the Upper Mississippi, or much of Mexico or California, where you can see a deer a long way off, you will often note a pace quite different from that

with which they play before a dog and vastly different from that with which they fly from some strange noise. It is because they know too well what is the matter, and there is no occasion for stopping to look back. Of course a cross current may at times enable you to walk within shot of a deer; but you can never rely on anything of that sort, and your first care should be to know the direction of the wind, however light it may be. Where deer are trying to escape you by hiding they are often quite indifferent to your scent, and letting them smell you is sometimes the only way you can make them move. But in the great woods of the north the cover is rarely dense enough to enable the Virginia deer to play this trick, and it is quite safe to calculate on his running at top speed long before you are within sight.

It is almost as hard to realize the acuteness of the hearing of a deer, and probably more deer are lost to the tyro through this than any other cause. For the great majority of those that elude even the best hunters escape unseen and generally unheard. Of these the tyro knows almost nothing, and it is some time before he can understand how he is left exploring with eager eyes the thousand lovely places for a deer to stand in that have no deer in them. It takes long to learn that you cannot afford to crack even the lightest stick, crush the softest leaf, or let even the softest snow pack too fast beneath your foot except where speed demands it. A certain amount of ground must be covered. This will vary so with the character of the country and the quantity of game that your pace may have to change many times during the day. But subject to this you can hardly move too quietly for even the tamest deer. And if deer are skulking or hiding from you where the cover is dense enough to enable them to do it you must not be misled by the fact that at such times they do not mind noise. When deer hide it is because they know what you are and know you cannot see them. But many a one instead of doing this will slip away and leave you far in the rear if you make the least bit of unnecessary noise in approaching. Only by finding many a place where the deer has scattered the snow or dirt in long leaps, over a ridge where he could not see you, and with a strong breeze blowing from him to you so that he could not smell you, can you begin to realize how keen the ears of the deer are and how well he knows the crack of the lightest twig beneath your foot or the scraping of the lightest brier against your clothes, though a thousand more may be rustling and crackling in the swaying of the trees beneath a strong breeze. Nay, it seems rather as if the more branches were creaking and twigs rattling in a high wind the more quickly the animal can detect your peculiar noise. So much is this the case that many a good hunter says a windy day is a poor one to hunt because the deer are so nervous with watching and listening. I have seen many a day that made me think they were correct. And after you have learned all this you will still wonder and wonder and wonder how deer still fly out of bed, over a ridge where they cannot see you and against a breeze so strong they cannot smell you. It will be long before you learn that it was not the crackling of any stick or the scraping of anything on your clothes, but the slow packing of soft snow under your moccasined foot you let so carefully into it. This sound is carried along the ground, and though heard more easily by deer in bed is still so quickly heard by one standing that you cannot be too careful.

You may, of course, have a very different experience and have the luck to run over several fool deer on your very first hunt. But if you match yourself a few seasons against the Virginia deer as found in the great forests of the northern part of the United States, instead of saying that I have overrated the acuteness of a deer's senses you are much more likely to find yourself wondering whether a deer has not a sixth sense. You will find so many

times when you have every condition just right, when a ridge lies between you and the game, when the wind blows strongly over it, and when the distance is so great and the nature of the ground such you feel certain the game could not have heard you that the game is suddenly gone with those long leaps which never fail to tell the tale. No matter how carefully you may have worked your foot down into the snow, eased off every twig that could make the slightest scratching on your coat or pants, or kept the strong breeze dead ahead of you all the time; no matter how long you may take to go that last quarter mile that you know will bring you to the game, before you can get in sight it is gone, and all you see is the long track of its flight. It is the most mysterious thing in the whole range of hunting, constantly upset-

"When deer hide it is because they know what you are and know you cannot see them."

ting the calculations of the most practised hunter. Yet it makes the most charming excitement the land beyond the pavement has to offer, and is the main reason why thousands are crazy over still-hunting.

If it were possible for the beginner to have a practical knowledge of these matters before entering the woods he would still have a long list of errors to go through. That strange persistency with which we take hold of a new subject by the wrong end is never so strong as when we try to match our own acuteness against that of the deer. The last thing the tyro will think of is the extreme importance of seeing the game before it sees him. Given two creatures in the woods, each in search of the other, the great advantage is with the one that happens to be at rest when the other moves within range of its eyes. As it is next to impossible to see deer when lying down in heavy cover they must be sought when on foot. The best time for this is when feeding, for then they are spending less time in watching for danger; although very little reliance can be placed on this, as at any second they may raise the head to look around. The tyro hears that deer feed early in the morning and late in the evening, but it is still hard to realize that when deer feed by daylight at all it is generally in the gray of dawn, all after that being a mere continuation on which one cannot always rely. So a few moments' delay in starting may easily cost one a good shot.

Reaching the ground a little too late because you had to have a decent breakfast you find nothing but signs of deer extremely fresh, with beds here and there showing that the tenants got up late and were not very much afraid of your camp. If this ground happens to be hardwood ridges with acorns falling you are likely to find signs enough to send a deluge of chills over your anatomy. But you have either arrived a few minutes too late or have in some way let the game know you are coming. Finding tracks so fresh and plentiful you little imagine the deer that made them may be half a mile or a mile away either looking back to see if you are following, or lounging about preparatory to lying down for the day if they have left the feeding ground before you were near enough to alarm them. You naturally tarry on the feeding ground where the

fresh signs are so abundant. This is well enough, for if the deer have merely wandered off without being alarmed there may be others there that are a bit longer about their breakfast. But this is not why you tarry. It is because you see fresh beds which make you think the game lives here all the time. But the chances are that these are night beds—a very different article from day beds. Night beds a deer will make almost anywhere, for he knows he is safe from man at night. But rarely will he lie down by day where you are likely to find him with ease, and seldom will it be on the ground where he feeds on some special thing such as acorns. Sometimes he may go but a short distance to the brushy point of some ridge where you cannot get within shot without making considerable noise. But more often he will roam a mile or so to some big windfall or extra heavy thicket, or the brushy head of some remote gulch, or the young forest of saplings and briers that is growing up where pine has been cut off. The daily life of a deer is simplicity itself, generally within a circle not over two miles in diameter and often much less where little disturbed. In the woods they find feed and water everywhere and spend most of the time lying down.

Your chances of finding a deer on foot in such a way that you can see him before he sees you are thus limited to a short period of early morning, though this period becomes longer with the approach of the rutting season, or "running time"; while at all times of the year some deer are on foot longer than others. The case is not very much improved in the evening, the time being then also short in which you have much chance to see a deer on foot before he sees you. Your remaining hope is, therefore, to "jump a deer"—that is, to bounce him out of bed and either catch him running as he skips away or possibly get a standing shot in case he is overcome with curiosity to know what the racket is about and stops long enough to give you a chance.

"Jumping a deer" is a highly attractive phrase, quite apt to make a tingling in the back hair of the tenderfoot who hears it for the first time. It is also intensely satisfactory to the chap who always has to shave before wooing nature. You may, indeed, get a good shot in this way, and it is generally the only way to see the grandest of all the sights of the woods; deer running through a windfall. To see the glossy curves of fur curl over the lofty logs that lie piled on each other in boundless confusion is well worth a trip to the woods, while for him who loves the rifle as I do, more for what cannot be done with it than for what can, there is no such target elsewhere. But for the tyro who is dying to get that first deer, " jumping a deer " generally means out of sight and out of hearing both. For the deer that goes off to lie down after feeding does not go to sleep but to ruminate and take life easy. Once in a great while one falls into a doze, but almost always the head is well erect and all senses keen for danger. And even if one is in a doze it may slip away without your suspecting its existence, for sleep deadens little of the senses of this wary animal. The man who " wouldn't shoot such an innocent creature as a deer " should by all means see one getting out of a heavy windfall, while the man who loves game that can get away can here find the attraction of the woods at its climax.

Next to the difficulty of comprehending the wonderful senses of the deer is that of understanding how one looks in the woods. Your ideas are necessarily taken from pictures or from stuffed deer or tame ones in a park. You are almost certain to be looking for a deer, whereas you might better be looking for almost anything else. In the woods you seldom see half of a deer and generally much less, often only a part of the shoulder, or only an ear over a log or a leg under it, a bit of rump projecting from a bush, or a head and bit of the neck reaching up for leaves. The arcade of maple lit up by the scarlet of the ginseng and bush cranberry, the little arbor where the wild hop is yellowing over the thorn apples on which half a dozen ruffed grouse are taking their breakfast, the edge of the pool where the trout flashes through the water over which the chelone is still nodding, or the darksome glade where the golden petals of the witch hazel are closing the floral march of the year, would all make lovely frames for that charming artist's deer with individual hairs all glistening, the dark dew claws shining, and even the split in the hoof flashing artistic light from its edges. But the glittering tines, the proud neck of the sculptured war horse, the shaggy chest and bulging rump with tail full of shining hairs are not there except at long intervals, when you may rout an old fool out of bed and get him twisted as to the points of the compass. And sometimes in rutting time a grand old buck may stop in his course within a few yards of you and make a handsome picture, and a doe may even do the same sometimes. But such things are so rare as to be utterly misleading when put in a picture. A deer as generally seen in such a way as to give a fair chance for a shot would be entirely invisible in a picture the size of this page. Even if he would stand for a time exposure with the best light you could wish the finest camera could rarely take him so that you could find him in five minutes on a picture a foot square.

Consequently a deer is about the last thing you need look for. Peculiar spots and patches of color shifting around the neutral grays, though ranging almost from white to black, are what must catch your eye. And the woods are already so full of these without any deer that it seems a hopeless task. But if the artist's deer is there you will have little trouble in seeing him, whereas if the real deer of the woods is there you will need the last bit of eyesight you have to see him before he sees you. Not only do you need good eyes but you need them well trained or the dim blur in the distant thicket may fail to catch them before it fades in a way you may never notice. So the distant horn that looks more like a broken stick or the few inches of shank seen below some log will at first escape you entirely. You must scrutinize a thousand things in vain, but instead of being a bore you will find it a constant delight.

It is much better when a deer is in motion, but even then it is a long way from the deer of the picture and from the deer running before the hounds. It may be but an upward wave of white flirting farewell to your hopes down the dark corridor of pine, seen but for a second as it goes over some log and then gone forever. Or it may be a rising curve of beamy gray shining full in the sun for a second and gone by the time you raise the rifle. The deer in motion looks more like the deer you expect to see, whereas if you should see him at rest and not alarmed he would probably seem awkward and angular like an old cow and of not half the height you expect a deer to have. But even when in motion you rarely see the whole body, and in quite open woods it is easy for a deer to run away from you in plain view without your seeing him, unless he makes noise enough to attract your attention.

The consequence is that while you are wondering where all the deer are, asking whether they have come down from the north yet, whether it is running time or not, and a lot of silly questions, they are all around you every day, half a dozen or more near enough for you to shoot at and as many more that might have been had you been more careful. But as the days go on you will learn that a deer can see out of a thicket much better than a man can see into it, that it is often better to go around a ridge than to go over it and that in general short cuts are dangerous because you are in a game in which you can afford to take no chances. And first of all you want to be alone, for the very charm of the Virginia deer especially is that he is game no "gillie" can point out for you. If your sole object is to say you have killed a deer and you have only a few days in which to do it a good hunter might hasten the time of getting a shot. But it is far more interesting to hunt alone, get left in good style, and then lie about it. In real still-hunting you want a part of the woods all to yourself. There are times when you can use a companion after you know the deer and the ground, but by your side is the last place you want him.

How expectation pants for the falling of the snow! Here it is soft and feathery, and now you can tell just where the game has gone and have no trouble in following it. The mysterious disappearance that has worried you so much on bare ground, and especially on the dry and rustling leaves of Indian summer, will trouble you no more. By the time it is light enough to see the sights on your rifle the ground is a network of tracks and the snow thrown out in front of them sparkles with freshness. Surely this big buck cannot be two hundred yards away. You cock your rifle and start on the trail with assurance playing havoc with your nerves. Surely you will see him, for are not the leaves all off so that you can see three times as far as you could before, and does not the fresh snow that still clings to the massive trunks and

festoons every natural arbor form a background against which the dark blue coat of the deer will stand out bright and clear? How your coat will stand out against the same background you do not inquire, but on you go up hill and down dale, finding where the deer has stopped to paw up acorns or to nibble the twigs of some shrub, all the time looking for the artist's deer. Here he has switched the snow off a log with his tail as he leaped it, yet not in alarm, for he goes on at a walk. Wonderful how far he is ahead of you so early in the day, isn't it? Wonderful rather how long a short distance seems when you are expecting to shoot every second and looking into every bush a few yards away as if you were hunting rabbits.

About the time you are positive he is just over the next log the track suddenly changes into jumps fifteen feet apart through bushes from which all the snow has been shaken and the bright red arils of the burning bush scattered around with the shining fruit of the inkberry. And this was on a flat which has been in your plain view for some minutes. And you did not even see him run. And you have been told, too, that bucks are fools at this time of year. Some are; but you must figure the other way.

And now you will follow him, of course, though you may have been told a hundred times it is useless unless you can follow on a dog trot till night, when you may possibly tire him enough to make him careless. But go on, for never shall you have a better chance to know how quickly the eyes of a deer can detect a motion. It matters little whether there is one deer or a dozen, whether the ground be rolling so that you can have plenty of ridges over which you can peep, or smooth so that you can see farther ahead; whether it is windy or still, cloudy or bright, the ground covered with snow or bare. If deer are still-hunted to any extent the chances are many to one that you can follow that deer from morning till night within a circle of three miles in diameter, and often much less, without ever seeing him again. But you will find many a place where he has stopped to look back and gone again with long jumps. Had you let him alone and taken the track several hours later you would have found that he soon stopped this, fell into a walk, straggled around a bit to feed, and then went off to lie down. But the fact that every place where he has stopped to look back he has left in hasty flight shows that he has seen you before running. He may, indeed, have smelt or heard you, but this was not necessary, for while watching his back track his eyes were good enough. And how can he thus see you time after time, a dozen times or more, and run away with such lofty bounds without your seeing even the flip of his tail? I give it up. But when you have had a bit of this experience you will know something about the eyes of the deer.

And you will try white clothes, will you, on the snow? All right. I could not take the word of any one for it and had to try it for myself. In open country, such as the bluffs of the Upper Mississippi, where there were still many deer when I lived there, this would sometimes work well. But the woods are full of gray and black, across which the motion of white clothes is plain and quite as alarming to the game, if not more so. And the amount of snow that may be falling from the trees makes no more difference than the motion of ten thousand branches helps you when in common dress. Where deer are hunted only with hounds they are often quite different. All this paper applies to deer that have learned what the still-hunter is.

A still greater surprise may await you when you conclude to work out the trail of a deer that has gone to lie down. It is late in the morning and he will be sleepy perhaps. You have the woods all to yourself, without another hunter in the township, and take the trail of a deer that has not been alarmed. After a vast amount of care in picking your way along without noise, keeping the wind in your face as much as possible, and straining your eyes for a sign of fur, you find as usual the signs of venison that has vanished in hot haste. Or may be you see a distant whirl of dark gray on the brushy point of some ridge, or from a huddle of brier-covered logs on the face of some slope, out of sight about the time you have the rifle from your shoulder. After being left in this way a few times you begin to wonder if deer do not watch the back track before being alarmed as well as after. It is certain that some do, the Virginia deer especially, where much hunted by still-hunters. As far back as 1867, when there were no hunt-

ers compared with to-day, they did this in those parts of Minnesota and Wisconsin where I used to hunt, lying down almost always where they could look back upon the trail. I never found the blacktail or the mule deer doing this, though they would probably learn it if much traced.

This is a difficult play to checkmate, about the only way being to work along the trail in half circles on the side, swinging in often enough to be sure you are on the course, then backing out so as to be out of sight. At the same time you must so select the ground as to keep out of reach of the deer's nose, must avoid descending ridges on the open slope toward the trail, but work around through the sags and other places where you are not likely to be seen. At the same time you must use the high points as vantage ground from which to see your game. All this is slow, of course, and often a failure, but when well worked is so often effective as to make it about the most exciting part of still-hunting. When you have done it a few times you will feel thankful that there is one kind of game that can keep you at your wits' end and cannot be called up by a guide for you to murder or pointed out by a clodhopper whose hobnailed boots scrape every rock, while his master's leggings scrape every bush. In this way I once got within six feet of a very wary buck, his horns being just visible over a log that I could touch with the rifle. I had located his whereabouts so exactly that I spent over an hour in making the last two hundred yards. Nothing but the softest snow and the greatest care in touching anything, the softest moccasins lowered most carefully would make it possible; but it was well worth the trouble. But such a thing is extremely rare even under the best conditions and no conclusions can be drawn from it except that it is advisable to work in behind a deer wherever possible, which means that you must keep off the trail all you can.

More than in any other subject it takes long to reach a practical realization of the simplest principles. You may be told, for instance, that though the deer can manage his feet well on the darkest night he still prefers moonlight for feeding, that when the moon is near the full he utilizes so much of it that by daylight he is full of stomach and somewhat weary of leg.

Therefore, he will go to bed earlier than usual for the day and in doing so will often go farther back than at other times. All this is quite reasonable, yet you will spend many a weary morning wondering what has become of the deer that have made so many fresh signs. Day after day and year after year you are likely to be left alone in the woods before you can realize that on much ground it is almost useless to hunt after daylight unless you can follow the game to where it has gone for its siesta.

All of this means that still-hunting is a science. Many a deer is killed by violating all its principles, but for one such fifty slip away unsuspected. One must not only study the daily life of the game, but must make oneself a bundle of good habits. It is just as easy to lower the gun from your shoulder before looking over a ridge as it is to keep it there to alarm game by its whirling flash. It becomes second nature to tread softly, to feel sticks through your moccasins before you let your foot down full weight, to go around bushes instead of smashing through them, and a score of similar things. Deer may be killed in spite of carelessness, as they may by a man with boots on instead of moccasins. But if you train your feet to wear moccasins so thin that you can feel every inequality of the ground you will soon discover that killing the Virginia deer without them is quite accidental where he is at all wild from still-hunting.

This subject is so vast that I can give but samples of what one must learn to realize the highest pleasure that can be drawn from still-hunting. With the wild Virginia deer it is the farthest from murder of all that is done with rifle or gun, the finest game of skill man ever plays, finer even than he plays against his fellow man. In " The Still-Hunter " I thought I had treated the subject too fully, but in looking it over twenty years after publication it seems as if I had not said enough. The vast range of the subject, the many ways in which you may be left alone, the intense care, eyesight, and knowledge of the game and the woods necessary for much success, make the hunting of the Virginia deer a joy to thousands who would not touch a gun for any other purpose, for beside it all other hunting is tame and even the pursuit of the blacktail and the mule deer often ridiculous in simplicity.

15.
HUNTING ALASKAN WHITE SHEEP WITH RIFLE AND CAMERA (1899)

Painted for OUTING by Jas. L. Weston.

IN CLOUD-SWEPT PASTURES.

MY CAMP ABOVE TIMBER-LINE.

HUNTING ALASKAN WHITE SHEEP WITH RIFLE AND CAMERA.

BY DALL DE WEESE.

IN the fall of 1897 I hunted the moose, the rare white sheep, and the huge brown bear in the Kenai Mountains of Alaska, and with my own gun secured a fine specimen of each. I returned to Alaska again last fall (1898) to procure specimens of large mammals for the Smithsonian Institute. On this trip I had provided myself with cameras suitable to photograph some of this wild game in their native haunts, which would give me more pleasure than shooting the animals. Never before had the *Ovis dalli* been caught in a sportsman's camera.

After a six weeks' trip of four thousand miles, August ninth found me in camp (with two packers, one white man and one Indian) on the Kenai Mountains, at timber-line, some ninety miles back of Cook's Inlet. At the start I had had three white men and five Indians in my party to assist me in getting my outfit up the rapids of the Kussiloff River and to the head of Lake Tuslumena. This consumed eight days of arduous labor, as we were compelled to pull the boat at the end of a one-hundred-foot line, wading the ice-cold water, passing the line under and around leaning timber; and many times it consumed three hours to make one mile, while the bloodthirsty mosquitoes sapped the life out of us and almost drove us frantic.

Mr. H. E. Lee, of Chicago, had accompanied me as far as Cook's Inlet and intended to continue, but while I was preparing for our trip to the interior he changed his mind, saying : "I would not go up that Kussiloff River and endure the hardships and dangers

145

and suffering from the infernal mosquitoes for all the game and gold in Alaska." I told him he could return to Homer and get good hunting within twenty-five miles of the beach. He so decided, and was very successful.

Mr. Berg, who was with me in 1897, also started with me, but the first night out from salt water he was taken with rheumatism in the limbs so severely that it was necessary for him to stay in the boat. His condition grew worse from day to day, and on reaching the lake I made camp for him, and detailed Mr. Singer to remain with him and do everything possible for his comfort, while I pushed on to the mountains. I kept two packers constantly on the trail between this camp and my line of camps to the summit of the range, so that I could get supplies, send meat down, and learn the condition of my unfortunate companion.

The next ten days I spent in making a map and collecting topographical data of the country, killing one white sheep for our larder. I now set about to get photos and the desired specimens, as the season had advanced to the proper time when the pelage of the sheep was in good condition, the old coat having been entirely shed and the new one out about an inch in length.

This rare wild white sheep is found nowhere in the world but Alaska, and few specimens for mounting whole have ever been obtained. This species, named *Ovis dalli* by Professor Dall, differs from his cousin, the Rocky Mountain big horn (*Ovis montana*), in color, *O. montana* being a dull brown in midsummer, changing to a grayish drab in winter, with a light ashy colored patch over the rump all the year, while the *O. dalli* is snow-white at all seasons; in fact, there is not a colored hair on any part of his body. He is not quite so stockily built as our "big horn," yet more trim and shapely. Two of my specimens stood forty-two inches at the shoulder. His limbs are not quite so heavy, and his horns will not average as large at the base, although quite as long. The horns of my largest specimen of 1897 measured 41¼ inches in length and 14½ inches in circumference at the base.

The flesh is the most delicious of all wild game. In the summer this sheep lives chiefly on the rich succulent growth of the *Asplenium septentrionale*, which grows in the crevices of the rock on the sunny slopes of this rugged range. This beautiful animal must endure great hardships to survive the winters of this icy North. Many of the higher peaks are snow-capped all the year, while on

A CAMP BELOW THE TIMBER-LINE.

the lower hills, that range in altitude from four to five thousand feet, there is a period of some six to eight weeks of partially open ground. The home of the *Ovis dalli* in this section of Alaska is on the high range where its frowning sides break into deep gashy cañons and precipitous walls to a mighty nameless glacier from ten to twenty miles long.

I had now made a side camp above timber-line and on a range of peaks never before visited by white men or Indians (so my Indians claimed). We had nothing to burn but a scrubby willow brush which we pulled up by the roots. The weather was very changeable at this altitude ; rain, heavy fog and spitting snow, with an occasional day of sunshine, and cold, frosty nights.

Early morning found me moving toward the glacier, intent on getting a photo of the sheep. I had pointed out a mountain about six miles to the east, and instructed my two packers to meet me at its base about noon, and to approach cautiously and watch out for me on their right, for it was a photo I more desired as I could get the animal later. I had traveled some two or three miles, stopping occasionally to scan the mountain sides closely with my field glass for a band of sheep. From the summit of a very broken ridge, I sighted a bunch of some thirty to forty quietly feeding and slowly moving toward a glacier. They were some three or four miles away and a little to the left of my course. I carefully took in the country and outlined my route.

The blood now began to quicken as I followed the ridge into the gulch and commenced the stalk to a favorable position where I could get an exposure that, as yet, had never been the privilege of man. When under the cover of a hillside, I ran up hill and down, then climbed out of a cañon from eight hundred to a thousand feet, with the perspiration saturating every stitch of clothing, yes, even through my moccasins. Upon rounding a ledge of rock, I caught sight of three sheep within a hundred yards, on my lee. I drew back quickly and circled to my left to cut them off from the bunch. This took me considerably out of my course and caused me to travel an extra two miles. Another climb of some six or eight hundred feet I thought would put me on a bench level with my quarry.

I now had the wind in my favor and cautiously approached a ledge of rock for a look. Oh, what a sight ! Through my glasses, it seemed but a hundred feet to the picture I would give five hundred dollars to have on the plate of my camera at a hundred-foot snap. About half of the bunch had gone out on the edge of the glacier while the rest were nipping the *Asplenium*. Occasionally an old ewe would start on a seemingly educating tour with her one or two half-grown lambs, rush about in a short circle, then back into the bunch again; while the great horned "fellows" seemed to gaze on the proceedings with delight, for the season had come when *they* leave their more lofty and secluded locality to visit the mothers and young.

I had fears that my two men would come in sight and alarm them; then I thought they would surely be on the lookout. On and upward I climbed among the rocks, with weary limbs, breathless and the perspiration dropping from my face like rain. A half hour more had passed, and I was within one hundred yards of the ridge between me and the band that I felt would soon make an impression on the film of my 5x7 camera.

I paused for breath in which to adjust my camera and climb to the spot for position that I had selected with my glasses an hour before. I suddenly cast a glance up the mountain on my left in line where I felt sure the boys would naturally pass. For some reason I had doubted what would be their tactics. Lo ! and behold, there they were about five hundred yards up and moving along that comparatively smooth mountain side. Cæsar's ghost ! Reader, can you imagine my disgust and wrath ? No, you cannot, unless you have had similar experiences. I was at the first glance paralyzed ; I chilled, the sweat seemed to run cold, and I felt my features contract and my jaws set. I gave the hat signal to drop down—I repeated it. I stared and clutched my rifle. Should I take a shot at them ? On they tramped as if going to a corn-shucking. In my wrath and despair I tore the grass from its bed and turned my finger-nails back clutching at the rocks. I gave the hat signal again and again. Finally to my intense relief they dropped.

I climbed along feeling convinced that the sheep had sighted my men at different times as they passed along the breast of the opposite mountain and had now disappeared over the glacier, and probably the only chance of my life to get a photo of a band of wild white sheep on a glacier had been foiled. With a spark of hope still left, I reached a higher point, thinking they had traveled upward. I peered over the rocks and I was not disappointed, for sure enough they were just moving out of sight near the crest of a low ridge. I was sick. I had noticed higher and to my right two rams seemingly taking in the situation, from a point among the rocks where they felt safe and whence they had watched the men making their way for the last half mile. Now, they had sighted me some three hundred yards from them and had commenced to move. They stopped, to pose for their pictures, of course, at that long range. Well, it was a fatal stop for the larger one, for in an instant I sent a ball through him and he rolled over dead. I took a running shot at the other ram, but missed.

My two packers came over to me. I will not write our conversation. Indian no sa ba, and I forgive them. I took photo, then measurements, dressed the noble game, then ate a cold lunch, and sent my men back with the head, skin and meat, instructing them to go to the camp at timber-line and care for the skin ; for the Indian to take a pack of meat down to camp number one to my sick man, and for Hobert, my white man, to bake bread the second day at camp number two, and for them both to meet me with bread and bedding for all at camp number three (above timber-line) on the evening of the fourth day.

My good Mr. Hobert did not like the idea of leaving me alone, but I assured him that I had often done this and would be careful, so we shook hands for a four-days separation. They slipped into their pack-straps and rose up with their heavy loads; and as they picked their way down the mountain homeward I started northward determined on getting another chance for the much-desired photo. Two hours of hard climbing brought me to the summit of this spur. Then a snow-squall set in. Soon the wind grew fierce, and the clouds of snow and mist surrounded me and sent a chill to the bone.

I commenced descending on the opposite side and began prospecting the mountain for mineral, as it was now evident that I could do nothing with my camera. I reached timber-line camp (number three) at nine o'clock in the evening, soaked to the skin with rain, which had changed from snow after I had reached a lower altitude. My faithful Hobert had placed my outfit under my rubber blanket and weighted it down with stones. He had also pulled some scrub willow and piled it near by. I added an extra sweater and a heavy coat to my wet body, and soon had a supper of boiled rice and raisins, broiled mutton chops, bread and tea.

The scrub willow was so scarce that I did not dare to use it in quantities for a fire sufficient to dry my clothing. My bed consisted of two caribou skins (undressed, which are the best thing on earth, for they really seem to generate heat), one camel's-hair blanket and rubber spread. I was soon snugly tucked in and at peace with all the world.

Next day at 2 P. M. I was far from camp and on a broken side of a rugged mountain. I now sighted a bunch of sheep some two miles away on my left, on a table of another mountain. Hope kindled anew, as the day was favorable, and being entirely alone on these grand old peaks I felt confident of success. To get in proper position it was necessary for me to make a long detour, on account of the wind and the lay of the country. I traveled rapidly, and soon reached a point from which I expected to lay out my line for the final approach. I reached the top of a break in the slide rock, and, looking over the ledge, I saw a fine old ram sitting (they will sit on their haunches like a dog) on the next ledge in front of me.

It is unusual for a ram to post as sentinel unless he takes a position from one to three hundred yards above his flock. An old barren ewe is invariably on guard. A careful survey of the country convinced me that the bunch was quite near him on a shelf immediately below. I retreated a few yards, divested myself of every superfluous article, including my old hat, drew my camera from its heavy case and adjusted it for a sixty-foot snap. I used a sixteenth stop, and set the time for a twenty-fifth of a second, in case of a running shot.

I crept to the ledge for another look. The old fellow had now lain down from his sitting position. No other sheep were in sight. I again retreated, and crept cautiously up the slope for a short distance, then to the edge and looked again. Over the back of the old guard I could now see the bunch about thirty yards below him. There were some fifteen to twenty; some lying down while others were feeding. I saw it was impossible for me to approach nearer from this point. I retreated below my first position. I now took another look ; the old ram was again in a sitting attitude, and some twenty yards above was the ever-watchful ewe that I had not been able to see.

My approach was now cut off from this direction also, and the situation became perplexing. I finally decided on a plan. I moved down the mountain until entirely out of sight of the old ram, but still where I could get a view of the ewe. I hammered some rocks together to attract her attention, and waved my red handkerchief over the ledge. She was up in an instant facing me. I did not repeat this, but watched. This was an anxious period.

After five minutes or so she slowly descended to the bunch. I now returned to my first position. The old ram was standing and turning his head in all directions. Not seeing anything, he seemed unwilling to leave his post, although his faithful mate had warned him and had returned to her charge. They certainly had decided to wait an alarm from him ; they had not moved off, for I could see them as there was only one way for them to retreat without passing me.

Ten minutes passed and still he stood with all the wary instincts of his nature aroused. What a picture, with his snow-white, graceful form, his head erect and crowned with massive, wax - colored horns that curved to a full circle. He seemed to have convinced himself that it was a false alarm, for he became more composed, and I felt that the flock had again quieted as their lordly sentinel still held his ground. Now was my time for the final effort.

My heart beat violently, almost loud enough for him to hear. I quickly stole to where I had left my rifle and cautiously returned to my position. He now stood facing me. To drop him dead on the spot was my desire, for as he lay there, I could make a dash to his ridge and get a snap at the flock before

it became aware of his fate. I knew that the report of my rifle would be so light that the flock would not be alarmed at that distance; besides I had the ridge and wind in my favor. I took careful aim and fired. He dropped as if stone-dead. I quickly laid down my gun, snatched my camera, rushed quietly as possible down the ridge and up the next, aiming to reach a position a little below him. Out of breath I reached the point and looking over, I saw that the old fellow had regained his feet, and was staggering into the flock, which had just begun to move away and was now about thirty yards distant. I raised my camera in position and pressed the bulb. I wound the film and made another exposure. I believe these to be the first negatives ever obtained of wild sheep alive on the mountains.

The flock were now fully alarmed, and it was marvelous to witness the agility they displayed in making their ascent among the crags and ledges. I went back for my rifle and returned to hunt the wounded ram, which I felt certain could not go far. I followed the trail across rocks and snow-drifts. Suddenly I saw a white object ahead and high on the cliffs. I adjusted my glasses and discovered it was a big ram, although I could not see the horns with the naked eye. It was a four-hundred-yard shot.

Bang—I missed. Bang—he started. Bang—he dropped and commenced rolling down, then getting up and rolling again. It was a hard climb to reach him, but on doing so, I found to my surprise it was not my wounded ram, although a very fine specimen.

It was now too late in the day to look for the lost one. I then took measurements and dressed my noble prize. I had my pack-straps with me, and started to my lonely camp, which I did not reach until eleven o'clock P. M., for I carried the whole skin, head and saddles of this sheep. Hunters, you have an idea of my load.

The next day it was necessary for me to repair my moccasins and climbing shoes, which I had worn through in several places. In the afternoon I made a trip to a glacier and saw sheep, but will not go into detail regarding them. The next day I started for a long, hard trip and to return where I expected to find my wounded ram, for I could not leave him there. After a long prospecting trip to the head of an enormous glacier, I reached a place where the precipitous cliffs joined the yawning crevasses of the walls of living ice. I saw several sheep out, crossed over the divide, and commenced the semicircular return to camp, yet keeping in mind the locality where I hoped to end the suffering of my quarry.

My route brought me to a very rough, steep slope on which a narrow arm of a glacier extended from the summit of the range down at an angle of about fifty degrees for some twelve to fifteen hundred feet below me. To go around this, either above or below, meant the loss of my course and the day as well. It was frightful; however, I put on my ice irons and slowly worked my way across, but solemnly promise I will never do so again.

Another hour of hard climbing brought me around this mountain, where I felt confident my game had hidden. I was yet a mile or more from it, but I noticed a suspicious looking, small white spot on a shelf of rocks and a little below me. I focused my glasses and found it to be a sheep lying down with head erect. I felt this must be my ram, for there were no others in sight and he was wounded. He had hunted seclusion among the rocks to die alone. I steadily advanced in open view for at least half a mile, when I noticed him get up. I stopped and adjusted my glasses. There he stood, looking in my direction. I sat down and watched for him to move. Presently he slowly turned around and began picking his way around the mountain, in the direction he had come two days before. I could plainly see him limp. When he came to the last ridge where he would disappear behind the mountain, he stopped for another look. I still remained quiet and watched his every move through my glasses. Finally he passed out of sight.

It was now eight P. M., and I knew I must act quickly. I scaled the mountain to its summit, crossed over and down the other side on a noiseless run, knowing about where I should get to head him off. I had traveled about half a mile and was watching on my right for his shapely horns, when suddenly on my left, and within sixty yards, on a low bench, I saw two fine old rams. We looked at each other a full minute. It would have been easy work to kill them both, but I passed on, for I felt that a shot might turn my unfortunate from his course.

A heavy mist or fog was now settling down over the peaks, and while descending through it, I caught sight of his head over the swell of a smooth, sloping ridge. He saw me at the same instant and bounded forward on a more level footing, running quartering from me and to my left. The distance was some two hundred yards. I quickly brought my rifle to place. Bang—he turned a little more to my left and increased his speed (overshot). Bang—I noticed him jerk his head backward (shot in front of him). Bang—and with the report he rolled over and over. I approached him and found that my shot of two days before had entered his breast and passed between the shoulder-blade and the ribs and made its exit at the loin, not having broken a bone or touched a vital spot. How he lived I knew not. My last shot was through the shoulders.

It was now nearly nine P. M., and the sun had just sunk behind Mt. Illimana. While I was glad of the prize, I was truly sorry for this beautiful animal. He was my last *Ovis dalli*.

16.
BIG GAME IN COLORADO
(1891)

THE KING OF THE CAÑON.

OUTING.

AUGUST, 1891.

BIG GAME IN COLORADO.

BY ERNEST INGERSOLL.

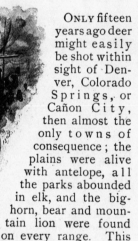

ONLY fifteen years ago deer might easily be shot within sight of Denver, Colorado Springs, or Cañon City, then almost the only towns of consequence; the plains were alive with antelope, all the parks abounded in elk, and the bighorn, bear and mountain lion were found on every range. This primitive condition of things has been greatly modified. Railroads thread many of the passes, the mountains are pitted with mines from base to apex, the charcoal burners have desolated some of the fairest hillsides, and the lumberman has cut away the coverts of the deer, while farms and hay ranches and the corrals and pastures of horses and cattle occupy the lush valleys where wild animals used to feed and bring forth their young.

Nevertheless this is a comparative rather than an absolute statement. The game of Colorado has disappeared, it is true, from its former haunts in the valleys and parks most populous and easily accessible, but in the remoter quarters of the State something of the old-time plenty, if not the pristine fearlessness, may be seen. Never again, probably, must travelers stop and drive the antelope away from their mule

train with stones, as happened more than once to the writer's party in Southern Wyoming in 1877. No longer can the hunter expect to meet elk and blacktail absolutely fearless of man, as were many which we saw that same year, but this feature the sportsman will not regret. He glories in a successful stalk or a skillful chase only when the game is alert and wary. He counts his reward of pleasure in the difficulties overcome rather than in the mere fact of final killing. He would find small satisfaction in walking up to and shooting an animal which was too ignorant to run away.

Colorado is a big State. You might hide away all New England in it. Large portions of it are entirely unsuitable for population outside of the mining industries, so long, at any rate, as irrigable soil remains to be occupied in the better parts, and that will be for a long time to come. The growth of railroads, which has been so rapid and apparently without end, has in fact confined itself either to the really limited regions where precious ores are dug, or else has followed certain river cañons in making through lines east and west. The eastern front of the mountains has been penetrated in almost every valley and bristles with towns, and the southwestern quarter or San Juan country, as far north as the Gunnison and Grand rivers, is well occupied; but a great area in the western central and northwestern quarters is as yet an untamed country, where the hunter may find work for his rifle.

The northwestern quarter of Colorado,

A WEIGHT CARRIER.

comprised in Garfield and Routt counties, still remains one of the wildest and most primitive regions of the great West. It is wholly west of the Rockies proper, and in a general way is a series of lofty plateaus gradually sloping down from the Park Range to the valley of Green River. But this plateau bears great numbers of short ranges and isolated peaks, many of which rise to snowy altitudes. Westward from these mountains flow two large rivers, the White, and further north the Yampah, as important feeders of the Green River, each having a host of tributaries that gather from rocky gorges and wind their way along pleasant valleys and parks.

Among the head waters of these streams are such mountains as Shingle Peak, Mt. Marvin, the Dome and Pagoda Peak, from which streams flow down not only into the White and Yampah, but southward into the Grand. The valley of the Grand, Egeria Park and the head waters of the Yampah have much open ground and have been pretty well settled on by farmers and cattlemen, whose operations have driven away the game to a great extent, though the settlers have more visits from bears and wolves than they like, and often get a shot at deer of various kinds. In the Elkhead and other mountains lying between there and North Park game is still to be found, including elk, but the peaks are exceedingly high, the foothills are rugged, snow comes early and the whole region is a difficult one to travel and hunt in.

At the western foot of these massive uplifts, however, along the upper White River, around Trapper's Lake, among the southern foothills of Dome and Pagoda peaks, over on Dodd's, Sage and the other creeks which go to form the Yampah, and down Williams River, as good and comfortable hunting is still to be had as anywhere in the West.

Few settlers have gone in there as yet and no ledges of precious ores tempt the invasion of the miner, while not a single railroad or wagon road penetrates the valleys or crosses the hills. There is plenty of timber, but this is scattered about, leaving every little valley open and many of the lower hills bare and grassy, while the higher slopes are clothed with dense forest, every gorge and stream side is lined with spruce and cottonwood, and all the parks are dotted with dense clumps of aspen and small shrubbery. No part of Colorado is prettier or affords more pleasant camping grounds or charming bits of scenery than this, and every one of the swift, sparkling, snow-fed streams is full of fish. In this healthful and beautiful region game abounds—elk, deer, bear, panther and small quarry of every sort—and the sportsman can get at it with the minimum of expense and waste of time and trouble.

The point of entrance to this region, and to a large extent the place for outfitting, is Glenwood Springs, a flourishing town at the junction of the Roaring Fork

PREPARING TO START.

with Grand River, which is the terminus of the Colorado Midland Railway.

This road is among the less known but most entertaining of the transmontanic routes. Its eastern end is at Colorado Springs, whence it enters the mountains by way of Ute Pass. The first part of the route, therefore, is along the northern base of Pike's Peak into South Park, a stretch of beautiful, grove-dotted, open land, where Virginia deer are still not uncommon and excellent trout fishing is to be had in the streams and lakelets. Reaching the valley of the Arkansas at Buena Vista, the railroad crosses to the foot of the Main or Snowy range of the Rockies, and begins to ascend the pass between Mounts Massive and La Plata.

By a strangely circuitous course it winds its way from spur to spur until it has climbed to the level of 10,000 feet, where it passes through the Hegerman tunnel to the Pacific Slope. The view backward from this point toward the east is one of the most spacious and sublime in the whole range of Western travel ; and the view westward as the tunnel is left behind and the wonderful descent of the Pacific Slope begins is of many grand mountains and deep valleys, among which the road finds its way down the valley of the Frying Pan and Roaring Fork — both famous trout streams—to Glenwood Springs, by some very clever expedients in engineering.

Glenwood Springs has grown to importance not so much because it is a good business point as because of the presence of some remarkable springs of hot mineral water which supply elaborate bathing houses and spacious pools. Here are handsome modern hotels, well supplied stores and every facility for outfitting a hunting party to good advantage. Glenwood therefore becomes an admirable starting point for an expedition into the northern game country. In fact it is the only starting point.

A wagon road runs northward from there as far as Trapper's Lake, but it is a pretty hard road, and the taking of a wagon is not advisable if a party means to do any earnest hunting, since they will need to go back into the hills where a wagon could not be driven without more trouble than the convenience was worth.

The better plan by far is to buy at Glenwood Springs riding horses and pack animals which can be taken as far into the mountains as anyone wishes, following old Indian trails or going where there is no trail at all. The riding animals will naturally be ponies, which may be purchased at from $35 to $50 apiece — the latter sum being an outside figure. The pack animals may be mules, ponies or donkeys. Mules will carry most, and are great climbers, but they cost high and need much care. Pack ponies may be had for $25 to $35, and are more commonly used than mules. For a hunting expedition, however, burros (donkeys) would probably answer all purposes better than either horses or mules. They cost only $15 to $20 a piece, and are easily loaded and cared for. One for each member of the party may seem to an Eastern man a small allowance, but that number ought to be enough to carry all the luggage and camp equipment required by men who want to hunt.

Riding saddles of the ranger pattern, which are altogether best for this kind of work, may be bought in Denver for about $25 apiece. Pack saddles or paniers will cost $4 apiece. For burros the panier is probably best. A guide, who will also be cook, care for the animals (as a tenderfoot would not know how to do well), and be general camp helper, may be hired for about $3 a day, you, of course, furnishing him board while he is with you.

The biggest of the big game of this region is, of course, the grizzly. He is the genuine Old Ephraim, too. The writer has known of some of the largest bears on record killed at the foot of Pagoda Peak. At midday they climb high up where it is cool, but at night they descend into the wooded heads of the gulches and spend the twilight in seeking food. Anything comes handy to their omnivorous palates, and no animal is more readily lured by bait.

Baiting, indeed, is the customary method of hunting them there. A deer or elk is searched for and killed in the locality where bears are hoped for. If it falls in a favorable position so much the better. Let it lie and do not go near it. If not, drag it with as little handling as possible to some place where rocks or other cover make a good stand to shoot from. This should be chosen, of course, with reference to the prevailing draught of the evening wind, which, as a rule, sucks down the gulch. Once placed, go near it as little as possible. The second evening will be time enough to examine whether it has been disturbed. After that keep watch between

SAM HAD HALTED IN A CROUCHING POSITION.

"I LEVELED ON THE LEADING BUCK."

sunset and the time when it gets too dark to shoot. If the day is rainy the bear may come as early as 4 or 5 o'clock. On clear and especially on moonlight nights he may not appear until long after dusk. The early dawn is another feeding time, when you may obtain him by watching. In broad daylight you will only stumble upon him, however, just as he might stumble upon you in wandering about at midnight. Black bears are numerous there, too, and some of them are almost as big as the grizzly, though hardly as interesting to tackle.

Elk and deer shooting needs no directions. Mule deer are abundant everywhere in the parks by September, when the bucks have renewed their horns and the fawns have grown. They come out to feed on the edges of the glades at sunrise, and slowly collect into little companies that move toward the warmer and more open valleys and plateaus as the autumn advances. The elk have similar habits, and are inclined to form large bands in the winter, those containing several thousand individuals having been seen in time past in this very region.

Now a band of more than a hundred would be noticeable, so rapidly has this noble animal succumbed to reckless hide hunters and market men.

Along certain creeks, where the country is open, antelope live, hiding away in the brushy ravines in summer and coming out with the earliest frost. As they are chased just enough to make them wary, the sportsman will find great sport in endeavoring to stalk these alert and swift-footed creatures, whose flesh is the best addition to the camp larder.

Where such animals as these, not to speak of beaver, badger, skunk, ground squirrel, etc., are numerous, beasts of prey may of course be looked for. The loud-barking coyote sneaks through every gulch and skirts the edges of the woods like the vagabond he is. More thoroughly a mountaineer, the large gray or timber wolf makes the crags echo with his howl, but is nowhere numerous enough to be troublesome. The little yellow wildcat, or bobcat, will be seen often enough, but the panther will rarely show himself, though if he is heard you may be able to tole him down to your bait and get him.

Few mountain lions have been shot in Colorado, however, except those which have been met by accident and dispatched by a quick shot controlled by steady hands and a cool head.

The region north of Grand River, reached from Glenwood Springs, is probably the best hunting ground in Colorado, but another district demands a little attention. West of the main range of the Rockies, in the very centre of the State, is a great group or chaotic spur of lofty peaks, known as the Elk Range, which fills the space between the Grand River on the north and its largest tributary, the Gunnison, on the south.

These mountains are, as a whole, lofty, rugged and snowy in the extreme. Composed largely of eruptive granite, their peaks are splintered ridges and sharp pinnacles of broken rock; they abound in amphitheatre-like cliffs inclosing barren areas above timber line, icy and difficult to reach, and their valleys are narrow gorges, thickly wooded and conducting torrents full of cataracts well fed by the snow banks. Viewed from the outside they present a massive, lonely and alpine grandeur as impressive as that of almost any group of heights in the State, while he who penetrates their fastnesses finds a picturesque and rugged scenery hardly surpassed even in the tremendous cañons and among the steep and towering peaks of the San Juan.

No mines are worked except on the outskirts of this great group, for even if ores exist in their interior ledges the cost of getting them out is too great to justify the attempt. The headquarters of the mining is in and about Aspen, a lively town near the head of the Frying Pan, where an outfit and guides can be procured for an expedition. It is manifest, however, that while the Elk Mountains offer an excellent opportunity for wild mountaineering adventures they do not promise so well for the sportsmen. Deer of both species undoubtedly occur among them but not so numerously as on the plateaus westward, of which the principal one is the Grand Mesa. Bear haunt their lonelier parts and not infrequently descend to the valleys, and of course lynx and a less number of panther may occasionally be encountered. The name

"THE LAST SAD RITES."

was given originally on account of the abundance of elk met with by the early explorers about their base. These have been largely, though not wholly, exterminated. A band of twenty-five or thirty was seen last season not far from Aspen, and doubtless other small bands find shelter in the remoter valleys, especially those which open toward the north and west. But it must be remembered that in summer the elk go high up to the alpine pastures at timber line, and remain there until driven down by the snow, and that this is a difficult region in which to follow them.

Bighorn are unquestionably numerous in the Elk Range yet, where they find safe retreats on the lofty crests that are so hard for hunters to climb ; but the law of Colorado forbids killing the mountain sheep during the next three years.

Taking all things into consideration, if you are in search of big game in Colorado, the best course seems to me to go to the very end of the Midland Railway and then strike northward on to the head of White River.

It was this direction that friends of mine took at the end of a three months' scientific tour in the fall of last year, and what chances there are for big game may be best learned from the report of my friends as I here repeat it :

While upon the broken plains and mesas and among the lower foothills there was work to be done for all but two, the exceptions being "Sam" and myself. But then we were privileged and tolerated by the kindly chief on two conditions—that we did not hinder the working of the staff and that we supplied the entire outfit with game and fish whenever and wherever possible.

When the work in hand was nearly accomplished two-thirds of the party were to move southward and report prior to disbanding for the winter, while the chief, "Sam," myself and needful helpers were to work into the mountains for a three weeks' exploring trip. Some of the "boys" had gone to bring up burros and pack horses, for no wagon could follow our route further. Early one morning a driver came in and reported having seen antelope in a valley a mile north of us, and "Sam" and I hastily got ready and loped away in pursuit. Reaching the valley we dismounted, and, advancing cautiously to a commanding point swept with the glass the long tongue of

grass stretching between steep, rough hills. We learned several welcome things by this scrutiny. In the first place the antelope were there—seven of them—and in the second place we discovered that the valley formed a sort of cul de sac, with no exit likely to tempt an antelope, save the gap immediately below us opening upon a great stretch of comparatively level prairie. In addition we saw that we held a great advantage in position, and that the game would almost certainly when alarmed make a dash for the open.

Hastily retreating to our horses, we mounted and rode quietly to the entrance and in along the north side of the valley for some four hundred yards. Here I halted behind some brush, while Sam quietly advanced several hundred yards farther. Where I was the valley was perhaps half a mile wide, and I could not see the game, but sat keenly watchful for the first sign of the expected stampede.

"Sam" had been gone nearly an hour when suddenly I heard a shot and then another and another. Standing bolt upright in the stirrups, I could command a long stretch of the valley, and presently heard another report and a distant cheer. Round a point, flying like the wind, came the frightened band, heading directly for the gap below me. I counted six only, and then bracing myself firmly I leveled on the leading buck, aiming just below the white crescents on his neck, and fired. At the shot he wavered slightly, halted, and his trained followers pulled up almost in their tracks, bewildered by the echoes from the hills. My buck stood broadside on and I fired again, aiming at the shoulder. This time they located me, and launching ahead like a flash they darted for the gap, my buck lagging behind. I fired two hurried shots as they drew almost abreast of my stand, and then wheeled my horse and spurred for the gap as if the fiend was at my back. The good nag grasped the situation ; he saw the bounding quarry and knew the call for speed and he buckled to his task right gamely.

On we flew toward the goal, the antelope seeming to fairly hurl themselves through the air, while my stout-hearted horse laid back his black ears and thrust out his eager nose and stretched away in a thundering gallop, faster and faster, till his girths fairly swept the grass. He was racing in dead earnest and enjoying it hugely, but he ran to defeat, for the game beat him out handsomely by good fifty yards, and once in the open the footing was too treacherous for reckless riding. With difficulty pulling up my thoroughly excited horse, I slid off him and pumped away vigorously at the rapidly vanishing antelope, but apparently all to no purpose; then remounting, I retraced our course to look for my wounded buck. He was standing motionless not far from where I had last seen him, and a great crimson stain upon his side told that he was sorely wounded. Even as I carefully approached he staggered forward a step or two, swayed from side to side, stumbled around in a semicircle and then lurched down into the grass, stone dead.

In time came "Sam," wearing a grin almost as broad as the valley, and across his saddle a fine young buck, and ere long a very triumphant procession acknowledged the cheers of the delighted camp.

Next day we made a final long stage westward to meet the boys with the horses and burros at a previously arranged point; two days later all was in readiness, and we began our climbing expedition.

Signs of game were about every water course and pool, and on two occasions I had capital luck with the trout, though the rod was merely a branch from the brush and the streams difficult to get at where we happened to reach them.

Gradually working our way upward, we finally reached an ideal camp ground—plenty of forage, shelter and good water close at hand—and we spent a week exploring the surroundings with good result. Deer and grouse could be found almost anywhere, and we saw plenty of bear sign and now and again tracks of "lions," but these latter gentry wisely kept their distance and, as usual, offered no chance for our rifles. But the crowning exploit—a feat that will remain ever green in the memory of "Sam" especially—was the killing of "Ephraim."

One of the boys came in at night and reported that he had found unmistakably fresh bear sign in a little ravine about five miles from camp. He said it was an extremely rough spot, walled in in places with ragged cliffs of naked rock, and that he was positive a grizzly, and a regular old snorter at that, lived in the ravine.

At sunrise we were ready, each man with a snack of lunch in his pocket, and we followed our guide down a great slope through the timber, then over a

steep crest which taxed muscles and lungs to the utmost, then down another long slope, and finally to the stream where he had seen the track. Following it upward for about a mile as best we could, a pool was reached, and its margin showed plainly the footprints of our guide and the track of a huge bear. Suddenly the guide exclaimed excitedly, "Look here, this is fresh!" and we found a great footprint, made so recently that we involuntarily glanced all round for the cause of it. But "Ephraim" had doubtless sought his domicile an hour before.

"Now, he's bin yer fur a drink," said the guide, "and has likely gone loafin' along up the ravine and by this time is in his den, snoozin'. It's among the rocks on that side, I reckon, an' we'll round him up 'fore long. We'd all best sneak along top of the cliff an' see what we kin see."

An hour later we had gained the summit of the cliff at a point above where the guide suspected "Ephraim" dwelt. Below us was a steep descent, marked with countless pinnacles, ledges and steps, and near the bottom fragments of rock were piled in chaotic confusion. We could work our way down readily enough, providing missteps were carefully avoided, for a fall would simply mean instant destruction. For many minutes three pairs of eager eyes searched every visible foot of the ravine and every crevice and cavern among the boulders. Not a sign of life was to be found nor was a tomb quieter than the rock-strewn prospect.

Presently a low hiss from our guide called our attention to him. His face was ablaze with half-suppressed excitement, and silently he came creeping to us and whispered, "I seen him!"

"Where?"

"Creep 'round yer and look down — right below yer. Ain't he an ole whaler?"

"Sam'" and I looked long and earnestly and with beating hearts, but saw no bear. Then the guide crept forward and took another look and whispered, "He war thar all right, fur I seen him. He walked 'roun' that rock and looked bigger'n a steer. We'll jest lay low fur a bit; he's as ugly lookin' an ole devil as ever yer seen, an' I reckon hez a den down under thar."

We waited for half an hour, watching intently. It was not more than seventy-five yards to where the guide had seen him, and a series of rock steps made it quite feasible for a man to descend to his level. Finally "Sam" signified his intention of going down. "Yer want ter be mighty keerful," said the guide; "if he gets his eyes on yer he'll go fur yer sure."

"Sam" said, "All right; you fellows place yourselves to cover me and I'll go down. I'm going to see that bear if it takes a leg." Forthwith he began a noiseless, carefully gauged descent, lowering himself from point to point and from ledge to ledge until he was barely forty yards from the supposed den. We waited and watched with rifles ready and nerves strung to the straining point. "Sam" had halted in a crouching position and was peering keenly down when the crisis suddenly arrived. A big piece of shaly rock, loosened by his movements, started to roll down and finally, followed by a small avalanche of pebbles and grit, lit with a crash upon the shelf-like level where the bear had been.

A moment later an immense rusty-brown head seemed to protrude from out of the solid rock, and "Ephraim" had come forth to see who dared invade his stronghold. He was immediately below "Sam's" point of vantage, and looked to be so close that he might have been almost touched with the rifle, though in reality the distance between them was about thirty yards. Before the grim brute saw his foes; before he even realized that the avalanche of stones was aught else but a natural slip, a .45 calibre bullet struck him fair and true in the back of his mas-

sive head and laid him dead in his very doorway. As "Sam" started to pump in another shell his treacherous foothold gave way a trifle, and he slid downward directly toward the bear for about ten feet or so; the next instant he was climbing like a scared cat upward as fast as hands and knees could carry him, while the expression on his face did our hearts good to see. He speedily rallied, however, and yelled to us to know could we see the bear. Then we all three went down to within twenty feet of our prize, where the guide drew a bead on the small, round ear and fired point blank into it. But "Ephraim" was a thoroughly dead bear, though the guide declared that he took no chances, and I believe rightly enough.

"Ephraim" proved to be a big, old he bear, much the largest our guide had seen. His enormous bulk—he was fat as a stall-fed ox—his great fangs and terrible curved claws were almost terrifying, even in death, and he certainly would have proved himself a dangerous customer had fate ordained he should have had half a fair chance. As it was, "Sam" had secured a magnificent trophy fairly enough, and took it all coolly and as a matter of course.

"Say, 'Sam,' how did you feel perched up there when his head showed; were you scared?"

"Not a bit."

"Then what the deuce made you climb so when you slipped."

A knowing wink was the sole answer.

17.
THE MAINE GUIDE
AND THE MAINE CAMP
(1901)

THE MAINE GUIDE AND THE MAINE CAMP

By Herbert L. Jillson

THE Maine guide, in the mind of every sportsman who has "done" Maine properly, is closely associated with memories of pleasant and successful days with the rod on lake and stream, or long tramps through the woods with the rifle. It is his guide, not the sporting camp proprietor or the people he meets, that the sportsman, after return to civilization, remembers most of all. This recollection is almost always tinged with tenderness, for "Charlie" is to the minds of a certain number of sportsmen, not only the best guide in the State, but the staunchest friend in the world; while, on the other hand, Charlie thinks no sportsmen come to Maine except Mr. So-and-So and a few others of his select coterie. All others lack much or little of being up to Charlie's ideal, and he loves to relate, with glowing eyes, in the presence of other guides, the achievements with rod and gun of the mighty Nimrods whom he guides. To the sportsman, on the other hand, all other guides than their own particular are just a bit "off." They talk too much or too little, paddle or walk too slow or too fast, or, possibly, the cooking is uncertain; but their Charlie hasn't a fault. It is a pleasure to converse with him or be in his company, his paddling and gait are just right, and the coffee never fails to be good, the trout cooked to a turn, the bread light, or the flapjacks brown and tender.

Some sportsmen are, indeed, wont to carry their enthusiasm so far as to quarrel about their guides much as children do about their papas, and while Mr. Gun admires Mr. Rod, personally, he cannot for the life of him understand how he can go into the woods with "that blockhead Tommy." Both seem to forget that a guide is much like a wife; what suits one man has no attractions for another. It is the old, old story where people fail to comprehend what there is in the mysterious word—companionship.

The typical Maine guide is just as much a product of the soil as are the mighty forests, and his replica is not to be found elsewhere. They are, of course, all human and differ in temperament. One may be nervous and excitable, another reserved and deliberate; a third, patient and forbearing, and a fourth, quick tempered and unreasonable; but, as a class, good guides are to a man, strong, willing, friendly and ever on the lookout to see that their "sporter" has the best there is to be got. They are good friends and, sometimes, bitter enemies, for their sense of justice is keen and they are ready to retaliate for a just and, sometimes, a fancied grievance. The majority are sober and honest, if one accepts the latter qualification by making allowances for the fairy tales which they are wont to spin for the entertainment of their city guests, and, often, they have told these over and over until they really believe them. Profanity is not a rule among them, although a moderate amount adds zest to their conversation on fitting occasions. With scarcely an exception they know their place and keep it, seldom mistaking kindness for familiarity or imagining that they are the sportsman and the sportsman the guide. They do not expect to be put on a basis of familiarity. They realize that the men they guide come from a world of which they know little, yet they are seldom envious. They only ask to be treated like men, nothing more.

Guiding is a business with them, devoid of all the frills the uninitiated enthusiast might attach, and taken season in and season out, it is about as hard work as one would wish to undertake. To tramp long miles carrying a heavy pack or an eighty-pound canoe over a rough trail, to paddle from morning until night, to be ever at the call of some one who is in the woods for enjoyment, and then to end the day by getting supper, chopping wood for the night, building a lean-to and boughing down the beds is no easy or unimportant task. If ever a class of men earned their money fairly and squarely it is the guides who are working for $2.50 and $3 a day. A good guide gives his employer the benefit of knowledge gained from years of experience in the woods—the art of woodcraft, the habits of fish and game. He does not hesitate, if need be, to risk his life for his employer, and the greatest personal discomfort is a pleasure to him if it only adds to the enjoyment of his party. Who else would sit in a canoe and paddle for hours in a hard rain drenched to the skin? Who else would pack a canoe half a dozen miles without grumbling, simply for the sake of a few hours' fishing? Who else would give up a blanket and sit by the fire that you might be warm, or go without food that you might not go hungry? No one but the guide is the answer of all who have been fortunate enough to be under the care of a good one while in the woods.

The guide does his best work for the man he likes. It adds pleasure to his occupation to have a man who is appreciative, kindly, and patient. The guide likes to be told that the cooking is good, that the day's sport has been satisfactory, and he appreciates any demonstration of personal interest. Above all things he hates a "kicker," and such a man has a hard time in the woods as soon as his failing becomes known. He admires a man who is a good shot or expert with the rod, and will do anything to assist such a one to obtain what he desires, for he feels, and justly, that half the glory of his employer's achievements falls upon him. After taking a man up close to a mammoth moose or big deer and seeing a whole magazine of cartridges fired without effect, or after paddling cautiously up to a fine trout pool and having the water pounded until the fish flee in terror, he gets discouraged, and it is not to be wondered at. He has done his best in every way, and to have grumbling is not pleasant. The guide admires the straightforward man. He can tolerate anything if he believes one is sincere in it. If a man can neither shoot nor fish he likes to know it, if things are wrong he would feel better to receive a friendly suggestion than to be told something he knew was not true.

First of all the sportsman who wants to enjoy Maine and see the State properly should secure a good guide, for the best fishing is not found on the brooks and lakes close to sporting camps, and the finest hunting is miles distant, even at the wildest and most remote of them. This can be best done by securing information from some old time Maine sportsman who knows such men. A registered guide is not necessarily all right, for there is little opportunity for the fish and game commissioners to investigate and mediocre men get certificates. After securing his guide, the sportsman must treat that guide "white," and there will be no trouble. The guide does not expect you to help paddle the canoe unless you so desire, for the "help" would probably flavor more of hindrance. If you care to "sack" part of the pack over the trail he will be grateful, but he does not expect it. He wants you to get all the pleasure you can and first, last, and always to be reasonable, not to expect more of him than flesh is capable of, to appreciate the good things he brings your way and to make the most of unavoidable discomforts. If you have money and choose to give him $5 or $25 at the end of your stay, as a tip, or a nest egg for the "little 'un," it will further cement his regard for you, for money is scarce in Maine, and people live plainly. If you cannot afford to do this, friendly acts and kindly interest will do just as well. Do whatever the heart prompts and the purse permits, and your guide will ever be your stanchest friend and most ardent admirer. Above all, make no promises of gifts when you "get home," if you are not in earnest. Always keep faith with your guide if you seek his faithful service and respect.

Photo by E. R. Starbird.

A CABIN INTERIOR.

ATTEAN LAKE—A VIEW FROM THE CABIN PORCH.

THE CAMP

THE Maine sporting camp, as it is in reality, is little understood by those who have not visited it. At the sportsmen's exhibitions, to be sure, one may have seen sample camps, but an impression formed from these imitations would be far from correct; they give a very inadequate idea. Within the past few years, comparatively speaking, sporting camps have been springing up at favorable locations all over northern Maine. The proprietors are generally guides who have seen a possibility to make money through the venture. Each camp has its "preserve," so called. The greater part of the wild lands of northern Maine are owned by men or companies of men, who, on account of their vast lumbering wealth, often will not sell at any price, and the figures set when the lands are on the market, are beyond the reach of any save millionaires. The land owners are willing, however, to lease "sporting privileges," so called, for a term of years at prices varying from $25 to $100 per year. This gives the lessee **right** to build cabins on the land and to

go over it, camping at will, cutting such wood as is necessary for cabins, wharves, rafts, fuel and the like. Others cannot camp upon the land without the consent of the lessee, but the State makes all lands and all water public so far as crossing them is concerned, and one may fish or hunt them at will, so long as he does not build fires or camp upon them. Each sporting camp has from one to five townships, each six miles square, in its preserve. This gives a large territory, numerous ponds and streams for fishing, waters where deer congregate in the summer and forests where big game roams in the autumn. The camp manager opens up this land. There is a "home camp" at a central point and as convenient to the main road as possible, and trails are cut to the best fishing and hunting grounds, where cabins and lean-tos are erected according to the nature of the territory. At the most important of these branch ponds canoes are placed in order to avoid the necessity of carrying them through the woods when guests desire to visit the places. If there is a mountain near at hand, or a place of especial interest, a trail is cut to that and a feature made of it as a tramp.

The ideal location for a sporting camp is at a point where a large mileage through rivers and lakes opens up for canoeing and at the same time a vast country for tramping from the nearby shores. If one can be fortunate in having a railroad close by another card is played, but these ideal locations are few, and the majority of the camps are not so favorably situated. The extent of territory enables the proprietor to handle a large number of people of varying tastes—those who desire the comforts of the home camp continually, others that want a little rougher fare, and the sportsman who desires nothing better than the lean-to or deserted lumber camp. The typical home camps are models in their way and every art and craft known to the backwoods, and much of civilization is used to make them attractive and comfortable. They are located on some river or pond, backed by the forest, and at a central point with a good view of water, forest and mountains. The number of cabins varies from six to twenty, and they are usually of two sorts, single and double.

The single camps are about 16 feet by 22 in size and some 6 feet high to the eaves. The roof is of "splits," shingles made by splitting cedar or pine with a "frow," and the floor is of boards if there is a sawmill near, and if not, of hewn logs. There are single sash windows on either side and the rough logs, chinked with moss, are often concealed from view on the interior, by a lining of splits or birch bark.

The furnishings consist of two wide beds located on either side at the extreme end of the cabin, a table, and comfortable easy chairs, of the folding pattern. Located in a corner at the front of the cabin is either a rustic fireplace made of stones, or a little wood stove. The former method of heating is the most popular, for there are few nights and mornings in Maine, spring, summer or autumn, when a fire is not comfortable and a cheery blaze is always very delightful to chat by, or to watch flicker on the ceiling after one has retired. These furnishings, home made and rustic, together with the cabin lining and the dim light let in by the small, low windows, make the interior of these cabins very unique and artistic. Bright colored curtains at the windows and draperies upon the shelves, together with guns and rods

CAMP AT LONG POND.

hung upon deers' feet and wooden pegs, further delight the artistic senses. There are numerous shelves to hold the many things the visitor needs, hooks for clothes made by nailing up forked sticks cut to the proper length, or driving in rough wooden pegs, and here and there little oddities; a match box of birch bark, an etching on a bit of fungus, and the like. A broad porch springs from the front of the cabin where one may sit or swing in a hammock. It will be seen that a man and his wife or a couple of sportsmen may be very comfortable in this little home, for a long or short stay, making headquarters for such trips as they desire to make from time to time.

The double cabins are much the same, only larger. There is a main living room in the center with the fireplace at the end, and four rooms, each with a bed, on the sides. The porch is larger and the roof higher, thereby letting in more light. These cabins hold four, supposedly, but they may hold eight comfortably, and the single cabins are adapted to four persons who are well acquainted. The dining-room is a large separate cabin joined on to a kitchen which rests at the rear. The rough tables are concealed with clean linen, and plain crockery and knives answer as well as silver and china. The interior of this cabin is lined and there are numerous trophies—mounted heads and fish, outlines of big trout, bits of moss, birds' nests, birds' wings, and the like upon the walls for decoration.

There is usually a separate cabin, or casino, for general assembly, social evenings, entertainments and the like. Here are card tables and chairs invariably, and oftentimes magazines, papers and sometimes a piano. A rustic fireplace is a central feature.

The food is good. In the summer there are toothsome fried trout three times a day if one wishes, and in the autumn plenty of venison. A cow furnishes milk, while a little garden supplies few or many vegetables according to its location. There are delicious berries during the summer. Sparkling spring water is always found.

It will be readily seen that the home camp is entirely "suitable for ladies," and it seems very queer to camp managers that this question is asked again and again each year, in letters.

The branch or back camps are not so luxuriously fitted out, but even ladies who are fond of roughing it often find their way to them and come back delighted. These camps have supplies, but a guide is necessary to visit them enjoyably. This personage does the cooking, paddles the canoe, shows where the fish and game are, and makes himself valuable as only a guide can. A cook stove helps the cuisine and one forgets that the table dishes are of tin, the dining table covered with oil cloth, the beds of boughs, and that blankets take the pace of sheets.

Farther "in" is the lean-to or tent and the meals are cooked by the camp fire, a portable baker being used to bake bread. The farther in one goes the rougher becomes the task and the less the larder affords, but the country is wilder and fish and game abound in astonishing numbers. Here is where the sportsman goes and stays after once tasting the wild life.

It is not strange that year after year Maine is becoming more and more a resort for people who seek rest and recreation as well as sport with fish and game. Rangeley and Moosehead have their hotels, golf links, tennis courts and every luxury to be found at any popular seashore or mountain resort, but the sporting camps seek to cater only to those who love the woods and their solitude, and the magnificent sport which is found all about, together with necessary comforts. For a place to rest and escape the noise of the city or the confusion of the overpopulated summer resort, the camps have no equal.

As long as satisfactory legislation holds in force there can be no doubt about the great future of northern Maine as a resort for all classes of people. The sporting season is from the middle of May until the last of June and from September 1st until December. During July and August the sporting camp is only such in name, and the proprietor strives to fill his cabins with family parties. Each year the numbers who come for weeks and months during this period are increasing. Maine sporting camps as "summer resorts" are as yet little known, but "loving friends" are good advertisers.

18.
THE FIELD TRIALS
(1907)

THE FIELD TRIALS

A CHAPTER IN THE BREEDING AND MAKING OF DOGS

BY CHAS. B. COOKE

PHOTOGRAPHS BY H. M. ALBAUGH

THE preliminaries all attended to, arrangements made for hotel accommodations, judges selected, horses and wagons all engaged, entry blanks printed and distributed and the entries all duly received with nomination fees properly attached, the all eventful day rolls around in the autumn, when the sportsmen gather with their dogs to "make good" with actual work the many boasts of superiority which have been made to fellow sportsmen throughout the year. It is a jolly good crowd and everybody is in for a good time. The Secretary, of course, is early on the ground, generally a day or two previous to the event, in order to see that everything is in shape for the opening day. The field trials are generally run adjacent to some country town which can furnish sufficient hotel and livery accommodations, and yet situated in a country sufficiently open and known to contain quantities of birds. The field trials are run on partridges, more familiarly known as quail or bob white. The object is to ascertain the best dog, the dog which has the best speed, range, style, stamina and bird-finding qualities. The judges selected have a very delicate as well as unenviable task in deciding these points.

The first duty of the Secretary is to send out about six weeks previous to the date on which the trials are to be held, an entry blank to all the members of the field trial association, and to all others who have applied. On this blank is entered the name of the dog, sex, pedigree, date of birth, and the stake for which it is entered—the Derby, the open All-age or Free-for-all, as the case may be. The nomination fee in each stake is usually $5.00, which must accompany the application for entering the dog. This being done, the next step is the assembling of the participants and professional handlers at the trials. On the night previous to the day on which the trials begin, those who have their dogs on hand ready to start are required to come forward and pay to the Secretary an additional fee, which is usually $10.00, known as the starting fee. When this fee is paid the name of the dog for which it is paid is written on a slip of paper, carefully folded and placed in a hat. When all of the dogs which are present and ready to run in a specified stake have qualified, the names are shaken up and drawn out one at a time—the first name drawn out of the hat is run with the second, and so on until all of the dogs are paired off. The names are then posted in a conspicuous place in the hotel where all interested can copy them for reference next day.

The drawing of the dogs, as this is called, is always attended with much interest, for frequently stakes are won or lost in the drawing, owing to the time of day at which a dog is fortunate or unfortunate enough to be put down. Sometimes the morning is cold and the ground frozen, and the brace of dogs which goes down first is handicapped, and again dogs may be drawn so that they will fall in the heat of the day, between twelve and three o'clock, which again is a handicap. All of these points are considered for or against a dog in a professional field trial.

The drawing over, and many pleasantries exchanged between old friends, the crowd is soon off to bed to be up with the lark,

On the road to the trial grounds.

Loading the dogs preparatory to making a start—an unusual crate.

ready to get away from town at an early hour, the horses and wagons being ordered from the livery stable to be ready by seven o'clock A. M. Next morning everything is hustle and bustle getting breakfast, loading the dogs into the wagons, and selecting riding horses for the day's trip. As a rule the crowd is late starting, and it is more like nine o'clock than seven when the party moves in the direction of the grounds which are probably from two to five miles distant from the town. It is indeed a most inspiring sight to see a long cavalcade of horses and the various types of wagons and buggies loaded with all sorts and conditions of dog crates, nearly every one of which contains a yelping canine anxious to be let loose for his hour's sport. The grounds being reached, the judges call for the first brace. They are soon brought up and the command given "Let your dog go." The two dogs are then cut loose by their respective handlers and the fun begins. If the brace happens to be a fast, wide ranging pair, the excitement is the more intense, and the crowd in its anxiety to see the dogs and watch their work is apt to become unruly. Here the field marshal comes into play; he commands the crowd to "hold back" and let the handlers of the dogs get out in front with their horses, if they happen to ride, for it is optional with them whether they ride or walk. The Judges follow the handlers on horseback, for their job is a tiresome one, and they must stay at it all day. The spectators are commanded to remain fifty yards in the rear of the judges, but this is seldom obeyed, and the marshal is continually yelling at the crowd to "hold back." All at once the thrilling, heart-piercing sound is heard, "point Judge" from a nearby covert. All hands make a break for the spot, throwing aside conventionality and forgetting the marshal's admonition of a few minutes before to "hold back." There stands the dog on a staunch point, his tail and head erect and every nerve tense; the other dog, which has made a wide cast in another direction, upon catching sight of the dog which is pointing, stops to a beautiful "back." The handler comes up, and when

" Keep off that wheat! "

"Are you ready? Let your dog go, Mr. Handler!"

the judges order him to do so, he walks in front of his dog, keeping his eye strictly on his charge, for fear it will make an error. The dog must stand perfectly rigid when the birds are flushed. "There they go," everybody cries, "watch 'em," for they must be followed to work the dogs on "singles." Both dogs behaved nicely when the birds were flushed and a gun fired over the point to ascertain if they be "steady to shot," which means they must not run in or "break shot," as such conduct is called. The gun is fired only for this purpose, for no birds are killed in a field trial. Retrieving is not a part of the training of a field trial dog; this may seem strange to the uniniated, but it is a big item in running the trials. If each dog were required to retrieve a dead bird it would take weeks to pull off a meet, which now consumes four to six days. Any sort of a dog can be taught to retrieve, but it cannot be made to smell and point birds. The birds are followed and nice work is done on the singles, possibly one dog gets all of the points, possibly honors are even, or may be the good

work of a covey find is offset by a dog running over and flushing all the singles and spoiling its chances, or "cutting their throats," as the expression goes. The judges look at their watches, for they have timed the dogs and if they have run their heat of forty minutes or over, they are "ordered up" and the second brace is called for. These may not be on hand, some wagon has been late getting started or taken the wrong road, and a wait is incurred until the wagon comes up, or is found.

The braces of dogs are run one after another in the order drawn until all have had a chance on game; then comes the second series, in which the judges, after comparing their notes, and from keen observation, select the dogs which have made the best showing and drop the others. These winners are paired off according to the discretion of the judges to be run a second time. Of course some good dogs are left out, but they have had their chance, and either took advantage of the opportunity given them, spoiled their chances or were outclassed. Each pair of dogs is not in a

Waiting for the wagons to come up with the next brace.

A few participants in the trials—"Attention, boys!"

Lunch out in the lot on the warm side of the barn.

race by itself. Sometimes both are taken into the next series, while another brace is left out entirely. A good high-class, wide ranging dog may have hunted industriously and been unfortunate in not finding birds, while a less attractive dog may have done a lot of bird work and is carried on, and right here comes the disappointment. A man knows what his dog can do, for he has seen him do it before, and it requires all the fortitude and manhood in him not to "kick" when his good dog is left out of a stake and another, not near so attractive, is given a place. But dear reader, we must not forget this is a trial of bird dogs, which by a peculiarly endowed trait are gifted with the wonderful power of running at high speed and instantly detecting the scent of a bird, and that the dog is trained to point and hold his point until you or I can get there and shoot the game for our own use. It is of course very delightful to see the fast, wide ranging dog go, and equally distressing to some of us to see the "duffer," through a streak of good luck, placed above him, but we are hunting birds, and bird-finding is the first requisite.

The happiest time of the day is luncheon when the tired, hungry crowd all gallop up to the appointed farm-house where the lunch wagon is waiting, the Secretary having instructed the hotel keeper what to prepare and where to send it. An impromptu table is erected behind the barn, in the sun out of the cold, wintry wind, which has a habit of blowing in the beautiful autumn days when most field trials are held. Coffee, turkey, sausage, cakes, biscuits, and all the good things are devoured by the waiting guests, and then come the cigars. After luncheon, the horses are mounted for the afternoon race. The same plan is pursued in the second series as in the first, then come the finals, when the two best dogs are put down to run for first and second place. Sometimes this is decided in ten minutes, sometimes it takes an hour, and it may have taken two days running to get to the last brace. Frequently there are from eight to fifteen braces of dogs in a stake. When eventide rolls around, the crowd makes a break for town, which may be anywhere from five to ten miles distant. The ride back is truly a free-for-all race, going at a full gallop in their anxiety to get back to the hotel to a

warm fire and hot supper. At night, generally, the annual meeting of the Association is held, when matters of business are attended to and new members are elected, also the drawing for the next stake takes place. Some associations run four stakes —a Member's Derby and Member's All-age, for members only, as well as an Open Derby and Open All-age for professionals as well as members; then there is a subscription or champion stake which calls for the best dogs of all. The entrance money is usually paid out as prizes; the club, however, guaranteeing a purse of about $400 to $600 in each stake, hoping to be reimbursed from the entry and starting fees.

The Derby stake is limited to puppies whelped on or after January 1st of the year previous to holding the trials. In the breeding of dogs for a Derby prospect, it is always the ambition of the owner to get a puppy, whelped as early in the year as possible, for the reason that it is old enough to receive a good preliminary training the following fall, and by the next summer is ready to show what is in it on prairie chickens, and, later in the fall, to make or lose its reputation on quail. The prairie chicken trials, which are generally held in the west or northwest, are of immense value in the development of the field trial dog. The broad prairie and flat country being conducive to range, the puppy being able to see its handler for a greater distance, creates in it a greater degree of confidence which it cannot acquire in a close, brushy country. The first thing necessary in field trial prospects is range and independent hunting. If a puppy shows these qualities to any degree, it can be encouraged, with the proper training. Then, if it has a nose to back up the speed and range, and can find birds, it is a good prospect and worth spending money on. Thousands of pointer and setter puppies are tried out each season, any one of which would make what is known as a good shooting dog, but very few measure up to the high standard necessary to landing in a winner's place in the field trials. An honest, expert professional handler will not take a patron's money for the training of dogs for field trial purposes when there is no chance for the dog to win. Of course there are many conditions which enter into the field trial

"Point Judge!"   A fine piece of work in the high grass by a prize winner.

The day's work over, supper is relished by the cracks that have produced the sport.

which make the best of dogs lose, but after the weeding-out process, and after sending back home many which have not come up to the standard, those which do compete in the field trials are generally of the highest order. These dogs are valuable—valuable because they have shown their intelligence and their high qualities by being able to hunt better, to go faster, to stay out longer, to hunt more independently, and to find more game than those which have been left at home. These dogs range anywhere in value from $100 to $5,000. Were it not for the field trial, for this weeding-out process, and the survival of the fittest, no such prices as these would ever have been heard of for a sporting dog, such as a pointer or setter. Strange to say, field trials are confined almost exclusively to pointers and English or Llewellyn setters. Very few Irish or Gordon setters have ever been able to stand up against these other breeds. Occasionally the Irish setter is seen in some small stake, but they have never seemed to develop the class, snap, and style necessary to make them of the winning breed.

The field trials which have been run in the United States for the last twenty-five years have developed the English setter and pointer to a high state of efficiency, and the field trials are on the increase. Nearly every season records the organizing of new associations, which form into circuits. These circuits are arranged with fixed dates as in horse racing, so that handlers may go from one to the other and participate with their string of dogs in a half a dozen different meetings, making it profitable for them in the winning of the purses put up by the various associations. As a rule, these purses range from $300 to $600 in each stake, and the money is divided into four parts, of which the first winner receives 40 per cent., the second place 30 per cent., the third place 20 per cent., and the fourth place 10 per cent. Should the handler be fortunate enough to have the dog which wins first in the Derby and first in the All-age, he has landed a nice sum of money. There are professional handlers, who have followed this business for years, whose income never falls below $2,500 a year and sometimes as high as $4,000. The usual charge for handling a dog is $12.50 per month during the training season, which includes feed and care, and if the dog is especially good, the handler may take him for a percentage of winnings, the owner to pay the nominating and starting fees which usually amount to $15.00 in each stake. The running of field trial dogs is not an inexpensive amusement by any means, but when one has a good dog that is worth spending money on, he is almost sure to be able to realize a large price, besides all of the pleasure and honor attached to its winning. There are, of course, as in all other forms of sport, the disappointments which fall to the lot of those who persevere and stick at it; the sportsman, however, is found year after year in the winning column. The greatest disappointment to all breeders of high-class dogs is the death list, or mortality of puppies; this is something fearful. Where one is raised successfully, probably twenty-five die, and we do not think we exaggerate in making this statement. The field trial dogs of the present day are generally inbred and are, therefore, delicate. On the theory that like begets like, patrons of field trials have mated the dogs which have proven themselves winners, until we now have a composite, high strung, nervous animal, subject to all the ravages of the many diseases known to the canine world.

It is indeed discouraging to raise a lot of puppies to the age of six months or a year, bright, intelligent fellows, any one of which you would choose for a companion, which you have nurtured and cared for, then to see them drop off one by one, with that most dreaded of diseases, distemper, yet, like a child having whooping cough, it is best for them to take the disease and get over it, for then one can spend his money on a certainty. It is disheartening, after you have educated a dog and made him worth $500 or $1,000, to have the disease take him off just at the time when you begin to enjoy the fruits of your labor. The field trial has been a great method of bringing out these high-class dogs. Were it not for the field trials, they would never have been heard of, and a peculiar thing about the field trial business is that every man is an enthusiast, every owner has the best dog, which is bound to win, and he enters his dog and pays his expenses, feeling sure that he will certainly carry off the

The veteran reporter—"My, that was a bad break!"

prize, but out of seventy-five or eighty entries in a field trial, only eight of them can win, as there are only four prizes in each stake. Somebody must lose. There is an element of luck, but luck cannot always be against your particular dog, and certainly in a half a dozen of these field trials, under possibly a dozen or more different climatic and field conditions, it will have all the opportunity in the world to demonstrate whether or not it is made of the winning stuff. The field trials can not be successfully run in a small broken territory, or in a country which is too much wooded. It requires a large area, from ten to twenty thousand acres of good bird country, because the dogs as a rule are very fast, wide ranging individuals and cover an enormous amount of territory.

Some of the largest field trial associations in the country, which have excellent grounds, are the Independent Field Trial Club, S. H. Sockwell, Sec., Indianapolis, Ind.; Illinois Field Trial Association, W. R. Green, Sec., Marshall, Ill.; The Continental Field Trial Club, John White, Sec., Hempstead, L. I.; The Eastern Field Trial Association, S. C. Bradley, Sec., Fairfield, Conn.; the United States Field Trial Club, W. B. Stafford, Sec., Trenton, Tenn., and, of course, our own Virginia Field Trial Association, which has possibly the largest individual membership of any association in the United States.

The running of field trials is the greatest and cleanest sport known to the lovers of outdoor life. There is nothing to compare with it. It has a certain fascination which no other form of outdoor amusement enjoys, and one out of which you get recreation and pleasure all the year round, for there is just as much pleasure in the anticipation as in the realization, and a business man can sit at his desk in any city in the United States and keep up day by day, week by week, with his dog as it travels from one point of the United States to the other, learning its lesson and receiving its education at the various field trials held between August 15th and February 1st.

19.
NEWFOUNDLAND
CARIBOU
(1903)

NEWFOUNDLAND CARIBOU

By RICHARD D. WARE

NEWFOUNDLAND and its caribou have become topics of increasing interest to American sportsmen of late years, and with good cause. It really takes but little more time, if any, to arrive at hunting grounds where it may be fairly said that success depends only on the man behind the gun, than it does to get into some of the supposedly more accessible moose and caribou country in New Brunswick, from which many a good man has returned with a full magazine of cartridges and perhaps an "If" story. The journey can be made entirely by rail, with the exception of the short run from Sidney to Port-aux-Basques, with unusual comfort; and when you have left the train you are on the trail, for in the caribou country something may happen the next minute.

My own experience a year ago is probably the common one. The great impression gained from the sources which were available was that as winter approached there was a great general migration of all the caribou from the northern part of the island, "where they feed and bring forth their young," to the southern part, and that in the spring they went back north again for the laudable purposes mentioned. The cause of these migrations was given as climatic, like the migrations of the birds. It seemed obvious from the authorities that during the summer the beasts were all as far north as they could get, which would mass them in the great peninsula which makes the northern end of the island, and that an intended hunting trip for the early part

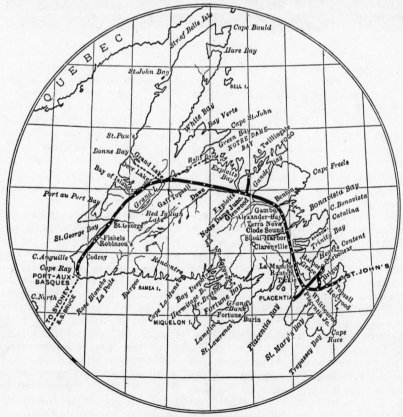

The Caribou Country in Newfoundland

Coming in from a Day's Hunting.

of September would have to be planned for that country.

By good fortune, in July, we learned that the friend of a friend was fishing near a station in the southeastern part of the island. This was a chance for something definite, and he was written to. He stated that he saw caribou nearly every day. That seemed impossible, for according to the migration theory there ought not to have been a caribou within three hundred miles of him, and he was cross-examined. He refused to be shaken, and advised us to take his guides and come and see for ourselves. We went, and on September first were on our way due west into the country with "Uncle John," the guide, and his men.

In September, caribou begin to appear in the "leads" in the Howley district, all working toward the south, mostly does, fawns and young stags, at first singly, or in twos and threes. As the season goes on they come in larger companies, as many as twenty or thirty, or even more, together. Some old stags will be with these companies, but they generally lag along behind as yet, as they are heavy and slow moving. This procession to the south-

ward keeps on well through October, and then gradually ceases. This is the time when Howley is in its gory glory. The shooters lie on the points in the lakes and ponds, which interrupt the line of march, and shoot the caribou as they swim by. They patrol Sandy Lake stream in boats, and shoot them as they cross. Back from the water courses they camp, as they did along the railroad track until the recent law was passed prohibiting it, on the leads down which the animals travel, and shoot them from the tent doors. If several parties are camped on the same lead, as is frequently the case, the appearance of a good stag is the signal for a free-for-all sprint across the bog for the first shot, a sociable but hardly ideal method of hunting such noble game. In the spring the animals go back again to the north through the same district. Here is the foundation of the migration theory.

The twelve caribou we saw the first day in our southern hunting grounds exploded it, and we sought for the truth from our guide, philosopher and friend. His statements, borne out as they were by what we were able to observe, show that it is this. There is no general migration of the caribou in the sense that they all go north at one season of the year, leaving none in the southern parts of the island, and all go south at another season, leaving none in the northern parts. Wherever there are great moss-producing barrens and bogs in the vicinity of woodland, there one will find caribou all through the year, north or south. As these conditions exist over practically the whole island, barring the mountainous west coast, one may put it more definitely, that one will find caribou over the whole island all through the year, the only qualification being that one will find them in the woodland country during one period, and on the barrens and bogs through another.

The young caribou is born in May or June in the woods, where the doe has betaken herself after the manner of most wild creatures when such events are approaching. The instincts and requirements which led to banding together in the open country in the fall have lost their force, and the desire to be alone is the ruling motive in both sexes. The doe with her fawn has all she can attend to, and wishes not to be disturbed. The stags, and the does as well, begin to grow their new antlers about this time, and their sore heads and tender horns make them sulky and unsociable.

About the last of August the does find their fawns are pretty sturdy youngsters. They can feed themselves and run from danger fairly well, and maternal solicitude consequently abates considerably. They think it would be pleasant to go out into the open country and see other does and their fawns, and things generally, most usual desires in the feminine which need no further exposition. The young stags, whose spike or pronged horns have grown more quickly than the great branches of their elders, are filled with vain desires to exhibit them to some appreciative doe or try them on another stag, and they, too, drift out into the barrens where they can see and be seen, joining the does and fawns which have preceded them. By the tenth of September, and generally a few days earlier, the older stags have stripped the last velvet from their antlers and polished them on the trees. One can almost always tell what the summer environment of a stag has been from the color of his horns. Those that are dark-colored have been rubbed on spruces or junipers, which have exuded pitch upon them, to which dirt has adhered and been rubbed into the horn. The light-colored antlers have been cleaned on alders or birches, and have absorbed their more liquid, greenish juices. The stags have had their horns literally on their minds all summer, and their purpose dimly begins to dawn on them. They are not yet the truculent beasts they become a few weeks later, for one often sees several old stags together at this season; but they are prepared for the coming frays, and come forth into the open country, where they join those already assembled, as they have picked up each other here and there as they wandered about.

By the first of October practically all the caribou have left the wooded country for the open, where the conditions for natural selection for the reproduction of the species are most favorable. The breeding season continues through October, with battles royal between the great stags for supremacy over the different herds, during which the younger stags avail themselves of all the opportunities which the contests of their elders make possible. Their duties to their race being accomplished, the beasts lay down their arms—or, to put it less metaphorically, their horns drop off—and settle down to more harmonious conditions for winter on the barrens, for here they find the deep gray reindeer moss which makes their favorite food supply, now that the woods have ceased producing. The winter winds blowing over the great expanses keep the snow from covering the moss too deep for the animals to get at it by pawing, a condition which is greatly helped by the fact that the first snow freezes into ice when it falls on the wet bog, making a glassy surface which prevents much drifting. They spend the winter wandering about looking for thin places to feed in, with an occasional meal of the black moss on the spruces when some fierce storm drives them to take shelter in the woods. The snow finally melts away, and the trees begin to leaf out again with the spring. One beast after another leaves the herd, goes back to some familiar haunt in the woodland and begins another cycle in its existence.

Of the caribou we saw on the first day,

eleven out of the twelve were does and fawns, not over three together. The one stag was a small one, by himself. All of them were feeding by the edge of the woods.

On September 3 we traveled most of the day through wooded country on the way to some new barrens, and started several does with fawns in the thick of it. When we finally reached the barrens, a single doe at the edge of the woods was the only sign of caribou for miles.

The next day nine were seen in the same

were counted that day. During the rest of our stay we saw an average of twenty-five caribou every day we hunted, with a good proportion of old stags among them. On September 11 we counted over fifty. From seeing no old stags at the beginning, it became so that we were able to pick our game. It is certain that the old stags are the last to leave the woods.

Our hunting ground was a long wide valley between two heavily wooded ridges, stretching away westward into the interior, and our camp was at the eastern end of it.

Our Camp in the Southern Hunting Grounds.

locality—does, fawns and one spike horn. On the fifth the first old stag was shot in a strip of woods, still in velvet, and this one and another with him were the only large stags of the twenty-seven caribou that were seen.

During the morning of the sixth we saw the first real herd, well out on the barren, a company of sixteen, does and fawns and two old stags, and in the afternoon came upon a trio of old stags traveling together. These three were out of velvet, as were all the stags we saw afterward. The does stay in velvet much longer. Thirty-three

Nearly every day caribou would be seen coming from the wooded country to the eastward, up through the valley. None came by from the opposite direction. One would have said from the conditions in our vicinity that there was a general migration of the animals from east to west, but on one trip a dozen miles or so to the westward we found the general line of travel to be toward the east. The fact was that our valley was the assembling ground for the caribou from the woodlands on all sides of us. Our guide had killed them there in former years in every month from October to April. We could see another great valley far in the distance beyond our northern ridge, where he had done the same thing. That was another assembling ground for the animals which spent the summer in the woods which surrounded it. One of our men said that he had recently gone ashore from a fishing vessel to a barren near the Straits of Belle Isle, and had found it strewn with innumerable caribou horns. As they do not shed their horns much before December, there must have been caribou at that north-

road through the Gafftopsail region as well. These barrens are the local place of assembly for the animals which do not have other barrens nearer their summer quarters. Those approaching from the south and east make no great showing, as they come in from a great circumference and have the whole wide country in which to travel. Those coming from the north follow along the northern slope of the mountains and converge through these valleys into this narrow space running due north and south between the lakes and

A Newfoundland Lake—Bordered by Wooded Caribou Country.

ern part of the island well into the winter. The so-called migrations amount to nothing more than the assembling of the caribou from all directions on the barren grounds which may be nearest their summer quarters, where they can find an ample food supply, and their subsequent dispersion to the woods in the spring.

The conditions at Howley are entirely consistent with this conclusion. The country lying north of Red Indian Lake, east of Grand Lake, and south of the railroad, is a great expanse of moss-covered barrens, extending north of the rail-

river and the bay, which act as natural barriers. If they wander to the east, the bay turns them back. If they strike the lakes or river, they follow along their shores instead of swimming them, as their course has the same direction as their own. Hemmed in, they assemble more rapidly.

There are half a dozen water-ways accessible from the railroad in the eastern part of the island which lead into country which is practically untouched. The hunting would be honest and sportman by stalking instead of mere killing in the water and on the runways.

20.
SHOOTING GROUSE IN MIDDLE NORTHWEST (1903)

"With an upward, noble rush the grouse leaped."

Drawing by Lynn Bogue Hunt.

OUTING

OCTOBER, 1903

SHOOTING GROUSE IN MIDDLE NORTHWEST

By H. S. CANFIELD

THE day was in late October and a veil of clouds was drawn across the sky, so the light was gray and good. The man knew that the bird lay concealed in the half acre of space in the heart of the woods. This space was covered with the short weed which bears the black seeds known as "beggar lice." He had flushed the bird a quarter of a mile away, and had missed because a tangle of branches interfered. Now he was sure that the quarry was his, for in the little space there were no trees to mar the aim, save that in its center a squat balsam stood fifteen feet high and eight feet through.

The man advanced slowly to the edge of the opening. He was eager, yet cool. The fore-end of his double-barrel was in his left hand, the gun nearly horizontal, the butt within six inches of his shoulder, and the safety slide upon his hammerless had been pressed forward, so that all was in readiness. As he emerged from the growth of timber which fringed the half acre, and paused for a moment, he had almost the trap position, looking keenly out over the brown weeds, as if he expected to hear the question, "Ready?" The thought even came to him that this was an unknown trap with an unknown angle, but a known target, and he intended to smash that target before its tumultuous wings bore it ten yards.

Moving slowly, placing one foot before the other softly, he advanced, every sense upon the alert. He marked the *rat-tatting* of a sapsucker upon a dead pine, and a red squirrel sprung his rattle in an irritating way. Five steps onward and the stillness was unbroken; ten, fifteen, twenty, and the squirrel's chatter ceased; twenty-five!

With an upward noble rush and a thunder of beating pinions, the grouse leaped. One second, and the right barrel spoke, the charge passing three feet under; a half-second, and the left barrel cracked. From the balsam floated gently down half a hatful of green plumes; the grouse was away.

The man stared blankly, then laughed. He was an old hand, and could pay tribute to the wiliness of his foeman, even in defeat. Belly to the ground, tail depressed, head humped upon back, from its unknowable hiding-place the grouse had watched him. Five brown weeds had bent over it, blending with its plumage; dead leaves lay along its sides, also blending. Only the developed negative of a photograph would have shown it crouching there. As the man advanced, its still round black eye had estimated his distance; it had estimated also the surroundings, the width of the open plot, the height and thickness of the balsam in

"A mass of pines, birches and spruces . . . the home of the ruffed grouse."

front. Once the bird had calculated that the balsam was too far away for its purposes, and it had moved forward quickly and stealthily for ten feet, without stirring a leaf or weed stem. It had flushed when the man was within five yards, had sprung upward with all of its strength, and had whirled behind the balsam like a dun-colored flash. That was all—an old trick of the grouse, but one that will prove effective eight times out of ten.

The man blamed himself, which was right. He had nothing to say about the choke being worn out of his gun, or the smokeless powder being old and therefore slow, or the shell being improperly loaded. Instead, he said that he saw the weedy space in which the bird had taken refuge, and he saw the balsam in the middle, and he should have entered the clearing from the other side and gone straight to the balsam, forcing the grouse to fly in another direction and give him a straight shot. That, however, was the hindsight which is always so much better than the foresight; so he tramped on, confident that before sundown there would be other birds, some of which would find their way into the wide pockets of his shooting coat.

The woods of the Northwest stretch for many miles east and west below Lake Superior, a vast mass of pines, hemlocks, balsams, firs, maples, birches, and spruces, and that is the home of the ruffed grouse. Down the still, solemn forest aisles it wanders, and as every four-footed neighbor, except the deer and rabbit is its enemy, it has learned through countless generations to take care of itself. Its caution has developed; its instinct amounts almost to reason; and at every season, save when the snow lies white on ground and tree, its protective coloration is a miracle. Next to the wild turkey, it is the noblest of our feathered game. Its strength of wing is superb, and its speed is greater than that of any other member of the gallinaceous family. Because of its habitat it has acquired a faculty of steering not short of the marvelous. In this respect it is not approached by any flyer, except, perhaps, the squealer duck of the South, itself a woods dweller. Flushed close at hand and badly frightened, the grouse will shoot away between trunks and through branches thick enough almost to obscure vision, with tilt of either wing darting to left or right, raising or lowering its flight and maintaining a speed of a hundred miles an hour, without grazing a feather. There is no instance of this bird injuring itself by flying against limbs or boles, save when struck in the head and blinded, or otherwise hurt desperately.

It has a hundred tricks of defense. It will sometimes lie still until the hunter is within a yard of it, then soar straight upward in his front, towering like a woodcock; again, it will rise forty yards away, and the sound of its wings is his only notice of its presence. It will cower upon a branch under which he passes, and his cap will not be more than a foot below it as he goes; and though it has seen him approaching, it will remain quiescent in frightful fear until his back is turned. It will flush then, and when he has slewed himself hurriedly around he will catch only a glimpse of a brown, broad wing far away. Wounded and falling in the open, it will be found—if it is found at all—with the telltale speckles of its breast against the trunk of some brown tree against which its feathers are indistinguishable, and the black ruff about the neck of the male will be laid against the darkest part of the bark. Often it will double like a fox; often, as man draws near, it will spring noiselessly into some spruce and hide until he passes, dropping then to ground and continuing its feeding; often, too, it will decline to take wing, though unhurt, and will run fast for a half mile—so fast that the most expert woodsman will be unable to keep pace with it. This it will do only on leafy ground, and never when snow would betray its tracks.

The man who pursues the ruffed grouse in his native fastness needs endurance, patience, a knowledge of woodcraft, and skill with his weapon. He will travel uninhabited territory, and must know how to find his way out of it with or without a compass. He will force his way through hazel brush as high as his head, and higher; he will climb over logs four feet through at the butt, and many of them; he will skirt the ends or edges of tamarack swamps; he will find himself in hollows so deep and dark that even at midday the sunlight filters through dimly; he will breast steep hills carpeted in leaves as smooth under foot almost as ice; he will work along the sides of ridges, where one foot will be half a yard below the other; he must be prepared to shoot in front, to left, or right, or behind him, and he will find that fifteen out of twenty shots are snapshots purely, with no time left him in which to calculate bird-speed, or distance, or how much to hold ahead, or anything else. If he bags two out of six shots, in and out, through the day, he will have cause at nightfall to take his right hand in his left and shake with himself as a grouse man worth talking to.

It is not a bad thing to be with an expert field shot when he is introduced to grouse in a grouse country. He will be used to the snipe zigzagging over open marshes, to the quail flying as straight as a string above level fields; even to the erratic, but not swift, woodcock in sunny thickets, or cornfields, or swamps, or canebrakes. Perhaps he will rather fancy himself as a handler of the shotgun, and he will be free about the camp fire to talk of fifteen straight quail bagged in southern Illinois, or eight woodcock out of ten in western New York. He will have the same gun and, if the season be early, he will have No. 8 shot chilled in front of pink-edged wads which cover the quickest powder— and he will not understand how a bird as big as a grouse can get up and get away from two barrels that he knows are held squarely on him. The expert field shot, experienced in other fields, who comes to camp after his first day in the woods, is not the man who left it in the morning. He is less chipper, and more silent. He eats his supper voraciously, throws out occasional remarks of an interjectory or exclamatory character, goes to bed soon and tosses uneasily in his sleep.

There are few cardinal rules to be observed in grouse shooting, but they are cardinal:

Hunt along the sides of hills; move softly; keep eyes and ears open; listen for drummers; explore thoroughly each opening which grows grass seeds or beggar lice; walk around each spruce tree, for the bird is fond of spruce berries; when the bird flushes pitch up the gun, keep both eyes open, and look only at the grouse, paying no attention to the barrels. That is snap-shooting, and it is snap-shooting only which counts. Eight grouse out of nine in the North woods are killed within twenty yards, and they will go the first twenty yards in less than a second. Perhaps the best possible definition of snap-shooting has been given by old George Hudson, a Mississippi River guide: "Shootin' a shotgun ain't nothin' but pointin' nohow." That definition is peculiarly applicable to grouse shooting. Point the shotgun as you would point a finger, and let go. So will you bag an occasional bird. Nobody ever yet killed anything by keeping the load in the gun.

Of course a man will find more birds with a good dog than without one, yet either pointer or setter is worse than useless in the North woods. They are wide-ranging animals; they will be out of sight nine-tenths of the time; they come to a stand, and stay on it; their owner knows nothing about it; when the covey flushes he may hear the burr of the wings, but that is all; the dog then goes on and finds another covey, and the same thing happens. With a pointer or setter of the best, a man will crowd so much exasperation into a day that he will want no more of it.

The only dog is the cocker spaniel. That animal will stay within reasonable distance, will hunt industriously, and will find birds. It will give tongue when the birds are close and, if the man is near enough to shoot, he may get in both barrels. In any event the spaniel will flush the covey, and then follow it. If it be well trained, and it soon trains itself from experience, it will mark the trees in which members of the covey alight, will hurry to them and bark furiously, much as if it were a "coon dog," and had a coon treed. Some of the best spaniels are practically infallible in thus marking trees. If the shooter is at a distance when the covey is found he will be drawn to its roosting birds by the dog's voice. He will then have his choice of very difficult shooting, or plain murder.

So long as the dog leaps about and barks the grouse will not heed the man. They will sit stiffly, looking down at the animal. The man may, if he chooses, pick off bird after bird, beginning with the one on the lowest branch so that the noise of the bodies falling through the limbs will not disturb the others. They will stay to be shot under these conditions—and it may be said here that a great majority of grouse killed in the North woods are killed

"Grouse are fond of the narrow roads and trails through the woods."

in this way, either by market-hunters or by alleged sportsmen. If the man be genuine, however, he will flush the birds from the tree and he will then have shots hard enough to suit anybody.

The grouse from its altitude of forty to fifty feet, springs outward and sails away at enormous speed, going commonly on a down-slant, and it will, if it can, place the tree-top immediately between itself and the shooter. All men who have shot at quail driven from a tree know how difficult this shot is, and the only way to make it is to have the bird showing cleanly above the barrels of the gun, with the muzzle leading it by a good foot and dropping steadily when the trigger is pulled. That is the receipt if the grouse goes outward and straightaway. Often, however, it will half-circle, and thunder among other tree-tops, and then the man must do the best he can and score another miss. Consolation is found in the fact that there is more pleasure in an occasional good shot of this character than in butchering a wagon-load of birds squatting in the branches and staring down at a dog. Between slaying them in this way and knocking down chickens in a farmer's barnyard, there is no difference at all. One shot is as easy as the other, and is as sportsmanlike.

For some reason grouse are fond of the narrow roads and trails through the woods, and will be found in greater numbers along them than elsewhere. They do not go to the roads only to dust themselves, as they frequent them whether they are wet or dry. Possibly they have some idea that along a road they can see approaching danger more clearly. It is not bad sport to take a single horse and buggy and drive slowly, looking keenly into the underbrush and firing at the birds as they get up. They always sail away into the woods as fast as they can go, and make difficult shooting for a man sitting down, whether the horse stop or not. Generally they will permit the buggy to come much nearer than a man on foot, often flushing within two yards of the wheels, and if the shooter have a good driver he need pay attention to the birds and to nothing else. They are plentiful, too, by running streams to which they resort to drink. Along the north and south forks of the Flambeau River, in Wisconsin, is great grouse coun-

try. Taking a canoe or double-prowed skiff, with a guide to pole it, a man may go for a dozen of miles down one of these streams, and on his way will see many grouse trotting down the bank to sip, or else resting quietly within two feet of the water, dozing. Sometimes they crouch in this fashion on little sand-bars, and may be the boat, noiselessly floating, will get close to them before they rise. In this case the shooting is exceptionally fair and fine, as the river is sixty yards wide and the grouse must cover at least thirty yards of open water before it finds shelter.

Late in the season, when six inches of snow is on the ground and the evergreen forest stands half dark and half white, one may have some sport with the grouse, a rifle of .22–caliber being the weapon. They are stalked then much as if they were deer, the hunter moving cautiously in rubber shoes, which come half way to his knee, with two pairs of heavy woolen stockings between him and the rubber. He may depend upon it that distinct as are the brown feathers on the snow, the bird will see him long before he sees it, and he will hear it rise. If he catches a glimpse of it in flight he will mark its line and follow on, inspecting the spruce trees. He must find his bird at thirty yards away, as it will probably flush again when he comes closer, and must make his shot at that distance. His target will be the head, and the head of a ruffed grouse at thirty yards is not easy to hit.

Near sunset the birds flock into the iron-wood trees, snipping off the buds. These trees grow generally in gulches or ravines, and a man making his way down a ravine will hear the clicking of their bills of a still winter evening a hundred yards away. Hiding himself as much as possible he will do his best to get within shooting distance of the tree. If he succeeds, he may use up a dozen shells, as the sharp spat of the little smokeless powder charges does not disturb them greatly. As it cracks, each bird, save the dead one, will rise to its full height on the branches, look sharply around, then resume feeding. There are men who have bagged a half-dozen grouse from a single tree in this way. When all is said, however, it is scarcely sport.

The shotgun, in the woods' tangle, with the swift and noble flyer soaring away, is the thing.

21.
SPORT ALONG THE
NORTHWESTERN
BORDER
(1890)

SPORT ALONG THE NORTHWESTERN BORDER.

BY A. B. GUPTILL.

THERE are those, doubtless, to whom the "drumming" of the partridge and the rhythmic cry of the wild goose, if possessing anything of melody, yet fail to suggest even a passing thought of possible sport. As for me, from the day when I was first granted the boon of carrying a game bag and playing "retriever" for a (sometimes) tolerably indulgent *pater familias*, the roar of whose old muzzle-loading fowling piece used to awake the echoes of Maine's rock-bound shores, where the festive and toothsome sand-piper and the George's Bank "fog mull" seemed to delight in passing the sultry months of summer, I longed for the time to hasten when I should be permitted to exchange a threadbare "roundabout" for the yellow-hued and fascinating shooting jacket and gratify to the full an innate love for hunting.

A quarter of a century has been added to the record of time since then, and the memories of coast shooting grow more and more dim as the years flit by. Instead of sailing for coots, "old squaws" and "whistlers" in Quoddy Bay, or essaying to decoy the wary black duck in the Scarborough marshes as of yore, I now plan to spend a few days, with the coming of Jack Frost and the red and gold of each recurring October, among North Dakota's lakes and wheat fields in pursuit of the garrulous "honker" and his traveling companions, the redhead, canvasback and lordly mallard, which the first "norther" sends hustling down from the lakes and inland seas of the far North.

Probably no part of the American continent offers a finer or more varied field to the sportsman than the vast northern belt of forest, lake, prairie and mountain stretching westward from Lake Superior to Puget Sound.

The extensive forests of Minnesota give friendly shelter to the black bear, the deer, moose and caribou. Several of the streams which flow into Superior are well stocked with trout, and its smaller lakes fairly teem with bass, pickerel, pike and muskallonge.

The broad wheat fields of North Dakota are the Mecca of the "wing shot" from the time that prairie chickens "ripen" until the quack of the last mallard and the honk of the last goose are drowned in the gusts of north wind which about the middle of November waft the grain-fattened gourmands southward to the "slews" of Texas, the rice fields of Georgia and the Carolinas, and the celery beds of the Chesapeake.

Then there are the famed *mauvaise terre*, or "Bad Lands," of Western Dakota and Eastern Montana, where the "rifle shot" may enjoy stalking the antelope, deer and big-horn (mountain sheep), with now and then a "brush" with a bear or mountain lion (cougar) to lend just a seasoning of hazard to his sport; while farther westward among the mountain fastnesses of the Rockies and Cascades the stately elk, the grizzly bear, the caribou, and the goat of milky whiteness challenge the nerve, skill and endurance of even the keenest sportsman. Almost numberless are the mountain streams that teem with trout, and the salmon trolling of the Columbia River and waters of Puget Sound is one, at least, of the piscatorial delights which New England lakes and Canadian rivers cannot rival.

In the fall of 188– I accepted an invitation to join a party of eight gentlemen — members of an Eastern rod-and-gun club—upon a hunting and fishing tour of the region traversed by the Northern Pacific, a railroad which penetrates some of the finest "game country" to be found anywhere in the West. This "outing" of six weeks proved so delightful, so spiced with exciting sport both with rod and gun, so varied in scenery, and, above all, so restful from the cares of business and so health renewing, that I doubt if its pleasant memories will ever be effaced from the mind of any member of the party, though another deer may never spring from cover before his rifle nor another trout rise to his deceptive fly.

Through the courtesy of Charles S. Fee, the general passenger agent of the North-

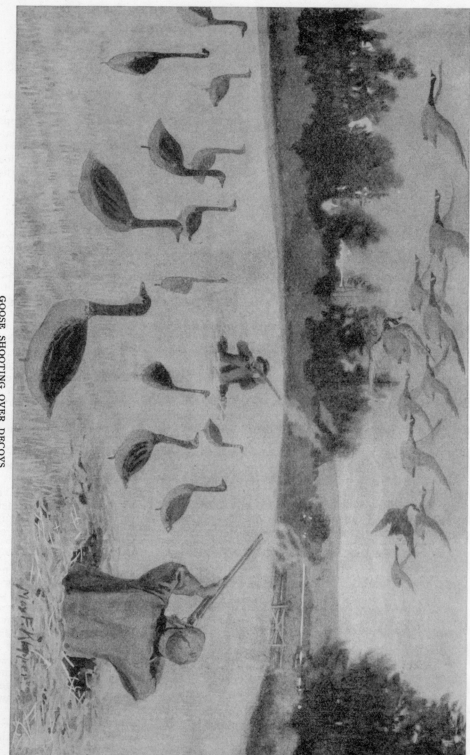

GOOSE SHOOTING OVER DECOYS.

THE FUSILLADE.

ern Pacific, an excursion car, equipped with cook and porter and provisioned for the entire trip, was furnished for the party's use. Time was when wheeled palaces of this sort, combining in luxurious comfort observation, hotel and sleeping accommodations, were placed at the disposal of high dignitaries of church and state only ; but in this generation of progressive ideas no arrangements calculated to conduce to greater comfort, and therefore pleasure, in connection with trips of this kind, are regarded as too elegant by Northwestern railroads, particularly as ladies often gladly lend their presence in making up parties of tourist anglers—aye, even gunners.

The long train which rolled out of the Union Depot in St. Paul on the afternoon of our departure bore upward of forty local Nimrods, one and all bound for the grain fields of Western Minnesota and Dakota

in quest of the gamesome prairie chicken, and an entire baggage car was given over to the comfort of as distinguished a company of pointers and setters as ever graced a bench show. The pages of one number of OUTING would be far too few for recording the thousand and one minor, but none the less pleasant, incidents of our jaunt — the eloquent discussions respecting the merits and demerits of rods and guns, the mirth-provoking reminiscences of previous hunting and fishing trips, the merry banter that passed from lip to lip, the contests at whist, and, when all else failed to amuse, the plantation melodies of Mistah Johnsing and his efficient coadjutor who presided in the kitchen.

At Detroit, Minn., 230 miles northwest from St. Paul, our car was side tracked to afford opportunity for fishing, and three days of this sport sufficed to stock our ice box with some two hundred pounds of pike, pickerel and black bass.

Lake Detroit, the largest of the several small lakes which dot the western confines of what is properly termed "The Lake Park Region of Minnesota," is a pretty little sheet of limpid, blue water, fringed with timber, its sandy shores here and there graced by tidy cottages of summer visitors, who find pleasure in boating, bathing and fishing and in driving about its shady avenues. From October 1, when flight ducks begin to arrive, until November 10 (often later) excellent pass shooting may be had in this vicinity, a fact of which we resolved to take advantage upon our return from the coast.

Satisfied for the time with fishing, an seemed like a golden sea of garnered sheaves. September 5 found us at Leonard, Dak., a station on the Southwestern branch of the Northern Pacific, twenty-eight miles from Fargo, where teams

Engraved by H. Pflaum.

THE TROPHY.

early morning ride of forty-seven miles through a region of rolling prairie brought us to the western boundary of Minnesota, the world-famous Red River of the North and its no less celebrated valley, whose broad and level miles of fenceless farms with drivers were secured and our initial "chicken shoot" was inaugurated, thirty-eight grouse and a brace of teal being the net result of the day's sport. The pleasures of the next four days were but successive chapters of a continued story,

"HOW OUR DECOYS BROUGHT THE DUCKS."

Sheldon, Verona and one or two points in the James River Valley being visited, the smallest bag secured for any one day being twenty-seven and the largest fifty-six birds.

Our traveling shooting box reached the main line again at Jamestown, Dak., on the evening of the 9th, and early next morning was attached to the Pacific Express, and we were given a 300-mile daylight ride over billowy prairie; across the broad Missouri, up the winding valleys of the Heart, the Sweet Briar and the Curlew; across the Little Missouri; on past "Sentinel Butte" (būte), whose flat summit still shows traces of rifle pits and breastworks hastily constructed by the lamented Custer and his Seventh Cavalry troopers when surrounded and besieged by the Sioux in the early '70's; through the weirdly grotesque "Bad Lands," reaching the historic Yellowstone Valley at Glendive just as the September sun was slowly sinking beyond the gilded battlements of "Iron Butte," seemingly reluctant to relinquish even a hemisphere to the sombre shadows of night.

Glendive is an admirable outfitting point for parties seeking deer, mountain sheep and antelope. Some sixty miles to the north lies the Missouri Valley, the country between being for the most part rough, rolling and treeless, characteristics which render it peculiarly adapted to the habits and preferences of the antelope;

while the O'Fallon, Cabin, Cedar, Glendive and other creeks, which wind about among the rugged buttes that flank the wide valley on the south, are all readily accessible, and rank among Montana's best resorts for mule ("black tail") and Virginia deer, as well as big-horn. Deer of this locality are, comparatively speaking, "easy game," even to the amateur sportsman; but he who would win the prize of massive horns proudly borne by the mountain ram must gird his loins for climbing "greasewood-" clad hillsides and craggy buttes and patiently bide his time.

This was one of the several favored and favorite game regions which our party had early settled upon visiting, but as the days were still warm, our larder in no serious need of replenishing with game, and the anticipated cooler weather of our homeward journey would be more favorable in every way for this kind of sport, it was decided that we should make a hasty tour of Yellowstone Park, view the heralded wonders of its hot springs and geysers, gaze upon the reputed charms of its lakes, falls, cañons and cascades, test the vaunted gamesomeness and delicacy of its mountain trout, and then proceed westward for a week's hunt upon the heavily-timbered slopes and among the barren, snow-capped peaks of the Bitter Root Range of the Rocky Mountains.

Pursuant to this plan of procedure, our westward journey was continued until next morning, when we reached Livingston, Mon., at the head of the main valley of the Yellowstone — midway between Lake Superior and the Pacific. Here our car was attached to the Park branch train and we were rapidly whirled southward up the narrowing river; through pretty "Paradise Valley" nestling in the shadow of the Snow Mountains; and rocky "Yankee Jim Cañon," to Cinnabar, terminus of the branch road, fifty-one miles from Livingston.

At this point we were transferred, along with forty-eight other passengers Parkward bound, to the waiting coaches of the Park Transportation Company and conveyed to Mammoth Springs, eight miles distant, reaching the hotel at the springs shortly after 12. A refreshing mineral-water bath, followed by a bountiful luncheon, served to put us in excellent humor for a stroll about the world-renowned springs in the vicinity, and after a few hours spent in sight seeing, rods

"A WHACKER!"

and flies were brought out, and the shady pools and dancing rapids of the neighboring Gardiner River pretty generally explored with gratifying success, forty-seven trout being caught, many of which would average more than a pound in weight. This is said to be one of the best trout streams of the "reservation," and we certainly felt no inclination to doubt the assertion.

We were astir bright and early next morning, and 7 o'clock found us climbing the long hill leading to "Golden Gate," on our way to Norris and the "geyser basins" of Firehole River. Space forbids even a bird's-eye sketch of the many grand and marvelous features of this almost fairyland, and when at 6 P. M. of the fifth day out our conveyance again rolled up to the wide veranda of Mammoth Hotel scepticism as to the proclaimed attractions of this vast pleasuring ground had given place to conviction that half the truth had not been told.

Next day we returned to Cinnabar and Livingston, and, continuing westward to Missoula, took there the Missoula and Bitter Root Valley branch railroad to Grantsdale, fifty miles south, where saddle horses, pack outfit and guides were employed; and September 18 found the party encamped a half-day's ride from the railroad upon the banks of one of the several charming little mountain streams which serve to swell the volume of Bitter Root River.

There are many fine game regions both in the main chain and divergent spurs of the Rocky Mountains, fairly easy of access from either the main line or branches of the Northern Pacific, and it is often a matter of no little perplexity to decide just where to go for the most satisfactory results. Generally speaking the time at one's disposal, considered in connection with the character of the game sought, materially assists in determining this important question. If grizzly bears are the game most desired and time be unlimited a better region than the Big-Horn Mountains of Northern Wyoming—one hundred miles up the Rosebud River from Forsyth—would be difficult to find, unless it be, possibly, the Wind River range farther to the southwest.

These mountains undoubtedly afford the best as well as the most dangerously exciting bear hunting to be found in the world; and elks, deer and mountain sheep are also plentiful.

For caribou, the Kootenai region of Northern Idaho probably excels any other mountain district; and it may be readily reached from either Hope or Sand Point stations; while moose are most abundant in the "basin" drained by the Big Hole River, sixty miles southeast of Grantsdale. Both caribou and moose still exist also, and in fair numbers, among the pine barrens and *muskeags* of Northern Minnesota.

Antelope may almost be said to be indigenous to the plains and foothills east of the Rockies, while sheep and goats are to be found in nearly every range of mountains from Livingston to the Pacific.

Splendid sport may be had, too, both in the way of hunting and fishing, in the country immediately to the north of Flathead Lake and the Indian reservation of the same name, in Northwestern Montana, a region which is reached from the railway station called Horse Plains, at which point Indian guides and bronchos for riding and "packing" may be obtained.

Three things combined in determining us to go to Grantsdale in preference to some of the other equally good and, in some instances, undoubtedly better game districts of which we were fully advised, viz.:

Our limited time, the proximity of the Bitter Root country to our base line, and the variety of game, as well as trout fishing, which it afforded. We had neither the time nor the inclination to make bear hunting anything more than a possible incident to other sport; in fact, if the truth were known, I doubt very much if any member of the party felt that he had suffered the loss of any bears the recovery of which might entail an exhaustive search.

Speaking for myself, though I have for several years enjoyed a more or less diverse and extensive acquaintance with the larger game animals of the United States and have ever held the .50 calibre Express bullet in high esteem as a deterrent and sedative potion when promptly backed by about 110 grains of good rifle powder, yet I fail to recall any animal among the varied fauna of North America which I wouldn't rather run afoul of in a region destitute of good-sized trees with limbs close enough to the ground to render expeditious climbing a matter requiring no special display of dexterity, than to be suddenly and unexpectedly placed in jux-

"UNBIDDEN GUESTS."

taposition to the often ferocious, always pugnacious Rocky Mountain grizzly.

"Under such circumstances," say our scientific theorists, who doubtless occasionally find a robust imagination a great help in the preparation of essays on hunting, and who often exhibit surprising "nerve" with the pen, "a good weapon, a quick eye, a tolerably accurate knowledge of vital and vulnerable parts, and a steady nerve are all that are required to insure the triumph of mind over matter in this dangerous pastime."

Now, as a matter of practice, it not infrequently occurs that, owing to the glancing of even a well-aimed bullet, or the wedging of a cartridge at the critical moment, a veteran, even, finds himself in the catch-as-catch-can embrace of one of these ponderous brutes ; and in such case, if succor be not at hand, the chance of future usefulness, nay, even of life, on the hunter's part may be measured with tolerable accuracy by the biblical standard of the rich man and the camel.

But, descending from the elevated plane of science and exhilarating atmosphere of theory to resume my narrative, our week's camp out in the Bitter Root range proved delightful and sufficiently productive of results, both in the way of

game and exciting sport, to satisfy all. Four large elks, three bears (two cinnamon and a "silver tip"), three fine goats, one mountain lion and two deer were secured, besides upward of two hundred pounds of large, handsome trout, not counting the dozen or more which were appropriated by a couple of bold, bad bears—and thereby hangs a brief tale.

One showery morning, while we were lingering about the camp fire hoping that the weather would soon clear, two of the party, Messrs. H—— and L——, thinking it a fine time to try the trout in the impetuous little stream upon which we were encamped, donned "waders" and rain coats and sallied forth rod in hand, leaving rifles behind. An hour's excellent sport had taken the pair perhaps a third of a mile down stream, when L——'s shrill voice, calling loudly for help, brought even the "packers" to their feet, and, catching up rifles, everybody was soon hurrying to the assistance of the anglers. Scarce half the distance had been covered when H—— hove in sight heading campward, his rod and creel cast aside and coat tails indicating great haste.

From him it was learned that two bears had suddenly come out of the dense tim-

THE FALLEN MONARCH.

"WHAT'S THAT?"

directed bullet. The capture of the cougar was likewise a matter of accident largely, he being discovered in a sunny nook among the rocks, high up the mountain side above timber line, by two of the party engaged in hunting goats.

Upon our return to Missoula arrangements were made to have such of the game mounted as was desired, and the journey coastward again resumed. The two succeeding days were passed amid new and interesting scenery, that of the Cascade Mountains being especially grand, while the grain fields, sheep ranches and well-tilled fruit and hop farms along the way attracted considerable notice and furnished not a little food for thought and discussion.

At Tacoma, terminus of the Northern Pacific and point of departure for Alaska tourists, the *City of Kingston*, one of the new steamers of the Puget Sound and Alaska Steamship Company, was taken for a short tour of Puget Sound points, and salmon fishing indulged in until the market fishermen of the Sound began to regard us with feelings of envy. Unlike their Eastern cousins, salmon of Pacific waters rarely rise to even the most skill-

ber close by L——, who was forced to drop his rod and seek safety in a tree top ; while he, being thirty rods or more farther up stream, promptly started for camp to—obtain aid. Guided by L——'s shouts, the now thoroughly excited party soon appeared upon the scene, to find a cadaverous - looking creature, with a shaggy, brown coat, quarreling with a half - grown cub over the mutilated remains of L——'s creel, which in the earlier stages of the proceedings had yielded its contents to gratify the epicurean taste of the freebooters ; the doughty fisherman meanwhile sitting astride a spruce limb, dividing his time between hallooing for help and wishing that his Winchester were within reach of his nervous fingers.

A couple of shots sufficed to quiet the cub's snarling, but the mother made a game fight, charging furiously at her assailants in spite of intimidating numbers, and receiving nine bullets before being brought to grass. This is how we came to bag two cinnamon bears. The "silver tip" was surprised at a banquet of "service berries" and killed by a single well-

"THERE THEY ARE!"

fully-wielded fly ; while, curiously enough, the glitter of a trolling spoon is almost certain to provoke a "strike," and once hooked, tackle, skill and patience are put to the test in landing these great silver-sided aristocrats of the finny tribes that often exceed twenty pounds in weight.

Delighted with our brief visit to the coast, and sincerely regretting that other engagements precluded the possibility of a more intimate acquaintance with the game of the Cascades than the display windows of the taxidermists afforded, our homeward journey was begun September 29, a stop being made at Eagle Gorge, a station fifty-two miles east from Tacoma, for a day's fly fishing in Green River, one of the excellent trout streams of the Pacific Slope.

Noon of October 2 found us again at Glendive with guide, wagons and camp plunder in readiness for an immediate start, and nightfall saw us snugly encamped upon the headwaters of Glendive Creek. A more charming spot for camping, or a region better adapted by nature for a deer park and mountain-sheep range, it would be difficult to imagine. A narrow vale, carpeted with nutritious buffalo

THE COUGAR WE CAPTURED. (PAGE 381.)

grass, watered by a shallow stream fringed with tall cottonwoods and thickets of willow, and flanked by picturesque buttes, here and there studded with fragrant groves of red cedar, and gullied by deep dry ravines or "draws" filled for the most part with a thick scrubby growth of black ash and bulberry bushes, combined to make up its landscape features ; while, as if to add to our entertainment, we had the vesper solo of an occasional coyote to accompany us to the Land of Nod, and the matin chatter of garrulous magpies to welcome our return.

If I ever spent a week of more unalloyed pleasure I certainly have no recollection of it. As for game, seven mule deer, four Virginia deer, two antelopes and three magnificent specimens of the big - horn family, besides some twenty

grouse and sage hens, were to us satisfactory testimonials as to the repute of the "Bad Lands" as a game region and of our own marksmanship. Nearly every ravine explored for miles around harbored one or more deer, and little difficulty was found in approaching within easy rifle shot, in most cases within buckshot range ; but antelopes and mountain sheep proved extremely wary, and though several small bands of both were seen, only by dint of the most patient stalking and the exercise of strategy were we able to get within even long-rifle range, except upon one single occasion.

This exception is connected with an amusing incident, which I cannot forbear relating, even at the risk of arousing the ire of the genial gentlemen who figured as companions in ill luck, and who were really pretty fair shots as well as anglers.

On the morning preceding the breaking up of camp a pair of mules and lumber wagon were sent across the rolling "divide" into a neighboring creek bottom, some four or five miles distant, to bring in a couple of deer which had been killed, dressed and "flagged*" by Doctor C—— and Mr. S—— the day before. It was, of course, necessary for one of the gentlemen to accompany the driver in order to point out the precise locality of the venison, and Mr. S—— cheerfully volunteered to perform that duty, leaving his friend to pack up his pill bags and other impedimenta preparatory to a return to the haunts of civilization. As the morning was calm and a cloudless sky augured an unusually pleasant day, two of the younger members of the party, Messrs. Adams and Natwick, who thoroughly enjoyed climbing buttes and were the proud possessors of established reputations for general frolicsomeness, decided

---

* The tying of a handkerchief or bit of cloth to the antlers of a slain deer to prevent molestation by coyotes, an efficient stratagem practiced by hunters upon the "plains" where trees are not at hand on which to hang venison.

to accompany Mr. S—— and sallied forth, rifles in hand and belts bristling with cartridges.

The racket made by the great lumbering wagon precluded the possibility of hunting on the way; but it had been planned that luncheon in the adjacent valley should be followed by a short foray among its buttes and ravines, and there was no telling with what sort of an adventure the trio might meet.

Slowly they picked their way over the rough country, now climbing a steep hillside, now following the sinuous course of a narrow " hog back," or descending the dry bed of a "washout," until the wagon halted at last upon the table-like summit of a high butte at whose base lay the valley sought.

How to get the team down there was the problem which the three hunters thought to solve, as they dismounted and strode forward to the brow of the hill; but an almost perpendicular bluff met their searching gaze. Mr. S—— was sure that the doctor and he had climbed this same butte the day before and at a point sufficiently sloping to afford fairly easy passage for wagons. Leaving the driver to await a signal should their quest prove successful, the three skirted along the edge of the bluff, "looking for the sign board," as Adams jokingly remarked, in speaking of the incident, "which should point the way to S——'s turnpike," when suddenly and simultaneously three pairs of eyes were greeted by a sight that sent the hot blood tingling through the veins and brought weapons into play in short order.

Standing upon a narrow, jutting point immediately below the hunters and less than a hundred feet distant, were a bouncing big mountain ram with massive curling horns, three ewes and as many half-grown lambs, all unconscious of danger. Bangety—bang—bang—bang! rang out the repeating rifles, and bangety—bang—bang! echoed the surrounding hills. The startled quarry, unable to determine at the moment whence came the sounds or the bullets which whistled just over their heads, stood like statues, though with every sense alert and every muscle ready for prompt action. It was a "surprise party" all around; and when at length the bewildered sheep, having located the hunters, had bounded (unscathed) out of sight, three very badly "rattled" marksmen (?) rested from their rifle practice and silently read the unutterable disgust betrayed by one another's countenances.

October 10, 11 and 12 were occupied in the delightful pastime of wild goose and sandhill crane shooting about Dawson, Dak., a very fine place for this kind of sport, the abundance of geese, both "Canadas" and Arctic or "snow geese," locally but incorrectly termed "brant," which frequent the lakes and wheat fields of this locality being simply phenomenal. A morning or evening's shoot from decoy-surrounded "pit blinds" in this vicinity is an experience to be remembered for a lifetime, and in our case proved an excellent "overture" to the three-days' royal duck shooting in the "Park Region" of Minnesota which practically terminated our outing.

22.
BEAR HUNTING
IN BRITISH COLUMBIA
(1896)

Painted for OUTING by Hermann Simon.

AT FORTY-YARD RANGE.

BEAR HUNTING IN BRITISH COLUMBIA.

By Wm. Edward Coffin.

THE desire to kill a grizzly bear was almost a mania with me. Fair success in big game shooting and several disappointments when after the grizzly had only made me the keener, so when the last holiday drew near it was not strange that my mind was full of the great plantigrade.

Correspondence with residents of British Columbia elicited the cheering information that Revelstoke was a promising point from which to start upon the hunt proper. In due time I reached the wonderful mountain region of which Revelstoke forms such a minute fragment.

My guide, Jack, and cook, Jim, announced with pride that with money I had forwarded they had purchased the provisions and camp outfit. These were already on board a little steamboat, the *Marian*, which would start early next morning bound down the Columbia River, and would leave us at Thompson's Landing, on the northeast arm of Upper Arrow Lake.

From Thompson's Landing to Trout Lake over the mountains, some twelve miles as the crow flies—at least thirty miles as a man walks—there is a rough trail, cut for the use of a pack train which carries flour, bacon, whisky and other supplies into a little mining camp at the head of Trout Lake. There we hoped to find a dug-out or boat of some description, in which we could paddle to the foot of the lake, some eighteen miles. Beyond that were the pathless mountains, and all our dunnage and supplies must be carried on our backs.

At Thompson's we were met by Charley, a packer, who proved to be a royal good fellow, faithful, even tempered, and with phenomenally good eyesight.

There are but two houses at Thompson's Landing, so on noticing the boxes, crates, and bags which were being unloaded from the steamer and piled on the lake bank, I inquired whom all these things were for. "Those are your provisions," said Jack the guide. "What, all these?" I said. "Yes, I thought you wanted to be comfortable, and expected me to spend the money," was the answer. Now, horses cannot be taken into the hunting ground. Forty pounds is all that a man can pack over the mountains. Twenty pounds, with gun, ammunition, and a rubber blanket, would be quite enough for me. Therefore our party, the guide, cook, packer and myself, could carry only one hundred and forty pounds.

There we were, thirty miles from a town, with tents, cooking utensils, and provisions weighing, as I afterward learned, thirteen hundred pounds. The situation was too absurd to be anything but laughable. Indeed, it is next to the best joke in my experience. The best comes later on. There was nothing to do but make the best of it, so a modest outfit was selected, and the balance left to be sent back at the first opportunity and sold for my account.

After making a bargain for pack horses to carry our outfit to Trout Lake the next morning, I ate supper and went to bed. To bed, but not to rest. The room, eight by ten feet, with a seven-foot ceiling, contained two beds, no sheets, no pillow-cases, the only covering a loose blanket. Two men were asleep in one bed; the other had been reserved for me. The one window was tightly closed. The night was hot and the atmosphere of the room was intolerable. I raised the window and the room filled with mosquitoes. They came in clouds. My room-mates tossed and muttered oaths in their sleep, but it was impossible to breathe with the window shut, so I tossed and muttered too. It was the last night spent under a roof that trip. Thereafter we pitched a tent, and behind mosquito netting slept in comfort.

Next morning we started on the twelve-mile tramp for Trout Lake. Declining the proffered hospitality of the

"Miner's Rest," we pitched our tent near the head of the lake, cooked supper and turned in. I was awakened at midnight by the noise of a pitched battle between two companies of prospectors, but I would not get up, even for a fight. We learned next morning that it was a drunken quarrel in which six or eight men had been engaged, several of whom were badly bruised. Gentle peace had been restored by the bartender, with a pick handle.

A prospector's life is full of hardship. An average kit contains one rough suit of clothing, worn by the man, no extra socks or shirts ; one half of an ordinary blanket, used as a shelter in rainy weather, as a covering in cold ; a small tin bucket, a tin cup, a revolver strapped to the waist, a miner's pick, a piece of bacon six inches square, one quarter pound of tea, two pounds of oatmeal, a little sugar, a little salt, and about thirty pounds of flour. Absolutely nothing else. This for two weeks.

The length of a trip is limited by the amount of flour a man can carry. Probably four days of the time is consumed in going to and from the supply store. A prospector commences at the foot of a mountain, working up the bed of a stream, looking for float or outcroppings. Many claims are located above snow line. One-half the time a man is standing in water or snow. Over-heated in the middle of the day, chilled at night, half clothed, insufficiently fed, he struggles on for the few years which suffice to reduce him to a wreck.

With it all, the people are law-abiding. In the United States, a like community would be ruled by the revolver. Though all of the men were armed, there was no shooting during the fight at the "Miner's Rest." One man drew a revolver, but was instantly disarmed by the bystanders. Crimes of violence are almost unknown. Theft is rare.

Revelstoke had no Justice of the Peace or other officer of the law. By common consent, disputes or misdemeanors were usually submitted to Jack Kirkup, the Government Mining Agent. He was a handsome young giant of herculean strength, whose severest penalty was to take a man by the shoulders and kick him out of town, with a warning not to return. One transgressor remarked that he would rather serve a sixty days' sentence than take another such kicking.

The only boat available was of roughly made boards, cut from the log with a handsaw, the green timber twisted and warped, the cracks in the bottom a quarter of an inch wide, the oars whittled out of cedar splits. We caulked the cracks with a pair of overalls and an old sack, loaded the boat, and rowed down the lake, making frequent stops to shift cargo and to bail out. Five hours' hard work brought us to camping ground.

The tent was pitched at the foot of the mountain, on a cedar-covered point projecting into the lake. The afternoon was spent in fishing. In three hours I caught nine silver trout, weighing seventy-three and one-half pounds. The tackle was a bass pole, one hundred and fifty yards of line, and a pickerel trolling spoon. The fish lie deep in the water. The spoon was held down by a heavy lead, and must have been a hundred and fifty feet below the surface. The fish were very gamy, jumping clear of the water from four to seven times, and making rushes which strained both pole and line.

Trout Lake is eighteen miles long and from half a mile to a mile broad. It winds between the mountains, with densely wooded and precipitous banks. Above the timber line rise peaks covered with snow, beneath which show the dark green ice of four large glaciers. The depth of the lake is unknown, but it must be great, as the water fills the gorge, and has no shallow margins.

Surrounded as this lake is by mountains, it is subject to sudden storms which sweep down the gorges, sometimes from one side, sometimes from the other. Indeed, at times the wind blows from a different direction at each end of the lake. These storms are accompanied by hail, snow or rain, as the case may be. They blow out in a few hours, but will raise waves of surprising size, and in a surprisingly short time. We were four miles from camp, and on our way back ran into a storm of great severity. The guide wanted to go ashore, saying he had been "capsized in this lake three times and had to swim ashore," adding that "swimming in ice water was cold work." Like the ostrich in the story, I knew it all, and promising to steer with a cedar split, which had been used for a seat, insisted on going ahead.

In a few minutes the pounding of the waves loosened the caulking in the bottom of the boat, and I had to stop steering to bail out the water which poured in. A mighty gust of wind gave the boat a twist, and one of the cedar oars broke in the middle. For a moment things looked serious, but Jack rose to the occasion. Shouting to me to bail for our lives, he brought the boat around, stern to the waves, but not until we had shipped two seas and were kneeling in six inches of water. By skillful steering and hard bailing we managed to reach the shore.

Jack first built a fire, then whittled an oar out of a cedar snag, while I dried my legs and cooked our only remaining fish—a two-pound silver trout. About three o'clock in the morning the wind ceased, the waves quickly subsided, and we were able to row to camp.

Next morning we started up the mountain. The ascent was difficult in the extreme. The lower slopes were covered with immense cedars, the ground strewn with prostrate trunks from four to seven feet through, between which grew a thicket of "devil's club." Devil's club is a giant nettle often six feet high, the stem, branches and leaves covered with spines, a wound from which is painful and, I presume, somewhat poisonous, as it makes a festering sore. Hours were spent in forcing a way through and climbing over logs. This forest passed, we came to jackpines, "thick as the hair on a dog's back," to borrow Charley the packer's expression. Remember, we had packs on our backs, the guide and myself carrying guns.

The small pines must be forced apart by main strength, the projecting branches catching the packs, and when released by the men ahead, slapping one in the face. Toward evening we started two black bear in a berry patch, but, owing to the thickness of the brush, did not get a shot.

A portion of our next day's journey was through a comparatively open forest, where we saw much bear sign. Above this forest we found running cedar, which lies flat on the ground and is very slippery and difficult to climb over. I had several hard falls here. Above the cedar were slides, places where avalanches had torn great gashes in the mountain side, which were over-grown with the alder thickets so common in the Maine and Adirondack woods. To go through the crooked and intertwined branches was almost impossible. They must be bent down and climbed over. These passed, we came to the moraines—rising in some places a thousand feet—composed of slate and shaly rock, which a touch will start to sliding. There is little solid rock in these mountains, the ledges are slaty; large pieces can be pulled out with the hand. As a result of this formation, and of the moisture from the melting snow, the mountain sides are seamed and scarred by earthslides.

Not a day passed without the rumbling, grinding roar of an avalanche. Fortunately, this was always at a distance. Above the moraines the glaciers and snow-covered peaks form a continuous frame, boldly contrasting with the blue background of the sky.

Our tent was pitched in a little clump of gnarled and twisted cedars, the extreme edge of the timber line. We had planned to hunt mountain goat first; afterwards, to try for bear among the berry patches, and caribou on the lower levels. Naturally we camped on the best available ground, and some idea of the character of the country will be given by the statement that to pitch a tent eight by six feet in size, a rough platform was constructed, which, resting against the mountain on one side, was over six feet above ground on the other. The cook dug a place on the hillside for his fire. As he stood at work his feet were upon a little platform, the fire being level with his chest.

The mountain goat is found in several parts of the Western United States, but seems to especially thrive in British Columbia. It has long, white hair, the only spots of color being the black horns, eyes, nostrils and hoofs, and is about three times the size of the ordinary domestic goat, which it closely resembles in general structure. It lives on the snow-line of the highest peaks.

Some hunters will say that it is the easiest of animals to kill. Probably that is true in a country where there has been little or no shooting, or if the goats are surprised while crossing from one range to another. My own experience has been very different. The mountain sheep, generally conceded to be the wariest of animals, is no more keen and alert than the goat we found. A stalk involved hours of arduous labor, and at the slightest evidence of danger the herd would take refuge in places where an approach without wings was well nigh impossible. For four days we hunted over the snow or watched from projecting points ; then taking Charley, the packer, who carried four blankets, an axe, tin bucket, and three days' provisions, we started to work along the divide, keeping near the summit.

We surprised a brood of noisy ptarmigans, and the guide caught a little chicken, and handed it to me that I might feel the heat of its body. I have never seen greater courage than was shown by the mother, who flew straight at my face. Although repeatedly pushed away with the open hand, she would not desist, until in pity I put the chicken down in the snow and left her in peace.

About noon of the first day out, Charley, who had made a detour, reported goats upon the other side of what he called "Nigger-head Mountain." With the aid of a glass, the herd, plainly visible to his naked eye, was located. The guide, turning to me, said, "There is rough climbing on that mountain ; do you think you can make it?"

Now for several days I had been writhing under a certain compassionate patronage in his manner, probably the result of my very poor showing at target shooting, or possibly because I insisted on always carrying two woolen shirts—one lasted him the entire trip. Here was my opportunity. "Can you make it, Jack?" I inquired. "'Course," said he. "All right, then, I can, too ; wherever you are man enough to lead, I am man enough to follow."

There was some nasty work in the first part of the climb, but after rounding the shoulder of the peak, we found a glacier, sloping from the summit at an angle of some forty-five degrees, and ending some hundreds of feet below in a precipice, over the edge of which could be seen the mist from a waterfall. From the brink of the precipice to the foot of the fall was, perhaps, a thousand feet.

When the sun shines, the snow with which the glacier is covered softens sufficiently to afford fair traveling, if the foot is stamped in at each step. If the sun is obscured, even for a few moments, this snow freezes, and to cross is difficult if not impossible.

The goats were quietly feeding near the waterfall on the opposite side of the canyon. We moved rapidly along, the packer in advance some fifty feet below me, the guide following.

Incautiously stepping into the shadow of the peak, where the surface was a glare of ice, I fell heavily and slid down the steep incline. The alpenstock in my hand broke like a twig. Instinctively swinging around, feet foremost, I pressed both heels and elbows against the frozen surface. Charley, the packer, heard the fall, and with a look of horror sprang out to catch me, but by that time I was going pretty fast, and his courage failed.

Down I went, faster and faster, the wind whistling by my ears, the loose snow flying in a cloud around me. Straight ahead was the precipice ; away below the canyon.

In a few moments I had slid four hundred feet. Fortunately the lower edge of the glacier was slightly cupped, and the loose snow from above had lodged in that little depression until it was about eighteen inches deep.

My speed slackened as this loose snow was reached, and digging my heels in for a last effort, I came to a stop, not fifty feet from the edge. Lying there, fearing to move, lest the snow banked in front of me should be loosened, I could look over the edge down into the depths of the canyon. If I close my eyes now I can hear the distant roar of the waterfall as it sounded then.

The two men soon worked down to a point whence they could cut footholds in the ice, and so, one on each side, they brought me out. The seat was out of my trousers and underclothing, the sleeves torn from my arms to the elbow, the snow stained with the blood slowly dropping from the bruised and lacerated flesh. My trousers and coat were so distended by the snow gathered on the way that I appeared to be blown up like a football.

So far as my own observation goes, it is the anticipation, not the danger, which unnerves a man. There is an exhilaration in the crisis itself which drowns all other feelings. The first impression was of amusement at the panorama of horror, resolution, and fear shown by Charley's face, as he saw me falling, started to catch me, and then jumped out of the way. Next, an almost impersonal thought that this would be my last hunt ; then a recollection of the " Uncle Remus " story, in which the terrapin complains that the buzzard taught him how to fly but not how to alight; and a thought as to how it would feel when I struck the bottom of the canyon. Last of all, as the trousers gave way, the absurdity of my appearance, coasting down the incline on nature's cushions. This seemed so very funny that I broke into peals of hysterical laughter, which lasted until, working along the ice, solid footing was reached ; then I sank on the snow in complete collapse, shaking like a leaf. Fortunately the gun was slung on my back, and my hat lodged in the snow, but my pipe went over the edge.

Disrobing sufficiently to dislodge the snow packed into my clothing, I rubbed my honorable scars with gun grease, and carefully caulked the hole in my trousers with a towel. The goats had disappeared.

Upon the mountain over which we started to follow them was an enormous moraine, or slide, perhaps fifteen hundred feet high, composed of small pieces of shale, and extending a quarter of the way round the mountain to impassable cliffs. This we must climb up and around. Once started, we must keep on or fall. Carefully working the foot in, a step forward was taken. As the weight was thrown on this foot, the slate would commence to slide. Another step must be made at once. As the foot was raised a mass of the loose material would slide down the mountain with a rumble, raising a cloud of dust.

Three hours were consumed in the painful ascent, with but a single rest. In one place, where the bed-rock projected, I threw myself down, and clasping the little crag with both arms, panted for breath. Nothing but pride kept me from crying—I felt like it ; but the shortest way out was over the summit, so on we struggled.

At the top of the slide we found a difficult cliff. At one place we could only work around a corner by clasping extended hands, as a protection against a misstep. Then we clambered up a twenty-foot snow wall, in which the guide cut steps as he advanced, until we gained the summit. We followed the trail over the snow for perhaps a quarter of a mile, then stopped for lunch, a rest and a smoke.

Charley, who had started off for a reconnoissance, returned, breathless, to report a goat in sight.

It was an easy stalk to about two hundred yards above where the animal was lying. That is a longer shot than I like to risk, and shooting downhill at a white object lying on a snow bank is not easy ; but there seemed to be no way of getting nearer without alarming the game. I fired, and missed. As the goat jumped I fired again, the ball striking just above the kidneys.

The goat ran across a knife ridge, dividing the chasm between two peaks. Down we rushed, the guide in advance, Charley hurrying back for his pack. Blood on the snow showed that the goat was hard hit, and Jack sprang upon the ridge, balancing himself with outspread arms as he jumped from rock to rock as lightly as a bird. "Come on !" he cried. I looked at the ridge. A tight rope would have seemed easier to walk, for that would have been comparatively straight. This ridge was broken, uneven, and looked sharp enough to split wood upon. On one side was a steep slide. A man falling would be torn to pieces by the sharp-pointed slate. On the other side was a glacier. It was too much. Humbled at last, I shouted across : " Jack, perhaps I could go wherever you lead, but I am not fool enough to try this. Please accept my apologies."

" Well, you run round the glacier. He may go straight through." This was called over his shoulder as he disappeared among the rocks.

With many misgivings I started around the mountain, on the glacier, which was some two miles in length, half encircling the mountain, and completely filling the canyon. Its surface descended in rolling benches, like a giant toboggan slide. The afternoon sun shone full upon it, and the crevasses were the only danger. There were many of these, but none too broad to be easily crossed.

The goat came in sight, slowly limping around the mountain side, half a mile away. As rapidly as possible, I followed. Although steadily gaining ground, I was still a quarter of a mile behind when the goat clambered around the shoulder of a cliff, which I could only pass by a partial descent of the mountain. Jack and Charley were both in sight, and as the sun was setting we decided to camp and to follow the trail next morning.

When we reached timber line, a pile of cedar boughs was cut for a bed, the ground being everywhere soaked with water from the melting snow. A few boughs were stuck upright for a wind break, and I sank into a dreamless sleep which the mountains always give me.

The night was very cold and our covering scanty, but the two men kept up a roaring fire, and I was greatly surprised next morning to find the ground frozen solidly.

We took up the trail at daybreak, and within three hundred yards we found the goat dead. He was a large buck, a perfect specimen in every respect. Although the carcass had lain over night without being bled, as a seeker after experiences, I decided to take the foreshoulder that we might taste the meat.

To reach the camp, we had to cross the mountains, and a hard day's work it was. The sun shining full in my eyes as we climbed, together with the glare from the snow, produced a painful inflammation. We were much concerned for the guide, who had an attack of vertigo, probably resulting from drinking the ice-cold water and exposure to the intense heat of the midday sun.

At last camp was reached and the goat meat cooked for supper. My curiosity was easily satisfied. One mouthful was enough. It tasted like a menagerie smells.

The next day I was compelled to spend in the tent with my swollen eyes covered with a wet bandage, which at last reduced the inflammation.

As bear was the main object of the trip, and time was limited, camp was moved back to the waterfall, half-way down the mountain. The tent was pitched in a place shaded by large trees, and with a background of rock covered with wild raspberries. On the benches near were many blueberry bushes, laden with ripe fruit, which was of two kinds—the ordinary mountain blueberry, and a species as large as a grape and tasting a little like a plum.

Charley started off to scout for promising ground. Jack and myself hunted to the left. We soon separated, following parallel lines, about three hundred yards apart, I taking the lower level.

By an enormous bowlder I paused to look. I heard the crack of a twig on the other side, and rushing around saw a medium-sized black bear disappearing in the bushes. The distance was not over forty yards. The bullet struck in front of the hind leg, and ranged forward through the body. The animal fell at once. Feeling sure it was a mortal wound, and not wishing to spoil the hide, I approached, holding the gun ready for another shot. With a snarl and glare of rage, the bear tried to rise, then fell back dead.

It was a three-year-old female, my first bear, not as big as it might be, and a black, not a grizzly; but still a sure-enough bear. While bleeding the carcass I noticed the peculiarly vicious expression, the eyes bloodshot, the lips curled in a snarl, with a feeling of pity for the gentleman bear who had such a vixen for a mate. Charley, the eagle-eyed, reported a distant view of a grizzly, for whom the succeeding day was spent in fruitless search.

On the third day we worked in the opposite direction. Two bear were started, black, as we found from the tracks; but the underbrush was so thick that we could not see them. Later in the day, while walking along the mountain side alone, I heard the cracking of a twig. In a moment a loose stone rolled, and I rushed through the dense bushes toward the sound. Unfortunately I looked the wrong way, for on examination I found the track of a black bear which had half-circled me. When my rush was made he had jumped at least ten feet, and made off up the mountain.

For convenience in reaching different points, we now moved camp to our old ground on the lake border.

During the next two days, while on scouting expeditions, the packer saw two black bear, and the guide a grizzly. From the lake we saw a large black bear away up on the mountain side. While ascending the mountain in parallel lines —the guide on one side, the packer on the other, myself in the center—we started two black bear, one running each way, quite near the men, but not within sight of me. The major part of these two and the succeeding day were spent in watching "wallows," places where the bear roll in the water, which showed signs of frequent use by both black and grizzly bear. On the last day the guide thought he heard a splash below us. Working cautiously down we found a pool completely hidden by the thicket, in which a large black bear had just been wallowing.

All this was most exasperating. To understand the difficulties under which we labored, imagine the mountain side, seamed by canyons and gullies, and densely covered with underbrush. There had been no real rain for ninety days, the occasional light showers blowing over in a few moments. Each twig, leaf, and the very ground itself, was so brittle and dry as to make movement without noise impossible. I have heard my guide moving through the brush a quarter of a mile away, and, of course, a bear's hearing is much better than mine. We had to depend entirely upon still hunting, as berries were so plentiful that the bear would not touch a bait. This may sound strange to an old hunter, but the fore-quarters of the goat, carried down the mountain with infinite labor, lay untouched, although the track of a bear passed within fifty yards. The carcass of the female bear had not been disturbed five days after it was killed. Nearly all the tracks and sign found among the berry patches were of black bear, and I think it safe to say that with a plucky and well-trained dog, we could have killed eight.

Watching bear wallows is dull work. For hours the hunter must sit perfectly quiet. To pass the time I commenced to study ants, watching their efforts to carry off, and their battles over, crumbs of bread or dead flies. Mosquitoes were not troublesome, but the flies were very bad. Ranging in size from a large species called "bull-heads," whose bite would bring blood, to a tiny midge, they were omnipresent and persistent. The bull-heads seemed to hunt in packs of three or five. At each change of location we were attacked, but after three to five had been killed, were left in peace.

Beyond a few "fool-hens," and an occasional "snow-grouse," we saw no members of the partridge family. The streams near the lake were full of brook trout ; but the overhanging underbrush made fly-fishing impossible. Fishing with the three-foot pole and six-foot line with which the cook kept the table supplied had no attractions for me.

Thinking that the grizzly bear might be living upon fish, we decided to move camp some four miles to the opposite side of the lake, near a creek which was resorted to every second year by countless numbers of a small, red fish, the name of which I did not learn. By this creek ran a well-beaten trail, upon which two years before my guide had within two days killed two grizzly and a black bear.

To give the berry patch one more trial, we mounted a little knoll to closely examine the mountain side. Hardly had Jack raised the glass to his eyes, when he put his hand on my knee, saying, "There is our grizzly. I saw his nose back of that clump of bushes." We hurried through a small swamp and up the opposite hillside. Moving with the utmost caution we approached the spot. The bear had gone. To our left lay a shallow ravine, filled with underbrush, extending for half a mile up the mountain.

"He must be in there. You run to the upper end. I will try to drive him out," said Jack. Up I ran with heart thumping and breath coming in gasps, from the exertion of running up hill in that thin air. At the head of the ravine was a large rock. Climbing on this I could see over the bushes.

Hardly had I looked at my gun to be sure it was all right, when in the ravine below a twig snapped. A moment later the bushes parted about two hundred yards away, and a large black bear started to climb over the edge of the ravine. My disappointment was keen, but there was something to take it out on, and aiming back of his shoulder, I fired. He fell, but immediately jumping up, commenced to run. Three more shots were fired at the black object, glancing through the bushes, one bullet going through the fleshy part of his leg.

I started in pursuit. The bear ran up hill about three hundred yards, then, circling, started down directly toward me. I could hardly believe my eyes. Had the bear been a grizzly, I would have understood it. Could it be that a black bear would show fight !

Some thirty yards above was a clump of small trees, which were directly between the bear and myself. Waiting until he emerged from these, I heard him crash into the underbrush ; then a gasping roar, and all was still. When I approached the trees a black paw stood up in the air. My bear was dead. What I had imagined to be a charge was only a blind rush down hill in the death agony.

He was a magnificent animal, large and very fat; the body coal black, the nose, from eyes down, a light brown. It was the brown nose that had deceived the guide.

After helping to skin the bear, and cut off the head, feet and hams, I started off for the lake, some two miles distant. The packer was to meet us with the boat at a point four miles from camp. Traveling light; I was to hurry on and send Charley back to help Jack with his heavy load.

The packer was fishing from the boat, far out in the lake. I fired a shot as a signal, then sat down to rest. It was a thoughtless act, for when hunting large game I never shoot either at small game or without an object, nor do I take the odd chance of firing at running animals if distant. During this entire trip, aside from a little preliminary target shooting, my gun was discharged but nine times. The men with me knew this.

Now, after my slip on the glacier, Jack's former condescension was exchanged for parental solicitude. Evidently he had doubts as to my safe return to civilization. In an incredibly short time I heard his shout, and he burst through the bushes, hatless, the perspiration streaming down his face. "Thank God," he said, as he saw me standing on a log, "when I heard that single shot I was sure you had stumbled on a grizzly, and he had got the best of you." His concern was so genuine, and his relief so apparent, as to make quite an impression on me.

The day's incidents were not through with yet. Leaving New York in a time of great business depression, I did not think it prudent to be entirely beyond the reach of a message. Having arranged for two telegrams to Revelstoke each Friday, one from my family, the other from the office, I engaged a man to bring them into the mountains. At an agreed-upon spot on the lake shore directions were to be left as to where we could be found. The plan worked well. When the second messages were received I inquired quite casually as to the expense, and was horrified to learn that I was paying sixty-five dollars for each trip, and was therefore liable for one hundred and thirty dollars. This was harrowing, but it was too late to save that money, so telegrams were written to the office and to my wife, who was in Chicago, asking them not to wire unless the urgency was imperative. This I had explained to the messenger, telling him it was hardly probable that any other message would be received, but if one came to bring it through regardless of expense.

After the return of the men with the bearskin and meat, we rowed toward camp. Imagine my horror as we neared the tent at seeing the messenger standing on the lake shore, waving two telegrams in his hand. My heart stood still as I sprang ashore and tore open the familiar brown envelopes.

The first was from the Western Union office at Chicago, a printed form, stating that the party to whom my message was addressed could not be found at 4761 Lake Avenue. The second, also a printed form, stated that the party addressed had been found, and the message delivered at 4671 Lake Avenue.

All that mental agony and the sixty-five dollars because of the transposition of a single figure. I keenly appreciate a good joke, and that was the best joke in my experience. The reaction from painful apprehension reconciled me to the loss of money, and we had a jolly evening after a royal supper on roast fool-hen, trout of two kinds, and bear paws. The last tasted like pigs' feet, but were much more dainty.

After moving our camp as proposed, we found that the red fish were not in the creek yet, and there was no fresh bear sign. I spent two days in an unsuccessful hunt for caribou, and then my time was up. Caribou are plentiful at times, but I saw none.

23.
DIVERSIONS IN PICTURESQUE GAMELANDS (1908)

SCRIBNER'S MAGAZINE

JULY, 1908

DIVERSIONS IN PICTURESQUE GAME-LANDS

GRAND BAD-LANDS AND MULE DEER

BY WILLIAM T. HORNADAY

PHOTOGRAPHICALLY ILLUSTRATED BY L. A. HUFFMAN

IT is an interesting but unaccountable fact that comparatively few American sportsmen ever have carried their rifles into really fine bad-lands. The particularly wild and picturesque bad-lands of Montana and Wyoming have for me the same fascination that arctic ice has for a a pole-hunter. When fully under the spell of their grim and uncanny grandeur, one seems to live in a Dantean world, wherein everything is strange and unreal. If you go about with open eyes, you will see that even such savage-looking wastes of land carvings as those of Hell Creek and Snow Creek are stocked with interesting animal life, queer vegetation and physical wonders. If you are a paleontologist—ah! then your finds are likely to surpass all others—as we shall see.

Unfortunately for the sight-seer, the bad-lands along our transcontinental railways are rather tame. The wild tracts do not generate much freight, nor many passengers. To see and feel the real thing, and have it dominate your senses with hypnotic power, go when nerve-weary to a place where you will find a Grand Canyon in miniature, and panoramas of wild nature that you can dream over all the rest of your life. For the time therefor, choose either October or November, of The Present year.

I think the finest bad-lands in all Montana are those on Snow Creek and Hell Creek, reaching southward from the Missouri River for a width of twelve miles. The trail trip northwestward, 120 miles from Miles City, is a good curtain-raiser for the real experience. The modest little buttes and coulees along Sunday Creek are just wild enough to convince the explorer that civilization has been left behind, and that the wrestle with Nature is really on. Six hours from the trail's beginning, "the next water." "firewood" and "grass" are topics for serious thought, especially between the hours of four and five in the afternoon.

At the head of Sunday Creek, the plain and simple bad-lands of that stream fade out, and you emerge upon a vast stretch of rolling prairie uplands, absolutely treeless, and drained by numerous small creeks. In days gone by that was one of the finest buffalo ranges in all the West. After the buffalo days, this side of 1884, it was a fine cattle range; but the awful sheep-herds have gone over it, like swarms of hungry locusts, and now the earth looks scalped and bald, and lifeless. To-day it is almost as barren of cattle as of buffaloes, and it will be years in recovering from the fatal passage of the sheep. That once-popular buffalo range extends northward over divide and valley, across the Little Dry, Sand Creek and the Big Dry, ninety miles at least, where it breaks into the awful bad-lands that scarify the country along the southern side of the muddy Missouri.

There were only four of us; and we left Jim's ferry on the Yellowstone on Oc-

Wolfer's Roost—The prettiest cabin in Montana.
Max Sieber's home on Hell Creek, at the edge of the bad-lands.

tober 2nd. Jim McNaney was with me on the historic Smithsonian buffalo hunt of 1886, even unto the day when we found and killed the big bull whose lordly portrait now adorns and illumines the face of our new ten-dollar bill.

Our souls had yearned so strongly for another look at our old haunts up Sunday Creek and beyond the LU-bar ranch that when he proposed a hunting trip to "the worst bad-lands in Montana," I had come all the way from the East to respond.

By good luck, our old friend L. A. Huffman, expert photographer, sportsman and all-around good fellow, had been persuaded to join us; and to the fighting strength of the outfit he had contributed his historic white horse, Jady, and a buggy to carry cameras and plates. The fourth member was Bert Smith, cook and wagon-driver. The other equine members of the party were Bull Pup, Sunfish, Easter Lily, Yellow Belly, and Louey.

Joyously we pulled up to the Little Dry, seventy miles from Miles. and made Camp No. 3. For supper the cook fried—most becomingly—the four sage grouse that Jim

shot in the shadow of the LU-bar Buttes. The pungent and spicy odor of the sagebrush—sweet incense to the nostrils of the Eastern sportsman—the swishing flame of the camp-fire, the snort of the tired horses thankfully feeding at ease, and the white oil-cloth spread on the clean buffalo-grass all gratefully combined to soothe the senses like an opiate. *Montana, again!* This is Life! In that glorious weather, we scorned the Sibley tent and slept in the open, triumphantly, as do men who for ten years and more have longed for the trail and camp-fire in buffalo-land. It was Layton Huffman's "first real big-game hunting trip since Ruth was a baby."

For seventy miles our spirits had mounted higher and higher every hour. The joy of it seemed too bright to last—and sure enough, it was! It was at our camp on the Little Dry that Calamity overtook us, sweating and weary from our all-night ride.

In the early morning, while we were hitching up for a fine start, Calico Charley slowly galloped into view from the south, rode up to our camp-fire and with a brief, "Hello, fellers!" stiffly dismounted. A

Our camp on the bank of Hell Creek.
At Sieber's ranch.

blind man could have seen that he had ridden hard and long.

Jim McNaney, Huffman and I were each of us married men; and each had given double hostages to Fortune. During a long half-minute of painful silence, we looked at Calico Charley, and at each other, without the courage to ask the fatal question. At last Jim managed to say, in a very low voice,

"Well, *which one of us is it*, Charlie?"

"It's you, Jim," said Charley, very gently. "Maggie's been took *awful* bad. The doctors say there's got to be an operation— right away. . . . It's to be at four o'clock this afternoon."

Maggie was Jim's wife, and the mother of little Jack. "Sorry" was no name for what we all felt at that moment.

"Well, boys," said Jim, quietly, "I'm awfully sorry to miss the hunt with you; but I must hit the trail back. Bull Pup will get me there by four o'clock, all right. . . . Now, the rest of you must go on, and have the hunt; and if Maggie gets well enough that I can leave her, I'll try to join you on Hell Creek, for a few days with you at the finish."

And so, taking a handful of cigars and a box of matches, he flung himself into his saddle, touched Bull Pup with a spur, and in an instant was galloping away on the seventy-mile run.

Three weeks later when he met us returning, again at the LU-bar Buttes, he told us briefly of the ride.

"Well, sir, that plucky little beggar of a Bull Pup took me to Miles by half-past three—and he *never turned a hair!* Blamed if I don't believe he could have brought me back again to the Little Dry by midnight! He's the best little cayuse I ever owned. . . . Yes, you bet, Maggie was glad to see me. . . . Oh, yes; the operation was fine, and she's getting on all right!"

When Jim galloped away from us, Layton Huffman and I conferred briefly, and took an inventory of our resources. Calico Charley could not go on with us. It remained for Layton and me to find the hunting grounds, somehow, kill our game, take our pictures, and get safely back again, on time. Jim told us that at Jerdon's, on the Big Dry, we could inquire the way to Egan's ranch; and once there, the ranch people would put us wise as to the hunting grounds, and "locate" us.

Before we moved out, Layton elected me foreman of the outfit. In that position, I did not have to work very hard, but as horse-wrangler-in-chief, I think I earned my keep.

Without the loss of a moment, we pulled on north, and on a level flat a mile above the ruined LU-bar ranch house we saw the spectacle of the sage grouse. It was a sight that neither sportsman nor naturalist could easily forget.

The flat was as level as a floor, and the closely cropped buffalo-grass upon it was as smooth as a tennis court. The ground looked like buff-colored manila paper. The plain was very thinly dotted with tiny clumps of young sage-brush, no larger than spring geraniums, and over numerous spaces even those were absent. As I rode in advance of the wagon, there arose a short distance ahead, but quite near the trail, certain sage grouse sentinels, which betokened the presence of a flock. As I slowly rode forward, the birds all stood at attention, and looked at me. Presently they began to stalk very slowly and majestically athwart the trail. Momentarily expecting them to take wing, I rode forward, pianissimo, in order to see how near I could approach the flock before it would explode into the air, and wing away.

Montana is a land of many surprises. In very open order, spread out over a quarter of an acre of ground, with heads held high and striding with regal dignity and deliberation, those twenty-four sage-grouse stalked up to the trail, and across it. At a nearness of thirty paces to the skirmishers of the flock, I drew rein to gaze; and presently our whole outfit halted close behind me, to look and wonder.

Each of those birds strutted as if he alone owned the whole of Montana. They gave us stare for stare, preserved their formation, and sauntered on across the trail as if there were not a loaded shot-gun within a hundred miles. It was the most magnificent series of grouse poses that any of us ever beheld, and we regretted that the exigencies of the trail compelled us to move on. The lofty heads, the big, plump bodies, and the long, marline-spike tails slowly and majestically stalked away into the easterly sage-brush, and never a feather stirred in flight.

Even to this day, I wonder how those birds *knew* that we would not "shoot them up!"

The trail was good, and our load was light; Jim's team was in fine shape, and we went forward at a rattling pace. By the time you have ridden from the Yellowstone through twenty miles of bad-lands, and across sixty miles of billowy divides, you stand on the hurricane deck of the lofty watershed that separates Little Dry Creek from the Big Dry. Incidentally, you also see your first solitary and scared prong-horned antelope, and it looks unspeakably lonesome. As you draw rein, and gaze in spellbound silence toward all points of the butte-filled compass, you think, "How *big* Montana is! This is indeed the top of the continent!"

Your vision takes in with one cycloramic sweep at least one thousand square miles of butte-studded country, and the mental and moral uplift of it all is worth the cost of the trip. Then, and not until then, is your mind in a proper frame to approach the weird wonderland that lies to the north, beyond old Smoky Butte, that looms up in the northwest, a grim and majestic sentinel.

We camped on Sand Creek, and in the gray dawn Layton kindly shot two blue-winged teal for breakfast. Immediately thereafter, by a very close shave we succeeded in heading back our horses after the whole bunch had decided to take advantage of their right to the initiative and referendum, and hit the trail back to the Yellowstone. Had they succeeded in giving us the slip we might have spent half a week in chasing them on foot.

We pulled on north to Jerdon's store and post-office on the Big Dry, forded a river of real water, and obtained careful directions for reaching Egan's ranch without a guide. The specifications were all right, but, as often happens after a contract has been let, the ground plan of the country didn't seem to fit them.

Beyond Jerdon's the trail was dim, and as it lengthened its dimness increased. We failed to find the turn-off for Egan's, and went straight on. When sixteen miles had been reeled off, we reached the crest of a lofty divide, crossed a high and level mesa, and from the western edge of it looked down upon a sea of rolling prairie, richly set in grass. We said, "The ranch may be

Under Panorama Point.

The sterility of the bad-lands immediately below the rich grass-lands.

The bad-lands of Snow Creek from Panorama Point.

on the creek that we see, away down yonder. Let us get there, even though we do go west."

We started on the down grade, and very soon the country on our right hand (north) went all to pieces into rugged ravines. We drove and rode, wound in and wound out, and just about sunset reached the bottom, and the creek. There was a sinuous chain of golden-yellow cottonwood trees, firewood to burn and water in the hole—but not the faintest trace of a ranch, past, present or to come.

Then and there we were unquestionably and shamefully lost; and since there did not appear to be any other human beings north of the Big Dry, nor any clue to our position, we went into camp, fed sumptuously and bade Dull Care begone. That night the coyotes serenaded us in old-time style, and we dreamed that we had come into our own wild domain, wherein no man might molest us, nor make us afraid.

The next morning at peep of day, I saddled Easter Lily—Jim's favorite mare, and my special mount—and galloped northward to look for hunting grounds. Three

miles along, I caught a glimpse of land ahead that quickly led me to halt and climb to the mast-head of a tall butte that rose conveniently near.

Glorious! Two miles beyond that point the grassy plain broke up into a wild revel of bad-lands, such as delights the heart of a mule deer, and a deer hunter. The whole landscape was hacked, and gouged, and cut down into a bewildering maze of deep canyons and saw-tooth ridges, all thinly sprinkled over with stunted pines, and junipers and cedars. As far as I could see, to right, to left and straight away, the wild and eerie bad-lands bespoke mule deer, and beckoned us to come on.

I hurried back to the outfit and reported.

"There are grand bad-lands ahead of us, and quite near at hand; and there must be deer in them. There surely is water in them, somewhere, and all we need to do is to work down to a good camping place, and make ourselves at home. There is no sign of a ranch, and we don't need any!"

Layton gave a defiant gesture with his free hand, and recklessly consigned Egan's ranch and Hell Creek to the Bad Place.

The mule deer that escaped from a mountain lion.
Right antler broken off, right ear torn, and wound on neck.   Shot from Panorama Point.

We hit a dim old wagon trail, and when Huffman saw the promised land, from Pisgah Butte, he smiled with satisfaction, and said that it was good.

"But where on earth does this wagon track lead to, anyhow? Let's follow it up, and see if it don't lead down to good wood and water."

We spurred ahead of the team for about two miles, and presently completed the ox-bow course he had been describing with the previous ten miles. Going due east at last, almost bursting with superheated curiosity, we reached once more the bank of our creek of the previous night—and suddenly came up against the prettiest little log cabin in all Montana! It had the lines of a Swiss chalet. There was a dug-out store-house, a pile of buffalo horns, a stable, corrals, and a fine but lonesome shepherd dog chained beside a nice, clean dug-out kennel.

There was no one at home but Shep; but he said he was mighty glad to see us; and wouldn't we 'light and stay awhile? We would. Huffman put up his hands, and peeked in at the window.

"Bachelor quarters; and everything as clean and neat as new pins!"

We eye-searched the country round, but saw no sign of the bachelor. At last we were mounting to ride away, when "spang!" came the call of a six-shooter from the throat of the bad-lands, northerly.

"There he is," said Layton. "He wants us to wait."

Ten minuter later, up came the habitant, breathing heavily, red of face, and looking none too pleasant. He was short of stature, sandy of beard, clad *in neat buckskins* and armed with both Winchester and Colt. He was Max Sieber, ex-buffalo-hunter and Texas cowboy, at present engaged in hunting wolves for the bounty on their scalps, and holding down a valuable water-hole for an increment. Huffman immediately voiced our curiosity.

"Well, now, will you tell us—*where* is Hell Creek?"

"*This* is Hell Creek," said Sieber, very emphatically. "And what are you going to do about it?"

"Well! Of all the Luck!"

By guiding ourselves, and opportunely

Buffalo-hunter's cabin at the edge of the grazing grounds.
Bad-lands of Snow Creek.

missing the Egan ranch—which was well out of the game country, eastward—our hunter's luck had led us to an ideal camping place at the very focus of the bad-lands we were seeking.

Behind us was the high and billowy "mesa" covered with unchewn grass a foot high, a domain that was worth thousands of dollars to any stockman. I never saw such grass elsewhere in the West. Sieber was mowing and stacking it, for his pair of monstrous horses, and their sides were ready to crack open with Prosperity. Eastward lay a strange region of high-level bad-lands; and northward, the labyrinth of canyons, and peaks, and ridges was fairly indescribable.

At first the grizzly old wolf-hunter was offish and suspicious; but Layton instantly divined the trouble, and took the situation in hand.

"Now, let me tell you, Sieber. My name's Huffman. I live in Miles, and I'm a photographer. This man is from the East, and he has come out here to kill one or two black-tail, and see how they live when they're at home. I'm going to take

pictures of the bad-lands. We don't own a hoof of range stock, and don't want to; and we're not looking for a range, or a ranch site, for anybody. This is a pleasure trip, old man, and nothing else,—honor bright."

That was ample. Sieber's clouds rolled away in a burst of sunshine, and the whole country became ours. Being of a sociable disposition, and also downright lonesome, Max was as heartily glad to see us as we were to meet him. He cordially invited us to camp near him, which we did; and from that moment until we parted from him, two weeks later, eight miles along the home trail, we were much together. To find so fine a "character," and precisely where a picturesque old-timer so perfectly fitted in, was great luck.

I wish I could set before the Reader an adequate impression of the fourteen halcyon days we spent in that wonderland; but it is impossible. The best that I can do in a few pages will give but a pale glimpse of the whole.

An early discovery, and one which gave us keen pleasure, was the fact that Sieber is an ardent game protectionist, and a con-

sistent hater of game-butchers. His indig-
nant recital of how certain ranchmen of the
North Side had slaughtered great numbers
of antelope and deer to feed their dogs, re-
ber's cabin—Hell Creek makes a picturesque bend, and in its encircling arm there
is an ideal camp-ground. The cut-bank
furnishes shelter; likewise horned owls and

Details of a cut-bank with the owl and swallow's nests.

vealed the real lover of wild animals. We
joined him in anathematizing all men who
kill female deer and fawns, and we pledged
each other that, come what might, *we* never
would do either of those disreputable things.
    Just below Wolfer's Roost—I mean Sie-
swallows. The plaza is covered with good
grass, and there is much good firewood in
the thin grove of cottonwoods two hundred
yards above. We brought down our outfit, pitched our Sibley tent, and settled down
to have the Time of our lives.

The outfit (all but the photographer) in the bad-lands of Sunday Creek.

Max kindly offered to go out with us for the afternoon, and we blithely accepted his company. Whenever he could go with us, he was *persona grata*, to the utmost.

We set out on foot over the plateau to seek the panorama of the bad-lands, with an edge on our expectations like that of country boys going to a circus. We footed it briskly westward along the edge of the high plateau, and after the shaven prairies of the sheep ranges farther south that wild-west grass was really inspiring. It was knee high, and rich as cream—mingled buffalo grass, grama grass and spear grass. Only its long distance from the nearest railway had preserved it immaculate. I mention it thus particularly because at that late day the existence of such a tract of virgin grass-land on the northern buffalo range was decidedly noteworthy. It is all occupied by cattle now.

There are several kinds of bad-lands. Those most commonly seen are usually tracts of dry and half sterile country, with low buttes scattered over them, always somewhat picturesque, but seldom grand. Usually, such tracts are of considerable extent, and you enter them by such slow degrees that your impressions of them arrive rather tardily.

But the Snow Creek bad-lands are very different. You could erect a hand-rail on the line where the rolling, grass-covered buffalo range breaks off into a wild chaos of rugged depths. In a series of jumps, both quick and long, the grassy coulees drop into ravines, the ravines into gulches, and the gulches into deep and gloomy canyons. Fertility ends as abruptly as sterility begins. Often at the spot where a grassy ravine drops sixty feet sheer into the head of a barren gulch, a lone pitch-pine tree takes root and grows up in the angle, as if trying to reach up and get a peep at the upper level.

Near the upper edge of sterility, dark-green masses of trailing juniper cling to the steep sides of the high ridges, as if to hold their barren soil from being further scored and washed down into the Missouri. In the blasted heads of the ravines and arroyos, usually where the ground all about is as bare as a brickyard, we often found growing rank clumps of the narrow-leaved mug-wort (*Artemesia tomentosa*), twin brother of the common sage-brush, and well beloved of the mule deer.

When we reached a view-point which opened up a particularly fine prospect, we indulged in a few exclamations of surprise and pleasure.

"And are ye really fond of scenery?" said Sieber, beaming with pleasure. "Then come with me, and I'll show you one of the finest sights you ever saw in your whole lives!"

We dared him to go on, and make good.

Turning abruptly northward, Sieber led us only half a mile along the level top of a lofty wedge of the table-land, which maintained its elevation out to a sharp point that terminated in mid-air. Afterward, for our own convenience, we named it Panorama Point.

It seems to me that no human being can stand on that spot and view that marvellous labyrinth of wild Nature without being thrilled by it. Instantly your thoughts fly to the Grand Canyon of the Colorado, as seen from Point Sublime, only this is in miniature. The fact that you stand on a sharp point, from which the world drops steeply away on three sides, is not the thing that is so profoundly impressive. It is the depth, the breadth, and the awful wildness of the maze of bad-lands into which you look. Before you, and on either hand, there stretch miles upon miles of ragged chasms, divided and walled in by a thousand fantastic cliffs, and buttresses, and domes of naked hard-pan that stubbornly defy the forces of erosion, and refuse to crumble down. In several places there are masses of earth architecture that remind one of the ruined castles on the Rhine. These bare walls are mostly of gray earth, not rock, and the carving of them has been most strangely done. It is only when you climb amongst them, and touch them, that the wonders of erosion are fully revealed.

The hard, dry earth has most stubbornly resisted the disintegrating action of water, wind, heat and cold, and there are hundreds of earth cliffs nearly as smooth and as perpendicular as the brick walls of Harlem.

I dislike to estimate the total drop of these bad-lands from the plateau to the waters of Snow Creek, but I *think* it is about eight hundred feet.

After the first moments of spellbound wonder and amaze, you begin to pick out the geography of what lies before you. You see that the axis of all this wild waste of carved and furrowed earth is the level and very narrow valley of Snow Creek, which

The author's coincidence mule deer.

High level bad-lands. About in the centre of this picture was found the Triceratops horn which led to the discovery of *Tyrranosaurus rex.*

From a photograph, copyright by L. A. Huffman.

A wild chaos of carved earth.

comes down from the west. You can easily trace its course eastward to the point where it bends abruptly northward and runs into the Missouri, parallel with the last eight miles of Hell Creek. In the creek bottom there is a sinuous string of cottonwood trees, aspens and willow brush.

The uttermost boundary of this sublime prospect was formed by "the breaks of the Missouri," on the northern side of that stream, and about twenty-five miles away. With a glass, the valley of the "Big Muddy" was plainly defined, and so were the "breaks," but no camera is able to seize and record those far-distant details. We absorbed them into our systems, but on the dry plates they do not appear. Every camera has its limitations.

All this while, I have been wildly impatient to record the occurrence of the first three minutes of that first view from Panorama Point. It will read like a shameless invention, but it is strictly true. I can furnish two affidavits, from white men, with recognizable names.

When the Wolfer led us to the Point, Layton and I seated ourselves on the outermost edge of the jumping-off place, and rested our feet on a little ledge that is conveniently placed below. Sieber seated himself directly behind me, on the left. We had taken only one good look at the panorama before us, and the choice adjectives were but beginning to loosen up, when Sieber excitedly exclaimed:

"Look there! Look! *There goes a dee-er, now!* Shoot, quick! Shoot!" (He always said "*dee-er*" for deer.)

A hundred and twenty yards below us, and to the left, on the steep side of our flat-iron, stood a really fine adult mule-deer buck, gazing up at us in mingled astonishment and curiosity. While Huffman scrambled to his knees, behind me, I turned on my rocky perch, and actually *waited for him to get ready!* Having given him what I regarded as time enough, our two rifles cracked together, so exactly in unison that a moment later, when I threw out my empty shell, Layton innocently exclaimed:

"Why—did *you* shoot, too?"

The buck kicked back with both hind feet, then turned and went bounding down to the bottom of the gulch. We saw on his side a fatal red blotch—which Huffman had made, not I.

"He's hit! He's hit!" cried Sieber.

The buck leaped across the dry bed of the ravine and started up the opposite ridge, intending to climb high over it and away; but half way up he fell, and quickly expired.

When we laid hands upon Huffman's prize, and examined it, a strange and interesting story of wild-animal life was revealed. About three months previously, that is to say about August 1st, that deer had been leaped upon, from above, by a mountain lion. Its right ear was fearfully torn, and there was a big wound on the top of the neck where the skin and flesh had been torn open. The main beam of the right antler had been broken off half way up, while the antlers were still in the velvet. The end of the broken antler had healed over in a way that enabled us to fix the date of the encounter with a fair degree of accuracy. Both the hind legs had been either clawed or bitten, but we could not surely determine which.

It is our opinion that when the mountain lion leaped and fastened upon the neck of his intended prey, the struggling buck either leaped or fell over a cut-bank and landed upon his back, with the puma undermost. Although he broke off the executive branch of his antler, he so seriously injured his assailant that the mountain lion was glad to escape without doing further damage. Some of the casualties to the deer are plainly visible in Mr. Huffman's photographs of the dead game.

A few days later we found about two miles above our camp, close beside the dry bed of Hell Creek, the story of another wild-animal tragedy. On a tiny bit of level bottom-land, which was well planted with thick clumps of tall sage-brush, there lay the well-gnawed remains of a mule deer. Close beside the skeleton there was a round hole in the earth, like a post-hole, made by the waters of the creek, about two feet in diameter and five feet deep. This hole contained about two-thirds of the hair that once had covered the deer. As sure as fate, that yawning hole, which lay like a hidden trap under the long grass and the drooping branches of the sage-brush, had been the undoing of the luckless deer. It seemed to us that while being chased by wolves, the deer had landed heavily on that spot, with *both its forelegs in the hole,* and before it could scramble out, a wolf, or several wolves, had pounced upon it, cut its throat in quick time, and afterward devoured the animal as it lay across the opening. In no other way could we account for all that hair on the sides and bottom of the hole.

In the hope that the wolves would return to those remains for a final gloat over them, Max Sieber generously provided three wolf traps to welcome the expected guests; but during our stay none were caught.

The weather during that golden October was supremely fine. When you have only two weeks to spend in your hunting-grounds, it is good that none of the time should be stolen from you by anything so cheap and commonplace as rain. It was a grand time for the cameras, and we revelled in the opportunity. Huffman's pictures were fine, but my seventy-odd kodaks did not develop as well as they should have done.

We hunted deer, also; but in reality our desire to shed blood was not very strong, and our rifles were useful chiefly as an excuse for ranging far and wide. One of our finest days was when Layton and I rode off alone, and took a wide circuit through the western bad-lands, worked down to Snow Creek, and climbed back by a new route. We discovered, well away toward the west, a long, round-topped ridge, richly set in grass, rising between two pine-filled canyons, and sprinkled all over its top with scattered pines and cedars. It was like a lovely dream park, and just when its serene beauty had filled our souls to the chin, we found the nymphs. Five fat and sleek mule-deer does suddenly appeared amongst the cedars just beyond our horses' noses, stood still, and gazed at us for the fleeting moment which is so fatal to that species. Even before they wheeled away, Huffman had mentally christened that ridge "The Doe's Pasture"—a very fit name, indeed. Then the does wheeled and calmly trotted away toward Snow Creek, leaving us wondering *how* they had so quickly learned of our solemn vow not to shoot female deer! That they *had* found it out (by telepathy?) I am sure I can prove, by Huffman.

We struck an old buffalo trail, and followed all its devious windings down the steep sides of a canyon, in and out, twisting and turning, until at last it landed us on the level floor of the valley of Snow Creek. It is a long, hard job to lead a horse either up or down between mesa and creek-bottom.

We forded the little stream and found a cosey shelter in the sun close beside the combination so dear to the frontiersman—wood, water and grass. There we off-saddled, let our horses graze, built a friendship fire, ate our frugal luncheon, and basked in the romantic wildness of our surroundings.

We found no bucks that day, and cared naught. Late in the afternoon, when we finally climbed out of the bad-lands, leading our horses, and following another old buffalo trail up to the grass-lands, we discovered in the head of a long valley a goodish bit of heavy pine timber. Just within the edge of that, and within pistol shot of the rich grass-lands where the buffalo millions fed fat as late as the early eighties, we found the half-ruined remains of a buffalo-hunter's cabin. No lazy man was he who built it, for it was well done, and had been a comfortable home. The roof had partially fallen in, but the walls were quite intact; and as Huffman and I poked about the place, we saw visions of long-vanished herds of shaggy black heads and high humps, hides drying on the snow, millions of pounds of fine buffalo beef going to waste, and the constant dread of "hostile Sioux" over all.

Along the edge of the buffalo range we found in many a grassy hollow and sheltered coulee the bleaching remains of buffaloes, now reduced to scattered bones, very white and clean. In 1886, we found between the Little Dry and Sand Creek thousands of decaying carcasses, lying intact just as the buffalo skinners left them, the hairy heads looming up black and big on the bare sod. But now, all those have so completely disappeared that it would take a long and wearisome search to find enough buffalo bones to fill a bushel basket. By diligent watchfulness, however, Sieber had accumulated nearly a hundred weathered buffalo horns, and had them piled on the roof of his store-house, waiting for a chance to dispose of them.

At Sieber's ranch, a dozen old buffalo trails converged, focussing upon the deep and permanent water-hole which constituted our friend's most valuable asset. So plain are they as they lead down the steep slope from the east that Mr. Huffman made a photograph to show three of them on one plate. What could be finer for wild bison than grazing grounds such as these, close beside perpetual water, and a labyrinth of ravines in which to shelter from the sweep of the blizzards!

Our camp was exceedingly comfortable, and also interesting. Our tent stood within seventy-five feet of the high cut-bank on the opposite side of the waterless creek, and in a cosy niche in the earthen wall there lived a fine old western horned owl. His pulpit was only about twenty feet up the wall, and there he sat, every day, meditating and blinking away the hours. His working hours were from sunset until sunrise. During the daytime he always seemed happy to meet those who called upon him, and occasionally hooted vigorously, *in broad day*—not necessarily for publication, but to guarantee good faith. I can hear even yet the hollow and sepulchral reverberations of his greetings as he called out:

"*Hoo*-hoo-hoo-*hoo*-HOO,—ah!
If you won't shoot *me*,
I won't shoot *you*,—ah!"

We accepted the trust the old fellow reposed in us, and throughout our stay the only service we exacted of him was looking pleasant while Mr. Huffman planted his largest camera at the shortest possible range, and took his picture. Quite near to him, and stuck against the bare wall of earth, were the mud nests of a colony of cliff swallows, but at that season the owners were absent for the benefit of their health.

The gathering of our supply of firewood, from the clump of cottonwoods in the bend above our camp, led to an episode with five small animals. Our cook hitched a horse to an ancient and very dry cottonwood log, snaked it down to our tent, and proceeded to cut it up. Being cottonwood, and old, it was necessarily hollow. In due time the inexorable axe revealed in the cavity a fine, ample and very proper nest, made chiefly of the feathers of wild birds, and containing five white-footed mice, snugly settled for the winter. Packed close against the side of the nest was about a pint and a half of fine, clean seed, like radish seed, evidently furnished by some weed of the Pulse Family. While the food-store was being examined

and finally deposited in a pile upon the open ground near the tent door, the five mice let us see how they run, and escaped to the sage-brush.

Now, in that rustic scene there was a bit of stage property which no one noticed at the moment, but which any old theatre-goer among those present might have known would be put to use before the play was played out. It was the old-fashioned buggy that belonged to Jady and Mr. Huffman.

At the end of the day, we promptly forgot the white-footed mice; but they made other arrangements. In the morning when Mr. Huffman lifted the cushion of his buggy, and opened the top of the box underneath, in quest of more dry plates, five cunning little heads bunched close together, five pairs of beady black eyes looked up at him in friendly curiosity, and politely asked him what he wanted. I heard a cry for help.

"Great—day—in—the—morning! Just come out, and look here!"

It was one of the drollest sights I ever saw. The mice were not in the least alarmed, and for some *minutes* they made no attempt to escape. They seemed to be consumed with curiosity, about *us!*

"Get your camera, *quick*, and take them where they are!"

The photographer flew for his machine, and actually brought it to bear upon the group; but its big, glaring black eye, so near and so fearsome, was too much for mice, and before the negative could be exposed they stampeded. They streamed down the wheels and again took refuge in the sage-brush.

On taking an account of stock, we found that those amazing little creatures had gathered up every particle of their nest, and every seed of their winter's store, and *carried all of it up into the seat of that buggy!* The nest had been carefully remade, as good as new, and the seeds placed close by it, as before. Considering the many journeys that were required to carry all those materials over the ground, up the shafts of that buggy and into the seat of it, both the agility and the industry of those tiny little animals was amazing.

By way of experiment, we again removed both nest and seed, and placed them all upon the ground near the tent, as before.

During the following night, those indomitable mice *again* carried nest and seed back into the buggy seat, precisely as before. Then we gathered up the entire colony, nest, seed and all, and finally took the whole collection back to New York, where they might be seen of men.

And yet there are people who doubt whether animals reason!

Directly eastward of our camp there was a stretch of bad-lands quite different in character from the great Panorama of Snow Creek. It was high land, but in places most gruesomely blasted and scarred, as if by raging fires. At intervals there rose isolated buttes, or groups of buttes, like so many volcanic islands in a sea of dead lava. Among those buttes there are patches of grassy grounds, and, what was more to the point, many clumps of narrow-leaved mugwort, white sage and cinnamon sage. Sieber said that in October the solitary mule-deer bucks approve that region, and are occasionally to be found there, at long range. He told me, with deep feeling and the self-abasement that marks the truthful hunter, how he once climbed to the top of a low S-shaped butte, saw a fine buck below him within fair range, fired at him with all possible confidence and a good rifle, but missed him, clean and clear! He would give twenty dollars to know *how* he came to miss "that buck."

On the third morning of our stay, we elected to investigate those bad-lands, and again Max Sieber recklessly volunteered to accompany us,—"hay or no hay." We got an early start, and were in our hunting ground at daybreak.

I now approach an incident before which the most hardened *raconteur* might well pause, and calculate his chances of being believed. When written down, it will read so much like a cheap invention that it might be wiser to leave it untold; but inasmuch as an "affidavit" is now supposed to be quite irrefragable "evidence" of the truthfulness of even the silliest pipe-dream about "nature," and Max Sieber is still at Jerdon, Montana, and able to make affidavit of the entire truthfulness of this story, I will make bold to set it down.

Layton, Sieber, and I together hunted through those bad-lands for two hours or more, without results; and then Layton left us to hunt alone through an isolated

group of buttes half a mile away. Sieber and I tramped about until we approached a low butte, and then he said:

"Now, here we are! If you will come up to the top of this butte with me, I'll show you right where I missed that fine big buck, last winter."

I thought (very secretly), "Oh, *hang* the big buck you missed last winter! What I want to see is a living buck, not the scene of a dead failure."

But Sieber blithely started up, and solely to humor a kind friend I sacrificed myself and climbed after him, without audible protest.

We reached the top of the queer hog-back, which really was like a capital S, three hundred feet long, and along its crest we walked. At its farther extremity it rose a hundred feet higher, in a bald, round dome of blasted earth. Up that also Sieber and I climbed, side by side, and presently overlooked its highest point.

Raising his right hand, he pointed down the farther slope, toward a ragged notch a hundred and fifty yards away, and said, reminiscently:

"That buck was standing right down in —*why! Look! Look! There's a dee-er there now!*"

Down he crouched,—sensible to the last, —hoarsely muttering, "But it's a doe!"

But I knew better; for I had seen the glint of high light on a fine pair of antlers. "*No!* It's a buck! *I see his horns!*"— Bang!

He leaped just twice, then went down to stay; and by the time we reached him he was lifeless. But really, the remarkable coincidence represented in the flesh and blood of that buck seemed almost incredible. It took minutes for us to adjust our minds to it, and make it seem real.

Sieber said to Huffman: "It was as purty a shot as I ever saw made—quick, close behind the shoulder, and a shore bull's-eye."

The death of that fine specimen, in a wild and rugged landscape, and by a single shot, gave me all the blood I cared to shed on that trip, even though it was, as Sieber said, "a mighty long way to come to kill one black-tail buck, saying nothing of the hard work and the expense." But it is not all of hunting to kill game.

That was a fine, large buck, with fairly good antlers,—fully developed and long, but not so massive as we like to have them. He stood 42 inches high at the shoulders. The contents of his stomach was totally different from what I expected. Instead of the grass that we all looked for, it consisted almost wholly of narrow-leaved mugwort (*Artemisia tomentosa*), which had been eaten to the exclusion of practically everything else. There was hardly a trace of grass. Later on, when we tasted the stems of that species of mugwort, and found how pungent and aromatic is the flavor, and how tender to chew, we did not wonder why the deer were partial to it.

Those buttes east of our camp were literally alive with cottontail rabbits. They loved the sunny nooks that were strewn with rocks, and it was a common thing to disturb a meeting, and see five or six rabbits wildly scurrying away in different directions, but all in sight at the same moment. The prairie hare was very scarce; and I saw only three individuals during the entire trip.

Gray wolves, and coyotes also, were rare, —thanks to the delicate ministrations of Wolfer Max and others. I saw only four wolves during the month that we were out. One spotted lynx was seen. Mr. Huffman and I came upon it on Hell Creek, finishing a repast of rabbit, and although my companion-in-arms wounded it, it managed to get into a wash-out hole in a cut-bank and escape.

We saw the fresh work of the western yellow-haired porcupine, on Hell Creek above our camp, where several cottonwood saplings had been denuded of their bark and small twigs, pro bono porcupine.

Sieber assured us that in the Panorama Bad-Lands there dwelt, even at that time, a band of about half a dozen mountain sheep; but we did not look for them. I did not doubt the report, because I once met the fresh head of a huge old ram who lived in bad-lands down in Wyoming which were by no means so deep or so high as these.

The most exciting feature of our story remains to be told.

Over in the easterly bad-lands, about in the centre of the landscape behind my dead mule deer, I found three chunks of fossil bone which when fitted together formed a horn-like mass nearly a foot long. It was the terminal third of *the right horn of a Tricer'-a-tops*, a huge three-horned, armored reptile of the Upper Cretaceous, that is as big as a rhinoceros, and looks like one, dead or alive! Then Max Sieber took me to a spot near by where he had found the badly weathered remains of what once had been a fossil skull, as large as the skull of a half-grown elephant. It lay quite free, upon the bare earth, in a place that looked very much like the crater of a volcano, it was so blasted and lifeless, and cinder-like. The skull was so badly weathered that nothing could be made of it, but near it lay several fragments of ribs in a fair state of preservation.

It was very evident that in the age of reptiles some gigantic species had inhabited that spot. There was no knowing, without a thorough examination by an expert collector of fossils, what that square mile contained; and so, with Professor Henry Fairfield Osborn in my mind I brought away the specimens which seemed likely to afford Science a clue.

On reaching New York, Professor Osborn was keenly interested. The Triceratops horn was considered of sufficient importance to justify the American Museum in sending Mr. Barnum Brown to the scene of the find, to make a careful reconnoissance of that locality. Halfway up the western face of the butte directly opposite Sieber's cabin, on the east bank of Hell Creek,—the very one which bears the two piles of stones which I erected to form the wild western "water sign,"—Mr. Brown found the remains of a new genus of gigantic reptiles—predatory, and carnivorous to the utmost. A skull, *six feet long*, and set with frightful teeth, was unearthed and sent to New York; and in due time the world was introduced to *Tyrranosaurus rex*, the Tyrant Lizard, late of Hell Creek

24.
HUNTING IN
BRITISH COLUMBIA
(1911)

VANCOUVER ISLAND DEER AT HOME

HUNTING IN BRITISH COLUMBIA

By BONNYCASTLE DALE

PHOTOGRAPHS BY FLEMING BROS.

A Land that Is Still Filled with Game, Large and Small, and Whose Waters Teem with Fish

EXTENDING from the boundary of the State of Washington on the 49th parallel clear up to the 54° the ever decreasing heights of the Rocky and the Cascade Ranges, and the wide, uninhabited plateaus between, form a hunting ground almost four hundred miles square. This is the mainland of British Columbia. There is also the huge Vancouver Island, eighty miles out to sea, with its backbone range of mountains, its length of three hundred miles, and its width of eighty, furnishing another immense hunting field.

Its woods are filled with blacktail deer and its northern valley with wapiti, the true American red deer, called here the American elk. Bear, panthers and wolves abound and the rivers are literally filled with salmon and trout. I use the word advisedly when I say filled as I have counted over a hundred salmon in a pool some fifty feet in diameter. These were spawning, but they are equally numerous off the river mouths and they take a spoon greedily, that is the Spring and the Cohoe do, but of this later.

The noblest animal that inhabits the huge valleys and plateaus of the mainland of British Columbia is the moose. Go to the Cassiar district if you want the finest moose hunting the world offers and remember that you will not be too late as these animals, under the care of the Provincial Government, are actually increasing in numbers. You can take but two bull moose but we give you four months, beginning in September to

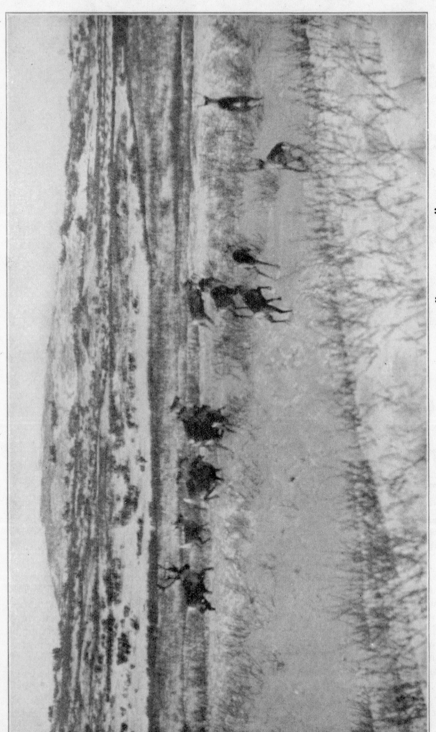

A BAND OF BRITISH COLUMBIA CARIBOU "ON THE JUMP"

DOE AND FAWN OF BLACKTAIL DEER

A BRITISH COLUMBIA WINTER SCENE THAT WILL GLADDEN ANY HUNTER'S EYES

get them, and we charge the regular license of one hundred dollars per hunter. If you get a bull close to a thousand pounds, with a forest of beams and branches that extend between five and six feet, really the inside cavity of the upper beam resembles a bone bath tub, you will feel amply repaid.

I wondered as a lad how they carried those mighty masses of horns through the underbrush, but if you have ever seen a moose place his horns lengthwise to his body you will notice that wherever the broad shoulders can pass the horns can follow. If you are going to hunt out here come early; July is none too soon to get north and get started, but by all means write to the game warden at Victoria, B. C., for pamphlets explaining everything.

You need not go as far north as Cassiar. If you come west by rail stop off at Lytton. North lies a parklike country. If you are fond of horseback work you can ride to your heart's content. One hundred miles from the main line of the railroad sheep and goat, deer and bear—grizzly and black—can be readily found, and guides are easy to get at the towns on the line.

I think of all the simple game our friend the mountain goat has place of honor. *Mazama montana* is a creature without knowledge of sanitary habits and when I tell you that we have come so close to him as most readily and disagreeably to discern his heavy odor, you will not wonder that good heads are obtained. Meet him suddenly on his own stamping ground and the old chap will stare at you much after the fashion of a tame goat. Suddenly the knowledge that curiosity is a dangerous thing comes over him and away he charges at the most impossible side of the hill—and he makes it too, with much clatter of displaced shale. Even these nimble, crafty, old warriors pick out "no thoroughfare." Sometimes several cases have been noted of a goat having wandered along a ledge until it became so narrow that it was impossible for it to turn. I have noted in all cases of mistakes made among the animals that panic seizes them, and although the animal inevitably falls from the cliff I do not think it leaps; rather

it falls off as soon as it begins to plunge. I have seen three sheep on closed trails, unable to go ahead, back up or turn. How long they could stand the strain is uncertain, but we saw them through the glass all of one day.

If you seek the myriad caribou (*Rangifer montanus*) go any place in lower and central British Columbia. You have the same four months to hunt him and the one license includes all game that wears hair, scales, or feathers. Within a day's trailing from the railroad you can get most excellent shooting, and those wondrous branching horns are not to be found of greater extent anywhere, at least so European sportsmen inform us. Steamboats now take the place of the more picturesque canoe but you will need the latter on side trips. Bands of ten to one hundred caribou are no uncommon sight after the snow flies. With the new modern high power rifles these lordly animals fall an easy prey. The ones pictured were in the Cassiar district.

Haunts of the Mule Deer

The mule deer (*Cariacus macrotis*) are to be found all over the lower mainland but not on the island; this is true of the white-tailed deer also, but the black-tailed deer are everywhere, both on island and mainland. My assistant and I never kill these small deer. Time after time we have essayed to capture them by hand. We have met them on the seashore where the tide shut off their retreat and the almost precipitous clay cliff prevented them climbing. As soon as we get near enough up flies the black tail, back goes the head and off up that seemingly impossible bank they go. The ledges in places are not more than an inch wide, yet they bound and leap and scramble from one to another.

One day I watched Fritz, my assistant, take the best (?) trail, while ahead of him leaped and plunged a fawn. The little yellow legs fairly twinkled in the shower of uptorn cliff it was sending down and my lad forgot his danger and, pressing his body to the cliff, kept on. He had to choose more practicable paths than the nimble fawn—he told me afterwards that it made its way up one place where there was no ledge at all. Finally the fawn rolled half way down and Fritz did not dare to follow.

It took him an hour's knife cutting and scraping to get to the top of the hundred foot cliff and then he arrived under the overhanging top of the bank and had to tunnel through. I have had one of these animals charge me rather than jump off a blind trail, at least he saw me standing there and came right along in huge leaps, bounding like an animated ball along a trail not a foot wide. I had to squeeze against the bank and let this buck pass. Another time I was glad to jump behind a tree—so if you want to kill a small deer the country is full of your game.

If it is sheep you seek, the story is different. We have no less than four varieties out here—and very much up in the clouds all of them are too. That magnificent sheep the bighorn heads the list. *Ovis montana* is well worthy of the trouble it takes to secure him. Right in the Rockies, not very far from where you leave your Pullman, but very much above you, bands of these nimble animals are feeding. A few hundred miles to the north, in Cassiar, *Ovis Stonei, Ovis Fannini* and *Ovis Balli* are to be found, but if you can get the bighorn never will the sweet-scented fragrance from the old briar pipe ascend after dinner is over and the den reached toward handsomer horns than grace the heads of these perfect animals.

If you are a naturalist bring your camera, a good focal plane shutter with the latest telephoto attachment and a good strong telescope and you can study this wild sheep while yet there is time, for notwithstanding the fact that the Government is establishing a mighty preserve in the Rockies, the fauna of America is passing out. My eyes have seen the light for but fifty years and in that brief space I have noted the extinction, the decimation, or at least the lessening of almost all the fauna, no matter whether it wears scales or hair or feathers, almost everything that was on this continent or in the water of its littoral at my birth is sadly decimated at this my fiftieth year. All must pass before the close cutting line of northward advancing civilization. These mighty masses of animals need mighty feeding grounds, so does the rapidly growing human race. It seems very sad, but perhaps it is better so, for every wild animal we have killed we have reared ten domestic ones to take its place.

No doubt many of my Eastern readers will want a bearskin for the kiddies' feet to patter on and increase the respect for that mighty hunter "dad." Notwithstanding the magazine stories to the contrary, you could send that kiddie of yours and if he could shoot straight enough he could bring home that bearskin. The bears are poor, cowardly grass eaters, berry feeders, mice catchers, aye, they even eat ants and grasshoppers, snails and slugs—and yet these nature-fakirs write about them as if their natural food was man, white preferred. I do yield respect to a grizzly that cannot get out of your road, or one that is wounded, but the average black bear, and it is plentiful all over British Columbia, will run like a grumbling pig, aye! even if the cubs are at her heels.

Bruin in a Comedy Rôle

We have some very funny things happen with the bears. Of course as soon as a boy stumbles up against one he expects to be eaten alive right off. One little lad, skating, sat down on a log for a rest and over he toppled right on top of a nice, big, smooth, black bear. Now you see this bear had never seen a magazine, so he did not know that boys were made for bear's food, so he jumped up and slapped away at the intruder. The scared boy ran out of the mess and his friend killed the bear with an axe.

I know of Indian boys less than a round dozen of years old killing one of these big, fat, lazy, vegetable eaters. But remember it is a big animal and if you sting it up well with a poorly directed shot, its teeth and claws are big enough to make a bad wreck of you, although even when wounded the chances are that it will run. I know of one Indian that wounded a grizzly; first he chased it, then the bear took a hand and chased him, it in turn became the pursued again. Ahead lay a river and over it a great hollow cedar had fallen. Into this the bear scrambled and after it loped the Indian, and, as he so graphically said later, "The hyas fool bear turned." The result of it all was that a hunter's dog found the pair. The bear was on top—dead—the Indian underneath almost smothered with gore from thirty-eight stabs he had up-prodded into the big, brown breast, and it managed to claw his hip and bite his shoulder badly before it died, but he killed it all the same with his skinning knife.

Wolves we have all over the province. I regret to announce that the British Columbia wolf does not prefer human beings for food. This big gray chap—he is almost black on Vancouver Island—eats things far smaller than a man. Anything that the keen eyes and clear scent can discover, anything that lives and moves and is small enough not to put up a good stiff fight is his prey. No doubt the old, the infirm, the dying, and the very young deer do fall a prey, but it would be a very poor buck that could not beat off a wolf with its sharp front hoof or beat it in a race.

It is the panther (*Felis concolour*) that does the most damage. Even in a stern chase this beast cannot catch a deer. (I write from notes carefully gathered all over the coast from hundreds of guides and hunters and from my own observation.) The deer must almost be delivered into his claws before he is sure of it. True, a very young fawn, or a deer that is ill, is sure bait for the long, lithe, sneaking, cowardly cat,—a cat so cowardly that it has never yet been recorded on this coast as attacking man, woman, or child. Many a time its evil yellow eyes have glared on the kiddies on Vancouver Island on their way to school, but none have been attacked; many a little innocent has seen a panther, as the trail later proved, but they do not feed on children out here.

Could it be possible that some notes from Mars about animals have fluttered down to this planet, for surely all the men who write these bloodthirsty animal tales cannot be liars, and none of the men that really study the wild animals have been killed or injured; or even

scared? Many's the night Fritz and I have slept under a tree, where the well pressed cedar told of a black-tail deer's bed and the only weapons we had in camp were our small pocket knives. There is no danger in the woods of British Columbia save from a falling tree.

If it should happen that your tastes lie toward fishing, this Pacific Coast has wonders to offer. Since I arrived here I have hardly ever gone out ostensibly to fish or shoot; we just put the rod and gun into the canoes and take whatever actually comes across our path. Steelhead trout that you cannot land under the half hour, the hardest fighting fish in the waters of this continent, abound. Cutthroat trout leap in every harbor, bay and fiord. Off the mouths of the rivers that debouch from the mainland and the island great Spring salmon, running from ten to eighty pounds, are found each spring month, and in the summer, too, waiting for us lucky fishers to go out and fight with them.

Later in the summer, Cohoes run, a fish of much endurance on the end of a hooked line, one that fights you all the time. These five to eight pounders run in schools of countless thousands. I have seen ten to fifteen thousand caught in one salmon trap in one day off these fishing grounds.

In the fall remaining until late spring hosts of wild fowl are with us, bucks of all breeds, most of which I can study from the desk window where I write this without leaving my typewriter seat. They feed and swim along or rest right on the shores before my bungalow—and in every other inlet and fiord on Vancouver Island and the mainland.

I do not write this to switch men from their old hunting grounds, but if, unhappily, these are being decimated, here is the last and greatest hunting ground on this continent. I have no retainer from any person, company, or government, but I have shot and fished all over the United States and you never charged me a cent in those days—and if what I have written here gives any man a good bag for a fair day's work I am satisfied.

25.
BIG GAME
IN THE ROCKIES
(1899)

BIG GAME IN THE ROCKIES.

BY JOHN N. OSTROM.

Our hunting party had been organized for business, and for that peculiar pleasure experienced by some in doing what is difficult, dangerous and perhaps foolhardy. Excepting myself, the hunters were all from beyond the Missouri, and experienced on the plains and in the mountains. I could not claim as much experience; but as I had frequently hunted in the Indian Territory I did not by any means consider myself a tenderfoot, and so far as endurance was concerned I believed myself as well able to follow the trail all day as any of my comrades.

I HAD been hunting bear and elk for six months, in my mind's eye, and when on September 16th I found myself actually dumped off at Berry's Ranch amongst a formidable pile of guns, ammunition and camp equipage, I realized that at last the campaign was actually to open with all its excitement, hardships and dangers.

Berry's Ranch is on the Eagle River, about fifty miles northwest of Leadville, and the mountains rise directly from the foaming river.

Mine host Berry is a born hunter. Although his gray hair and wrinkled

259

face indicated his age to be some sixty years, his eye was keen and restless, and he had that peculiar habit in walking of raising the feet high up and putting them down softly as though not to scuff dead twigs and leaves—the sign of a successful game stalker.

The next morning's train brought my cousin Hub and two of his friends, completing our party. We had expected that Berry would accompany us as guide, but as harvesting had begun he could not get away. His neighbor, Dutton, however, came to our rescue, and proved a veritable old sleuth-hound on the trail.

I turned out in the morning before the sun, for in hunting I like to get an early start, but it availed me nothing in this instance, for Jennie was late with her breakfast, although it was a most excellent one when we did get it. We should have been off at sunrise. Dutton led the column with the pack-horse "Nibs;" then came little long-eared Jenny, covered under a mass of white canvas, bags of provisions, and general camp fittings; then Smith, riding the black horse Nig, and carrying my camera outfit; then George, mounted on the sorrel Pete, and bringing up the rear came Hub and I on foot. The day was beautiful, and we got along for nearly the whole ascent without serious trouble. I frequently stopped to look back, for the sight was an inspiring one. Many miles away, across the Eagle, rose the majestic Mount of the Holy Cross. It cannot be advantageously seen from the valley, but two or three thousand feet up, on the opposite range, its white cross and clustered peaks rise in enchanting beauty. About sunset we reached a beautiful spring in a bunch of green pines, pretty well toward the top. It was the first water we had seen since leaving the ranch, and we stopped long enough to get a drink and to eat a mouthful of snack, carried in our pockets. The camp-fire chat was not very animated, as we were all very tired, and no one had tried to hunt, though we had seen abundance of old "signs" of elk and deer on top of the divide.

In the morning I slipped out at daylight, and took a circle around on the divide. It had snowed a little during the night and frozen, so that stealthy walking was impossible, and I knew that I should probably not sneak onto any game, as I had hoped to. But the landscape was grand. Across the Piney, in the far distance, the Gore Range rose snow-capped, and without a cloud to obscure it. This sight alone was worth the hard climb of the day before.

The peculiarity of the country here is alternate patches of green pines about a foot in diameter, dead ones in windfalls, and interspersed with bare patches of good range. The wind being down the mountain, Dutton advised descending through the openings and coming up through the green pines, so that we might have the wind of the game we hoped to find there. After we had descended cautiously about a mile in the open we heard a crash in the timber to our right. The rattle of horns through the limbs meant that he was in there, but had no use for our company, so we kept on down the open for about half a mile further, and then swung around to the right into the timber, and headed up the mountain. We had not gone far when we struck the perfectly fresh trail of a big bull elk, which settled the identity of the fellow we had flushed half a mile above. But he was making straight down the slope, and Dutton said it was useless to trail him. It was too bad to give him up, but there was some consolation in hearing him run and seeing his ox-like track. After this we scrambled around through the pines up the mountain for a while and then separated. In about an hour I heard a couple of shots above me, which braced me up somewhat with the anticipation of a steak for dinner; but on reaching camp I met a disgusted party with only a groundhog and a grouse.

Just as the sun was going down I set up my camera and shot the Gore Range, which had come out clear and bold, with a background of azure, dotted with a few cumulus clouds, in a very striking manner. We cooked a good supper of hot biscuit, slapjacks, boiled potatoes, fried grouse and pork, and coffee. I noticed that it took perceptibly longer to boil potatoes than at usual altitudes, and I judged that we must be about 10,000 feet above sea level. While at supper we decided to move camp a day's ride further along the divide.

In the morning I made some exposures of Camp Piney, and we then packed up. We had not gone more than half a mile before we struck the trail of a bull elk and two cows, all apparently made the night before. The trail took us down the mountain through a succession of green pines and openings covered with good range grass. It certainly was an ideal place for deer and elk, and I fully expected to jump a bunch of them in every new opening we struck. We followed the old bull's trail for about four hours, crossing a stream and climbing a mountain opposite, when his track again swung down toward the Piney, and it was evident, from the lay of the bald knob we were on, that he was making for the green pines at least eight miles below. We were now several miles below the summit, and Hub knew there was a small lake somewhere above us in a niche called the Devil's Slide. I noticed that within sight, and at the head of the run we were on, the water came over a quite broad crest of rock, and it occurred to me that the lake might be back of it. I therefore suggested making the climb, which we did, finding the lake.

We had scarcely struck its little outlet before I stumbled onto a bear "sign" so fresh that it made my heart thump. A big fellow had been wallowing in the run so recently that the water was yet roily. The rocks and green pines were thick around us, and a sort of swamp grass, about shoulder high, grew along the run. It was a veritable den. The trail led directly through the tall grass, and the track was so large and fresh that we were afraid to follow it without reconnoitering with great care. With this end in view, Hub proposed to go around the patch of grass to see if the trail passed out anywhere, for if it did not we knew that our game was probably lying down asleep inside. I got back a little way from the grass and took a position behind a sort of rocky bulwark, so that there were several yards of clear opening between me and the point where the trail entered the cover. As the wind was in my favor, I knew that I should not be scented, and if the bear came out on my side I should have a fair shot. Hub then began his circle around the swamp grass, which was about 100 yards in diameter. When he had got about one-quarter of the way around, I heard a sort of snorting grunt, and almost immediately after a frightful-looking grizzly rose up on his hind feet in the grass, about fifty yards

off. He had not seen me, but had scented Hub and was looking towards where I knew him to be and standing broadside to me. As I raised to fire my arm trembled so that it was impossible to hold a steady bead, for the bear was so much larger than I had ever dreamed of meeting, and the danger was so great if I missed, that it completely unnerved me. I knew it was my time, though, and, holding as nearly under his huge shoulder blade as I could, I pulled. My heart fairly jumped into my mouth on the instant, for I was conscious that I had pulled off to the right from my intended aim. With an awful roar the bear disappeared in the grass, and then began the most furious exhibition of frenzied rage that I had ever witnessed. I could only see the grass swaying violently, but the beatings of the ground with his huge paws, the roars and growls and whines, were perfectly frightful. I had evidently got in a shot, however, that made it impossible for him to more than roll around in a small circle. Finally, as everything had been quiet for some minutes, we began closing in on him cautiously, but in what proved to be a most foolhardy undertaking, for I had not gone more than fifteen yards within the cover before, with a fierce roar, the bear's head showed in the grass immediately in front of me, in a mad charge. I whirled immediately and ran for the rocks. As I bounded through the intervening opening, I heard Hub's rifle crack twice in quick succession, and not hearing the bear immediately behind me, I looked around and saw him reared up on his fore-paws, just out of the grass. I then saw what I had suspected before, that I had fortunately broken his back. Every few seconds he would rise up on his fore-paws and gnash his teeth in a perfectly terrible manner. Thinking to put an end to him, I shot him again directly in the hollow between the shoulders, as nearly as I could judge. The bullet knocked him down, but he rose again, when Hub, who had approached on his flank, shot him sidewise through the neck, just below the ear, from which he sank, and, stretching out with a convulsive shiver, died.

Coming to examine his wounds we found that my first bullet had crashed completely through his backbone about six inches below the shoulders, while the second one had just missed the heart and had ranged clear through him, being found in one of the hams. But neither of the 45-caliber 500-grain bullets had killed him, and my chances would certainly have been slim if the tremble in my arm had not deviated the shot to the most vulnerable spot I could have chosen. Hub's first two bullets, when the brute was charging me, had gone through his lungs, and the last one had broken his neck.

We had been so much excited and interested during the operation as to forget about time, when all at once we realized that night was closing in on us. Hub said we were about four miles from our proposed camp, and that the ground was very rough, being cut up with deep gulches. As we were both about played out, therefore, we decided to make the best of it and camp in the den. We therefore dragged the skin around to the other side of the lake, which we found about 150 feet in diameter, and selected a nice place in the pines some 100 feet from the water. Hub made a fire and brought some bear steak, while I made a good soft bed of "Colorado feathers" by cutting off the tips of the pine boughs from the trees around.

It was now as dark as Egypt, except from the red glare of the pine fire, and being in a dangerous place we determined to take alternate turns of sleeping and watching. I won the morning watch by guessing the nearest on our northern bearing, decided by my compass. Then I crawled under the bear-skin, on top of the feathers, and was soon lost in sleep.

About three o'clock, feeling thirsty, I went down to the lake for a drink. While lying down drinking I heard a dead twig snap directly on the opposite shore from me, and, looking over intently, without rising, I soon saw, low down near the water, a pair of eyes in the darkness. Although considerably startled, I determined to try a shot at them, the slight sound convincing me that it was a lion, and I knew that he could not spring upon me before I could get back to camp. I therefore rested my elbows on the beach and held up my gun to see if I could catch a bead. The low camp-fire being directly to my back, I found that I could dimly see the front sight, and taking deliberate aim about six inches below the eyes, as nearly as I could estimate, I fired. At the crack there was a frightful scream, followed by a rustling noise, as though the animal were bounding off through the grass. I knew at once that it was a lion, but decided not to reconnoiter until morning.

PINEY LAKE.

Just before daylight I heard a snarling and snapping in the direction of the bear carcass, and knew at once that the wolves must be at work there. I therefore awoke Hub, and as he confirmed my belief we decided to try and sneak on them for a shot.

When morning came it was necessary to find our camp as soon as possible, and after hanging up the bear-skin in one of the pines we pulled out. Upon emerging from the timber surrounding the lake the great Gore Range came again in view, and now we could fairly see at its base Piney Lake, the head of the Piney River and the home of speckled trout. Hub had already told me of it, for he had been there the July before on

PACKING OUR BUCK.

BERRY'S CABIN.

a fishing trip. We were now in sight of our objective camp, but to reach it we had two deep forbidding gulches to cross.

After we had crossed the first gulch we met Dutton, who, thinking that we were lost, had started out in search of us. We then hurried on to camp. The boys had just finished breakfast and were evidently relieved at seeing us once more safe and sound. Hot coffee, bread and potatoes were certainly an agreeable substitute for unsalted bear steak, and besides we had some nice juicy venison,

Eagle and the Piney, and the view was superlatively grand. To the right the Mount of the Holy Cross loomed up through the clouds, while by going 500 yards to the left the saw-tooth edge of the Gore Range rose in bold relief.

According to agreement Hub and I saddled up in the morning, and, taking camera and guns, laid our trail for the lake. We reached it after a four hours' hard ride, and my anticipations of pleasure were more than realized upon looking upon its placid surface from the shore. It certainly is a worthy subject

CAMP PINEY.

Dutton having killed a yearling buck on the trail the day before.

I was very anxious to visit Piney Lake, and this would take a day from our present camp. It was therefore agreed that Hub and I should start for the lake in the morning, while the others should return to the ranch. Dutton agreed to be back by the second morning to take in the pack.

As the sun had been shining all the morning the light snow was gone, so that hunting for the balance of the day was unfavorable, and I therefore decided to unpack my camera and take some views of Camp Gore before breaking up. We were now camped on very nearly the highest ground between the

for a poet's dreams or an artist's touch. It has been so frequently used by camping parties that the underbrush is all cut out; in fact, we found two tents pitched there, but the owners were out. The lake is about five hundred yards in diameter and nearly round, and, like the outlet, abounds in brook trout, but it was out of season.

We made the trip back without incident, reaching the tent about dark and finding it unmolested. After a hearty supper we turned in.

As Dutton had not returned in the morning by the time we were ready to start, we determined to leave the tent for him to pack in and start ahead with the horses for the ranch through a promising deer country which Hub knew of. In about two hours we came to the head of June Cañon, which empties into the Eagle not far from our destination, and sat down on a log in the thick pines, thinking that our game might come to us, as is frequently the case in such circumstances. We had not been resting more than twenty minutes before we heard a rattle in the timber ahead of us, and we could soon see through the pines a large buck. When about one hundred and fifty yards off he stopped suddenly, turned around and lay down quickly, with his head toward what had frightened him. He had not scented us, as the wind was in our favor, and his attention was attracted in the other direction. Hub told me to shoot first, and he would try him on the run if I missed. As he was lying, I could only see his neck and shoulders, and being endwise to me it was by no means an easy shot ; but, resting my elbow on my knee, I drew close down on the base of the neck and fired. Without even raising his head he fell forward, and upon coming up we found a six-prong buck still in death. The bullet had struck squarely in the base of the neck and broken it. As we had two horses with us we decided to pack the buck in, and after a hard lift succeeded in landing him across old Nibs' saddle and binding him on with the lariat. We

now heard steps ahead of us, and soon saw Dutton coming along with the horses. He had flushed the buck about a mile below us, and was following his trail. As the old man agreed to go back for the pack alone, we gave him our extra horse, and then started out with the buck. It was very troublesome work until we got out of the pines, and old Nibs seemed on the point of bucking a great many times when the horns swung around into his ribs, but for a wonder he did not, and we finally reached the ranch in good order.

The time of year to choose for a trip to the high Rockies varies with the nature of the game you most desire. If you want trout at their best and bears, at least in the district we were in, then I should say select July.

If you want comfort go in September. If you are after elk and deer, then later, in October, and though that noble game has been thinned even in the Rockies, you will find a sufficient remnant to satisfy all legitimate sportsmen. What you will need to be, however, in addition to a good shot, is a good climber, and in good condition.

Do not in any event go high up on the divide, for the risk of sudden storms is great there, and it is not prudent to challenge pneumonia to a race in those altitudes. You might lose.

26.
SHOREBIRD SHOOTING
IN NEW ENGLAND
(1892)

SHORE-BIRD SHOOTING IN NEW ENGLAND

BY H. PRESCOTT BEACH.

O UT into the cold, gray mist, into the fog and spray, into the dimness of dawn, we followed the crooked, stony path from the village to the sea. We crossed a field of tangled briars and weeds, soaking our leggins with the heavy dew, and bending past a row of little fishermen's huts, came out upon the shore. Around us the brown sands, strewn with shells, seaweed and stranded drift — for the tide was near the end of the ebb — seemed to stretch endlessly away through the vapor. The spires and roofs of Milford were hidden, and only the ghostlike form of old "Stratford Light" stood out in the distance to mark the western end of the curving line of trees and brush that follow the banks of the Housatonic to its mouth. To the eastward a two-mile strip of level shingle skirted the coast, running far out to

sea, and on this pool-paved strand innumerable shore-birds, when the tide went out, flocked to feed. As the rising water drove them landward, they would come sweeping in with the gulls and terns to wing up the inlets and creeks that crawl through the meadows.

"Pete," our English setter, sniffed the morning air with eagerness, eyeing us impatiently while we paused to slip in shells. He was longing to course out over the beach after a bunch of ring-neck plover huddled by the edge of a tide-left shallow, but he caught my eye and subsided reluctantly, crouching at my feet. How cautiously he sneaked after us when we crept down the shore, knowing well he would have no part in the sport that day, save to fetch in the dead birds like the sterling, good retriever he is !

Then they all rose, sounding a shrill

alarm and flickering off, leaving us away out of range. By their hasty and prolonged flight they must have been shot at lately. With them a pair of Wilson's plover were startled (rare birds in New England nowadays, though common enough on the sand-shores of the Gulf States), and these two came circling back to hover high above us. Bang! from Withers' piece, and— bang! from mine as one bird faltered, and the other darted past like a flash. It was a clean miss for me and a bad one, albeit the bird was a fast flyer and quartering. Withers' choice came flopping slowly down some thirty yards away in a tangle of eel-grass, whence Pete, a moment later, snatched it stone-dead. We stopped to admire the rare, pale-gray bird with its luminous black crescent on the forethroat and breast of spotless white, and, while admiring it, almost lost a shot at a passing flock of knots or robin-sandpipers. Together we wheeled with fingers still on our seconds, and fired with one report; then, both still holding on the flock, pulled the firsts, only to find empty right barrels respond to the snap. Apparently we did not reach the "knotty subjects," as the Colonel called them; but Pete was off on the wings of the wind toward the water's edge till, following the birds, he was lost in the mist. His keen eyes had seen a wounded bird flying with difficulty, and he knew it would drop ere long. Back he came on a canter with two big knots in his mouth, both heavy birds, wonderfully well fleshed for the season, and neither had been hit hard. A knowing dog that Pete!

"Whew!" gasped the Colonel. "I am getting hot even in this cold air. It makes me perspire just to see that dog work. I am going to sit down on this piece of timber awhile and rest my gun. You can go on."

Just on the very water's edge I came upon a dozen or more dowitchers, or redbreast snipe, making a breakfast among the barnacles and the periwinkles, and missed them with both barrels in some unaccountable way. The Colonel started up with renewed ardor and bagged one as they whirled by. They settled again only a few rods below, and there we got in some killing work, Withers dropping three when they got up and I taking four a moment after. The scattered survivors, few and frightened,

fluttered across the channel toward the Charles Island bar.

By this time the sun was well above the ridges and lit up the whole shore until we could apparently see for miles in the clear air and could mark in the distance birds feeding, birds flying, birds resting. Sandpipers, curlews, tattlers, singly or in pairs, or in flocks of hundreds, flitted hither and yon. The playful terns, far out beyond them, frolicked in the sunlight, pursuing and again pursued by a solitary osprey, diving and dodging and darting—mere flecks of white against the dark green.

"Do you see those sanderlings just lighting under the clay bluff?" called Withers some time later as we wended our way along the sand. "Well, it's a large bunch, and I am going over to raise them. Come on!" So off we set, floundering through the little ponds and slipping across the intervening patches of mud till we came to hard sand and good footing along close under the bluff. When we were not more than twenty yards away, they all straggled up by twos and threes. I barely got in my two shots, but Withers reloaded in time to drive at the rear detachment twice more with deadly effect, both of us counting eight out of that flurry.

We overtook them again and killed one at every shot, reloaded and missed entirely in the wild hurry to save time. Some curlews went whistling past, and Withers almost looked glum with disappointment at not being loaded. They never stopped, but bore on across the channel and settled down on the bar. "Let's go up to the canoe and lunch under a sail; this seems so infernally hot," proposed Withers—"and after a bite '—t' and a swallow," I providently added, interrupting, "we'll go over to the bar. Everything is taking wings in that direction."

For two hours or more we lounged under the awning, and the sun burned down on the sand, and then a hurrying flock of spotted sandpipers or "tip ups" glimmered past, heading for the island, and that aroused the Colonel. "Hurry up, old boy; let's run this craft across the flat and launch her now—the tide is coming in fast!" he cried with a grab at the painter while I pushed at the stern.

We slid her over the shingle and into

the water, while I coaxed the rebellious Pete aboard. Pete is no sea-dog, and he knows his weak point. Once well in, my gun in hand, I watched Withers lay his down, and all at once—whang! whang! and both barrels went off at a stray plover overhead, while whang! whang! went the Colonel's round head against the thwart, and his gun-muzzle was thrust into the mud.

With great labor I unsnarled him from the coils of rope and pieces of twine in the bottom of the canoe, and taking charge of his gun, bade him paddle for dear life.

Our boat had barely grated on the gravel of the bar, when the Colonel snatched his gun and let go right and left at something pretty nearly in line with my ear, I judged, from the deafening whiz. Then he yelled in glee, "A pair of ruffs—bagged both!" Pete, as if to atone for his recent land-lubberly attack of seasickness, plunged in and brought the birds to us in grand style.

A lonely blue-stocking, the first of its kind I had seen in many a year, stood motionless by a bed of rock-weed, where he had been feeding. He rose, and I captured him with the second barrel. A beauty he was, too, when Pete bore him to me—a big white fellow, with cinnamon on his head and neck, ashy-gray on tail, and wings of blue-black. His long legs were of dull, lustrous blue, whence his name. This wader, a relative of the European avocet, and extremely rare on the eastern coast, particularly North, is common on the alkaline lands of the West, notably in the Yellowstone region.

Pete, unobserved, rushed off ahead and flushed some turnstones, one of which by merest accident turned in the Colonel's direction and was shot. The others disappeared up the island, to be seen no more, and Pete received a thrashing, which he took with unqualified approval, wagging his tail with great appreciation at each whack.

The tide was coming in so fast now, we forsook the bar and followed up to the island itself, about an acre in extent, rocky and high, except at one end, where on low ground a dismantled house stood. South of the ruins, in a marsh, was a little muddy pond surrounded by cat-tails and rushes. Thither we took our way through long, clinging grass, and

peering through the bushes and sedge, saw hundreds of birds feeding around the edge. There were kill-deer and golden plover, bullheads, a pair of stilts, peeps and godwits without number, and piping plover and a horde of willets. Hardly had we gained the place when the willets, the sentinels of the shore, raised an unearthly tumult. They woke the whole swamp with piercing calls; a hoarse bittern in the bog chimed in, and pandemonium reigned.

In the midst of this we opened fire, and while the frightened denizens wildly circled in uncertain flight around us, we loaded and reloaded many times. The air was blue with smoke, and quivered with the shrill cries of the willets, the scared whistle of the plover, the squeaking call of sandpipers, and, over all, the thunder of the guns.

Slowly the smoke cleared, and Pete dashed in to garner the harvest of death. From every tussock of swamp-grass, from bog and brake, from the osiers and cat-tails, he brought them in. They were floating in the pond, lying on its muddy margin, struggling in the brambles hard by. Pete, with a wisdom born of many years afield, retrieved the slightly wounded first, then the hard-hit, leaving the killed for the last. We fell to and helped gather them in ourselves, laying them in a pile on the bank, a mass of lovely color. Fawn, buff, tan, chestnut, cinnamon, rusty brown and olive, blended with white, pale lemon, sulphur, ash, drab, silver, gray, steel blue and black, flashed in the sunlight from fallen crests and folded wings, and dabbled over all the fatal flecks of crimson.

One by one the Colonel laid them down, and as he finished called "Sixty-eight!" Slowly the game was carried down to the canoe and packed under the seats; the guns were stowed in, and Pete persuaded to embark. The tide was way up now, and a brisk wind from the southwest drove us in, raising the white caps around us. Past the oyster-boats at anchor, and over the sunken "Sou'west Ledge," round the rough stone breakwater where the current boiled and eddied, past the low-lying huts on the shore, we glided with our beautiful birds in the bow, and faithful, tired old Pete with paws on the guns fast asleep.

27.
A CAMP HUNT
IN MISSISSIPPI
(1885)

A CAMP HUNT IN MISSISSIPPI.

In Tunica county, Mississippi, on the banks of a sluggish bayou leading into one of those beautiful lakes which was once, doubtless, the bed of the Great Father of Waters, is my favorite hunting-ground.

Annually, as soon as the early frost has killed the miasmatic germs of the swamp atmosphere, I am accustomed to visit these wild forests in search of sport.

This season the alluvial deposits of last spring's overflow covered the bottom-lands with a rich coating from the fertile hills and valleys of the far North. The undergrowth on the lowlands had been destroyed by the deep overflow, and the high-water

"B'AR SIGN."

marks in dark circles belted the tall cottonwood and gum trees in mud-stained rings twenty feet overhead. Along a ridge beside the bayou, where only the highest water reached and quickly passed off, the vegetation was rank and luxurious. The cane, in impenetrable masses, made a lair

for the bear, wildcat, and panther which found in its tangled labyrinth refuge from human foes.

Along the bayou, where the tall cypress fringed the shores with crisp, brown foliage, among the cypress knees, whose roots insured a safe foothold in the treacherous bog, were the footprints of the numerous denizens of the swamps that had slaked their thirst in the bayou. A large track, which led into the canebrake, broader, if not so long as a human footprint, was evidently made by some large animal, which often came and went, always using the same path. It was noticed by a tall hunter, walking stealthily along the bayou, who smiled grimly, as he ejaculated, " B'ar sign ! "

A little farther on was another and smaller track, and the quick eye of the hunter sparkled as he examined it carefully. It was like that of a cat, only much larger, but there was no mark of claws, as in the bear-track.

The long, sharp claws of the *Felidæ*, by a beautiful, structural conformation of the bones, ligaments, and muscular parts, are always preserved without effort from coming in contact with the ground, and are retracted within a sheath, so as to be kept sharp and ready for use.

" Painter," muttered the hunter, bending low and looking intently at the footprints, mentally calculating how large the animal must be to fit such a track, and how long a time had elapsed since it had passed along the banks of the bayou. He was a tall, raw-boned man, with clear, gray eyes, a long chestnut beard, and a complexion, once fair, but now so bronzed by exposure to the sun and the miasma of the swamp as to wear, almost, the swarthy hue of the Indian. His lonely habits had caused him, when revolving some question in his mind, to hold converse with himself. " Painter," he muttered again, " and been here less than an hour ago. Now, Wash, you must keep a look-out. You ought to kill that ar' varmint ! "

Along the bayou the hunter followed the track until it entered the dense canebrake. " I'll find out if you makes your home in thar," he said, as he shouldered his rifle and walked along the margin of the cane.

A couple of hours later he had walked entirely around the canebrake, which covered several hundred acres, his object being to discover whether the panther had passed out and gone elsewhere, or was making its lair in the cane. As there was no track going from the cane he argued that the panther was still there.

"Now, if I had the dogs I would soon git him out of this," he muttered; "but it's no use to tackle a painter in his den, in a canebrake like this. I like elbow-room when I fight a painter, any-how. I'll go and try them turkeys I saw on the other side of the cane, to pass away the time till ole Asa gits here with the dogs."

Wash Dye wended his way quietly along the banks of the bayou until he reached the place where he had scattered a flock of turkeys while looking for the panther, and then he sat down by a huge cottonwood-tree, in the bed of a dry bayou which never had water in it except during an overflow.

Although the cane lined its banks in tangled masses not a sprig of it grew in the ravine in which he was seated. Taking from his pocket a hollow, bugle-shaped, wooden instrument about six inches long, with a small reed for a mouth-piece, he placed it to his lips, and, sucking the air through it, imitated the note of the wild-turkey calling its companions.

COTTON-MOUTH.

The *yelp*, or call, was answered by a gobbler, and in a few minutes the hunter saw it cautiously slipping along the open ravine close beside the cane. It was nearly within gunshot, and he sat in eager expectation of securing his prey, when, like a ray of light, the descending body of a huge panther flashed before him, — leaped from the canebrake embankment, — snatched up the turkey, and sprang back as quickly as it came. It disappeared so suddenly the hunter scarcely realized the fact that the animal he had been so anxious to find had watched him pass and repass, had taken advantage of his *yelping*, and being an expert turkey-hunter himself and knowing the habits of this bird, had placed himself, between the turkey calls, in a position to spring, thus outwitting his foe and capturing the turkey.

"Cuss that painter!" ejaculated the hunter; "if that wa'n't the most impudent thing I ever saw. Wa'al, Wash, to think of your being outgineraled by a painter!" and the hunter vowed vengeance on his foe with the feelings of one having a personal wrong to avenge.

He went to the spot where the panther had leaped upon the turkey, and noted the ground very carefully; then he cautiously followed it into the canebrake. A few feathers was all the sign he could discover. In such a mass of tangled canes and vines it was not possible to follow an animal that might take it into its head to defend its lair, and a hand-to-hand fight in a canebrake with a panther would be no pleasant undertaking. Already was he so tied up in vines that he was compelled to cut his way out with his hunting-knife. Regaining the opening at last, he resumed his position, and again began to call turkeys. The *yelping* of the flock was heard now in various directions, and a hen, coming within range, was fired at and killed.

"Wa'al," said the hunter, as he picked it up and started for camp, "I've got my supper in spite of that varmint, dod rot him! I'll make him pay yet for cheating me out of my gobbler."

On reaching camp he was greeted by two other hunters, who had kindled a fire, and were seated in the door of the tent quietly smoking their pipes. These were the writer and a man familiarly known throughout the bottom as old Asa, the bear-hunter.

Wash Dye had preceded us some hours, to examine the country for "b'ar signs." I had a business engagement which delayed me, but had followed with old Asa, bringing horses and camp equipage to the spot designated as a camping-place, where about twenty rough, ungainly-looking mongrels of every color and description lay around the camp-fire. A bear dog belongs to no particular breed; he is an accident. The bear-hunter gathers together every kind of dog he can pick up, and out of a large number he occasionally finds one that, as old Asa remarked, "takes to b'ar."

"What have you found, Wash?" asked old Asa, as the hunter threw down his turkey, and dropped languidly upon a blanket by the fire.

GOING!

The expression of his countenance forboded that he would predict a poor prospect for a hunt.

"I found a flock of wild turkeys," he replied, laconically.

"Then why didn't you kill a gobbler?" asked old Asa, good-humoredly. "A hen is a mighty inconvenient fowl; too much for one, and not enough for two."

"I got beat out of a gobbler," replied Wash, "by a tarnation, impudent cuss of a painter." Then he related his adventure in the tone of a man who was highly incensed at the disrespect paid him by the forest robber.

GOING!

"Why didn't you shoot him before he got back in the cane?" I asked.

"Shoot him!" replied Wash. "I had as well attempt to shoot at a flash of lightnin'. I have been so mad ever since, I've jist been b'ilin' over. Dod rot the critter!"

"I had lots of fun here, once," remarked old Asa, "watching a painter and an old he-b'ar disputin' the right of way across the bayou on yonder big cypress log."

"How was it, Asa?" I asked.

"Wa'al, you see that ar hollow log lyin' on the bank, amongst the cane thar?"

"Yes," I replied.

"Wa'al, I found a wolf-den in thar, bout two years ago, with a lot of wolf-puppies in it, so I clomb up into yon hackberry-tree, that's kivered over with muscadine vines, to wait for the old she-wolf to come in, so I could git a shot at her. While I was settin' up thar an old he-b'ar come waddlin' along the bayou, and started to cross on that cypress log. I was jist drawin' a bead on him when I saw the biggest old he-painter I ever seed jump up on the

t'other end of the log. The b'ar was about half-way across when he saw the painter; but he jist sot up on his haunches and worked his fore-paws like he war waitin' for toll. The painter bowed his back like a big Thomas cat and growled. The old b'ar just sot thar, looking like a black, woolly nigger bossin' a toll-gate. The painter crouched low, like a cat creeping along arter a rat, until he got close up to the b'ar, when old Bruin gave him a slap side the head with his paw which sent him off the log into the bayou. I was so full of tickle I jist laid back ag'in the tree and larfed till I like to fell out, I shook so. The painter wa'n't cooled off a bit by his duckin', and instead of goin' 'long off about his business, when he could jist as easy have swum out on t'other side, and let that b'ar alone, he jist swum to the eend of the log he was on first, and went at the b'ar ag'in, with his ears all laid back, his jaws stretched open, his teeth shining like dogwood blossoms, and his tail lashing his sides, that glittered like a lady's moryantike silk dress. I tell you he war a prutty thing!

"But thar sot old Bruin, smilin' sorter contemptuous like, not skeered a bit, until the painter made a jump at him, and got another slap in the face which sent him

GONE!

tumblin', curchug, to the bottom of the bayou. I thought that ar' painter war mad afore, but when he landed on the bank, a-spittin' and a-screechin', with every wet har a standin' the wrong way, mad don't begin to express the sentiments of that ar painter; he war in a perfect rage! And thar sot old Bruin, holdin' the fort, sorter smilin' like.

"I shook so a larfin', I had to hold on to a limb, to keep from fallin'.

"But the painter didn't keep old Bruin waitir long, but instead of going up in reach of his paw, he jumped about fifteen feet in the air and lit on his back, and, Lord! what a tussle thar war!

"The b'ar tried to shake him off, but it war no go; so he rolled off the log into the bayou, and presently they both riz and come to the surface, and made for shore, whar they clinched ag'in. The painter got a grip on the side of the b'ar's head, and the bar give him a hug that made him loose his grip; but he wa'n't makin' nothin' er squeezin' that ar painter, for the long, sharp claws on his hind-feet war rakin' and tearin' into his bowels. They rolled over and over until the bar give it up, and fell over dead; the painter's hind toes had scratched into his vitals. The painter, himself, was lyin' on the ground with every rib broken, when I concluded I'd end the show by sendin' a rifle-ball through his heart, and he tumbled over dead.

"I waited about an hour longer for the wolf, and was jist about to give her up when I heard her howl, and soon arter I saw her slippin' in with a pig she had stolen; so I let drive at her, as she stood broadside, and cut her down. Then I clomb down, and went to look at the scene of battle. The b'ar war literally torn to pieces, disemboweled by that ar rantankerous painter; and the painter would likely have died too, if I had not put an end to him with my rifle.

"I built a fire and stayed there all night. I knowed the wolves would eat up my

b'ar-meat if I left. So I skinned them all, quartered the meat, and hung it up in trees, and went home next morning for help to carry in my game. I caught the wolf-pups and sold them to some passengers on a steamboat, at Helena, about a week arterwards. I suppose they wanted 'em for pets."

It was early fall, and we kept the air filled with the fumes of tobacco-smoke to ward off the execrable mosquitos which infest the swamps.

THE TURKEY CALL.

These beautiful lakes and bayous, filled with fish, and surrounded by every variety of game, have some serious drawbacks. Along their margin one must be careful where he treads, for the slimy moccasin and deadly cotton-mouth lie in their coils ready to strike their envenomed fangs into the foot of the intruder. But in many respects it is a lovely country. The venomous reptile can be avoided, and will pass away to his winter retreat as soon as the chilly breath of autumn opens the season for game; but the summer months are hot and unhealthy in the bottom-lands. The woods are festooned with vines, filled with the fragrant odor of the wild-grape and honeysuckle; but the poisonous malaria floats inperceptibly on the odorous breeze, tainting the air with poison and filling the system with disease; then a horrid chill creeps over the body, shaking the bones until the teeth chatter with ague, followed by a fever that seems to boil the blood, leaving the frame prostrated, and the eyes and face yellowed with jaundice. A glorious land for the negro to cultivate the cotton-plant,—in climate not unlike his native Africa; a paradise for the hunter, when the summer months have passed; a most enchanting winter climate; but the trail of the serpent is over it all, for the deadly miasma guards this beautiful Eden with the sword of death.

The night fell dark over the quiet camp, the stars became dim and clouded, and

sharp hoofs, while he tore the branches of an overhanging limb with his tall antlers. "If one of us will wait here long enough," he continued, "we will git a shot; this is a regular *runway* for deer. See, how thick the tracks are along the edge of the bayou!"

"You remain here, Wash," I said, "and I will follow on after the buck."

I kept carefully on the track of the deer; it turned off from the bayou into a wide, open wood, where the overflow had destroyed all vegetation except the bamboo and green-briar vines, which had put out after the water had fallen. Looking far

BEAR DOGS.

before morning the rain fell in torrents. Old Asa arose at the first pattering rain-drops, and housed his dogs in the huge, hollow gum that had once been a wolf-den.

When morning came the woods were wet and dripping. "No painter to-day," said Wash, as he looked out through the mist.

"A fine day for a still-hunt for deer," I remarked.

"You and Wash go out and try the deer," old Asa suggested. "I will have to stay in camp to keep the dogs quiet."

After breakfast, although it was still misting, Wash and I started off up the bayou after deer. We had walked about a quarter of a mile when we found a fresh buck-scrape.

"This fellow is not far off," said Wash, as he carefully examined the sign where a big buck had scraped the earth with his

ahead, I saw the buck quietly feeding, and, keeping well to windward, slipped carefully along after him.

As I peeped from behind a large cotton-wood tree a panther noiselessly crept across the opening, intently watching my buck, but approaching from a different direction. As it passed behind a clump of large trees, stooping low, I ran as quickly and silently as I could to a tree that was in gunshot. I stepped beyond the tree, and was within fifty yards of it, but, treading upon a dry stick, which snapped, startled, it turned half round, exposing its chest to my fire. I quickly threw my gun to my shoulder, and fired at a dark spot upon its breast. At the crack of the gun it rolled over, but, instantly recovering, darted away among the timber, and I saw it no more. Going to the spot, I found I had cut a large bamboo vine which was across its chest, mistaking it for a dark mark upon its tawny hide. The tough vine had broken the force of my ball, so I had not killed it, although I knew from the marks of blood I had given it a severe, if not a fatal wound.

While following the bloody trail, I heard Wash's rifle, and as I needed help to follow the wounded panther, I sounded a signal on my horn for him to come to me. He answered promptly, and in a few minutes I saw him rapidly approaching.

"What's the matter?" he questioned.

"The matter is I have shot a panther, and wounded it."

We followed the track until it entered the canebrake, and in the wet cane it was impossible to follow it farther.

"What did you shoot at, Wash?" I asked.

"I killed a very nice yearling doe."

"Then let us return to camp and get the dogs, and try to get this fellow of mine out of the cane. It will not go far I know; it is badly hurt."

Wash assented, and we started for camp. When we reached the spot where Wash had shot the doe, the deer was gone. The marks on the wet earth, where she had struggled when she fell, and the spot of blood, where Wash had cut her throat, were all that was left to show where a deer had been.

Wash gave a long, low whistle, then an exclamation of indignation.

"Dod rot that painter, he has come and stole my deer!"

This was the only solution of the mystery, for there were the footprints of the panther going and returning from the canebrake, but there was no sign of the deer being dragged off. If it had been a bear, we could have followed it easily by the marks of the body on the ground; but the panther carries off his game differently. He seizes it by the neck, and throwing the body over his back, so balances it that it does not touch the ground, and thus carries it off by main strength.

"Wa'al, I'll be dod rotted!" ejaculated Wash, "if that ar' painter haint got the best of me ag'in. He

stole my turkey, and now he has got my deer!"

We pushed on to camp, to get old Asa and the dogs, and soon returned to the spot. I wished to follow my wounded panther first; but Wash was so exasperated at being beaten by a "tarnation varmint," as he called it, he would not listen to my proposal. So we put the dogs on the trail, and in a few minutes they broke forth in full cry. We followed, cutting our way through the wet cane as fast as we could, and in a short time heard them baying.

"They've treed him," said old Asa; "be keerful how you approach; if it sees you it will jump out."

We pushed on and were almost near enough for a shot when out it sprang. We heard a howl and a crash through the cane, as it bounded off pursued by the pack. As we passed the spot where it

"CUSS THAT PAINTER."

had taken the tree, we found a dead dog, which it had literally torn to pieces when it leaped out; for it had sprung upon the dog's back, and sinking its huge tusks into its neck had disembowelled it with its hind claws, and then sprung off into the canebrake. Around and around through the dense thicket it ran, pursued by the pack, until it treed again. We were all scattered through the canebrake, and I was pushing on towards the tree where the dogs were baying, when I heard the sharp crack of a rifle and the rush of the dogs, as the panther leaped to the ground; then all was quiet for a moment; and then I heard Wash's shout of exultation, as he sounded on his horn the note of victory.

When I reached the spot I found Wash sitting upon the body of the huge beast he had slain, and the dogs panting on the ground beside him.

"I've got him," said Wash, "the tarnal thief! He's the very rascal that stole my gobbler yesterday, and my deer to-day. The impudent thief! to think that Wash Dye was a-goin' to act as commissary agent for such a yellow cuss as he is!"

We were not far from the bayou, and with our knives we hacked a path so that we could get a horse in to drag out the body.

"Now, Wash, we must get the other one," said I.

"All right!" he replied. "I'm in for exterminatin' the hull gineration."

Reaching the place where my wounded panther had entered the canebrake, we put the dogs on the trail, and they soon ran into it. We heard them howling, and when we reached them, found two badly crippled, and the rest baying at the foot of a tree. Old Asa threw up his gun and fired; the panther ran up the tree some twenty feet higher, clutching at the limbs in a death-struggle. I knew it would fall, but, to make sure it should not injure the dogs, I sent a shot into its side, as it lay exposed to my fire. It gathered itself convulsively, clutched at the limbs, then fell crashing through the branches to the earth. It was a large female, and the one I had wounded, as we found my bullet deeply embedded in its chest.

"You've got her!" exclaimed Wash, coming up, "and I've found my deer too. I jist accidentally ran on it in the cane."

We cut another trail out to the camp, and, getting our horses, selected a gentle one belonging to old Asa, accustomed to carry all kinds of game, and, by taking the panthers one at a time, and tying them to a halter attached to the horse's tail, dragged them out of the canebrake.

We secured the deer in the same way. The panther had only made one dainty meal from the carcass, and covered it with leaves to prevent the buzzards from finding it. We succeeded in returning to camp with all our booty, — wet, tired, hungry, and jolly.

Notwithstanding the prejudice against eating panther flesh, as being too cattish, it is almost as white and nice as the breast of a turkey. And I assure the reader we made a very enjoyable supper, after the fatigues of the day, on wild turkey, venison, and panther steaks.

James Gordon.

28.
FOLLOWING
DEER TRAILS IN
NORTH WESTERN WOODS
(1904)

On the Runway.

FOLLOWING DEER TRAILS IN NORTH-WESTERN WOODS

By H. S. CANFIELD

PLACE a fly with wet sticky legs on a pane of glass and let him wander for an hour. When he is ended and dead he will have left a map of the trails of these woods. Some of them are tote-roads to lumber camps; some are logging roads; some are roads that stroll along the banks of streams apparently with no particular purpose; some are Indian trails; but eight out of ten of them are deer-trails, or runways. The difference between an Indian trail and a deer-trail is that the deer-trail is straighter. It is characteristic of the Indian to make a trail ten feet out of the way around the end of a log not more than six inches through; the deer would step over it.

That is a vast extent of forest which runs from the eastern part of Michigan on the right to the western part of Minnesota on the left, as you stand looking at the map on the office wall and wishing for the good time to come. Maples and

basswoods and birches, hemlocks, spruces and pines shadow its ground; hills clothed to the summits throw up high rounded shoulders to the sky; rivers wind through it, creeks rush down to the rivers; deep-bosomed in trees, a thousand lakes flash like mirrors in the sun; and often a great tamarack swamp blocks the foot-farer forbiddingly, impenetrable save to the wild life of the region. Above the woods through late September and all October is an arch of fleckless blue; the frost lies white of mornings; the air gets into the blood, an air cool and resinous to the nostrils; the trees in a hundred contrasting but harmonious tints, running the gamut of browns, yellows, greens and reds, back and forth, again and again, are a glory But when November comes the sky is gray; snow flurries pale the outlook; the leaves of autumn are marching a million strong through the forest aisles.

It is to be said of deer-shooting in the

lakes region that mostly it is sport in its high form. There if anywhere the man matches his trained skill and intelligence against the inherited cunning of the animal and not infrequently loses. For it is generally still-hunting that is followed and the conscientious still-hunter earns all that he gets. There is run-way shooting, which is the second highest form of the sport. In using it and obtaining game the man, at least, demonstrates his marksmanship if not his woodcraft. He takes the stand selected for him by his guide while the guide makes a detour in the hope of scaring up game. The chances are that he will do it and when he does the animal, having been disturbed and frightened, will take to the runway at speed. It may pass the hunter belly to the ground, or it may be in full gallop, or it may be trotting rapidly, throwing back its head occasionally in an effort to discover its pursuer. At any rate it will not be strolling along half dreaming, and it offers a mark of more or less difficulty in proportion to the rate of its progress and the amount of vegetation which intervenes. A deer moving even at a trot through the trees seventy-five to a hundred yards away is not a sure target for the rifle, not to count "buck-ague," sights raised too high, too sudden pressure of the trigger and other things which go to make up the shooter's mishaps.

He only is a deer hunter, however, who goes after the deer unaided, and only when he has killed his buck unaided is he entitled to call himself of the blood brotherhood of the rifle. This is the true sport. All others are weaker variations of it, or base imitations, or worse. The man has his gun and his knowledge of the woods and the animal's habits; the deer has a greater knowledge of the woods, keener eyesight, wonderfully sensitive nostrils, protective coloration, tremendous speed and great endurance. In every natural sense it is the man's superior. The match is not an equal one; its advantages are too heavily on the side of the deer. This is shown in the proportion of successes and failures of even the most expert of shots and trailers. The best hunter that ever struck the woods has not been able to average one deer knocked down to five followed. It is the man's persistence which gets him a deer finally.

People going to the woods for the first time are sure, before starting, that they will get at least two deer apiece. They have a sneaking idea that they will smash the law, if they get the chance, and kill three or four, or six or a dozen. They spend two weeks with or without guides and go back home without seeing a deer. They say that there are no deer in those woods and the camp proprietors and the guides and the magazine and sporting writers are all liars. They go back the next year, however, and the year after and in time they get so that they kill a deer a season, or maybe two, and are satisfied. The trouble is not the scarcity of deer, but the scarcity of "deer-sense."

All of the heavily wooded States of the North and Northwest now protect deer to the limit. The shooting season is short; the number of animals any man may take is two. Deputy game-wardens are active. Fines are heavy; imprisonments are not infrequent. The territory is ideal for deer-breeding and conservation. It is huge, it is tangled; its swamps, unless frozen, are not to be hunted at all. So favored, the deer have increased enormously. In no part of the world are they so plentiful as now in the northwestern woods. Wolves kill many more of them than hunters do, but they are able to hold their own against natural foes. So long as the governments continue to restrain men the deer will continue to multiply.

Go into the woods in the month of October before the shooting opens. The ground is brown with leaves, the air is cool, all conditions are pleasant. A man with an ordinary pair of eyes in his head shall not walk a mile before he sees deer signs; tracks or droppings, or beds, or marks upon trunks where the bucks have rubbed the last dried velvet from their antlers. The farther he goes the more signs he will see. He will stumble upon a runway that is a Fifth Avenue of promenade for them. The track is as beaten as a country road. Now and then he will hear a crash in the hazel brush where some buck or doe has seen him and leaped. The chances are that he will even catch glimpses of a brown form or two darting between the great boles.

These conditions will continue to the opening of the hunting season. They will continue in rapidly modifying degree

He only is a deer hunter who has killed his buck unaided.

for three or four days after the season opens. Then deer will be hard to get. The reason is simple: Distance is nothing to these animals. They will travel twenty miles between sunrise and noon without special effort, stopping to feed on the way. When they decide to quit their ranges they go fast. Seeing the woods full of hunters they leave those woods, going either to woods which hold fewer men or, if in the search of a day or two they are unable to find free spaces, they go into the swamps where they know that they are secure. Any man who has spent a season or two in the forest knows that his best chance to get the two bucks allowed to him by law lies in reaching the ground promptly. The guides say that the deer smell powder and leave. They can not, of course, smell the nitrate in an unexploded shell, but they can see the man carrying the shells, and when they have been disturbed twice or thrice by these enemies they have enough of it.

Yet the man who knows how, can get his allowance of two deer within a week and select bucks at that. He may even refuse bucks that have badly developed antlers and insist that his game wear the complement of prongs or "points." Some years are required to bring him to a pitch of excellence where he is sure of his quarry and himself, but once he attains to it he has a valuable knowledge, a knowledge that no man can take from him. The pursuit of the deer legitimately, rifle in hand and sandwich and compass in pocket, requires every quality which goes to make up the true sportsman: patience, endurance, woodcraft, good-nature, courage, quick eyes and steady nerves. It requires that the woods shall be a book to the man; a book in which is recorded all things that happen within the woods confines, and the successful hunter must be able to read it as he walks.

He must deduce from sign how much time has elapsed since the deer passed; for sign twenty-four hours old is of little more value than no sign at all. He must know from tracks not only how old they are, but how fast the deer moved when they were made, whether the deer is buck or doe, whether it was travelling with set purpose, or fleeing, or merely strolling. He must know the ground and then the tracks will tell him that the deer was going

to water, or to feed, or to its lair. If he starts the animal and fails to get a shot he must know what runway it is likely to take and then, travelling at a long trot, he must make for that runway and intercept the fugitive, or he will see it no more. He must know where the deer stay in warm clear weather and cold dark weather and what becomes of them in light snow or rain. He must know their feeding hours and places and sleeping hours and places and at what times they go back and forth. When he knows all of these things and a hundred others and has tested his knowledge time and again, he will find ten deer in a day where the inexperienced man would not find one, and if he is lucky he may get one out of the ten.

The good hunter is cautious. He does his best to move without stirring a twig. He prays that the night may be damp so that the leaves will not rustle under him. He asks for a light snow so that the trails may be more easily followed. There are many times when he gets these favoring conditions. Let him go forth then and ply his craft to the uttermost. Let him move like a brown ghost between the trees, working slowly up wind. Let him have ears trained to catch the lightest sound of the forest and eyes to dive through the darkest shadow and see the dun skin beyond. Let him be eager yet slow, with no thought for anything, save the object of his chase, his attention unattracted by the partridge which whirs up near him, his mind undiverted by any of the thousand sights and sounds. Let him be all hunter from top to toe, a "fell hunter," as Thoreau phrases it, with the accumulated wisdom of years of effort stored in him, yet shall five deer move off from him, more ghost-like than he and he shall know nothing of their going; five more shall watch him from covert with round lustrous eyes, not the tip of an ear exposed, and turn again to grazing when he has passed, and if he fires at all the chances are five to one that he will fire at a buck or doe in full speed flying from him before he saw or heard it mo e. So he will need to be a quick and accurate shot as well as a stalker, and it will take him nearly as long to learn to shoot the rifle correctly at flying targets among the trees as to learn to find the targets. From these unchangeable

Any track worth following will be damp to the forefinger.

natural conditions have come two kinds of still-hunters, one the stalking kind, who moves with care and trails his game to the end like an old hound, and the other the rapidly going kind, who glides swiftly through the forest, following a fresh trail at the top of his speed, not hoping to steal upon the deer while it is feeding or lying down, but desiring only to go so fast and easily that he will be within shooting distance when it sees him and jumps. This man will cover much more ground in a day than the other and will get more shots. He will average possibly as many dead deer. Both of them hunt across wind, or up wind, and both must be imbued with deer-lore or any killing they make will be accidental.

There are certain fundamental rules of deer-shooting—beginners' rules—which may be quickly stated: Deer feed early in the morning and late in the afternoon, generally in open places. Between ten o'clock in the morning and four in the afternoon they are in covert, lying down mostly. They should never be hunted down wind. Keep off twigs and leaves if they are dry. Take long strides and put the foot down softly. Look cautiously over the top of any hill before showing the body. Let the eye explore the tops of dead fallen trees or slashings before drawing near to them. The edges of any deer-track worth following will not have crumbled and fallen in; if made on ground they will be damp to the forefinger. If nearing a lake be cautious and when a view is had of the opening run the eye thoroughly around the shore-line; look near at hand with a double closeness. Any deer started, unless it has decided to leave the country, may be counted upon to circle and come back near to the starting point inside of an hour or two. Therefore in returning by the same route in the afternoon be watchful of places where deer were in the morning. Never—and this rule should be printed in type a foot long— never shoot at anything unless its identity is thoroughly established. Rigid observance of this rule would have saved a hundred homicides within the past five years.

In drawing on a deer the experienced hunter will endeavor to shoot it squarely through the shoulders. That shot will stop it inside of twenty feet every time. If the animal is shot through the heart and has just taken a full breath it will run from twenty-five to a hundred yards. Hit back of the heart through the body, it is likely to go almost any distance from one mile to ten. A bullet through the head or neck bones or spine will stop it, of course, but nobody shoots at those marks of intention. They are too difficult. The hunter does not always have choice of shots. He is often forced to shoot at the animal when its rump is turned toward him, or when it is facing him. He may get his deer or may not, even if the bullet strikes fairly, for there is then no certainty of inflicting a fatal wound. The modern high-powered small-calibred rifles will throw through a deer from end to end, but often the bullet is deflected by a bone and goes out without reaching a vital spot. There is much outcry against the use of these rifles, but in the hands of a careful man they are very efficient weapons; in the hands of one not careful almost any sort of rifle will do to kill another hunter with. Men are slain in the woods because the men who slay them mistake them for deer, not often because the rifles carry too far. Imagination plays strange tricks with the untutored or exciteable. Last year in the Adirondacks a man shot a woman sitting by the side of a trail; not long ago, in the same region, a guide paddling a boat along a lake was shot and killed by a hunter standing in the woods fifty yards away; two years ago in Wisconsin a child standing on a rock in the middle of a shallow river was shot by a "sportsman" who came unexpectedly to the bank two hundred and fifty yards distant. A patch of brown coat-sleeve seen through the trees or undergrowth, a section of brown back, a glimpse of brown leggings are often sufficient to cause the snuffing out of humanity's brief candle. Invariably the survivor is " crazed with remorse "— which does the dead one a lot of good. He ought to be jailed for twenty years.

Yet to the man who loves the open, the spice of danger acts rather as incentive than deterrent. The deer are there, swift, beautiful, cunning and timorous, the miles of massive woodland, the balsamic airs, the keen and friendly emulation, the strenuous endeavor, the tired muscles, the gnawing appetite, the dreamless sleep —sleep so deep that it is no longer sleep but slumber. Pan has on the garb of early winter and whistles shrilly among the rushes where thin ice has formed. Against the dead pine the giant woodpecker smites his iron bill. The song birds have gone south and at dusk the brown owl quests for the partridge. Around the inner walls of the shack the firelight leaps ruddily and falls on contented faces.

29.
CAMPS AND CRAMPS
ON THE LITTLE SOU'WEST
❀ ❀ ❀
THE WIZARD OF
THE WETLANDS
(1902)

CAMPS AND CRAMPS ON THE LITTLE SOU'WEST

By WILLIAM J. LONG

DRAWINGS BY J. N. MARCHAND

TEN years ago, Phil and I took our hardest camping lesson in the school of hard knocks—a school which, by the way, has a reputation for turning out good graduates.

During previous trips we had heard much of a big unknown lake lying somewhere about the headwaters of the Little Sou'west Miramichi. A hard, dangerous river led up to it; the lake itself was said to be haunted, and certainly had a bad reputation among the Indians—partly because of the difficulty of getting there, and partly because of the few people that had ever visited it, some had been drowned, and some killed, and some never came back.

"He would * * * nose around * * * till he found a lily root, drag it up, and stand chewing it with huge satisfaction."

Naturally such a lake excited our lively interest. We inquired about it in the settlement far down the river. There everybody discouraged us; nobody could be hired to go as extra canoeman. We rode twenty miles to see an old hunter who had tramped up to the lake on snowshoes, and trapped there one early spring. He said we could never reach it in a canoe; that such an attempt on our part would be madness. Then we decided to go.

For Phil the expedition was to be chiefly scientific. He had been for several years collecting and classifying specimens for a work on the Ichthyology of Canada. For me the trip was one of pleasure—just to fish, and camp, and study the wood folk, and incidentally to help my friend during the summer vacation. Both of us relished immense the wild free life and the touch of adventure implied in such a trip.

During the winter we planned ceaselessly, and wrote long letters full of schemes and advice. He discovered by good chance that a gang of lumbermen were working, that winter, on the lower reaches of the river, and that by sending our whole outfit by team to their camp we could save some sixty miles of desperately hard upstream work. It would involve a tramp of thirty miles, in midsummer, through an unbroken forest, over the dimmest of trails; but we took the alternative instantly.

That spring, on the last sledding, we sent in a big Micmac canoe and an abundance of provisions, with careful directions to the lumbermen as to storage. Then Phil bethought himself, and sent in another messenger with directions to swing the canoe up to the beams of the log stable. That was a wise afterthought. Otherwise the porcupines, when they came out hungry in the spring, would have eaten half the bark from our canoe, and rendered it useless.

The Fourth of July found us united at the last settlement on the Miramichi, brimful of enthusiasm for the conquest of the river. We had found one Indian, less superstitious or more needy than the rest, who agreed to go with us for extra wages. He had been in to the lumber camp during the winter, and knew the trail, he said. At the last moment Phil decided to take a boy also, whom we called Gillie, to help about camp while we were off on our

scientific investigations. He came from another river, knew nothing about the lake, and was crazy to go.

Noel, the Indian, was a most valuable man, though a great grumbler. Without him we could never have reached the lake. He was a perfect canoeman, magnificently daring on the river, and timid as a rabbit everywhere else—scared of his own shadow when night fell and the loons began to cackle like idiots.

As for Gillie, I am glad to put the responsibility for his hiring on Phil's shoulders. He was absolutely useless about camp, though willing enough, and forever in trouble. He ate like a young robin, which eats its own weight every day. All this, of course, we found out afterward.

From the settlement we drove twenty miles, as far as the road went, then struck into the forest afoot on what had been a tote-road in winter, over six feet of snow, but which was now scarcely to be distinguished from the surrounding forest. We carried our packs, containing clothing and various articles which we were unwilling to send in earlier, my gun, rifle, and fishing rods, and three days' provisions. Two days' easy tramping, we judged, would bring us to the lumbermen's camp.

At noon of the second day we came to the place where two old trails crossed the one we were following. Phil took out a paper, upon which a lumberman had sketched our route, and argued as to the right way. That confused the Indian, who, if left to his instincts, might have brought us through all right. We camped that night a good fifty miles from where we had entered the forest, and still no signs of a camp or recent cuttings.

Next morning, instead of going back and trying another trail, we started through the woods by compass. That was the beginning of sorrows. Nobody but a timber-cruiser has any business to attempt walking in a New Brunswick forest in summer; a worse place can scarcely be imagined. The great trees above shut out all sunlight; beneath, the foot sinks deep out of sight in moss; fallen trees lie across each other in hopeless confusion; underbrush opposes every step; there is no opening anywhere. Worst of all, flies, midges, and mosquitoes swarm over one in myriads; and in climbing or forcing a way, one has

"Phil caught up * * * a nest of tin plates * * *
and hurled them with a mighty yell."

no spare hand to brush them away. We camped that night hopelessly lost.

Bad as the first day's wanderings had been, the next two were inexpressibly worse. We ran into a great burned district, where the fallen trees were multiplied a thousand-fold; between them stiff blackberry and raspberry bushes forced a way, and a scratchy vine ran riot everywhere. When I think now, sometimes, of the possible horrors of the wilderness, it is never of intense cold, or starvation, or maddening loneliness, but of those two days in which we staggered on, climbing through and over and under endless windfalls beneath a July sun, sweating under our packs, torn by briers, eaten by insects, ready to drop at every step from hunger and exhaustion.

The fourth and fifth days we lived on berries and small birds which I shot; on the fifth night we slept in the green forest again, huddled close together with belts drawn tight by a fire. In the morning Phil shot a red squirrel, and I snared four tiny trout from a brook. That was all we ate till evening, when, from a tree on a mountain, Noel gave a mighty shout and came scrambling down to tell us that the camp was just ahead.

Two days rest with plenty to eat made us fit again; though Gillie had a swollen hand from grabbing at a big porcupine, which he mistook for a bear cub. The canoe and provisions were found in excellent condition; and one day's hard work carried them all over an intervening mountain and left them by the river bank. That night we slept with the roar of the heavy rapids in our ears. It was our lullaby as long as we were on the river.

Then began our struggle against the worst river we had ever met in the wilderness. We were three weeks overcoming it, wading in cold water daily, often for hours at a stretch, when our muscles were not equal to the task of driving the canoe by the poles. In all that time we seldom slept dry, and never warm; for in the gorges the nights were cold. Several times ice formed on the bottom of our upturned canoe.

One day, I remember, we worked like beavers, only harder, from daylight to sunset to make less than a mile of progress. Twice that day we upset in bad water, luckily while provisions were ashore being portaged round dangerous rapids. I don't know how many times we were near to drowning. Once Phil saved us a hundred-mile tramp by following the upturned canoe to the very verge of a rapid, in which nothing could live; once Gillie, who could not swim, lost his footing and I had to swim after him.

So we fought our way up, keyed by continual excitement, and somehow getting fun out of an experience which would have been worse than penal servitude to anyone that did not like it.

Once, after being rained on for two successive days, we camped in a beautiful spot, a high bluff, overlooking a salmon pool and splendid stretches of river. Some of our provisions had begun to mould, so we decided to stay here a few days to dry them. Incidentally we wanted to let a little sunshine soak into our own skins.

At noon of the second day's rest we were all off searching the elements of a dinner, Phil with a fly-rod, the Indian with a big pail, for berries, and I with a gun. Our sugar, flour, and hardtack were spread in the warm sun to dry. At the last moment Gillie was sent back to watch them.

Some time about two o'clock we drifted back. Phil had two little trout, lean and lathy from hard living in quick water; Noel had a handful of wild currants rattling over the bottom of his tin pail; and I had a young partridge somewhere in a side pocket. As I came in sight of camp, I saw Phil plunge out of the underbrush across the open, shouting and swinging his hat. Down by the tent Gillie lay with his head under the fly, the rest of his body in the warm sun, the whole of him sound asleep. Just beyond was a huge bear that wandered out on the bluff to see what civilization could furnish to a jaded woods appetite.

He had eaten all the sugar, and was mouthing at the hardtack when Phil appeared. The bear looked up, wondering at the outcry; he had never seen a human being before. Phil caught up the first thing at hand—a "nest" of tin plates, eight or ten of them—and hurled them with a mighty yell. They separated, of course, and when the bear found his wits the place was full of big flashing missiles, some flying straight at his head, others rolling at him with a great bang and clatter. He seemed to me to just turn a somersault,

"Phil took out a paper, upon which a lumberman had sketched our route, and argued as to the right way."

then hurtled away toward the woods, whimpering like a scared puppy, volleying dirt and chips behind him in his desperate hurry.

Just as he got to the woods Noel appeared, dead ahead. There was another wild yell; the pail flew at the bear's head, scaring what wits he had left completely out of him. The Indian went up a tree; the bear down the bluff, jumping with a mighty *souse* twenty feet sheer down into the river. There he swam across, like a muskrat, and I could see the underbrush twitching violently as he flew up the opposite hill for the big timber.

Next day Gillie went fishing at the foot of the bluff, taking my little trout rod. Suddenly there was a wild outcry. We jumped to the bluff and plunged down headlong, barely in time to fish Gillie out of the salmon pool, where he was clinging with precarious hold to a slippery rock. Just below, the rapids were roaring like fiends for their victim. It turned out that, while trailing his fly for little trout, a thirty-pound salmon had followed it up and hurled himself out of water at Gillie's

feet, which startled him so that he lost his foothold and tumbled over backward into the current.

"He *joomped* at me; he *joomped* at me," was all he could sputter when we dragged him half lifeless to the bank.

We reached the lake at last, tired, thin, and hungry, but happy as schoolboys at having proved an impossibility possible. The first thing to greet us was a seagull—which surprised us, for till then we had never known of them going so far inland. The moment our canoe appeared round the point at the outlet she came flying down the lake, accusing us shrilly of having robbed her nest. We followed her as she hovered just ahead, so near that I could have touched her at times with the paddle, till she led us to her nest on a solitary rock. The eggs had all been eaten—by a thieving mink, probably—while she was away fishing.

We assured her, as best we could, that we were innocent. She seemed to understand, too, for she stopped her crying and came close to us fearlessly, complaining softly of her loss. It was a lonely place, one of the loneliest I have ever seen. I have wondered since if she felt it so, and came to us for a crumb of sympathy. She was quite alone on the lake, and came often near our camp as long as we stayed.

The lake turned out well scientifically; but what it furnished otherwise kept us still thin and hungry. Trout were very scarce, and small game kept itself well hidden. Frogs were plenty and delicious, but poor Noel, who could not be induced to touch frogs, kept pulling his belt tighter, cutting new eyelets at intervals, till he grew troubled and came to me for an old pair of suspenders.

"I don' want pull-um belt no tighter. 'Fraid he crack-um backbone," he announced seriously.

Our devices for helping out our larder were at times ingenious; and a fine touch of excitement was seldom lacking. Down the outlet, a little way, was a pool in which were plenty of salmon; but the water was too warm; they would not rise to a fly. Late in the afternoon some of the big fish would sometimes begin jumping in sport, throwing themselves high out of water. I used to sit on a rock at the foot of the pool for hours at a time, my gun ready, waiting to catch my fish in the air—as one would cut down a woodcock in thick cover, in the swift moment when he rockets above the brush, and says *wheep!* and whirls down again out of sight. It was good sport and honest, and much more exciting than fly fishing. One had never more than a second in which to sight his fish and shoot; and he was always coming up in unexpected places. After the report he would disappear, but would presently come struggling back to the surface, when the second barrel, into the water close beside him, would stun him till I could slip the landing-net under him. I got four good salmon that way; and never were fish of mine eaten with such solid satisfaction.

Another device proved even more successful; though we tried it but once, when necessity proved her inventiveness to be stronger than the game laws. Phil and I were catching specimens with a ring-net, one evening, when a cow caribou with a good sized calf came out on a point below. We had no weapon; but the sight of that calf made us fearfully hungry. It was ten days since we had tasted fresh meat—

and that was muskrat. We landed at once, crept down just inside the brush, and rushed out on the point, shouting wildly. As we had calculated, the caribou bolted one way, the calf another, both into the water, which was fortunately deep. Before the calf had fairly found his legs I swam ahead of him and turned him to shore, where Phil had him. He made very good veal, and being hungry we ate it thankfully.

A few days before we left the lake I came near wrecking the expedition and bringing us all into most serious straits by a bit of carelessness. I had been still-fishing in deep water. Later in the afternoon, as I paddled along shore toward camp, I doubled a point and came upon a bull moose feeding in the water just ahead. He would plunge his head deep in the water, nose around for a moment till he found a lily root, drag it up, and stand chewing it with huge satisfaction, while the muddy water poured down over his face. Then he would go fishing again after more roots, which moose, by the way, like better than anything else.

I had often seen the animals feeding before, but always at a distance. Here, at last, was a chance to get close to one and to see how he would act.

Waiting till he plunged his head under, I moved toward him, "fanning" the canoe along silently without lifting the paddle from the water. When his head began to come up, I sat motionless, low in the canoe, till he finished his lily root and ducked for more. Then I crept toward him again.

Three or four times this was repeated successfully, till I was within twenty yards and the great brute, still facing away from me, was utterly unconscious that anybody was near. Then, as I crept still closer, his head came up unexpectedly; his keen ears, which were not under water that time, had caught the ripple at the bow of the canoe. He whirled like a flash, with a bound and a snort and a mighty splash. His ears pointed at me, his nostrils twitched, his jaw fell, the root dropped, and he stood staring in intense astonishment, from nose to tail just one huge interrogation point. Like the bear, he had probably never seen a human being nor a canoe before.

For a long half minute we watched each

other, motionless as two statues. Then a breath from the lake began to drift me in nearer and nearer. Still he made no motion to run away; instead it seemed to me that the mane on his neck began to bristle. I worked my wrist slowly, "fanning" the bow outward. That brought me still nearer. He took a slow step in my direction, his muscles all a-quiver. Then the red light blazed out in his eyes and he plunged straight at me—one, two bounds, and the big velvet antlers were shaking just over me.

There was a rifle in the canoe, but not a second of time in which to use it. I rolled over, away from him, upsetting the canoe between us, and struck out for deep water. When I turned, at a safe distance, the bull had plunged one forefoot through the bottom of the canoe, crushing bark and cedar ribs as if they were eggshells, and was now trying to pull it out awkwardly. He seemed to be frightened a bit at the queer thing which gripped his leg, for he snorted in excitement and thrashed his antlers. But he was getting madder every moment.

A great fear swept over me that he would ruin the canoe and leave us to face the awful river below in a spruce bark of our own building. I swam ashore hastily below him, and began to shout and splash the water. He made a jump or two in my direction; whereupon I took to the water again, the bull following up to his shoulders. It was muddy bottom and he trod gingerly. When he would come no farther I swam rapidly to the canoe and tugged it away into deep water. The bull watched me meanwhile, astonished at the strange sight; but he made no effort to follow till I landed at a point above, and righted the canoe, and tipped the water out. Then he came swinging along shore, gritting his teeth and choking fiercely; but before he reached me I had stuffed my shirt into the hole he had made in the bark and was again afloat.

Luckily I had formed a habit, years before, of always having the paddle fast to a cord when hunting or trying experiments in a canoe. It is a good habit; one can drop his paddle at an instant's notice with no fear of losing it.

Failing provisions drove us from the lake soon after this. Moose were plenty, but Phil and I both objected to killing one of the noble beasts for a few pounds of flesh. Besides, meat is no diet for a summer outing. We left the place most reluctantly, for we had grown to love its wild loneliness. The seagull followed us, calling softly—was it to bring us back?—as we drifted down the lake into the outlet.

The run down the river was quick and exciting, through numberless rapids, up which we had toiled at a snail's pace. Running a river is much more dangerous than poling up; but we did it safely, with only an accident or two. Spite of the hardship, we voted the trip a success; and before we said good-by we had planned another trip through the same waters, to explore the inlet and a couple of unknown lakes far above.

"I used to sit on a rock,
* * * my gun ready,
waiting to catch my fish
in the air."

THE WIZARD OF THE WET LANDS

By EDWYN SANDYS

DRAWINGS BY CLARE ANGELL

HY a wizard? Yankee fashion I might retort with, Why not? When a bit of brown bird life only about eleven inches long can cause a six foot man to do all sorts of crazy stunts I should say the wee fellow at least possessed peculiar powers. That the snipe can make a lazy, heavy sleeper rise at gray dawn and go toiling across weary leagues of bog, morass, and muddy mess for perhaps eight or ten hours at a stretch is a well known fact. That he can make a temperate man drink, a truthful man lie, an accurate man miss, and a good man curse, he has repeatedly proved, while at the same time with a mere wave of a wing he can cause a sinking heart to leap with joyous pride and a weary eye to flash with sudden fire. These things, and a few others which need not be dwelt upon, backed by a flight of the now - you - see-it-now-you-don't — the-quickness-of-the-wing-deceives-the-eye order, appear to warrant the title herewith bestowed.

And with all his eccentricities he is a good little wizard and one of the best loved of all our lesser game. Once a snipe shooter always a snipe shooter might be truly said, for it is questionable if even the quail has more valiant champions than stand ready to defend the honor of the long-billed, bent-winged master of the mud.

The snipe, properly Wilson's snipe, *Gallinago delicata*, but commonly known as English snipe and wrongfully called half a dozen other names, is a widely distributed species. It visits every state at some season; its northward migration extends within the Arctic Circle, while it is known to go southward to northern South America and the West Indies. Comparatively few of the birds which move northward from February until May breed south of the international line. It is quite true there are breeding grounds at various points of the Northern States, but the great breeding range extends from latitude 42° north to some undetermined point much nearer the Pole than most sportsmen will venture.

Some time in September the first south-bound birds pass below the Canadian grounds, and soon most of the suitable marshy bits of East and West have their share of long-billed prizes. Then begins an astonishing attack which extends from ocean to ocean and generally sweeps southward from Canada to California. Probably tons of lead, half of which is wasted, are fired at the artful dodger.

The sexes are alike, the description being as follows: Top of head, black, with three buff stripes; neck, buff, lined and spotted with black; back, black, feathers barred and margined with rufous and buff, the latter giving a striped effect; rump and upper tail coverts, rufous, barred with black; wings, sooty black, feathers barred with rufous and margined with white; primaries, blackish, web of first white nearly its length, edged with white at tip; tail, usually of sixteen feathers, the three outer whitish with narrow black bars, the others black with rufous bar and tipped with pale buff; chin and upper part of throat, pale buff, lower throat and breast, buff, spotted with sooty brown; flanks, white, barred with black; abdomen, white; under tail coverts, buff, barred with sooty black; bill, legs, and feet, greenish. Length, 10½ to 11½ inches; wing, about 5 inches; tail, 2¼ inches; bill, 2½ to 3 inches.

Many sportsmen of the gray-headed brigade still insist that, like the woodcock, the snipe lives by what they term "suction." Better informed people, of course, know that both birds eat worms and an astonishing number of them, and that the worms are secured mainly by probing (boring) for them with the peculiarly sensitive bill, the upper mandible having a very flexible tip by which the worm is felt, seized, and drawn from the earth. By this, however, is not meant that snipe and cock invariably bore for their food. Both will take worms crawling upon the surface and

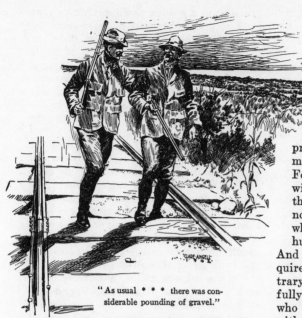

"As usual * * * there was considerable pounding of gravel."

nights to bring in northward bound birds is dark and damp with a puff of warm breeze from the south and a dash of warm rain. Upon such a night I have seen the snipe pour in so that wings or voices were audible nearly every moment. Must have been pretty good snipe grounds, do you remark? They were. When "Frank Forrester" first tramped over them, he with a muzzle loader could bag twenty, thirty, and forty brace in a day, and not so many years ago the keen men who worked that ground took each one hundred shells for one day's sport. And this did not mean that each bird required a deal of shooting. On the contrary there were men who might average fully three-fourths of all their birds and who were able to grass bird after bird without a mistake upon days when things worked just right. I have seen a private match at twenty shots a man result in a straight score for the winner while the loser missed but twice.

While the great flight of snipe extends well to the northward of New England, occasional nests have been found in Connecticut and Pennsylvania. A slight hollow in the ground or a tuft of rank grass holds the three or four eggs, which are olive-gray washed with dull brown and spotted and scribbled on the larger end with deep brown and black. The courtship is peculiar, the male and female frequently rising high in air and sweeping about in swift circles, then diving earthward at full speed, at the same time producing a queer rolling sound impossible to represent on paper. This "drumming," as it is termed by sportsmen, is also frequently performed by single birds and late in the season as well as during the period of courtship. A drumming snipe not seldom ascends until almost invisible, then seemingly flies straight down at an amazing rate, whereupon is heard a loud humming, presumably caused by the rushing of the air through the primaries. An empty corkless ink bottle swiftly thrown will produce a similar sound, and the old schoolboy trick of "making a nail hum" is no bad imitation.

both frequently feed in thickets and almost dry ground, where they secure the prey by turning over fallen leaves.

When migrating the snipe travels by night, and while some excellent authorities have claimed that a moonlit journey is necessary, or at least preferred, my experience has taught otherwise. More times than can now be recalled I have cat-napped through the black monotony of a steamy spring night so as to be on precisely the proper spot when the first flight of geese came in to feed at gray dawn. And at intervals throughout such nights I have heard the wings and voices of myriad snipe hissing and rasping athwart the black mystery as the first comers of the year sped to the fat muck of thousands of acres of wet lands. Moreover, I have toiled till dusk over fenceless fields of black tenacity and seen never a bird, nor a boring nor a chalking, nor anything that is his; have turned in dead beat at some farm house about 8 P. M., been literally hauled out, against the grain but in accordance with positive instructions, before dawn, and have later found the birdless ground of the previous evening to be swarming with silent, skulking snipe, which if not weary from a long flight certainly acted like resting new arrivals.

I have heard snipe moving by moonlight and that many times, but the night of

The snipe occasionally takes to some

large, horizontal limb, more often alights upon the top rail of a fence, a stump, or big log, and I once saw one standing on the top of a stout post which supported wire. Another bird was seen to pitch on a small stack which was surrounded by water and yet another upon the roof of an old outhouse. There was no mistake in either case, for I flushed and killed the bird on the stack and had a close view of the other before it left the roof.

The names by which the snipe is known in various localities are rather numerous and some of them quite curious. While the correct one is Wilson's snipe, we find " American snipe," " common snipe," " snipe," " meadow snipe," " little wood- " snipe," " English snipe," " bog snipe," " marsh snipe," " Jack snipe," " alewife bird," " shad spirit," " shad-bird," and " gutter snipe." It is " a snipe or snite, a bird lesse than a woodcocke," in Baret's Alveary, 1580; and in Drayton's *Owl*, 1604, occurs, " the witless woodcock and his neighbor snite." Other sometime crumbled old parties speak of " simpes " and " simps," and I sincerely trust their shooting was a lot above the average of their spelling. The name " Jack snipe," so persistently used by some writers who ought to know better, is misleading, as it rightly belongs to a smaller bird which so far as may be learned from authentic records has been taken only upon the other side of the Herring Pond. One excellent authority refers to it as " a twiddling jack " and unworthy of the notice of sportsmen.

The flight of the snipe is swift, vigorous, and usually for the first few yards erratic. The bird gets under way smartly and as a usual thing goes boring up-wind in a style rather suggestive of a feathered corkscrew. A series of electrical zigzags get him to top speed, whereupon his progress steadies a bit and he darts away in something more like a straight line. As a general rule, a flushed bird springs a few feet into the air, hangs for the fraction of a second, then begins to twist and dodge as though the Old Boy was at his tail. It would be very interesting could we discover the original cause of the dodging. Possibly some ancient foe, now long extinct, was best baffled by that mode of flight, for there usually is some such explanation for peculiar actions by wild things. Because the flight happens to be

puzzling to a gunner is no guarantee that the bird dodges for that purpose—such an explanation would imply a deal more intelligence than the entire tribe of snipe are possessed of. Snipe, of course, dodged on the wing long prior to the appearance of firearms, and it is extremely unlikely that the erratic flight has anything in the nature of protective tactics against the devices of human foes.

The fame of the bird as an object of the sportsman's pursuit has been fairly earned. Swift, small, erratic, he presents the most difficult mark of all our game of shore and upland. In my opinion only teal and canvasback are harder propositions, and with them the real difficulty is apt to be more of weather conditions and the methods usually employed rather than the speed of the fowl, great though it be. The shooting of the snipe is unlike that of any other bird. Some men attain truly wonderful skill at it and as a rule such men are referred to as " crack snipe shots," instead of the broader term " crack shots."

To me there is a trifle too much of sameness about it. I am no shirker in the field, yet there is a tinge of monotony about marsh lands and unending mud and water which cannot hold me as does the infinite variety of conditions, the marvelous beauty of turning foliage, and the clean, vigorous action of sport on the uplands. In point of fact I could enjoy six days per week of grouse, quail, and cock, but it is questionable if the charm of snipe shooting would wear equally as well.

And now the actual shooting. The best gun is a light twelve-gauge—the handiest all-round gun ever made. It should be a close, hard shooter because the mark is swift and small and half the chances at longish range, the average rise being yards further than is the rule in quail shooting. I use number eight shot, because to my notion the popular number ten is apt to mean too many pellets in the meat and consequently too much lead for busy teeth later on. The quantity of smokeless powder will depend upon the gun—I believe in using plenty, all the gun can burn properly, for the large percentage of long shots demand all possible power. When birds are few, a free-ranging pointer or setter is an invaluable helper; where birds are very plentiful, a reliable spaniel, that will keep at heel until ordered out, is all the dog required. I am not very fond of running a fine pointer or setter all day on wet mud. It is hard for his feet and coat, and unless he be carefully washed and thoroughly dried so soon as the shooting has ended, he is apt to have a miserable time of it during a long ride home and be all stiffened up in the morning. Very frequently, too, a fine dog, unless broken on snipe, is apt to try to get too close to his birds and so cause flushes. When snipe are wild, as often happens, a dog must point at long range. Dogs broken on quail and in every way reliable on the uplands, could not be expected to understand this, and some of them require days to master the peculiarities of the long-bills.

A great many men employ quail tactics when after snipe, especially in regard to beating up-wind. This I do not advise, because it means a lot of birds boring into the wind's eye and dodging like blazes while offering the smallest possible marks. A cross section of a snipe going straight away is much smaller than many people imagine. The vitals of a bird so going might be covered by a silver dollar, the head is apt to be covered by the body, while only the edges of the wings are exposed, which means an extremely narrow surface.

Because the bird loves to bore up-wind I walk down-wind, thus securing a quick chance as he curves into the wind in front, or else a square crossing shot as he passes up-wind at either side. In either of these positions the effect of his dodging is minimized, while I still retain the privilege of making a half turn and using the second barrel at a straightaway, or almost a straightaway bird that has got through his dodging and is trusting solely to his speed. In all these shots the gun has a better chance in the straightaway after the turn as just mentioned, while, of course, the side shots mean all one side of the bird and most of the long wings fully exposed. This gives the gun a rather large target instead of a very small one and practically does away with the saving erratic flight.

The reason why some men work up-wind is because they imagine the straightaway shot to be easier. They fail at crossing shots, not because the shot is difficult, but because they have not learned how to make it—in other words they never have mastered the highly important points—allowing a fast bird plenty of lead and pulling trigger without checking the steady swing of the gun. Unless one is holding a tremendous distance ahead, to stop the swing of the gun means to miss through shooting behind. Quickly as shot travels there *is* a fractional loss of time between the beginning of movement by the trigger finger and the arrival of the pellets at any point—for convenience, say thirty or forty yards from the muzzle. During that interval, brief though it be, a snipe will travel a certain distance, and that distance is precisely what the gun should be ahead of him when the trigger finger starts to pull.

Those who have not actually experimented with the pattern of guns and the matter of leading fast birds according to distance, might with advantage make a few patterns at twenty, thirty, and forty yards, using a thirty-inch circle upon large sheets of paper. The results will show a spread of pattern as the distance is increased, and let us hope an even and fairly close distribution of the pellets, for that means a useful field gun. The twenty-yard pattern will show the shot so closely bunched that no snipe within its circle could escape instant death. At the distance, then, the one necessary thing is to get any part of that pattern on him, but correct shooting would demand his being exactly centred. To insure this the gun would have to be held just ahead of him and kept swinging at exactly his speed and not stopped as the trigger was pulled. At thirty yards it is still more important that he be centred, because the charge has loosened considerably while the most pellets, hence the smallest gaps in the pattern, are in the centre. For the same reason that necessitated holding just ahead at twenty yards, the lead must now be increased one-half to insure the best result at the ten yards of increased range. At forty yards, the pattern has opened sufficiently to allow free passage to an object the size of a snipe at several points toward the outer limit, yet there remain enough closely placed pellets at the centre to do the work. If a second smaller circle be now described, which includes all of the paper which shows no dangerous gap, the deadly portion of the charge will be determined. To make sure of a snipe, that portion must cover him at forty yards, and to insure its reaching the proper spot at the exact moment, the gun must be held ahead just twice the distance which the twen-

ty-yard range demanded. In other words, as the shot leaves the muzzle the latter should be some inches ahead of the bird and swinging in true time with the mark. At greater distances the lead must be increased in proportion, but other possibilities now creep in, because, as the charge spreads more and more too large gaps may appear almost anywhere, which means the extreme reliable range of the gun has been passed.

A few, possibly successive, extremely long shots prove nothing beyond the fact of the gun's being a hard shooter, as at the same time the patterns might be poor. I have killed snipe when they seemed beyond the range of the gun; but such kills are merely accidental. No wise man would dare wager upon such shots because he knows the pellets might not again find the mark once in ten attempts although given the proper allowance for the distance.

There are two deadly methods of shooting straightaway snipe. One is lightning-fast, the next thing to out-and-out snap shooting. The other is to wait until the bird has completed his shifty first flight and give it to him the moment he steadies. Both are scientific. I prefer the former, because, being naturally very quick with my hands, I can get on a bird before he has time to begin dodging. Were it not

for this I certainly should wait. A man to shoot at all evenly *must* do one or other, for any attempt at a compromise will leave him neither quick nor slow and prone to fire at precisely the wrong moment, when the wizard of the wet lands is in the midst of his little trick wherein the quickness of the wing deceives the eye.

And now a glimpse of snipe shooting in which the characteristic sameness" of leagues of wide wet lands and successive springing, dodging, *scaiping* sprites was a bit varied. Unto me spake long Tom and his words were crisp and as follows:

"Now *will* you be ready at 3 A. M. and game to foot it out?"

"I *will!*" said I.

I meant it, and I had need to, for when long Tom got through with you, other things also seemed long, notably that awful final homeward mile. Our campaign necessitated a gray dawn start, because it began with a six-mile tramp in cold blood along a railroad track. We might have driven to one corner of the ground, but to take a horse also meant that which we both detested—a fixed point to which we would have to return at evening. And when you take a horse snipe shooting the birds invariably are most abundant farthest from where you tie the brute, and at nightfall you are apt to find yourself only five miles from home, but eight miles from the horse. Then, of course, you have to—but reader, you understand!

We started at dawn and so soon as we had reached the railroad Tom tersely remarked:

"Come, shake those long legs. I've got you where I want you now!"

This was pregnant with fell intent, and I grinned defiance, for we were about the same age and weight, in fact, six-foot, two-hundred pounders, and about even all around. As is usual when a couple of behemoths get to playing, there was considerable pounding of gravel.

Before us spread miles of ground, of all degrees of consistency between semi-liquid and putty-like stiffness. A strip of it, perhaps two miles long by one-half broad, began near our feet and ended near a dim blue mass which betokened higher ground and forest, and near those trees was a broad creek.

"Come on! I've *got you now!*" chatted Tom, and I thought of Kilkenny cats and sighed for the things which I knew would happen and unwittingly for one thing of which neither of us dreamed. For half a mile the footing was fairly good, and as we both wore ordinary walking boots and leggings, we escaped the harrassing drag of the customary waders, which are good enough when one intends to *drive* home, but worse than useless for a long tramp on dry going. Presently we began to get a bit anxious and to more than half wish for the canines left securely kenneled at home. Upon such ground, with birds plentiful, dogs are unnecessary, but where, as sometimes happens, the snipe are broadly scattered, the conditions are reversed.

We were some thirty yards apart when suddenly I heard the well known whip-hip-hip of bent wings and the "*Scaip-sca-ip!*" as an artful dodger flushed before Tom. Old "Take-your-time" was a picture as he flashed the beautiful twelve into position then waited those straining seconds till the dodging ceased. Then came the puny "*squinge*" of smokeless, and somebody's long bill was settled in full. Breaking the gun as he went and never taking his eyes off that one spot of a thousand similar spots, Tom moved forward thirty yards and retrieved. The whole performance was a perfect illustration of the deliberate method of which he undeniably was a master.

"That long brute's dead-on to-day," was my inward comment as I moved ahead.

"*Whip-hip!* *Whip-hip — Scaip sca-ip!*"

A brace of unpatented corkscrews were ready to bore holes in the whence, but the light gun just cleared its throat a couple of times and both birds hearkened to the warning and that before the second had time to make one decent twist.

"I'll mark the last one," said Tom as I went to the first bird. Right well he knew how I'd completely lose track of one the moment I left the firing point, and he followed the best method, to stand in his tracks and keep his eyes on the spot and direct the search for the second. When shooting alone, or far from a comrade, and a double is made, I reload before stirring a foot. This leaves two empty shells on the ground to indicate my exact position and this, with the memory of the turn or partial turn made for the second, gives a close line on its whereabouts. Very frequently this saves a bird and valuable time, for at the worst it will guide to within a few yards of the game, and every yard saved in beating foot by foot through grass is important. Hat or handkerchief dropped at the firing point also makes a useful mark when grass is tall. A snipe breast upward is easily seen, but only about half of them fall in that position. Back upward the striped effect blends curiously with grass and its shadows, and a winged

"'Here is your life-line' * * * I ventured as I tossed him one leg of the trousers."

CLARE·ANGELL 1902

or otherwise wounded bird seems to know this and act accordingly. Men trained on the wet lands acquire a marvelous knack of marking down, and a mighty useful accomplishment it is.

Moving on, Tom flushed a brace on bare mud and served, the last bird falling full fifty yards from the gun. I marveled, for it was a long clean kill. Before he reached these two single chances were offered and accepted, and a third bird went careering away, rising higher and higher till it looked like a wind-driven leaf. As Tom's birds were down on easy ground I kept my position more from habit than with any idea of being of service. A wave of his hand directed my attention to the late towering bird, which, as they frequently will, had decided to return. Like a plummet it fell some thirty yards away, and, as an experiment, I held about four feet under it, and it hit the mud with a resounding spat. It was a great shot, and Tom's emphatic "Broke its own neck!" was merely his way of expressing keen appreciation.

For an hour after this there was very pretty shooting. The birds were nicely distributed, rising singly and well within range and only a trio finding any truth in the oft repeated "scaip-scaip!" Finally a missed bird pitched in a broad patch of short stuff which showed a spring-like greenness, and Tom turned after it:

"Look out there! Where are you going?" I yelled; but it was too late. In an instant it seemed he was down and floundering and the whoop he uttered might have been heard for miles. If any of my readers have attempted to run in snipe ground they will understand my task. Fortunately the distance was short. To skin out of the coat, drop gun and hat upon it, and start for him was the work of very few seconds.

His face was ghastly white and the treacherous ooze was up to his belt and he was slowly sinking. After his first wild scramble he had wisely ceased all effort, but he was scared clear through. So was I for that matter, for it was a nasty situation. He had his gun, but I dared not venture near enough for that to be of use; besides I question if either of our grips would stand the pull upon such smooth holding.

The belt and the corduroys! Glory be! It was a noble inspiration—Nay! the very thing I was *panting* for. Those who have taken off leggins and trousers while trying to stand upon snipe ground, will understand why I presently cursed and sat down upon cool, moist mud; but the legs were long and the material stout. The *seam* never would stand the strain, but the good old belt, made fast to the upper part of one leg, carried across the seat and again made fast, would take the direct strain. In a minute the tackle was ready and I reached for his gun. He hated to let go of it and I didn't blame him.

"Here's your life-line, and remember *they* cost a ten spot." I ventured as I tossed him one leg of the trousers. The way his hand clutched on the cloth was a marvel to see. "Steady now: wiggle your legs a bit," I grunted as I cautiously put on the strain. There was one moment of agonizing doubt; then Thomas began to come and finally, with a sort of regretful sucking-sigh, the awful trap let go and he came slithering out of that.

Mud! I mined into a pocket till I got pay dirt—otherwise his flask, cleaned it with grass, and we halved the contents. Then we looked at each other and laughed in a semi-hysterical sort of way, for each knew, and well, too, how serious a thing had passed.

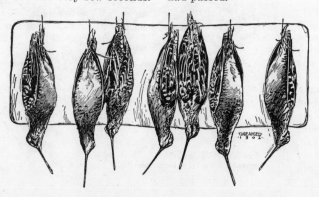

30.
SPORT: PAST, PRESENT AND FUTURE
(1888)

A PAIR OF POACHERS.

OUTING.

DECEMBER, 1888.

SPORT--PAST, PRESENT AND FUTURE.

BY ALEXANDER HUNTER.

IT may be a pleasant task for the sporting antiquary or the historian of some future period to trace the rise and fall of shooting in the section where the Potomac bursts foaming through its narrow bed at the Great Falls to Point Lookout, where the wide, majestic river mixes its fresh waters with the brine of Chesapeake Bay. But retrospection only brings sadness and regret to the sportsman of to-day, who sees the finest shooting-ground for wild fowl on the American continent now denuded of its game, except in scantiest quantities.

Potomac in the Indian dialect signifies "The River of Swans." A pleasure or health seeker as he passes down the bay *en route* to Old Point, or a tourist on a pilgrimage to Mount Vernon, admires from the steamer's deck the fine scenery, the bold headlands, the sweeping curves of the shore, and the ever-shifting scenes of the beautiful river, but he will never catch a glimpse, in a lifetime's travel, of the stately birds that were so plentiful that the river was named after them.

All the observant traveler now sees is the settling of, perhaps, a dozen broad-bills in the water, or the alighting of a solitary shuffler or mallard. He will learn with surprise that not many years back the steamer literally ploughed its way through vast flocks of ducks, who only took wing when the sharp prow was within a few yards of them, while every creek, stream and run that poured its waters into the river was alive with waterfowl of a dozen different species, scurrying to and fro, circling high into the air, or striking into their native element with an explosive splash. On a windy day the river was so black with them that the bosom of the deep seemed to have been changed into an undulating, many-hued meadow.

Across the river from Mount Vernon was one of the most famous ducking blinds on the Potomac. The steamboat passengers notice with curiosity what appears to be a small island directly in the centre of the river, which at this point is about two miles wide. It is a miniature Loch Leven

The Willet

Ox Eyes

Castle, and the ruins of a small stone edifice makes it a romantic picture in the varied panorama that unfolds as one passes down the "River of Swans." Right across on the Maryland side is one of those old colonial brick houses that tell of days when his Majesty was "prayed for" by fox-hunting parsons, and where the King's health was drunk before each toast by the cocked-hat gentry. The house, which stands on a high hill, and faces Mount Vernon across the river, is the manor-seat of the Chapmans, a family whose name is connected with every public enterprise or "high emprise" from the conversion of the colony of Maryland into a commonwealth.

General John Chapman was a great lover of both rod and gun, and some thirty years ago he conceived the idea of making comfort and sport go hand in hand. Having made his soundings, he kept his slaves steadily at work, during odd days and off hours, hauling rocks in flat-boats, and dumping them into the rolling river. He kept his own counsel, and his neighbors began to fear he was going crazy. At last his island was completed. Like the Old Point "Rip-Raps," it arose sheer from the water, and was composed entirely of loose rock. Chapman Island, as it was called, had an area of about a quarter of an acre, and was shaped like a cigar—the smaller end gradually decreasing in height and breadth until the narrowing ledge disappeared in the water. At this point the decoys—rarely under a hundred, often

double that number—were placed. At the large end of the island was the hunting-lodge, at a distance of about seventy-five yards. It was built low, but the walls were thick, and a coal stove kept it comfortable in the stormiest, coldest days. It is doubtful whether there ever was a blind in all America that surpassed in attractions this artificial island.

Ducks, as a general thing, when moving in great numbers, choose the middle of a river, and seeing a large flock (the decoys) floating near the point, they would invariably swirl aside and join them. At a time when the river was full of waterfowl, some idea may be had of the royal sport, without any terrible exposure and endurance; a warm fire, refreshments of all kinds within a minute's walk, and the ducks raining down in a ceaseless stream from the sky—that was the very poetry of sporting.

In the fall and winter months General Chapman had his house filled with the men whose names are household words in America, and his oyster roasts, canvasback and terrapin stews were as widely known then as were the dinners of the great lobbyist and gourmand, Sam Ward, a quarter of a century afterwards.

From the traditions handed down, it is known that General Washington was an enthusiastic rider after hounds, and it was at one of the meets that he first met Mistress Betty Custis; but he never was a devotee of the gun. There are several letters written by him to his patron, Lord Fairfax, of Greenway Court, which are, or were a few years ago, in the possession of Mrs. Custis, of Williamsburg, Virginia. In them the young surveyor tells in glowing language of the fine runs he has had and the brushes he has taken.

Opportunity makes the right man; but for the Revolution, George Washington, of Mount Vernon, Virginia, would have been a hard-riding fox-hunter, a shrewd bargainer at a horse-trade, and a vestryman of the Pohick church.

Washington's nearest neighbor was famous George Mason, whose statue adorns Capitol Square in Richmond, Va. He lived a few miles down the river at Gunston Hall, which, next to Greenway Court, was in its day the most celebrated hunting resort in Virginia, and was the scene of many a glorious meet long after girder, rafter and roof of Greenway Court had mouldered in the dust.

Gunston Hall of to-day is the same building as that of over a century ago. It was built for comfort and not for show, for the walls are very thick, making the rooms warm in winter and cool in summer. It was erected in 1739, and every brick was brought from England as ballast. The plantation originally comprised 5,000 acres, and was, without exception, the finest game preserve in the country. Colonel Mason was an ardent sportsman, and cherished and protected the game on his land. At his river front the wild celery grew in the greatest profusion. If those old walls of

ON THE BANKS OF THE POTOMAC.

Gunston Hall could talk, what entrancing tales they could tell of men of iron mould and giant minds, and maidens "passing faire"! There is a porch around the ancient mansion, religiously preserved, though it is in the last stages of dilapidation, where on the south side of the hall Washington and Mason were wont to sit during the long summer evenings, their senses lulled by the fairy-like scene, their eyes ranging over the grand, circling sweep of the river, and their conversation freshened by many a decoction of pounded ice, fresh mint, and Jamaica brandy. By the way, there are comparatively few people who ever tasted a real Virginia mint julep. The decoction, hastily mixed and as hastily drunk, is called a julep. Bacchus, save the mark! It is as different from the royal mint julep as corn whisky from the imperial cognac. It does not take five minutes, an hour, or a day to properly brew this wonderful drink, but a year at the very least. Here is the way Colonel Bob Allen, of Curl's Neck, on the James River, used to prepare the julep. In the early spring, gather the young and tender mint, have your demijohn three-quarters full of the best whisky, and into its mouth drop the mint, rolled into little balls, and well bruised—about a quarter of a peck, loosely heaped up, to each gallon of liquor. Next, enough loaf sugar is saturated in water to melt it, and sweeten the whisky *ad lib.* This fills the demijohn, which is then sealed tight, and kept for the future, being rarely opened for at least two years.

The preparation of the drink is simple, and yet artistic. First, a julep ought never to be mixed but in a silver flagon—there is such a thing as a "perfect accord." The demijohn being opened, the fragrant liquor is poured into the mug, with a double handful of *crushed* ice—not pounded, but crushed until it is like hail or snow ice—(a stout towel and a few blows against a brick wall will accomplish this result); add a few sprigs of fresh mint, a few strawberries, a tablespoonful of Jamaica rum, and you will have an elixir worthy of Jove to drink and Ganymede to bear.

But the swans from whom the Potomac takes its name, what of them?

In my boyhood I have often heard the

A POT-HUNTER WAITING FOR DUCKS.

septuagenarians and octogenarians of the lowlands speak of the vast migratory flocks of swans and geese that would whiten the river for miles. So many were they that in the spring-time, when the imprisoned frost was released from the ground and the surface of the earth became soft, vast numbers would swoop upon the fields of winter-wheat, and ruin the crop in a single day. It was a common thing for the farmers to employ every supernumerary on the place to guard the young and tender wheat.

But when the steamboat appeared on the scene, both swan and wild geese vanished, never to return.

Memory carries me back to my old ancestral home on the Virginia side of the Potomac, directly opposite the Washington Navy Yard.

In those days, a planter was an epicure by blood, a gourmand by breeding, and as long as his digestion remained unimpaired he could revel in the best of living on the choicest viands; and were he a devotee of the gun, he could amuse himself by killing a variety of game in such quantities that satiety would be apt to ensue.

Yes, the noble river furnished an unfailing supply of succulent food to the dwellers on its banks. The number of fish that swam in the clear waters of the Potomac would seem incredible in these times of purse-ponds and gill-nets. Our overseer used to devote one week in the spring to hauling a small seine, and would catch an abundance of fish to last the plantation the ensuing year, and there were enough herrings salted in barrels, and smoked shad in kits, to half fill our huge cellar that ran underground the whole length of the house. Fresh fish was on every table of the plantation nine months out of the year as a matter of course. The troll lines, set a short distance from the shore, yielded a steady supply of catfish, eels, perch, tobacco-boxes and fresh-water terrapin, or "tarrapin," as they are called—a luxury only second to their cousin the "diamond-back." As for the ducks and geese that made their home during winter on the flats between Washington and Alexandria, their number was simply astounding. I have hunted in the last decade from Havre de Grace to Tampa Bay, but never have seen such apparently limitless numbers of ducks as circled in the very sight of the Capitol's dome some thirty years ago.

The channel was on the Maryland side. It varied from one hundred to one hundred and fifty yards across. For a mile and a half the water was rarely over two feet on the flats at low tide, and not over a fathom at the high-water mark. On these shallow bottoms there grew in the greatest luxuriance a peculiar quality of indigenous plant, called celery-grass, which wild fowl preferred to any other food. About the middle of November the birds began to congregate in such huge flocks that on a clear morning, when suddenly disturbed they took to wing, they made a noise like rolling thunder.

There were sportsmen, of course, at that time in the two cities of Washington and Alexandria, but they confined themselves to the laziest mode of shooting, and followed the creeks and streams that bordered or led into the river. Here the wild fowl afforded fine sport, with but little hardship.

As a general rule, the family on the plantation soon became tired of eating wild ducks; even the incomparable canvas-back palls at length upon the palate, as much as the partridges that are devoured on a wager, one each day for a month. The products of the poultry yard in the end were always preferred to the spoils of the river. Frequently, when company were coming to dinner, it was desirable to have a plentiful supply of game on the table; so my aunt, a famous housewife, would call up Sandy, who, being lame in one leg, was the general utility man of the plantation, one who could turn his hand to anything except regular labor, which he hated as a galley slave his oar, or as much as Rip Van Winkle did to earn an honest living. Sandy resembled Rip in more ways than one, though, fortunately for him, he had no sable Gretchen.

"Take Brother Bush's gun, Sandy," my aunt would say, "and go down and bring me some ducks."

"How many does you want, Miss Jane?"

A mental calculation, and the number was given; then Sandy hobbled off with a matter-of-fact air, as if he were merely bound to the barnyard to slaughter half a dozen chickens. It was just as easy an undertaking, and one infinitely more to his taste. Calling one of the house-boys, he would go with him to the shore, a couple of hundred yards or so distant. Then the couple would walk in single file for some

large tree bordering the river. The ducks feeding on the wild celery close to the shore would on their approach swim lazily from the banks out of gun-shot. Sandy would take his position behind the trunk of the tree and lie close. His companion would leisurely walk back to the house. The wild fowl, seeing the cause of their alarm disappear, would slowly circle back, and Sandy, waiting till they were well bunched, would let go both barrels; then, denuding himself of his breeches, he would wade in and bring out his game. The ducks never seemed to "catch on" to this dodge, and Sandy rarely failed to fill his orders, as the drummers say, " with promptness and dispatch."

There was only one pot-hunter in the neighborhood of Washington thirty years ago—an old, grizzled, weather-beaten man, named Jerry, who anchored his little schooner in a snug cove on our shore every winter, and such was the unfailing supply of wild ducks that Jerry was rarely forced to up-anchor, set his sails and speed farther down the river. Old Jerry was assisted by his son, young Jerry, a chip of the old block. Every Saturday these two would put their game in canvas bags and carry them to their regular customers in Washington.

I became a fast friend of these two

A KICKER.

pot-hunters, as much, indeed, as a boy of twelve years could with matured men. I suppose I imbibed from them that over-mastering love of sport that has made me a wanderer for a score of years. I was of practical use to them; the sentiment and the benefits were all on my side, for I made the gardener give them regular rations of turnips and cabbages. In return, I was allowed the run of their cabin, a little cuddy at which the meanest, poorest slave on the plantation would have turned up his nose.

Jerry was one of the few pot-hunters who possessed a swivel—a monster ducking gun, with a solid, uncouth stock, fastened

THE CURLEW.

to a barrel some ten or twelve feet long, with a bore as large as an old twelve-pounder Napoleon. This "thunderer" was loaded with twenty or twenty-five drachms of powder, and between thirty and forty ounces of shot.

Old Jerry would be in his skiff at the earliest dawn of day, and would cruise from Washington to Alexandria, closely followed by his son and heir, some hundred yards in the rear.

As soon as old Jerry saw a closely bunched flock of ducks, he would lie flat in the bottom of the skiff, and take his creeping paddles, which were about two feet long, two inches wide by a quarter of an inch thick, made of the best hickory, and painted a neutral color. With his arms hanging over the sides of his skiff, and a paddle in each hand, he could make his way evenly along, hardly raising a ripple. As he would approach closer the ducks would get more and more restless, swimming backward and forward, and gazing with alarm at what seemed a log with a

queer, indescribable motion on each side. At last, when the woolen cap of a man could be seen, and underneath it the glittering eyes could be detected, then it was that the flock would rise from the water and take wing. That was the moment old Jerry was waiting for, with the stock resting against his shoulder, which was protected by a bag or pillow stuffed tight with feathers to break the recoil, and his eye ranging along the black barrel just as an artilleryman sights his piece before giving the word. A quick jerk of the trigger, the click of the flint striking the pan, the flash of the priming powder, then the deafening roar of the swivel, followed by a flash of flame, an encircling volume of smoke, the swirl of the water as the skiff was rocked by the kicking gun, and the deed was done. Old Jerry would rise up, grasp his double paddle, and make for the shore to reload, while the younger Jerry would come up in hot haste to pick up the dead, and dispatch with his double-barrel the crippled ducks.

Many a day have I played truant, and half the darkies on the plantation would be searching for me, while I, in the seventh heaven of delight, was with Jerry in his skiff following up the diving ducks whose wings were broken. I had a little single barrel that would make the water splash, and that was about all.

It was my one thought by day and dream by night to possess a gun big enough to kill the ducks at a fair distance—not a swivel by any manner of means—I had not the slightest desire to be behind that huge piece of ordnance when it went off. I wanted one that could strike a flock at eighty and a hundred yards. I never divulged my thoughts at home. I was that unfortunate "ne'er do weel," known as the only son, and such an intimation would have raised hysterics at the female end of the house, and something worse at the male end of the mansion, for my paternal ancestor was a retired officer of the navy, and when he was excited his speech savored of the forecastle more than the cabin, and his actions became alarming.

A kind fate threw into my hands just such a weapon as my soul longed for, and I look back to it now with the same affection that a man of many *affaires de cœur* recalls the memory of his first love.

To make a long, rambling story short, my father bought, as a curiosity, a long Dutch ducking gun, that was intended to be fired from the shoulder by a man of stalwart build. Loading it carefully, the captain told the overseer, named Robinson, to fire it. This individual was a tall, ungainly lopsided man, who got sideways over the ground like a crab. He had a slatternly wife, with the most vivid, burning red hair I ever saw, and a large, callow brood of vividly headed children.

I suppose Robinson fired the gun, for it was brought back by his eldest hope, who said something about "Dad's laid up; somethin' or nuther kicked him;" but no attention was paid to what he said.

My father, accompanied by his youthful likeness, set out to try the gun himself. He made me fasten a piece of paper to the side of the ice-house, and then raised the long weapon slowly until he caught sight, and then pulled. I saw him spin around from the force of the blow, and utter the most blood-curdling curses against the gun, and next seizing the harmless piece and striking it against a tree, he broke the stock short off, then throwing the barrel down, he walked wrathfully away. I picked up the pieces tenderly, and carried them to Uncle Peter, the plantation carpenter, and told him I would give him a quart of that liquor he most loved in the world if he would patch it up. Uncle Peter agreed, if I would pledge myself to keep his share in the affair secret. Of course I promised.

What with braces, screws, clamps, rivets, the old piece was reconstructed, and I was as proud of it as a girl of her first long dress, or a spinster with a beau. It was about eight feet long, with a bore about the size of a Queen Anne musketoon. The barrel was slightly curved outside. The trigger was hard to pull, but the springs were good, and every time the flint fell a handful of sparks would be generated.

But, shades of Vulcan, how that ancient gun did kick! No vicious army mule, no bucking broncho, no Five Points billy-goat ever were productive of more sudden shocks. While the recoil was not so great as that of the famous gun that left the load stationary while it lodged the man who fired it in the fork of the tree two hundred yards in

the rear, yet, like a champion pugilist, it sent every one to grass who tackled it. Uncle Peter was laid out. Sandy, steadying himself with his crutch planted firmly in the ground—a human tripod —was spun around and hurled to mother earth, as Hercules threw Antæus. Jack, the giant of the plantation, who led the cradlers in the harvest field, and pulled one end of the seine against six on the other side, tackled that weapon, and he, too, for the first time in his life, was vanquished. Though this piece could not quite rival the matchlock that belonged to Artemus Ward's grandfather, which would not only knock the shootist over, but club him when he was down, still it put every man who fired it on the invalid list for the balance of the day.

I would not have put that gun against

OLD JERRY AND THE DUCK GUN.

my shoulder and pulled the trigger for a month's holiday. Uncle Peter, however, did the trick, and fixed the gun so that it was as harmless as a copperhead with its fangs drawn. He got the blacksmith to rivet a couple of iron rings close to the muzzle and another on the breech just above the pan. Next, he put a massive staple in the prow of the skiff, and another and a smaller one on the front seat ; a chain with a catch passed through staple and ring, and held everything tight. When the gun was fired the staples received the shock, and no kicking could loosen them.

Uncle Peter finished the job Saturday night, and Sunday morning a mysterious message came from the overseer's son, Sam, that he was waiting to see me in the shuck-house. I no sooner laid my eyes on him than I knew his mind was full of something.

"Well, Sam, what is it?"

"Mister"—Sam called every white man and boy mister—"I done hearn pop say as you were a-goin' to use that air big gun."

"Yes, I am ; but you keep your mouth shut about it. You hear, Sam?"

"I ain't a-goin' to tell, but you'd better leave her alone."

"Why?"

"Cause it'll kick yer liver lights out, that's why."

"How do you know?"

"Ef you cross yer heart, an' say, 'I hope I may die,' I tell yer."

This mystic process having been complied with, Sam commenced :

"One evenin' I slipped home from the brickyard, an' thar warn't anybody at home 'cept the child'en. Pop was gone to market, an' tuk mam wid him. I seed the big gun sittin' in the corner, but pop had tole me that ef I ever tortched it he'd knock thunder outen me. So I dassent handle it. Jest then a big hawk lighted on the barn, an' I jest grabbed the gun, meanin' to shoot that bird, thrashin' or no thrashin'. I crept behind the corn-house, an' run the muzzle through the logs, an' I tuck aim at the hawk that was watchin' fer

a chicken. I tried to draw back the hammer to a full cock, when the hammer slipped, and it went off. At first I thought that something had busted, then that Mose, the brindled bull, had butt me, or that Toby, the old blind mule, had kicked me, an' I commenced a hollerin', an' jus' then, by gum ! pop an' mam druv up, an' mam thought as how I was killed, an'—" Here Sam stopped to take breath.

"Well, Sam, what did your father do? Did he scream, too?"

"Scream !" answered Sam ; "pop ain't that kind. No, he picked up the big gun with one hand, an' tuk hole on me with the other, an' dragged me home, me a-kickin' an' a-tryin' to break away all the time, an' then he got that cowhide that hangs over the chimbly, an' almost tanned the hide offen me. But you jus' see where that big gun kicked me," and Sam opened his shirt and showed me his narrow pigeon-chest that was bruised black and blue.

"Now I mus' be goin', mister. You mine me, don't you tortch that air big gun ; as sure as yer do she'll knock yer cold."

Sam's tale frightened me, and I pulled the trigger, with my heart in my mouth, the first time ; but Uncle Peter had done his work well, and if it kicked I never felt it.

I remember through this long vista of years the ecstatic pleasure of creeping up to a huge flock early one morning, and the thumping of my heart that beat like a trip-hammer against the bottom of the skiff— for I was lying close, and using the creeping paddles. At last, at last ! and as the flock cleared the water I let drive, and was rather astonished to find myself safe and afloat.

So in the Old Dominion the fox-hunter followed his hounds, and took timber as it came. The partridge-hunter discharged his right and left shots in the stubble. One fine morning in April, 1861, they awoke from their easy-going, rollicking existence, and dropping the shotgun and sporting rifle, grasped instead the sabre, the lanyard, the sword, or the musket.

SPORT—PAST, PRESENT AND FUTURE.

BY ALEXANDER HUNTER.

PART II.

OR four years the game in Virginia, all undisturbed, increased and multiplied at an astonishing rate. There was no shot to be had in the Confederacy, and the only way an ardent sportsman, when home on furlough, could take a shy at the game, was to hammer out from a leaden bullet long, square blocks, and then cutting off the ends with a knife, to use a brick to roll these bits on the floor until each pellet became round enough for use. It would take a man a day, and exhaust all his patience, to make one pound of shot; and he would naturally be very chary about using his ammunition, and rarely pull a trigger except when certain of his game. In most sections of Virginia to fire a gun was a dangerous pastime, for what with raids, irruptions, incursions and forays, the people were in a state of siege, and the report of a firearm was as likely as not to be followed by a bullet from some traveling soldier, prowling bushwhacker, or passing cavalryman, thrown just for good luck in the direction of the sound. Then, if it should happen that a raid was in progress, the shot would attract the videttes and scouts, and the luckless gunner would find himself in hostile hands; and if too old or too young for military service, he might consider himself lucky if he were allowed to depart minus his fowling-piece and dog.

In the mountains of Virginia the wild turkeys were more numerous than they ever were before, the various bivouacs furnishing them in winter with an ample supply of food, while, best of all, they were allowed to feed unmolested. The waterfowl on the Potomac kept up their ratio of increase, for except the officers of the gunboats patrolling up and down the river, none dared to fire a gun. There were hunters of men in those times scattered along the banks, as well as floating on the bosom of the blue water. The explosion of a sportsman's gun, and its smoke, might serve as an admirable target for the boatswain of an iron-clad with a crew nearly dead with listlessness and *ennui*, and glad to get an excuse to blaze away at anything.

In the fall of 1865, those Virginians who loved sporting, and had the good luck to return to the homes of their youth with their arms and legs intact, had a rare and royal time among the fur and feather, and a moderate shot would return in the evening and show such a bag as the result of the day's sport as would last the family for a week. A couple of sportsmen living about ten miles from Culpeper Court House, Virginia, killed, in one day, eighty-four rabbits and fourteen wild turkeys. If a gunner can start even half a dozen cotton-tails now in a long day's tramp he considers himself fortunate, and he won't see a wild turkey in a season's shooting. I well remember a hunt that I had in the autumn of 1865, just after the war ended. It was a perfect day in November, with the morning mists still hanging around the tree-tops. I had borrowed a double-barrel from one friend, and a good, staunch pointer named "Josh" from another. I climbed the fence of an orchard, and put the dog out in a huge field near Warrenton Junction, where portions of both armies had often encamped. Josh had not gone seventy-five yards before he came to a dead stand, and with beating heart I advanced and hied him on. As the birds rose I let fly both barrels, and—did not touch a feather! Loading up, I again sent Josh careering over the stubble. In ten minutes he had pointed a covey, and I again emptied the gun with the same result as before. If ever a dog's face expressed contempt Josh's was surely the one. His dewlaps curled up, and he absolutely showed his teeth, whether in anger or derision I never found out. The third time I approached a covey that Josh had cornered in a big patch of briers, and two more loads were sent harmless as Macbeth's sword "cutting the intrenchant air." This

was enough for that disgusted dog. He sneaked off, and I never laid my eyes upon him again.

It was no great matter, the birds were so plentiful that I had merely to walk up and down the field, and I banged away most lustily. All in vain! I could not touch one. I fired with both eyes open, then with one shut, and still no partridge lingered on that account. I became superstitious and fired with both eyes shut. I doubled the charges, until I swept that meadow with leaden pellets, as a field is cleared by grape-shot. But there were no dead. At last, in my despair, I would shoot even if the bird was half a mile off. I went home that evening, after shooting away about ten pounds of shot, with one solitary partridge in my game-bag, and this bird, when I flushed him suddenly, was so scared that he flew from the edge of the field across a fence and against the trunk of a black-jack tree with such force as to knock himself silly, and before he could hustle himself away I had jumped the fence and wrung his neck.

There was apparently enough fur and feather in Virginia just after the war to supply the whole of America with small game, but in one decade the state of the case was completely altered. First came the invention of the breech-loader, which enables one to shoot all day without intermission. The game stood but little chance against these machines of perpetual destruction. But worse even than the breech-loader was the old army musket, loaded with a handful of shot, with a lately enfranchised freedman behind the big end of it. The darkey is a nocturnal prowler,

SHOOTING OVER DECOYS.

as much so as a 'coon or 'possum, and his prowls through meadow, woods and fallow cause him frequently to stumble on the wary turkey that forgets his cunning as he struts around preparatory to flying to his roost, generally a dead limb on a lofty tree. He bags many a molly cotton-tail loping down the road to get his evening drink at the branch. But it is when "our friend and brother" catches sight, in the shades of the evening, of a flock of partridges settling in some field for their

loader as a great orator does upon the garrulous, loquacious youth who talks upon every subject at any time, and at any length, while he only opens his mouth to make knock-down arguments, or to utter words of great import that thrill and convince. When the reverberating roar of that old A. M. was heard, it was safe to bet that something that did not come from the barnyard would fill the shooter's iron pot that night.

A weather-beaten old darkey said to me

RED-HEAD DUCKS AT HOME.

night's rest, that he becomes dangerous. It is then that the old army musket is converted into a terror, and when its muzzle bears upon the whole covey squatted in a space that can be covered by a bandana handkerchief, and its contents are turned loose, every bird will be either killed or crippled.

The freedman's musket, battered and patched though it be, must look down upon the handsome, resplendent breech-

once : " It dun cos' me nearly five cents to load that air musket, countin' powder, caps, shot and everythin', an' I ain't gwine to let er off 'less I knows I'se sartin to make by de shot."

The baybird-shooting in the summer, and the duck-shooting outside the Virginia capes, was at its zenith some fifteen years ago. Then, too, the canvas-back, that king of water-fowl, before whose name the gourmand bows in homage, still

POTOMAC SHOOTING—OLD STYLE.

fill of shooting every day at the baybirds. They were so plentiful that all along the Virginia Broadwater every oyster-bar or mud-flat would be covered with them, and all the shooter would have to do would be to make a blind out of sea-grass, place his decoys around him, and then try his hand on singles, doubles and flocks, striking them on the turn, while a hundred pair of yellow-legs, or willet, would not be considered anything out of the way. As it is now—well, the finest shot in the country could not kill that many snipe in a week, simply because they are not there to kill. The vast flocks of robin-snipe that tarried in their migrations along the shores of the Chesapeake and the Broadwater of the Atlantic coast have entirely disappeared. The curlew still haunt their favorite places, but have become so wary that neither blind nor decoys can lure them, except, indeed, at the earliest dawn of day, before their eyes are wide open. Half a dozen curlew, between sunrise and sunset, in the blinds, is something for a sportsman to be proud of, for no crow is keener-eyed, more suspicious, and keeps a sharper lookout than these birds. Fifteen years ago I have often killed from thirty to fifty from sun to sun, at Smith Island or Cape Charles, but now

lingered in the tributaries of the Chesapeake Bay, but now it is nearly extinct. A sportsman may gun for a whole winter in the bay and not kill half a dozen "canvasbacks," but, if a good shot over the decoys, he can count on the kind known as the "red-head"—and if he knew how to pull out a few feathers, as does the professional pot-hunter, he could easily follow that gentleman's example and sell them at fancy figures for "canvas-backs," which in another decade will be as utterly annihilated as the dodo. Still, great is the culinary *chef's* art, and if he can, by the magic power of his sauces, herbs and seasonings, pass calf's head off for green turtle, and the skillpot for diamond-back terrapin stew, then nobody is hurt. His patrons enjoy it just the same, and to the average man the red-head duck tastes as well with his champagne as its incomparable relative.

Fifteen years ago—even ten years—many an amateur would pack his trunk with ammunition, and taking steamer for Old Point Comfort, disembark there, and after a few hours' wait at the Hygeia Hotel, proceed on his way to the eastern shore of Virginia by crossing the Chesapeake Bay. Or he would go outside the capes, and stop at Cape Charles, or Cobb's Island. Once at his objective point, he could be certain in the right season of having his

ROBIN-SNIPE.

one has to load his shell with No. 3 shot to bring down the high-circling, distrustful curlew.

The willet is still fairly plentiful. They lay their eggs and rear their young in the neighboring sea-meadows, and though preyed upon by crabs, snakes and raccoons from the time the egg is laid until the bird is able to fly, they still hold their own. They are such sociable birds that whenever a flock of snipe is fired into, one of the dead is almost certain to be a willet.

The ox-eye, another variety of the snipe family, is found in abundance on the shores and sea-meadows, and they owe their preservation, like the sandpipers, to their insignificant size. There are no birds in existence that keep so close together when on the wing as these ox-eyes. A large flock resembles a solid mass, and dire is the de-

POTOMAC SHOOTING—NEW STYLE.

struction that a double-barrel makes as it pours forth its contents of No. 8 shot at point-blank distance and strikes them on the turn. I asked old Nathan Cobb, of Cobb's Island, which is outside the Virginia capes—a pot-hunter of half a century's experience, who has grown independent from the proceeds of his gun—what was the greatest number of snipe he had ever killed by one discharge of his double-barrel.

"Wal," said Nathan, with his Eastern Shore drawl, "I was out gunning one spring, about thirty years ago, and had a No. 8 muzzle-loader that would hold comfortably six ounces of shot. I ran in on a solid acre of robin-snipe on the beach, and fired one load raking them as they fed,

giving them the other barrel as they rose. I picked up three hundred and two."

I next asked him the greatest number of brant he had ever killed in one day over the decoys, with single shots.

"I bagged," he answered, "about ten years ago, one hundred and seventy brant, and nearly every one of them was a single shot."

I can easily believe this, for I have shot in blinds with many sportsmen, at red-head, shufflers, black duck and brant, and I never yet saw amateur, professional, or pot-hunter, whose aim was so unerring and deadly at the flying ducks as Nathan Cobb's. I do not believe this score has ever been beaten in this country.

At the present day this same story of the disappearance of the waterfowl on the Virginia coast and along the Capes becomes dreary from repetition. It does not pay the sportsman to go to Cobb's Island now. I spent three seasons there in the winter, during the "Eighties," and found that the brant were so wild that they would not stool. Then I went to Cape Charles, just outside the Capes, and, though it is a most inaccessible place, the brant would not come near the decoys.

Two winters ago, I tried Currituck Sound, and found palatial club-houses open all about that noble sheet of water. Some of these houses are so splendid in appointment that when you glance around the elegantly furnished rooms, with their damask curtains, Brussels carpets and open grates where the anthracite is piled high, it is impossible to imagine that just outside roll the dark waters of the Sound, while miles upon miles of barren sea-meadows, marshes and swamp separate the house from civilization. All of these club-houses are owned by Northern men—rich in world's gear, of course—men who count their incomes by thousands, where ordinary bread-winners of the professions count their earnings by tens. Think of having in the magazine of a club-house thirty thousand dollars in guns! Gordon Cumming, starting for a ten years' game hunt in the jungles of Africa, or Stanley, setting out to fight his way through the "Dark Continent," with countless hordes of savage "Wawangi" disputing his passage, never had that amount invested in weapons—and all to kill the wary geese and swift-flying ducks.

Even with such perfection of outfit—with guns of every imaginable make from the 12 to the 4 bore, and trained gunners to oversee every arrangement, the clubmen were talking gloomily about the sport fast deteriorating. Pot-hunters, "duck pirates," countrymen, freedmen—all who lived or robbed along the shores of the Sound had their shy at the ducks, day in and night out, and such a fusillade was never heard since Burnside stormed and carried Roanoke Island, some miles below, in the glinting spring days of 1862. I found good enough sport on the private point of a friend who lived on a large farm by the shores of the Sound. Still the birds were thinning rapidly.

Last winter's experience with Currituck made me determine never to go to that spot again for sport. I do not think I overstate matters when I say that wildfowl-shooting on the finest grounds in the world is doomed. Gone are the vast flocks, decimated are the swans and geese that were so plentiful in certain localities even three short years ago, and indigo blue are the rich sportsmen who quaff their champagne in silence and puff moodily at their twenty-five cent cigars as they think of the meagre bags they have made, and how matters, now so bad, are always getting worse, thereby proving the old saw which saith "Nothing can be so bad that it cannot be made worse." The club men should, however, be glad that the snipe will always be with them.

For keen trading, guileless equivocation and general deviltry commend me to the "cracker" of the North Carolina Coast. He could discount the Jersey Yankee upstairs and down-stairs. The typical specimen is slab-sided and always thin; I never met a fat one yet. Their complexion shows that they have wrestled for years with "chills," and their cheeks are as yellow as a newly-pulled gourd; they drawl in their speech, look at you with half-shut eyes, are afraid of neither man nor devil, have no hero-worship in their composition, and are as familiar with the captain of a yacht as with the roustabout. They are as keen as a brier, despite their listless, indifferent air, and to them more than any other cause is due the extermination of the

wild fowl in Currituck Sound. They cleaned out the wild geese by setting steel traps on the bars. What they did not catch they frightened away.

Mr. William Palmer, the superintendent of the Palmer Island Club, states, moreover, that the number of sportsmen who come to Currituck to shoot has increased twenty-five per cent., while the natives have crowded the Sound with their blinds, and every male "cracker" who can hold a gun straight is on the watch.

It is true that there are stringent State Laws against the illegal killing of wild fowl, and also a close season. If these rules were enforced there would be first-class shooting in Currituck Sound for years to come, but the laws seem to be completely ignored; there is not even a pretense of observing them. The law makes a strong provision against a gun being fired at a duck after sunset, but there are numbers of murderous, greedy natives who have their skiffs hid in the woods and swamps in which are the huge ducking guns already referred to. Every hour during the night can be heard the sullen boom of these swivels floating across the waters, and the true sportsman, as he listens to the echoing roar, can only grind his teeth with rage, for he knows what a slaughter is going on, and how the survivors will take wing and abandon the Sound for good and all.

But the worst remains to be told. As if steel traps and big guns were not enough to destroy the wild fowl, the ingenious natives make fires on the banks of the creeks that run through the marshes, and, as the ducks float in ricks up to the illuminated waters, the ambushed assassin gets in his deadly work. Unless the sportsmen who own the club-houses on the Sound, by concerted action and vast outlay, can prosecute the offenders, then "Othello's occupation's gone."

My own idea is that these clubs are too exclusive. They should make it a point to cultivate the *entente cordiale* with the sportsmen of the State of North Carolina, and thus, by gaining their co-operation, they could induce the State authorities to take stringent action against the law-breakers. Unless this is done the sporting code will remain a dead letter as far as Currituck is concerned. The people shrug their shoulders when the subject is mentioned and say, "Those fancy Northern sportsmen don't want a North Carolinian to kill a North Carolina duck in North Carolina waters," and so on, and so on. Had I the arranging and the forming of a game protective association of the club men in Currituck, I would extend a pressing and standing invitation to every member of the Legislature and every officer of the State Government to make the club-houses their own, and the Governor and his staff should be kidnapped every winter, and be made to enjoy the gilt-edge sport of the " Yankee " clubs.

Seeing in a State paper that the Lighthouse Board intended to abandon the Pamlico (N. C.) Light-house, I applied to the Treasury Department to turn it over to me for a " shooting box." This was done, and I hope to have some good sporting in the future.

Southward the sportsmen must make their way, and find more inaccessible spots than Currituck to establish club-houses. This being the case, the topography and charts of the regions lying south of Currituck become interesting to the handlers of the gun. Four miles across the mainland is that grand sheet of water, the Albemarle Sound, some fifteen miles wide. Though this sound cannot compare with Currituck for the number and variety of its waterfowl in past years, at the present time it is filled with the birds that have been driven by night-shooting away from Currituck to find safer quarters there. Undoubtedly there will, in the next few years, be erected many club-houses in Albemarle Sound. Some twelve miles as the crow flies across the peninsula, another sheet of water is encountered. This is the Crotan Sound, apparently of about the area of Currituck. There is an abundance of waterfowl here, and but few, if any, clubhouses, which will, however, soon follow.

Ten miles southward, across a swampy, barren pine country, there appears the largest and grandest sound of all, the Pamlico. I have no data to furnish the exact size, but the steamer travels over 100 miles before it arrives at Pamlico Point

light, at the spot where the Pamlico River enters the Sound. Here is the home and haunt of the swan, and, as they have been but comparatively little hunted, they furnish fine sport to those who have their own yachts and plenty of time. There are no spots at Currituck that can afford more exciting sport or show a greater abundance of all kinds of waterfowl than Pamlico Point, Porpoise Point, about five miles distant, or Brant Island, some twelve miles away. The inaccessibility of the place prevents the shore pot-hunters from disturbing the game, and the "duck murderer," with his nightshooting, has not yet put in an appearance.

The water of Pamlico Sound is neutral to the taste ; sometimes fresh, again decidedly saline, but, for most of the time, it is simply brackish. This condition arises from the fact that the Neuse and Pamlico Rivers pour fresh waters into its area, while New Hatteras and Oregon inlets and Core Sound admit the salt waters of the ocean. This mixture of fresh, brackish and salt waters in a common receptacle naturally attracts every variety of waterfowl. The red-head and shuffler haunt the mingling of the fresh-water rivers with the Sound waters, while the black duck, mallard, and that king of aquatic birds, the gamest of all—the brant, stay in the vicinity of Oregon Inlet. In my opinion, within a few years Pamlico Sound is destined to be the greatest sporting-ground in the country, and the costly and expensive club-houses at Currituck will be discounted by the new ones at Pamlico Sound.

How long it will be before the breechloader in the hands of the natives and the swivel gun, killing in the night, will drive the wild fowl out of that extensive region is a question that none can answer. Many sportsmen who have been forced southward and still southward during the past years in quest of game hope that Pamlico Sound will furnish winter sport to last them at least the balance of their days.

31.
THE STORY
OF THE SHOTGUN
(1903)

THE STORY OF THE SHOTGUN

By W. B. ASHLEY

PHOTOGRAPHS BY T. C. TURNER

MAKERS of things have a universal tendency to immediately get out an improvement, thereby fostering a standing demand for something better than whatever is. The first gun-makers, instead of stopping with the original product of their brains and unskilled labor, instantly set about improving that long tube, thoughtfully fastened to a stick for convenience in handling, which fired its load of powder and stones by a torch. The clever idea of shaping the wooden handle of that artillery so as to fit the shoulder, meanwhile reducing the barrel from eight feet long by sixty pounds throughout to four feet by fifteen pounds, was succeeded by the first gun to employ the principle of priming, hammer and trigger; the last borrowed from the crossbow. The priming was in a flash-pan at the side of the barrel, the trigger was the other end of the hammer, and that was a holder for the slow-burning match or fuse which, on premeditated or accidental contact with the priming, effected what the modern firing-pin does.

Then came the wheel-lock, which, by its serrated edge, struck sparks from a corresponding piece of steel in the flash-pan, and was revolved when wound up by a key and released by a peg.

A happy substitute was soon found in the power of flint to get sparks from steel, and thus by one stroke the chance of misfire was greatly lessened and a better ignition secured. The flint was held in the head of the hammer and made to strike the spark as it descended into the flash-pan; the cost of the gun was cheapened and its use began to be general. Then guns were got up with a combination of flint and match-locks to insure certainty of fire, unless both missed.

Barrels were gradually lightened and lead shot was substituted for junk. The idea of preventing misfires continued popular and baffling. Guns were put together for a time with several chambers that revolved by hand power, carrying their flash-pans with them; they were not repeaters, but still they saved time. Repeaters were made by dividing the rear of the barrel into from three to eight compartments, separated by two leather wads, and each supplied with its own trigger, hammer and pan. The proud possessors of those guns could surely have no cause to envy the owners of four-barreled affairs that were operated in the same way, nor to covet the strange arm coming into notice as a breech-loader, in which the charge was placed in the rigid butt of the breech when the double barrels were moved either vertically to the left or brought down at a clear right angle.

And so, step by step, and now and then a stumble, the shotgun advanced toward its end of being as nearly automatic as possible, convenient to handle, easily loaded and quickly fired. The simple change from a wooden to an iron ramrod hastened matters, and then came the percussion cap, and presently the cartridge carrying its own priming.

It is a remarkable coincidence that the catalogue of gun essentials was completed and machinery to take the place of hand labor in their manufacture was devised about the same time; and in the development of the shotgun there is no more interesting stage than this: as, in fact, present-day improvements are mostly such as are made possible by the more accurate and uniform working of machinery and add little, if any, to the working principles

stock and forearm, which reach the factory from the sawmill, cut in the bare outline of the part to be made. The wood is chiefly of American growth, black walnut predominating, and the best grades go naturally to the gun factories. It is seasoned sometimes for three years. The first lathe it reaches, which cleverly compels the cutting tool to follow any sort of irregular pattern by means of a revolving model that automatically guides it, completely shapes the gunstock as you see it. After that, other lathes attend to the digging out of the bed for the lock-plate, inserting the proper holes and notches and slits for magazine, mountings, lock and butt-plate. The smoothing down of the roughened surface and subsequent polishing and varnishing are all machine done, but the checking is dexterously filed out line by line by young

Brazing. " The ribs are brazed to the pair."

of the gun. Even the hammerless was attempted in the far past, as was also a magazine in the stock.

Once the wide-eyed boy could stand unmoved by band or baseball, watching the skilled craftsman turn out a gun-barrel just a little better than his last, and finally cutting in his initials and the date. To-day that boy had needs have a hundred eyes on independent muscles to watch the making of a gun.

You begin with the wooden sections, the

women. Guns made by hand were often most elaborately carved and engraved, elegantly mounted, and in exterior adornment made works of art, things of great beauty and value; to-day the cost and time are put into the interior, and the question of decoration is left largely to individual selection. In another and quieter room you will see a workman bending over a barrel vised in the engraving block, deftly cutting out by the pattern before him some design that will match what he has

Bluing the Barrels.

already engraved upon the receiver and action lever and the wooden parts. But very few guns in proportion to the output go through those trained fingers.

It is enticingly claimed for some guns that the sportsman needs only a screwdriver with which to take the arm apart for cleaning and repairs. This speaks well for simplicity. It has taken upwards of twelve hundred operations to make an entire gun of about ninety-five parts, of which most are contained in the receiver. To make these parts, special machines, or, more accurately, in many cases special tools to fit machines, have been devised by each factory. The steel comes in from the foundry, like the wood from the mill, roughly shaped to its purpose. The forges grab these pieces when at a white heat, pound them into submission and better shape

Matching and Pairing the Barrels.

for the work ahead, and pass them along to the machine room. You are immediately deafened by the sound of chewing and grinding and the breaking of steel bones, and presently the myriads of small pieces of steel are spit out of these mighty jaws with nothing left to them but what is needed for their use in the gun. It may be the butt plate or the receiver shell or a tiny sear; whatever it is, it is complete. These machines are many and varied, and are in charge of men who become expert in their particular lines; and, when the milling and edging, the boring and threading, the grooving and the polishing have each had its turn at those pieces of metal, they go by tray and boxful to the assembly room.

It was not idle italicizing to advise sportsmen using "care to replace parts to the same place from which they came and in their original positions." Experienced men are paid good salaries to do that original placing in the first assembly room. Inside that dug-out piece of steel called the receiver must be stowed upwards of ninety pieces, according to the gun, all interacting upon each other, aiding, restraining, supplementing. Here two springs acting in perfect harmony must set in motion bolts and slides and pivoted bars that effectually lock the gun at full and half cock, and, at the fall of the hammers, instantly permit its opening for reloading by hand or lever.

"The engraver deftly cuts out the pattern on the barrels."

And then here is a button which disengages all this at will of the operator. In the repeaters must be placed the frictionless, effortless carriers of the cartridges, so adjusted that they work in unison with the nimble extractor and ejector of the used shell, and place the new load in position, all in response to the same pressure that cocks and locks the hammers until the carriers have done their work. Locking a gun is like locking anything else—it secures the contents against intrusion from without and prevents their egress by the wrong way. In the double-barreled must be placed a scientifically cut bolt that with nineteen assistants locks the gun tight, or at the proper pressure permits the barrels to swing down on their equally scientifically constructed pivot until caught just at the right place by the stops, and then bolts and tumblers and hooks and pins are all set in motion by perhaps one pressure on an outside lever, and perform their duties noiselessly in an instant of time, even recording on the upper face of the tang that all is "safe."

In addition to the expedition gained in completing guns, we owe to machinery the invaluable ability to replace any one of these parts as readily as we would buy another shoe-string, and it can be inserted more easily.

Many shotgun barrels are bored through the solid rods that are received by the factory somewhat over the right length and diameter; bored by powerful machines that carry their keen tools through the thirty to forty odd inches of steel as one might an auger through a two-inch plank; bored, perhaps, by what is called a chucking machine, driving from four to six cutters through in succession to obtain the proper caliber, with a final bore for absolute trueness, that stops about three inches from the muzzle, when a special tool shaves the remainder so as to diminish the size of the bore at the muzzle by about 33-1000ths of an inch, and that is called the choke. These are the barrels that have no fancy figure on their surfaces nor in the catalogues; and, if your barrels are beautifully marked with a curling, interlacing tracery, they were made by a very different process, and those delicate lines are the evidence of foreign manufacture and the acme of metalworking for lightness

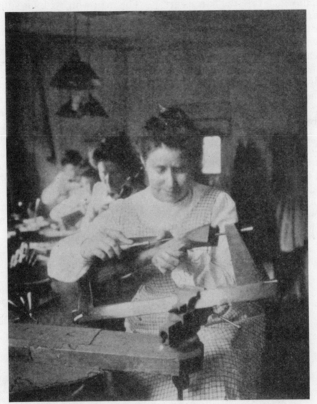

"The checking of the stocks is filed out by young women."

and strength, and not the chemical action of some mysterious acid upon ordinary gun steel, as many suppose.

Narrow sheets of iron and steel piled in alternate layers are welded into a solid bar which is drawn down into rods about a quarter of an inch square. These rods are twisted, rope-like, sixteen to twenty turns to every inch of length, laid together in sets of threes, with the twists in opposite directions, again squared, and then welded

into ribbons of widths from one half inch up. The ribbons are coiled about a mandrel of the required diameter and welded into a seamless tube. The entire process, particularly at this stage, requires great skill, for the correct contour of the barrel, as well as the evenness of the figure, depends upon the hammering. It is by the different alternations of iron and steel in the piling and the subsequent twisting that the different figures in the barrels are produced, the white marks of which are the iron, the dark, steel.

The boring machines get in their fine work on these barrels just the same as in the common kind, and all barrels go into the hands of the straighteners. This is a good old pastime still much in vogue with gunmakers, and one cannot but wonder at the opportunities it affords for keeping a job whether or not there is anything to do. Hanging between the workman and the light is a piece of ground glass with a small bar or rod vertically across its center. The straightener man rests the muzzle end of the barrel on an upright and focuses on the bar. Instantly, at least so he says, he can detect the slightest variation from perfectly straight reflected lines on the polished interior. He quickly lowers the barrel to an anvil and strikes it a quick blow with a hammer at just the spot where the alleged variation was. Thus perhaps once, perhaps several times, and the barrel is straight. It is then put in charge of a lathe that rough-turns the outside to the required diameter, two tools cutting away considerable material. There is no trusting these lathes to handle the barrel on the square, however, so again the man with the perfectly straight face does the hammer act, and the lathe is given another round, using four tools this time; and then the hammer and anvil again, and then a single turning of the lathe to finish the exterior, after which the straightener once more. This is his last chance at the barrel unless the gun has two, in which case the barrels are now paired and finally straightened. The pairing offers no difficulties, excepting in the figured metal, when only the matching of a team can be compared to it for skill and patience required; the scientific adjustment of the two barrels to each other is done after the final straightening.

Now are brazed on the lugs or metal pieces that take notching and drilling and grooving so as to work into the firing mechanism and receive the grip of the forearm; and then, in the double-barreled, the under and top ribs are brazed to the pair, which must be set together with great nicety and strength.

After the polishing, done with shaped emery wheel and hand tool called striker, a many-toothed metal affair, the barrels are treated to a homœopathic dose of preventive against rust, which means they are purposely rusted by a very simple process which you *think* you fully understand. This browning and bluing of the barrels requires from four to six baths in a preparation of acids, with intermediate rubbings down; a hot-room drying, and final oiling afterward; and this is what brings out the figure in all its delicate coloring and gives the plain barrel elegance of color and finish.

The man who, with his sufficient equipment of a screw-driver has confidingly taken apart his gun, reassembles it in a somewhat different manner from what now characterizes that work in the factory where the gun gets together quickly and surely, and then goes to the testing room to be shot off from three to fifteen times for accuracy of aim and perfection of manipulation, the barrel having been tested alone for strength by an excessive charge earlier in its career. It is an old story with the factory expert, who merely signs the tag that accompanies each gun, telling who did what, and when.

There is the secret of the modern gun; it is made without a hitch and to work that way.

Where the Finished Barrels are Kept Ready for Assembling.

32.
WILD DUCKS
AND TAME DECOYS
(1896)

WILD DUCKS AND TAME DECOYS

BY HAMBLEN SEARS.

PRACTICALLY speaking, Henry Eldridge was a genius; and if his lines had been cast in smoother places he might, and no doubt would, have astounded humanity by his inexhaustible resources. As it was, Henry, nominally a builder of carriages, also built himself houses in which, one after another, he lived; and many a time have I seen him pause in the midst of his work—he paused often—to take a huge and ancient bull-fiddle from its corner, and for half an hour play some absurd jig upon its decrepit strings. At certain periods in the prosecution of his decayed wheelwright trade, his fiddling, and his house-building, he would descend into the cellar of one of the houses, carefully open a locked cupboard, and pour out half a tumbler of the most magnificent home-made elderberry wine that ever touched the lips of wheelwrights or of fiddlers. This he would look at long and fondly. Then filling the rest of the tumbler with Jamaica rum, he would drink it off at a gulp, and snatch a short twenty minutes from his many occupations to sit upon a barrel head and gaze with unswerving thoughtfulness upon the cheeses and rafters of the roof.

This, however, was not by any means the limit of Henry's versatility. It had no limit. His genius suited itself to the season. On the appearance of the first black duck sailing over the dunes of Cape Cod, Henry would calmly and seriously close the door of his wheelwright shop, tenderly lay away the bull-fiddle, and leave the last unfinished house to stand or fall as it should decide. The time had come for other things; and taking one more sip of the wine of his heart, he would call to him his thirty tame ducks, put them in their movable crib, and urging his worn-out, moth-eaten steed, make all haste to reach Cliff Pond and his shooting-box. Once there with the ducks flying, he would remain till late winter, making uncertain descents upon his home and family for food, but always returning as soon as possible to the "pawnd."

It did not trouble Henry, if it ever occurred to him, that Cape Cod, and especially Brewster, had been shot out years ago; that ten to fifteen brace of duck was an enormous day's work. He did not shoot to kill; he had the truest sporting spirit, the spirit that enjoyed tricking the game; and he was as satisfied with one duck well shot as with a hundred merely slaughtered. What did cause him to pour forth the vials of his wrath, however—bitter vials they were, too, accompanied by a most extraordinary variety of language—was to find that he had harbored in his bosom, that is to say, in his shooting-stand, a tenderfoot, a man who did not know enough to refrain from sneezing when ducks were in the pond, or who insisted on slapping his freezing ears at the moment an enormous gander was walking deliberately over the waves into gunshot. Then neither ducks nor geese, neither courtesy nor the tender senses of those present, were considered by Henry. Everything was forgotten in the immediate necessity he felt for stating in his high nasal tones the views he entertained as to the propriety of such persons being in warmer places than Cliff Pond, or even the earth upon which that pond rested.

It was not a surprise to me, therefore, to receive an epistle from Henry one cold January day, to the effect that if I would leave New York at once and make all haste to Brewster, I would find "that the" —and at this point in the letter there appeared a peculiar drawing resembling a number of jack-stones arranged in the form of an irregular "v"—"were flying." Knowing Henry's humorous vein, I surmised that this must be his method of referring to geese, and forthwith I departed.

It was a cold, bleak night when the laboring train, tired with its many stops and starts, pulled up at the Brewster station. Darkness had come on, and as the lights of the cars disappeared to the eastward and the gloom settled down over the little

lonesome station, the wind whistled and moaned through the telegraph wires, and I could see nothing but the bleak, uneventful landscape of stunted firs and stone walls melting off into the darkness. It might have been a hundred miles to the nearest human being, except for one light down the rutted road, the particular house which Henry, his wife, and seven children happened at that moment to be occupying. There was nothing for it but to trudge through the sleet and melted snow, with my two guns in one hand and a big grip in the other.

I found on arriving at the house that, as is their wont in this heart of Puritanism, events and circumstances had conducted themselves in their own original fashion. It appeared that the geese had suddenly departed, but that in their place had come red-heads and mallards and black ducks; and thus I began a fortnight of duck-shooting over Henry's tame decoys.

II.

Many a sportsman of the better sort continues to condemn the practice of shooting game over tame decoys. It would be useless to deny his argument. Frankly speaking, the only sportsmanlike conduct in hunting shore birds, as in hunting other game, is to crawl up on them by sheer sporting skill, and kill them in their own country, so to speak, with every chance on their side. Shooting over wooden decoys, however, has come to be acknowledged as allowable to sportsmen. The wooden 'coys are set out on a point; the flying birds see them, swing above them for a first look, and are shot with one barrel as they light, with the other just as they start to fly away. Shooting over tame ducks is simply a much more exciting, vastly more skilful piece of work of the same kind. For a spot where ducks fly constantly these tame birds are not necessary, but on such shot-out ground as Cape Cod they add greatly to the science of the sport.

Henry had a carefully regu-

RECREATION.

EDUCATIONAL FLIGHTS.

lated plan for training his decoys, and it was a constant source of surprise and interest to me to watch the workings of this peculiar system. When carefully nurtured, the intelligence of such a stupid bird as a barn-yard duck is something extraordinary. But the training must be constant and daily, and before a bird is fit for decoy-work practically two seasons have been consumed. The lessons begin and turn on the question of food. Henry made it his first study to compel his friends to trust him so thoroughly that he could pick them up and put them in his pocket head downward at any time, with the certainty that on being returned to the ground they would simply rustle their feathers and shrewdly cock one eye up at him to await the never-failing handful of corn. It has always been a question with me whether he himself had not more of the duck in him than the human being, for he could imitate duck calls of all kinds in a manner that would not only attract wild game, but would bring the gun to your shoulder as you walked along the shore in his vicinity. One good sportsman, who used to call himself my friend, not only shot (and afterwards paid for) one of Henry's decoys as she stood tied to a rock, but actually lay among the stones of the beach half an hour one early morning under the impression that Henry's constant calls came from a flock of birds just behind the stand.

After bringing these strange waddling pets of his to a maudlin state of tameness, he never failed to set up a most complicated and continuous series of duck quacks and calls whenever he threw out their food. It was not long, therefore. before the birds associated corn with Henry's extraordinary imitations of duck Bedlam, and as any self-respecting bird is bound to quack vociferously immediately upon seeing food, it became a consequence quite within the compass of the duck mind to infer that whenever Henry quacked, corn was near at hand and shortly to be forth-coming. The result was an instantane-ous symphony. Consequently by the end of the summer a duck of reasonably high birth was sure to set up a hyster-ical song the moment he or she caught the sounds of Henry's voice. Whether Henry actually understood duck language and discussed points of interest with the birds I do not know. At all events, he understood a system which brought forth calls and shrieks from every one of his thirty pets whenever he saw fit to put it in operation.

Having proceeded thus far, it became his next duty to teach the birds to fly—a sufficiently original occupation to illus-trate the extensive scope, the many-sided character of Henry's genius. This he practised gradually with each bird in his barn-yard, always appealing to the duck's appetite. He would grasp one of them around the body with both hands, her head meantime pointing outward. Then bend-ing his knees and lowering the neophyte close to the ground, he would rise steadily but swiftly and hurl the bird into the air. Instinctively she put out her wings and circled around the barn-yard, descending gradually, and at the same time setting up a most hopeless racket, naturally start-ing the other twenty-nine, who fancied this was Henry calling them to dinner.

As the duck's wings were clipped, she naturally could not fly away; hence she soon alighted near by, and waddled com-fortably back into the yard to secure the handful of corn. Here was another long and weary stage of training, during which Henry's remarkable persistency and en-ergy, his "infinite capacity for taking pains," were constantly to be noted. The decayed wheelwright trade and the strug-gle with the half-completed houses were not, in Henry's opinion, sufficiently enno-bling occupations to demand an exhibi-tion of this capacity which lay within him. It required something extraordi-nary, something like teaching birds to fly.

After months of trial and tribulation, with sometimes a broken back and a con-sequent duck funeral, the birds grasped the meaning of this peculiar flight; and Henry could then stand behind his barn-yard fence and, by throwing up one bird after another, give you and any stray wild ducks flying past the impression that there was a duck Valhalla in the vicinity.

At the time of my arrival all this had been finished. Henry was shooting day after day at the old stand, which he maintained physically while several of us maintained it financially. The birds themselves were by this time just as much at home going through their duties at the pond as they had ever been in the farm-yard. Henry regretted, he said, that the geese were elsewhere collecting some oth-er sportsman's shot in their feathers; but ducks were filling the pond every morn-ing, and they might serve my purpose. This was what I heard after Mrs. Eldridge had kindly taken off my coat and the elder daughter had put my grip in the one unused, and therefore abnormally cold, room in the house. Henry's son re-lieved me of both the guns, promptly took them out of their cases, and, putting them together, sat in a corner fondling and ad-miring them until after twelve that night. Meanwhile Henry and I sat with our feet on the stove, while the children brought me all their choice possessions out of the one room which five shared jointly. And all this while the New England north-east wind whistled along over the sand hills outside.

In an indefinable way there were com-fort and hospitality about the whole place, something that made you feel thankful you were born a New-Englander, and that New England Yankeeism was still running along better than a good third in the race. Henry had perhaps as little *politesse* as any human being could have, and yet his very lack of it, his gruff fa-miliar manner, his offer of his worst— that is to say, his best—black stub of a clay pipe, was distinctly hospitable. Here were his seven children and wife within one room talking to me on all sides. Yet none was sent away. There was nothing to be ashamed of in them. They were all his. The dirt upon their faces was his. He had with his own hands put every board in its proper place on the walls and roof that sheltered us. To-morrow we would drive to the pond in a carriage made by himself, and though he had not built the horse, he had at least paid for it. Henry had little or no money, but he owed not a cent; and he could look any man, whether from New England or old England, or from the South or West, in the eye, telling him he was as good as he, and no mistake. Even Henry's stories were his own. They had a picturesque, original charm that is indescribable. They were of ducks and guns and sometimes of men. They included good shots and bad misses, and a shrewd word or two on your dealings with men, and your safest plan of being honest with a fellow as the best way of making him honest with you.

As time wore on and the stories grew to that delicious type wherein the "pawnd"—which is two miles long—"were covered s' thick with ducks th't yer couldn't see the water, 'nd I wuz just on th' point uv pulling both barrels, when"—as this time of the evening approached, Henry, with his serious air and silent tread, disappeared down the perpendicular stairway into his cellar, to return ten minutes later with some of that homemade elderberry that would have made the eyes of the hot stove water if it had had any. And as I sipped my portion and Henry gulped his down, it dawned upon me that it was eleven o'clock, and that at two in the morning I was to be bundled out of bed to begin the six-mile drive to Cliff Pond.

III.

There is nothing that could be more disagreeable than to be waked at 1.30 in the morning of a January day, or rather night, with but three short hours of sleep to your credit; and yet after a hopeless regret that I had undertaken the journey at all, and a bitter yearning for New York city and five hours more of repose, I managed to get out of bed, wash and dress by candle-light, and drink a cup of coffee before two. Then the day began. We proceeded to the barn-yard, and while I harnessed the horse by candle-light, Henry caught the ducks and put them into their box, which was thereupon loaded upon the wagon. By twenty minutes after two we were under way for Cliff Pond, and then any yearning for home that in a weak moment the flesh might have felt was changed to congratulations by the cold night breeze. For the drive through the silent firs and pines six miles up into the Cape set the blood tingling in my body. Henry smoked and said nothing. He was already beginning to feel the excitement of the sport, and the presence of the softly squeaking ducks, the guns, the uncertainty of what might be already resting upon the pond, were quite sufficient to make me excited too.

It was after three when we came with-

THE BLIND—SCALING DUCKS.

in a quarter of a mile of the pond. Then every sound ceased about our caravan, except the soft conversations and occasional arguments of the uncomfortably crowded birds. Henry indicated, partly by whispers and partly by motions and pushes, that I was to descend. The horse was silently secured to a tree in a sheltered ravine. Henry took the ducks on his shoulders, and I carried the four guns and the cartridges as we silently stumbled up over a rising ground through the snow.

The journey through the trees continued for five minutes without other noise than the softly whistling wind and the movements of the ducks, who had been considerably upset during their transfer from the wagon to Henry's shoulders. It was so dark in the woods that at times I failed to distinguish Henry's form from the surrounding trees, and it was with some surprise, therefore, that I suddenly bumped against him. He had stopped before the door of what seemed to be a one-room shanty, and was in the act of unfastening the padlock. As we stood there I heard a peculiar lapping noise, which resolved itself a moment later into the sound of small waves on a gravel beach. But nothing of water nor of beach was to be seen.

Henry now had the door open, and we entered—ducks, guns, and all. He then conveyed to me in whispers the information that we must station the ducks at once, as day would break in about half an hour, and naturally everything must be done before then. Whereupon he opened a door at the opposite end of the hut and let the ducks out of their cramped position. Following them through the door, I found, principally by the sense of touch, that we were in a species of chicken or duck yard, some ten feet wide and twenty-five feet long, running down into what soon turned out to be the waters of the pond.

This stand was of the usual pond or lake type. The hut had been set back among the pines and cedars, and as they had no leaves to shed in winter, they completely covered the little house from top to bottom. The yard, or stand proper, was surrounded by a five-foot board fence, banked up outside with small firs and pines to imitate an enormous pile of brush. And Henry had brought his architectural gray matter into requisition

to construct gates leading out to the beach at either side, with small openings in them through which the ducks could enter or leave the stand. At the end of the yard which abutted on the water's edge he had drawn on the military portion of his inexhaustible store of knowledge and constructed two bastionlike wings, one of which permitted the gunners to fire eastward, and the other westward, while the stand itself faced to the north. By running a low bench along this lower end he had made it possible for those inside to kneel and fire one barrel through the loop-holes, and then jump up and take the second barrel on the wing over the top of the stand.

All this was observed largely without the use of eyes while Henry was opening the gates and taking some of the ducks outside. And in this bitterly cold water, which froze on the ducks' feathers as soon as it touched them, we tied those unoffending creatures by the leg to a cord which ran out on the water and disappeared in the darkness. It appeared that this glacial cord was a "runner," and that it extended out into the pond four hundred feet to a pulley in the end of a long pole, which was anchored in such a manner as to be held just under the surface. The line running through this returned to the stand, passed through a small hole to the inside, and out again through another, until, at the end of its eight-hundred-foot journey, it joined itself and formed a circuit.

To this the ducks were tied one by one with a leather noose. As one bird was fastened and dropped into the icy water I pulled in on the other part of the rope, and gently forced Mistress Duck three or four feet out on the black water. Thus in a few moments we had what to any wild duck, to say nothing of any tame man, would appear to be a flock of birds swimming about at random and raising a horrible racket in all this silence of the night. The thing was repeated with more ducks, on another and similar endless runner, which ran to another spot on the pond.

This done, Henry directed me to pull first one and then the other flock out to the pulleys, while he moved up and down the beach and stationed eight or ten solitary ducks at intervals, after the manner in which any other mortal would have tied dogs or anchored boats. Each of these had a yard or more of rope, and each could paddle in the water or climb up the beach, squawking all the time to her heart's content.

The exterior preparations having been completed, we returned to the stand and thrust the rest of the educated thirty into boxes. Everything was now ready, then everything about the place seemed to have a lifting motion. Trees began to stand up; the water rose as the horizon widened. The light to the eastward changed from gray to white, and I could make out the opposite shore, a long black line. Finally the white changed to red,

WAITING FOR THE WORD.

and still the night was as dark as ever. Henry betook himself to the shanty to lie down, but I could not leave the night. There was nothing to do but wonder what manner of bird, and how many, might be still further out in the pond, and to listen to the sound of the little waves singing to an accompaniment of the soft night breeze in the firs and the startling quack of those frozen ducks out on the water.

At last it came almost suddenly, a great streak to the eastward; then a little more; deeper and deeper, and rising ever higher. All sorts of noises seemed to wake, and everything, even the sky, went on rising slowly and gracefully.

Suddenly I felt a keen vise grasping my arm just above the elbow, and turned to see Henry's sharp face looking out into the middle of the pond, with one of his long fingers pointing through the branches at something which in time resolved itself into a black line on the water.

Ducks, surely ducks, and seven—eight

—nine—ten of them, too! Neither of us breathed more than was necessary for a moment. Then Henry became a duck—that is to say, he emitted quacks by the dozen—and the birds on the runners, those anchored along the shore, and those in the boxes at our feet set up an answering note that must have told wonders to their wild cousins out in the pond. The work was fairly begun now, and it lasted two long hours. Each of us took up a duck and scaled her, waiting after each "cast" to watch her circle around the stand until she flew shrieking out on the water. Another and another followed until they were all gone. Then, as the corn Henry threw out attracted their attention, they trotted back through the holes in the fence and came forward to be scaled again and again. One bad scholar grew obstreperous, and evidently decided on going over to the enemy. But Henry took Aunty in his arms—Aunty, it should be understood, was his duck of ducks—and after conversing with her for a moment, hurled her into the air. She circled and screamed and settled on the water as the others had before her, but she had no sooner touched the surface of the pond than she swam straight out after the deserter, passed him, headed him off, and pecked at him until he gave up the spree and returned homeward in disgrace.

Meantime we kept a glass on the mystic ten, and gradually became more and more certain that they were moving over to see what extraordinary feeding-grounds their cousins must have found.

Five hundred yards, by the mark! Three hundred and nearer!

Henry paused and loaded the four double-barrel guns without making a sound, jerked the runners to start the two flocks singing again, and then returned to the charge. Still they came on, until they were within fifty yards of our birds on the runners. Then something happened. Possibly we struck the barrel of a gun against the side of a loop-hole. Perhaps the click of a cocking hammer reached them. At any rate, the mystic ten turned and swam away. Tears came into my eyes so that I could not see, and I heard Henry muttering to the bushes words and phrases and things one would rather have left unsaid. But the ten waggled their tails in our faces as they continued to move off.

A punch from Henry and a jab he made

at a duck caused me to grasp another, and the business of hurling these unoffending creatures into the air was resumed.

The wild ones turned again and started back. The distance lessened moment by moment, and at last we had them in the very midst of the decoys on the east runner. A method of procedure arranged between us beforehand was now put into effect. Henry took the left side of the stand, and slowly and cautiously pulled in on the runner. The decoys, whether they would or no, were forced to move in also, and with them came the wild birds, as if fascinated. In an instant they were a little less than fifty yards away, and with the most feverish care each man took his gun by the butt as it lay ready in position pointed through the loop-hole. Each covered his side of the flock and waited.

Henry directed the charge, and I was to delay till I heard him count "one"—"two"—firing at the time when he should say "three." It seemed a very long wait. First he was forced to delay till the wild birds separated themselves completely from the tame; and even then he waited until the former had grouped themselves into comprehensive range. That delay was a strain on one's nerves, and it was almost in a dream that I heard his husky, whispered count begin. I pulled mechanically, and in the smoke jumped upon the bench. Catching a glimpse of a black object rising off to the right, I fired a snapshot. But he came down like a plummet, and as the smoke of the second charge cleared away eight birds lay dead on the water, one was swimming directly away, and the tenth was trying to fly. The second guns came into play, and two reports settled the ninth and tenth birds; and Henry's little water-spaniel had a deal of swimming to bring them all in.

If you are a sportsman, you are saying at this moment, "That is no sport; it is slaughter." In a measure, judged by the highest standards, that is true; but you deceived the duck when you crawled up on him, and I deceived him when I made him crawl up on me. It is not in the strictest sense the ideal of sport; but, on the other hand, it is neither mean nor unworthy of a good sportsman. And the study, preparation, time, money, and excitement of it all are not to be compared with the practice of crawling up on the bird or of shooting over wooden 'coys.

Twelve o'clock found us again at Hen-

POTATIONS.

ry's home, in the midst of Henry's family, and before Mrs. Eldridge's boiled turnips, boiled potatoes, boiled beef, and boiled coffee. We had scarcely finished when Henry beckoned me to follow, and with the entire family looking the other way, we descended those sacred cellar stairs. There was the cupboard, there was the row of small demijohns within, and as this was a special occasion, I sipped my portion while sitting on a soap-box, and watched Henry indulge in an extra bumper. And then suddenly I was gone to make up for lost time and to sleep for hours, while Henry went out and unlocked his shop door to see if any of the wheels had gone round during his absence.

IV.

At six we were all at supper, even to the baby, who insisted on preferring my food to hers. One of the mystic ten graced the table, but he did not taste as

that boiled beef and boiled coffee had at noon. Henry considered the whole history a famous one, and before he had finished telling it the fifth time, it was quite evident that a week hence the story would take its place among those which began with the usual statement that the water in the pond was invisible, owing to the number of ducks on its surface. Mrs. Eldridge seemed to appreciate this fact, for she frequently suggested to Henry that it would be wiser for him to eat more and brag less, and requested me to refrain from crediting all his "fearful lies."

It was a good supper, however, and as Henry and I resolved ourselves into two spokes of a wheel, with the stove for the hub, the seven children again proceeded to produce their possessions and hold them up for my admiration, laboring under the impression that I had failed to notice them the night before. Henry talked on again in his keen, half-generous way of ducks and guns and men, and told new stories of all, and made new and equally original criticisms on the last of these three intimates of his. When I attacked his live-decoy shooting from the sportsman's point of view, he had enough of the true sport in him to agree that it was, or at least had been, frowned upon deservedly. But, as he said, " It's killin' of 'em by deceivin' 'em, and that's what th'other, the wooden kyind, is too, some-'at." As we sat there he advanced his idea of sport and of slaughter, and then we drifted off, as anybody will under such circumstances, into discussions on religion, business, and politics. Through it all ran that same Yankee, practical view which seems to go so well with a sharp nose and big kindly eyes, which is satire in its best sense rather than sarcasm, which seems to grasp the pith of a matter, and to have a rugged integrity that demands for itself considerate and honest attention, whether the question be of politics or religion or ducks.

So the tenth and twelfth pipes were smoked out, and the lamps began to splutter, when I told Henry that I must have a full three-hours' sleep that night, or he might not be able to get me up at two in the morning a second time. But as I stood up to take a candle from the mantel, he quietly forced me back into my seat, deliberately replaced my feet on the rim of the stove, and with his serious mien descended his ladderlike cellar stairway, reappearing again with two tumblers of that same elderberry.

One lamp went completely out, as if disgusted; but we stood by the stove in the light of the other, and I sipped and he gulped again. Then both of us sat down, and gazed at the rafters and the cobwebs of the roof for full twenty minutes, and I felt that such a day was one that gave a suggestion of the value of living; and that, after all, it is a good thing to be out in the woods of New England shooting ducks, drinking home-made elderberry wine, and having the infinite satisfaction of being a New-Englander yourself.

THE SHOT.

33.
THE STORY OF A NORTH CAROLINA TURKEY HUNT (1907)

Painting by Lynn Bogue Hunt.

"Revealed himself in his majesty .... a princely egoist
swollen in his self-admiration."

IN QUIET COVERS

THE STORY OF A NORTH CAROLINA TURKEY HUNT

BY MAXIMILIAN FOSTER

WITH A DRAWING IN COLOR BY LYNN BOGUE HUNT

ANUARY'S sun came riding over the edge of the distant hills, filling all this Carolina land with its bland and glowing radiance of cloudless dawn. Frost had fallen in the still, clear night; the fields gleamed with it, and in that quick air of early morning one looked far and near, every detail of the rolling landscape minutely shown — the acres of flowing broom, golden yellow; the browned, rusty scars of harvested cotton patches; the hollows chapped with the gullies of red, raw earth, and against this sweep of open country, a flank of the Hebron woods rising like a shore of cliffs —woods where the wild turkey ranged. An abandoned cornfield stood beside the woodland's edge, a piece of tilled ground now overgrown with ragweed and a few lean stalks springing from last year's crop; and toward this corner, in the growing light, Buell and I ranged our way, the far-famed 'Bijah padding onward in the lead.

"You'll excuse me, suh," said Buell, with a quick glance at the sky, "you sut-tenly will, suh, if I ask you to hurry. Suntime 'pears to be a little early this morning, and if you'll jest nudge up that jinny mule, suh, I'll be obliged to yuh."

I nudged, as requested, and clapping heels to his own mule, Buell forged ahead at a hand gallop. Behind us lay the last of habitations—a squalid negro cabin of logs, mud-chinked, a drove of lean, flea-ridden razorbacks rooting around the dooryard on terms of intimacy with its flock of pickaninnies, and tied to the fence, a mangy rabbit hound that yowled at Bije dismally. Buell, with his old-fashioned muzzle-loader slatting to and fro on the pommel, urged on down the slope, his clumsy mount brushing a way through the frost-glistening sweep of broom-straw; and I followed. For time and tide and turkey wait for no man; if we hoped to find our birds in the open we must hasten before the growing sunlight drove them deep into the almost impenetrable tangle of cane-brakes reaching along the river's oozy curves—blind covers chosen shrewdly by the all-wise turkey gangs.

We came to a tumble-down snake fence, and Buell drew rein. "If you'll alight, suh," said he, getting down, "we'll turn these yeah mules into the field, and let them shift. Yondah's where I saw the gang, there by that peaked 'simmon tree. Bije—hey, you—*Bije!*"

Bije, discouraged in his chase of an alert Molly Cottontail, came to heel, and with a lolling tongue, and sad, innocent eyes watched on his haunches while we unsaddled and turned out the mules. Then Buell, shouldering his piece and calling to the dog, struck down along the fence toward the ragged corner of tilled ground lying under the shadow of the trees.

"Yes, suh," he said, pointing forward, "there was seven in the party—one as large a gobbler as it has been my fortune to see. I failed to get him, however. Bije, you, *suh!*"

Bije, at command, ranged on ahead, and Buell, after another sharp scrutiny of the field before us, stalked on after him. "Yes, suh, a turkey cock with a baird as long as a yellow gal's pigtail. I assure you, suh."

But how and why Buell, a noted hand among the turkeys, failed to get his amazing fowl, I was not to learn. "I and Bije, suh, scattered the flock mighty nice, and at the first yearp from the blind, I heard and then saw him. Bimeby, I took aim, suh—careful aim, I declare, my fowling piece leveled right on—— Hey—sshsh! *You—Bije!*"

The dog, plowing along the slope before us, evinced sudden signs of excitement. His tail, sprung high in the air, lurched back and forth above the tips of the ragweed, and circling broadly, he struck up for the edge of the woods. Game had been there; one glance at Bije told the story.

Buell, too, showed an answering alertness. "If I am not mistaken, the birds have been here, suh."

"*Oip!*" babbled Bije, suddenly giving tongue.

A hand gripped me by the wrist. "Down, suh—on the ground. Don't move!"

Buell, already had sunk to the ground, and with the grip of his hand on my arm, there was nothing but to plump down beside him. Turkey shooting I'd seen before, but Buell's method was peculiar to this section of the south. Bije, it appeared, was to have full swing for a while, to yoip and babble as he liked.

"Yi—oi—oi!" yelped Bije again.

A lone scrub oak was our cover. Buell pushed aside the stiff, prickly foliage and peered. "There they go!" he whispered suddenly, his grasp tightening excitedly on my arm, "three hens—there's another. See! See—there's the big gobbler—two more over there. See them run!"

I looked, and saw nothing at all.

"Look—over there, suh—by the peaked 'simmon."

I peered again. A sudden movement, a quick view of dark shapes sliding through the ragweed toward the woods.

"Oip—yi-hi-hi!" yelled Bije, and burst into full tongue.

A roar of wings answered. I saw a heavy shape of black lurch into the air; another followed, and with flapping wings lumbered toward the wood. Then all up and down the front of the wood, the air seemed filled with these flapping, clumsy shapes, a fresh clatter of song bursting from Bije as he viewed the cherished game.

"Four—six—seven!" counted Buell under his breath, "there's another on the ground—see it run!"

Then the last bird, running like a shadow, gained its speed, and with another roaring flutter of wings sprang into the air, pumped across the interval, and clattering among the twigs and foliage was gone into the thickness of the woods.

Buell arose with twinkling eyes. "Indeed, suh, you are fortunate. If I am not mistaken, we shall have tukkey inside the hour. Is your piece loaded, suh?"

Yes, my piece was loaded. I assured him so, and Buell, arising leisurely, surveyed the front of the wood with a critical eye to pick and choose its likeliest point of attack. Far in its depths, Bije yapped finally; then silence fell, and shouldering the muzzle-loader, Buell moved slowly toward the trees.

For this was his method—fair or otherwise, I would not say. The willing Bije, turned loose upon the range, had routed up the game; the gang was scattered broadly, and now, in due time, we were to lurk behind the cover of a blind and yelp up, the timid yet—sometimes—credulous birds. Poor sport, you'd say—yes!—but if properly undertaken, the one legitimate way. You cannot stalk them openly—or may not, since the law discourages tracking on the snow as a means too brutally successful.

Then, again, it snows infrequently in this Carolina country, and on the bare, open ground there is a wide difference between a turkey track and the slot of heavy game—a white-tail, or a thousand-pound moose, perhaps. Nor is there much sport in marching through a turkey range, seeking to kick up some unwary bird at random. If you see him first, the chances make for a slaughter, but usually it is the other way—the turkey sees you and you do not see it at all; and, as in moose-calling, yearping has its merits, its forgiving refinements—a fair excuse if you match wit against wit—and I mean by that, if you do the calling yourself. So I was to call—to *yearp* them up, as Buell expressed it, and I will not tell you how many hours I had sat with Buell on the back porch, the long gallery overlooking the quiet evening fields, the sweep of rusty cotton land and the corn and beyond this stretch of dark and sleeping woods, Buell sucking at his corncob, and I, with a turkey bone, playing Pan-like the tune that was

—or *not*—to lure from their hiding the alert timid birds. All sounds came from that woodland pipe—notes too fine or shrill, or, on the other hand, sucked forth with a sudden, alarming coarseness—every note but the right one, till, in the end, the knack came of itself, suddenly, and Buell admitted dubiously it might do.

Buell strode along; the gobbler and a small hen had gone in at the crest of the rise some way to our right. Lower down, three others spreading out, had ploughed their way through the under branches, while still further down the rise, one other followed by the last bird rising, had swung in over a clump of laurel, and, after this short flight, had taken to their legs and scooted through the brush afoot.

"The hollow there seems good," I ventured, suggestively, "it's wide and clear of brush."

Buell nodded. "Yes, suh, that's a mighty good chance. But if you'll pardon me, suh, we cain't see down there as far as from the raise in yondah. There's a draw at the foot, too, and it'll be laike these yeah tukkeys'll come along the aidge without trying to cross. That will bring them up to position, suh, if you'll excuse me."

I laughed. When Buell talked turkey, as the saying is, it was a good time to listen. I saw the logic of his choice. Bije, emerging from the wood, eyed us with a pensive, disappointed air—again, with the never-ending pain of it, Bije had failed to run down the flapping, tantalizing quarry, almost caught, yet always getting free. But Bije had never lost heart, and now, but for Beull's sharp command, Bije would have plunged back into the cover to make another desperate, never-despairing effort.

"Bije—you, Bije, *suh!*"

Dejectedly Bije came to heel, and in silence we made our way among the trees.

The raise on which we stood, dipping sharply to the right, lifted from a gully into a broad, open sweep of hardwood, clear of brush, a solitary jack-pine at the crest, and beside it, a fallen log gray-green with its shield of moss. On the left, a scattering clump of laurel grew upon the incline; and beyond this, the hill plunged down abruptly, the canebrake at its foot and the circling wall of foxgrape raising its ropy barrier between.

Buell halted. "Well, suh, we cain't do better. There's a gunshot on every side, and if you laike, suh, we'll try that gobbler right hereabouts."

A few branches cut from the nearest jack-pine made a screen, and with this blind raised before us, Buell crouched down beside me, one elbow on the ground and his long legs stretched out before him. Then we waited, a long interval of suspense. We made no talk, but sat and listened, our ears strained for the lightest sound, and hearing many—the scurry of a mouse along the leaves—the scratching clatter of squirrels racing along the tree trunks—the thumping of a woodpecker busy on his morning's quest. Far away in the broom straw a bob white called shrilly—*boy-see—boy-see—boy-see!*—then all was still.

"Hark!" said Buell suddenly.

He sat upright, his head fixed tensely.

"There! Do you hear that, suh?"

I heard it, too. "Keep close, suh!" warned Buell, peering over his shoulder toward the left. Again—tuh—*tub*—Tuh—TUH! in rising inflection. It was close by, somewhere beside the screening wall of the canebrake. Buell shook his head as I lifted the bone turkey call toward my lips. "Too close," he whispered, "there—down by the draw—a young bird!"

He had hardly spoken when the turkey showed itself, a small hen, as he said, lonely and agitated. It came out from behind the bole of a hickory, its snaky neck jerking back and forth, peering with beady eyes on every side, and one foot set carefully before the other. There was craft and suspicion and watchfulness, the matchless qualities that had saved it and its kind from extinction. For a while it strutted forward along the sunlit glade, and we let it go unscathed, slim, wary, suspicious. Then it dodged suddenly into cover, and was gone.

I called. The rasping notes of the cry yelped their summons loudly in that quiet, and Buell raised a warning hand.

"Not so coarse, suh. A little lower."

We listened; nothing answered. A woodpecker beat his loud tatoo on a deadwood below in the swamp; far away a quail piped jubilant, and Bije, curled up at our feet, stirred and breathed deeply.

"Try it again, suh," advised Buell, after a long interval.

Again the pipe sucked out its scraping

note. Buell raised his warning hand. *"Listen!"*

We had the answer. Somewhere in the distance, the piping, rasping note of the call brought forth a quick response—or was it only echo? "Yearp him again," whispered Buell, "there's your gobbler."

After a long wait—a period of watching—of waiting in that same tense silence, it was time to yearp once more. The pipe held loosely between the opened hands, sent forth its softened, modulated *chirk—tchirk—tchirk—tchirk*—a subdued, close seductiveness, low and confidential. It sounded on the woodland quiet appealing and discreet—ended echoless, and then with our ears sharpened for the first warning, our eyes watching sharply, we sat there motionless, waiting, listening, intent.

There! Above the hill something walked on the dry, noisy carpeting of the leaves. Buell's hand, outstretched, reached for his muzzle-loader—again that scuffling rustle among the fallen leaves, but on the side away from the coming gobbler. Then something stalked through the undergrowth, vaguely disclosed—paused, and stepped along the slope. "Sho!" exclaimed Buell, beneath his breath—only another hen, fat and plump, not the big gobbler we looked for in our eagerness.

Tuh—tuh—Tuh—TUH!—in rising inflection—*tuh—tuh—Tuh—TUH!* clucked the hen softly.

It was a strong temptation to see that fat, toothsome bird go stalking off unscathed, but we let her go. For a shot, rumbling through the woods at this stage of it, would have put an end to the game. Tuh—tuh—Tuh—TUH! she clucked again, and, as if in answer, a new scuffle below warned us to be on the lookout.

Bije stirred uneasily at our side. Buell, frowning, laid a hand on the dog's back, and again Bije lay close. A minute passed. I saw Buell straighten out a forefinger; he was pointing forward as if to draw my attention to the front. Then his lips moved in a half-heard whisper.

"Over there—behind the jack-pine."

A light scuffle among the leaves—a touch of moving color within that screen of foliage. *Tuh—tuh—tuh—tuh!* muttered the hen above us on the hillside. No need now, for the Pan-pipe to rasp out its cheating note—Nature was helping us more ably

to the appointed end than we could avail ourselves. Once again—and then into the open stepped our game!

He showed himself—suddenly—without noise. Turning the fallen log, one strut brought him into open view, cautious, slinking, almost mean in his crafty wariness. His snaky neck, lean and long, perked to and fro in watchfulness, and even at the distance, we could see his beady eyes shine as they spied nervously about him.

He paused—stood motionless a moment; then revealed himself in his majesty. One other strut forward brought him beneath the shaft of sunlight, and like royalty, his fears allayed, he thrust back his head with a bridling, swelling movement of pride, his feathered bigness inflating slowly and his head more haughtily withdrawn. There I had the picture to remember—the sun streaming down upon him through the wood's leafy roof, bland and disclosing, the great bird ruffling himself majestically, proud, overconfident, a princely egoist, swollen in his self-admiration, puffed out that others might admire. For the moment, he poised himself magnificently; then came the swift and abject change.

The dog, uneasy, stirred noisily at our feet. At the sound, the wattled head shot forward with a thrust of startled inquiry. One foot raised itself, and his feathers gleaming as if of bronze, smoothed abruptly into place, molding flatly against his long and lean, tapering gauntness of form. Then, with a sudden dart, a movement quick and swiftly unexpected, he fled for cover, streaking it along the leafy flooring, his head and neck stuck forward like a running grouse.

The gun, roaring upon that quiet air, filled all the wood with its thunder. Echo boomed crashing from the hill behind, and with a flurry of beating wings, he launched himself in flight. But again the gun roared; a cloud of feathers sprang upward, drifting slowly on the listless air, and in the depths of the canebrake below we heard the crash of breaking branches, a heavy thud, and then the beating flutter of heavy wings. Bije, leaning forward through the tangle, yapped once, then all was still.

"I believe, suh," said Buell, with a shining eye, "that Bije has yo' gobbler down yondah by the cane there!"

34.
STILL HUNTING
THE GRIZZLY
(1885)

IN THE BIG HORN MOUNTAINS.

[DRAWN BY R. SWAIN GIFFORD, ENGRAVED BY R. A. MULLER.]

THE grizzly bear undoubtedly comes in the category of dangerous game, and is, perhaps, the only animal in the United States that can be fairly so placed, unless we count the few jaguars found north of the Rio Grande. But the danger of hunting the grizzly has been greatly exaggerated, and the sport is certainly very much safer than it was at the beginning of this century. The first hunters who came into contact with this great bear were men belonging to that hardy and adventurous class of backwoodsmen which had filled the wild country between the Appalachian Mountains and the Mississippi. These men carried but one weapon, the long-barreled, small-bored pea-rifle, whose bullets ran seventy to the pound, the amount of powder and lead being a little less than that contained in the cartridge of a thirty-two-caliber Winchester. In the Eastern States almost all the hunting was done in the woodland; the shots were mostly obtained at short distance, and deer and black bear were the largest game; moreover, the pea-rifles were marvelously accurate for close range, and their owners were famed the world over for their skill as marksmen. Thus these rifles had so far proved plenty good enough for the work they had to do, and had also done excellent service as military weapons in the ferocious wars that the men of the border carried on with their Indian neighbors, and even in conflict with more civilized foes, as at the battles of King's Mountain and New Orleans. But when the restless frontiersmen pressed out over the Western plains, they encountered in the grizzly a beast of far greater bulk and more savage temper than any of those found in the Eastern woods, and their small-bore rifles were utterly inadequate weapons with which to cope with him. It is small wonder that he was considered by them to be almost invulnerable and extraordinarily tenacious of life. He would be a most unpleasant antagonist now to a man armed only with a thirty-two-caliber rifle, that carried but a single shot and was loaded at the muzzle. A rifle, to be of use in this sport, should carry a ball weighing from half an ounce to an ounce. With the old pea-rifles the shot had to be in the eye or heart, and accidents to the hunter were very common. But the introduction of heavy breech-loading repeaters has greatly lessened the danger, even in the very few and far-off places where the grizzlies are as ferocious as formerly. For nowadays these great bears are undoubtedly much better aware of the death-dealing power of men, and, as a consequence, far less fierce, than was the case with their forefathers, who so unhesitatingly attacked the early Western travelers and explorers. Constant contact with rifle-carrying hunters, for a period extending over many generations of bear-life, has taught the grizzly by bitter experience that man is his undoubted overlord, as far as fighting goes; and this knowledge has become a hereditary characteristic. No grizzly will attack a man now unprovoked, and one will almost always rather run than fight; though if he is wounded or thinks himself cornered he will attack his foes with a headlong, reckless fury that renders him one of the most dangerous of wild beasts. The ferocity of all wild animals depends largely upon the amount of resistance they are accustomed to meet with, and the quantity of molestation to which they are subjected. The change in the grizzly's character during the last half century has been precisely paralleled by the change in the characters of his northern cousin, the polar bear, and of the South African lion. When the Dutch and Scandinavian sailors first penetrated the Arctic seas they were kept in constant dread of the white bear, who regarded a man as simply an erect variety of seal, quite as good eating as the common kind. The records of these early explorers are filled with examples of the ferocious and man-eating propensities of the polar bears; but in the accounts of most of the later Arctic expeditions it is portrayed as having learned wisdom, and being now most anxious to keep out of the way of the hunters. A number of my sporting friends have killed white bears, and none of them were ever even charged. And in South Africa the English sportsmen and Dutch boers have taught the lion to be a very different creature from what it was when the first white man reached that continent. If the Indian tiger had been a native of the United States, it would now be one of the most shy of beasts.

How the prowess of the grizzly compares with that of the lion or tiger would be hard to say; I have never shot either of the latter myself, and my brother, who has killed tigers in India, has never had a chance at a grizzly. Owing to its bulk and muscular development being two or three times as great, I should think that any one of the big bears we killed on the mountains would make short work of a lion or a tiger; but, nevertheless, I believe either of the latter would be much more dangerous to a hunter or other human being, on account of the immensely superior speed of its charge, the lightning-like rapidity of its movements, and its apparently sharper senses. Still, after all is said, the man should have a thoroughly trustworthy weapon and a fairly cool head who would follow into his own haunts and slay grim Old Ephraim.

A grizzly will only fight if wounded or cornered, or, at least, if he thinks himself cornered. If a man by accident stumbles on to one close up, he is almost certain to be attacked, really more from fear than from any other motive,— exactly the same reason that makes a rattlesnake strike at a passer-by. I have personally known of but one instance of a grizzly turning on a hunter before being wounded. This happened to a friend of mine, a Californian ranchman, who, with two or three of his men, was following a bear that had carried off one of his sheep. They got the bear into a cleft in the mountain from which there was no escape, and he suddenly charged back through the line of his pursuers, struck down one of the horsemen, seized the arm of the man in his jaws and broke it as if it had been a pipe-stem, and was only killed after a most lively fight, in which, by repeated charges, he at one time drove every one of his assailants off the field.

But two instances have come to my personal knowledge where a man has been killed by a grizzly. One was that of a hunter at the foot of the Big Horn Mountains who had chased a large bear and finally wounded him. The animal turned at once and came straight at the man, whose second shot missed. The bear then closed and passed on, after striking only a single blow; yet that one blow, given with all the power of its thick, immensely muscular fore-arm, armed with nails as strong as so many hooked steel spikes, tore out the man's collar-bone and snapped through three or four ribs. He never recovered from the shock, and died that night.

The other instance occurred, two or three years ago, to a neighbor of mine, who has a small ranch on the Little Missouri. He was out on a mining trip, and was prospecting with two other men near the headwaters of the Little Missouri, in the Black Hills country. They were walking down along the river, and came to a point of land thrust out into it, which was densely covered with brush and fallen timber. Two of the party walked round by the edge of the stream; but the third, a German, and a very powerful fellow, followed a well-beaten game-trail leading through the bushy point. When they were some forty yards apart the two men heard an agonized shout from the German, and at the same time the loud coughing growl, or roar, of a bear. They turned just in time to see their companion struck a terrible blow on the head by a grizzly, which must have been roused from its lair by his almost stepping on it; so close was it that he had no time to fire his rifle, but merely held it up over his head as a guard. Of course it was struck down, the claws of the great brute at the same time shattering his skull like an egg-shell. The man staggered on some ten feet before he fell; but when he did fall he never spoke or moved again. The two others killed the bear after a short, brisk struggle, as he was in the midst of a most determined charge.

In 1872, near Fort Wingate, New Mexico, two soldiers of a cavalry regiment came to their death at the claws of a grizzly bear. The army surgeon who attended them told me the particulars, so far as they were known. They were mail-carriers, and one day did not come in at the appointed time. Next day a relief party was sent out to look for them, and after some search found the bodies of both, as well as that of one of the horses. One of the men still showed signs of life; he came to his senses before dying, and told the story. They had seen a grizzly and pursued it on horseback, with their Spencer rifles. On coming close, one had fired into its side, when it turned with marvelous quickness for so large and unwieldy an animal, and struck down the horse, at the same time inflicting a ghastly wound on the rider. The other man dismounted and came up to the rescue of his companion. The bear then left the latter and attacked the other. Although hit by the bullet, it charged home and threw the man down, and then lay on him and deliberately bit him to death; his groans and cries were frightful to hear. Afterwards it walked off into the bushes without again offering to molest the already mortally wounded victim of its first assault.

At certain times the grizzly works a good deal of havoc among the herds of the stockmen. A friend of mine, a ranchman in Montana, told me that one fall bears became very plenty around his ranches, and caused him severe loss, killing with ease even full-grown beef-steers. But one of them once found his intended quarry too much for him. My friend had a stocky, rather vicious range stallion, which had been grazing one day near a small thicket of bushes, and towards evening came galloping in with three or four gashes in one haunch, that looked as if they had been cut with a dull axe. The cowboys knew at once that he had been assailed by a bear, and rode off to the thicket near which he had been feeding. Sure enough a bear, evidently in a very bad temper, sallied out as soon as the thicket was surrounded, and, after a spirited fight and a succession of charges, was killed. On examination, it was found that his under jaw was broken, and part of his face smashed in, evidently by the stallion's hoofs. The horse had been feeding, when the bear leaped out at him, but failed to kill at the first stroke; then the horse lashed out behind, and not only freed himself, but also severely damaged his opponent.

Doubtless the grizzly could be hunted to advantage with dogs, which would not, of course, be expected to seize him, but simply to find and bay him, and distract his attention by barking and nipping. Occasionally a bear can be caught in the open and killed with the aid of horses. But nine times out of ten the only way to get one is to put on moccasins and still-hunt it in its own haunts, shooting it at close quarters. Either its tracks should be followed until the bed wherein it lies during the day is found, or a given locality in which it is known to exist should be carefully beaten through, or else a bait should be left out and a watch kept on it to catch the bear when he has come to visit it.

During last summer we found it necessary to leave my ranch on the Little Missouri, and take quite a long trip through the cattle country of south-eastern Montana and northern Wyoming; and having come to the foot of the Big Horn Mountains, we took a fortnight's hunt through them after elk and bear.

We went into the mountains with a pack-train, leaving the ranch wagon at the place where we began to go up the first steep rise. There were two others besides myself in the party: one of them, the teamster, a weather-beaten old plainsman, who possessed a most extraordinary stock of miscellaneous misinformation upon every conceivable subject; and the other, my ranch foreman, Merrifield. Merrifield was originally an Eastern backwoodsman, and during the last year or two has been my *fidus Achates* of the hunting field; he is a well-built, good-looking fellow, an excellent rider, a first-class shot, and a keen sportsman. None of us had ever been within two hundred miles of the Big Horn range before; so that our hunting trip had the added zest of being also an exploring expedition.

Each of us rode one pony, and the packs were carried on four others. We were not burdened by much baggage. Having no tent, we took the canvas wagon-sheet instead; our bedding, plenty of spare cartridges, some flour, bacon, coffee, sugar, and salt, and a few very primitive cooking utensils, completed the outfit.

The Big Horn range is a chain of bare rocky peaks, stretching lengthwise along the middle of a table-land which is about thirty miles wide. At its edges this table-land falls sheer off into the rolling plains country. From the rocky peaks flow rapid brooks of clear, icy water, which take their way through deep gorges that they have channeled out in the surface of the plateau; a few miles from the heads of the streams these gorges become regular cañons, with sides so steep as to be almost perpendicular. In traveling, therefore, the trail has to keep well up towards timber-line, as lower down horses find it difficult or impossible to get across the valleys. In strong contrast to the treeless cattle plains extending to its foot, the sides of the table-land are densely wooded with tall pines. Its top forms what is called a park country,— that is, it is covered with alternating groves of trees and open glades, each grove or glade varying in size from half a dozen to many hundred acres.

We went in with the pack-train two days' journey before pitching camp in what we intended to be our hunting grounds, following an old Indian trail. No one who has not tried it can understand the work and worry that it is to drive a pack-train over rough ground and through timber. We were none of us very skillful at packing, and the loads were all the time slipping. Sometimes the ponies would stampede with the packs half tied, or they would get caught among the fallen logs, or, in a ticklish place, would suddenly decline to follow the trail, or would commit some other of the thousand tricks which seem to be all a pack-pony knows. Then, at night, they were a bother; if picketed out, they fed badly and got thin, and if they were not picketed, they sometimes strayed away. The most valuable one of the lot was also the hardest to catch. Accordingly, we used to let him loose with a long lariat tied round his neck, and one night this lariat twisted up in a sage brush, and in struggling to free himself the pony got a half-hitch round his hind leg, threw himself, and fell over a bank into a creek on a large stone. We found him in the morning very much the worse for wear, his hind legs swelled up so that his chief method of progression was by a series of awkward hops. Of course, no load could be put upon him, but he managed to limp along behind the other horses, and actually, in the end, reached the ranch on the Little Missouri, three hundred miles off. No sooner had he got there and been turned loose to rest, than he fell down a big wash-out and broke his neck. Another time, one of the mares—a homely beast, with a head like a camel's — managed to flounder into the very center of a mud-hole, and we spent the better part of a morning in fishing her out.

We spent several days at the first camping-place, killing half a dozen elk, but none with very fine heads. All of these were gotten by still-hunting, Merrifield and I following up their trails, either together or separately. Throughout this trip I used a buckskin hunting-suit, a fur cap, and moccasins. Not only was this dress very lasting, but it was also very inconspicuous in the woods (always an important point for a hunter to attend to); and in it I could walk almost noiselessly, the moccasins making no sound whatever, and the buckskin reducing the rustling of branches and twigs as I passed through them to a minimum. Both of us carried Winchester rifles. Mine was a 45-75, half-magazine, stocked and sighted to suit myself. At one time I had bought a double-barreled English Express, but I soon threw it aside in favor of the Winchester, which, according to my experience, is much the best weapon for any American game.

Although it was still early in September, the weather was cool and pleasant, the nights being frosty; and every two or three days there was a flurry of light snow, which rendered the labor of tracking much more easy. Indeed, throughout our stay in the mountains, the peaks were snow-capped almost all the time. Our fare was excellent, consisting of elk venison, mountain grouse, and small trout, the last caught in one of the beautiful little lakes that lay almost up by the timber-line. To us, who had for weeks been accustomed to make small fires from dried brush, or from sage-brush roots, which we dug out of the ground, it was a treat to sit at night before the roaring and crackling pine logs; as the old teamster quaintly put it, we had at last come to a land " where the wood grew on trees." There were plenty of black-tail deer in the woods, and we came across a number of bands of cow and calf elk, or of young bulls; but after several days' hunting, we were still without any head worth taking home, and had seen no sign of grizzly, which was the game we were especially anxious to kill for neither Merrifield nor I had ever seen a wild bear alive.

One day we separated. I took up the trail of a large bull elk, and though after a while I lost the track, in the end I ran across the animal itself, and after a short stalk got a shot at the noble-looking old fellow. It was a grand bull, with massive neck and twelve-tined antlers ; and he made a most beautiful picture, standing out on a crag that jutted over the sheer cliff wall, the tall pine-trees behind him and the deep cañon at his feet, while in the background rose the snow-covered granite peaks. As I got up on my knees to fire he half-faced towards me, about eighty yards off, and the ball went in behind the shoulder. He broke away into the forest, but stopped before he had gone twenty rods, and did not need the second bullet to which he fell. I reached camp early in the afternoon, and waited for a couple of hours before Merrifield put in an appearance. At last we heard a shout — the familiar long-drawn *Ei-koh-h-h* of the cattlemen — and he came in sight, galloping at speed down an open glade, and waving his hat, evidently having had good luck ; and when he reined in his small, wiry cow-pony, we saw that he had packed behind his saddle the fine, glossy pelt of a black bear. Better still, he announced that he had been off about ten miles to a perfect tangle of ravines and valleys where bear sign was very thick ; and not of black bear either, but of grizzly. The black bear (the only one we got on the mountains) he had run across by accident. While riding up a valley in which there was a patch of dead timber grown up with berry bushes, he noticed a black object, which he first took to be a stump ; for during the past few days we had each of us made one or two clever stalks up to charred logs which our imagination converted into bears. On coming near, however, the object suddenly took to its heels ; he followed over frightful ground at the pony's best pace, until it stumbled and fell down. By this time he was close on the bear, which had just reached the edge of the wood. Picking himself up, he rushed after it, hearing it growling ahead of him ; after running some fifty yards the sounds stopped, and he stood still listening. He saw and heard nothing until he happened to cast his eyes upwards, and there was the bear, almost overhead, and about twenty-five feet up a tree ; and in as many seconds afterwards it came down to the ground with a bounce, stone dead. It was a young bear, in its second year, and had probably never before seen a man, which accounted for the ease with which it was treed and taken. One minor result of the encounter was to convince Merrifield — the list of whose faults did not include lack of self-confidence — that he could run down any bear ; in consequence of which idea we on more than one subsequent occasion went through a good deal of violent exertion.

Merrifield's tale made me decide to shift camp at once, and go over to the spot where the bear-tracks were so plenty, which was not more than a couple of miles from where I had slain the big elk. Next morning we were off, and by noon pitched camp by a clear brook, in a valley with steep, wooded sides, but with good feed for the horses in the open bottom. We rigged the canvas wagon-sheet into a small tent, sheltered by the trees from the wind, and piled great pine logs nearly where we wished to place the fire; for a night-camp in the sharp fall weather is cold and dreary unless there is a roaring blaze of flame in front of the tent.

That afternoon we again went out, and I shot another fine bull elk. I came home alone towards nightfall, walking through a reach of burnt forest, where there was nothing but charred tree-trunks and black mold. When nearly through it I came across the huge, half-human footprints of a great grizzly, which must have passed by within a few minutes. It gave me rather an eerie feeling in the silent, desolate woods, to see for the first time the unmistakable proofs that I was in the home of the mighty lord of the wilderness. I followed the tracks in the fading twilight until it became too dark to see them any longer, and then shouldered my rifle and walked back to camp.

That night we almost had a visit from one of the animals we were after. Several times we had heard at night the calling of the bull elks, a sound than which there is nothing more musical in nature. No writer has done it justice; it has in it soft, flute-like notes, and again chords like those of an Æolian harp, or like some beautiful wind instrument. This night, when we were in bed and the fire was smoldering, we were roused by a ruder noise,—a kind of grunting or roaring whine, answered by the frightened snorts of the ponies. It was a bear, which had evidently not seen the fire, as it came from behind the bank, and had probably been attracted by the smell of the horses. After it made out what we were, it staid round a short while, again uttered its peculiar roaring grunt, and went off. We had seized our rifles and run out into the woods, but in the darkness could see nothing; indeed, it was rather lucky we did not stumble across the bear, as he could have made short work of us when we were at such a disadvantage.

Next day we went off on a long tramp through the woods and along the sides of the cañons. There were plenty of berry bushes growing in clusters, and all around these there were fresh tracks of bear. But the grizzly is also a flesh-eater, and has a great liking for carrion. On visiting the place where Merrifield had killed the black bear, we found that the grizzlies had been there before us, and had utterly devoured the carcass with cannibal relish. Hardly a scrap was left, and we turned our steps toward where lay the second bull elk I had killed. It was quite late in the afternoon when we reached the place. A grizzly had evidently been at the carcass during the preceding night, for his great foot-prints were in the ground all around it, and the carcass itself was gnawed and torn, and partially covered with earth and leaves; for the grizzly has a curious habit of burying all of his prey that he does not at the moment need. A great many ravens had been feeding on the body, and they wheeled about over the tree-tops above us, uttering their barking croaks.

The forest was composed mainly of what are called ridge-pole pines, which grow close together, and do not branch out until the stems are thirty or forty feet from the ground. Beneath these trees we walked over a carpet of pine-needles, upon which our moccasined feet made no sound. The woods seemed vast and lonely, and their silence was broken now and then by the strange noises always to be heard in the great forests, and which seem to mark the sad and everlasting unrest of the wilderness. We climbed up along the trunk of a dead tree which had toppled over until its upper branches struck in the limb-crotch of another, that thus supported it at an angle half-way in its fall. When above the ground far enough to prevent the bear's smelling us, we sat still to wait for his approach; until, in the gathering gloom, we could no longer see the sights of our rifles, and could but dimly make out the carcass of the great elk. It was useless to wait longer, and we clambered down and stole out to the edge of the woods. The forest here covered one side of a steep, almost cañon-like ravine, whose other side was bare except of rock and sage-brush. Once out from under the trees, there was still plenty of light, although the sun had set, and we crossed over some fifty yards to the opposite hillside and crouched down under a bush to see if perchance some animal might not also leave the cover. To our right the ravine sloped downward towards the valley of the Big Horn River, and far on its other side we could catch a glimpse of the great main chain of the Rockies, their snow-peaks glinting crimson in the light of the set sun. Again we waited quietly in the growing dusk until the pine-trees in our front blended into one dark, frowning mass. We saw nothing; but the wild creatures of the forest had begun to stir abroad. The owls hooted dismally from the tops of the tall trees, and two or three times a harsh, wailing cry, probably the voice of some lynx or wolverine, arose from the depths of the woods. At last, as we were rising to leave, we heard the sound of the breaking of a dead stick from the spot where we knew the carcass lay. It was a sharp, sudden noise, perfectly distinct from the natural creaking and snapping of the branches,—just such a sound as would be made by the tread of some heavy creature. "Old Ephraim" had come back to the carcass. A minute afterward, listening with strained ears, we heard him brush by some dry twigs. It was entirely too dark to go in after him; but we made up our minds that on the morrow he should be ours.

Early next morning we were over at the elk carcass, and, as we expected, found that the bear had eaten his fill at it during the night. His tracks showed him to be an immense fellow, and were so fresh that we doubted if he had left long before we arrived; and we made up our minds to follow him up and try to find his lair. The bears that lived on these mountains had evidently been little disturbed. Indeed, the Indians and most of the white hunters are rather chary of meddling with "Old Ephraim," as the mountain men style the grizzly, unless they get him at a disadvantage; for the sport is fraught with some danger and but small profit. The bears thus seemed to have very little fear of harm, and we thought it far from unlikely that the bed of the one who had fed on the elk would not be far away.

My companion was a skillful tracker, and we took up the trail at once. For some distance it led over the soft, yielding carpet of moss and pine-needles, and the foot-prints were quite easily made out, although we could follow them but slowly; for we had, of course, to keep a sharp lookout ahead and around us as we walked noiselessly on in the somber half-light always prevailing under the great pine-trees, through whose thickly interlacing branches stray but few beams of light, no matter how bright the sun may be outside. We made no sound ourselves, and every little sudden noise sent a thrill through me as I peered about with each sense on the alert. Two or three of the ravens which we had scared from the carcass flew overhead, croaking hoarsely; and the pine-tops moaned and sighed in the slight breeze — for pine-trees seem to be ever in motion, no matter how light the wind.

After going a few hundred yards the tracks turned off on a well-beaten path made by the elk; the woods were in many places cut up by these game-trails, which had often become as distinct as ordinary foot-paths. The beast's footprints were perfectly plain in the dust, and he had lumbered along up the path until near the middle of the hillside, where the ground broke away and there were hollows and bowlders. Here there had been a windfall, and the dead trees lay among the living, piled across one another in all directions; while between and around them sprouted up a thick growth of young spruces and other evergreens. The trail turned off into the tangled thicket, within which it was almost certain we would find our quarry. We could still follow the tracks, by the slight scrapes of the claws on the bark, or by the bent and broken twigs; and we advanced with noiseless caution, slowly climbing over the dead tree-trunks and upturned stumps, and not letting a branch rustle or catch on our clothes. When in the middle of the thicket we crossed what was almost a breastwork of fallen logs, and Merrifield, who was leading, passed by the upright stem of a great pine. As soon as he was by it he sank suddenly on one knee, turning half round, his face fairly aflame with excitement; and as I strode past him, with my rifle at the ready, there, not ten steps off, was the great bear, slowly rising from his bed among the young spruces. He had heard us, but apparently hardly knew exactly where or what we were, for he reared up on his haunches sideways to us. Then he saw us and dropped down again on all fours, the shaggy hair on his neck and shoulders seeming to bristle as he turned towards us. As he sank down on his fore feet I had raised the rifle; his head was bent slightly down, and when I saw the top of the white bead fairly between his small, glittering, evil eyes, I pulled trigger. Half rising up, the huge beast fell over on his side in the death-throes, the ball having gone into his brain, striking as fairly between the eyes as if the distance had been measured by a carpenter's rule.

The whole thing was over in twenty seconds from the time I caught sight of the game; indeed, it was over so quickly that the grizzly did not have time to show fight at all or come a step towards us. It was the first I had ever seen, and I felt not a little proud as I stood over the great brindled bulk, which lay stretched out at length in the cool shade of the evergreens. He was a monstrous fellow, much larger than any I have seen since, whether alive or brought in dead by the hunters. As near as we could estimate (for of course we had nothing with which to weigh more than very small portions), he must have weighed about twelve hundred pounds; and though this is not as large as some of his kind are said to grow in California, it is yet a very unusual size for a bear. He was a good deal heavier than any of our horses; and it was with the greatest difficulty that we were able to skin him. He must have been very old, his teeth and claws being all worn down and blunted; but nevertheless he had been living in plenty, for he was as fat as a prize hog, the layers on his back being a finger's length in thickness. He was still in the summer coat, his hair being short, and in color a curious brindled brown, somewhat like that of certain bull-dogs; while all the bears we shot afterwards had the long thick winter fur, cinnamon or yellowish brown. By the way, the name of this bear has reference to its character, and not to its color, and should, I suppose, be properly spelt grisly,—in the sense of horrible, exactly as we speak of a "grisly specter,"—and not grizzly; but perhaps the latter way of spelling it is too well established to be now changed.

In killing dangerous game steadiness is more needed than good shooting. No game is dangerous unless a man is close up, for nowadays hardly any wild beast will charge from a distance of a hundred yards, but will rather try to run off; and if a man is close it is easy enough for him to shoot straight if he does not lose his head. A bear's brain is about the size of a pint bottle; and any one can hit a pint bottle off-hand at thirty or forty feet. I have had two shots at bears at close quarters, and each time I fired into the brain, the bullet in one case striking fairly between the eyes, as told above, and in the other going in between the eye and ear. A novice at this kind of sport will find it best and safest to keep in mind the old Norse viking's advice in reference to a long sword: "If you go in close enough, your sword will be long enough." If a poor shot goes in close enough, he will find that he shoots straight enough.

I was very proud over my first bear; but Merrifield's chief feeling seemed to be disappointment that the animal had not had time to show fight. He was rather a reckless fellow, and very confident in his own skill with the rifle; and he really did not seem to have any more fear of the grizzlies than if they had been so many jack-rabbits. I did not at all share his feeling, having a hearty respect for my foes' prowess, and in following and attacking them always took all possible care to get the chances on my side. Merrifield was sincerely sorry that we never had to stand a regular charge; we killed our five grizzlies with seven bullets, and, except in the case of the she and cub spoken of farther on, each was shot about as quickly as it got sight of us.

The last one we got was an old male, which was feeding on an elk carcass. We crept up to within about sixty feet, and, as Merrifield had not yet killed a grizzly purely to his own gun, and I had killed three, I told him to take the shot. He at once whispered gleefully, "I'll break his leg, and we'll see what he'll do!" Having no ambition to be a participator in the antics of a three-legged bear, I hastily interposed a most emphatic

veto; and with a rather injured air he fired, the bullet going through the neck just back of the head. The bear fell to the shot, and could not get up from the ground, dying in a few minutes; but first he seized his left wrist in his teeth and bit clean through it, completely separating the bones of the paw and arm. Although a smaller bear than the big one I first shot, he would probably have proved a much more ugly foe, for he was less unwieldy, and had much longer and sharper teeth and claws. I think that if my companion had merely broken the beast's leg he would have had his curiosity as to its probable conduct more than gratified.

We tried eating the grizzly's flesh, but it was not good, being coarse and not well flavored; and besides, we could not get over the feeling that it had belonged to a carrion-feeder. The flesh of the little black bear, on the other hand, was excellent; it tasted like that of a young pig. Doubtless, if a young grizzly, which had fed merely upon fruits, berries, and acorns, was killed, its flesh would prove good eating; but even then it would probably not be equal to a black bear.

A day or two after the death of the big bear, we went out one afternoon on horseback, intending merely to ride down to see a great cañon lying some six miles west of our camp; we went more to look at the scenery than for any other reason, though, of course, neither of us ever stirred out of camp without his rifle. We rode down the valley in which we had camped through alternate pine groves and open glades, until we reached the cañon, and then skirted its brink for a mile or so. It was a great chasm, many miles in length, as if the table-land had been rent asunder by some terrible and unknown force; its sides were sheer walls of rock, rising three or four hundred feet straight up in the air, and worn by the weather till they looked like the towers and battlements of some vast fortress. Between them at the bottom was a space, in some places nearly a quarter of a mile wide, in others very narrow, through whose middle foamed a deep rapid torrent of which the sources lay far back among the snow-topped mountains around Cloud Peak. In this valley, dark-green, somber pines stood in groups, stiff and erect; and here and there among them were groves of poplar and cottonwood, with slender branches and trembling leaves, their bright green already changing to yellow in the sharp fall weather. We went down to where the mouth of the cañon opened out, and rode our horses to the end of a great jutting promontory of rock, thrust out into the plain; and in the cold clear air we looked far over the broad valley of the Big Horn as it lay at our very feet, walled in on the other side by the distant chain of the Rocky Mountains.

Turning our horses, we rode back along the edge of another cañon-like valley, with a brook flowing down in its center, and its rocky sides covered with an uninterrupted pine forest—the place of all others in whose inaccessible wildness and ruggedness a bear would find a safe retreat. After some time we came to where other valleys, with steep grass-grown sides, covered with sage-brush, branched out from it, and we followed one of these out. There was plenty of elk sign about, and we saw several black-tail deer. These last were very common on the mountains, but we had not hunted them at all, as we were in no need of meat. But this afternoon we came across a buck with remarkably fine antlers, finer than any I had ever got, and accordingly I shot it, and we stopped to cut off and skin out the horns, throwing the reins over the heads of the horses and leaving them to graze by themselves. The body lay near the crest of one side of a deep valley or ravine which headed up on the plateau a mile to our left. Except for scattered trees and bushes the valley was bare; but there was heavy timber along the crests of the hills on its opposite side. It took some time to fix the head properly, and we were just finishing when Merrifield sprang to his feet and exclaimed, " Look at the bears!" pointing down into the valley below us. Sure enough, there were two bears (which afterwards proved to be an old she and a nearly full-grown cub) traveling up the bottom of the valley, much too far off for us to shoot. Grasping our rifles and throwing off our hats, we started off as hard as we could run diagonally down the hillside, so as to cut them off. It was some little time before they saw us, when they made off at a lumbering gallop up the valley. It would seem impossible to run into two grizzlies in the open, but they were going up hill and we down, and moreover the old one kept stopping. The cub would forge ahead and could probably have escaped us, but the mother now and then stopped to sit up on her haunches and look round at us, when the cub would run back to her. The upshot was that we got ahead of them, when they turned and went straight up one hillside as we ran straight down the other behind them. By this time I was pretty nearly done out, for running along the steep ground through the sage-brush was most exhausting work; and Merrifield kept gaining on me and was well in front. Just as he disappeared over a bank, almost at the bottom of the valley, I tripped over a bush and fell full length. When I got up I knew I could never make up the ground I had lost, and besides could

hardly run any longer. Merrifield was out of sight below, and the bears were laboring up the steep hillside directly opposite and about three hundred yards off; so I sat down and began to shoot over Merrifield's head, aiming at the big bear. She was going very steadily and in a straight line, and each bullet sent up a puff of dust where it struck the dry soil, so that I could keep correcting my aim; and the fourth ball crashed into the old bear's flank. She lurched heavily forward, but recovered herself and reached the timber, while Merrifield, who had put on a spurt, was not far behind.

I toiled up the hill at a sort of trot, fairly gasping and sobbing for breath; but before I got to the top I heard a couple of shots and a shout. The old bear had turned as soon as she was in the timber, and come towards Merrifield; but he gave her the death-wound by firing into her chest, and then shot at the young one, knocking it over. When I came up he was just walking towards the latter to finish it with the revolver, but it suddenly jumped up as lively as ever and made off at a great pace — for it was nearly full-grown. It was impossible to fire where the tree-trunks were so thick, but there was a small opening across which it would have to pass, and collecting all my energies I made a last run, got into position, and covered the opening with my rifle. The instant the bear appeared I fired, and it turned a dozen somersaults downhill, rolling over and over; the ball had struck it near the tail and had ranged forward through the hollow of the body. Each of us had thus given the fatal wound to the bear into which the other had fired the first bullet. The run, though short, had been very sharp, and over such awful country that we were completely fagged out, and could hardly speak for lack of breath. The sun had already set, and it was too late to skin the animals; so we merely dressed them, caught the ponies — with some trouble, for they were frightened at the smell of the bear's blood on our hands — and rode home through the darkening woods. Next day we brought the teamster and two of the steadiest pack-horses to the carcasses, and took the skins into camp.

The feed for the horses was excellent in the valley in which we were camped, and the rest after their long journey across the plains did them good. They had picked up wonderfully in condition during our stay on the mountains; but they were apt to wander very far during the night, for there were so many bears and other wild beasts round that they kept getting frightened and running off. We were very loath to leave our hunting grounds, but time was pressing, and we had already

THE DEATH OF OLD EPHRAIM.

[DRAWN BY A. B. FROST, ENGRAVED BY S. P. DAVIS.]

many more trophies than we could carry; so one cool morning, when the branches of the evergreens were laden with the feathery snow that had fallen overnight, we struck camp and started out of the mountains, each of us taking his own bedding behind his saddle, while the pack-ponies were loaded down with bear skins, elk and deer antlers, and the hides and furs of other game. In single file we moved through the woods and across the cañons to the edge of the great table-land, and then slowly down the steep slope to its foot, where we found our canvas-topped wagon. Next day saw us setting out on our long journey homewards, across the three hundred weary miles of treeless and barren-looking plains country.

Theodore Roosevelt.

35.
IN THE CASCADES
(1899)

IN THE CASCADES.

BY R. L. WARNER.

"I am still a lover of the woods and fields
 and mountains,
And of all that we behold from this green
 earth;
Of all the mighty world of eye and ear,
Both what they half create and half perceive;

Well pleased to recognize, in nature and the
 language of the sense,
The anchor of my purest thoughts,
The nurse, the guide, the guardian, of my
 heart and soul,
Of all my moral being."

—WORDSWORTH.

THAT'S the way I always feel when I temporarily cease camping on the trail of the dollar, light my brier pipe, and, through the wreaths of gray incense, review the scenes of days spent in communion with our gentle mother, Nature, in the far West. I think that when a fellow once has had a real taste of Western life under favorable conditions, he never quite gets over wanting to hit the trail toward the setting sun.

There is no better hunter or woodsman in Washington or Oregon than John Davis. Thoroughly good-natured, obliging to a degree, full of dry humor, a tireless and patient hunter, he is hard to beat as a guide and companion for weeks in a country where even blazed trails are exceptional and you mostly have to feel your way cautiously along as you go.

I was going through a lot of old photo prints and picked up a little bunch marked "Southern Oregon." They bring back to me recollections of one of the happiest hunts which it was my privilege to enjoy with John Davis and the "chosen few." Two of the boys are now in Alaska, two are helping to hold down the Atlantic seaboard, and of all the five, John Davis, the faithful, alone resorts to the scenes of our former joys.

The memorable autumn, of which these pictures partly tell the story, was spent in the Cascade Range in Southern Oregon. Our base of supplies was a little town, where we engaged a native of the Emerald Isle to transport our outfit sixty-five miles into the mountains. The road lay for twelve or fifteen miles through a beautiful farming country with wide expanses of wheat stubble, dotted here and there by the orchards which have made Oregon famous as the land of the big red apple; then rising gradually into the hills, we followed the course of one of the many river valleys which form the Pacific water-shed of the Cascades.

Many of the brilliant-hued Mongolian pheasants, or "Chineys," as they are locally called, were seen running in the fields or passing on noisy wing to some bit of dense cover, and, as signs of civilization became less frequent, our old friend, the blue grouse, was occasionally met with, and two or three of them were gathered into the wagon for future reference.

The native grouse has had a hard time of it in Oregon since the Mongolian emigrant began to possess the

WE WERE FOUR.

365

Painted for Outing by C. Rungius.

THE BLACK-TAIL AT HOME.

land. The Chinese pheasant is very hardy, multiplies with astonishing rapidity, and is, withal, such a greedy monopolist and pugilist, that he has wiped out almost everything else in his class, frequently not even drawing the line at the barn-yard cock.

About noon we arrived at the ranch of Monsieur Pierre Peppiet, where we put up for dinner. M. Peppiet was something of a hunter himself, and had, the previous year, captured and domesticated a fawn, which, after some persuasion, consented to stand for his picture. One of the most inspiring events of the day was enacted by our "native" pilot with the assistance of his team of half-broken cayuses, which served as motive power for the buck-board, upon which we sat at short intervals throughout the day. These demure-looking, rawhide-covered, equine motors had figured it all out that they were not going to accompany that buck-board any farther than M. Peppiet's ranch, and when they came to be hooked up after dinner, they resented the indignity vigorously. After an hour's work, upon the part of seven men, we got enough harness onto the brutes to keep them within hailing distance of the buck-board, and six of us held them while their sandy little proprietor mounted the bridge and yelled to us to stand from under. When they were released they started for headquarters on their front feet, employing their rear extremities the while in a well-directed effort to dissolve partnership with the buck-board. Swaying and plunging, the outfit disappeared down the road, with the master of ceremonies magically sticking on and plying the long whip with a liberal accompaniment of profanity. After the space of a quarter of an hour, during which time bets were freely offered, with no takers, that the combination would not again be seen intact, there trotted into view a humiliated-looking team of yellow cayuses, the buck-board and proprietor following triumphantly in their wake. We secured from Monsieur Peppiet the loan of a pack pony named Spilley and resumed our journey, with the same in tow.

The country became wilder, with only a little ranch nestling in an open valley here and there, and soon we were buried in one of those great forests of Douglass, fir and cedar, with which the Oregon slopes of the Cascades are covered. Emerging, late in the afternoon, into a little open prairie of a few acres, which had been roughly fenced by the pioneer who had "taken it up," we jumped a white-tailed doe just at a point where the road passed between the fence on one side, up hill, and a steep slide below. She started with great leaps, trying to take the fence, but could not, and after trying several times, stopped a moment, bewildered, then whirled around and dashed back directly past us, not twenty yards away. She was a beauty, her sides shining red in the sunlight, the picture of grace.

Six miles beyond this point, just at dark, we arrived at the head of navigation for buck-boards and camped for the night. Before daylight the next morning we had had breakfast, and, with our outfit packed on the three horses, were following the trail, which was to bring us to a little meadow in a pocket of the mountains, six or seven miles further up. A dense fog filled the valley, but the trail was steep and we soon emerged from it, coming out upon a high point into the clear upper atmosphere, just as the first hint of dawn appeared.

Turning, we looked back across the great sea of white fog which stretched away from our feet in mighty billows, rolling on until the eye could follow no further. The rose light in the east grew stronger, putting out the night lamps, one by one, till only the morning star remained on high, above the snowy cap of a lofty peak, like a spark of incense before God's altar. The dark outline of the Cascade Range stood like a silhouette against the lightening sky, its great shadow falling over us onto the white sea of fog, fifty miles away. And then the morning came swiftly on, shedding its rich light upon this glorious scene and waking the first notes of the forest birds.

We located our meadow in due course and dismissed our guide with his two treacherous mustangs, retaining Spilley as a packer for side trips. By nightfall we had constructed a substantial camp, thatched with shakes split out of a fallen cedar. An ice-cold spring afforded an abundance of delightful water, and Spilley munched the grass in the little meadow with evident satisfaction. An attractive feature of this camp was the abundance of late huckleberries. Great patches of the blue and brown fellows were to be found all through that part of the range and were appreciated by the bears no less than by ourselves. Bear sign was plentiful about these berry patches, many of the bushes being broken down and stripped of fruit by Bruin, who knows a good thing when he sees it.

I have never seen deer sign so plentiful anywhere as on this range. You would have said there were thousands of deer, and there must have been, for their trails were everywhere, and numerous fresh tracks were to be seen every morning, even along the rivulet which flowed out of our spring, down through the meadow, not a hundred yards from camp. Nevertheless, it was not until the evening of the fourth day that we had any venison, for it was the light of the moon and the deer were feeding at night, lying close during the daytime among the great beds of thick fern, which made still-hunting, under such circumstances, well nigh impossible.

These great ferns are characteristic of the Cascade forests, growing often to the height of a man's head and filling in the spaces between the huge tree trunks so completely that, though we frequently jumped up bedded deer, it was rarely that a fair shot could be had. John Davis, however, succeeded, as usual, in circumventing regularly enough venison to keep the camp well supplied. John could go out and get a deer where nobody ever heard of deer before. He "don't hunt 'em perticlerly, jus' kinder goes out and looks round till he sees one and shoots it." But in time we all got our deer, and I my first one, by the way, although this was by no means the first occasion on which I had gone out to "look round for one."

In the course of our peregrinations we had discovered a lick crossing on the river a couple of miles below our camp, and we were dead certain that, if it only had not been in the light of the moon, we could have got more deer than you could shake a stick at. I had watched the crossing faithfully two evenings till dusk and no deer, but, on returning in the morning, would find that from five to twelve deer had been there during the night.

A third evening I had stayed a little later than usual, and was just going to pull out for camp when there appeared across the river the head of a doe; then there was a doe there, and then another, two beauties, one of them drinking, the other standing just at the edge of the water looking up the stream, broadside toward me. I couldn't see them come out of the woods; they just seemed to happen there without coming at all. I kept cool enough to draw a careful bead well down on the shoulder of the first one and unhitched my Marlin 40–60. That doe disappeared instantly, and I felt sure I saw her go into the river. Then I began to pump cartridges into the gun and blaze away like mad at the remaining doe, succeeding in throwing five shots into the scenery around her before she could make up her mind into which direction she wanted to run.

I fooled around about an hour in the growing darkness, trying to find the doe I had "killed," but finally had to give it up and make for camp. The next morning I was back at the crossing about as soon as it was light, and, sure enough, there was my deer ashore on the edge of an eddy, about fifty yards below where she had been shot. After this our luck began to improve, and, in the course of two weeks, we had jerked as much venison as we felt we could comfortably take out with us.

I don't know whether the fellows who go hunting down in Maine, and elsewhere in the "East," ever "jerk" venison or not, but if they don't they miss a good deal. It is very easy to jerk the meat so that it will keep for a year, and jerked venison isn't half bad either.

One day I created a little diversion for myself by getting lost, although I think this is the first time a public confession of the fact has been made, for I succeeded in flimflamming the rest of the crowd as to how it all happened. It was our custom to hunt alone, each fellow filling out his own programme for the day. On this day I had gone into a new part of the range, about six miles from camp, which was especially blessed with huckleberries, in the hope of finding a bear After pottering around there nearly all day without meeting my bear, I started to return. I had the general directions of things all right, but, somehow or other, a country like that looks a whole lot different at five P. M. from the way it does at nine A. M., and I got lost.

I was about three miles from camp when I got off my bearings and headed through the wrong gap down toward the river. When I struck the river it was pretty dark, and the going was difficult. I managed to cross, however, and then started down stream, away from camp instead of toward it. The more I worked along the less familiar the bank of the river seemed, but I attributed this to the darkness and kept picking my way down stream through the great tree trunks and over dry beds of small boulders in bends of the river, all the time expecting to find the big fallen cedar across the stream, which would give me the bearing for camp.

After about an hour of this, I came out upon the high bank of a dry creek bed, which had been cut deep by the spring freshets. While everything about me was pretty dark, I could distinguish the big tree trunks fairly well, and could mark the course of the river by the foaming rapids and constant roar, but, as I peered down into this black creek bed, I began to feel a little bit creepy, for it was darker than a pocket down in there.

While I hesitated and tried to decide whether to cross or turn back, there came suddenly, from out that inky blackness, the sound of pebbles crunching together and the cracking of a stick, as if made by the movement of a heavy body. I have heard it variously disputed as to whether a fellow's hair will actually rise with fright, and I believe that the weight of scientific opinion is against the phenomenon, but I am sure that, at that moment, all the hairs of my head individually *tried* to stand on end. I could feel them tingle clear down into the roots.

I don't say that I was actually scared as I backed away from the edge of the bank, grasping my rifle tighter, all ready to fire at the slightest provocation; but when I had got back thirty or forty yards, and faced up stream again, I felt that irresistible desire to flee from an unseen danger behind, which instinctively comes over you when you go down alone through a long, dark corridor, which you know is absolutely empty.

After working up stream to the starting point, I had about decided to build a fire and lie out all night, when three rifle shots, in quick succession, from over the ridge to the north, away up stream, revived my ambition, and an hour later I was in camp. I lounged into the firelight as unconcernedly as possible, ungratefully inquiring whether they were afraid to stay in camp alone, whether they supposed that I couldn't take care of myself in an open country like that, etc., but I believe it was three days before I altogether recovered from that creepy feeling.

The "artist" had possessed himself of a brand-new camera for this trip, and a very large majority of his time was put in cruising around getting the scenery to sit for him. His insatiable activity in this direction came near resulting in his taking home a punctured skin, and, although the incident afforded us unbounded joy at his expense after it was all over, it was pretty ticklish at the time. A spike buck had been killed late one evening and hung up not over a mile from camp. In the morning it was found that a cougar had visited the carcass during the night and helped himself freely. One of the boys volunteered to go down to the nearest settler's cabin, twelve miles below, and enlist the coöperation of a hound, which we had seen there while passing through, so the next morning we all returned to the spot prepared for a real cougar hunt.

The cougar had dined plenteously on venison, and the hound took up his trail at once, working along through the high ferns out into a windfall and up along the side of a bald butte. The artist, who was a corker in fast going through such country, kept close after the hound with his camera in position for quick action, and, when we finally heard the dog baying, high up among the rocky benches of the butte, he and John Davis were the only ones within range of the game. It seems that at this juncture the man of the camera came up and found the big cat at bay on a shelf of rock, with the dog camped out ten or twelve feet below him. Climbing carefully up along a dead tree trunk, in order to get within range, the artist brought his focusing battery to bear on the enemy.

That plate, however, has not yet been developed, for the cougar, mistaking this for a hostile move, cut the sitting short by making a flying leap at the camera man, knocking him off the log to the ground four or five feet below, where he landed on top of the camera. Just at this moment John Davis put in an appearance, and took a crack at the cat, which had remained upon the log, growling viciously. All he said, as he finished carefully skinning the beast, was, "folks what ain't got no more sense than they need in town, ought to stay there!"

But our artist redeemed his reputation, with interest, a couple of days later, and the big white bear's tooth, which swings on the latch-string of my den, is a constant reminder of his triumph.

Four of us were to spend a few days on a goat hunt on the eastern slopes of the range, leaving in camp one of the boys, who had a short line of traps set down the river. With our commissary department lashed upon the back of the patient Spilley, we trailed up through the head of the valley, out toward timber line, until nearly noon. At this time we were following the edge of a deep and heavily wooded cañon, our artist in the lead, *sans* camera, but equipped with his Marlin 45–70 by way of consolation.

The going was very rough and two of us, with the cayuse, had fallen pretty far to the rear, when we heard a shot from up in front, followed at the space of twenty seconds by another. Hurrying forward, as fast as we could get Spilley over the logs and through the bare pines, we found the other fellows complacently viewing the remains of a large black bear.

It seems, as Louis climbed onto a log and paused, raising on his knee, the bear came up over the edge of the cañon and, without seeing him, moved along toward him not twenty paces distant. With perfectly steady nerve, the converted camera cruiser placed 405 grains of lead through the bear's nose into his neck, killing him instantly. The second shot had been fired into his head, just to make sure that he was not playing possum. This bear was in very good condition, and bear steaks formed a welcome addition to our larder. He was in poor fur, however, and the hide could not be saved.

About the middle of the afternoon we came out into the bare upper country, between timber line and snow. Here our trail, if such it might be called, lay over beds of lava, sometimes fairly even, sometimes broken into great blocks, the interstices filled with pumice

and a little scant soil which sustained a few small herbs. Now and then was heard the long, clear whistle of our old friend, the hoary marmot, and occasionally we saw him at a distance scampering across the rocks. Other signs of life were few, and there prevailed that clear stillness which is found only in the rare altitudes above timber line and which has caused these regions so aptly to be called, "the country of the silence."

Toward night we descended a little and camped in the head of one of the coulées which draw into the cañons about the bases of these mountains. Early the next morning we pushed on again, working into a wilder and more forbidding country, scarred with bare cañons, which had been cut hundreds of feet deep by the waters of the glaciers which they have drained through the long centuries since the flight of years began. While crossing the bed of one of these cañons we came upon unmistakable signs of goat. Three or four ewes with kids had been through there early in the morning. Their tracks were easily discernible in the wet sand, and they had evidently come out of the timber at dawn and passed across to the higher benches of a peak which rose three or four thousand feet above us.

This was encouraging. None of us, barring John Davis, had ever killed, or even seen, a goat, and here were goats within two or three hours' travel, at most, from the spot where we stood. Late in the afternoon, just as we were going into camp, we saw, far up on the mountain, what at first appeared to be a couple of white rocks, but when they moved closer together we knew that they were the real thing which we had come to see.

In the morning we divided, John and Otis making for a spur on the west slope of the mountain, while the rest of us passed on to the northeast side. After an hour of the hardest kind of climbing, we reached a point of rock which jutted out, overlooking, on one side, the bare, steep slope of loose volcanic matter across which we had come, and on the other commanding a view of a sharp, crevice-like cut in the side of the mountain, the opposite cliff being somewhat lower than the point on which we stood. Here we remained for some hours.

At one time we thought we could hear distant shots, but finally ascribed the noise to falling rock. Late in the afternoon we cruised along around the mountain and then down into camp, without having seen a living thing the entire day. At camp, however, we found a different story. Otis had scored; he got goat, sure enough. Only a little one it was—a kid, in fact, we assured him—but a goat nevertheless. I have heard of a well-known sportsman who went goat-hunting, killed three or four goats, the heads and skins of which were preserved, all the time living on sowbelly and flapjacks, having no meat. He did not think that g o a t was g o o d to eat. Well, maybe it isn't, but if a n y b o d y tells you that Rocky Mountain kid isn't good to eat, don't you believe him. The meat of this kid suited us first rate. It was sort of a cross between mutton and venison, not at all the d r y, tasteless, tough

On the Trail

One of us

article which goat meat is g e n e r a l l y cracked u p to be.

J o h n and O t i s h a d worked up to a bench about sixteen hundred feet above the c a m p, when t h e y found

the very identical band of ewes and kids whose trail we had crossed the day before. John had made a long detour to get above them, and had, he firmly declared, killed a ewe, but could not find her, she having run a little way and fallen into some deep crevice in the rocks. The band started down the mountain and Otis opened fire, turning all but one kid, which passed down over a little ridge one hundred yards above him, he firing as it ran. Running up to this point, he looked over and saw the animal apparently leaning against a great boulder thirty yards distant, facing away from him. It occurred to him that the kid was wounded, and he conceived the brilliant idea of catching it alive, so he got the boulder between himself and the innocent object of his strategy and crawled up till he could make a spring around the rock and grab it by the legs. It was stone dead, having been hit by one of his shots while crossing the ridge, and had died leaning up against the rock with legs rigid. John Davis, who witnessed this tableau, related the minutest details with much flourish, and ceased not from that time forth to assure every one that Otis need hereafter carry no rifle on his goat hunts; he could "just catch 'em easy with his hands."

This was all the goat we had to show for four days' patient hunting, although we were satisfied that John had killed his ewe, by the sight of a flock of ravens, those croaking undertakers of the upper country, circling about that corner of the mountain.

The story of our hunt would be incomplete without some reference to our camp followers. Chief of these was Spilley, our little yellow cayuse, who, whether he looked at you with his pink eye or his blue eye, always looked the same demure, patient, abused little bargain-counter remnant that he was. But Spilley, like the famous singed cat, felt better than he looked, and he knew a great many things that some people who live long and useful lives never find out. He knew, to the fraction of an inch, just how far the pack bags stuck out from his sides, and we soon learned that if, in his judgment, it was not advisable to attempt a passage between two certain trees, it was best to let him go around, and whenever he started to make his way through an opening which appeared too narrow to his less intelligent human guide, he always came through with everything on and generally an inch to spare.

When he was cinched up in the morning, he knew just how to swell himself up, roll his eyes and groan in a manner that would have brought tears to the cheeks of an S. P. C. A. officer; and after you had gone away and left him cinched up in this fashion for five minutes, you could go back and throw a dog between him and his cinch without half trying. He was an expert in getting over logs. Instead of getting his front feet clear over, as a city horse would do, and then scraping his shins trying to bring up his rear guard, Spilley would put his front feet on top of the log and then clamber up with all fours, like a cat, jumping off on the other side. We became very much attached to him, and it was with genuine sorrow that we bade him good-bye and left him with his urbane owner, Monsieur Peppiet.

The Canada jays frequented our camp, watching for scraps of meat, while their more noisy blue-coated brethren flew about among the high tops of the firs.

Two glossy little chipmunks afforded us much pleasure by their comical games of tag back and forth about the camp, and we became very well acquainted with them indeed before we left. Such free life near to Nature's heart endears to one amazingly these dumb creatures.

There was another little contemptible winged insect, namely, the yellow jacket, which took the liveliest interest in our jerking venison and seemed to appreciate the spare scraps of meat hardly less than did the familiar whiskey jacks.

It has always been our rule on these hunts to imitate, as nearly as possible, the primitive savage, taking with us no extras and depending upon our own resources for everything but the merest necessities; in short, going right back to first principles. Even hats are tabooed much of the time after we quit civilization, and it is surprising how comfortable you can be, in all sorts of weather, without any head covering save that which Nature has provided.

The last morning finally came and with it Riley and his mustangs. Camp was broken; the last frying-pan was tied onto the pack, and, as we paused, before plunging into the thick forest, for a parting look across the little meadow, some one, in happy vein, pronounced a benediction upon the scene, in Shakespeare's lines:

" And this our life, exempt from public haunt,
  Finds tongues in trees, books in the running
      brooks,
  Sermons in stones and good in everything.
  I would not change it."

36.
BIG GAME HUNTING IN THE WILD WEST
(1888)

BIG GAME HUNTING IN THE WILD WEST.

BY THE LATE BRIGADIER-GENERAL RANDOLPH B. MARCY, U. S. A.

Author of "Prairie Traveler," "Thirty Years' Army Life on the Border," "Border Reminiscences," etc.

ROCKY MOUNTAIN GOATS AND SHEEP.

BY far the rarest mammal in America, with the exception of the musk-ox, is, probably, the mountain goat.

Its range is so circumscribed and so difficult of access to the naturalist or hunter, that its peculiarities and habits have been less observed or understood than those of any other game quadruped (excepting the musk-ox) upon this continent.

It is herbivorous; selecting its pasturage upon the loftiest and most inaccessible mountain peaks, where, in security, it crops the tender herbage contiguous to the perennial snows, and never descends to the lower valleys unless it be during the severest winter weather, when the deep snows cover its food upon the mountain tops and compels it to seek subsistence in the sheltered valleys, where it is hunted by the Indians, and occasionally with considerable slaughter.

Rocky Mountain goats are seldom gregarious, but roam in groups of four or five, and are so suspicious and watchful in their proclivities that it is difficult to approach them, unless they happen to be near cover. And, as their pasture-grounds generally border precipitous bluffs, if wounded by the hunter they are very likely to run or fall among rocks or into deep chasms where they are lost or cannot be reached.

Indeed, before hunting them I was assured by a veteran mountaineer that within his experience he had been unable to secure more than about one-tenth of those he had killed.

The range of this mountaineer extends from Northern Montana, through the western part of Oregon and Washington Territory, into Alaska and British Columbia, as far as the head of Mackenzie's River, and, before the Canadian Pacific Railroad was completed that far, they were quite abundant around the head-waters of the Saskatchewan River, in the vicinity of some of the Hudson Bay trading-posts. There are a few of these animals still remaining in the mountains around the head-waters of Sun River, above Fort Shaw, as well as upon the mountains bordering other tributaries of the Missouri, and some can be found near the head of Bitter Root River, where I hunted in 1885.

They are about the size of the domestic goat, and some of their propensities are analogous to those of that animal. They are both addicted to climbing upon rocky localities and are very sure-footed, but in most other respects they are different — in instincts, habits and appearance.

Several distinguished physiologists have classed this goat as belonging to the genus *Capra;* but more recent examinations have induced some naturalists to believe that in all its essential features and affinities it is an antelope, pertaining to the genus *Aplocerus,* which may be a correct scientific classification, but in its habits, features and affinities it differs materially from the prong-horned antelope of our prairies. The goat, for instance, has a much heavier, longer and finer double coating of silky wool, its horns are permanent and solid, while those of the antelope are deciduous; its figure and the contour of its head and body are as unlike as possible.

The mountain variety have short stocky legs, with feet admirably adapted to their

ROCKY MOUNTAIN GOAT.

alpine habitats, as they are provided with rubber-like soles or pads that are tough and elastic, somewhat like the frogs in horses' hoofs, which do not wear off and become flat, but permanently retain their convexity, which, with the tough, horny, but elastic exterior edge of the hoof, accommodates itself to the irregularities in rocky surfaces, and enables them to grip and hold on to the smoothest and most vertical slopes without slipping or falling.

They have an outer fleece of long, pendent, soft hair, and under this is a short, close coat of a silky texture, which is said to equal in fineness that of the Cashmere goat, and both coverings are as pure white as new-fallen snow, without the slightest intermingling of color.

Their horns are persistent, only about five inches long and one inch in diameter at the base, corrugated about half way from the head, and terminating in a smooth sharp-curved point, the whole coal black.

Although this animal has been known to the Hudson Bay Company's people for two hundred years, yet, in accordance with their exclusive policy of keeping all information concerning affairs within the vast area of their jurisdiction from the knowledge of the rest of the world, they have paid but little attention to natural history or any-

thing else save the acquisition of the enormous profits resulting from their fur traffic, which for one hundred and ten years amounted to one hundred per cent. per annum upon the par value of their stock.

According to Sir John Richardson they did, however (probably with the anticipation of enhancing the value of their assets), shortly after their first trading-post was established upon the Columbia River, send the wool of this goat to an expert for examination, under the direction of the Wernerian Society, of Edinburgh, and it was reported as being of great fineness and superior to that of the domestic sheep, in that it was wholly and uniformly fine, while that of the sheep was various in quality and texture on different parts of the same individual.

The first authentic account we had of the mountain goat was furnished by Lewis and Clarke, after their return from their wonderful exploratory journey to the Pacific Ocean, in 1804–5. They reported that the animal was found in many mountain localities, but in greater numbers upon the Pacific coast ranges passing the Columbia between the falls and the rapids.

The goat is doubtless the most fearless mammalian climber of the mountains.

Audubon says of him: " He wanders over the most precipitous rocks, and springs with great activity from crag to crag, feeding on the grasses, plants and mosses of the mountain sides, and seldom or never descends to the luxuriant valleys, like the Big Horn.

" He indeed resembles the wild goat of Europe, and is very difficult to procure. Now and then the hunter, after fatiguing and hazardous efforts, may reach a spot from whence his rifle will send a ball into the unsuspecting goat. Then he rises from his hands and knees, and taking deadly aim pulls the trigger, and at the crack of his rifle he sees the goat, in expiring struggles, reach the verge of a dizzy height and roll over and over, and disappear in a cloud of dust into the yawning abyss beneath, where a day's journey around the gorge would hardly suffice to bring an active man to where the bruised quarry lies."

For several years I heard so much about the difficulties of finding and stalking the rare and wary mountain goat, that my ambition was incited to attempt adding one of these animals to my stock of trophies, and I resolved to take advantage of the

STALKING THE MOUNTAIN GOAT.

first favorable opportunity that presented for gratifying this fervent aspiration.

In 1885, two friends, who were ardent sportsmen and had hunted with me several seasons in the Rocky Mountains, joined me, and about the first of September we left New York for Montana, *via* St. Paul and the Northern Pacific Railroad, and after crossing the "Great Continental Divide" above Helena, stopped at Missoula, a thriving town of about 2,500 people, near which there is a garrisoned post called Fort Missoula.

We were received here most kindly by the officers, who did all in their power to make our stay pleasant, and gave us all the information and assistance they could to aid us in our contemplated excursion into the mountains, and one of the officers, Lieutenant Thompson, a capital hunter and a most agreeable gentleman, was kind enough to offer to join our little party.

After enjoying the hospitality of the officers at that most delightful post, and making all preparations for a comfortable mountain excursion, we started out from the fort and traveled for two days up the Bitter Root Valley, which was quite densely settled by farmers, who produced abundant crops. When we reached a point where the mountains approached near the river and presented some quite lofty ranges

and peaks, the summits of which were capped with perpetual snow, we pitched our tents upon the river bank near the base of the mountains, on the summits of which our guide (a very respectable citizen of Missoula) informed us we would be tolerably certain to find goats and other large game.

The Bitter Root River at our camp was about eighty yards wide, with clear cold water, which issued from the adjacent snowy mountains and flowed with a swift current over a rocky bed that looked so favorable for trout that two of the party took out their tackle and proceeded to the rapids, from whence they returned in a short time with their creels filled with beautiful speckled trout of a large size, which had risen to their flies with most gratifying avidity and afforded a substantial addition to our larder.

The following morning we forded the river and drove to the outlet of a large cañon, in which we were to make our first efforts to find the mountain goats.

Our packing equipage was all overhauled and put in order that night, and early the next morning, after several of our unbroken broncos had balked, kicked and "bucked" for some time and not succeeding in extricating themselves from the tightly girthed *apparahoes*, had by suspending then their antics and beginning to graze, signified their willingness to give up the contest and go ahead, we started out, leaving a proper guard with the wagons.

Our route through the cañon led us over an exceedingly rough, rocky and tortuous Indian trail, along near the banks of a rapid, clear stream, which was shut in on both sides by elevated mountains, rising nearly vertically from their bases to an altitude of many hundred feet, some of them capped with perpetual snow, and it was near these white-caps that the guide expected to find the goats, but we did not discover any during the first day.

We bivouacked that night in the gorge, and the following morning continued on

espied, near the summit of a very lofty mountain, three goats that were grazing along near the snow-line, but they soon moved off from us over the crest of the sierra, and as their position was so difficult of access, in consequence of the abrupt intervening slope of the mountain, we did not think it worth while to attempt the ascent.

Once after this we saw two others, which two gentlemen of the party, going in different directions, undertook to reach by resorting to zigzag courses in scaling the steep acclivities.

One of them succeeded in getting a shot and killed his goat, but it rolled down the mountain over the rough and jagged rocks so far that when he found it, after a long

OUR PARTY IN CAMP WATCHES OUR ASCENT.

up the stream for several miles, when we heard an elk call in advance of us, and two of the party hurried on, and in a few minutes we heard two shots, which on reaching the place we ascertained were fired by the men ahead, who had killed a large bull elk; and this was the only large game we met with that day.

On the following morning, however, we

search, the body was so much mutilated that he did not think it worth preserving.

In returning to our permanent camp the next day, as I passed by the place where we had hung the elk meat, I saw upon the tree a pine-martin, which I shot; and as this was the first time I had ever met with one of these animals in the woods I was very glad to place it among my trophies.

We returned to camp after a hard ride the following day, not at all satisfied with the result of our extremely laborious excursion.

After this we moved our permanent camp to the outlet of another very long cañon, in which our guide was of the opinion we might be more successful than we had been in the other.

Mr. B——, one of our companions, was not well enough to make another rough jaunt at this time, but Dr. Seward, of Orange, N. J., and myself resolved to try the new cañon, and after getting our packs in proper order we set out with the guide and two soldiers up the tortuous windings of a narrow defile similar to that in the other cañon, but the ground more broken and difficult to traverse.

After about five miles we arrived near a small lake, where we saw some elk tracks, tolerably fresh, and stopped to lunch.

Shortly afterwards two country boys rode up, one about eighteen and the other probably fourteen years old. It appeared they had come out for a hunt, and seeing our tracks had followed on to join our party. They were bright, hardy fellows, armed with magazine rifles, and mounted upon good ponies.

As they came up the eldest boy said to me, "Where are you fellers going?" I replied: "We fellers are about making an excursion into these Alpine sierras for the purpose of bagging a few of those wary quadrupeds, the American chamois. Permit me to ask where you fellers are bound; are you also out on a sporting excursion?" To which the youngest made the abbreviated response of "You bet, ole pop!"

We did not invite them to join our party, but they continued on with us all the afternoon, and when we stopped to encamp for the night they also made their fire near us.

We had been in camp but a few minutes when our attention was drawn to three white spots near the summit of a lofty mountain spur directly in front of our camping-place, and on looking at them with a glass we discovered they were three white mountain goats, quietly grazing near the snow. Whereupon I resolved to make the attempt of reaching them, although it was then near sundown, and they were at least 2,000 feet above us. Accordingly, I directed the guide to leave his rifle behind and go with me, and in five minutes we were ascending the base of the acclivity, through trees and brush, toward the white

spots, and after we had made about one-third the distance they appeared more like live animals, and shortly afterwards we could see them plainly walking around while feeding.

When we reached the timber line we were about half-way up to them, but from this line the face of the mountain was bare and rocky, with here and there a few fissures or broken inequalities affording some little cover, but the slopes were so abrupt and smooth that we could not walk while standing upon our feet, and were obliged to crawl along upon our hands and knees. This method of stalking we found not only tardy but extremely irksome, as we were so much exposed that we had to carry our heads and bodies as near as possible to the rocks, in order to screen ourselves from the goats.

Besides, the altitude of our position was then so great that I found it difficult to breathe the attenuated atmosphere unless we moved very slow and halted often to relieve our breathing.

We continued on, however, until at length the goats seemed to have finished their suppers and laid themselves down upon the rocks for a *siesta*, after which we were not so much exposed to their observation, and in a few minutes, by cautious crawling, we succeeded in getting within moderate rifle range, I in advance and the guide directly behind me; but too much out of breath at that instant to hold my rifle steadily, I motioned the guide to keep quiet until I had recovered a little, when, aking deliberate aim at the most distant one that had likely got the wind of us and was running away, I fired, but shot over him.

I then turned the other barrel upon the next and shot it through the body, and quickly reloading shot the third; both the last staggered for a moment, then tumbled over and rolled down the mountain out of sight. The guide, at the last shot, slapped me on the shoulder, with the exclamation of "Hurrah for you, General!" Indeed I think he was fully as much if not more gratified at my success than I was myself.

We then took the trail of the two wounded goats, which were when shot some distance apart, and followed them down the mountain by the blood for about 200 yards, where we found them lying as evenly side by side as if they had been placed there by hand.

After disemboweling and hanging them up in a tree we hurried down to the camp, where we fortunately arrived just at dusk. If we had been much later we would have found it difficult to descend the abrupt, slippery mountain after dark.

The Doctor and soldiers had, with their glasses, watched all our movements, even to the hanging the carcasses upon the tree.

Early the next morning the soldiers and the oldest boy hunter climbed up and brought the sheep into camp, and their heads and skins are now in my trophy-room at Orange.

We ate some of the meat, but did not find it very palatable — nothing like as savory as the flesh of the mountain sheep or antelope.

In one of the reports upon explorations for the Pacific Railroad it is stated that the white goat of the Rocky Mountains is, in all essential features and affinities, a true antelope, having little in common with animals of the type of the domestic goat beyond what belongs to all ruminants of its family. Their jet-black, polished horns, upon both sexes, are small, short and uncinated, like those of their diminutive brethren of the Alps, the chamois, which, in fact, seem to connect the genus with the American antelope.

Major Long, in a communication to the Philadelphia Agricultural Society, said : " The mountain goat inhabits that portion of the Rocky Mountains between the 48th and 68th parallels of latitude."

Godman, in his natural history, says : " They are found in great numbers about the head-waters of the North Fork of the Columbia, also near the sources of the Marias, or Muddy, and on the Saskatchewan and Athabasca rivers."

FIVE distinct species of wild sheep have been recognized by naturalists as having their habitats within the different lofty mountain ranges of the world, namely : the Argali (*Ovis ammon*, Linn.), of Asia ; the Corsican Moufflon (*Ovis musimon*, Pal.); the African variety (*Ovis tragelephus*, Cuv.); the Burrhal (*Ovis burrhel*) of the upper Himalayas, and the American Big Horn, or Rocky Mountain Sheep, sometimes called the " Cimmeron " (*Ovis montana*, Cuv.), which is indigenous exclusively to our continent.

In this paper I only propose to present facts concerning the habits and peculiarities of the last-named species, with which my extended practical experience has made me thoroughly acquainted.

In view, however, of the coincident fact that the Argali of Siberia seems to approximate more nearly to the American Big Horn than any other foreign species, a brief notice of some of the most prominent characteristics of that animal appear important in this connection.

It is described by naturalists as being a conspicuously majestic and beautiful animal, nearly as large as an ox, with horns four feet in length and nineteen inches in circumference at the base, and other proportions of corresponding magnitude and symmetry.

Its strength, agility and fleetness are said to be astonishing for so large an animal.

Its feeding grounds are near the summits of the loftiest mountain ranges, and when disturbed it makes for the most broken and inaccessible crags, over which it skips with marvelous ease and celerity, where the hunter finds great difficulty in following it.

It is very true these characteristic traits assimilate very closely with those of the American Big Horn, but the latter animals do not always ascend to the tops of the higher mountains for their pasturage, as has been represented. Indeed, they generally graze in lower locations, as I will presently show.

The color of the adult ram is in the autumn a dark, rich brown, while that of the ewe is a lighter rufous grey, both sexes having a white disk upon the rump.

THE AMERICAN BIG HORN, OR ROCKY MOUNTAIN SHEEP.

Horns are common to both male and female ; they are transversely corrugated, and supported upon osseous piths or bases of exceeding tenacity and hardness, which gives them great strength for their butting encounters, and when they strike together in their fierce battles the sharp sonorous detonations can be heard for great distances.

Some have supposed that the bruises often found upon the front of the horns of the rams were caused by the animals jumping down the walls of cañons and alighting upon the horns instead of upon their feet. But I am confident this is erroneous, as, besides my own observations, I have questioned many old mountaineers upon this subject, and they all concurred in the opinion that there was no foundation for such a belief. Moreover, they said the Indians, who are the most acute observers of the habits and peculiarities of animals, had never witnessed any such magical achievements in lofty tumbling as that mentioned, but they were in perfect accord that the battered horns were the results of their fierce battles during the rutting seasons.

An average pair of horns upon a full-grown ram will weigh from 15 to 20 pounds, and measure from 12 to 14 inches around the base. I have several such in my collection, but I have one pair which surpass in dimensions any I ever saw, and measure 17⅛ inches in circumference where they come out of the head.

I was told by a friend that an Englishman in Wyoming had offered $500 for a pair of mountain sheep horns that would measure 18 inches. I think he was safe in offering this extravagant premium, as the only pair of horns I have ever known of that size were many years ago brought by Captain Stansbury, of the U. S. Engineers, from the Rocky Mountains, and as the animal is hunted so much nowadays, I do not believe any such giant appendages will ever again be found.

There has been some diversity of opinion concerning the habits of these animals among writers who perhaps have not hàd opportunities for observing their peculiarities within their native ranges. For example, several have represented them as resorting to and procuring their sustenance exclusively from near the summits of the loftiest mountain sierras, and that rarely, unless driven by severe winter storms, do they resort to lower localities.

This, however, is not in accordance with my experience deduced from close observation during eight seasons hunting within favorable localities, where I saw large numbers, under the most auspicious circumstances for studying their habits, and I seldom found them near the tops of elevated mountains ; on the contrary, they were generally near the lower rocky cañons, and grazed upon the adjacent slopes and valleys, but considerably beneath the altitudes of the higher peaks.

They are, like their domestic namesakes, decidedly gregarious, and when they have not been disturbed by the hunter, or by carnivorous quadrupeds, it is not uncommon to find ten or fifteen together ; and occasionally I have seen much larger flocks, composed of rams, ewes and lambs, and this during the September and October months.

They are persistently local in their proclivities, and after having been scattered by shots, or by fright, will soon return to their customary grazing grounds.

We hunted them in one locality on Sheep Creek, Wyoming, during several different seasons, and never but once failed to find them within a mile of the same place.

In one herd I counted twenty-nine, led off by two large rams ; and at another time I am confident I saw a flock of from eighty to one hundred, but I was so situated that I was unable to count them accurately.

When this large flock was first discovered I was upon a low spur of the Casper mountain range, with a companion whose keen eyesight enabled him to see upon the side of an opposite hill, about two miles distant, what he took to be a flock of Big Horns lying under a rocky ledge, and with the aid of our field-glass we could distinguish them plainly. As they had the wind of us we were obliged to make a very wide circuit to get upon the lee side of them, which, by smartly galloping our horses, we soon accomplished without disturbing the sheep.

Then tying our horses securely out of sight, we cautiously approached toward the game under cover of a rocky projection, and as we came near, we took off our caps and softly crept up and cast our eyes over the crest of the crag, expecting to find the sheep where we last saw them. But instead of this they had disappeared, probably having heard us, or taken the wind from us, and run around the hill ; and as their tracks indicated this, we hurried back to our horses, mounted, and galloped around upon the opposite side of the hill, hoping we might head them off as they came around; and when we reached a narrow defile, where we thought it probable

"AND I AFTER HIM AS FAST AS MY HORSE COULD RUN."

they might attempt to pass, we dismounted, and leaving our horses, walked noiselessly forward until we discovered the heads of the large flock of at least eighty mountain sheep, lying quietly down among the rocks about 150 yards off, whereupon we instantly dropped upon our hands and knees and crept cautiously forward until we secured a good position behind the rocks. Then, taking deliberate aim, we

fired together, at which the terrified flock jumped up, and not seeing where the shots came from, became confused and ran around in different directions, giving us good opportunities to make several other running shots which were effective; and when at last they ran out of range they left with us five of their number stretched out upon the ground before us.

Although this was during the rutting season, the flock embraced rams, ewes and lambs. The following season we shot seven more near the same ground.

At another time, our guide, Little Bat, after looking carefully in all directions from the crest of a high bluff bordering a deep, precipitous cañon, informed us that he saw one sheep lying down under a tree upon the slope of an adjacent gorge. I directed the glass to the spot and could discern the tree, but not the sheep, which he saw with the naked eye.

As these gorges were for the most part impassable for horses, we were, in order to reach the position of the sheep, compelled to traverse two or three miles around to head the one we were upon, which took us entirely out of sight of the sheep we were after, but our admirable guide led us direct to a spot overlooking the position of the wary Big Horn, and we secured him without difficulty. After which we started for camp, but had not gone far when another sheep leaped upon a high rock overhanging a deep cañon, and with its head raised to its highest limit, seemed to look me directly in the face and challenge me for an encounter. My shot knocked him over the rock, and he rolled several hundred feet into the bottom of the cañon, where he managed to get upon his feet again, but a second shot finished him, and we were about to move on again toward camp when twelve or fifteen more sheep made their appearance at the bottom of the gorge, out of which we shot five more, that fell among holes in the rocks, where we were unable to find them all. As we were, while firing, some six or eight hundred feet directly over the sheep, which obliged us to draw an almost vertical line of sight upon them, they did not at first discover us, and ran around in the utmost confusion and bewilderment, which afforded several easy shots before they became conscious of our presence above them.

At another time, while we were taking our lunch upon Sheep Creek, with our horses grazing around us, we suddenly heard a rattling in the rocks above us, and

mounting our horses, we took their trail and picked up four sheep that we had wounded, but they did not drop until they were some distance.

We each packed one of the animals upon our horses and returned to the lunching-place, quite well satisfied with the achievement. But as I pulled off the one from my horse the docile old beast turned and kicked me several feet, knocking me over violently, but fortunately did not hurt me seriously. He seemed much frightened at the appearance of the sheep as it was taken from his back.

One day, while hunting sheep in the Casper Mountains, I had the pleasure of witnessing a most striking illustration of the wonderful fleetness, sureness of foot, and muscular powers of that animal.

As I was riding slowly along over the crest of a cañon, I discovered a sheep directly in front of me, standing upon a

THE DOCILE OLD BRUTE TURNED AND KICKED ME.

soon a small flock of mountain sheep that had taken alarm at something, came rushing over the bluffs, and crossing the creek about 100 yards below us, came in sight as they ascended the hill upon the opposite side.

We seized our rifles and fired several times before they were out of range. Then

rock part-way down the gorge. I fired at him from my horse, and from his appearance supposed I had wounded him, but soon discovered my mistake, as he immediately started off at full speed over the hills, and I after him as fast as my horse could run. But he gained upon me, and turned into the cañon, taking the vertical slope diagonally down until he landed upon the upper edge of an immense smooth-faced rock, where I expected him to drop every instant, but instead of this the momentum acquired by his rapid flight carried him over the rock with lightning velocity, and when he reached the lower side I felt certain he would fall, still believing him severely wounded; but, making an astonishing upward leap, he landed upon another smooth rock, over which he slid in the same rapid manner as before, and thus he continued on until I lost sight of him.

It was certainly one of the most beautiful and intensely interesting exhibitions of animal strength and agility it had ever been my fortune to behold, and I enjoyed it exceedingly. Moreover, this was corroborative evidence of the opinion I had before entertained, that the flight of the Big Horn as he scaled the rocky gorges of his native habitat was sufficient to baffle all pursuit by man or horse.

The first well-authenticated mention made by any writer on this animal was by Father Picola, the first Catholic missionary to California, as early as in 1797. He said "they were a kind of deer with a sheep-like head, about as large as a calf one or two years old."

He adds, "I have eaten of these beasts; their flesh is very tender and delicious."

This animal was for a long time supposed to be identical with the Siberian Argali.

The eminent naturalist Baron Cuvier regarded it the same as the *Ovis ammon*, and in many respects their habits are closely analogous. He was of opinion that the Argali crossed Behring's Straits upon the ice, from which species originated the American Big Horn variety, so generally distributed over our territory.

Audubon does not concur in this, as he says our animal is considerably the largest; whereas other writers represent the Argali as being nearly as large as an ox, with horns four feet in length, which is much larger than any Big Horn found in this country: so that if Cuvier's theory is correct, the Argali must have degenerated considerably in our climate.

Mackenzie says that during his long sojourning and explorations in the northern part of British America he heard the species spoken of by the Indians as "white buffaloes," and Lewis and Clarke say that at one time during their protracted expedition in 1804, when provisions were scarce on the head-waters of the Missouri, they saw plenty of wild sheep, but found them too wild for successful hunting.

Now, the "white buffaloes" alluded to by Mackenzie could not have been mountain sheep, as this species is dark brown. But there is another species, the mountain goat, which is perfectly white, and is to this day more abundant in that section of country about the head-waters of the Saskatchewan and Mackenzie rivers, where Mackenzie spent a long time, and which were doubtless the animals referred to by the Indians.

Those spoken of by Lewis and Clarke may have been the mountain sheep or the mountain goat, as both varieties are still inhabiting the head-waters of the Missouri, where they passed and wintered.

37.
GRIZZLY BEAR LORE
(1902)

GRIZZLY BEAR LORE

By HENRY G. TINSLEY

OF ALL the beasts that roam the field —in America, at least—none has had anywhere nearly so much prominence in adventurous literature as the hulking, clumsy grizzly bear of the Rockies and the Sierras. He has been invaluable to the writers of the old-fashioned dime novels, and what a wealth of material his ferocity and prowess have furnished story tellers. Consider what almost infinite quantities of Western fiction have depended for thrills and hair raisings on a gory hand-to-hand struggle between the hero of the narrative and a fuming, gnashing grizzly bear.

It is less than a century since the grizzly bear *(Ursus horribilis)* was known outside the undiscovered West. The beast first became well known in 1816, when London made a great ado over the arrival of two enormous grizzly bears (" Mr. and Mrs. Martin ") sent by the Hudson's Bay Company as a gift to the English King. For weeks people flocked to see the new and savage beasts, confined in extra strong pits in the London Zoölogical Gardens. British writers of cheap fiction seized upon the American grizzly and his Indian and white hunters, away off in the solitary mountain fastnesses of the vast West, as rich material for building an original style of fictional adventures. Hunters and trappers for the Astor Fur Company, on the Pacific Coast, and others for the Hudson's Bay Company in British Columbia, occasionally came back to civilization from the wilds of the continent. Their stories of fearful tussles with powerful grizzlies and of the ferocity of the enraged beasts, were fresh supplies for the makers of the most salable fiction of the day—even if it was not so high class. For longer than a generation Luther Jenkins and Brigham Lawrence, of London, and Captain Mayne Reid, of New Orleans, kept at top notch the novel reading public's opinion of the prowess of the American grizzly. A score of other English writers of adventure have profited largely by their use of the grizzly bear as a most belligerent character among wild animals.

A commonly mooted point among hunters of big game in the West is whether the early hunters and trappers after the grizzly bear did not exaggerate Old Ephraim's ferocious ways, his terrifying aspect, and his extraordinary endurance, or whether the grizzly bear of to-day is a degenerate scion of a powerful sire. All hunters after western big game agree theer is a wide difference in temper, stature and ferocity between Old Ephraim as hunted to-day and the grizzled old fellow that used to appear in thrilling Western fiction, and of which Kit Carson, Jim Bridges, and other plainsmen told so thrillingly in other days. Some philosophic souls argue that early hunters had reason for magnifying the terrors of following after Old Ephraim. He was the biggest, fiercest, and ugliest beast they had ever tried conclusions with, and armed only with their crude weapons it was indeed a mortal risk to rouse his ire. The first pale-faced hunters who encountered grizzly bears were in the Lewis and Clark expedition up the Missouri River and across the unexplored region to the Columbia River. That was in 1804 and '06. In the official reports of the expedition are several paragraphs descriptive of the towering mien, the marvelous muscularity and the intense fierceness of grizzly bears. Later, when frontiersmen east of the Mississippi pushed across the river and over the prairies and plains, finally coming upon the Rocky Mountain grizzlies, the beasts must have seemed appalling big and terribly dangerous by the side of the biggest game the hunters had ever seen before.

Small wonder it is that the grizzly used to be considered marvelously invulnerable and tenacious of life. The bear hunters of fifty years ago were armed with a long, single-barreled, small-bored pea rifle, in which the bullets ran seventy to the pound. A modern thirty-two calibre rifle carries a slightly heavier ball than the rifles of the early bear hunters. The oldtime muzzle-loader was so crude and uncertain of fire that there is nothing with which to compare it in these days of breechloading repeaters, scientific ammunition, and fine adjustment of missiles to the bore. One may understand then what courage it must have taken to confront the biggest and savagest of American wild beasts, and run chances of inflicting a painful wound only, that would instantly transform the smarting grizzly into a concentrated bestial fury and vengeance. Captain Sutter, famous because the first gold discovery in California happened on his estate near Sacramento, has written that he has known a wounded grizzly bear to dash into the very faces of a party of hunters and to kill them all before they could escape.

Other veteran hunters insist that the ferocity and strength and tenacity of life in Old Ephraim has degenerated by his contact with mankind. They opine that several generations of grizzly bears have had bitter experiences with increasing numbers of rifle-carrying hunters, until the beasts have come to know that the days when they were ruthless, swaggering monarchs of hill and dale, forest or plain, have

passed and that man now hunts them with sure and deadly weapons. There are numerous reliable statements of grizzly bears having attacked men, but nowadays the grizzly does not seek out his human victims, as there are credible statements that his forefathers used to do. Neither does he lie in wait, and, pouncing upon a hunter, tear him into bloody shreds in delighted fiendishness, as the old time stories used to tell. The change in the grizzly's disposition is likened by veteran hunters to the change in the character of the white cousin of the grizzly, the polar

" He has the same broad head and the same broadness across the top as all other bears."

bear of the Arctics. When the stations for the Hudson's Bay Company were established, the diaries of the men there often referred to the fright of attacks by polar bears. Many a navigator in the Arctic seas has been clawed and chewed to death by polar bears. But for nearly a century the polar bear has not been regarded as so very fierce and nowadays it is looked upon as a cowardly beast. Association with armed men has modified the polar bear's disposition.

The hunter after grizzlies in these times must climb high up mountain sides, and have stout legs and more than usual

He is Double the Size of His Black Cousin, and His Paws, Teeth and Claws Are Very Much Larger and Stronger.

breathing capacity. The home of the grizzly is a cavern or shelter beneath a ledge far up a mountain. Civilization has driven the beast to higher altitudes and farther from the haunts of man. The Spanish lore of California abounds in stories of grizzly bears commonly seen in the valleys sixty and seventy years ago, while the diaries of the first American settlers in California and Oregon contain frequent references to grizzly bears that have slain or been slain in the pastures or along a stream in the valleys. As late as 1862, when Leland Stanford was Governor of California, a bounty of $10 was given by the State for each grizzly bear scalp, and several hunters each got more than a hundred scalps in one year. A party of five professional hunters spent a whole year in hunting for grizzlies only in Oregon in 1848, and they brought to Sutter's Fort at Sacramento over 700 pelts.

All grizzlies interbreed and this obliterates some characteristic marks of the several species. On the southern Pacific Coast the two gray species—the light and the mud grays—of grizzlies are closely allied. The light gray is seldom seen north of the forty-fifth parallel or as far east as the continental divide. It is the most common of all. The silver tip is the largest, and most hunters agree that it is quite the most formidable and dangerous of all the bear race. Its numbers have been severely decimated during the last half century, and nowadays it is only found among the highest and most solitary parts of the Rockies of British Columbia and northernmost United States. Once it roamed over the wilderness of the Northwest, in bands of ten and twelve. The original silver tips sprang from grizzly and brown bears, and they combine all the ferocity and prowess of the former with the agility and stubbornness of the latter. The Lewis and Clark expedition gave the world its first knowledge of the silver tip, and it is somewhat laughable now to read that the frightened hunters in the expedition believed they saw silver tip grizzlies that stood six feet high on all fours, and weighed even a ton or two each.

In form the grizzly is like all other members of the bear family. He has the same wabbly gait, the same little beady eyes, the same swaying of his head, accompanied by bellowing when he rages.

He has the same broad head and the same broadness across the top as all other bears. He is double the size of his black cousin, and his paws, teeth, and claws are much larger and stronger than in any other bears. The fur is abundant, coarse, and long. The species gets its name from the grizzled hue of the fur. In weight, mature grizzlies range from 800 to 1,300 pounds. The published statements of the finding of 1,800 pound bears do not have credence among veteran hunters. The famous grizzly bear that Henry ("Grizzly") Adams went about the West exhibiting thirty years ago, was an unusually large specimen, and it weighed 1,500 pounds.

Unwieldy and clumsy as the grizzly appears, it is at once quick in motion and of overpowering strength. It has been known to overtake a fleeing bison, beat and claw it to death, drag the 1,200-pound carcass several miles over boulders and through forest, and then dig a hole for burying the bloody mass until there was fit opportunity for devouring it. A grizzly bear killed a two-year-old cow on a ranch in the Sierra Nevadas a few years ago, and carried it eleven miles up a very steep mountain side, over crags and fallen trees, through dense brush and across several ragged gulches between 10 o'clock at night and next dawn.

In the old days of the Spanish occupation of California, a common amusement on fête days was a fight between a grizzly bear and a bull. Oldtime residents, who witnessed the barbarous contests, say that the grizzly came off victor. Some bears have dispatched five and six bulls in an afternoon. The maddened bear would always rise upon his hind legs as the attacking, bellowing bull, with head lowered, came prancing toward the grizzly. The bear would await the attack, then at a favorable moment, quick as a flash it would deal the bull a staggering blow between the eyes. This blow was sometimes so powerful that the bull dropped dead with a crushed skull. Anyhow, the blow from the bear's paw was always so heavy that the bull was groggy for a few minutes and stumbled on its forelegs. Meanwhile the grizzly would cling to the bull, striking its razor-like claws deep into the bovine flesh, while it bit and chewed the bull to death. At some of these Spanish contests bears have broken bulls' legs as if they were pine sticks.

"The best illustration I ever knew of a grizzly's powerful forearms and quickness of motion occurred at a bear and bull fight in San Gabriel, Cal., in the early forties," said Señor Don Aguilar recently. "In the excitement of the mortal fight between the beasts, a man accidentally fell over the railing to the floor of the pen below. In a second the big hulking bear dove from the bull straight at the man, striking one paw at his head. The man was literally and instantly scalped, and in a second more the grizzly had torn the man into a horrible mass.

"I have known young grizzly bears to carry carcasses of heifers," said Captain Dan Fuller, of Portland, Ore., "for more than fifteen miles just as fast as most men can run. Once I saw an old grizzly carrying a dead pig, weighing about 150 pounds, in its forepaws and mouth as easily as a boy would carry a cat. Three summers ago I was in the Coast Mountains and I saw a she grizzly bear carrying a yearling cow home to her cubs. I had a place on a mountain side where I could see every movement of the bear in the sparsely timbered valley before me. She carried the dead cow in her forepaws for about three miles, across sharp rocks, over logs, around the rocky mountain sides, where even a jackass could not get a foothold, to a narrow trail up the steep mountain. She never stopped to rest for a moment, but went right along. I followed her, and just about half a mile from her lair I laid her out."

The diet of this hulking, intractable despot of the mountains is the most elastic of any creature in natural history. No other beast has so many and such diverse varieties of foods as the grizzly. The omnivorous tastes of black and cinnamon bears are well known, but the grizzly relishes many more articles of diet. All kinds of fruit, grubs, some vegetables, and all kinds of flesh except human flesh are palatable to the beast. Old Ephraim will knock a cow or a horse down at one blow of his powerful forepaw, and tear the carcass to pieces, feeding upon it until he can scarcely walk. He dotes on acorns, fish, ants, and crickets. He eats peaches and apples with the same relish as pork, and he will run great risks with his car-

cass to feed upon a colt. He will go long miles and endure fatigue to lap wild honey from a tree. He loves a mess of field grubs, and he will eat watermelons and green corn by the bushel. He dotes on the entrails of deer, digs up and eats raw potatoes, and will risk his life to snatch a porker from a pig sty and go hastening home with it. He has a fondness for horse and mule meat, and he will climb trees, rob birds' nests and eat the eggs there. He can make a meal off a colony of ants, and he will sit for hours on the bank of a mountain stream and watch a chance to snatch a fish from the water. If the forest or the field do not furnish his food, he may turn with equal relish to the orchard, where he can devour plums and peaches. He will climb a fruit tree, and strip whole branches of ripe fruit with his huge paws and claws, and then on his way home will finish off the meal with a toad or a lizard. It is one of the anomalies of natural history that a great, ferocious, powerful half-ton beast like the grizzly, which delights in slaying an ox and stripping its bones clean, should find any satisfaction in lapping up insects and tiny vermin.

Even if there are no tracks visible, a veteran bear hunter knows well when a grizzly bear, anyhow several bears, have recently passed that way through a forest. A thousand and one things make that fact clear. Here and there are the bruised and bent limbs of trees where bruins have hauled down the limbs in search of birds' nests. There are tree trunks of rough bark where the bears have scratched their backs, bushes where the beasts have stripped away every berry, and oak trees beneath which every acorn has been carefully picked up. If there are any wild or orchard fruit trees in the locality, they surely bear the marks of a visit by grizzlies, if the beasts have been that way. Wide acres, where all stones the size of a man's head have been overturned by bears in their search for grubs and crickets, tell the story of bruin's meanderings. But the principal evidence of grizzly bruin's passage that way will be seen in the demolition of any ant hill in the locality. A grizzly loves to feed on ants. With a swoop of a forepaw he will tear away the dome of an ant mound. A network of galleries, inhabited by myriads of teeming ants is laid bare. The beast then pokes his great nose and mouth down into the open hill, and by inward breathing, like a huge suction pump, draws the whole ant population into his open maw. A half-dozen strong inward breaths and a grizzly bear will have drawn into his mouth and digestive apparatus every vestige of life in the greatest ant hill.

One would naturally think that an animal with such an extraordinary range of appetite and such a hearty one, too, would be the very easiest kind of lure into a baited trap. But the grizzly is really the most difficult game to catch. While black bears, panthers, cougars, are all comparatively easily trapped, the grizzly is the wariest of all about traps and guns. The lore of the hunters' camps in the Sierras abounds in anecdotes of the sagacity of grizzlies when traps have been laid for them. The entrails of deer and field mice are, strange as it may seem, generally the most tempting trap morsels, but these have no effect unless careful strategy is exercised by the trapper. A grizzly's scent is very keen. He has been known to smell a man even half a mile away, and he scents fresh meat farther than that.

"When we set our bear traps," said a veteran hunter to the writer, "we are always careful to leave nothing about the trap that will inform the beasts that human beings have been that way. I have known an old hat or a pair of shoes, carelessly left near a bear trap, to frighten away the animals. Several years ago when my partner and I were trapping and hunting bears and foxes in the Siskiyou Mountains in southern Oregon, we were after three big grizzlies that we knew went across an open field every few days. We rigged up a deadfall trap of timber, and we baited it with venison. We found next day that the bears had been there, had smelled, at a safe distance, at the baited trap. We next baited very carefully with honey and pork, and withdrew from the scene. The bears came that night and smelled and went away. Then we tried, one at a time, half a dozen other kinds of bait that had sometimes been useful in tempting bruins into our traps. But all without success. What made it most exasperating was the fact that we knew the grizzlies remained in that region, and came at night and at least sniffed at our

baits. We baited still once more, and just as we were about to leave the scene, I saw that we had carelessly left an old discarded pair of overalls in some bushes nearby the trap. We carried the old overalls away, and the next time we went to our traps we had a whopping big bear caught. Those overalls had shown the beasts that man had had something to do in placing the food there for them, and no delicacy could tempt them from their suspiciousness."

The vitality of a mature grizzly is almost beyond the belief of one who has had no hunting experience among them. Nearly every veteran hunter and trapper in the Western mountains tells his own pet anecdote of personal knowledge of Old Ephraim's marvelous vitality. Instances of the beast having traveled one or two hundred yards after having been shot straight through the heart are commonly related, and there are undoubted instances of grizzlies, shot even several times through the heart, and possessing enough vitality to still charge savagely at their attacker. Mason D. Edwards, once a State Senator in Oregon, has told how a grizzly bear, into whose heart he had shot four heavy rifle balls, still kept enough vitality to climb over fallen logs and dash through a dense chapparal, only to sink to the ground as it had tried to deal its hunter a blow with its forepaw.

Some one has called the black bear the comedian of the brute creation; the grizzly bear is a vindictive, dyspeptic creature. The Blackfeet Indians know him as "the great cross devil in fur." He has none of the fun-loving traits of his smart cousins. He is the meanest sort of a parent, and will even slay his own offspring, if the mother does not hide her progeny and stand guard over it until its infancy is passed. Very few grizzlies have ever been trained to do tricks like the common ones of black or cinnamon bears, and the only grizzlies that were ever trained for public performances were the two great beasts that accompanied "Grizzly" Adams from town to town in the far western country many years ago.

While the ferocity of the monarch of American wild beasts may have popularly been exaggerated, Old Ephraim is undoubtedly the most dangerous and formidable animal on this continent with which hunters have to reckon. The mountain camp lore of the West is full of stories of grizzly bears that have attacked men in sheer vengeance. There are some reliable stories among the oldtime hunters in the Rockies and Sierras of grizzly bears which have singly and alone charged upon groups of armed hunters, for some slight provocation, and have never desisted until they have clawed and chewed the hunters into shapeless masses of bleeding flesh. Kit Carson used to say that the grizzlies he and his comrades encountered in the West during the thirties were the most awful things ever known on four feet, beside which modern grizzlies are gentle and refined.

While the grizzly has no share in the clownish character of his little black cousin, there are occasions when he appears grotesquely humorous. One of these is when he is a fisher. The sight of the clumsy old fellow sitting solemnly on the bank of a mountain pool intently looking down into the water for hours at a time awaiting a chance to splash his big forepaw into the water and to catch an unwary fish in his sharp claws is always funny. Old Ephraim is no mean adept at fishing. If another and less thoughtful grizzly enters the pool, where the fisher is patiently watching and waiting, and roils it so that the fisher bruin cannot see his game, a gamut of growls and, quite likely, some blows result. Another funny situation for Old Ephraim to assume is robber of a honey tree. The grizzly, having located a hollow tree trunk in which his marvelously accurate smell has told him from a long way off that wild bees have stored honey, goes straight to the tree. Several taps with his long claws upon the bark inform bruin by the hollow sound, the exact location of the sweet store. No matter if a swarm of angry bees issue forth and sting him in many places at the same time, he does not desist in clawing and chewing a hole in the trunk. Then the grizzly thrusts his furry forepaw through the aperture and into the honeycomb. The sight of a big shaggy beast, with an enormous mouth, rudely thrusting a forepaw into the honeycomb and then licking the dripping, sticky liquid mass from his paw, while he savagely fights as best he can with his other paw a swarm of buzzing, stinging pestiferous bees, is one of the things hunters in the Western mountain camps laughingly describe.

The old saying in the West that " A man's a fool to go arter b'ar alone," was spoken of grizzly bear hunting. While Old Ephraim will seek every opportunity to escape from man, he is very quickly and unexpectedly transformed into an animated, crashing, and frightful automatic tornado. Hunting guides never permit tenderfeet, who go out to the mountains to hunt bears, to shoot a grizzly until a safe avenue of escape from an enraged beast is determined upon, in case the bullets do not kill. An experienced hunter knows before he aims what he will do and where he will go after the shot has been fired. A wounded bear will charge a battery of Gatling guns. The moment he feels pain, he becomes a horror in fur and claws. Rising on his two hind legs, with forepaws extended, head swaying from side to side, big red mouth open, uttering terrifying bellowings, the brute goes straight at his attacker. Only a wall of boulders can hold him back, and his death alone will check his efforts to get to tearing his enemy to pieces. And all this solely for vengeance, for a grizzly bear has never been known to eat human flesh. The bears that devoured the youths who made improper remarks concerning the bald pate of patriarchial Elisha were certainly not of the grizzly variety.

The most raging, dangerous mood of a grizzly bear is when one of its paws has been caught in a steel trap and the beast is maddened by pain and desperation. There can be scarcely anything in brutish anger more awing than this! The monster bellows and grunts; it gnashes its big teeth until it does not seem a sound tooth can be left in the jaws; it claws the earth with its three free paws, and it pounds the trap about frantically. If it can get the trap loose from the mooring chain, it goes crashing, smashing, bellowing through the forest with the clumsy trap on the foot. The agony of the tight grip of the trap on the caught paw increases every moment, and the bear bellows and roars the louder. Woe to the man who falls into a grizzly's clutches at such a time. One can scarcely imagine a more sanguinary fate at the claws of a brute. Once in a while the grizzly will tear and chew his paw loose from the gripping teeth of a steel trap, leaving the bleeding paw in the trap. Several bears with a pawless leg have been shot in Southern California.

In August, 1896, James B. Holmes, of Pasadena, Cal., was chatting with a hunting guide up among the Coast Range Mountains, in Kern county, in San Joaquin Valley, California. As they talked they heard a crackling of twigs behind them. "I believe it's deer," said Mr. Holmes. The guide said "no." A moment later the crackling became louder. Both men then thought surely deer were coming down the mountain side, and they leaped to their feet.

"They're deer, sure; look out," said Holmes softly.

Both men stepped aside and waited. Mr. Holmes had a rifle in his hands, and he and the guide stood watching the thicket above them, whence the crackling sound came. As they looked, the gray nose of a grizzly was protruded through the foliage, and Mr. Holmes and the guide stepped backward while they caught their breaths. Mr. Holmes is a crack shot, but he had never had experience with grizzlies. The nose of the bear made a fine mark, and Mr. Holmes raised his rifle to blaze away. He was about twenty yards from the bear. Just as he was going to fire there was more crackling of brush, and two other and larger grizzles thrust their heads through the thicket toward the men. The guide turned pale.

"For heaven's sake, don't shoot," he called. Mr. Holmes lowered his rifle.

"Run for the hill! Run for your life!" yelled the guide.

Mr. Holmes heard him yell "run!" but did not catch the instructions to go for the hill. Near the crest of the hill was a clump of trees and Mr. Holmes made a rush for them with the idea that he might find a hiding place or some place of shelter. The bears gave vent to frightful bellowings and went bounding over stones and chapparal after Mr. Holmes. He afterward said it was the most awful moment of his life. He stretched every nerve and exerted every muscle. The bellowings of the three grizzlies close behind told him there was one chance in a million for him to escape alive.

The bull grizzly bear was nearest. Just as Mr. Holmes felt the hot breath of this beast upon his hands, he resolved to do something desperate. He wheeled around quickly. The grizzly towered above him. He made a last effort to get his gun in position and fired. At that moment he was knocked down. The bull bear buried his teeth in his right leg just below the hip, tearing open the flesh. The pain was wellnigh killing. The female came up and made a vicious snap at his ribs, but only succeeded in grabbing his coat and driving her teeth through the cloth and through a pasteboard match box, igniting the matches. The female gave an angry roar, shook her head and snapped at Mr. Holmes' face, and he gave his head a feeble jerk. It was just in time. He heard the teeth snap in his face with a sound like that of closing a steel trap.

Mr. Holmes swooned. He was unconscious for three or four minutes, and then, slowly rising, reconnoitred the situation. He saw the bears with the cub trotting at their feet disappearing in the brush. Peeping over the brow of the hill he perceived the guide, pale and trembling. When he arose the guide sprang to his feet and rushed toward him, saying:

"Thank God, sir, you're alive. It's the narrowest squeeze I ever saw. The box of burning matches scared the bears off."

There is a deal of discussion among hunters after big game in the mountains concerning the sort of fathers and husbands grizzly bears make. The consensus of opinion seems to be that bruin is an unfaithful, heartless spouse, and a contemptible father. He will help Madame Bruin seek a cave or an opening in the rocks or mountain side, where their cubs may be born, and he will carry a dainty morsel, such as a sheep, a calf, or a part of a cow's carcass there for his mate's food. However, a few days after the cubs are born in the family circle, he will leave the home, probably never having any further acquaintance with his spouse and her offspring. Thereafter, Madame Bruin must make her own way and provide for her cubs. Unlike the black bear, which is a jolly, fun-loving father that rolls and frolics with his baby children, the male grizzly will have nothing to do with the cubs. Madame Grizzly and her children are companions for two summers and they hibernate, rolled together in a ball of fur for about one hundred days, during the coldest days of winter. The mother bear and her young travel far and wide—moving principally at night. Kit Carson said that the wide range of a family of healthy grizzlies in a summer season is almost incalculable. He had reason to know of a mother grizzly and her two cubs that once left their hibernating cave among the southern spur of the Rocky Mountains in New Mexico one spring in the forties, crossed Colorado and Wyoming, were seen in the mountains in Montana and were back in New Mexico again for another winter before the following October.

Nowadays the settlement of the West has curtailed the restless roaming habits of grizzlies.

The beasts are gregarious. Bands of fifty and more of them were frequently found in other days, when the animals were many and hunters were few. Sometimes a band of this size would be together for a month or two. Localities far removed from the presence of human beings, where berries grow in plenty, where the wild honey bee makes honey in an old hollow tree trunk, where an occasional excursion may be made to a ranch pig pen, and where there is a pool of water in a setting of mud, are ideal summering spots. When the bears have filled their stomachs with any of the large variety of foods to their liking, they will spend hours in rolling in the soft mud and shallow water. At such times the cubs are most playful, but veteran hunters all agree that a veteran male grizzly was never known to be sportive, and the mother grizzlies seldom romp and frolic with their young as all female felines and all other varieties of bears do.

The maternal instinct, however, is as strong in the she grizzly as in any other animal. There are numberless instances of mother bears giving up their lives to save their cubs from danger. Only recently the writer heard a hunter tell how a grizzly cub got in one of his steel bear traps, and how the mother came and clawed and bit and scratched at the vice-like jaws of the trap in a vain hope of freeing her young. When daylight came and the hunter, rifle in hand, approached, the mother grizzly, in her rage and her love for her cub, charged straight at the hunter and was shot down.

The cuteness—sagacity, some observers call it—of grizzly bears is shown in hundreds of different ways. The bear lore that is always retailed about a campfire of hunters and trappers in the mountains is filled with stories and observations of this sense, which seems to belong to grizzly bears alone among the great family of bruins. All hunters have had experiences in which they have been led many miles from camp, across mountains, over wide areas of boulders and through rocky canyons by some smart old grizzly that seemed to have a human mind in teasing the hunter along and at the same time adroitly keeping out of range of rifle when there was an opportunity for the pursuer to shoot. The bear that knows it is hunted and sees a chance to escape will do so every time. It will climb hastily into spots most inaccessible to a man, and when it has surveyed the field from behind a titanic boulder or in a dense chapparal, where the hunter cannot shoot, it will decide upon a course of escape. If there is a she bear in the band and her cubs are along, she will drive the little fellows on ahead a few feet and defend them in the rear. When bruin knows there is a chance for a bullet from a hunter's gun to come that way he will hasten as fast as possible, not stopping to rest until some protection is afforded from bullets by rocks or timber. Many she bears, in their anxiety to save their cubs, have been seen to pick them up in their forepaws and trudge clumsily along.

The sagacity of grizzly bears is very often shown by their manner of seeking food. A ranchman in the foothills of the San Bernardino Mountains a few years ago found that a little pig disappeared about every week from his pens. The print of bears' paws told what was carrying away the little porkers, but the pen was surrounded by such strong and high paling that the ranchman could not imagine how any beast ever got in there. An all-night watch showed him that a grizzly bear came that way, climbed a live oak tree that grew near, and, walking out on a branch that grew over the pig pen, dropped to the ground within the paling, snatched a terrified pig, and making for the gate, that could be opened from the inside only, hastened to the family den miles away up in the canyon.

38.
PRESIDENT ROOSEVELT'S
MISSISSIPPI
BEAR HUNT
(1903)

PRESIDENT ROOSEVELT'S MISSISSIPPI BEAR HUNT

By LINDSAY DENISON*

PHOTOGRAPHS BY THE AUTHOR

IN THE margin of so much of the chronicles of the present national administration as have to do with Mr. Roosevelt's recent bear hunt in Mississippi, common opinion has entered the comment that it was a failure. And surely it did seem like a failure when a hunter, who for years, as private citizen or public officer, had made his outings conspicuous by the luck and skill with which he brought down the big animals which were his particular pursuit, went with a special train and a considerable retinue into a land full of bears, only to return without having himself dealt out death to a single half-grown cub — without having burned a grain of powder. But down in the Yazoo delta, in Mississippi, the President's bear hunt will never be remembered as a failure.

"He got three bear," they will tell you in Sharkey County. So at the very outset it is necessary to appreciate fully that the Mississippi bear hunt proper is a communal and not an individual sport, and that the man for whom the hunt is organized is credited with all the killing done by his company and the pack. It was something of a blow to the sense of Southern hospitality — which is no stronger anywhere than in Sharkey County—to find that the President had a vigorous desire to kill a bear himself. It was even more of a blow to find, after this prejudice of the distinguished guest had been discovered, and a bear had been captured at least half-alive to await his pleasure, that he refused, with something very like scorn, to put the finishing bullet into it.

From the moment the President declined to act as executioner for a bear which was tied to a tree and was too much exhausted to stand on its feet, the Mississippi hunters made up their minds that it was almost beyond possi-

bility to meet the peculiar bent of Mr. Roosevelt as a sportsman. They regarded the entire expedition as abnormal; and, for that matter, it was.

Indeed, one of the leading Mississippi newspapers went so far as to announce, on the second day of Mr. Roosevelt's presence in the state, that he and his hosts had "outraged all the ethics of bear hunting" by arbitrary restriction of the membership of the hunting party. It must be acknowledged that this dread charge may have been inspired by the discovery that this particular newspaper's reporter was not to be permitted to follow at the President's heels from dawn to sunset as long as the camp lasted. But fairness compels the admission that the accusation had in it the warp and the woof of truth. The "ethics" of the traditional Yazoo delta bear hunt could hardly be made to conform with that privacy and safety which must hedge about any presidential diversion. Really, it is very difficult for a president to play. One is reminded of a Sunday morning, in the Little Sunflower camp, when the President rode off into the woods alone and without a gun, to rejoice himself with that luxury of solitude which a president enjoys more rarely than any citizen of these United States; he had hardly crossed the ford into the tangle beyond the river, when one of his hosts ordered Holt Collier, the negro guide, to follow and keep him in sight.

"I suppose," the President said afterward to a friend, "that the dear kind folks were afraid something would jump out of the woods and bite me."

The President's first invitation to join a Mississippi bear hunt came from Governor Longino, of Mississippi. He was informed that Governor Heard, of Louisiana, and some twenty or thirty other distinguished statesmen and planters and business men of Louisiana, Tennessee, and Mississippi, would

---

* Mr. Denison was one of three special correspondents to accompany the President's party.

The President.

President Roosevelt Fording the Little Sunflower River to Begin the Day's Hunt.

be of the party. With the most cordial desire to become acquainted with these representative southerners, the President could not bring himself to contemplate their invitation approvingly. It is even reported that he compared the prospect of the projected hunt to the leading of a charge of cavalry on a herd of cattle in the stockyards. As has been admitted before, there

wondering how he could go hunting down there without taking a great crowd along, to him came Stuyvesant Fish, president of the Illinois Central Railroad. Mr. Fish knows his railroad from Chicago to New Orleans, as well as the farmer's boy knows the path from the barn to the cow pasture. He knew all about the bear country. He knew bear hunters, and he then and there invited the Presi-

Holt Collier, the Famous Negro Scout, Guide, and Bear Hunter.

are some forms of sport against which Mr. Roosevelt seems to have an unreasoning prejudice.

But the invitation set him to reading over again Wade Hampton's chronicles of Mississippi black bear chasing. From them he gathered that there was still, fairly close at hand, an opportunity to enlarge his experience in hunting big game. While he was still

dent to enjoy a bear hunt without political complications, and without becoming one of an invading army in the swamps. The President accepted gladly. Mr. Fish wrote to Mr. John M. Parker, of New Orleans, a cotton factor, whom he knew had hunted in the delta. Mr. Parker wrote to E. C. Mangum, of Sharkey County, who owns and manages four cotton plantations on the edge

The Presidential Hunting Camp on the Little Sunflower.

of the bear cane brakes. Mr. Mangum wrote to Holt Collier, the negro guide, former Confederate scout and a marked character through all the delta; to Major George Helm, to Hugh Foote, and to Leroy Percy, all crack shots and all familar with jungle hunting, as every planter and Mississippi gentleman must be. Mr. Fish wrote to Judge Dickinson, the general solicitor of the railroad. Mr. Roosevelt, asked to invite a guest, sent for John McIlhenny, a young man of New Orleans, who had been under his command in Cuba. It was, of course, understood that the Secretary to the President, Mr. Cortelyou, and the President's surgeon, Dr. Lung, should accompany him. It will be seen, therefore, that with the sincerest desire in the world to keep down the membership of the party, there were already ten white men in it. What would have been the number if there had been forty hosts, most of them men whose political situation was such that they could not afford to alienate a friend by declining to issue an extra invitation, would require a census expert to determine.

Of course, the President cannot stir from Washington without a following of stenographers, for his own emergencies, and federal guards and press reporters. Only one stenographer went down to Mississippi, and he was left at the railroad to receive despatches at the telegraph station. As no anarchists or lunatics inhabit the Sunflower wildernesses, the federal guards likewise remained at the railroad. The number of reporters had been officially cut down to three, representing the three news agencies, which, between them, supply news to every newspaper in the world, and these three were furnished with passes to the camp, but necessarily made their headquarters at the telegraph station. The absence of the President in the woods makes it possible for wicked and malicious persons to make money in Wall Street by circulating false information of startling importance unless rumor is forestalled by the knowledge that the press associations are as closely in touch with the President as anybody can be, and will send out the first news concerning anything that he does and anything that may happen to him.

But against all the rest of the world, the road between Smedes' plantation and the Little Sunflower camp was guarded by negroes armed with repeating rifles. These pickets

were armed not only with guns, but with "white man's orders," which made the guns more than empty threats. This was demonstrated. A young man of Vicksburg contemptuously facing the muzzle of one of these rifles on the outskirts of the camp, remarked meaningly that it was a new thing in Sharkey County for a negro to presume to raise so much as his little finger against a white man.

"Dass all right," stammered black Wallace, trembling with a peril which he knew right well was not a whit less than that of the young man in front of him, "*but I done got mah ordahs fum white folks.*"

And the young man turned in his tracks, went back to Vicksburg, and wrote of "outraged ethics."

They told us at first that we would come to a horrible end, if we attempted to follow the trail to the camp without a guide. They told us painful stories of men lost in the jungle, with nothing but lizards and snails to eat and bayou water to drink. It was, to be sure, hardly as plainly a traveled road as Broadway, but we were unable to discover any reason why one wide enough awake to see a blazed tree a hundred feet ahead should ever lose himself on it. The road from the Smedes siding ran for four miles through Smedes and Kelso plantations, wide stretches of cotton-fields once picked over, but now white again with the opening of late maturing bolls. Back of the fields were the gaunt tracts of "deadened" timber, which defined the planter's next step into the frontier between swamp and cultivated land. Along the road, in the middle of the fields, and back in the "deadenings," were the white-washed cabins of the negroes. Now and then a black woman appeared at a cabin door. There were no men in sight, either about the houses or in the fields at work. They were all over at Smedes, standing along the siding, regarding the President's special train with awestruck eyes. Leaving the plantations, the road wound through four miles of open forest, carpeted with a brier tangle knee high, which made travel anywhere out of the trodden trail almost impossible. Here all the trunks were much darker in color for fifteen feet from the ground than they were above, showing the effect of the annual flood, which about Smedes is referred to only as the "Yazoo backwater." Explaining the marks on the trees, Jim, the guide, waxed eloquent in describing the prowess of a Mr. Hamilton, who used to hunt bears through these woods in boats in the backwater season.

Then came Coon Bayou, a four-mile-long mud gully, where the flood water caught and lay stagnant through all the summer and fall, attracting bear and deer and raccoons. A deer went trotting back into the bushes as we slid down the slimy incline into the bed of the bayou. A flock of mallard ducks rose with a roar of wings and a flash of white, fifty feet beyond. Scrambling up the other side, we were in the real delta swamp. Briers and creepers were knit together between tree trunks and saplings, so that it seemed as though a sickle or a scythe must have been necessary for one who would leave the trail. There were banks of brier tangle twenty and thirty feet high, and from fifty feet to an eighth of a mile in length, looming up in the forests on either side. Time and again there were places where the trail had been cut out with axes, like a tunnel, through the jungle. In another mile we were in the camp.

It was a simple enough camp. Four A tents in a row, on the edge of the slope down to the river; a big shelter tent for the negroes, back in the edge of the clearing; piles of fodder and bedding for the mules and horses tethered in a wide semi-circle between the two; in the middle of the open space a great cypress log, against which the camp-fire was built, and a bench burdened with water-pails and tin washbasins; at the end of the row of white men's tents another bench, the dining-table, just too high for a man to eat from in comfort if sitting, and just too low for one who would eat standing, and the cooking shanty; dogs everywhere, followed about by negroes armed with blacksnake whips, and shouting protests about the uttermost impossibility of teaching any four-footed creature the deference due to the President of the United States.

The river itself, on the bank of which stood the camp, is a fast-flowing, mud-banked stream. The water is quite clear, and, according to report, is full of small-mouthed bass, which it pleases the Sharkey County citizens to call "trout." The feverish anxiety of everybody in camp to make a bear face the President, however, was so intense that no one had any time for serious attention to fishing. Across the river was a jungle like that which hedged about the camp on the civili-

zation side, and extending for several miles over to the main Sunflower River. Into this jungle Holt Collier started his dogs.

They were a pack without monotony. Old Remus, who has been on his last hunt as often as Patti has made farewell tours, was a gaunt and clean limbed, if decrepit, beast, with a foxhound's body and a bloodhound's head. Then, there were more or less pureblooded foxhounds, plain "yaller dogs" of the conglomerate and unlimited variety that hangs about every negro cabin, and one lone "fice dog." One never sees "fice dogs" at a dog show, somehow, but the breed is plainly enough defined in the South, and is maintained with some purity. It is more like the Yorkshire terrier in conformation than any other breed; the color is usually a careless mixture of black, gray, and tawny yellow in varying proportions. There are invariably long, piratical whiskers hanging over the lower jaw, and if there was ever a fice dog of decent temper, his name has not been embalmed in tradition. That there was but one fice dog in Holt Collier's pack was a serious deficiency, because the bear hunter relies upon the fice to harry the bear and bite his flanks, and run away to bite again as soon as the bear has turned his head. Jocko, Holt's fice, was a valiant little scoundrel, but not equal to the emergency that confronted him the first time the pack came up with a bear. He fell, sorely wounded, in the conflict and was brought back to camp a helpless invalid. Thereafter none of the fights between dogs and bear were long enough sustained to allow the hunters time to catch up. Had there been ten more, or even five more, dogs like Jocko, there would have been no such opportunity as there has been for funny editorials.

But that was a great fight while it lasted; that fight with the first bear. The dogs had found his trail early in the morning, and had chased him four miles down the Little Sunflower and four miles back. It was a warm day, and the pace was fast. The bear was very, very tired. Because the bear was so far ahead of the dogs, and the President was not used to cane-brake riding, he was taken, against his protest that he wanted to ride with the dogs, to a spot past which Major Helm and Mr. Foote told him the bear must surely run. They waited there all the morning and late into the afternoon, while the tooting of the horns of Holt Collier and Mr. Parker, and the yapping and baying of the pack died out of hearing. Now and then they heard it again, but never apparently approaching them. At last they came back to lunch. When they had been gone from the spot two hours or more, though, the bear did return. It was a sorry return. He was wearied nearly to death, and was looking for a water hole. Behind him, in front of him, all around him, was the angry and frantic pack. Spurring his horse almost over him was Holt Collier, shouting and cursing.

"Gwan, you fool bear!" he yelled, "Gwan up a tree. Gwan up a tree, or I'll kick you up one!"

Now and then the grim, bearded, black face would be turned to Mr. Parker, who was riding close behind, and indignantly complain:

"Mr. Parker, sah, can't you please, sah, come forward an' tell dis yer bear in polite language dat he'll have some regyard for our feelin's and dat he is desired to get up a tree whilst we all goes and gets de Colonel?"

But the bear lacked all the instincts of true southern hospitality, and kept straight on to his water hole. He fairly fell into it when he found it. The dogs piled on top of him, Jocko first. There was a flashing confusion of black, hairy fore feet beating them off—of white teeth snapping here and there at the squirming mass; squeals of wrath and pain from the dogs were lifted in a deafening chorus. Then the bear rose straight up on his hind legs and stood waist deep in the water. In the grasp of his mighty fore legs he had a curly yellow cur that was Holt Collier's especial pet.

"Leggo mah dog, bear!" howled Holt, leaping from his saddle, rifle in hand. Bear and dog fell back into the muddy pool. Holt could not shoot without the risk of killing two or more of the pack, as well as the bear. He clubbed the rifle and leaped into the battle.

"Leggo mah dog!" he shouted again, and swung the stock of his gun through an arc that landed at the base of the bear's skull, and twisted the steel frame of the stock. The bear let go of the dog; but it was too late; the dog was dead. The bear, too, seemed to lack further interest in the proceedings; but he was not dead, and Holt tied a rope about him and dragged him up the edge of the pool and tied him to a tree. Five or six disabled dogs, including Jocko, were helped ashore. Then Holt sent a negro boy, who had come trailing after, running to camp to "tell the Colonel we done got de bear at bay an' are a' waitin' for him."

The close of the tragedy is now historic. Every newspaper reader knows how the President stopped short when he saw what was expected of him, and between laughter and indignation requested Mr. Parker to end the victim's life with a hunting knife. The President's hosts were very much chagrined.

"Why, sir," said one of them to me afterward, "if I'd had the slightest idea he was going to feel that way about it, sir, I'd 'a' had those ropes cut off that bear long before he came in sight."

After this unhappy experience the President begged in vain to be allowed to ride with those who were following the hounds. It wouldn't do, the old hunters told him. It wasn't the way. If he really wanted to meet a bear, while the bear was still enjoying complete energy and fighting capacity, he must put himself in the hands of one who could tell by experience which way the bear was going to run, and so head the beast off. For four days this plan was tried. The guide invariably guessed wrong. There were terrific rides through briers and tangles—rides which covered the face and hands with scratches, and almost dragged one from the saddle at every jump of the horse; there were nervous waits in the gloom of the woods, when the bear seemed to be coming straight to destruction. But every bear went the other way in the end. One cub, to be sure, was run down and killed by the dogs; another was chased nearly ten miles and killed by Tom McDougall, one of Mr. Mangum's clerks, when there were but three dogs left in the pursuing pack, and not another man within six miles. The others ran until they were safely away, for there were no Jockoes to stop them.

But even though he did not bring back a bearskin punctured with a bullet hole from his 30-30, and even though he had never a chance to bring the butt of the gun to his shoulder, Mr. Roosevelt and Mr. Fish, and those who accompanied them into the swamp, came out much richer than they went in. Aside from the complete freedom from official cares, and indeed, from a knowledge of what was going on in the rest of the world— that stenographer at Smedes was a most wise and valuable young man, and what little filtered through him went to Mr. Cortelyou and not to the President—there remained the memory of the long talks around the camp-fire at night, when Collier, sitting apart, as he felt that a dependent should, but speaking simply and fearlessly, as became one who knew, despite his color, he was no less of a man than any of the officials or planters or lawyers or brokers about him, told the wonderful story of his life as a "white man's negro"—how at white men's bidding he had killed white men and had gone unscathed; how he had met Union soldiers in hand-to-hand conflict; how he fought off a band of vigilantes that had planned to take his life without just cause. The homely figure of Swint Pope, cook and justice of the peace, stands out as he came to the dinner-table wiping his hands and asking Mr. Fish to excuse him for a moment while he went to the outposts and signed some papers which had been brought out to him from civilization, explaining: "They's some appeal bonds in some cases I decided against yo' railroad, suh." There was the memory of Swint's cooking, sweet potatoes fairly candied with their own sweetness, and pork gravies and turkey hashes, whose odors, floating through the wilderness, were a more certain recall signal to the hunters than all the horns ever taken from cows' heads. There was the instructive picture of Holt Collier and of some of the white men, too, dipping their horns into the water hole where the first bear had

died, and drinking their full of a purée of bear and dog and mud, all held in solution in water that had been standing for at least eight months. A northern bred man would have found such a dose a deadly sure summons to swamp fever. Then there was the wonderful privilege of meeting these gentlemen, typical of the modern South, with all the courtesy and consideration of the old days, and all the shrewdness and the positive progression of the new. It will be long, indeed, before any of the party forgets the frank conversations that passed up and down the line as they rode through the cool of the early morning, down bridle paths walled with hanging green, each man balancing a rifle on his hip, and the dogs ranging through the briers underfoot.

The President's bear hunt was a great success, even though it was a very different success from that which he may have anticipated when he accepted Mr. Fish's invitation. And Mr. Roosevelt was sufficiently initiated into the nature of Yazoo Delta hunting to declare that, before he is three years older, he will go back to the Little Sunflower, and, with Holt Collier as his only guide, will chase bears until he comes up with one and kills it, running free before the dogs. And then, he has declared, he will invite all his hosts of this last fall's hunt to come join him and be his guests, and, to the full bent of their kind hearts, protect him from dangers and hardships that he does not want to escape.

39.
DUCK SHOOTING
ON SAVANNAH RIVER
(1896)

OUTING.

MARCH, 1896.

DUCK SHOOTING ON SAVANNAH RIVER.

By "Dick Swiveller."

WITH December's opening week came the chosen date for a trip down the Savannah river after ducks, which my good friend Sam and I had promised ourselves, just as soon as business would allow us to get away.

We were admirably equipped, having a roomy tent, plenty of blankets, and an ingeniously arranged camp chest for holding needful provisions. There were, of course, numerous other things in the camp outfit to aid comfort, for when one walks in a boat he can carry many conveniences not found in a saddle or pedestrian outfit.

Two splendid boats had been provided; one a large bateau, to carry all the camp duffle; the other was used to shoot from and carry our ammunition and the "kit" containing changes of clothes and rubbers, for the duck shooter on the Savannah not only gets ducks, but occasionally duckings as well. The bateau was commanded by Nigger Joe, a prince of camp cooks, while Aleck, his black friend, guided the shooting craft skillfully down the current, past the bending willows under which the wild fowl are found and flushed at the approach of the boat.

This kind of sport is very exciting, giving the shooter great opportunities for scientific work in all directions for the second barrel, the first generally being used as the birds rise from the edge of the water presenting the sides of their bodies.

It was a crisp morning of white frost when old Sol peeped over the hills and found our boats launched on Horse creek, four miles from the Savannah, and one mile south of Augusta.

Concluding our first camp breakfast on the banks of the creek, we manned the boats and were whirled away on the swift current, the objective point being the mouth of the narrow stream where it empties into the historic Savannah river.

A little after twelve, Sandbar Ferry, on the Savannah, was reached, and we camped on the Georgia side. The wind had piped around to nor'east by nor', and the air was damp and penetrating. The boats were beached and securely fastened to a heavy stake driven in the ground. Well it was that this precaution was observed. Sam and I pitched the tent and stowed guns, ammunition and camp equipage inside, while Joe made an inspection of cooking utensils and began preparations for dinner. Aleck soon had a splendid fire blazing, and in an hour Joe had a good dinner ready and spread on the mess chest, which was so built as to convert the top into a table. Two small camp-stools were brought forth, and Sam and I pulled up to the board.

I had just finished my third waffle when—"scaip! scaip! scaip!" sounded the cry of a snipe.

We arose and, limbering up our guns, seized a dozen cartridges each of No. 10 shot, loaded for the woodcock we expected to find at Sisters' Ferry, a hundred miles south. We crossed over

Painted for OUTING by Hermann Simon.

"THE SKY WAS FULL OF THE FLYING."

the sand bar between the tent and a corn-field, from whence came the cry of *scolapax*. Climbing the rail-fence, we advanced but a short distance when three snipe arose. For three-quarters of an hour we had good sport, and returned to the camp with sixteen birds.

By five o'clock the rain had fairly set in, and bid fair to continue all night. We had hopes that the morning would dawn bright. All night it poured. I awoke two or three times and listened to the steady patter on the canvas, and at last would be lulled to sleep again with that feeling of security that comfortable quarters bring.

Daybreak revealed a dull leaden sky and steady rain; it was useless to go further until the storm abated, as it was, at least, one day's paddling to reach the shooting grounds; we therefore concluded to remain in our present camp until the clear-up. All day Thursday the downpour continued, and there was no intermission Thursday night or Friday. Friday, at about five P. M., we found the river coming up a little, but, as we were encamped at least fifty yards from the water, we had no grave apprehensions of being flooded out that morning.

Friday afternoon, bunches of ducks, mostly mallard, and a few black ducks, were marked winging their way south. Occasionally a phalanx of geese appeared high overhead bound for the shores of tropical islands. As the birds were en route with us we felt that in a day or so we might form a closer acquaintance with them.

Night shut down like the lid on a pot, amid a steady rain and moderately high wind; the latter had, however, cut around more to the west of north. So, snugly housed, we lounged and smoked until nine o'clock, when *taps* was sounded, the fire heaped up, lanterns extinguished, and, rolled in our blankets, we slept.

About two o'clock I heard my friend go out, but I immediately dozed off. A moment after he tore open the tent and shouted, in great alarm:

"Dick, for Heaven's sake get up, haul out Aleck and Joe; the river is within a hundred feet of the tent; I fear the boats will be lost—quick—quick, man, we must work for our lives!"

Sam started a big blaze at once. I yelled at the darkies, and as they did not move fast enough, I tramped over them, throwing on my clothes the while. The boys, being fully aroused, made a rush through the darkness and storm for the boats, while Sam and I struck the tent and began to pack.

"We can't reach de boats," came from the darkness, in Aleck's voice. For an instant Sam and I gazed at each other, then I seized a lantern in one hand and a faggot in the other and rushed toward the sound of the voice, and in water up to their waists found the negroes twenty feet from the boats and in dreadful fear of going further. The angry waters were coming higher with awful rapidity. I could just see one of the boats almost submerged by the pull down of the rope that fastened it to the stake. I made a rush that way—a heavy hand was laid on my shoulder, "Mars Dick, hit hain't yer time yit; yer doan' know these yer waters," and Aleck's powerful hand hurled me back. Something glittered in the torchlight, and Aleck made a spring for the boat with his hunting-knife in hand to cut the rope, but ran foul of the stake and found it quite loose. Springing in the shooting boat he threw to us a good sized coil of rope that lay at the bottom. I caught the coil, then the two brave men pulled up the stake. I ran in shore with my end of the rope, towing both boats and niggers to the sand. It was quick work and a brave act on the part of Aleck, for he risked his life in the plunge for the boat. Had his grip on the side of the boat broken he would have been swept away on the flood, out in the blackness and storm beyond help.

In the bright glare of the fire on the bank we literally tumbled our camp equipage into the boats in an incredibly short time. The water came on and up, curling over the sand, and when Sam boarded the bateau with his gun-case in one hand and the frying-pan in the other, I saw the flood extinguish the remnant of our fire.

We had two lanterns, giving but feeble light in the pitch darkness. As the boats floated they would be pushed on the sand until well grounded. This operation was repeated every few minutes, as the water rose rapidly. Before us was the goal that morning light would reveal in the shape of a corn-field bank; behind us, the angry river—almost certain death if we should miscalculate and push off into it. Several times I consulted my compass to be assured that we were headed for the bank and not veering southward down stream with a likelihood of being carried away.

The rain continued more or less until three o'clock and then ceased altogether. Presently we discerned a rift in the clouds, which broadened and increased until a star was seen by our wary eyes, then another and another, until at last we felt sure the storm had spent itself and a bright morning was in store for us.

We four mariners, soaked to the skin, hungry, weary with watching, looked on these heavenly signs with pleasure, and our spirits rose proportionately.

The boats were now near enough to the bank to permit our longest line to reach. We accordingly tied up, and all hands assisted Joe to prepare breakfast. Wood was close at hand, the hatchet quickly cut the heart out of a stick, and piling up a few splinters, a dry rag from my gun case, into which powder was rubbed, quickly ignited from the flame of the match, was applied under the little pile of splinters; small shavings were added, and soon the fire became a fact; wood in small pieces was added, then longer pieces, and behold the fire ready for Joe, his coffee-pot and frying-pan.

Warmed and cheered by a substantial breakfast, we stowed everything safely and comfortably in the boats, and as the sun came rolling up beyond the eastern forests, we cast loose from the shore, and were whirled south on the bosom of the flood. Aleck's paddle simply kept the boat's prow straight. Borne along on the swift current, the motion was exhilarating, and seated on top of the mess chest with my twelve-gauge in my lap, I enjoyed the scene. On and on we swept, passing great forests, far back into which, at some points, the high river could be seen, suggestive of hiding-places for duck; or again, near the shore, rounding the points under great limbs draped in funeral moss.

Boom ! Boom ! "Ha, there's Sam's ten-gauge."

"Mark to de left ahead ober de trees, Mars Dick."

A quick motion of the paddle, and the boat shot nearer the shore. Five mallard came swinging out toward the river, and in an instant they were forty yards away, almost overhead. I threw my gun to my face, and holding four feet ahead of the leader, pressed the trigger. Not waiting to see the result, I pulled the left barrel on another dimly seen through the smoke. He collapsed —killed clean.

"Missed wid yer fust."

"Yes ; I held too far ahead at that angle."

The mallard was retrieved, a fine, plump drake, insuring us a *morceau* of duck for dinner at least.

At eleven o'clock Silver Bluff was sighted, half a mile below, where we went into permanent camp until the river should fall a few feet, it being quite useless to look for ducks at such a high stage of water under the willows.

My friend had killed three mallard, two with his first barrel and one with the second. Joe began at once to dress the four birds for dinner, not any more than enough for two half-famished white men and two hungry negroes. Any one who has had any experience in the way of providing for the average Southern "dark," is well aware of his prodigious gastronomic organization and the amount of "rations" that can be stored in his apparently illimitable stomach.

Sam and myself were not at all dainty or dyspeptic, or inclined to mince over homeopathic doses from the top of that old camp chest. On these camp hunts it was generally a bird apiece and other things in proportion.

Sunday morning the river was booming and rising, making it unnecessary to try further down stream, even if we desired. The day was spent in drying the camp outfit thoroughly. The following day we had some good quail shooting in the immediate vicinity of camp. We were indebted for this to a gentleman living near, who kindly visited us and went with us, working a pair of pointers.

Thursday morning at daylight we cast off from the shore, Aleck at the paddle, Sam and I forward, with guns in our laps and cartridges handy. Two miles below camp we found a bunch of mallard. They were feeding under the willows, close to the water's edge. We marked them a moment before we were discovered, and when within about thirty yards they rose. My friend's gun thundered, while I arose from behind him and covered a bird that was climbing up through the timber and doubled him up.

"Mars Dick, mark to the right." I looked and saw a greenhead coming up the river, forty yards away, and at right angles to the line of fire. I held well ahead of him—he wilted in mid-air and tumbled over and over to the water in that style that carries peculiar pleasure to the sportsman when he realizes a clean kill. Four ducks were retrieved. Rounding a point a quarter of a mile further on, we flushed a bunch of teal not twenty yards away. There were probably a dozen or so in the flock. Sam killed three with his second barrel, and I made as fine a double as I could wish for. Two of the birds flew on either side of the boat and passed it up stream. They were too near to shoot in passing, but I faced about and killed the one to the left as he was making for the woods, and dropped the one on the right possibly forty-five yards away, and both birds fell to the water without a flutter. Shortly afterward, Sam's keen eye detected a bunch of black ducks floating in a small inlet or arm of the river. There was a tongue of land between us and this little bay, skirted on the right by the forests. The boat was quickly beached and my friend took to the woods, making a detour of some distance in order to get a shot. The black duck is very timid and wary. Sam approached with great caution, and well screened. Aleck and I watched with anxiety. Some moments passed, when the birds flushed and separated somewhat, but in a moment we saw two puffs of smoke and two of the birds pitched down to the water—a beautiful and scientific double and clean kill. Of the remaining ducks two of them separated and one came directly for our position. It was an exciting moment. Straight as a bullet he came, on swift, even pinion. The nigger held his breath as

the butt of the gun slipped to my shoulder, the muzzles caught the duck's breast and were carried up, and at that instant, when he was for a moment hid by the barrels, I pressed the trigger. I saw the bird pitch forward and downward, and the momentum carried him within arm's length of the boat. Aleck held him up and yelled, and an answering hurrah came from Sam, who had watched the shot. When my big friend came, we shook hands in exuberance of spirits. At the next point below, a solitary black duck flushed from the shore and was killed by Sam's second barrel. We judged this to be the last one of the four.

We made camp about five o'clock in a very good location on the Carolina side and were glad to reach the shore and stretch our cramped bodies and legs. My score book shows thirty-one ducks killed that day. Joe prepared us a fine dinner of mallard and teal, with baked potatoes, biscuits, waffles and coffee. Then came the soothing smoke, and through the curling wreaths the events of the day were discussed. What would camp be without tobacco ! What real solid comfort we find as, stretched on the blankets or seated before the cheery blaze, we rest, smoke and talk ! There are many possibilities in a day's shooting, resulting in a diversity of things to talk over, and under the influence of the pipe there is a pleasure added to conversation that mere words fail to describe.

In the morning I awoke and found Sam gone, and while listening to an animated discussion between Joe and Aleck, who were preparing breakfast, I heard the boom of a gun away off in the forest. "Who is that shooting, Joe ?"

"Recon hits Mars Sam; 'e said thar wuz powerful right smaat o' squirrel about yer; 'e bin gone right smaat time."

Twenty minutes later my companion returned with a half-dozen of what proved to be the toughest varmints that ever went into a hunter's pot. We threw them aside in disgust and finished our breakfast of broiled duck, which in most cases is good enough.

It was nearly noon, and we had but little shooting since ten o'clock. The boat was being paddled close to the

Carolina shore, when we heard, far away in the woods, "duck talk" from what seemed myriads of the birds. The water at this point had set far back, and the wild fowl were in there feasting on the acorns and mast. We forced the boat far back between the trees, and at last found our passage barred by a large fallen trunk. We could see hundreds of ducks away out of range; we were well "blinded," and had not been discovered. Still, there we sat feasting our eyes on mallard, blue-bill, broad-bill, and teal, not knowing how we would get a shot. Presently Joe and his bateau came to our signal. Joe was an old river man, and knew of a creek a short distance above that would permit the entrance of a boat.

"Yer see, Mars Sam, I'll jest teck de boat yous all is in, kase dat ain't so all fired heavy as dis yer one, an I'll go up the crick and meck a gran' sneak aroun' de raft o' duck, and easy like kome in on dem from de opersite side, an' all you smaat folks has to do is jist ter lay orful quiet an' saliwate 'em."

"Joe, you are a smart boy and the thing may work. Hustle in the boat, work carefully, and we will do our part," said I.

In a few minutes Joe disappeared, and we filled in the time eating lunch, smoking and watching the ducks far off in the forest. It was probably an hour and a half after Joe's departure when we noticed a perceptible movement among the fowl toward the open river. They came swimming very slowly in solid lines and great bunches. Thick masses were in our immediate front, and the long lines, rank on rank, extended far to the right and left of us. They came nearer and nearer; it was a great sight. In all my experience I had never beheld anything like it, and scarcely so great a number of ducks of so many varieties in one vast flock—a magnificent spectacle to the eye of the sportsman. We crouched low, guns ready and second guns handy. On came the birds, paddling away from the enemy far in their rear, loath to take wing in the thick woods and to leave good feeding grounds. Safe in the distance between them and the creeping bateau, but riding into the jaws of death, nearer and nearer approached the beautiful birds. "Sam," said I in a whisper, "Are you ready?"

One heart-breaking half minute. "Now!"—boom—boom—boom—boom! I caught my second gun. Earth, air and sky were full of the flying, whirling ducks; and such a roar and thunder of wings and confusion I will probably never witness again. The excitement was superb; and when the major part of the flock had winged their way out of the woods, ducks continued to get up here and there singly and in pairs, keeping us busy for the next two or three minutes. One fool mallard flew safe into the open; then in his blind excitement and fright flew back within five yards of the boat and, as he turned down the river, was killed by Sam. The battle was over, and our suppressed excitement gave out in broad smiles, and the yells of the darkies answering each other. We killed the cripples and gathered in sixteen fine birds. Crossing the river, camp was made.

Duck shooting on the Savannah has a charm that the sport offers in few other places. On this Southern river we float down, running point after point from one shore to the other, surprising bunches of ducks here and there, offering all kinds of shots. Then there are the constant changes of scenery and a new camp almost every night, and usually fine weather just cold enough to stir the blood, if the expedition is projected—say the middle of December. There are also points where a permanent camp can be made, in the vicinity of which good woodcock, quail and turkey shooting can be enjoyed.

When the trip is finished, you can simply wait for an up-river steamer, load boats and camp duds generally on board, and settle down to enjoy another phase of the trip, life on a Savannah river steamer, which, to the writer, is a constant source of amusement.

40.
A Glance at the Grouse
(1903)

A GLANCE AT THE GROUSE

By EDWYN SANDYS

DRAWINGS BY MARTIN JUSTICE.

THE fame of the game red bird oversea is too well known to require any comment here. Besides, in the matter of grouse, we have troubles not a few of our own. That the British bird is a grand fellow goes without saying, but the question if he be the head of his race from the sportsman's point of view, is quite another matter.

Enthusiastic mortals, who have been so fortunate as to enjoy fine sport upon carefully preserved moors, never weary of praising the British bird, and in justice to them, there is a deal of truth in their claims. Driving grouse finds no parallel among our sports. This is owing to the broad difference of conditions which govern sport here and in Great Britain. But let not the free American scoff at his British brother. John Bull, with all his peculiarities, is a mighty good fellow and a true sportsman withal, and, considering his opportunities, he quite frequently is a rattling good shot. If he does prefer an exceedingly heavy bag, sometimes secured in what some might term an exceedingly heavy way — that's *his* affair, not mine. I don't much fancy his grouse driving. I like to tramp far, to cover country, to see other things besides grouse, to enjoy the infinite variety of field-

"Another form of grouse-shooting is still-hunting, or trailing the birds on the snow."

shooting; but let not my readers for one moment imagine that I would sneer at the drive. Driven grouse, as a rule, go like the wind; they will carry a deal of shot, and only a master hand can score heavily.

Ahead of good dogs, the red grouse affords sport which, on favorable days,

who know the prairies at mid-autumn, and later, know our plains grouse at their best. The early season, as a rule, means sweltering days and fat, logy birds, which may flush from your very foot. This is the time when most sportsmen see our grouse in action, and I feel free to state that at this

"To slowly pace the length of this corridor

could hardly be surpassed. Our nearest approach to it is chicken-shooting on the plains. Both our sharp-tail and pinnated grouse are easier marks than the red fellow, and it is only toward the end of the season that our sport rises to the level of the other. And I say this in all fairness. Only those

time the birds are too easy to afford genuine pleasure to a *keen* sportsman.

But later in the season — ah! then it was different. There was grouse-shooting that *was* grouse-shooting, and the man who scored clean on half his birds was entitled to respect, even among good shots. Then come sweet, windless, Indian-summery days, when big, strong birds lie well. No more the lying to your boot, the unsteady, flustering flush, the meadow-lark-like flight. Grown shrewd and strong through much pursuit, big, hard-feathered fowl flush with a leap and a roar at half your gun's range, while fast, wide-ranging dogs beat the ground so far ahead that only a sharp lookout could promptly detect the long, impressive roading and the final confident pause. Two white spots on a distant slope told the story which the ponies, too, could read. A sharper gait, a sudden halt, a hasty dis-

while the good dogs wormed through the low cover."

and go steaming away as though Auld Hornie were at their fat sterns. Then only your quick man and your good gun can stop them, and when fairly cut down they hit the dry grass with a thump.

Many a time and oft have I ridden for miles behind a team of knowing ponies, mounting—perhaps, instead, a quick double from the rig, and, if you had held right, were near enough, and so on, you had the satisfaction of dropping one big bird; maybe two.

And the survivors? Away at electric speed over the grassy sea, perchance for a mile before they pitch to the shelter of some bluff. Then sport indeed, as you beat them up, singly if you be fortunate, in a bunch if Fate be unkind. And, in any event, you need not be afraid of shooting too straight, or too hard, for these fellows are ⸱ badly scared the second flush, and a scared old chicken is a mighty long way from a fricassee.

But there is another grouse, — gleam now the eyes and stir the pulse of sportsmen! — a brave, shy beauty, to whom pen of mine cannot do justice. This bird, the ruffed grouse, is by many considered the king of our feathered game. Nor is the grouse unworthy of the honor. While, to my notion, all things considered, the quail is our best game, I should feel like ranking the grouse an honorable second.

He is indeed a noble fellow. Beautiful in life, crafty and strong in eluding pursuit, and very palatable upon the board, he is all that a choice game bird should be. His sole fault is that there is hardly enough of him in any one place. His pursuit, except in a few favored localities, is a bit too uncertain to satisfy the average sportsman — too long between drinks, as it were. Yet I have seen ruffed grouse shooting which, in spots, was as full of action as quail-shooting. But such memorable occasions are rare. Perhaps a dozen times, during a shooting career of about a quarter of a century, it has been my blessed fortune to blunder into a red-hot ruffed grouse corner. I say "blunder" advisedly, for no man has a license to say when and where he will find such sport.

In the "popple" region of Michigan, in the beautiful glades of Wisconsin, in the flat forest lands of Western Ontario, in the northern wilds of that province, and in some covers of the Red River Valley, I have occasionally found grouse in numbers and in cover which rendered possible some really lively shooting. Among the picturesque Pennsylvania hills, too, if memory serves me aright, there were certain hasty things like ruffed grouse which slanted away down deep ravines in defiance of shot.

The grouse of the Pennsylvania hillsides is a problem to be tackled by that man who can with one arm perform two motions at the same instant. I am ambidextrous, but I did not greatly injure the Pennsylvania brand of grouse. I would scale a grand hillside, up and up, amid trees from which the foxgrape hung like living rigging. Now

and then would sound a booming whur-r and a glorious something would leap from the hillside and fairly dive for the brush so far below. Most of the time I shot at this something — shot behind it, above it, to one side of it, but, I suspect, never below it. Six, seven, eight times, this something roared and leaped and dived. The *ninth* time I happened to catch it full amidships. There was a gust of shattered feathers, and the something went a whirling down clear to the trout stream away below. I climbed down after it and eventually bagged a bouncing big grouse. After laboriously climbing all the way back again, I learned that there were no more birds on that particular hillside, so the bag consisted of one.

That sort of grouse-shooting is exactly the thing for those who love the exercise of the sport, and who dislike slaughter. I will cheerfully guarantee them all the exercise they can stagger home with, and this with no cruelty whatever and the minimum of slaughter. Out upon the slaughter of grouse under such conditions! It would be most reprehensible, and the man who could slaughter one-third of his birds ought to be made president!

But ruffed grouse shooting is not always like this. I can see a marvelous Wisconsin ravine, a winding corridor, hung with rich tapestry of painted leaves supported by close-standing columns, amid which the snowy birch gleams like marble. 'Tis an ancient roadway, and for two miles it runs between the misty hills. Beside it whispers a foamy rill with smiling pools, where elfin trout tilt at the larvæ clinging to floating leaves. Along the roadway proper the footing is smooth enough, but the path is narrowed by crowding briers, among which the ripe haws glow like points of flame. To slowly pace the length of this corridor while the good dog wormed through the low cover was an experience long to be remembered. Ruffed grouse love such places, and birds driven to the heights and not followed would, if flushed in the morning, surely work back by late afternoon. So I had two beats per day.

That sport was as good as any I have seen. About ten o'clock — there was no advantage in going earlier — I would begin operations. There were two large broods, and each appeared to have its own section of the cover. Owing to the nature of the ground most birds flushed slightly up the

His First Grouse.

sides, then darted into the corridor and hummed around the first curve, to pitch at uncertain points beyond. The first day the broods rose almost like quail. I got a double shot at the first, and a double and two singles at the second; but on the next visit, a few days later, the birds were strung all along the corridor, and only twice did two rise together.

Now, this was indeed a notable day. The dog knew the ground and worked as steadily as a clock, merely trotting from point to point. And there I was fit and keen, moving along what looked like a gigantic picture-gallery, while the dog drew from side to side as the scent led. A pause, and a grand bird would roar up amid a whorl of leaves, twist in his flight to buzz straight away a trifle higher than my head. Most of those that escaped owed their salvation to the fact that they happened to flush very near a bend in the corridor, around which they whisked too soon for accurate work.

One trip through settled the business until late afternoon. At the farther end I lay at ease, and smoked and talked with the dog until creeping shadows told that it was time for the return trip. Then again the measured advance, the beautiful dog work, the roaring flush, the clean kill, or miss, as the case happened to be. I did not fail too many times. The conditions were too favorable and the whole thing entirely too enjoyable to allow of any serious bungling.

This assuredly was grouse-shooting as one seldom enjoys it, yet had I been a bit wiser more of it would have been my reward. After having practically cleaned out this spot, I sought far and wide for others like it, and to a certain extent was successful. Sometime later I found myself near the corridor, and decided to beat through it on the chance of picking up a straggler. The leaves were nearly all down and the cover was a mere trifle.

Somewhat to my astonishment, the dog at once made game and presently a thunder-wing fellow rose at about thirty yards. I dropped him, and as he hit the brush, another and another bird rose and darted —not along the corridor, as heretofore, but straight up the bank and into the dense woods. As I advanced birds kept rising at long range, all but the few I succeeded in stopping going like mad for the woods. In the two miles I must have flushed nearly thirty, of which I got a half dozen, not one of which fell within thirty-five yards.

My neglecting the corridor for so long had been a serious error. It was a choice spot, and I should have remembered that what is good for one lot of birds will doubtless prove as attractive to others after the original tenants have been destroyed. While I was seeking other grounds the leaves fell and so changed the conditions that birds would no longer lie reasonably close.

There were other places — in Michigan. One was what the natives term the "popple" country — it offering what sportsmen of the eastern states would call easy brush-shooting. There were plenty of birds, too — fifteen to a gun being a good but by no means extraordinary bag. But my fairest Michigan memory is of another spot — a couple of hundred acres of easily rising ground — just enough slope to furnish life to a couple of sweet-voiced brooklets. All of this slope was snarled with briers and ringed by unbroken forest. To beat the open uphill, and stop the grand fellows as they stormed out of the brush and streaked away up the long slope, was a joy which would make a man forget his home, his wife, his ox, and his ass — in fine, every-thing that was his except dog and gun and the privilege of being on that ground!

Nor did that mine peter out. It was good for two days a week, because it was an ideal ruffed grouse ground, and the solemn woods all about held unnumbered birds in nearly absolute safety. The keenest of men and the truest of guns could do little in the heavy standing timber. Your grouse, in such a range, has a nasty habit of whisking behind the first convenient trunk and then keeping that trunk between himself and the gun until he has whizzed past the danger zone.

I tried the woods a few times, only to win vexation of spirit and almost deadly doses of disappointment. There is no fun in filling tree-trunks full of shot, and the birds almost invariably treed a couple of hundred yards away. To follow these, to crane one's neck till it hurt, to finally detect a bird sitting bolt upright upon some lofty limb and to deliberately pot the said bird on its perch, was at best a stupid performance. Away with it! Such work *might* be all right for a small rifle, but not for the gun. I will frankly admit having shot dozens of treed grouse, nor would I now hesitate to cut the head off a big fellow treed in cover which forbade a fair flying chance. In heavy woods, too, I will shoot a running bird without compunction—I have missed lots of them—but to deliberately start into a cover in which a flying shot would be the exception would hardly be interesting.

And there is another form of grouse shooting for which I confess a weakness. This is still-hunting, or trailing the birds on the snow. I'm afraid that sportsmen who scoff at this hardly understand the game. There is much more in it than meets the ordinary eye. You, of course, use no dog. When a new snow falls, the woods are like so much clean paper, and the furry and feathered folk are so many unintentional scribblers. To the man who knows, the scribbling is easy and most interesting reading. Here a woodmouse dotted along, dragging his tapered tail; yonder a hare passed at speed, scared by the red rascal that made these dog-like tracks. Small triangles show where squirrels have traveled from nest to storehouse, and larger triangles betray where the cottontails held conference till a soundless-winged owl broke up the meeting. Nor did it adjourn *sine die*—for one fat unfortunate *died* where you see that big mark. Alongside a log, in at a knot-hole, through the hollow and out at the end, run queer small prints in pairs. A snaky, white weasel left that sign, and if you carefully followed it, 'twould lead to the scene of a tragedy. By the stream are larger reproductions of these prints, where the mink has trailed the night long on murderous quest.

And here, amid the tan-leaved dwarf beeches, is something. Oho! The very sight of it makes you grasp the gun tighter, and you begin to peer ahead and to breathe a bit faster. Those trim prints running yonder in true line were made by a grouse. He may be twenty yards away, or anywhere, and you follow with beating heart and tense muscles. 'Twill be a rush and a roar and a glimpse of brown, and you know it.

What's this—the end of the track? Yes, and see yonder—Reynard was careless that time. The dainty trail ends with a few marks much farther apart and with streaks between. He ran to the takeoff.

Here is another grouse track leading to the clump of briers. Careful, now—it's fresh as—Look! Did you not see that brown thing dart from the stump to that tuft of dried fern and brush? Steady, now! he must be right there before you and he'll go straight away to——

"Whur-r-r!"—almost behind you.

"Why, how the dev"—? Bing!—Bang!

Good boy! The first load's in that maple fifteen yards from your nose, but the quick second did the business. As to how the— ahem! he got almost behind you when you had seen him directly in front—that's a way he has. He saw you as he ran and before he started to run, so he played a card which usually wins. Go get him, he's a beauty and stone dead.

What are you breathing so fast for and why do your eyes flash? 'Twas a thriller, and you know it, and you're prouder of that bird than you'd be of three killed over a dog.

A Pair of Mongrels.

41.
ANTELOPE HUNTING THIRTY YEARS AGO AND TODAY
(1903)

ANTELOPE HUNTING THIRTY YEARS AGO AND TO-DAY

By GEORGE BIRD GRINNELL

DRAWINGS BY CARL RUNGIUS

IT IS difficult for the man of to-day to realize the abundance of game in the West thirty or forty years ago. Up to the time of the building of the Union Pacific Railroad, and indeed for a few years after that, the great game of the plains was almost as numerous as it had ever been. Hitherto the larger herbiverous animals had been exposed to attack only by people who sought them for food, and the number destroyed for this purpose did not equal the annual increase. The Indians and the few white travelers through the country made practically no impression on the herds. In 1873 I hunted in eastern Nebraska, on the Cedar, a tributary of the Loup River, not more than 130 miles west of the city of Omaha, and saw a number of bands of elk. A little further to the west and south, buffalo were plenty, and antelope were everywhere abundant. In those days the three noticeable animals of the prairie in central Nebraska and further to the westward were the buffalo, the elk and the antelope. To the north and to the south of the Platte River these animals still abounded.

In those old times the antelope never seemed so numerous as the buffalo, the difference in size and color of the two beasts accounting in part for this. Nevertheless their numbers were very great; and on their winter range, where they gathered together in herds of hundreds, or even thousands, one received an impression of their numbers which in the present day we can never get.

In the old times the traveler over the plains was seldom out of sight of the antelope. As he passed over each swell of the prairie he was likely to see before him a little bunch which, as he approached, became alarmed and ran off to one side, to wait and watch until the travelers had passed along, and then to resume their feeding.

The antelope's curiosity has become proverbial and was a great danger to it. Though the most keen sighted of animals, it never seemed quite satisfied with what it saw, and often insisted on taking a closer look, until finally it ap-

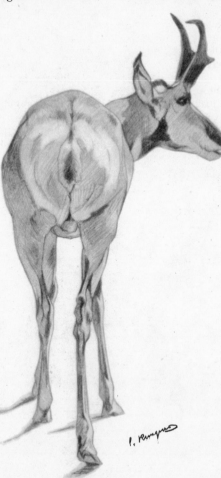

The antelope's curiosity has become proverbial.

proached within shot of the hunter. In early morning a tent or wagon would so puzzle a nearby antelope that it would walk up close to the strange object to discover what it was. On a number of occasions I have killed antelope from the camp, and again while stopping in the middle of the day to cook a little food have had them come to the hilltop, look for a time, and then gallop toward me until finally I killed one within forty yards of the fire over which the coffee pot was boiling.

When hunting one season in Colorado, the camp being absolutely out of meat, I set out one morning before daylight, on foot, to kill an antelope. No game was seen until, just as the sun was rising behind me, I walked up out of a ravine on a flat, and saw, about three hundred yards off, two buck antelope staring steadily at me. They looked, and looked, but did not seem alarmed. The distance was too great for a sure shot, and I decided to disregard them, hoping to find others within easy range. I walked up in plain sight, and toward the antelope, both of which stood looking at me. I continued to walk toward them, and they did not move, and at last when I was within a hundred yards of them I fired at the largest, and killed it. I have always believed that the

Doe, July.

antelope, which were looking directly at the sun, had no idea what sort of an animal it was that was approaching them. No doubt they recognized a moving figure, but no doubt, also, they were absolutely ignorant as to whether it was man, cow, or elk.

In somewhat the same way I have paddled up to deer feeding on the beach on the British Columbia coast, when the sun was low in the west and at my back. All the western deer, and the elk and buffalo as well, when unable to get scent of a strange object will stare at it long and carefully, striving to learn by the eye just what it is.

I learned to hunt from the Indians, or from men who themselves had been taught to hunt by the Indians, and usually have killed my antelope by stalking. I early learned that if meat was needed, the one quality necessary to secure it was patience. Often I have looked over a hill and seen a bunch of antelope feeding well out of range, and so stationed that there was no apparent way of approaching them ; but a study of their position usually showed that somewhere not far away there was a ravine or a hillock which would afford cover, and often an hour or two of waiting resulted in such a shifting of the lit-

Old Buck, in Rutting Season

White Fawn, October.

white hairs of the rump, so that the rump spot became much larger than usual, and after a little would let the hairs fall down to their normal position. The erection of the hairs seemed a sign of alarm. Now and then a doe would lie down, folding her slim legs under her very deliberately; but most of the animals continued to move about, and if they went a little way from one that had lain down, she stood up and followed them. Several times I thought the whole band were going to lie down well out of rifle shot, but they did not do so, and at last, when the sun began to decline toward the west they began to work nearer to the hill on which I lay. They did this very slowly, and an eager hunter might have grown weary of watching them; but I was well content with what I saw. Usually, the does seem to lead the band, the bucks following along behind, sometimes grazing, sometimes scratching heads and necks against a sage bush, or even pretending to fight it.

Gradually the old does worked nearer and nearer to where I was, until at last they were all within easy range. The bucks were still a little further than I liked, but after a time they also came within range, and I picked up my rifle, which had been lying by my side, and loaded it. Then I began to debate with myself whether or not I should kill one of these antelope. I had watched them so long that I really felt more or less in-

tle herd's position as to bring them into a situation where they could be approached.

It is but a few years since I had an experience of this kind. A bunch of antelope were accustomed to feed in a wide flat at the foot of a considerable mountain near the ranch, and one morning I rode in this direction, and when three-quarters of a mile from the place where the animals were to be looked for, crept up to the top of a ridge, and saw that they were in their usual place. Making a long round I rode under cover of another ridge to a pine-crowned ledge of rock above the antelope; but when I crept up to the top of the hill and looked over, I saw that they were far out of range, but feeding undisturbed. I had the whole day before me, and from my point of concealment I watched their movements. It was interesting to see the little band living their every-day life. There were several kids, half a dozen does, and a couple of bucks. They were safe and careless, yet always alert, and always graceful. The little kids were playful and quick, sometimes chasing one another here and there, again nibbling a bite of grass, or perhaps going close to the mother and lying down, only to rise again to their feet to resume their play. Sometimes when one was chasing the other, the one pursued would erect the

Young Buck, July.

Missed!

terested in each of the little band, and I inquired of myself whether it was worth while to shoot at and frighten them merely to satisfy myself that my hand and eye had not entirely lost their cunning. The more I thought of it the more I hesitated; and while I did not absolutely determine that I would not shoot at them, I put down the rifle, and took the cartridge from it. And then those absurd antelope, as if aware of my dubitation, kept coming closer and closer, climbing the hill toward me, until at length all the does but one lay down not more than forty yards from where I was. The bucks were still pottering around, and I felt a little like shooting one, but the meat was not actually needed; and at last, just before sunset, I backed away from my point of observation, went to my horse, cinched up the saddle, and, mounting, rode back to the house. I really have never regretted it.

Patience was called for when I killed the largest and fattest antelope I ever saw. This was in western Nebraska, on the range.

In the early days of cattle raising in the trans-Missouri country, the antelope fed in great numbers among the herds of cattle, as, since the beginning of time, they had fed among the buffalo; and in those days the few ranchmen, whose herds grazed on the prairies of Colorado and Nebraska, depended largely for their flesh food on the antelope. There were plenty of deer and elk, and occasionally a few buffalo to be had, but the antelope were the most abundant, and, in certain localities, the most easily killed of all the game of those prairies.

The killing of this big buck took place in the sandhill country of Nebraska, and gave me an early lesson as to the watchfulness of the antelope, the value of patience in hunting it, and the knowledge of its habits, which might be acquired by long practice.

With my friend, Captain North, the brother of Major Frank North, so famous twenty-five years ago as the white chief of the Pawnees, and the invincible leader of the Pawnee scouts, I was riding across a broad flat, beyond which high bluffs rose steeply. Suddenly against the sky line, above these bluffs, we saw rise, like two curving spider lines, the horns of a buck antelope, and my friend and I at once slipped from our saddles, on the side opposite the buck, and lying on the ground, permitted our horses to feed near us. The buck was a very large one, but there was no hope of approaching him so long as he remained where he was. I said this to Captain North, who replied that we were in no hurry, and might as well wait to see what the animal would do. The antelope stood there for some minutes, taking a long and careful survey of the country, dotted with feeding cattle and horses, and then, turning about, walked away from the edge of the bluff, out of sight. I asked my friend if it were worth while to try to creep up on him, in the hope that he had stopped not far away from the crest of the hill, but Mr. North said, "Let's wait a little longer and see what will happen." We had sat there perhaps ten minutes when the buck again appeared, and once more for a long time looked over the country. Then he disappeared again. This was repeated the third time, after a still longer interval, and when the animal went out of sight this time, Captain North said to me, "Now, go and see what you can do." I hurried across the flat, and climbed the side of the bluff, and when I peered over its edge through a bunch of weeds, I saw the old buck, head down, and apparently half asleep, chewing his cud, near a large doe. My shot was a lucky one, and the buck raced by me and down the steep bluff, and when I followed down where he had gone, I soon came upon him lying in the grass at the foot of the hill.

It long remained a deep mystery to me how Captain North knew that the antelope would come back to look twice and not three times, or how he knew that he would come a second time, after we saw him first. I know now that there was something in the animal's action when it withdrew the last time that told the practiced hunter what might be safely done. Although I had not then wit enough to observe it, I know now that the last time that the antelope went away from the edge of the bluff his lowered head and unconcerned walk showed that he was finally satisfied that no danger threatened from the flat, and that for the time he might leave that side unwatched.

While antelope were formerly so abundant that usually it made no great difference whether the man in need of meat got his shot early in the morning, or at midday, or in the afternoon, this was not always the case; and sometimes food was needed very badly. When hunting I commonly rode almost to the crest of each prairie swell and then dismounting, and removing the hat, advanced very slowly toward the ridge, stopping every two or three steps and carefully scrutinizing the ground that came in view be-

made except when their heads were down and they were feeding. Often his whole head might be in plain sight, and if, when the antelope looked at the hunter, he remained motionless, it would stare long and then put its head down and resume its feeding. There was thus often time to select the animal, and even to wait until it had put itself into the precise position desired. A side shot was always preferred, for there was then no danger of spoiling the meat, and I long ago learned

"Usually the does seem to lead the band, the bucks following along behind, sometimes grazing, sometimes scratching heads and necks."

yond the ridge. If an antelope was seen it was likely to be one of several, and the more there were in the bunch the greater likelihood that one of them would detect the hunter. After creeping forward as far as possible, the head was raised very slowly until it was so high that the eyes could cover much of the slope which began to fall away just beyond it. The important thing was to move very slowly, studying each foot of the ground as it appeared. If there were one or two antelope now in plain sight, no motion was

to shoot at the little curl of hair just back of the elbow, through which the black skin shows. As in most herbivores, the heart in the antelope lies low, and usually the creature drops to a well-placed ball. At the same time I have seen an antelope run four hundred yards with its heart torn to pieces.

If a man on foot suddenly comes in view of antelope not far off, and they see him, he may often bring them within shot by dropping immediately to the ground and lying flat. They see something—

they know not what—and after more or less running backward and forward and circling about are likely to come within range.

Everyone who has hunted antelope at all knows very well that after one of these animals has been startled and has run to the top of the hill to watch, it is useless to attempt to approach it. As soon as the hunter disappears from his sight, the antelope runs to another hill, and watches from there. On the other hand, I have several times killed antelope which were watching the wagon in which I was driving, by jumping from the wagon on the opposite side, lying flat for a time, and while the animal's attention was directed to the wagon I have been able to get under cover and within shot. In the same way I have occasionally, when riding with another man, dropped from my horse and let my companion go on with both horses, he holding the animal's attention until I had got under cover.

The hunter of course finds that no two sets of conditions which he has to meet are quite alike, and a good hunter will adapt himself readily to the necessities of any given case.

The antelope's tenacity of life, and his ability to escape pursuit, even when desperately wounded, is well known, and so many grewsome tales exemplifying this have been told that I will not add to the number.

Perhaps more remarkable shots have been made at antelope than at any other American game. This is natural, of course, since, being usually in plain sight, they were often shot at from great distances; and many a man, making a lucky guess at distance, and holding just right, has been enormously proud of a very long shot that killed. Of such long shots few were successful; but those that were so, often made for the rifleman who fired them a great—but wholly undeserved—reputation. I myself made the most extraordinary shot at an antelope that I ever heard of, which, however, has nothing to do with good shooting, but rather with the erratic course that a rifle ball may take. With several scouts, white men and Indians, I rode over a hill, to see three or four buck antelope spring to their feet, run a short distance, and then stop to look. I made a quick shot at one,

which dropped, and on going to him I found him not dead though desperately wounded. The animal had been standing, broad side on, his face toward my left. The ball had struck the left elbow, splintering the olecranon, passed through the brisket, broken the right humerus, turned at right angles, and gone back, cutting several ribs, broken the right femur, then turned again at right angles and came out through the inside of the leg, and struck the left hock joint, which it dislocated and twisted off, so that it hung by a very narrow string of hide. I never again expect to see so extraordinary a course for a rifle ball.

Antelope coursing, once a favorite sport in the West, especially at army posts, has, of course, passed out of existence with the passing of the game that was pursued. The antelope was the swiftest animal of the plains, yet among the antelope there is as much difference in speed and endurance as exists among horses. Some are swift and some slow; some long winded and some easily tired; so that, while some antelope could be readily overtaken by greyhounds or even horses, others were never approached. Perhaps the best record made by a greyhound was that of General Stanley's dog Gibbon which during the Yellowstone expedition of 1873 caught unaided twenty-one antelope.

The antelope is rapidly decreasing in numbers and is distinctly in danger of extermination. This danger is being recognized, and the statutes of several States forbid the killing of antelope.

In my time antelope were very abundant in the western Indian Territory, in Kansas, Nebraska, all of what was then Dakota, and to the westward. In the last three States, hundreds—often many hundreds—were seen in a day's march. Now they are practically exterminated from those States, except a very few in the dry country on the extreme western borders of each; but these survivors are to be numbered by hundreds—not more. In Montana, Wyoming, Colorado, and New Mexico there are still a few antelope, confined chiefly to the high dry portions devoted to range cattle. Similarly in Oregon, Nevada, Utah, and Arizona there are antelope, and no doubt a few in southern California; while in Texas, Mexico and lower California they are more numerous.

The Chrysanthemum.

California, Colorado, Idaho, Montana, New Mexico, the Dakotas, Oklahoma, Texas, and Utah protect the antelope, either unconditionally or for a term of years; the close time in New Mexico expiring in 1905. Curiously enough Kansas has no law on the antelope, although a few probably exist along her western borders. Besides this absolute protection, several States limit the number of antelope to be killed; Nebraska, which has a very few left in the northwestern corner, permitting one antelope and one deer, or two antelope or two deer, to be killed in a season. Nevada protects the female antelope, but permits the killing of three males. In Wyoming two antelope may be killed in each open season; in Manitoba two antelope in a season. The Northwest Territories, though limiting the killing to "three deer of any one species" in any one season, has no specific provision about the number of antelope to be killed in any season.

It is a hard matter to protect the species, for in regions where there are many antelope, there are not many men, and violations of the law are quite sure to go unpunished. However, it is not the rifle of the hunter that will exterminate the antelope, but another and greater danger. The radical remedy for the decrease is, however, obvious. If the United States Government will take up the matter and provide for the species' protection; if Congress will authorize the President to set aside, in such of the forest reservations as he may see fit, game refuges where no hunting shall be permitted, the antelope, and indeed all the other species of American large game whose fate is now trembling in the balance, may be preserved for all time. Surely the antelope, the only existing species of its extraordinary family, ought to be worth protecting. It has no near relatives, but stands alone among mammals. It is the one hollow-horned ruminant which sheds its hornsheaths, and if it shall become extinct the world will have lost not only a species, but a genus and a family, which nature has taken some millions of years to develop.

Except man, the only enemy that it need dread is the domestic sheep, which is now devastating the West, driving out the game, ruining the old horse and cattle ranges, exterminating the plants native to the country over which it passes, and leaving in its path a sandy or dusty waste, from which the wind picks up the soil powdered by the multitude of hoofs, carrying it away, and leaving only the rock and gravel behind. Over much of the western country the domestic sheep has driven the antelope from regions where it formerly abounded, and as the sheep press northward and eastward, the range of the antelope will necessarily become more and more contracted. It is to be hoped that the forest reservations which have been set aside will be protected by governmental order from the ravages of the sheep, and that within their limits the antelope may still have a chance to feed. And when, if ever, game refuges such as have been spoken of shall be set aside, each one should hold an ample territory suited to the life of the antelope.

No species of American game is likely to respond more easily to protection than the antelope. If it can be freed from persecution by man it will speedily re-establish itself. Its natural enemies are few, and if it has to contend only with them in its struggle for existence, it will survive and do well. It is most at home in many wide stretches of arid land where the farmers' fences can never interfere with it. It can live and thrive among the herds of cattle that feed upon these high plains, and the amount of grass that it consumes will never be large enough for it to be a menace to the stockman.

Female Fawn, July.

42.
WITH THE
IOWA CHICKENS
(1892)

Painted by Hy. S. Watson.

WITH THE IOWA CHICKENS.

"*Half a dozen birds buzzed away.*"

WITH THE IOWA CHICKENS.

BY ED. W. SANDYS.

IT was an eventful outing in more ways than one, and probably not one of the six who enjoyed it will forget the experience as long as he is able to swing the tapered tubes into position.

Like the famous "little cottage girl" we fancied that we should be able to say, "We are seven," but alas! when we met on the appointed evening in Milwaukee, instead of the seventh big-hearted friend who was going to share our luck, according to original intent, we received only a note—and not even a promissory note either! It ran as follows:

"Awful sorry. G. M.'s showed up and I can't possibly get away. Take the car and everything. I have made all arrangements and given necessary orders. Think of me when you're in the thick of it. Good luck! Yrs., UNDER-BRUSH."

Here was a pretty go, but there was no help for it. We knew right well that nothing but stern business could keep him from a shooting trip, so we six, with many expressions of sincere regret, boarded the private car and started.

It will not be necessary to dwell upon details of outfits. Our car was an excellent one and thoroughly well appointed, our *chef* a wizard, and each member of the party had his own favorite weapon. We had one dog — "Buster," a laverack of mighty fame, and the promise of a pointer to help with the work when we reached our destination, which, by the way, was Patterson, a small, open-faced town with grass side-whiskers, located somewhere in northwestern Iowa.

The members of the party may as well be briefly described as they appeared after dinner the first night, as we whizzed westward. From one corner of our parlor rose two mighty, aggressive streams of smoke, and somewhere behind the smoke were tangled up the Doctor and the Lawyer. Two inseparable chums and enthusiastic admirers of Nimrod; and what they didn't know about shooting would have filled the car and left enough over to load the whole train. Near them sat the Parson, above whose head rose the thin continuous thread of the connoisseur in smoke. These three formed, as it were, one side of the house, but the Parson didn't know quite as much about sport as his two cronies.

On the other side were ranged the Captain, the Brewer and the Scribe, or — as the Parson was given to calling them — "the world, the flesh and the other fellow." The Captain and the Scribe were the best shots and keenest sportsmen of the party, though the Brewer was by no means a bad performer a-field.

The first important event of the pilgrimage occurred at the boundary between Wisconsin and Iowa. The car was outfitted for a long siege, and the Brewer, fearing doubtless that the Parson's stock-in-trade might possibly become exhausted, had stored away a goodly stock of spiritual consolation, which he stoutly averred could knock the fiddle-strings off the Parson's brand, both for elevating influence and sure results. Just how all this pleasant accessory was to be got into Iowa's sinless prairie was rather an anxious problem as we neared Prairie du Chien.

The Brewer assumed all responsibility, and when at last an official of some kind appeared, the man of malt promptly took him in hand before he ever saw the inside of our house on wheels. We fancied that we saw the Brewer's hand slyly approach the side pocket of the official's coat as he said:

"Just a shooting-party, my dear sir; a few of the right sort going in to have a look at your noble prairies, and," he added in a tremendous whisper, "wealthy men, sir—liable to invest at any point that strikes their fancy!"

"Yes, that's all right; but I presume you people have a lot of liquor in that car, eh?"

"Nothing of the kind, my *dear* sir. Only a trifle for sickness. The great bulk of our stuff is *root beer.*"

"Root-beer?"

"Exactly, my *dear* sir. Allow me," and the Brewer stretched forth his hand again toward the stranger's pocket and lifted from it a small flask of our best brandy.

"Just the same as this that you carry yourself, sir—root beer, an excellent beverage; and he replaced the flask, while the official grinned knowingly and muttered: "Well, I'll be danged! But why do you call it root-beer?"

"'Cos we play roots with it. See?" and our car rolled away, bearing a much better satisfied party.

In due time we reached Patterson, and the car was safely sidetracked. We soon learned that chicken were abundant, and that we were certain of rattling good sport. The man who had promised to lend the pointer appeared with the dog early next morning, and gave us a long account of the brute's many virtues. It had been a good dog enough in its day, but showed every sign of age, so the Brewer, the Captain and the Scribe decided to stick to valiant Buster, and allow the professional gentlemen to shoot over the pointer, which, as they didn't know any better, they readily agreed to do; and so it came about that next morning the Captain and the Scribe started away over the prairie with Buster. The Brewer had a lazy fit and refused to join the morning shoot, and the learned trio arranged a little trip of their own, to try the new dog; the two parties to meet at about eleven at a farm-house some five miles away.

Buster was wild with delight at obtaining his freedom for an old-fashioned day's jaunt, and he sailed away over the grass in splendid form. Half a mile from the car he pinned a large covey of chicken, near some long grass, and a sportsman's eyes never looked upon a finer picture than the stanch black-and-white hero made. The background of rank grass served admirably to set off his shapely form and handsome coat, as he held his point nobly for good twenty minutes without a quiver.

The Captain and the Scribe both felt proud of their gallant friend as they carefully approached, and their eyes beamed with approval as the dog dropped like a flash as a big chicken burst with a thunderous roar of wings from the grass.

"Take him! load quick!" Bang! and the chicken went down in a cloud of feathers. Singly and by twos and threes, the birds flushed from about twenty square yards of cover, and the guns cracked as fast as two experts could pull triggers and shove in fresh shells. It was an illustration of perfect chicken shooting; birds getting up seconds apart, and affording just time enough for lightning work on the part of the sportsmen.

"Whurr—urr—burr! Bang—crack—bang—crack! Guns leaping to shoulders and dropping to be loaded like magic, and both men holding dead on and grassing their birds clean and well without a mistake.

Presently half a dozen birds, the last of the covey, roared up and buzzed away, and the two friends looked at each other and laughed loud, for it had been a fast thing and hot while it lasted, and honors were easy.

Buster, at the word, rose from his charge and bustled about, securing the fallen, and when men and dogs had completed their retrieving, ten grand chicken were piled together.

"By George! old chap, it's going to be a job, lugging these fellows about. We should have brought a buckboard—but aren't they beauties?"

"Best I ever saw so early in the season—but let's put 'em in the slings and beat on."

As anticipated, the weight of five fat birds to each man did not add to the comfort, but it couldn't be bettered, and they worked steadily toward the farm-house rendezvous.

Before half a mile had been covered Buster settled again on a beautiful point, and three more birds were grassed, one of the Scribe's requiring the second barrel to stop it.

The shooting was so good that long before the farm-house was reached Buster was ordered to heel, and the bag totaled twenty-one birds.

As the two entered the barn-yard

they beheld a spectacle which halted them in their tracks for two astonished minutes, and then, shocking though the the truth was, sent them into fits of laughter.

Near the center of the yard stood an old wooden pump and horse-trough; working the handle of the pump was the Lawyer, his face ashen with terror and his arms nervous with haste. Hard by, in an attitude of limp dejection, stood the Parson, goggling feebly at the horse-trough, in which lay the borrowed pointer half covered with water. Over the dog bent the Doctor, his face showing an agony of apprehension, and his hands busy rubbing and bathing the dog's body.

As the Captain and Scribe stared at this strange performance, the Doctor shouted: "Pump! pump! for God's sake, man, pump, or he'll croak!" at which the Lawyer worked the pump-handle so fast that it looked like a haze.

"Say, you fellows, whatever the mischief have you been up to? Has the old dog been sunstruck?"

The three started guiltily, and the look on their faces forestalled the dragging explanation: "No-o; Doc s–sh–ot him b–by mistake!" The scene, the tone of voice and the expressions of the men's faces were so utterly absurd that the Captain and the Scribe almost fell down for laughter, and, tragical though it was, the unfortunate dog added to the absurdity by raising his head when the laugh was loudest, giving a dismal howl, and promptly expiring.

It appeared that the dog had worked very well and at last pointed a covey. The Doctor was nearest, and when the birds flushed he got rattled and the gun exploded before it was at his shoulder, and the charge, or the greater portion of it, struck the poor old dog in the side.

There was no help for it; so the victim was buried, and for many a night afterward the trio were roasted unmercifully and frightened no end by the tales they were told of what the owner of the dog would do when he found out the truth. It may as well be explained here that the owner of the dog demanded five hundred dollars as compensation, but after considerable argument about the dog's age and limited usefulness, he compromised for an old French breech-loader which happened to be a

part of the car's outfit; and so the matter was amicably arranged. For ten long, happy days the car remained at Patterson, and the party enjoyed royal sport. More than one choice lot of birds was sent to friends, and at last the sportsmen realized that they had enough chicken-shooting for the present, and it was decided to have the car hauled into southeastern Dakota, where duck abound on countless lakes.

The season was too early for geese and swan, but they found duck so plentiful that it was difficult to avoid killing too many. At the first lake tried they had an experience with another borrowed dog, fortunately without serious results.

The Captain found track, in some mysterious manner, of a noted retriever, a spaniel, for which was claimed the honor of being the very best dog for duck in all Dakota. One evening the valiant Captain came to the car, leading the spaniel on chain, and he confided to the Scribe and the Brewer that he had secured a prize. Said he: "Just look at those ears and that coat! Thoroughbred, every hair of him; and as good as he's pretty. Here, 'Flash!'" and he shied a potato off into the grass. "Fetch it, good dog!" and Flash retrieved the potato in faultless fashion. Then the Captain further remarked: "Now, see here, you dog-killing mudheads; no shooting of this spaniel by accident. The man values him at a thousand, and I'm responsible. He's in my charge, to be used by me alone, and when you chaps get a lot of duck knocked down I'll bring Mr. Spaniel around and show you how a white man's dog retrieves; and I won't have to shoot him either!"

Next day every gun was posted on a long, narrow, very muddy lake, and tied to the cover at the Captain's side was the valuable spaniel. Duck were everywhere, and the Captain confided to his nearest neighbor, the Scribe, that he daren't let the dog loose with five guns blazing away, for fear of accident; but he would go round and have the dog gather in birds just as soon as a decent number had been knocked down.

The shooting was capital and the guns barked steadily for over an hour; the Captain and Scribe were in great form, and presently had about twenty dead duck floating on the water, while every now and then others were seen falling to the weapons of the quartet.

In time the flight ceased, and the Brewer, the Doctor, Lawyer and Parson came to the Captain's stand and suggested that, as so many duck were down, it would be a good scheme to have the spaniel secure them.

"All O. K.," said the gallant Captain. "We'll just have him retrieve the lot here first, and then put him to work on yours. Here, Flash, show your stuff!" And he released the dog.

"Fetch 'em, boy, good dog!" But Flash didn't move.

"Why, you dod-ratted fool! Get in there and bring 'em out!"

Still Flash didn't enthuse, and the crowd smiled shyly. The Captain looked warlike, but he picked up a root and hurled it into the water among a lot of dead duck. Like an arrow from a bow, the spaniel sped in and clove his way through the water. "Ha! ha! he didn't understand — now see 'im go!" exclaimed the Captain. "There's a swimmer for you!"

The Scribe watched an instant, then took the Captain's and his own gun and walked away to a safe distance, flung himself down and roared with uncontrollable mirth; for the spaniel coolly swam over half a dozen duck and brought back — the root!

One could have heard that party laugh clear to Milwaukee, but the spaniel would touch no duck. The Captain was wild, and if his gun had been in reach the spaniel's career would have ended then and there, but wiser counsel finally prevailed. Now, the Captain was game to the core, and after remarking, "Well, boys, the laugh's on me," he peeled off to his shooting-boots, and waded about for over an hour until everybody's game was safely landed, when he came ashore and remarked, "Keep that brute out of my sight, or I'll tamper with his brains. No more borrowed dog in mine!"

A week later the car rolled eastward, bearing a browned and happy party, but to this day any mention of borrowing a dog will cause a hearty guffaw.

43.
CARIBOU HUNTING
IN QUEBEC
(1895)

CARIBOU HUNTING IN QUEBEC.

By the late Edmund P. Rogers.

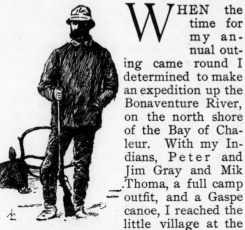

WHEN the time for my annual outing came round I determined to make an expedition up the Bonaventure River, on the north shore of the Bay of Chaleur. With my Indians, Peter and Jim Gray and Mik Thoma, a full camp outfit, and a Gaspe canoe, I reached the little village at the mouth of the river and secured quarters at Mons. Peletier's hostelrie, on the beach.

At roll call, next morning, Mik reported very drunk, he having somewhere in the night got hold of a bottle of "fire-water." This I had expected, as Mik always began work about two-thirds full. When he was in the woods, no better or more sober man could be found. I never had to conceal what little whiskey I carried, when once fairly started; on the contrary, I always gave him his "tot" with the rest.

After portaging the canoe and stores over to the river, we camped at night about twelve miles up. We put in the next day hunting over the blue-berry flats after bear, but those pests of the woods, the black flies (and strange as it seems, they are worse as you strike north), were so numerous, and my neck and face were so inflamed from their bites, that we concluded that no bear would repay us for the suffering. Even the Indians, accustomed as they were to the attacks of the insects, gave in, and we started on the back track. Evening found us again at Mons. Peletier's.

Fortunately a telegraph line passed through the village, and I wired to Campbellton for a tug, and to Mons. Horace, at St. Alexandre, to have teams ready Monday morning to portage canoe, stores, etc., over to St. Francis Lake. The little French operator was greatly excited over so many messages and their answers. She told me she had not taken in so much money in months.

At 8 o'clock, A. M., Sunday, we heard the tug's whistle, and, loading up our traps in a two-wheeled cart, we drove out to her. To our Yankee notions of navigation this appeared to be a strange procedure; but so shallow is the water, and so gradual the fall of the beach, that the cart is by far the handiest means of transportation. We reached our destination, St. Francis Lake, without further adventures.

We portaged to the foot of the lake, and, after engaging Michel and Ernest Blier and their dug-out, started down the St. Francis River, which forms the boundary line between Maine and Canada, and thence through Beau Lakes, the little St. John's and Four-mile Lake. All were lovely, with their studdings of islands and brightly-tinted shores. Duck were plentiful, and I shot enough to feed all hands.

Upon stopping to pick up my guide, Sandy Stripes, I found he was off "cruising" (i. e., hunting up good timber tracts), so I left word for him to join me as soon as he came in. We poled up the St. John's, through several swift rapids, and about midday we struck the mouth of the Allegash, where we stopped to "boil the kettle." While resting, to our surprise we saw, coming round a neighboring bend, two of the canvas canoes frequently used by the Maine hunters. The party included two young men from Cincinnati, Ohio, who had come from Moosehead Lake, and were bound down the St. John's.

After portaging round the Heavy Falls, some ten miles up, we bade adieu to Michel and his brother, as all was now plain sailing to Harvey's, where we intended camping. On the way I killed a nice lot of duck and a fine mess of trout. I also tried a shot at a deer crossing the river about four hundred yards off.

We concluded to put in some time here on Long Lake, caribou signs being encouraging. Deer and grouse were also plentiful. The Indians and settlers frequently kill the grouse with sticks or stones. The spruce partridge abounds here. Though not quite as large as the grouse, it is handsomer, the plumage being more decidedly marked, and the male bird having bright red wattles. The Indians call them "fool birds," so easily are they caught.

On one occasion, while paddling up the Bensacook Brook, we saw a male and two females on a small strip of beach. The male was parading up and down, with tail spread and wings sweeping the sand.

"You ketch 'em alive, Mr. Rogers," said Peter.

· Following his instructions, I placed the end of my trout-rod in the bowman's hand. He made a running noose in the line, which I passed over the bird's head. A yank brought him safely aboard. These grouse are not so palatable as the ruffed variety, the meat being brown and somewhat bitter from the spruce berry.

We made an expedition to McAuliffe Lake, which is surrounded with numerous barrens. Here we found the caribou roads at least six inches deep, and evidently used daily to and from water. While skirting the shore I saw a fine bull leisurely trotting along, some three hundred yards distant, and evidently oblivious of our presence. Peter decided to paddle closer in under the lee of a small island, which would put us within about one hundred and fifty yards of where the bull should pass. This was successfully accomplished, and we watched his progress as he moved down the trail, disappearing for a moment or so in the clumps of balsam that dotted the barren.

"Peter, I fear we will lose him. Had I better not chance it ?"

"No; he come near when he cross creek."

And so it proved. He easily cleared the creek by a jump of about twelve feet.

"Now, give him shoot," said Peter.

Standing up in the canoe I cut loose. At the report the bull stopped short, with head erect and pointed ears. He was evidently endeavoring to wind the source of the noise. I fired a second shot, and when the smoke blew to leeward I could see nothing.

"You got 'im," yelled the men, as they sent the canoe flying for the shore. The ball, a 50-express, had broken his neck at a clean one hundred and fifty yards. This was a satisfactory result of a standing-up shot in a frail canoe. He had a fine head, with brow points almost crossing each other. His coat was a beautiful mouse color, verging into pure white at his neck, and he had a fine bell—*i. e.*, long, hanging white hair under the throat. His head I see at this writing, and his fur coat has protected me in many a succeeding raid.

The next day a fine bull actually charged through the camp, but was off before I could reach my rifle. A few evenings after another came to Sandy's call, and we could hear his short, sharp bark, a quarter of a mile off, but drawing each minute nearer. Crouching near the canoe, with rifle at ready, we watched the beach. One of the Indians whispered, "There he come ;" but though we could hear him, we could not place him under the shadow of the bank. At last I made him out, or rather a moving dark mass now close to us. Aiming as near as I could judge for his shoulder, I fired, and heard the thud of the ball as it struck. We ran to the spot, and soon saw, by the trail of blood, that he was hard hit. We followed the trail on the sand till the tracks turned into the woods, then we decided to defer further search till morning. We took up the trail at sunrise, and soon discovered where the bull had lain upon a bed of blood-soaked leaves. We now felt assured that he was not far off; and so it proved a little later. A shout from Sandy drew us to the spot where lay our quarry, stiff in death. He had only a fair head.

To me this style of night hunting has no attraction. Its sole pleasure is the paddling for miles through these lovely lakes, the intense stillness, broken only by the weird call of Peter or Sandy, and the excitement (that is natural) of the answering bellow. I have known as many as five bulls to be called down in a week, and all circled round us without offering a shot that could be relied on. Far more satisfactory and exciting is the stalking on a crisp October day, with the track of your game showing plainly on the few inches of snow.

We decided to start for the settlement, and were soon once more near Beau Lake. As we entered its south end I heard a hail, "Are you Mr. Rogers?" Upon my answering, the man added, "Sorry not to see you as you went down; could have shown you lots of caribou." I consulted with Peter, and he advised me to put in a day, as our new friend, old McDonald, was a first-rate scout. He led us about nine miles back from the lake, to some excellent ground.

We began to hunt at daybreak, and about noon we were on the summit of Beau Mountain, having seen several bunches of cows on the route. We had something to eat, and then Peter tried a call. Like an echo came a response from some bull, and we crouched and waited. In a few minutes I saw a pair of horns towering over the bushes. Stepping to the left I discovered him, head on, his white, massive neck showing plainly through the brush. I took a careful aim and fired, but with no apparent result. Peter called again, and the bull uttered savage grunts, moved some ten yards, and again came to a stand. I now had him in plain view, broadside on, and tumbled him in his tracks. He was a noble brute, weighing some five hundred pounds, and having enormous branching antlers. The brow-points almost reached his nose before turning up, and both they and the main branches ended in broad and perfect palmations. Shocking to relate, we three old duffers, two of us well past sixty years, joined hands and performed a vigorous war dance around our prize.

"Mr. Rogers," said Mac, "I will bet all this fall crop you have the finest head in the United States."

It was indeed a noble head, and now hangs on the walls of Crumwold Hall, among the many trophies of elk, bear, mountain sheep, moose and deer, that have fallen to the rifles of my son, Archy Rogers, and myself.

44.
THE WHITETAILED VIRGINIA DEER AND ITS KIN
(1906)

Crouching Whitetail Fawn.
From a photograph by Elwin R. Sanborn.

THE WHITETAILED (VIRGINIA) DEER AND ITS KIN

ODOCOILEUS AMERICANUS (ERXLEBEN, 1777)

BY ERNEST THOMPSON SETON

ILLUSTRATIONS BY THE AUTHOR

NE Thomas Hariot, an English mathematician in the service of Sir Walter Raleigh, visited Virginia in 1584, and in his account of the Colony (pub. 1588) he says: "Of Beastes"—"Deare, in some places there are great store; neere into the sea-coast, they are of the ordinairie bignes as ours in England, & some less; but further up in the countrey where there is better feed, they are greater. They differ from ours only in this, their tailes are longer, and the snags of their hornes look backwards."

There is no doubt that Cartier saw the Whitetail in 1535, but Master Hariot, the mathematician, has given us the first identifiable description of the species, and it is by good right called Virginia Deer.

In speaking of it the early travellers use expressions that tell of astounding numbers. Thus Cartier's "great stores of Stags, Deere," etc., Hariot's "great store." Mor-ton, writing of New England and its Deer (1637) says: "There are in the countrey three kindes of Deare, of which there are great plenty, and those are very useful."

Just what writers meant by "great plenty," I have endeavored to ascertain.

In the season of 1895 the official returns showed that 4,900 deer were killed in the Adirondacks. It is notorious that official returns are far below the actual slaughter, for we must add those killed illegally during or out of season, as well as those that were killed and not found. There is also a proportion destroyed by natural enemies, so that we need not hesitate to accept the Chief Protector's estimate that 10,000 deer were killed in the Adirondacks during the season of 1895.

But this must have been far less than half their numbers, otherwise they could not stand the drain, as they evidently do. I have heard hunters estimate that under the most favorable circumstances, the Deer do not add more than a third each year by actual

451

increase. If, therefore, more than a quarter are killed in a season, it means a falling off. But the Adirondack Deer are holding their own, and I should therefore estimate their numbers at 40,000, or, roughly, three to a square mile.

The official report for Maine gives 7,579 Deer killed in 1899, which we are to believe means a destruction of at least 12,000 Deer. But they have ample room and are steadily increasing, so that I put those in Maine at not less than 60,000, or about two to the square mile in 1900. Mr. W. T. Hornaday* gives the estimate of Deer in Maine at 100,-000, or three to the square mile in 1904.

But the accounts of the hunters put the Whitetail far in advance of all other small Deer in point of numbers. Therefore I feel satisfied that ten to the square mile is a safe estimate of Whitetailed population in its true region, the immediate Mississippi Valley and the country to the east of it. This area was roughly 2,000,000 square miles—that is, it was the home of not less than 20,-000,000 Whitetailed Deer.

Even ignoring the other 100,000 square miles of Whitetail range to the westward, as it certainly was much less thickly stocked, we still see that the Whitetail was probably the most abundant large game of temperate

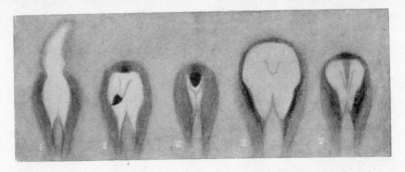

The tails and discs of: 1. New England Whitetail. 2. Colorado Mule Deer. 3. Oregon Coast Deer. 4. Wyoming Wapiti. 5. British Red Deer.

All records agree, however, that the Deer in the Adirondacks and Maine now are as nothing to those of days gone by; thus Morton says of those in New England (1637): "There is such abundance that 100 have been found at the spring of the year, within the compass of a mile." But even this we are told was far surpassed by the "incredible hosts" of the Middle States east of the Mississippi and of Texas. In the last State about 1850, I am credibly assured by many old hunters, "500 in one bunch" were commonly met with in the half-open country. Thousands could sometimes be seen in a day; they were there in tens of thousands.

The numbers in Kentucky were so great that it was believed impossible to exterminate them.

In the mountains of Colorado I have seen Mule Deer so plentiful that ten to the square mile would have been a very low estimate, indeed, and twenty would be safe for the region.

*"Am. Nat. Hist.," 1904, p. 131.

North America, excepting the Buffalo, and possibly ranking after that and the Caribou among all the big game of the continent.

Although the map of to-day shows a wide distribution, it is on a very different basis from that of two hundred years ago. The Adirondacks, northern New England, northern Michigan, northeastern Texas, and the dry parts of Florida, aggregating 100,000 square miles, may yet show an average of three Deer to the square mile. But we must consider the species absent from Ohio, Indiana, Illinois, Iowa, Nebraska, Kansas, Kentucky, the northern half of Missouri, and the southern halves of Minnesota, Wisconsin, Michigan, New York, and Ontario, a total area of about 600,000 square miles of their best country. And the rest of the region marked for Whitetail in present times is so nearly without them that one Deer to five square miles would be a liberal estimate. These figures would make the entire Whitetail population north of the Rio Grande somewhere about 500,000. The State of Maine, therefore, has now one-fifth

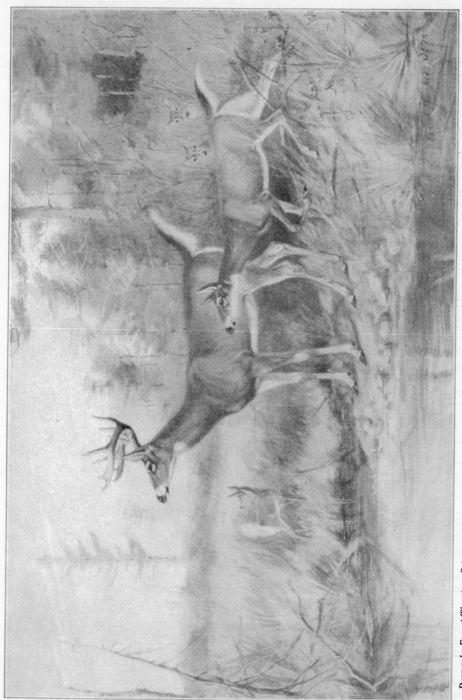

Drawn by Ernest Thompson Seton.

Whitetailed Deer.

of the Deer in the country, because she has learned that they are worth keeping.

The map illustrates an interesting fact in Whitetail distribution—while the species has lost much territory in the east and center of its range, it has also gained a great deal in the north and west. The reason for this will be seen in its habits, especially in its adaptability to agricultural conditions.

Had the map been made in 1890 instead of 1900, it would have given a still smaller range; 1890 seems to have been the low-ebb year for much of our wild game east of the Mississippi. Twenty years ago the Deer were exterminated in New England, except in the remote north woods. Now they have repossessed the whole country, even to the gates of New York City. Within the last year wild Deer have been seen about Greenwich, and even in Yonkers.

On the map I have not attempted to show the limits of different races or species of Whitetail now recognized by naturalists. There are some twelve of these, graded from very small in Florida and Mexico to very large in Maine and Manitoba, and from very dark in the Southeast to very pale, with greatly enlarged white areas, in the Northwest.

Bucks of the Florida Deer (*O. osceola*), rarely weigh over "110 pounds" (Cory), and ordinarily as low as 80 pounds (*C. A. Brambly*); the does are proportionately less. This represents the Southeastern extreme of size.

In the north we have a very different animal (*O. A. borealis*).

This is commonly said to attain a maximum weight of 350 pounds, but I find good testimony for much higher weights. Mr. John W. Titcomb, of the Bureau of Fisheries, says that two bucks weighing respectively 370 pounds and 420 pounds were killed in Vermont in 1899.

The most remarkable Adirondack buck that I can find authenticated is described by Mr. James M. Patterson in Colonel Fox's Forestry Report. It was killed by Mr. Henry Ordway in 1890. "Weight before being dressed 388 pounds [bleeding must have robbed it of 8 or 10 pounds, so that its live weight was about 400 pounds], height over withers 4 feet, 3 inches. There are 9 prongs on one antler and 10 on the other. Length of antlers, 32 inches; distance

between antlers, 26½ inches; length from tip of nose to tip of tail, 9 feet 7 inches."

To this Mr. A. N. Cheney adds: " I have talked with Mr. Patterson, who is a brother of ex-District-Attorney Patterson, of Warren County, since his letter was printed, and he added to the figures given that the Deer measured 37 inches around the neck, back of the head, and that the longest spike on one beam was 13 inches. The buck had been seen on several occasions during two or more years before it was killed, and a number of sportsmen had made special efforts to kill it. It appeared to have no fear of dogs that were put on its track, and on one occasion attacked and drove off two."

But these are the giants of their kind. The average dressed weight of 562 Deer shipped out of the Adirondacks by the Express Company in 1895 was* only 109½ pounds—a live weight of 136¼ pounds—each; but this included many small Deer and August specimens of all ages and sexes. An average full-grown buck of the region is about 200 pounds live weight, and the average doe 150 pounds.

The other extreme is found in a Mexican species of which Caton says: "The smallest of the North American Deer which I have studied is the Acapulco Deer. Some of the specimens which I have had weighed only about 30 or 40 pounds."

There is another interesting dwarf, or myth, to be considered. A curious battle has raged for long between two parties—the hunters in the West and the scientists in the East—over the Gazelle, Cottontail or Fantailed Deer. Every old hunter that I have asked assures me that in the early days of the West there existed a dwarf Whitetail in the thickets along the mountain streams of the upper Missouri.

It resembled the Texan Fantail (*O. texensis*, Mearns), which is found in the high mountains of the Texas and Mexican country. The scientists deny that any such creature ever existed, excepting in the far Southwest, and pointedly demand the production of hair, hide, skull or foot—anything, in fact, except a lot of gauzy camp-fire tales.

I could give some interesting extracts from the trappers' stories, but will content myself for the present by stating that all

* According to Colonel Fox's report.

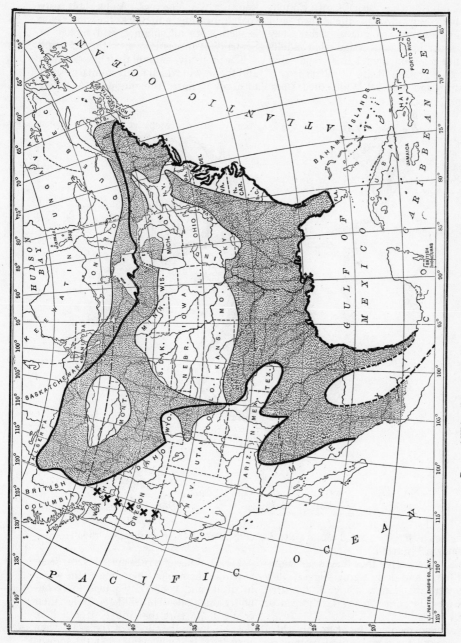

Range of Whitetail in primitive times and in 1900, by Ernest Thompson Seton.

The heavy line shows the original range—not fully worked out in Mexico. The tint shows the range in 1900. In the three large white areas, comprising the Atlantic coast, the Middle States and the far Northwest, the species has been exterminated, but in northern Canada and New England it has followed the settler and gained much territory. The recent extension into Utah is due to irrigation making more country possible for the species. No attempt is here made to demark the various species or races. Outlying or doubtful records are marked with a cross (x). In compiling this map I have used all available data in the records of several hundred ancient and modern travellers.

the old hunters believe in it. They say it looks like a Deer, is a little bigger than a Jack Rabbit, and has the habits of a Cottontail, bounding through the brush and squatting as soon as out of sight; they have shot them and found that adults with five tines on their horns weigh only 50 or 60 pounds and are in all respects a miniature and graceful Whitetailed Deer.

coats each year: a long thick coat, put on in September and worn till May; this is known as the *blue coat*. And a short rusty coat, appearing in spring as the winter coat is shed, worn all summer, and molted in September; this is known as the *red coat*.

The protective value of their blended tints and the way in which many animals turn it to account raises the question, Are they

Whitetail Buck with remarkable palmations.
Killed at North Lake Reservoir, town of Wilmurt, Herkimer County, N. Y., fall of 1891.
Drawn from photographs by Mr. Egbert Bagg, of Utica, N. Y.

The scientists say that these are fawns of common Whitetail.

The hunters reply that they wear many-tined horns and do not grow bigger; they never were abundant and have disappeared from most localities in the last fifteen or twenty years.

If anyone reading this can forward a skin or skull for examination, he may do good service to science.

Many careful observations have given scientific exactness to the old-established hunter belief that the Deer has two distinct

conscious of their adaptation to surroundings?

Mr. D. Wheeler writes me: "Deer seem to realize their color, they come to the water to drink and commonly pause to reconnoitre among dead brush that matches their coat. I am sure that the Northern hare does so, for in the spring of the year, when they are still in white and when the snow is in patches, they *invariably* squat or rest on the snow."

Mr. R. Nicholas of Portland, Ore., maintains that "ptarmigan in white always squat on the snow if the ground be bare in places." I have frequently watched Snow-shoe rabbits and white-jacks which were in full winter livery, though there was no snow at the time; twice I saw a white-jack crouch on a white rock, but I many times saw them crouch in brownish grassy places where they were ridiculously conspicuous.

On the bare ground they are of course more visible, and here they were very shy; though this might be explained by the absence of cover. I am not yet satisfied that these animals realize their color.

The sportsman hunter, however, pays little heed to the colors and fine distinctions on which the scientist founds his races. He usually lumps the twenty odd species and races of small American Deer as Deer, and carries a general impression of a deer-colored animal, paler on the under parts. This is a true impression as far as it goes, and I do not know of any color feature on the animal's trunk that will distinguish the species. But nature has added a label to each, and as though by kindly plan, this is the last part of the animal that the hunter sees as it disappears in the woods, saying in effect: "Well, good-by; I am so-and-so that you did not hit." If every sportsman would bring the tail of his Deer, or failing that, make a sketch of it, with a note of its length and the locality, we could tell with fair certainty the species he had got. The tail and disc of Deer show characteristics as distinctive as those of the skull.

There is a tendency to albinism among the Deer in some parts of the country, usually islands and isolated corners where it seems to be a consequence of inbreeding. Albinism is a freak or disease by which the coloring matter is left out of the hair on those parts of the body that are affected, and the hair there comes white. Sometimes it covers the entire animal, in which case usually the hoofs are white and its eyes pink. It is not by any means certain that the albino of this year will be an albino next year also. The affection is sometimes associated with internal worms.

There is one other very important detail

of anatomy that should be noted, and that is the glands on the outside of the hind leg. These are diagnostic of the species. They are sufficiently set forth in the illustration.

But the sportsman is quite sure to devote chief attention to the head and antlers. Here are two marked types. These repre-

Typical antlers of Whitetail (1) and of Mule Deer (2).

sent average horns of full-grown bucks. In general style the Coast Deer horns resemble those of the Mule Deer, but are more slender. A Whitetail buck has spikes the first year, and afterwards adds snags in proportion to his vigor, *when normal*, but antlers are usually abnormal. Mr. J. W. Titcomb states that a tame Deer which he knew, grew on its second autumn antlers (its first pair) that were a foot long and had three points on each. A pair with many snags *probably* belonged to an old buck, and yet again an old buck may have mere spikes. Thus it will be seen that anyone pretending to tell the age, by the horns alone, is sure to err. Some of the most remarkable variations are here shown.

The record for points still rests with the pair owned by Mr. Albert Friedrich, of San Antonio, Texas. These are of such super-abundant vigor that 78 points appear. The 42-pointer from the Adirondacks and the 35-pointer from Minnesota claim second and third places.

Hariot calls attention to the unique fact that the snags of the horns "look backwards." Caton adds, "thus enabling the animal by bowing his head in battle, as is his habit, to present the tines to the adversary in front. When two meet in the shock of battle thus armed, these antlers form such a complete shield that I have never known a point to reach an adversary." (P. 224.)

But they have an off-setting disadvantage. More in this than in any other American species do we find fatally interlocked antlers. Two bucks struggling for the mastery have in some way sprung their antlers apart, or forced them together, so that they are inextricably intertangled, and death to both combatants is the inevitable finish. It often comes by starvation, and those antler-bound bucks may think themselves lucky if found by their natural enemies and put to a merciful death.

Mr. Stanley Waterloo writes: "In November, 1895, Mr. F. F. Strong, a well-known Chicago business man, and an ardent sportsman, was, with a small party of friends, hunting near Indian River, in Schoolcraft County, Michigan. One day when the party was out, ravens were noticed hovering noisily over a certain spot, and, attracted by curiosity, the hunters sought the cause. Emerging into a comparatively open space in the wood, they made a discovery. For the space of nearly an acre the ground was torn and furrowed by the hoofs of two bucks, and near the centre of the open space lay the bucks themselves, with their horns inextricably locked. One of the Deer was dead and the hungry ravens had eaten both his eyes, though deterred from further feasting by the occasional spasmodic movements of the surviving combatant, whose eyes were already glazing." (*Recreation*, Sept., 1897.)

I remember reading an account of a hunter finding two bucks thus locked, one dead, the other nearly dead. He was a humane man, so went home for a saw and

The Bonnechere Head.
From a Topley Studio photograph supplied by Mr. Norman H. H. Lett.

cut the living one free. The moment it felt at liberty it turned its feeble remaining strength on its deliverer and he had much ado to save his own life before he could regain his rifle and lay the ingrate low. I am unable to find the record and give due credit for the story.

Audubon and Bachman tell of *three pairs* of antlers that were interlocked, and a singular case is reported from Antigo, Wis., where Mr. Matt. J. Wahleitner found two pairs of antlers locked together around a five-inch sapling. The photograph shows the horns to be in each case above average size.

An accident of kindred nature is illustrated in the drawing made for the specimen in New York State Museum. It shows the antler of a Deer driven through a tree. (Page 339.)

The feet are much less subject to aberration than the horns, but Dr. E. Coues (Bul. U. S. Geo. Surv.) has described a solid-hoofed Virginia Deer that was sent him by Mr. Geo. A. Boardman, of Calais, Me. In this freak the two central or main hoofs were consolidated as one. A somewhat similar peculiarity has often been seen in pigs, but never before recorded for the Whitetailed Deer.

The hearing and scent of Deer are marvellously acute, but their eyesight is not of the best.

Audubon and Bachman actually considered it imperfect.

"As we have often, when standing still, perceived the Deer passing within a few yards without observing us, but we have often noticed the affrighted start when we moved our position or when they scented us by the wind. On one occasion we had tied our horse for some time at a stand;

In riding through the woods at night in the vicinity of Deer we have often heard them stamp their feet, the bucks on such occasions giving a loud snort, then bounding off for a few yards and again repeating the stamping and snorting, which appear to be nocturnal habits. (Aud. and Bach.)

They have also a louder, coarser snort or challenge, as noted later. Mr. Franklin T. Payne describes some Park bucks that he shipped as "bawling with rage when captured." (*Rec.*, May, 1898.)

"In all our experience, extending over about forty years, we have never but once heard a Deer make use of the voice when seeking a lost mate. This occurred when upon one occasion, having shot at and scattered a band of stags, one of the number, not having seen or scented us, turned back, evidently seeking his leader, and passed close by, making a low, muttering noise like that sometimes uttered by the domestic ram." (A. Y. Walton, *F. & S.*, June 15, 1895.)

Seventy-eight-point Whitetail killed in Texas.

Spread, 26½ inches.
From photograph by their owner, Mr. Albert Friedrich, of San Antonio. Texas.

on his becoming restless we removed him to a distance. A Deer pursued by dogs ran near the spot where we were standing, without having observed us."

It seems to class all motionless objects down-wind as mere features of the landscape. The hunters take advantage of this weakness to stalk the animal when it is in the open. They run toward it without concealment as long as it is grazing, but the moment it shows by shaking its tail that it is about to raise its head they "freeze"—crouching low and still. The Deer takes its customary look around and lowers its head to feed again, whereupon they repeat the open approach, and thus continue until within easy shot.

I have heard of this trick often and have several times proved it a failure with Antelope. I never tried it on Whitetail Deer, but did it with complete success on a pair of Red Deer in Europe some years ago.

"The Deer is the most silent of animals and scarcely possesses any notes of recognition. The fawn has a gentle bleat that might be heard by the keen ears of its mother at the distance, probably, of a hundred yards. We have never heard the voice of the female beyond a mere murmur when calling her young, except when shot, when she often bleats like a calf in pain. The buck when suddenly started sometimes utters a snort, and we have at night heard him *emitting* a shrill whistling sound, not unlike that of a Chamois of the Alps, that could be heard the distance of half a mile."

The enemies of the Whitetail are, first, the buckshot gun with its unholy confederates, the jacklight and canoe. We hope and believe that two or three years will see them totally done away with—in Deer sport; classed and scorned with the dynamite of the shameless fish-hog. Next is the repeating-rifle of the poacher and pothunter. Third, deep snow. It is deep

Thirty-five-point Whitetail from Minnesota.
From photograph by K. H. C., *Recreation*, June, 1897.

snow that hides their food, that robs them of their speed, that brings them easily within the power of the cougar on his snowshoes; and the human cougar, who, similarly equipped for skimming over the drifts, is mentally as sanguinary and improvident.

The wolves rank high in the list of foes. They have long played seesaw havoc with the Deer in the north. The Deer came in with the settlers on the upper Ottawa. The wolves followed because in the Deer they found their winter support. In the summer the Deer were safe among the countless lakes, and the wolves subsisted on what small stuff they could pick up in the woods. But winter robbed the Deer of the water safe-havens, and then the wolves could run them down by the trick of relay chasing; thus they wintered well.

But wintering well meant increasing; the wolves became so numerous that they destroyed their own support, and starvation, followed by extinction, was their lot. Again the Deer recovered locally or drifted in from other regions, and again the wolves increased to repeat their own destruction. This has been the history of the Deer population along most of our frontier where winter is accompanied by deep snow. If we could exterminate the grey wolf we should solve half the question of Deer supply; but there is no evidence that we shall ever succeed in doing so. I find that Mr. E. T. Merrill, after much experience in Deer and wolf country, discredits the stories of wolves running down Deer. He says:*

"I have not yet seen the race between wolves and a Deer that lasted over ten minutes. Either the Deer gets to water or some clearing or road where the wolves will not follow, or else he is killed at once. Very often they drag a Deer down within a few jumps of where he starts. Deer in

Michigan and Wisconsin during the winter generally feed along the edge of a swamp under thick hemlocks where there is plenty of ground hemlock, and the wolves generally come in on them from two ways and drive them towards the swamp, and they will nearly always kill them within 40 rods of where they start." This is readily understood in country where Deer and other game animals abound. The wolf knows very well that the Deer is far fleeter than himself and if he fails in that first dash, it is easier for him to go elsewhere and try to surprise or trap another Deer. But when desperately hungry in regions where Deer are not so plentiful the wolves will stick to the one they start and follow to a finish, be it never so far. I have heard the accounts of many old Ontario hunters that entirely support this belief. These views, it will be seen, do not oppose those of Mr. Merrill.

Forty-two-point Adirondack Buck.
Redrawn from photograph in New York State Fish and Game Report, 1896.

In my own journal I find an instance in point, related to me by Mr. Gordon Wright, of Carberry, Manitoba. During the winter of 1865 he was shantying at Sturgeon Lake, Ontario. One Sunday he and some companions strolled out on the ice of the lake to look at the logs there. They heard the hunting cry of wolves, then a Deer (a female) darted from the woods to the open ice. Her sides were heaving, her tongue out and her legs cut with the slight crust on the snow. Evidently she was hardpressed and had run for some time. She was coming toward them, but one of the men gave a shout which caused her to sheer off. A minute later six timber wolves appeared, galloping on her trail, heads low, tails horizontal, and howling continuously. They were uttering their hunting cry, but as soon as they saw her they broke into a louder, different note, left the trail and made straight for their prey. Five of the wolves were abreast and one that seemed much darker was behind. Within half a mile they overtook the Deer and pulled her down; all seemed to seize her at once. For a few moments she bleated like a sheep in distress; after that the only sound was the snarling and crunching of the wolves as they feasted. Within fifteen minutes nothing was left of the victim but hair and some of the larger bones, the wolves fighting among themselves for even these. Then they scattered, each going a mile or so, no two in the same direction, and those that remained in sight, curled up there on the open lake to sleep. This happened about ten in the morning within three hundred yards of several witnesses.

Mosquitoes, ticks and deerflies are to be listed among the foes of the Deer. The mosquitoes bother them just as they do us. At times they avoid these plagues by sinking themselves in the mud and water. Blue ticks of the Ixodes species are a well-known pest. Mr. G. M. Martin tells me that in the Adirondacks during June and July, he has often seen such hanging on the Deer's leg, sucking their blood. They do not torment them much, but must be a great drain when present in numbers. The deerflies (*Œstrus*), however, are the most annoying of their small enemies.

Catesby says (1731): "Near the sea the Deer are always lean and ill-tasted, and subject to botts breeding in the head and throat." The hunters assure me that this same complaint is found in the north. The worm is known to be the larva of the gad-fly, or deerfly.

Many a man on first seeing Deer dash through the dangerous mazy wreck of a storm-track has wondered how they could escape with their lives. As a matter of fact, they suffer many accidents in their haste. I suppose that not one adult Deer in ten but will show by the scars on legs and belly that it has been snagged many times. One of the strangest cases of the sort is recorded from Montana by Mr. R. C. Fisk.* He shot a doe Whitetail that had driven into her body a "fir branch over a foot long and over half an inch thickness." It had entered between the fourth and fifth ribs on the right side, missed the right lung, pierced the top of the diaphragm and the point of the liver and rested against the under side of the

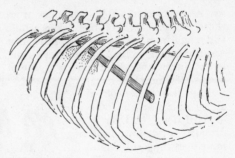

The Snag.

Redrawn from Mr. F. C. Fisk's sketch.

back bone. "That the animal met with this accident while it was yet young," says Mr. Fisk, "I am thoroughly convinced, for the end at the ribs had been entirely drawn into the opening of the heart and lungs and had thoroughly healed on the outside. The skin which I now have shows only the faintest trace of a scar.

"There was not a particle of pus or inflammatory matter of any kind; in fact, the limb, covered as it was with the white skin, exactly resembled one of the long bones of the leg. The animal was healthy and fat and the meat was fine."

The ordinary gait of the Deer is a low smooth bounding, with an occasional high jump. This low bounding is, at its best, I should estimate, according to our scale of speed as set forth in the Antelope, about twenty-seven or twenty-eight miles an hour. The ease with which they cover great spaces is marvellous. I have known a buck clear a four-foot log and fifteen feet of ground in one leap. The high jump taken occasionally is like the spy-hop of jack-rabbits and springbok, for purpose of observation.

In the water the Whitetail are very much at home. They can go so fast that a canoe-man must race to overtake them, which means that they go for the time being at over four miles an hour. They are so confident of their power that they invariably make for the water when hunted to extremity. There are many cases on record of Deer so pushed, boldly striking out into the open sea, trusting to luck for finding another shore.

There is a record* of a Deer captured at

sea near Portland, Me., five miles from shore, and another * of one taken a mile and a half from Sachuest Point, R.I., as it was swimming at full speed away from land. In regions where there is plenty of open water the Deer have little to fear from wolves and nothing at all from unaided dogs. A Deer in summer swims low, little more than the head showing, and when shot usually sinks. In late fall it swims much higher, the back showing. This is due partly to the recently acquired fat which has added more to its bulk than to its weight, but chiefly to the growth of the coat, each hair of which is a little barrel of air adding its flotation to the Deer. As Merriam says: "When the blue coat, which grows very rapidly, is an inch in length, it will, as a rule, float the Deer that carries it and this length is generally obtained about the first of October."†

The tracks that are here figured were drawn on the sandy shore of Big Dam Lake, forty miles from Kippewa, Quebec, September 15, 1905, and show the buck, doe, and fawn. The tracks of pig and sheep also are shown in contradiction of the state-

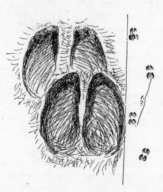

Right feet of Pig.   August 6, 1903.

No clouts.   Mud one-half inch deep.

ment that their tracks may often be mistaken for Deer tracks even by the expert.

In the mating season the Red Deer of Europe makes what is known as a "*soiling pit.*" In some open glade he digs a hole in which the rain collects. This he paws and messes till it is what our backwoodsmen would call a regular "dope." With this he plentifully besmears himself, rolling and grovelling in it like a hog that has only partly learned how to wallow. This habit we have seen repeated in our Moose and Wapiti, but it finds an even better development in the Whitetailed Deer.

All our ruminants have a great fondness for salt. They doubtless need it for a tonic and eagerly seek out anything of a salty nature that they can find in their native range. A great variety of soluble minerals seem to satisfy this craving. Merriam calls attention to a place in the Adirondacks where "the Deer had licked the clay, possibly obtaining a trifle of potash, alumina and iron derived from sulphates, decomposing pyrites."

Why they need it, or how often, or whether any individuals form a "habit" and so injure themselves, has not yet been ascertained.

* F. & S., April 4, 1896.

† "Mam. of Adir.," p. 130.

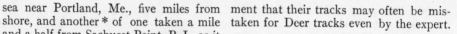

How large is the home locality of a Whitetail? Smaller probably than that of any other of the family in America. A Moose or Mule Blacktail may pass all summer on a square mile, but a doe Whitetail "is usually found in the same range, or drive, as it is called, and often not fifty yards from the place where it was started before." (Aud. and Bach.) These same

Tracks of Whitetail.   Quebec, September 15, 1905.

A. Buck running after Doe. From A to D he cleared, at one bound, 15 feet, and passed over the log X where it is 4½ feet from the ground. B. Doe, coming dripping out of water, steps here about 18 inches, farther on she trotted and the steps are 2½ feet long. Her tracks register well; that is, the hind foot falls in the mark of the front foot. C. A half-grown fawn with the Doe. For some reason its tracks do not register at all. Registering is better walking and especially lends silence to the tread.

naturalists remark with surprise on their finding a band of Deer that bedded at one place and fed nightly at another "nearly two miles off," and a third case of Deer that daily covered four or five miles between bed and board. These, however, are very exceptional.

All the Ottawa guides that I have consulted agree with me in giving to the individual Whitetail a very limited range. In the Rockies I know that two or three hundred acres will often provide a sufficient homeland for a whole family of them the year around, for the Whitetail, unlike the Wapiti or the Mule Deer, seems to be entirely non-migratory.

A. Hind foot of Whitetail at full speed. B. Track of right fore foot—Whitetail Buck at full speed; 5½ inches in length.

If we begin in the early spring to follow the life of the Whitetail on its Northern range, we shall find that in the month of January the does and bucks are still in company, although according to Audubon and Bachman, it is only during the mating season that the sexes herd together. Many exceptions indeed will be found to their general statement. I think that both males and females are found in the Deer yards throughout the winter and the young bucks may follow their mothers all the year round.

But the melting snow sets all free again. The older bucks go off in twos or threes; the does go their own way in small groups, accompanied by their young of the year before.

All winter they have fed on twigs, moss, evergreens, and dry grass; now the new vegetation affords many changes of nutritious diet, they begin to grow fatter, and the unborn young develop fast. The winter coat begins to drop out and a general sleekness comes on young and old. May sees the doe a renovated being, and usually also sees her alone, for now her six months' gestation is nearing its end. Some day about the middle of the month she slinks quietly into a thick cover, perhaps a fallen tree-top, and there the young are born. They vary in number, according to the age and vigor of the mother. "The first time she has one fawn. If in good order, she has two the following year. A very large and healthy doe often produces three, and we were present at Goose Creek when an immense one, killed by J. W. Audubon, was ascertained on being opened, to contain four large and well-formed fawns. The average number of fawns in Carolina is two, and the cases where three are produced are nearly as numerous as those in which young does have only one at the birth." (Aud. & Bach., "Quad. N. Am.," p. 226.) I have never heard of anyone seeing a doe actually accompanied by *four* fawns, or even *three*. And this recalls a fact that I have often noted. The average number of embryonic young found in

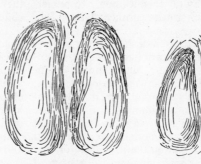

Sheep tracks, front and hind, different sized sheep.

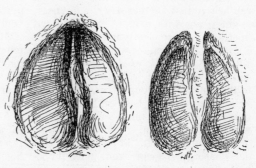

Buck and Doe.

mammals is greater than the average found in the nest even at an early date.

The Deer Family do not make any pretence at a nest. The home of the young is the *neighborhood* where they are born. They may consider the old fallen tree-top their head-quarters, but they will lie in a different part of it every day. Moreover, in Texas, "we have never known them to lie at this stage of their life as the young of sheep and goats do, almost touching one another, but they lie with more or less distance separating them, never very far apart and never very close together." (A. Y. Walton, *F. & S.*, June 15, 1895.) Their weight at birth is about 4½ pounds (Hornaday). Mr. J. W. Titcomb gives the weight of one at 3¾ pounds (*F. & S.*, March 18, 1899).

The mother visits them perhaps half a dozen times a day to suckle them; I think that at night she lies next them to warm them, although the available testimony shows that in the daytime she frequents a solitary bed several hundred yards away. I suppose that it is only in search of water that she really goes out of hearing of their squeak. If found and handled at this time they play dead, are limp, silent, and unresisting. This is purely instinctive behavior.

Their natural enemies now are numerous. Bears, wolves, panthers, lynxes, fishers, dogs, foxes, eagles, are the most dangerous of the large kinds. But their spotted coats and their death-like stillness are wonderful safeguards. Many hunters maintain that now the fawns give out no scent. Doubtless this means that their body scent is reduced to a minimum, and since they do not travel they leave no foot scent at all. There is one more large creature that some would put on the fawns' list of enemies, so far as I can learn without good reason, and that is—*their own father*. I can believe that another doe coming near, might resent with a blow the attempted liberties of a fawn clearly not her own, but I know of no reason for supposing that in a wild state the buck would injure his offspring, and I do know of several reasons to the contrary; although I have not been able to secure the best evidence of all, namely, proof of a buck going out of his way to defend a fawn.

The mother is ready at all times to render what help she can; and, unless hopelessly overmatched, she is wonderfully efficient. Her readiness to run to the young at their call of distress is, or was, often turned to unfair account by the hunters in the Southwest. They manufactured a reed that imitated the fawn's bleat, and thus brought not only the anxious mother, but sometimes also the prowling cougar and lynx within gunshot.

Natural questions that arise are: Does the mother never forget where she hid her young; can she come back to the very spot in the unvaried woods, even when driven a mile or two away by some dreaded enemy?

In the vast majority of cases the mother's memory of the place enables her to come back to the very spot. Sometimes it happens that an enemy forces the little one to run and hide elsewhere while the mother is away. In such cases she sets to work to ransack the neighborhood, to search the ground and the wind for a helpful scent, listening intently for every sound; a rustle or a squeak is enough to make her dash excitedly to the quarter whence it came. It is probable, though I have no proof of it, that now she *calls* for the fawn, as does a cow or a sheep whose young are missing.

In most cases her hearty endeavors succeed. But there is evidence that sometimes they end in a tragedy,—the fawns, like the children of the story, are lost in the woods.

The Moose and the Wapiti may hide their young two or three days, the Antelope for a week, but the Whitetail fawn is usually left in its first covert for a month or more.

At this age their rich brown coats are set off by rows of pure white spots, like a brown log sprinkled with snow-drops or flecked with sun-spots. This makes a color scheme that is protective as they crouch in the leaves and exquisitely beautiful when displayed on their graceful forms, later on, as they bound or glide by mother's side to the appreciative mirror furnished by their daily drinking-pool.

At four or five weeks of age they begin to follow the mother; this is about the beginning of July, but I examined a fawn that Mr. H. G. Nead found hidden in the grass near Dauphin Lake, Manitoba, on the 22d of August.

Analogy would prove that they begin to eat solid food at this time. They develop rapidly, and become very swift-footed. Some hunters assure one that the young are even swifter than the parents, but this, I think, is not so. As already noted, it is a rule that of two animals going at the same rate, the smaller always *appears faster*.

Their daily lives now are as unvaried as the Deer can make them. They rest in some cool shelter during the heat of the morning; about noon they go to their drinking-place. This daily drink is essential, and yet the map shows the Whitetail to be a dweller of the arid plains where no water is. Here, like the Antelope, they find their water-supply in the leaves and shoots of the provident cactus, which is among plants what the camel is among beasts, a living tank and able to store up in times of rain enough for thirsty days to come.

Quebec Whitetail.
From photograph by Norman H. H. Lett.

After a copious draught, sufficient to last her all day long, the mother Whitetail, with her family, retires again to chew the cud in their old retreat, where they escape the deer-flies and heat, but suffer the mosquitoes and ticks. As the sun lowers, they get up and go forth stealthily to feed, perhaps by the margin of the forest, where grow their favorite foods, or to the nearest pond where the lily-pads abound, and root, stem, or leaf provides a feast that will tempt the Deer from afar. They munch away till the night grows black, then sneak back to some other part of the home covert—rarely the same bed—where they doze or chew the cud till dawn comes on, when again they take advantage of the half-light that they love and go foraging, till warned by the sunrise that they must once more away.

This is a skeleton of their daily programme in the wilderness, but they modify it considerably for life around the settlement. The noonday visit to the watering-place is dispensed with. Instead they come by night. Foraging in daylight hours is given up. Secret and silent as the coon, the Whitetail family lurk in their coppice all day, and at night go not to the lily-padded shore, but to the fields of grain or clover, turnips or garden truck. Lightly the alert and shadow-like mother approaches the five-foot fence; behind in her track are the two fawns, not even shadowy, for *they are invisible* in their broken coats. A moment she listens, then with a bound she clears the fence, and, followed by the young, she lands in the banquet spread.

These visits are never during the day, nor are they during the hours of black darkness, for even the Deer require some light to see by. Their favorite time, then, for such a frontier foray is in the moonlight.

The rising of the moon is in all much-hunted regions a signal for the Deer to go forth, and many supposed irregularities in their habits will be found explained on reference to the lunar calendar.

As September wanes there are two important changes in the fawns: first they are weaned, second they shed their spotted—their milk-spotted—coat; they are now fawns of the year. As Caton says, they "are weaned about four months of age, but continue to follow the dam—the males for one year, the females for two years." (P. 308.) The exception to this rule is during that interesting first month of the little ones' lives. Then the older sisters or brothers may be lurking in the neighborhood; they may join the mother at the drinking-place, but during the nursing hours she does not want them near, and if need be takes rude means to prevent their coming.

In September, too, there is a disposition to reunite.

The bucks shed their antlers in January —even earlier, if very vigorous; weeks later, if puny. Mr. J. W. Titcomb's tame buck in Vermont shed one antler on the 26th of February, and the second on the 1st of March. When the melting snow leaves the sexes free to seek or shun each other at their will, these turn their unantlered heads from the social herd, and wander off, usually two together, as with most of our horned ruminants.

Bare ground with its sprouting grass and shoots now supplies bountiful food. The surplus energies of the does go to the unborn young, of the bucks to their budding antlers. These appear two to six weeks after the old ones are dropped.

Their growth goes on with the marvellous rapidity already noted for antlers. During the early stages they are so soft as to be almost plastic and every accident is recorded in their shape. By August they are complete, though still in velvet, and by the middle of September the buck has scraped and polished them clean. Until the last two or three weeks the horns have blood-vessels throbbing with blood, have nerves, and are sensitive integral parts of the animal's body. They are of course doomed to die and drop, but in that three months when really dead they are to discharge the office for which they were created. This is well known, but Judge Caton, our great Deer authority, makes a surprising additional statement: "The evidence, derived from a very great multitude of observations, made through a course of years, is conclusive that nature prompts the animal to denude its antlers of the covering at a certain period of its growth, while yet the blood has as free access to the covering as it ever had." That is, while yet the horn is living and sensitive the deer voluntarily subjects itself to the painful operation of skinning them.

Why? There must be a good reason. I can only suppose that the earlier his antlers are cleaned, the sooner he can enter the arena in which wives go to the winner, with obvious advantage to his strain.

All summer he has been living as quietly as the doe, sometimes frequenting the same places, but not seeing her if they chance there together. The margins of the forest and of the lake have powerful charms for him now, not only for their food supply, but because there he knows he can protect himself at once from the torment of the flies and the fiercest summer heat. In Audubon and Bachman we find a most interesting case which shows his method of doing this, as well as the cunning of the old buck. "To avoid the persecution of mosquitoes and ticks, it occasionally, like the Moose in Maine, resorts to some stream or pond and lies for a time immersed in the water, from which the nose and a part of the head only project. We recollect an occasion, when on sitting down to rest on the margin of the Santee River, we observed a pair of antlers on the surface of the water near an old tree, not ten steps from us; we were without a gun, and he was therefore safe from any injury we could inflict on him. Anxious to observe the cunning he would display, we turned our eyes another way, and commenced a careless whistle, as if for our own amusement, walking gradually toward him in a circuitous route until we arrived within a few feet of him. He had now sunk so deep in the water that an inch only of his nose and slight portions of his prongs were seen above the surface. We again sat down on the bank for some minutes, pretending to read a book. At length we suddenly directed our eyes toward him, and raised our hand, when he rushed to the shore, and dashed through the rattling canebrake, in rapid style."

Late September is the season of nuts, and nuts are to the Deer what honey is to the bear. Acorns in particular are its delight and the groves of oaks a daily haunt of the reunited family. The effect of such rich food in quantity is quickly seen. "Indeed," says Caton, "it is astonishing to me how rapidly the buck and the doe will improve as soon as the acorns begin to fall. Ten days are sufficient to change a thin Deer to a fat one, at the time when the summer coat is discarded and the glossy winter dress appears." (P. 308.)

In view of their fondness for acorns it is interesting to note that Sargent's map of the distribution of oaks in America east of the Rockies practically coincides with the range of the Whitetailed Deer.

If the Whitetail had any games or places of meeting we should find them used at this season, when all are fat and free from care. But so far as I have been able to learn they do not slide, play "tag," or "king of the castle," plash or chase each other in circles, or in any way show that they have taken the first steps in the evolution of amusement.

As October comes on, another change sets in with the bucks; their necks begin to swell to extraordinary size and their mating instincts to rouse. Hitherto they have been indifferent to the does when they met by but this Deer made altogether a louder and different noise from either." (*F. & S.*, Oct. 5, 1895.)

George Crawford and Linklater, guides of Mattawa, assure me that at this season

Abnormal antlers of Whitetail.
Redrawn from Caton's figure.

chance, but now they set out to seek them, and of this I saw some signs on the Ottawa as early as the 15th of September.

The buck does not gather around him a band of does like the successful bull Wapiti, and it is sometimes said that he does not issue any sort of a challenge. But the following curious paragraph by "Bachelor" shows that he has both the disposition and the voice to challenge at times. "Some years since . . . I was still-hunting in Arkansas. . . . I had been standing several minutes when I heard three successive sounds or noises that were much louder and coarser than the whistle or snort of any Deer I had previously heard. At first I thought it some other animal, but presently he was in sight, and when within about 200 yards of me he ran into a flock of turkeys. He would single one out and chase it away, then another, until he had chased off nine or ten, likely all of the flock, when he returned to the line or track he was following and came on, part of the time trotting and part of the time walking, but all the time travelling as if he were tracking something. When within eighty yards of me he came on my track and stopped, turning half around, giving me a fine shot. He was only a three-point buck, and rather small for a three-pointer, but he seemed to be on the war-path, judging by the way he chased the turkeys, and he seemed to care very little for me. Now I have frequently heard Deer whistle when frightened, and have heard them snort from the same cause,

the bucks utter a peculiar call like a sheep bleating or like the creaking of two trees rubbing together. As November, the true rutting time, draws near, "the necks of the bucks become enormously enlarged. As early as the last week in October, I measured the neck of a buck that was thirty inches in circumference, only ten inches behind the ear [ordinarily it would have been about twenty around]. The maximum development is attained about the middle of November." (Merriam, p. 116.) Col. Fox speaks of a buck whose neck was thirty-seven inches around.

Their whole nature seems to undergo a corresponding change, and by November they are ready to fight one of their own or

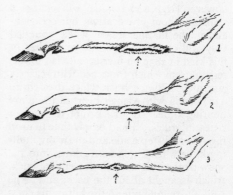

Left hind leg of Mule Deer (1), Coast Deer (2), and White-tail (3), to show the size of the metatarsal glands, respectively 5, 3, and 1 inch long.

any other kind that seems likely to hinder their search for a mate.

"At this season the bucks not only fight among themselves, but occasionally attack man, and more than one unfortunate person has been gored to death by them. In battle they make use of their horns, and also of their fore feet, whose sharp hoofs are capable of inflicting terrible wounds. I was once sitting quietly on a log in a Deer park when a buck approached, and, making a sudden spring, dealt me such a powerful blow on the head, with the hoofs of his fore feet, as to render me unconscious. No sooner was I thrown upon the ground than the vicious beast sprang upon me, and would doubtless have killed me outright had it not been for the intervention of a man, who rushed at him with a club and finally drove him off." (Merriam, "Mam. Adir.," p. 117.)

Mr. J. Parker Whitney relates a similar experience in Maine:

"It is very rare," he says, "that a buck, however large and savage, will charge a stalker without provocation, but occasionally in the mating season when wounded they will charge. I had an encounter of this kind in 1859 on my second visit to this region, from which I escaped with scarcely a scratch, killing a buck which dressed up 230 pounds, with a single heart thrust of my hunting-knife. It was before the day of repeating-rifles. I had barely time to drop my rifle and step aside and draw my hunting-knife when I was borne down into the snow by the weight of the descending buck, which I caught about the neck, and as he rose, drove my knife to the hilt in his chest at the junction of the throat, severing his windpipe and splitting his heart. Death

Two Whitetail Bucks with locked horns.
Redrawn from Mr. Stanley Waterloo's photograph in *Recreation* for August, 1899.

was instantaneous. I had difficulty in withdrawing myself quickly enough to escape the red torrent of life-blood which gushed forth." (*F. & S.*, Dec. 26, 1898.) If, however, the Deer is the conqueror, he never ceases to batter, spear, and trample his victim as long as it shows signs of life.

Several hunters have related to me how, when downed in the snow by some furious buck, they have saved their lives by feigning death.

Their stillness convinced the stag that his revenge was complete, and he slowly withdrew, casting, nevertheless, many a backward glance to satisfy himself that truly his foe was done for.

But it is for the rival of his own race that his weapons are sharpened and his deadliest animosity poured out, and Mr. Whitney's picture of a battle-ground is almost as telling as an account of the veritable fray. "The Deer, timid as supposed, is possessed of an indomitable and persistent courage in conflict with its own kind, and will fight to the extremity of weakness and even death before yielding. I have witnessed a number of scenes this season, where the trampled ground and broken shrubs indicated desperate encounters. One spot, a few miles from the lake, and as lately observed as December 11th, indicated a meeting of particular ferocity. I had tracked a large buck through eight inches of snow. The buck had evidently found several others in conflict, and being a free lance, had a free fight, and had immediately engaged. The snow was completely crushed and tumbled over an area somewhat larger than an ordinary circus ring, and it was decidedly apparent that a stag circus of unusual magnitude had occurred without the supervision of a ring master or the encouraging plaudits of spectators. I counted five departing trails, and the performance had probably terminated several hours in advance of my arrival. Probably one by one the vanquished had departed, until the acknowledged champion held the field. Such seems to have been the case, as the trails were diverging. One champion exhibited the hasty and ludicrous method of his exit by leaping over a broken tree six feet in height, when a projecting fracture had creased his body the whole length in passing, leaving a bountiful handful of hair and fragmentary cuticle in evidence. This might be accounted a feeling instance of the P. P. C. order of etiquette with the *Cervus* family. The trampled area was flecked with enough hirsute scrapings to fill a good-sized pillow, with occasional spatterings of scarlet coloring." (J. P. Whitney.)

Judge Caton's description of a battle is, I think, fairly representative. There is much effort but little slaughter; still the affair is a success because it decides what they set out to learn, namely, which is the better buck:

"The battle was joined by a rush together like rams, their faces bowed nearly

Deer horn embedded in oak.

Specimen in New York State Museum. Drawn from photograph supplied by the Director of the Museum.

Inscribed: "This portion of an oak tree with a Deer's head and horns was taken from a forest in the State of Michigan. It is believed that the tree was between 40 and 50 years old. Presented to the Museum by the Hon. William Kelly, of Rhinebeck, Nov. 24, 1859."

to a level with the ground, when the clash of horns could have been heard at a great distance; but they did not again fall back to repeat the shock, as is usual with rams, but the battle was continued by pushing, guarding, and attempting to break each other's guard, and goading whenever a chance could be got, which was very rare. It was a trial of strength and endurance, assisted by skill in fencing and activity. The contest lasted for two hours without the animals being once separated, during which they fought over perhaps half an acre of ground. Almost from the beginning both fought with their mouths open, for they do not protrude the tongue prominently, like the ox, when breathing through the mouth. So evenly matched were they that both were nearly exhausted, when one at last suddenly turned tail to and fled; his adversary pursued him but a little way. I could not detect a scratch upon either sufficient to scrape off the hair, and the only punishment suffered was fatigue and a conciousness of defeat by the vanquished."

Many observations and inquiries lead me to conclude that the buck Whitetail is usually seen with one doe, sometimes with two, rarely with three, never with more; so that, though far from monogamous and very flagrantly bigamous, he is still the least polygamous of our Deer.

In this connection I note with interest that often the buck is seen leading the band, whereas in the polygamous Wapiti and Red Deer, the leader is usually an old doe. One naturally asks the question, Is female lead-

Antler of Virginia Deer embedded in tree trunk.

Locality New York State.
From photograph of specimen in New York State Museum, by courtesy of Director John M. Clarke.

ership a penalty of polygamy? It would seem an inevitable outcome of the approved doctrine—that the majority must be right.

In mid December, after this the climax of their lives is over, the jealousies, the animosities, the aspirations of the males, the timidities and anxieties of the females are gradually forgotten.

The Mad Moon has waned, a saner good fellowship persists, and now the Whitetails, male, female, and young, roam in bands that are larger than at any other time of year. Food is plentiful, and they fatten quickly, storing up, even as do squirrel and beaver, for the starvation time ahead, only the Deer store it up in their persons where it is available as soon as needed, where it helps to cover them from the cold, and whence it cannot be stolen except over their dead bodies and by a burglar stronger than the householder himself.

Thus they wander in their own little corner of the wilderness till deepening snows cut down their daily roaming to a smaller reach, and still deeper till their countless tracks and trails, crossing and recrossing, make many safe footways where the food is best. Though round about them twenty feet away is the untrodden and deep-lying snow, that walls them in and holds them prisoners fast, until its melting sets them free to live these many chapters over again.

Experience shows that young Whitetails taken after they have begun to run with the mother are so fully possessed of the feral nature that in spite of all efforts, they remain wild and distrustful for the rest of their days. But caught during the hiding period of infancy, they are as easy to tame as puppies. Nevertheless, those who are tempted by opportunity should be warned that a Deer is the most treacherous of pets. The only change that domestication makes in them is to rob them of their fear of man. Their fierce combative disposition is there and ever ready to break out. Not only children and women, but many strong men have met with tragic ends from some tame Deer—doe as often as buck—that was supposed to be the gentlest, loveliest creature on earth.

Merriam says: "Both my father and myself have been knocked flat on the ground by being struck in the abdomen by the fore feet of a very harmless looking doe." (P. 117.)

I recollect a case that happened during my early life near Lindsay, Ontario. A tame Deer was confined in a certain orchard. The grandmother from the next farm was paying a call and chanced to take a short cut through that orchard. Hours afterward they found the shapeless remains of her body, cut and trampled to rags by the feet of the pet Deer that she had fed a hundred times.

One might easily collect scores of instances to show that our American species, not only the bucks in autumn, but bucks, or does, in spring, summer, autumn or winter, after the second year may become dangerous animals, and are almost sure to do so if not fully inspired with fear of man.

It is the opinion of all who have studied them that a tame Deer is more dangerous than a tame bear; a bear one knows is to be watched, and he has some respect for his friends; a Deer is always unsafe for everyone, and no man in his senses will ever expose himself or his family to the possible treachery of such a pet.

There is no probability that the Whitetail will ever serve man in any domestic capacity, but it may in a different way. By reason of its singular adaptability and gifts, it is the only one of our Deer that can live contentedly and unsuspectedly in a hundred acres of thicket. It is the only one that can sit unconcernedly all the day long while factory whistles and bells are sounding around it, and yet distinguish at once the sinister twig snap that tells of some prowling foe as far away, perhaps, as the other noises. It is the only one that, hearing a hostile footfall, will sneak around to wind the cause, study its trail, and then glide, catlike, through the brush to a farther haven, without even trying to see the foe or give him a chance for a shot. It is the least migratory, the least polygamous, the least roving as well as the swiftest, keenest, shyest, wisest, most prolific, and most successful of our Deer. It is the only one that has added to its range; that in the North and West has actually accompanied the settler into the woods, has followed afar into newly opened parts of New England and Canada, that has fitted its map to his, that can hold its own on the frontier. I shall always remember a scene at a mining camp in Gilpin County, Colorado, some years ago. The Whitetail Deer was known to have come into the region quite recently and the Mule Blacktail was growing scarce. A man came in and said as he stamped off the snow, "I just scared up a couple of Deer on the ridge." An old hunter there became interested at once; he was minded to go, and reached for his gun. But stopping, he said, "Whitetail or Blacktail?" "Whitetail," was the reply. "That settles it, a Blacktail I could get, but a scared Whitetail knows too much for me."

He sat down again and resumed his pipe.

The Whitetail is the American Deer of the past, and the American Deer of the future. I have no doubt that whatever other species drop out of the hard fight, the Whitetail will flourish in all the region of the plough, as long as there are sentiments and laws to give it a season of respite each year.

In some ways it is no better game than others that could be named, but its habits fit it in an unusual degree to continue in all parts of the country.

As a domestic animal it is a failure; but it may have another mission. The hunter makes the highest type of soldier, and the Whitetail makes the highest type of hunter that is widely possible to-day. The Whitetail trained the armies of the Revolution—even as the Antelope of the Veldt trained the Boers, and may supply the vital training of the country's armies in the future. When this people no longer has need of armies, when the nations learn war no more, and men cease to take pleasure in beautiful wild life—then only can we afford to lose the Whitetail Deer.

45.
HUNTING
THE BIG HORN
(1900)

HUNTING THE BIG HORN

IN THE COLORADO DESERT.

By E. E. Bowles.

THE most wary and timid of all the big game animals of America is that branch of the Rocky Mountain sheep (or Big Horn) family having its habitat in the mountains of that isolated and little-known territory designated on maps of the southwest as "The Desert of the Colorado;" a territory bounded on the east by the Colorado River, on the west by the Sierra Madre Mountains, on the north—well, by the southern line of Nevada, and on the south by the Mexican line; possibly 150 miles from east to west, and 250 from north to south.

As the coming of the white hunters, with their long-range guns, drove the Big Horns of the Rockies to the higher peaks, so the rush of the "boom" in southern California forced the sheep out into the fastnesses of the desert mountains, a literal *terra incognita*, save to prospectors and an occasional Indian. There they have remained comparatively undisturbed for years, increasing, until they are quite numerous, more plentiful than deer indeed, and as their present haunt is a waterless, treeless, barren waste of sand and rocks, there is no immediate prospect of their extinction. There are but few persons aware that in a day's ride from Los Angeles one can be in the heart of the mountain sheep country.

Some claim that the Big Horn of the Sierra Nevadas and the Rocky Mountains of the North are not so much larger than the wild sheep in the mountains of the southern desert, but as I have shot bucks, or rams, as you please, in the latter country having horns ranging from nineteen to twenty-three inches in circumference at the base, and from three to over four feet in length on the outer curve of the horn, it may be accepted as a fact that they are at least "big" enough to create an interest in their hunt and afford exciting chase.

Conceal their horns and they resemble nothing so much as an antelope, their dark gray coat of short hair shading to a light fawn, or almost white on the rump and belly. However, I believe they are heavier than an antelope; one big buck that we got last spring on a scratch shot at 250 yards, dressed over 200 pounds; this, of course, without the head or horns. They must have derived their family name from their horns, for in no other respect do they resemble a sheep more than does an elk, deer or antelope. However, in the winter season I have often found, close to the pelt, a fine, soft, short gray fur, it cannot be called a fleece, it is too fine and soft; this is in addition to their heavy coat of short straight hair.

Not only are they wary and timid, but unlike a majority of wild animals, they are devoid of curiosity. Tie your bandanna to your cleaning rod, stick it in the sand or in the crevice of a rock and then lie back and wait for their curiosity to bring them within range, and you will never see a sheep; yet this trick is often successful with antelope, but with sheep, the result is similar to the experience of our little Japanese cook, whom we had taught to handle a shot-gun; on his return from a weary and unsuccessful tramp after jack-rabbits his excuse was, "No ketchum, go quick."

Mountain sheep have the keenest sight and most delicate sense of smell and hearing of any animal it has ever been my good fortune to hunt, and I have hunted almost everything edible in the wild game line, except the caribou of the North. I am not a market hunter, my experiences having been confined to the necessity of supplying the usually scanty larder of a gold miner with fresh meat; therefore, anything I write is not from the view of an expert or a dead shot, but from that of an amateur who will take up any old gun and go into the hills after anything that will furnish his camp-fire with a roast or broil. I have read of these dead shots—read of them when I was a boy in books that I never left lying about the house, but whose contents I devoured at school behind the friendly cover of my geography. Those books told of men who, without a tremor, saw a grizzly stand upright, and

" Watched the sway of the shoulders,
    The paunch's sag and swing,"

until the monster was within eight or ten feet of them, and then "coolly and deliberately planted a bullet in his eye." Since those trustful and believing days of childhood hero-worship I have met his bearship on his native heath, have roused the "grizzled monarch" from his lair, and I now say after mature deliberation that no cinnamon, silvertip, or brown grizzly bear is going to get within 10 feet or 100 feet of me, provided always, of course, that I see him first ; but there is nothing sneaking or underhand about a grizzly bear ; he will give you a fair stand-up fight if you are looking for a fight ; the greatest fault I find in them is their extreme sensitiveness, their liability to take offense without just provocation. The report of a gunshot anywhere within the hearing of a grizzly is quite likely to cause him to hunt you up to ascertain if you were shooting at him. On the other hand, I have watched a grizzly pass within less than fifty yards of me, in an open bit of country, and all the attention he paid me was a sidelong glance which convinced him of my firm neutrality, so marked as to border on friendliness. I was not hunting bear. I patted my astuteness on its bald spot after he had passed and I had measured his nineteen-inch track. I remember once—but this is a story about sheep, not bears. However, here is a query I would put to professional hunters : Why is it when you take your shot-gun and go after quails, grouse, squirrels, or other small game, you are continually jumping deer, sheep, bears, or mountain lions, and the reverse happens when you take your rifle?

The mountains of the Desert of the Colorado are the most difficult hunting country of any I was ever in. The desert is not a level sandy plain ; it is diversified with mountain ranges from eight to ten miles apart, the intervening country being sandy valleys covered with cactus, greasewood, ironwood and wild sage. The mountain ranges have a general trend from northwest to southeast, rocky, barren and precipitous, rising almost abruptly from the sandy plain to a height of from 2,500 to 5,000 feet. Entirely devoid of soil, waterless,

treeless, with here and there, in crevices of the rocks, a bit of stunted herbage or bunch grass on which the sheep wax fat. No forest or underbrush to aid one in approaching his game unseen ; nothing but the bare, sun-burned rocks, under a brilliant sunlight and in an atmosphere so clear that with the naked eye a man may see another walking at a distance of five miles. Under such conditions to successfully stalk a Big Horn, with their sense of hearing, smell, and sight developed to such a remarkable degree, is a feat of which one may well be proud. I never did it—intentionally that is. I have "ran onto" bands of them with the wind blowing strong in my face, and it was then difficult to decide which was the more surprised.

The mountains are covered with bits of broken rock, which the elements have chipped from the massive formation, and one goes slipping, sliding, clattering along, and in the deathlike stillness of the desert, so absolute as to be oppressive, sound carries far. There is no soughing of the wind among the trees, no song of birds nor scream of hawk nor brawl of mountain stream ; nothing but inanimate, grewsome, horrible silence, that has turned more than one poor fellow's brain, whose mummified remains we have found later, his swollen tongue protruding between his blackened lips, his clothing torn from his body in frenzy, his features terribly distorted in his last agony.

Knowing the customary haunt of the sheep you intend stalking, and with moccasins on your feet, you may be successful ; I know it has been done ; I have seen Indians do it. The grazing being sparse the sheep feed from bunch to bunch, some constantly moving, and the least sign of motion on the part of another object of that inanimate nature will arouse their suspicions. When the big buck leader tosses up his head and looks in your direction, you may be 1,000 yards away, lying prone upon your face, pasted on the rocky face of the mountain, scarce daring to breathe, but you are in for it for he will stand like a statue for possibly an hour, never taking his eyes from you while the others feed on. You may resemble the many slabs of granite lying about, but I believe that he knows there was no rock or boulder in the exact spot you are occupying when he looked a short time before.

You watch him out of the tail of your eye from under your hat brim, and oh, how you want to sneeze, or scratch, or change your position, but you dare not; in dropping to the ground probably your rifle is under you, to give no gleam of metal, and now the hammer is eating into your thigh—you must move, ever so little—but it is enough; the statue stamps its foot and whirls, facing the direction the band must go and it never looks, but goes; you see a flutter of white flags and they are gone, only the leader, standing on the highest peak on the verge of the precipice to make sure —then he is gone. But do not allow him to make sure; remain motionless

.proaching water, so it is better to select a spot some distance away along their trail which is always well-defined. Let them get broadside on, pick your animal, aim at the forequarters and let drive; if you do not get it then "pump lead," pump hard and fast, you may cripple one and get it later; if one drops behind or goes in a direction independent of the band, follow it, it is your meat; you have winged it; if the band goes out of range in a bunch you may as well indulge in any expletives that your religion permits or the occasion warrants, and go back to camp. The best time to find them under such conditions, although it does savor of pot

"PASTED ON THE ROCKY FACE OF THE MOUNTAIN."

for a short while until he disappears after the band, then you may follow, possibly with better success, but more probably not.

There are a few water holes and tenejos (tanks) scattered through the mountains, but only wild sheep, Indians, and prospectors know their location. If it is fresh meat you are after the surest way of securing a supply is to post yourself within easy range of some high ridge leading to the water; they always select the highest ground. You might take station near the water, but I have also tried that without success. Sheep redouble their caution when ap-

shooting, is between early dawn and a little after sunrise. In the winter months they generally go without water for several days, but in the summer months they usually hunt water once a day.

As an illustration of their keenness of sight and evident memory I will relate one incident. A friend of mine, Joe Davis, from Llano County, Texas, a good man with a horse, rope and gun, and a good man to have with you under any circumstances, and I, were prospecting and found a water hole in the Dos Palmas Mountains, where it was evident Big Horns had been watering for ages, judging from the appearance of their trails. The small alkali spring was in a park-like place surrounded by mountains. This park was full of barren little knolls or hillocks from twenty to forty feet in height. About thirty feet up the side of one and commanding the water-hole, forty yards away, was a narrow shelf or bench covered with broken slabs of schist.

On this bench we erected a rude wall about four feet in height and with only two small loopholes, less than three inches in diameter, for our rifles. The cleavage of the rocks was smooth, and one flat stone on another made the wall close and firm. A few dwarfed greasewood bushes were growing around the base of the knolls, and, breaking the tops, we concealed the wall behind their red and green foliage. Then we went out on the trail one hundred yards and inspected our work ; it was satisfactory ; we had built blinds before, and we could only discover it by knowing its exact location. Understand that a blind was absolutely necessary, for the knolls were round and barren, save for the stunted greasewood, which afforded no more protection than would a currant bush in December.

The next morning we were behind our blind and the muzzles of our rifles in the loopholes before the dawn peeped over the curtain that night had looped up to the peak which towered above us on the right. With our backs against the rock we waited patiently for developments, and longingly fingered our pipes, but a smoke was out of the question, although the wind was in our favor. Through half-closed lids I watched the kaleidoscopic changes of the peak from pearl gray to rose, rose to pink, and from pink to silver just as Joe laid his hand on my arm. Silently he pointed up the ridge ; there, a full mile away, silhouetted against the clear morning sky, was a magnificent buck. Motionless he "viewed the landscape o'er," and the prospect being evidently satisfactory he moved on, followed by one. two, three, four, five, six others from under the ridge, three ewes, two young bucks and a lamb.

On down the trail along the "hogback" they came prancing, gamboling, and now and then stopping to nibble at some juicy bit of herbage ; for half an hour we watched them, possessing our souls in patience until they should be within range. Four hundred yards away the trail crossed a "saddle" in the ridge, hiding the quarry momentarily from our view ; taking advantage of this we shifted our positions to a "ready," careful to keep the muzzles of our rifles within the loopholes.

Up they came out of the saddle, and for an instant the wary old leader stopped, looking straight at our cleverly constructed blind. Literally holding our breath, we watched him through the very narrow space in the loopholes not filled by our rifle barrels ; one of the younger bucks, growing impatient, started on, but the old "boss" stamped his foot, whirled about, and the next instant they were out of sight only to reappear on the opposite side of the saddle going at full speed up the trail, and in less time than it takes to write it they had disappeared over the high ridge where we first sighted them. Silently Joe and I looked at one another ; customary expletives could not meet the occasion, but as we drew out our pipes he said : " Don't that rasp you ?" Then we went back to bacon and beans.

Now what frightened those sheep ? It was simply impossible for them to see us behind our blind, a solid wall of rock hidden by bushes. A strong morning breeze was blowing directly from the sheep, so it was not possible for them to have winded us ; several coyotes, that certainly have a keen scent, came down to the water hole, within forty yards of us, drank and played about for a time utterly oblivious of our presence. Later a huge wildcat also came and drank, rolled in the sand, then deliberately sat and made its toilet after the manner of a house cat ; none of these keen-nosed animals scented us, even at that short distance, and, of course, we did not shoot at them.

The only plausible theory that I can advance is that the sheep recognized some change in the landscape, that the bushes had been moved, that yesterday or the day before none had been growing on the site of our blind ; they were certainly not frightened at the presence of any other animals, for coyotes will not attack a mountain sheep unless it is disabled from wounds or age. I once witnessed a fight between a full-grown mountain lion and a big horn buck. The lion, after repeated "jolts," crawled away bruised and whimpering, and, admiring the big horn's nerve, I allowed him to pursue his victorious way. Two or three rods farther on, in answer to his call, a ewe and lamb came down an almost precipitous bluff. It was a grand fight and I can testify was strictly "on the square."

Joe had one failing that at times was fatal to his success in bringing down his game, but only when there were a number of animals together; that failing consisted in shooting at one and watching the others at the same time. The day following our fiasco at the blind I

for he came directly toward us. His horns measured twenty-two inches in circumference. That an animal of their size can carry such horns seems almost incredible. Frequently I have seen the old bucks throw their heads back, resting their horns on their shoulders and swallow space at a terrible rate. The old story that they leap from high precipices and alight on their horns I believe to be a myth. I have chased many of them and watched for that spectacle, but in vain, although I believe they might do it without breaking their necks; but they are very sure-footed, and will go where you cannot follow, leaping and bounding from point to

A FAVORITE HAUNT OF DESERT BIG HORNS.

saw him bring down a lone lamb at 250 yards, and a few days after a ten-pronged buck deer on the run at 200 yards. However, we congratulate ourselves that we got the big buck that discovered our blind. Several days later we were going up the broad arroyo and discovered him industriously feeding on an ironwood bush in a bank about 200 yards ahead of us. We both fired, my bullet going into the bank just over his back and Joe's evidently passing between his fore legs. He leaped to the top of the bank, but Joe's second shot struck him squarely on the horn, turning him around, evidently crazing him,

point and shelf to shelf, where you cannot find a foothold.

Sportsmen may be curious as to what guns we use. Those who live in the mountains are not particular, any old gun will do; I have been using an old 44-caliber, black powder model of '73; it answers my purpose. I have taken the shot out of a 12-gauge cartridge, rounded a stick the size of a lead pencil, punched holes in a cake of soap, melted the No. 6 shot, poured it in the holes in the soap, and reloaded the cartridges with the slugs. With these I have killed both sheep and deer. I cite this only as an instance of what necessity compels a man to do. But to take up the rifle.

The new smokeless powder, 30-30 or 30-40 models, are meeting with great favor, but I am one of those that love old friends the best. The new models are certainly good guns, but when one is after meat—I have my doubts. My objections are not those of an old comrade of mine, who said that the "drotted things killed so far that he had to salt the bullets, for fear the meat would spoil before he got to it." Neither that of another, who feared "a thousand-yard range might strain the gun." My objections are, that the small caliber steel or hard-pointed bullet, while it certainly penetrates, leaves such a small aperture that the wound does not bleed outwardly, making it almost impossible to trail your game, and unless struck in the spine, heart, or head, a wounded animal will sometimes go a long distance. On the other hand, the soft-pointed bullet shatters too much; it goes to the other extreme. I saw a running deer struck in the rump with one at three hundred yards, the ball coming out at the shoulders; only one ham was worth taking to camp.

There are yet numerous bands of Big Horns in the desert mountains of southern California, especially in the eastern portions of the counties of Riverside, San Diego and San Bernardino; no one hunts them save an occasional Indian or a prospector wanting a change from the everlasting bacon (Chicago quail), and he does not kill wantonly, only one for his own consumption. As an illustration that they are yet numerous I will relate one instance: Last spring two Chemihueva Indians came to my camp and wanted to buy or borrow some cartridges; they had two 44-caliber carbines, but had only nine cartridges between them. Of course, I refused them, as I was not at all anxious that they should hunt in that vicinity. They went into the Pinto mountains, three miles east of my camp, and the next night returned with the meat of seven sheep and one cartridge, and

yet an Indian is "no good" with a rifle at over 100 yards. There is not the slightest taste of mutton to the meat, and I prefer it to venison, which it very much resembles, only in my opinion it is more tender, sweeter and better flavored.

The desert has one advantage over the mountains of the north, and that is in the matter of climate; here one may sleep out of doors the year round without discomfort. Three pairs of good woolen blankets—one pair for a mattress and two for covering—together with a strip of 12-ounce or 16-ounce duck six feet wide by fifteen long, is ample bedding for the coldest winter months; in the summer—well, one may say that any bedding at all is superfluous. From November to April is the best hunting season; the other six months in the year are too hot. I have seen the thermometer in June register from 105 at midnight to 125 and 130 at noon in the shade in the coolest spot we could find about camp, and this for weeks at a time. One can have no idea of the power of the solar rays until he spends a summer on the desert. Of course, there is no humidity in the atmosphere to speak of, else man or animal could not live twenty-four hours.

If you are going into that country take burros; a wagon and team are troublesome, and one cannot get into the heart of the game country with a wagon. Take burros to pack your bedding and supplies, and another to ride, and you can go to the summit of almost all the mountain ranges, and the favorite feeding-grounds of the Big Horns. But under no circumstances enter that region without a guide; an Indian will do, and he will at the same time educate you in the mystery and delicate finesse of Big Horn stalking. The desert of the Colorado is an innocent-looking little blank spot on the map, but on the surface of what it represents lie the bleaching bones of many men. There are correct maps of it, but they are seared on the brains of a few prospectors. You must be wary in the Colorado desert.

ABANDONED—TWO DAYS FROM WATER.